NEW ISSUES FACING CHRISTIANS TODAY

FULLY REVISED EDITION

John Stott

President, the Institute for
Contemporary Christianity

Marshall Pickering

An Imprint of HarperCollins*Publishers*

Marshall Pickering is an Imprint of
HarperCollins*Religious*
Part of HarperCollins*Publishers*
77–85 Fulham Palace Road, London W6 8JB

First published in Great Britain in 1984 by Marshall Pickering
Second edition first published in 1990
This edition published in 1999

5 7 9 10 8 6

A catalogue record for this book
is available from the British Library

ISBN 0 551 03172 7

Printed and bound in Great Britain by
Creative Print and Design (Wales), Ebbw Vale

Abbreviations

The biblical text quoted is normally that of the New International Version. If another text is used, this is stated.

Arndt-Gingrich	*A Greek-English Lexicon of the New Testament and Other Early Christian Literature* by William F. Arndt and F. Wilbur Gingrich (University of Chicago Press and Cambridge University Press, 1957).
AV	The Authorized (King James') Version of the Bible, 1611.
JB	The Jerusalem Bible (Darton, Longman and Todd, 1966).
NASB	The New American Standard Bible (Moody Press, Chicago, 1960).
NEB	The New English Bible (NT 1961, 2nd edition 1970; OT 1970).
NIV	The New International Version of the Bible (Hodder & Stoughton, NT 1974; OT 1979; revised edition 1984).
RSV	The Revised Standard Version of the Bible (NT 1946, 2nd edition 1971; OT 1952).

CONTENTS

Part III Social Issues

Part IV Sexual Issues

Conclusion

PREFACE TO THE
FIRST EDITION (1984)

One of the most notable features of the worldwide evangelical movement during the last ten to fifteen years has been the recovery of our temporarily mislaid social conscience. For approximately fifty years (c. 1920–70) evangelical Christians were preoccupied with the task of defending the historic biblical faith against the attacks of theological liberalism, and reacting against its 'social gospel'. But now we are convinced that God has given us social as well as evangelistic responsibilities in his world. Yet the half-century of neglect has put us far behind in this area. We have a long way to catch up.

This book is my own contribution to the catching up process. Its source may be traced to 1978/9, when Michael Baughen, now Bishop of Chester, but then Rector of All Souls Church, invited me to preach a series of occasional sermons under the title *Issues Facing Britain Today*. Several of these chapters began their life in the pulpit, and subsequently grew into lectures at the London Institute for Contemporary Christianity, whose *raison d'être* is to help people develop a Christian perspective on the complexities of the modern world.

I confess that several times in the course of writing I have been tempted to give up. I have felt now foolish and now presumptuous to attempt such an undertaking. For I am in no sense a specialist in moral theology or social ethics, and I have no particular expertise or experience in some of the fields into which I trespass. Moreover, each topic is complex, has attracted an extensive literature, only some of which I have been able to read, and is potentially divisive, even in a few cases explosive. Yet I have persevered, mainly because what I am venturing to offer the public is not a polished professional piece but the rough-hewn amateur work of an ordinary Christian who is struggling to think Christianly, that is, to apply the biblical revelation to the pressing issues of the day.

For this is my concern. I begin with a commitment to the Bible as 'God's Word written', which is how it is described in the Anglican Articles and has been received by nearly all churches until comparatively recent times. Such is the basic presupposition of this book; it is not part of my present purpose to argue it. But we Christians have a second commitment, namely to the world in which God has placed us. And our two commitments often seem to be in conflict. Being a collection of documents which relate to particular and distant events, the Bible has an archaic feel. It seems incompatible with our western culture, with its space probes and micro-processors. Like every other Christian I feel myself caught in the painful tension between these two worlds. They are centuries apart. Yet I have sought to resist the temptation to withdraw from either world by capitulation to the other.

Some Christians, anxious above all to be faithful to the revelation of God without compromise, ignore the challenges of the modern world and live in the past. Others, anxious to respond to the world around them, trim and twist God's revelation in their search for relevance. I have struggled to avoid both traps. For the Christian is at liberty to surrender neither to antiquity nor to modernity. Instead, I have sought with integrity to submit to the revelation of yesterday within the realities of today. It is not easy to combine loyalty to the past with sensitivity to the present. Yet this is our Christian calling: to live under the Word in the world.

Many people have helped me develop my thinking. I thank the 'apostolic succession' of my Study Assistants – Roy McCloughry, Tom Cooper, Mark Labberton, Steve Ingraham and Bob Wismer – who have compiled bibliographies, assembled groups for the discussion of sermon topics, gathered information and checked references. Bob Wismer has been specially helpful in the final stages, reading the MS twice and making valuable suggestions. So has Frances Whitehead, my secretary for 28 years. She and Vivienne Curry typed the MS. Steve Andrews, my present study assistant, has been meticulous in proof correcting. I also thank friends who have read different chapters and given me the benefit of their comments – Oliver Barclay, Raymond Johnston, John Gladwin, Mark

Stephens, Roy McCloughry, Myra Chave-Jones and my colleagues at the London Institute, Andrew Kirk (Associate Director) and Martyn Eden (Dean). I am particularly grateful to Jim Houston, founding Principal and now Chancellor of Regent College, Vancouver, whose vision of the need for Christians to have an integrated world view has stimulated both my own thinking and the founding of the London Institute.

J S
June 1984

PREFACE TO THE
SECOND EDITION (1990)

Six years have passed since the publication of *Issues Facing Christians Today*, and in this brief period the world has witnessed many changes. Detente between the superpowers has dawned, and disarmament has begun. Freedom and democracy, undreamed of only a year ago, have taken root in Eastern Europe and the Soviet Union, even while brutal repression has trampled on these tender plants in China. Old debates (like the nuclear threat) have moved on, while new debates (like the AIDS epidemic) have arisen.

Hence the need for a second and revised edition of this book. The statistics on armaments, human rights violations, other religions, unemployment, divorce and abortion have all been brought up to date. It has been necessary to read and reflect on newly published books on almost every issue. A number of these have been written by evangelical authors, which is an encouraging sign of our developing social conscience. Another sign of this is the merger of the London Institute for Contemporary Christianity with the Shaftesbury Project for Christian Involvement in Society in order to form 'Christian Impact', and so combine research, education and thought with action. Yet other signs are the stronger commitment to social action explicit in the Manila Manifesto, which was adopted at the conclusion of the second 'Lausanne' Congress on World Evangelization (1989), and the 'Salt and Light' project sponsored by the British Evangelical Alliance.

This second edition of *Issues Facing Christians Today* also incorporates new material on many topics – on the rapid growth of the green movement and its warnings about ozone layer depletion and the greenhouse effect; on the Brundtland Report, *Our Common*

Future, and its concept of 'sustainable development'; on the burdens of debt borne by many nuclear families in the West and – to a crippling degree – by Third World countries; on three important Christian documents recently published in South Africa; on further thinking by evangelical Christians about the role, ministry and leadership of women; on human fertilization and modern reproductive technologies; on the theological, moral, pastoral and educational aspects of AIDS; and on the effectiveness of Christian social protest and witness.

I express my cordial thanks to Toby Howarth and Todd Shy, my former and present study assistants, for painstakingly rereading the whole book and making numerous suggestions; to Marty Eden, Elaine Storkey, Roy McCloughry, Maurice Hobbs, John Wyatt and Stephen Rand for perusing individual sections or chapters and proposing changes; and to Frances Whitehead for much retyping and some really skilful 'scissor-and-paste' editing.

In conclusion, I feel the need to restate what I wrote in the Preface to the first edition, namely that *Issues* represents the struggles of a person who lays no claim to infallibility, who is anxious to go on increasing his Christian integrity over against the pressures of a largely secular society, and who to that end is continuously seeking fresh light from Scripture.

J S
January 1990

PREFACE TO THE
THIRD EDITION (1999)

Issues Facing Christians Today was first published in 1984, and its second, updated edition appeared in 1990. Since then eight more years have passed, and a third, revised edition is already overdue. It is extraordinary that in the topic of every chapter the debate has moved on, and in some cases the situation has changed significantly.

With the collapse of Euro-Marxism, following the demolition of the Berlin Wall, much of the map of Europe has had to be redrawn. The end of the cold war has made possible some international disarmament treaties. The 'Earth Summit' at Rio in 1992 both mirrored and stimulated growing public alarm over ozone layer depletion and global warming. New policies of development and proposals for debt cancellation have brought realistic hope to the poorest nations. The conciliatory leadership of President Mandela and the dismantling of apartheid shine brightly against the increase of racially motivated violence and the re-emergence of nationalism in Europe. Christians are also disturbed by the influences which undermine marriage and the family (especially cohabitation and same-sex partnerships) and which challenge the sanctity of human life (especially abortion and euthanasia).

Ten consultants, each a specialist in his own field, have been kind enough to read the chapter of their expertise and then to recommend changes to make, books to read and new issues to consider. I am most grateful for their criticisms and suggestions. They are (in alphabetical order) Sir Fred Catherwood, Martyn Eden, Dr David Green, Gary Haugen, Sir John Houghton, Roy McCloughry, Dr Alan Storkey, Pradip Sudra, Dr Neil Summerton and Professor John Wyatt.

I reserve my special gratitude for John Yates, my current study assistant. Not only has he given himself the chore of reading the book's second edition several times over, made his own insightful suggestions, and updated the statistics, but he has also followed up our consultants' proposals, done some redrafting himself and advised me which books and articles I needed to read and ponder myself. I cannot speak too highly of his conscientious work.

J S

Autumn 1998

PART I

CHRISTIANS IN A NON-CHRISTIAN SOCIETY

Chapter 1

INVOLVEMENT: IS IT OUR CONCERN?

It is exceedingly strange that any followers of Jesus Christ should ever have needed to ask whether social involvement was their concern, and that controversy should have blown up over the relationship between evangelism and social responsibility. For it is evident that in his public ministry Jesus both 'went about ... teaching ... and preaching' (Matthew 4:23; 9:35 RSV) and 'went about doing good and healing' (Acts 10:38 RSV). In consequence, 'evangelism and social concern have been intimately related to one another throughout the history of the Church ... Christian people have often engaged in both activities quite unselfconsciously, without feeling any need to define what they were doing or why.'[1]

The evangelical heritage of social concern[2]

There were some remarkable examples of this in eighteenth-century Europe and America. The Evangelical Revival, which stirred both continents, is not to be thought of only in terms of the preaching of the gospel and the converting of sinners to Christ; it also led to widespread philanthropy, and profoundly affected society on both sides of the Atlantic. John Wesley remains the most striking instance. He is mainly remembered as the itinerant evangelist and open-air preacher. And so he was. But the gospel he preached inspired people to take up social causes in the name of Christ. Historians have attributed to Wesley's influence rather than to any other the fact that Britain was spared the horrors of a bloody revolution like France's.[3]

The change which came over Britain during this period was well documented in J. Wesley Bready's remarkable book, *England Before and After Wesley*, subtitled 'The Evangelical Revival and Social Reform'. His research forced him to conclude that 'the true nursing-mother of the spirit and character values that have created and sustained Free Institutions throughout the English-speaking world', indeed 'the moral watershed of Anglo-Saxon history', was 'the much-neglected and oft-lampooned Evangelical Revival'.[4]

Bready described 'the deep savagery of much of the 18th century',[5] which was characterized by 'the wanton torture of animals for sport, the bestial drunkenness of the populace, the inhuman traffic in African negroes, the kidnapping of fellow-countrymen for exportation and sale as slaves, the mortality of parish children, the universal gambling obsession, the savagery of the prison system and penal code, the welter of immorality, the prostitution of the theatre, the growing prevalence of lawlessness, superstition and lewdness; the political bribery and corruption, the ecclesiastical arrogance and truculence, the shallow pretensions of Deism, the insincerity and debasement rampant in Church and State – such manifestations suggest that the British people were then perhaps as deeply degraded and debauched as any people in Christendom.'[6]

But then things began to change. And in the nineteenth century slavery and the slave trade were abolished, the prison system was humanized, conditions in factory and mine were improved, education became available to the poor, trades unions began, etc., etc.

'Whence, then, this pronounced humanity? – this passion for social justice, and sensitivity to human wrongs? There is but one answer commensurate with stubborn historical truth. It derived from a new social conscience. And if that social conscience, admittedly, was the offspring of more than one progenitor, it nonetheless was mothered and nurtured by the Evangelical Revival of vital, practical Christianity – a revival which illumined the central postulates of the New Testament ethic, which made real the Fatherhood of God and the Brotherhood of men, which pointed the priority of personality over property, and which directed heart, soul and mind, towards the establishment of the Kingdom of Righteousness on earth.'[7]

The Evangelical Revival 'did more to transfigure the moral character of the general populace, than any other movement British history can record'.[8] For Wesley was both a preacher of the gospel and a prophet of social righteousness. He was 'the man who restored to a nation its soul'.[9]

The evangelical leaders of the next generation were committed with equal enthusiasm to evangelism and social action. The most famous among them were Granville Sharp, Thomas Clarkson, James Stephen, Zachary Macaulay, Charles Grant, John Shore (Lord Teignmouth), Thomas Babington, Henry Thornton, and of course their guiding light, William Wilberforce. Because several of them lived in Clapham, at that time a village three miles south of London, and belonged to Clapham Parish Church, whose Rector John Venn was one of them, they came to be known as 'the Clapham Sect', although in Parliament and in the press they were mocked as 'the Saints'.

It was their concern over the plight of the African slaves which first brought them together. Three days before his death in 1791, John Wesley wrote to Wilberforce to assure him that God had raised him up for his 'glorious enterprise' and to urge him not to be weary of welldoing. It is largely to the Clapham Sect (under Wilberforce's leadership) that the credit belongs for the first settlement of freed slaves in Sierra Leone (1787), the abolition of the trade (1807), the registration of slaves in the colonies (1820), which put an end to slave smuggling, and finally their emancipation (1833). It is true that 'the Saints' were wealthy aristocrats, who shared some of the social blindspots of their time, but they were extremely generous in their philanthropy, and the range of their concerns was extraordinary. In addition to the slavery question, they involved themselves in penal and parliamentary reform, popular education (Sunday Schools, tracts and the *Christian Observer* newspaper), Britain's obligation to her colonies (especially India), the spread of the gospel (they were instrumental in the founding of both the Bible Society and the Church Missionary Society), and factory legislation. They also campaigned against duelling, gambling, drunkenness, immorality and cruel animal sports. And throughout they were directed and motivated by their strong evangelical faith. Ernest Marshall Howse has written of them: 'This group of Clapham friends gradually became knit together in an astonishing intimacy and solidarity. They planned and laboured like a committee that never was dissolved. At the Clapham mansions they congregated by common impulse in what they chose to call their "Cabinet Councils" wherein they discussed the wrongs and injustices which were a reproach to their country, and the battles which would need to be fought to establish righteousness. And thereafter, in

Parliament and out, they moved as one body, delegating to each man the work he could do best, that the common principles might be maintained and their common purposes be realized.'[10]

Reginald Coupland in his biography of Wilberforce justly commented: 'It was, indeed, a unique phenomenon – this brotherhood of Christian politicians. There has never been anything like it since in British public life.'[11]

Anthony Ashley Cooper was elected to the British Parliament in 1826, aged 25. First in the House of Commons, and then in the House of Lords as the seventh Earl of Shaftesbury, he concerned himself successively with the plight of lunatics, child workers in the factories and mills, 'climbing boys' or chimney sweeps, women and children in the mines, and the children of the slums, more than 30,000 of whom in London were without a home, and more than a million of whom in the whole country were without schooling. His biographer Georgina Battiscombe, who is often sharply critical of him, nevertheless concludes her account of his life with this generous tribute: 'No man has in fact ever done more to lessen the extent of human misery, or to add to the sum total of human happiness.'[12] And he himself felt able to claim that 'most of the great philanthropic movements of the century have sprung from the Evangelicals.'[13]

The same story can be told of the United States in the nineteenth century. Social involvement was both the child of evangelical religion and the twin sister of evangelism. This is clearly seen in Charles G. Finney, who is best known as the lawyer turned evangelist and author of *Lectures on Revivals of Religion* (1835). Through his preaching of the gospel large numbers were brought to faith in Christ. What is not so well known is that he was concerned for 'reforms' as well as 'revivals'. He was convinced, as Donald W. Dayton has shown in his *Discovering an Evangelical Heritage*, both that the gospel 'releases a mighty impulse toward social reform' and that the Church's neglect of social reform grieved the Holy Spirit and hindered revival. It is astonishing to read Finney's statement in his 23rd Lecture on Revival that 'the great business of the Church is to reform the world ... The Church of Christ was originally organized to be a body of reformers. The very profession of Christianity implies the profession and virtually an oath to do all that can be done for the universal reformation of the world.'[14]

It is hardly surprising to learn, therefore, that through Finney's evangelism God raised up 'an army of young converts who became the troops of the reform movement of his age'. In particular, 'the anti-slavery forces ... were drawn largely from the converts of Finney's revivals.' Chief among these was Theodore Weld, who gave his whole life to the anti-slavery struggle. He was converted under Finney's ministry and worked for a time as his assistant.[15] Not that Weld was the American equivalent of Wilberforce, however, for he was not a parliamentarian. In fact, 'the agitation [that is, the anti-slavery agitation in America] was accomplished not so much by heroes of reform as by very numerous obscure persons, prompted by an impulse religious in character and evangelical in spirit, which began the Great Revival of 1830.'[16]

The nineteenth century is known also for the enormous expansion of Christian missions which it witnessed. It must not be imagined, however, that the missionaries concentrated exclusively on preaching, or indeed that their social concern was restricted to aid and relief, to the neglect of development and even socio-political activity. It is doubtful if these distinctions have ever been neatly drawn in practice. The American missiologist Dr R. Pierce Beaver has written:

Social action in mission can be traced from the time of the apostles ... Concern was never limited to relief. The itinerating missionary carried with him a bag of medicines, new or better seeds and plants, and improved livestock. Nevius introduced the modern orchard industry into Shantung. The Basel missionaries revolutionized the economy of Ghana by introducing coffee and cocoa grown by families and individuals on their own land. James McKean transformed the life of Northern Thailand by eliminating its three major curses – smallpox, malaria, and leprosy. Wells and pure water often came through the help of missionaries. Industrial schools were stressed through the nineteenth century, and industries were established. In addition, the missionaries were constantly the protectors of the native peoples against exploitation and injustice by government and commercial companies ... They played a very important part in the abolishing of forced labour in the Congo. They resisted blackbirding in the South Pacific. They fought fiercely for human rights in combating opium, foot-binding, and exposure of girl babies in China. They waged war against widow-burning, infanticide, and temple prostitution in India, and above all broke the social and economic slavery of the caste system for the low and outcaste peoples.[17]

Reasons for 'The Great Reversal'

It seems, therefore, to be an established fact that at least during the nineteenth century, not only in Britain and America but also through the agency of missionaries in Africa and Asia, the gospel of Jesus Christ produced the good fruit of social reform. But then something happened, especially among evangelical Christians. At some point during the first 30 years of the twentieth century, and especially during the decade following World War I, a major shift took place which the American historian Timothy L. Smith has termed 'The Great Reversal', and which David O. Moberg investigates in his book with that title.[18] Although Dr Moberg does not attempt a thorough analysis of the origins of the evangelical renunciation of social responsibility, they seem to have included the following.

The first cause was the fight against theological liberalism, which at the turn of the century was seeping into the churches of Europe and America. Michael Cassidy has called this 'The Great Betrayal' (the liberal neglect of the gospel); it occasioned 'The Great Reversal' (the evangelical neglect of social responsibility). For evangelicals felt they had their backs to the wall.[19] Understandably, they became preoccupied with the defence and proclamation of the gospel, for nobody else seemed to be championing historic biblical Christianity. This was the period (actually 1910–15) when the series of 12 small books entitled *The Fundamentals* was published in the United States, from which the term 'fundamentalism' arose. When evangelicals were busy seeking to vindicate the fundamentals of the faith, they felt they had no time for social concerns.

Secondly, evangelicals reacted against the so-called 'social gospel' which theological liberals were developing at this time. Its most popular spokesman was Walter Rauschenbusch, who was Professor of Church History at Rochester Seminary, New York, from 1897 to 1917. He had come face to face with oppressive poverty during his 12-year Baptist pastorate in New York City (1886–97), and this experience shaped his message. In his first book, *Christianity and the Social Crisis* (1907),[20] after tracing the social compassion of the Hebrew prophets, Jesus and the early Church, he criticized capitalism and advocated a simple kind of 'communism' or Christian socialism.[21] He also contrasted 'the old evangel of the saved soul' with 'the new evangel of the Kingdom of God'.[22] 'It is not a matter of getting individuals into heaven,' he wrote, 'but of transforming the life on earth into the harmony of heaven.'[23] Again, the 'essential purpose of Christianity' is to 'transform human society into the Kingdom of God by regenerating all human relationships.'[24] These quotations are enough to disclose his two errors, which led evangelicals to condemn the 'social gospel' and so hindered the development of an evangelical social programme. First, he identified the Kingdom of God with 'a reconstruction of society on a Christian basis'.[25] Secondly, he implied that human beings can establish the divine Kingdom by themselves (whereas Jesus always spoke of it as a gift of God). Though he said he cherished 'no Utopian delusion',[26] he nevertheless believed that 'it rests upon us to decide if a new era is to dawn in the transformation of the world into the Kingdom of God.'[27] The 'common aim' of church and state, he affirmed, 'is to transform humanity into the Kingdom of God'.[28]

It will be clear from this unguarded language that *Christianity and the Social Crisis* was not a work of serious theology. Nor was Rauschenbusch's second book, with its misleading title, *Christianizing the Social Order* (1912). His third book gave the game away, however: *A Theology for the Social Gospel* (1917).[29] He began it with these ingenious words: 'We have a social gospel. We need a systematic theology large enough to match it and vital enough to back it.' Indeed a 'readjustment and expansion of theology' is necessary in order to 'furnish an adequate intellectual basis for the social gospel'.[30] Thus Rauschenbusch betrayed himself. First, we formulate our social gospel, and only then do we hunt round for an intellectual or theological justification for it! He finds it in the Kingdom of God. 'This doctrine is itself the social gospel.'[31] For 'the Kingdom of God is humanity organized according to the will of God.'[32] 'The Kingdom of God is the Christian transfiguration of the social order.'[33]

But the Kingdom of God is not Christianized society. It is the divine rule in the lives of those who acknowledge Christ. It has to be 'received', 'entered' or 'inherited', he said, by humble and penitent faith in him. And without a new birth it is impossible to see it, let alone enter it. Those who do receive it like a child, however, find themselves members of the new community of the Messiah, which is called to exhibit the ideals of his rule in the world and so to present the world with an alternative social reality. This social challenge of the gospel of the Kingdom is quite different from the 'social gospel'. When Rauschenbusch politicized the Kingdom of God, it is understandable (if regrettable) that, in reaction to him, evangelicals concentrated on evangelism and personal philanthropy, and steered clear of socio-political action.

The third reason for the evangelical neglect of social responsibility was the widespread disillusion and pessimism which followed World War I, because of its exposure of human evil. Earlier social programmes had failed. Human beings and human society appeared to be irreformable. Attempts at reform were useless. To be sure, because of the biblical doctrines of original sin and human depravity, evangelicals should not have been taken by surprise. But between the wars there was no evangelical leader to articulate the providence and common grace of God as grounds for persevering hope. Historic reformed Christianity was in eclipse.

Fourthly, there was the spread (specially through J.N. Darby's teaching and its popularization in the Scofield Bible) of the premillennial scheme. This portrays the present evil world as beyond improvement or redemption, and predicts instead that it will deteriorate steadily until the coming of Jesus, who will then set up his millennial reign on earth. If the world is getting worse, and if only Jesus at his coming will put it right, the argument runs, there seems no point in trying to reform it meanwhile. 'Adopting political programs is "like cleaning the staterooms on the Titanic after it has hit the iceberg ... It is far more important simply to preach the Gospel and to rescue souls for the next life".'[34]

The fifth reason for evangelical alienation from social concern was probably the spread of Christianity among middle-class people, who tended to dilute it by identifying it with their own culture. This is without a doubt one of the factors underlying the American sociological findings reported by Milton Rokeach in 1969 and summarized by David O. Moberg. These were highly critical of the negative social influences of organized religion.

> The general picture that emerges from the results presented ... is that those who place a high value on *salvation* are conservative, anxious to maintain the *status quo*, and unsympathetic or indifferent to the plight of the black and the poor ... Considered all together, the data suggest a portrait of the religious-minded as a person having a self-centred preoccupation with saving his own soul, an other-worldly orientation, coupled with an indifference toward or even a tacit endorsement of a social system that would perpetuate social inequality and injustice.

David Moberg tells how this report brought a storm of protest on the ground that the research methodology was faulty, but he adds that altogether to ignore these findings and conclusions 'would be a serious mistake.'[35] Although I have been able earlier to mention some fine examples of social action in the eighteenth and nineteenth centuries, there have certainly been other situations in which the Church has acquiesced in oppression and exploitation, and has taken no action against these evils, nor even protested against them.

This 'Great Reversal' is explicable for these five reasons. We do not blame our evangelical forebears; in their place we would probably have reacted to contemporary pressures as they did. Not that all evangelicals mislaid their social conscience at the beginning of the twentieth century and between the wars. Some soldiered on, deeply involved in social as well as evengelical ministries, and thus retained this indispensable outworking of the gospel, without which evangelicalism loses part of its authenticity. But most turned away. Then during the 1960s, the decade of protest, when young people were rebelling against the materialism, superficiality and hypocrisy of the adult world they had inherited, the evangelical mainstream recovered its morale, and the process of 'Reversing the Great Reversal' (as David Moberg entitles his final chapter) got under way.

Probably the first voice to recall the evangelical constituency to its social responsibilities was that of the American Christian scholar Carl F.H. Henry, the founding editor of *Christianity Today*, in his book, *The Uneasy Conscience of Modern Fundamentalism* (1947). Not many seemed to listen. But gradually the message caught on. And in 1966, at the conclusion of an American conference on world missions, the participants unanimously adopted the 'Wheaton Declaration' which firmly bracketed 'the primacy of preaching the gospel to every creature' and 'a verbal witness to Jesus Christ' with 'evangelical social action', and urged 'all evangelicals to stand openly and firmly for racial equality, human freedom, and all forms of social justice throughout the world'.

In Britain in the sixties a number of evangelical leaders began to grapple with the social application of the gospel. Most of them were laymen in professional and business life, and prominent among them were George Goyder (*The Responsible Company*, 1961), Fred Catherwood (*The Christian in Industrial Society*, 1964) and Professor Norman Anderson (*Into the World*, 1968). This incipient groundswell of social concern found public expression at the first

National Evangelical Anglican Congress at Keele University in 1967. There Anglican evangelicals publicly repented of their tendency to withdraw from both the secular world and the wider Church, and committed themselves to conscientious involvement in both. As for the scope of mission, the Report produced by the Congress said that 'evangelism and compassionate service belong together in the mission of God.'[36]

The turning-point for the worldwide evangelical constituency was doubtless the International Congress on World Evangelization held in July 1974 at Lausanne, Switzerland. Some 2,700 participants gathered from more than 150 nations under the slogan 'Let the Earth Hear His Voice', and at the conclusion of the congress endorsed the Lausanne Covenant. After three introductory sections on the purpose of God, the authority of the Bible, and the uniqueness of Christ, its fourth is entitled, 'The Nature of Evangelism' and its fifth 'Christian Social Responsibility'. The latter declares that 'evangelism and socio-political involvement are both part of our Christian duty'. But the two paragraphs stand side by side in the Covenant, with no attempt to relate them, except for the statement in paragraph 6 that 'in the church's mission of sacrificial service evangelism is primary.'

During the years which followed the Lausanne Congress, there was a certain amount of tension within the evangelical movement, as some emphasized evangelism, others social activity, and all of us wondered how according to Scripture we should spell out the relationship between the two. So in June 1982, under the joint sponsorship of the Lausanne Committee and the World Evangelical Fellowship, the 'Consultation on the Relationship between Evangelism and Social Responsibility' (CRESR) was held in Grand Rapids, and issued its report entitled *Evangelism and Social Responsibility: An Evangelical Commitment*. Although of course we did not see eye to eye on every point, God led us to a remarkable degree of consensus. Social activity was said to be both a consequence of and a bridge to evangelism, and indeed the two were declared to be partners. Besides, they are united by the gospel. 'For the gospel is the root, of which both evangelism and social responsibility are the fruits.'[37] The Report also has a chapter on 'History and Eschatology' and a final more practical chapter entitled 'Guidelines for Action'.

A significant consultation was held in Britain in November 1988 entitled 'Salt and Light'. Jointly sponsored by the Evangelical

Alliance, Tearfund and the Evangelical Missionary Alliance, it brought over 300 people together from a wide variety of backgrounds in church, culture and experience. Twenty-one specialist groups reviewed the major contemporary issues of social ethics. In spite of participants' different theological and political perspectives, they expressed a common commitment to the integration of evangelistic and social concerns and to promoting this holistic vision among Christians.

Eight years later, in November 1996, the National Assembly of Evangelicals brought 2,700 evangelical leaders together. The Bournemouth Declaration, endorsed at its conclusion, included the following unambiguous statements: 'We recognize that no area of life is outside God's sovereign rule. We take the incarnation and transforming work of Christ as our model for engagement. We affirm our commitment to releasing Christian people for involvement at all levels of society …'. Moreover, these are no mere pious aspirations. For example, 'UK Action' (a joint initiative of Tearfund and the Evangelical Alliance) is enabling an increasing number of local British churches to develop holistic ministries among the urban poor. In order to encourage more informed prayer and political action, the Evangelical Alliance now produces *Westminster Watch*, a bulletin of news and Christian comment from the Palace of Westminster. And a number of evangelical Christian leaders and organizations were involved in the founding in 1990 of 'The Movement for Christian Democracy'. Its ideals are given a fine biblical expression in its *Westminster Declaration*. Its purpose is 'to further Christian understanding of social and political matters, to initiate appropriate forms of action, to stimulate informed discussion, and to influence policy-making'.

The Church and politics

It will have been noted that the Lausanne Covenant speaks not just of 'social responsibility' but of 'socio-political involvement'. It is the use of the word 'political' which causes red warning lights to flash in the minds of many evangelicals. They have always engaged in humanitarian work, especially in medical and educational programmes; it is political activity of which they have often fought shy. Indeed, opposition to it is much wider than the evangelical constituency. Whenever the Church (or any branch of it) becomes politically embroiled, a howl of protest can be expected from both within its membership and from outside. 'The Church should steer clear of politics,' people cry, and 'Religion and politics don't mix.'

Several different issues are involved in this controversy, and the waters of the debate are muddied by a failure to distinguish between them. The first is the definition of the word 'politics'. The second concerns the relationship between the social and the political, and why they cannot be kept apart. Thirdly, we need to consider the reasons why some people oppose the Church's involvement in politics, and what it is they are trying to safeguard. Then fourthly we need to ask to whom Christian political responsibility belongs.

First, we must define our terms. The words 'politics' and 'political' may be given either a broad or a narrow definition. Broadly speaking, 'politics' denotes the life of the city (*polis*) and the responsibilities of the citizen (*politēs*). It is concerned therefore with the whole of our life in human society. Politics is the art of living together in a community. According to its narrow definition, however, politics is the science of government. It is concerned with the development and adoption of specific policies with a view to their being enshrined in legislation. It is about gaining power for social change.

Once this distinction is clear, we may ask whether Jesus was involved in politics. In the latter and narrower sense, he clearly was not. He never formed a political party, adopted a political programme or organized a political protest. He took no steps to influence the policies of Caesar, Pilate or Herod. On the contrary, he renounced a political career. In the other and broader sense of the word, however, his whole ministry was political. For he had himself come into the world, in order to share in the life of the human community, and he sent his followers into the world to do the same. Moreover, the Kingdom of God he proclaimed and inaugurated was a radically new and different social organization, whose values and standards challenged those of the old and fallen community. In this way his teaching had 'political' implications. It offered an alternative to the *status quo*. His kingship, moreover, was perceived as a challenge to Caesar's, and he was therefore accused of sedition.

Secondly, we need to consider the relation between the 'social' and the 'political', now using this word in its narrower sense. In its final chapter the Grand Rapids Report addressed itself to this question. It distinguished between 'social service' and 'social action', and helpfully drew up the following table:

Social Service

- Relieving human need

- Philanthropic activity
- Seeking to minister to individuals and families
- Works of mercy

Social Action

- Removing the causes of human need
- Political and economic activity
- Seeking to transform the structures of society
- The quest for justice[38]

The Report went on to delineate socio-political action in these terms: 'It looks beyond persons to structures, beyond the rehabilitation of prison inmates to the reform of the prison system, beyond improving factory conditions to securing a more participatory role for the workers, beyond caring for the poor to improving – and when necessary transforming – the economic system (whatever it may be) and the political system (again, whatever it may be), until it facilitates their liberation from poverty and oppression.'[39]

It seems clear, then, that genuine Christian social concern will embrace both social service and social action. It would be very artificial to divorce them. Some cases of need cannot be relieved at all without political action (the harsh treatment of slaves could have been ameliorated, but not slavery itself; it had to be abolished). To go on relieving other needs, though necessary, may condone the situation which causes them. If travellers on the Jerusalem–Jericho road were habitually beaten up, and habitually cared for by Good Samaritans, the need for better laws to eliminate armed robbery might well be overlooked. If road accidents keep occurring at a particular crossroads, it is not more ambulances that are needed but the installation of traffic lights to prevent accidents. It is always good to feed the hungry; it is better if possible to eradicate the causes of hunger. So if we truly love our neighbours, and want to serve them, ✓ our service may oblige us to take (or solicit) political action on their behalf.

Why, then, is there so much hostility to the idea of the Church becoming politically involved? This is our third question. An articulate criticism was made by Dr Edward Norman in his 1978 Reith Lectures, *Christianity and the World Order*.[40] He was not actually denying either that 'biblical teachings have social consequences' ('they obviously do,' he said, p. 74), or that the love of God will involve Christians in 'corporate social and political action' (p. 79). His concern was rather over 'the politicization of Christianity', by which he meant 'the internal transformation of the faith itself, so that it comes to be defined in terms of political values' (p. 2). Dr Norman was surely right that Christianity cannot be reduced to or identified with a political programme. But it seems to me that he overreacted to this tendency and so gave many people the impression that he thought the Church should be entirely apolitical.

Yet the 1978 Reith Lectures contained at least four warnings, to which we will be wise to give heed, albeit critically. I will collate them in my own way:

1. The contemporary Church's political *emphasis*, that is, its frequent preoccupation with political issues, tends to eclipse what should be its central concerns, namely the individual ('personal redemption', p. 78), the inward ('the indwelling Christ', pp. 72–85) and the eternal ('the ethereal qualities of immortality', p. 2). Dr Norman is right that *some* churches have lost these dimensions altogether. Yet in retaining them, the Church must not overlook its corporate, external and temporal responsibilities. Christians are citizens of two kingdoms and have responsibilities in both. To love God with all our being is indeed the 'first and greatest' commandment; but to love our neighbour as ourselves is 'similar'. Each is askew without the other.
2. The contemporary Church's political *opinions* are nothing but 'the moral and political idealism of the surrounding culture' (p. 32), whether this is western bourgeois liberalism or Marxism. All the Church does is 'tag along, offering a religious gloss' to borrowed ideas (p. 4). It conforms, instead of criticizing.
3. The contemporary Church's political *contribution* is amateurish; it lacks the necessary expertise to participate.
4. The contemporary Church's political *expectations* are naive, because it tends to forget human fallibility and sin.

It will be observed that all four criticisms are levelled at the particular behaviour of *some* churches (though Dr Norman tends to generalize), and not at the concept itself that the Christian Church does have socio-political responsibilities.

To whom do these responsibilities belong? That is our fourth and last question. Failure to ask and answer it is one of the main reasons for the current confusion over Christian political involvement. We need to distinguish between Christian individuals, groups and churches. All individual Christians should be politically active in the sense that, as conscientious citizens, they will vote in elections, inform themselves about contemporary issues, share in the public debate, and perhaps write to a newspaper, lobby their member of parliament or take part in a demonstration. Further, some individuals are called by God to give their lives to political service, in either local or national government. Christians who share particular moral and social concerns should be encouraged to form or join groups which will study issues at a deeper level and take appropriate action. In some cases these will be exclusively Christian groups; in others Christians will want to contribute their biblical perspective to mixed groups, whether in a political party, a trade union or a professional association.

Granted the propriety of political thought and action by Christian individuals and groups, however, should the Church as church involve itself in politics? Certainly the Church must teach both the law and the gospel of God. This is the duty of the Church's pastors, teachers and other leaders. And 'when the church concludes that biblical faith or righteousness requires it to take a public stand on some issue, then it must obey God's Word and trust him with the consequences.'[41] Whether we think the Church should go beyond teaching and take corporate political action of some kind is likely to depend on whether we adhere to the Lutheran, Reformed or Anabaptist traditions within Protestantism in relation to church and state. At least we can agree that the Church should not enter this field without the necessary expertise. But when church leaders do their homework thoroughly, and take time and trouble to study a topic together in order to reach a common Christian mind and recommend common Christian action, their informed and united stand is extremely influential.

The biblical basis for social concern

What, then, is the biblical basis for social concern? Why should Christians get involved? In the end there are only two possible attitudes which Christians can adopt towards the world. One is escape and the other engagement. (You could say that there is a third option, namely accommodation. But then Christians become indistinguishable from the world and on that account are no longer able to develop a distinctive attitude to it. They simply become part of it.) 'Escape' means turning our backs on the world in rejection, washing our hands of it (though finding with Pontius Pilate that the responsibility does not come off in the wash), and steeling our hearts against its agonized cries for help. In contrast, 'engagement' means turning our faces towards the world in compassion, getting our hands dirty, sore and worn in its service, and feeling deep within us the stirring of the love of God which cannot be contained.

Too many of us evangelicals either have been, or maybe still are, irresponsible escapists. Fellowship with each other in the Church is much more congenial than service in an apathetic and even hostile environment outside. Of course we make occasional evangelistic raids into enemy territory (that is our evangelical speciality); but then we withdraw again, across the moat, into our Christian castle (the security of our own evangelical fellowship), pull up the draw-bridge, and even close our ears to the pleas of those who batter on the gate. As for social activity, we have tended to say it is largely a waste of time in view of the imminent return of the Lord. After all, when the house is on fire, what is the point of hanging new curtains or rearranging the furniture? The only thing that matters is to rescue the perishing. Thus we have tried to save our conscience with a bogus theology.

'Do you realise,' a student asked Tom Sine during one of his futurology seminars in the United States, 'if we start feeding hungry people, things won't get worse, and if things don't get worse, Jesus won't come?' She was utterly sincere, writes Tom Sine. He continues: 'The response of the (student) ... reflects what I call the Great Escape view of the future ... The irony of (this) approach to the future is that, while it claims to take God seriously, it unwittingly moves God outside history, insisting that even he is powerless "in these last days" ... It unintentionally fashions him into an impotent absentee landlord, who has lost control of his world and of human history ... The Great Escape becomes an incredible copout from all Christ called us to be and to do.'[42]

Instead of seeking to evade our social responsibility, we need to open our ears and listen to the voice of him who calls his people in every age to go out into the lost and lonely world (as he did), in order to live and love, to witness and serve, like him and for him. For that is 'mission'. Mission is our human response to the divine commission. It is a whole Christian lifestyle, including both evange-lism and social responsibility, dominated by the conviction that

Christ sends us out into the world as the Father sent him into the world, and that into the world we must therefore go – to live and work for him.

Still, however, we come back to the question 'why?' Why should Christians get involved in this world and its social problems? In reply, I propose to marshal five great doctrines of the Bible, which all of us already believe in theory, but which we tend to cut and trim in order to make them fit our escapist theology. My plea is that we have the courage to hold these doctrines in their biblical fullness. Any one of them should be sufficient to convince us of our Christian social responsibility; the five together leave us without excuse.

(1) A fuller doctrine of God

To begin with, we need a fuller doctrine of God. For we tend to forget that he is concerned for the whole of humankind and for the whole of human life in all its colour and complexity. These universals have important consequences for our thinking.

First, the living God is *the God of nature as well as of religion*, of the 'secular' as well as of the 'sacred'. In fact Christians are always uncomfortable about this distinction. For everything is 'sacred' in the sense that it belongs to God, and nothing is 'secular' in the sense that God is excluded from it. God made the physical universe, sustains it, and still pronounces it good (Genesis 1:31). Indeed, 'everything God created is good, and nothing is to be rejected if it is received with thanksgiving' (1 Timothy 4:4). We should be more grateful than we usually are for the good gifts of a good Creator – for sex, marriage and the family, for the beauty and order of the natural world, for work and leisure, for friendships and the experience of inter-racial, inter-cultural community, and for music and other kinds of creative art which enrich the quality of human life. Our God is often too small because he is too religious. We imagine that he is chiefly interested in religion – in religious buildings (churches and chapels), religious activities (worship and ritual) and religious books (Bibles and prayer books). Of course he is concerned about these things, but only if they are related to the whole of life. According to the Old Testament prophets and the teaching of Jesus, God is very critical of 'religion', if by that is meant religious services divorced from real life, loving service and the moral obedience of the heart. 'Religion that God our Father accepts as pure and faultless is this: to look after orphans and widows in their distress and to keep oneself from being polluted by the world' (James 1:27). The only value of religious services is that they concentrate into an hour or so of public, vocal, congregational activity the devotion of our whole life. If they do not do this, if instead we say and sing things in church which have no corollary in our everyday life out- side church, at home and work, they are worse than worthless; their hypocrisy is positively nauseating to God.

Secondly, the living God is *the God of the nations as well as of his covenant people.* We Christians sometimes make the mistake which Israel made in the Old Testament when they concentrated exclu- sively on the God of the Covenant, who had chosen them out of all the nations to be the holy nation, and who had pledged himself to them, saying, 'I will be your God and you shall be my people.' To be sure, this was a glorious truth. The notion of 'covenant' is a major biblical theme; the biblical revelation is unintelligible without it. But it is a dangerous half-truth. When Israel overemphasized it, they diminished the living God. They reduced him to the status of a tribal deity, a petty godling. He became Yahweh the god of the Israelites, more or less on a par with Chemosh the god of the Moabites and Milcom the god of the Ammonites. They also forgot the other nations, or simply despised and rejected them.

But the Bible begins with the nations, not Israel; with Adam not Abraham; with the creation not the covenant. And when God chose Israel, he did not lose interest in the nations. Amos bravely gave voice to the word of the Lord: 'Are not you Israelites the same to me as the Cushites [or Ethiopians]? ... Did I not bring Israel up from Egypt, the Philistines from Caphtor [Crete] and the Arameans from Kir?' (Amos 9:7). Similarly, the arrogant emperor Nebuchadnezzar had to learn that 'the Most High is sovereign over the kingdoms of men and gives them to anyone he wishes' (Daniel 4:32). He rules over the nations. Their destiny is under his control. Although Satan is called 'the ruler of this world' and is *de facto* its usurper, God remains the ultimate governor of everything he has made. 'From heaven the Lord looks down and sees all mankind; from his dwelling place he watches all who live on earth – he who forms the hearts of all, who considers everything they do' (Psalm 33:13–15). More than that, he has promised that in blessing Abraham and his posterity he will bless all the families of the earth, and that one day he will restore what the Fall has marred, and bring to perfection all that he has made.

Thirdly, the living God is *the God of justice as well as of justification.*[43] Of course he is the God of justification, the Saviour of sinners, 'the compassionate and gracious God, slow to anger, abounding in love and faithfulness' (Exodus 34:6). But he is also concerned that our community life be characterized by justice.

> He upholds the cause of the oppressed
>   and gives food to the hungry.
> The Lord sets prisoners free,
>   the Lord gives sight to the blind,
> The Lord lifts up those who are bowed down,
>   the Lord loves the righteous.
> The Lord watches over the alien
>   and sustains the fatherless and the widow,
>   but he frustrates the ways of the wicked.
>
> (Psalm 146:7–9)

This does not mean that he does all these things invariably, but rather that this is the kind of God he is.

Moreover, God's concern for justice, although he expects it particularly among his own people, extends beyond them to all people. Social compassion and justice mattered to him in the nations as well as in Israel. There is no clearer evidence of this than in the first two chapters of the prophecy of Amos. Before Amos rebuked Judah for rejecting God's law and turning to idolatry, and Israel for crushing the poor and denying justice to the oppressed (2:4–8), he pronounced God's judgement on all the surrounding nations (1:3–2:3) – on Syria for savage cruelty, on Philistia for capturing whole communities and selling them into slavery, on Tyre for breaking a treaty of brotherhood, on Edom for pitiless hostility to Israel, on Ammon for atrocities in warfare, and on Moab for desecrating the bones of a neighbouring king.

Several of the prophetic books similarly contain a section of oracles about or against the nations. That God is the God of justice, and desires justice in every nation and community is particularly evident from the Book of Nahum, which is a prophecy against Nineveh, the capital and symbol of Assyria. Yahweh's denunciation of Assyria is not just because she was Israel's long-standing enemy (e.g. 1:9ff.; 2:2ff.), but because of her idolatry (1:14) and because she is a 'city of blood, full of lies, full of plunder, never without victims' (3:1). Twice Yahweh says the terrible words, 'I am against you' (2:13; 3:5), and the oracle ends with the rhetorical question (3:19): 'Who has not felt your endless cruelty?'

It is clear from these Old Testament passages that God hates injustice and oppression *everywhere*, and that he loves and promotes justice *everywhere*. Indeed, wherever righteousness is to be found in our fallen world, it is due to the working of his grace. All human beings know this too. For we have an inbuilt sense of justice, to which the child's expostulation, 'It isn't fair!' bears eloquent witness. It is solid evidence of Paul's teaching that God's moral law is written on the human heart (Romans 2:14, 15). Both God's law and God's gospel are for our good.

Here then is the living God of the Bible. His concerns are all-embracing – not only the 'sacred' but the 'secular', not only religion but nature, not only his covenant people but all people, not only justification but social justice in every community, not only his gospel but his law. So we must not attempt to narrow down his interests. Moreover, ours should be as broad as his.

John Gladwin sums up this argument in his *God's People in God's World*: 'It is because this is God's world, and he cared for it to the point of incarnation and crucifixion, that we are inevitably committed to work for God's justice in the face of oppression, for God's truth in the face of lies and deceits, for service in the face of the abuse of power, for love in the face of selfishness, for cooperation in the face of destructive antagonism, and for reconciliation in the face of division and hostility.'[44]

(2) A fuller doctrine of human beings

All our philanthropic work (that is, work inspired by love for human beings) depends on our evaluation of them. The higher our view of their worth, the more we shall want to serve them.

Secular humanists, who are sincere in describing themselves as dedicated to 'the human case and the human cause',[45] sometimes appear more humane than Christians. But if we ask them why they are so committed to humankind, they are likely to reply with Julian Huxley that it is because of the human potential in the future aeons of evolution. 'Thus the development of man's vast potential of realizable possibility,' he wrote, 'provides the prime motive for collective action.'[46] The inadequacy of this as a basis for service is obvious. If the unimpeded progress of evolution were our chief concern, why should we care for the senile, the imbecile, the hardened criminal, the psychopath, the chronically sick, or the starving? Would it not be more prudent to put them to sleep like a well-loved dog, lest they hinder the evolutionary process? Compulsory euthanasia, not compassionate service, would be the logical deduction from the humanists' premise. The fact that they draw back from this abyss indicates that their heart is better than their head, and their philanthropy than their philosophy.

Christian people have a sounder basis for serving their fellow human beings. It is not because of what they may become in the speculative future development of the race, but because of what they already are by divine creation. Human beings are godlike beings made in God's likeness, and possessing unique capacities which distinguish them from the animal creation. True, human beings are fallen, and the divine image is defaced, but despite all contrary appearances it has not been destroyed (Genesis 9:6; James 3:9). It is this which accounts for their unique worth and which has always inspired Christian philanthropy.

For these human but godlike creatures are not just souls (that we should be concerned exclusively for their eternal salvation), not just bodies (that we should care only for their food, clothing, shelter and health), nor just social beings (that we should become entirely preoccupied with their community problems). They are all three. A human being might be defined from a biblical perspective as 'a body-soul-in-a-community'. For that is how God has made us. Therefore if we truly love our neighbours, and because of their worth desire to serve them, we shall be concerned for their total welfare, the wellbeing of their soul, their body and their community. And our concern will lead to practical programmes of evangelism, relief and development. We shall not just prattle and plan and pray, like that country vicar to whom a homeless woman turned for help, and who (doubtless sincerely, and because he was busy and felt helpless) promised to pray for her. She later wrote this poem and handed it a regional officer of *Shelter*.

> I was hungry,
>   and you formed a humanities group to discuss my hunger.
> I was imprisoned,
>   and you crept off quietly to your chapel and prayed for my
>   release.

I was naked,
   and in your mind you debated the morality of my appearance.
I was sick,
   and you knelt and thanked God for your health.
I was homeless,
   and you preached to me of the spiritual shelter of the love of God.
I was lonely,
   and you left me alone to pray for me.
You seem so holy, so close to God
   but I am still very hungry – and lonely – and cold.

Motivated by love for human beings in need, the early Christians went everywhere preaching the Word of God, because nothing has such a humanizing influence as the gospel. Later they founded schools, hospitals, and refuges for the outcast. Later still they abolished the slave trade and freed the slaves, and they improved the conditions of workers in mills and mines, and of prisoners in jails. They protected children from commercial exploitation in the factories of the West and from ritual prostitution in the temples of the East. Today they bring leprosy sufferers both the compassion of Jesus and modern methods of reconstructive surgery and rehabilitation. They care for the blind and the deaf, the orphaned and the widowed, the sick and the dying. They get alongside junkies, and stay alongside them during the traumatic period of withdrawal. They set themselves against racism and political oppression. They get involved in the inner city, the slums and the ghettoes, and raise their protest against the inhuman conditions in which so many are doomed to live. They seek in whatever way they can to express their solidarity with the poor and the hungry, the deprived and the disadvantaged. I am not claiming that all Christians at all times have given their lives in such service. But a sufficiently large number have done so to make their record noteworthy. Why have they done it? Because of the Christian doctrine of man, male and female, all made in the image of God, though all also fallen. Because people matter. Because every man, woman and child has an intrinsic, inalienable value as a human being. Once we see this, we shall both set ourselves to liberate people from everything dehumanizing and count it a privilege to serve them, to do everything in our power to make human life more human.

The film *The Elephant Man* made widely known the extraordinary story with which every English person was familiar at the end of the nineteenth century. It was in 1884 that Frederick Treves, a young surgeon and lecturer in anatomy at the London Hospital, found the Elephant Man in a rented shop opposite the hospital entrance. When Treves first saw his hunched-up form, he thought him 'the embodiment of loneliness'. He later described him as 'the most disgusting specimen of humanity' he had ever seen. He had an 'enormous misshapen head', with a huge bony mass projecting from his brow, and another from his upper jaw which gave him an elephantine appearance. Spongy, evil-smelling skin, like fungus or brown cauliflower, hung in bags from his back, his chest, the back of his head and his right arm. His legs were deformed, his feet bulbous, and he had hip disease. His face was expressionless, and his speech spluttering, almost unintelligible. His left arm and hand, however, were as shapely and delicate as a young woman's.

To add to his suffering, he was treated like an animal, hawked from fair to fair, and exhibited to the curious for twopence a look. Treves wrote: 'He was shunned like a leper, housed like a wild beast, and got his only view of the world from a peephole in a showman's cart.' He received less kindness than a dog, and, terrified of staring eyes, he would creep into a dark corner to hide.

When he was abandoned by the circus showman, Treves had him accommodated and cared for in a room at the back of the London Hospital where three and half years later he died in his sleep, a few days after he had received his Easter Day Communion.

Treves had imagined that he was an imbecile, probably from birth. But in hospital he discovered that he was a human being, Joseph Merrick by name, in his early twenties, highly intelligent, a voracious reader, with a passion for conversation, an acute sensibility and a romantic imagination. He was also a 'gentle, affectionate and lovable creature'.

When the first woman visited Joseph Merrick, gave him a smile and a greeting, and actually shook him by the hand, he broke down into uncontrollable sobbing. But from that day his transformation began. He became a celebrity, and many notable people visited him. Gradually he changed 'from a hunted thing into a man', wrote Treves. But actually he had always been a man. Treves may never have articulated the Christian doctrine of human beings made in the image of God. Nevertheless, it was his remarkable respect for Joseph Merrick which enabled him to lift up his poor misshapen head, and gain some measure of self-respect before he died.[47]

(3) A fuller doctrine of Christ

There have been many different reinterpretations and reconstructions of Jesus. Indeed, it is right that every generation of Christians should seek to understand and to present him in terms appropriate to their own age and culture. So we have had Jesus the ascetic, the sufferer, the monarch, the gentleman, the clown, the superstar, the capitalist, the socialist, the revolutionary, the guerrilla, the wonder drug. Several of these portraits are mutually contradictory, of course, and others have little or no historical warrant.

We need then to recover an authentic picture of him whom the Lausanne Covenant calls 'the historical, biblical Christ' (para. 4). We need to see him in his paradoxical fullness – his sufferings and glory, his servanthood and lordship, his lowly Incarnation and cosmic reign. It is perhaps the Incarnation which we evangelicals have tended to neglect most, in both its theological significance and its practical implications.

The Son of God did not stay in the safe immunity of his heaven. He emptied himself of his glory and humbled himself to serve. He became little, weak and vulnerable. He entered into our pain, our alienation and temptations. He not only proclaimed the good news of the Kingdom of God, but demonstrated its arrival by healing the sick, feeding the hungry, forgiving the sinful, befriending the dropout and raising the dead. He had not come to be served, he said, but to serve and to give his life as a ransom price for the release of others. So he allowed himself to become a victim of gross injustice in the courts, and as they crucified him he prayed for his enemies. Then in the awful God-forsaken darkness he bore our sins in his own innocent person.

Should not this vision of Christ affect our understanding of his commission, 'As the Father has sent me, I am sending you' (John 20:21)? For if the Christian mission is to be modelled on Christ's mission, it will surely involve for us, as it did for him, an entering into other people's worlds. In evangelism it will mean entering their thought world, and the world of their tragedy and lostness, in order to share Christ with them where they are. In social activity it will mean a willingness to renounce the comfort and security of our own cultural background in order to give ourselves in service to people of another culture, whose needs we may never before have known or experienced. Incarnational mission, whether evangelistic or social or both, necessitates a costly identification with people in their actual situations. Jesus of Nazareth was moved with compassion by the sight of needy human beings, whether sick or bereaved, hungry, harassed or helpless; should not his people's compassion be aroused by the same sights?

Leonidas Proaño was formerly Roman Catholic bishop of Riobamba, about a hundred miles south of Quito, Ecuador. Basing his thinking on the Bible, he was strongly committed to social justice in his country, not least for the Indians whose culture he wanted to see preserved against those who were threatening to erode and even destroy it. Although he refused to identify himself with Marxism, and was in fact not a Marxist, he was critical – indeed defiant – of the political and ecclesiastical systems in his country. He opposed feudalism and the oppressive power of the wealthy landowners. It is perhaps not surprising that he was threatened with assassination. At all events, after the overthrow and death in 1973 of President Salvador Allende of Chile, Bishop Proaño preached at a mass for Marxist students in Quito. He portrayed Jesus as the radical he was, the critic of the establishment, the champion of the downtrodden, the lover of the poor, who not only preached the gospel but also gave compassionate service to the needy. After the mass there was a question-time, during which some students said: 'If we had known *this* Jesus, we would never have become Marxists.'

Which Jesus do we believe in? And which Jesus do we preach? Is it possible that in some parts of the Church such a false Jesus ('another Jesus' – 2 Corinthians 11:4) is being presented to the young people, that we are repelling them from him and driving them into the arms of Karl Marx instead?

(4) A fuller doctrine of salvation

There is a constant tendency in the Church to trivialize the nature of salvation, as if it meant no more than a self-reformation, or the forgiveness of our sins, or a personal passport to paradise, or a private mystical experience without social or moral consequences. It is urgent that we rescue salvation from these caricatures and recover the doctrine in its biblical fullness. For salvation is a radical transformation in three phases, beginning at our conversion, continuing throughout our earthly life and brought to perfection when Christ comes. In particular, we must overcome the temptation to separate truths which belong together.

First, *we must not separate salvation from the Kingdom of God*. For in the Bible these two expressions are virtual synonyms, alternative models to describe the same work of God. According to Isaiah 52:7 those who preach good news of peace are also those 'who proclaim salvation, who say to Zion, "Your God reigns!" ' That is, where God reigns, he saves. Salvation is the blessing of his rule. Again, when Jesus said to his disciples, 'How hard it is to enter the kingdom of God,' it seems to have been natural for them to respond with the question, 'Who then can be saved?' (Mark 10:24–6). They evidently equated entering the Kingdom with being saved.

Once this identification has been made, salvation takes on a broader aspect. For the Kingdom of God is God's dynamic rule, breaking into human history through Jesus, confronting, combating and overcoming evil, spreading the wholeness of personal and communal wellbeing, taking possession of his people in total blessing and total demand. The church is meant to be the Kingdom community, a model of what human community looks like when it comes under the rule of God, and a challenging alternative to secular society. Entering God's Kingdom is entering the new age, long promised in the Old Testament, which is also the beginning of God's new creation. Now we look forward to the consummation of the Kingdom when our bodies, our society and our universe will all be renewed, and sin, pain, futility, disease and death will all be eradicated. Salvation is a big concept; we have no liberty to reduce it.

Secondly, *we must not separate Jesus the Saviour from Jesus the Lord*. It is little short of incredible that some evangelists teach the possibility of accepting Jesus the Saviour, while postponing a surrender to him as Lord. But God has exalted Jesus to his right hand and made him Lord. From that position of supreme power and executive authority he is able to bestow salvation and the gift of the Spirit. It is precisely because he is Lord that he can save. The affirmations 'Jesus is Lord' and 'Jesus is Saviour' are almost interchangeable. And his lordship extends far beyond the religious bit of our lives. It embraces the whole of our experience, public and private, home and work, church membership and civic duty, evangelistic and social responsibilities.

Thirdly, *we must not separate faith from love*. Evangelical Christians have always emphasized faith. *Sola fide*, 'by faith alone', was one of the great watchwords of the Reformation, and rightly so. 'Justification', or acceptance with God, is not by good works which we have done or could do; it is only by God's sheer unmerited favour ('grace'), on the sole ground of the atoning death of Jesus Christ, by simple trust in him alone. This central truth of the gospel cannot be compromised for anything. But, although justification is by faith alone, this faith cannot remain alone. If it is living and authentic, it will inevitably issue in good works, and if it does not, it is spurious. Jesus himself taught this in his 'sheep and goats' description of Judgement Day. Our attitude to him, he said, will be revealed in, and so be judged by, our good works of love to the least of his brothers and sisters. The apostles all lay the same emphasis on the necessity of good works of love. James teaches it: 'Faith by itself, if it is not accompanied by action, is dead … I will show you my faith by what I do' (2:17, 18). So does John: 'If anyone has material possessions and sees his brother in need but has not pity on him, how can the love of God be in him?' (1 John 3:17). And so does Paul. Christ died to create a new people who would be 'eager to do what is good' (Titus 2:14). We have been re-created in Christ 'to do good works, which God prepared in advance for us to do' (Ephesians 2:10). Again, 'the only thing that counts is faith expressing itself through love … Serve one another in love' (Galatians 5:6, 13). This, then, is the striking sequence – faith, love, service. True faith issues in love, and true love issues in service.

It is specially those of us who are called 'evangelical' Christians, who need to take this New Testament emphasis to heart. We have to beware of magnifying faith and knowledge at the expense of love. Paul did not. If he were able to 'fathom all mysteries and all knowledge', he wrote, and if he had 'a faith that can move mountains', yet had no love, he would be nothing (1 Corinthians 13:2). For saving faith and saving love belong together. Whenever one is absent, so is the other. Neither can exist in isolation.

(5) A fuller doctrine of the Church

Many people think of the Church as a kind of club, rather like the local golf club, except that the common interest of its members happens to be God rather than golf. They are religious people who do religious things together. They pay their subscription and are entitled to the privileges of club membership. In that frame of mind they forget William Temple's perceptive phrase that 'The church is the only cooperative society that exists for the benefit of non-members.'[48]

In place of the 'club' model of the Church, we need to recover the truth of the Church's 'double identity'. On the one hand, the Church is a 'holy' people, called out of the world to belong to God. But on the other it is a 'worldly' people, in the sense of renouncing 'otherworldliness' and being sent back into the world to witness and to serve. This is what Dr Alec Vidler, following a lead of Bonhoeffer's, has called the Church's 'holy worldliness'.[49] Seldom in its long and chequered history has the Church remembered or preserved its double identity. Sometimes, in a right emphasis on its 'holiness', the Church has wrongly withdrawn from the world and become insulated from it. At other times, in a right emphasis on its 'worldliness' (i.e. its immersion in the life of the world), the Church has wrongly become assimilated to the world's standards and values, and so become contaminated by them. Yet without the preservation of both parts of its identity, the Church cannot engage in mission. Mission arises out of the biblical doctrine of the Church in society. An unbalanced ecclesiology makes mission unbalanced too.

Jesus taught these truths himself, not only in his famous expression, 'in the world but not of it' (see John 17:11–19), but in his vivid metaphors of the salt and the light. 'You are the salt of the earth,' he said, and 'you are the light of the world' (Matthew 5:13–16). He implied (as we shall see more fully in Chapter 4) that the two communities, the new and the old, the Church and the world, are as radically different from one another as light from darkness and salt from decay. He also implied that, if they were to do any good, the salt must soak into the meat, and the light must shine into the darkness. Just so, Christians must penetrate non-Christian society. Thus, the double identity and responsibility of the Church are plain.

In a similar way the apostle Peter describes the members of God's new people on the one hand as 'aliens and strangers in the world' and on the other as needing to be conscientious citizens in it (1 Peter 2:11–17). We cannot be totally 'world-affirming' (as if nothing in it were evil), nor totally 'world-denying' (as if nothing in it were good); we need to be a bit of both, and we particularly need to be 'world-challenging', recognizing its potentiality as God's world and seeking to conform its life increasingly to his lordship.

This vision of the Church's influence on society is best described in terms of 'reform' rather than of 'redemption'. As A.N. Triton has expressed it, 'Redemption is not an infection of social structures … It results in individuals restored to a right relationship to God. But that sets up horizontal shock waves in society from which all of us benefit. These benefits are in terms of *reforming* society according to God's *law*, and not *redeeming* it by the death of Christ.'[50]

The effectiveness of the Church depends on its combination of 'holiness' and 'worldliness'. We shall return to these images later.

Practical action

I have assembled five doctrines and pleaded that we hold them in their biblical fullness – the doctrines of God (Creator, Lawgiver, Lord and Judge), of human beings (their unique worth because made in God's image), of Christ (who identified with us and calls us to identify with others), of salvation (a radical transformation) and of the Church (distinct from the world as its salt and light, yet penetrating it for Christ). These five doctrines constitute the biblical basis for mission, for both evangelistic and social responsibility. They lay upon us an obligation to be involved in the life of the world. But how?

Take the individual Christian first. In general terms, every Christian is called to be both a witness and a servant. For each of us is a follower of the Lord Jesus who both witnessed a good confession and said 'I am among you as a serving man.' Thus *diakonia* (service) and *marturia* (witness) are inseparable twins. Yet different Christians are called to different specialist ministries, just as the Twelve were called to the ministry of the Word and prayer, while the Seven were called to take charge of the daily distribution to the widows (see Acts 6). The metaphor of the Church as the Body of Christ enforces the same lesson. Just as each member of the human body has a different function, so each member of the Body of Christ has a different gift and so a different ministry. At the same time, whatever our specialist calling may be, emergencies will override it. The priest and the Levite in the Parable of the Good Samaritan could not excuse their shameful neglect of the man who had been assaulted and robbed by saying that their calling was to work in the Temple. If we are called to a predominantly social ministry, we still have an obligation to witness. If we are called to a predominantly evangelistic ministry, we still cannot say that we have no social responsibilities.

As for the local church, the versatility of its outreach can be greatly increased if full use is made of all its members with their different gifts and callings. It is a very healthy thing for the local church's oversight or leadership to encourage people with similar concerns to coalesce into 'special interest' groups or 'study and action' groups. Some will have an evangelistic objective – house-to-house visitation, a music group, a world mission group, etc. Other groups will have a social concern – sick and welfare visiting, a housing association, community or race relations, the care of the natural environment, pro-life, anti-abortion campaigning, the needs of an ethnic minority, etc. Such specialist groups supplement one another. If an occasional opportunity is given to them to report back to the church membership as a whole, the representative nature of their work will be affirmed, and they can receive valuable support from their parent body in terms of advice, encouragement, prayer and financial backing.

No one Christian could, or should try to, get involved in every kind of ministry. But each local church (at least of any size) can and should get involved in as many as possible, *through its groups*. The groups make it realistic for the church greatly to diversify its concern and action.[51]

I end this chapter with what may be a rather surprising reference to the Roman Catholic mass. The word 'mass' is said to be derived from the final sentence of the old Latin rite, *ite missa est*. In polite English it might be rendered, 'Now you are dismissed.' In more blunt language it could be just, 'Get out!' – out into the world which God made and God-like beings inhabit, the world into which Christ came and into which he now sends us. For that is where we belong. The world is the arena in which we are to live and love, witness and serve, suffer and die for Christ.

Chapter 2

COMPLEXITY: CAN WE THINK STRAIGHT?

L et us suppose we are agreed that our doctrines of God, human beings, Christ, salvation and the Church commit us inescapably to becoming socially involved – not only in social service, caring in Christ's name for the victims of oppression, but also in social action, concerned for justice and social change. To be thus strongly motivated is essential, but it is not enough. Any contribution we may hope to make will depend on our comprehension of the issues. We will be wise not to blunder unprepared into the minefield of social ethics. As I once heard the late John Mackay say when he was President of Princeton Theological Seminary, 'Commitment without reflection is fanaticism in action, though reflection without commitment is the paralysis of all action.'

We should certainly not underestimate the complexity of the issues which confront humankind today. True, every generation has felt baffled by its contemporary problems; so it is not surprising that we should feel the same way. Yet the number, scale and gravity of the questions facing us at the turn of the millennium do seem to be unprecedented, owing particularly to the scientific revolution. For example, the problem of war and peace has always troubled the Christian conscience, but the international stockpiling of nuclear weapons has greatly aggravated it. Similarly, the birth of the internet and of sophisticated information technologies have brought basic questions of identity and privacy to the forefront of discussion. And the cloning of a sheep in Scotland and of monkeys in the United States has jolted the world into a recognition of the need for serious thinking in the still young field of bio-ethics.

Clearly individual Christians cannot make themselves authorities in all these areas, and it is also doubtful whether the Church as such should be recommending particular and detailed policies. William Temple, who has certainly been the most socially concerned Archbishop of Canterbury in the twentieth century, made much of the need to distinguish between principles and policies. Writing in 1941 of continuing poverty and malnutrition in Britain, and of 'the industrial life of the country … disgraced by chronic unemployment', he went on: 'The Church is both entitled and obliged to condemn the society characterized by these evils; but it is not entitled in its corporate capacity to advocate specific remedies.'[1] Instead, the Church should inspire its influential members (whether politicians, civil servants, business people, trade unionists or leaders in other areas of public life) to seek and apply appropriate remedies. 'In other words, the Church lays down principles; the Christian citizen applies them; and to do this he utilizes the machinery of the State.'[2] Again, 'The Church cannot say how it is to be done; but it is called to say that it must be done.'[3]

The following year, in his better known book *Christianity and the Social Order*, Temple was still emphasizing the same distinction. 'The Church is committed to the everlasting Gospel … it must never commit itself to an ephemeral programme of detailed action.'[4] Readers of Temple will know that he was very far from saying that religion and politics do not mix. His point was different, namely that 'the Church is concerned with principles and not policy'.[5] The reasons why he believed the Church as a whole should refrain from 'direct political action' by developing and advocating specific programmes could be summed up as 'integrity' (the Church lacks the necessary expertise, though some of her members may have it), 'prudence' (she may prove to be mistaken and so be discredited) and 'justice' (different Christians hold different opinions, and the Church should not side with even a majority of its members against an equally loyal minority).

Even if we agree with this clarification of roles, and concede that not all Christians are responsible for working out policies, we still have to grapple with the principles, and these are by no means always easy to formulate.

Some Christians in this situation give up in despair. 'The age-long problems such as war, economics and divorce,' they say, 'have always divided Christians. There have always been pacifists and non-pacifists, capitalists and socialists, lax and rigid attitudes to divorce. And our modern problems, being more complex, are also more divisive. Besides,' they continue, 'there's no such thing as "the Christian view" on any of these problems; there is a whole spectrum of Christian views. Even the Bible does not always help us; it was written in such ancient cultures that it does not speak to our modern problems. So let us leave it to the experts and give up hope of finding a Christian answer ourselves.' Such despair denigrates God, because it denies the usefulness of his revelation as 'a lamp to our feet and a light for our path' (Psalm 119:105). To abandon hope of having anything Christian to say may even be mental laziness in the guise of a false humility.

True humility will lead us to sit patiently under the revelation of God and to affirm by faith that he can bring us to a substantially common mind. How can we believe in the Word and Spirit of God, and deny this? What is needed is more conscientious group study in which (1) we learn to pray together, (2) we listen attentively to each other's positions, and to the deep concerns which lie behind them, and (3) we help each other to discern the cultural prejudices which make us reluctant and even unable to open our minds to alternative viewpoints. This kind of discipline can be painful, but Christian integrity demands it. As a result, we shall refuse to acquiesce in superficial polarizations, for the truth is always more subtle and sophisticated than that. Instead, we shall undertake some careful mapwork, plotting (and emphasizing) areas of common ground, and clarifying residual disagreements with which we will continue perseveringly to wrestle.

If despair is one reaction to the complexity of modern ethical problems, its opposite is a naive over-simplification. Some Christians (particularly evangelical Christians, I fear) have tended to jump in head first. Either unwilling or unable to grasp the issues, we have sometimes denied that there are any. Or we have reasserted our evangelical watchword about the 'perspicuity' of Scripture (namely that its message is plain or transparent), as if this meant that there are no problems. We have then given glib answers to complex questions, and have treated the Bible as if it resembled either a slot-machine (in goes your penny, out comes your answer) or that extraordinary Victorian almanac entitled *Enquire Within*, which offered information on everything.

Certainly, the way of salvation is plain or 'perspicuous', which is what the Reformers meant by the term. But how can we assert that

Scripture contains no problems when the apostle Peter himself declared that in his brother apostle Paul's letters there were 'some things that are hard to understand' (2 Peter 3:16)? Applying God's ancient Word to the modern world is also hard. To deny this is another way of denigrating God, this time by misunderstanding the nature of his self-revelation.

Thus, we dishonour God both if we assert that there are no solutions, and if we offer slick solutions. For on the one hand he *has* revealed his will to us, and on the other he has *not* revealed it in a set of neat propositions.

A Christian mind

There is a third, better and more Christian way to approach today's complicated questions, which is to develop a Christian mind, namely a mind which has firmly grasped the basic presuppositions of Scripture and is thoroughly informed with biblical truth. It is only such a mind which can think with Christian integrity about the problems of the contemporary world.

This proposal immediately provokes opposition, however, from those Christians who have assimilated the anti-intellectual mood of today's world. They do not want to be told to use their minds, they say. Some even declare that it is 'unspiritual' to do so. In response, we draw attention to Paul's injunction to the Corinthians: 'Stop thinking like children. In … your thinking be adults' (1 Corinthians 14:20). The fact is that a proper use of our minds is wonderfully beneficial. (1) It glorifies God, because he has made us rational beings in his own image and has given us in Scripture a rational revelation which he intends us to study. (2) It enriches us, because every aspect of our Christian discipleship (e.g. our worship, faith and obedience) depends for its maturing on our reflection, respectively, upon God's glory, faithfulness and will. (3) It strengthens our witness in the world, because we are called like the apostles not only to 'preach' the gospel, but also to 'defend' and 'argue' it and so 'persuade' people of its truth (e.g. Acts 17:2f.; 19:8, 2 Corinthians 5:11; Philippians 1:7).

Towards the beginning of Romans 12 Paul uses the expression 'the renewing of your mind'. He has just issued his famous appeal to his Roman readers that, in gratitude for God's mercies, they should present their bodies to him as a 'living sacrifice' and as their 'spiritual worship'. Now he goes on to explain how it is possible for God's people to serve him in the world. He sets before us an alternative. One way is to 'be conformed' to this world or 'age', to its standards (or lack of them), its values (largely materialistic) and its goals (self-centred and godless). These are the characteristics of western culture. Moreover, the prevailing culture (like the prevailing wind) is not easy to stand up against. It is easier to take the line of least resistance and bow down before it, like 'reeds swayed by the wind'. Contemporary secularism is strong and subtle; the pressures to conform are great.

Paul exhorts us, however, not to be conformed to the world, but instead to 'be transformed' by the renewing of our mind with a view to discerning God's pleasing and perfect will. Here, then, is the apostle's assumption both that Christians have or should have a renewed mind, and that our renewed mind will have a radical effect on our lives, since it will enable us to discern and approve God's will, and so transform our behaviour. The sequence is compelling. If we want to live straight, we have to think straight. If we want to think straight, we have to have renewed minds. For once our minds are renewed, we shall become preoccupied not with the way of the world, but with the will of God, which will change us.

For Christian conversion means total renewal. The Fall led to total depravity – a doctrine rejected, I suspect, only by those who misunderstand it. It has never meant that every human being is as depraved as he could possibly be, but rather that every part of our humanness, including our mind, has become distorted by the Fall. So redemption involves total renewal (meaning not that we are now as good as we could be, but that every part of us, including our mind, has been renewed). The contrast is clear. Our old outlook led to conformity to the crowd; our new outlook has led us into moral non-conformity, out of concern for the will of God. Our fallen mind followed the way of the world; our renewed mind is engrossed with the will of God, as revealed in the Word of God. Between the two lies repentance, *metanoia*, a complete change of mind or outlook.

Paul writes not only of a 'renewed mind' but also of 'the mind of Christ'. He exhorts the Philippians: 'Let this mind be in you which was also in Christ Jesus' (2:5). That is, as we study the teaching and example of Jesus, and consciously put our minds under the yoke of his authority (Matthew 11:29), we begin to think as he thought. His mind is gradually formed within us by the Holy Spirit, who is the

Spirit of Christ. We see things his way, from his perspective. Our outlook becomes aligned to his. We almost dare to say what the apostle could say: 'we have the mind of Christ' (1 Corinthians 2:16).

'The renewed mind'. 'The mind of Christ'. 'A Christian perspective'. 'The Christian mind'. It was Harry Blamires who popularized this fourth expression in his book of that title, which since its publication in 1963 has had widespread influence. By a 'Christian mind' he was referring not to a mind occupied with specifically 'religious' topics, but to a mind which could think about even the most 'secular' topics 'Christianly', that is, from a Christian perspective. It is not the mind of a schizoid Christian who 'hops in and out of his Christian mentality as the topic of conversation changes from the Bible to the day's newspaper'.[6] No, the Christian mind, he writes, is 'a mind trained, informed, equipped to handle data of secular controversy within a framework of reference which is constructed of Christian presuppositions'.[7] Blamires laments the contemporary loss of Christian thinking even among church leaders: 'The Christian mind has succumbed to the secular drift with a degree of weakness and nervelessness unmatched in Christian history.'[8] Having deplored its loss, Harry Blamires sets about canvassing its recovery. He wants to witness the rise of the kind of Christian thinker who 'challenges current prejudices ... disturbs the complacent ... obstructs the busy pragmatists ... questions the very foundations of all about him, and ... is a nuisance'.[9]

Mr Blamires then goes on to list what he sees as the six essential 'marks' of a Christian mind: (1) 'its supernatural orientation' (it looks beyond time to eternity, beyond earth to heaven and hell, and meanwhile inhabits a world fashioned, sustained and 'worried over' by God); (2) 'its awareness of evil' (original sin perverting even the noblest things into instruments of 'hungry vanity'); (3) 'its conception of truth' (the givenness of divine revelation which cannot be compromised); (4) 'its acceptance of authority' (what God has revealed requires from us 'not an egalitarian attachment, but a bending submission'); (5) 'its concern for the person' (a recognition of the value of human personality over against servitude to the machine); and (6) 'its sacramental cast' (for example, recognizing sexual love as 'one of God's most efficient instruments' for the opening of man's heart to Reality).

Dr David Gill, formerly of New College, Berkeley, in his *The Opening of the Christian Mind*, proposes an alternative cluster of six characteristics which mark the Christian mind – namely, it is (1) 'theological' (focused on God and his incarnate Word), (2) 'historical' ('informed by the past, responsibly alive in the present and thoughtful about the future'), (3) 'humanist' (deeply concerned for persons), (4) 'ethical' (submissive to God's moral standards), (5) 'truthful' (committed to God's self-revelation in nature and Scripture), and (6) 'aesthetic' (appreciative of beauty as well as truth and goodness). Thus the Christian mind's 'basic contours' relate to 'God, history, persons, ethics, truth and beauty'.[10]

Both lists of six characteristics, Harry Blamires' and David Gill's, are true and valuable. But I have personally found it yet more helpful to adopt the framework provided by Scripture as a whole. For the truly Christian mind has repented of 'proof-texting' (the notion that we can settle every doctrinal and ethical issue by quoting a single, isolated text, whereas God has given us a comprehensive revelation), and instead saturates itself in the fullness of Scripture. In particular, it has absorbed the fourfold scheme of biblical history. For the Bible divides human history into epochs, which are marked not by the rise and fall of empires, dynasties or civilizations, but by four major events. – the Creation, the Fall, the Redemption and the Consummation.

First, *the Creation*. It is absolutely foundational to the Christian faith (and therefore to the Christian mind) that in the beginning, when time began, God made the universe out of nothing. He went on to make the planet earth, its land and seas and all their creatures. Finally, as the climax of his creative activity, he made man, male and female, in his own image. The Godlikeness of humankind emerges as the story unfolds: men and women are rational and moral beings (able to understand and respond to God's commands), responsible beings (exercising dominion over nature), social beings (with a capacity to love and be loved), and spiritual beings (finding their highest fulfilment in knowing and worshipping their Creator). Indeed, the Creator and his human creatures are depicted as walking and talking together in the garden. All this was the Godlikeness which gave Adam and Eve their unique worth and dignity.

Next, *the Fall*. They listened to Satan's lies, instead of to God's truth. In consequence of their disobedience they were driven out of the garden. No greater tragedy has befallen human beings than this, that though made by God like God and for God, they now live without God. All our human alienation, disorientation and sense of meaninglessness stem ultimately from this. In addition, our relationships with each other have become skewed. Sexual equality was upset: 'your husband ... will rule over you' (Genesis 3:16). Pain came to haunt the threshold of motherhood. Cain's jealous hatred of his brother erupted into murder. Even nature was put out of joint. The ground was cursed because of man, the cultivation of the soil became an uphill struggle, and creative work degenerated into drudgery. Over the centuries men and women have slipped from the responsible stewardship of the environment entrusted to them, and have cut down the forests, created deserts and dustbowls, polluted rivers and seas, and fouled the atmosphere with poisons. 'Original sin' means that our inherited human nature is now twisted with a disastrous self-centredness. Evil is an ingrained, pervasive reality. Although our Godlikeness has not been destroyed, it has been seriously distorted. We no longer love God with all our being, but are hostile to him and under his just condemnation.

Thirdly, *the Redemption*. Instead of abandoning or destroying his rebellious creatures, as they deserved, God planned to redeem them. No sooner had they sinned than God promised that the woman's seed would crush the serpent's head (Genesis 3:15), which we recognize as the first prediction of the coming Saviour. God's redemptive purpose began to take clearer shape when he called Abraham and entered into a solemn covenant with him, promising to bless both him and through his posterity all the families of the earth – another promise which we know has been fulfilled in Christ and his worldwide community. God renewed his covenant, this time with Israel, at Mount Sinai, and kept promising through the prophets that there was more, much more, to come in the days of the Messianic Kingdom. Then in the fullness of time the Messiah came. With him the new age dawned, the Kingdom of God broke in, the end began. Now today, through the death, resurrection and Spirit-gift of Jesus, God is fulfilling his promise of redemption and is remaking marred humankind, saving individuals and incorporating them into his new, reconciled community.

Fourth will come *the Consummation*. For one day, when the good news of the Kingdom has been proclaimed throughout the whole world (Matthew 24:14), Jesus Christ will appear in great magnificence. He will raise the dead, judge the world, regenerate the universe and bring God's Kingdom to its perfection. From it all pain, decay, sin, sorrow and death will be banished, and in it God will be glorified for ever. Meanwhile, we are living in between times, between Kingdom come and Kingdom coming, between the 'now' and the 'then' of redemption, between the 'already' and the 'not yet'.

Here, then, are four events, which correspond to four realities – namely the Creation ('the good'), the Fall ('the evil'), the Redemption ('the new') and the Consummation ('the perfect'). This fourfold biblical reality enables Christians to survey the historical landscape within its proper horizons. It supplies the true perspective from which to view the unfolding process between two eternities, the vision of God working out his purpose. It gives us a framework into which to fit everything, a way of integrating our understanding, the possibility of thinking straight, even about the most complex issues.

For the four events or epochs we have been thinking about, especially when grasped in relation to one another, teach major truths about God, human beings and society which give direction to our Christian thinking.

The reality of God

First, the reality of God. The fourfold biblical scheme is essentially God-centred; its four stages are disclosed from his point of view. Even the Fall, though an act of human disobedience, is presented in the context of divine commandments, sanctions and judgement. Thus, it is God who creates, judges, redeems and perfects. The initiative is his from beginning to end. In consequence, there is a cluster of popular attitudes which are fundamentally incompatible with Christian faith: e.g. the concept of blind evolutionary development, the assertion of human autonomy in art, science and education, and the declarations that history is random, life is absurd and everything is meaningless. The Christian mind comes into direct collision with these notions precisely because they are 'secular' – that is, because they leave no room for God. It insists that human beings can be defined only in relation to God, that without God they have ceased to be truly human. For we are creatures who depend on our Creator, sinners who are accountable to him and under his judgement, waifs and strays who are lost apart from his redemption.

This God-centredness is basic to the Christian mind. The Christian mind is a godly mind. More than that, it understands 'goodness' above all in terms of 'godliness'. It cannot describe as 'good' a person who is 'ungodly'. This is the clear testimony of the Bible's Wisdom Literature. The five books of Wisdom (Job, Psalms, Proverbs, Ecclesiastes and the Song of Songs) all focus, in different ways and with different emphases, on what it means to be human, and on how suffering, evil, oppression and love fit into our human-ness. The Book of Ecclesiastes is best known for its pessimistic refrain, 'vanity of vanities, all is vanity', well translated by the NIV as 'meaningless, meaningless, utterly meaningless'. It demonstrates the folly and futility of a human life circumscribed by time and space. If life is restricted to the average brief lifespan, is overshadowed by pain and injustice, and culminates for everybody in the same fate, death; if it is also restricted by the dimensions of space to human experiences 'under the sun', with no ultimate reference point be-yond the sun – then indeed life is as profitless as 'a chasing after wind'. Only God, Creator and Judge, Beginning and End, by adding to human life the missing dimensions of transcendence and eternity, can give it meaning, and so turn folly into wisdom.

Over against the pessimism of Ecclesiastes we read the oft-repeated maxim of the Wisdom Literature, namely, 'The fear of the Lord – that is wisdom [or its 'beginning' or 'principle'], and to shun evil is understanding' (Job 28:28; cf. Psalm 111:10; Proverbs 1:7, 9:10; Ecclesiastes 12:13). Here are the two major realities of human experience, God and evil. They are not equal realities, for Christians are not dualists. But they dominate life on earth. The one (God) brings human fulfilment, even ecstasy; the other (evil) human alienation, even despair. And wisdom consists in adopting a right attitude to both: loving God and hating evil, 'fearing' God with the worship which acknowledges his infinite worth, and 'shunning' evil in the holiness which despises it for its worthlessness. It is because God has made us spiritual and moral beings that religion and ethics, godliness and goodness, are fundamental to authentic humanness. Hence the tragedy of 'secularism', the closed world view which denies God and even glories in the spiritual vacuum it creates. T.S. Eliot was right to call it a 'waste land', and Theodore Roszak in *Where the Wasteland Ends* to characterize it as a desert of the spirit. 'For what science can measure is only a portion of what man can know. Our knowing reaches out to embrace the sacred.' Without transcendence 'the person shrinks'.[11] Secularism not only dethrones God; it destroys human beings.

If, because of the reality of God, the Christian mind is a godly mind, it is also a humble mind. This is another consistent theme of Scripture. When Nebuchadnezzar strutted like a peacock round the flat rooftop of his Babylonian palace claiming for himself instead of God the kingdom, the power and the glory, he went mad. Only when he acknowledged the rule of God and worshipped him, were his reason and his kingdom simultaneously restored to him. Daniel pointed out the moral: 'Those who walk in pride he is able to humble' (Daniel 4:28–37). It is a sobering story. If pride and madness go together, so do humility and sanity.

Jesus' contemporaries must have been dumbfounded when he told adults that they had to become like children if they wanted to enter God's Kingdom, and (even worse) that greatness in the Kingdom would be measured by childlike humility. We are too familiar with this teaching; it has lost its power to shock or stun. Yet Jesus not only taught it; he exhibited it. He emptied himself and humbled himself. So now, Paul adds, 'let this mind be in you which was in him'. The medieval moralists were right to see pride as the worst of the 'seven deadly sins' and as the root of the others. There is nothing so obscene as pride, nothing so attractive as humility.

Probably at no point does the Christian mind clash more violently with the secular mind than in its insistence on humility and its implacable hostility to pride. The wisdom of the world despises humility. Western culture has imbibed more than it knows of the power philosophy of Nietzsche. The world's model, like Nietzsche's, is the 'superman'; the model of Jesus remains the little child.

Thus the reality of God (as Creator, Lord, Redeemer, Father, Judge) gives to the Christian mind its first and most fundamental characteristic. Christians refuse to honour anything which dishonours God. We learn to evaluate everything in terms of the glory it gives to, or withholds from, God. That is why, to the Christian mind, wisdom is the fear of God and the pre-eminent virtue is humility.

The paradox of our humanness

I turn now from God to man, from the unalloyed splendour which characterizes whatever is 'divine' to the painful ambiguity which attaches to everything 'human'. We have already seen that the biblical understanding of humankind takes equal account of the Creation and the Fall. It is this that constitutes 'the paradox of our humanness'. We human beings have both a unique dignity as creatures made in God's image and a unique depravity as sinners under his judgement. The former gives us hope; the latter places a limit on our expectations. Our Christian critique of the secular mind is that it tends to be either too naively optimistic or too negatively pessimistic in its estimates of the human condition, whereas the Christian mind, firmly rooted in biblical realism, both celebrates the glory and deplores the shame of our human being. We can behave like God in whose image we were made, only to descend to the level of the beasts. We are able to think, choose, create, love and worship, but also to refuse to think, to choose evil, to destroy, to hate, and to worship ourselves. We build churches and drop bombs. We develop intensive care units for the critically ill and use the same technology to torture political enemies who presume to disagree with us. This is 'man', a strange, bewildering paradox, dust of earth and breath of God, shame and glory. So, as the Christian mind applies itself to human life on earth, to our personal, social and political affairs, it seeks to remember what paradoxical creatures we are – noble and ignoble, rational and irrational, loving and selfish, Godlike and bestial.

Perhaps I can best illustrate this dialectic by taking two examples, first our sexuality and secondly the political process.

It is pertinent to begin with our sexuality, partly because we are all of us sexual beings, and partly because, of all the social revolutions which have taken place this century, the sexual revolution may well be the profoundest. Sexual roles (masculinity and femininity), the context for sexual intercourse (in or out of marriage), whether the traditional understandings of marriage and the family can (or even should) survive the option of homosexual partnerships, contraception, *in vitro* fertilization, artificial insemination by donor, abortion and divorce – these are some aspects of human sexuality about which radical questions are being asked today. Although the Bible gives clear instructions on some of them, we will be far better placed to grapple with individual issues if we first gain a bird's-eye view of sexuality in general by seeing it in the light of Scripture's fourfold scheme.

According to Genesis 1 and 2 God created humankind male and female in his own image from the beginning, and told them to be fruitful. Although he pronounced creation 'good', he needed to add that, 'It is not good for the man to be alone.' And he went on to ordain that the sexual complementarity of men and women was to be con-summated in the mysteries of the 'one flesh' experience. Thus human sexuality, marriage, sexual intercourse and the family are all part of the creative purpose of God. Marriage (a publicly pledged, perma-nent, exclusive, heterosexual union) is not a human but a divine insti-tution, which therefore in itself is not affected by changing culture. Sexual intimacy within marriage is a good gift of a good Creator.

But after the Creation came the Fall. Sin has distorted our sexu-ality, as it has every other human instinct, faculty and appetite. Sex has surely become a far more imperious drive than God originally intended. Unnatural sexual deviations have arisen. Although sexual love can still be enjoyed, and even wonderingly celebrated as in the Song of Songs, nevertheless it is also often spoiled by selfish de-mands, fears, exploitation and cruelty.

The redeeming work of Christ through his Spirit has made pos-sible a whole new attitude to sex. This includes (in addition to a recognition of the Creator's purpose and gift) the control and sanc-tification of our sexual drive, a vision of self-giving love in marriage as a reflection of the relation between Christ and his Church, and a partnership between the sexes which, while not denying the respon-sible and caring headship which God has given to man (rooted in creation, not culture), also rejoices that in the married couple's rela-tionship to God 'there is neither male nor female', since they are now equally justified in Christ and equally adopted into God's family (Galatians 3:26–9). At the same time, Jesus taught that for a variety of reasons some will remain single (Matthew 19:10f.; cf 1 Corinthians 7:1ff.).

What about the Consummation? In the next world after the resurrection, Jesus said, 'they will neither marry nor be given in marriage; they will be like the angels in heaven' (Mark 12:25). So, although love is eternal, marriage is not. Procreation will no longer be necessary. Relationships of love will transcend the physical, and will probably be less exclusive (though surely not less rich) than in marriage. The importance of adding this fourth stage should be clear. It contains a message both for the married (lest the union be-come selfish to the point even of idolatry) and for the single (that marriage is not indispensable to the attainment of full humanness).

As we try to respond Christianly to the radical sexual challenges of today, we will find it easier to struggle with particular issues within this general biblical framework.

My second example related to 'the paradox of our humanness' concerns the political process. The nature of man (i.e. what it means to be human) has arguably been the basic political issue of the twentieth century. It has certainly been one of the chief points of conflict between Marx and Jesus, and therefore between the East and the West, namely whether human beings have any absolute value because of which they must be respected, or whether their value is only relative to the community, for the sake of which they may be exploited. More simply, are the people the servants of the institution, or is the institution the servant of the people? As John S. Whale has written, 'ideologies ... are really anthropologies';[12] they reflect different doctrines of our humanity.

Christians should be careful not to 'baptize' any political ideology (whether of the right, the left or the centre), as if it contained a monopoly of truth and goodness. At best a political ideology and its programme are only an approximation to the will and purpose of God. The fact is that Christians are to be found in most political parties and are able to defend their membership on conscientious Christian grounds. Thus, to indulge in a blunt oversimplification, both the main political ideologies in western societies appeal to Christians for different reasons. Capitalism appeals because it encourages individual human initiative and enterprise, but also repels because it seems not to care that the weak succumb to the fierce competition it engenders. Socialism appeals, on the other hand, because it has great compassion for the poor and the weak, but also repels because it seems not to care that individual initiative and enterprise are smothered by the big government which it engenders. Each attracts because it emphasizes a truth about human beings, either the need to give free play to their creative abilities or the need to protect them from injustice. Each repels because it fails to take with equal seriousness the complementary truth. Both can be liberating. But both can also be oppressive. A wit has put this well: 'The difference between Capitalism and Socialism is that in Capitalism man exploits man, while in Socialism it's the other way round!' It is understandable that many Christians dream of a third option which overcomes the present confrontation and incorporates the best features of both.

Whatever our political colour may be, all Christians tend to advocate democracy, which was popularly defined by Abraham Lincoln as 'government of the people, by the people, for the people'.

Not that it is 'perfect or all-wise', as Winston Churchill conceded in the House of Commons on 11 November 1947. 'Indeed,' he continued, 'it has been said that democracy is the worst form of government – except for all those other forms that have been tried from time to time.' The fact is that it is the wisest and safest form of government yet devised. This is because it reflects the paradox of our humanness. On the one hand, it takes the Creation seriously (that is, human dignity), because it refuses to govern human beings without their consent, and insists instead on giving them a responsible share in the decision-making process. On the other hand, it takes the Fall seriously (that is, human depravity), because it refuses to concentrate power in the hands of one person or of a few people, and insists instead on dispersing it, thus protecting human beings from their own pride and folly. Reinhold Niebuhr put it succinctly: 'Man's capacity for justice makes democracy possible; but man's inclination to injustice makes democracy necessary.'[13]

The future of society

A third sphere to which it may be helpful to apply the Bible's fourfold scheme is that of the possibility of social change. What expectation should we cherish that society can be improved? On this issue Christians of different traditions are to be found along a broad spectrum.

'Liberal' Christians have tended to be social activists. Because of their almost boundless confidence in human achievement, they dream dreams of building Utopia (sometimes mistakenly identified as 'the Kingdom of God') on earth.

'Evangelical' Christians, on the other hand, have tended – at least earlier in the twentieth century – to be social quietists. Because of their gloomy view of human depravity, they lack confidence in human beings (at least until they have been born again). They therefore consider social action a waste of time and social transformation all but impossible.

I have deliberately expressed both positions in their more extreme forms. Stated thus, the polarization fails to hold together the two parts of the human paradox.

Because human beings are made in the image of God, and the divine image (though marred) has not been wholly lost, they retain some perception of the just and compassionate society which would please him, and some desire to bring it about. On the whole, all humankind still prefers peace to war, justice to oppression, harmony to discord, order to chaos. So social change is possible, and indeed has happened. In many parts of the world we can see rising standards of hygiene and health care, a greater respect for women and children, the increasing availability of education, a clearer recognition of human rights, a growing concern to conserve the natural environment, and better conditions in mine, factory and prison. Much of this has been due (directly or indirectly) to Christian influence, although by no means all social reformers have been committed Christians. But whenever God's people have been effective as salt and light in the community, there has been less social decay and more social uplift. In the United States, for example, after the early nineteenth-century awakening associated with Charles G. Finney, 'born-again Christians were in the forefront of every major social reform in America ... They spear-headed the abolitionist movement, the temperance movement, the peace movement, and the early feminist movement.'[14]

Because human beings are fallen, however, and inherit a twist of self-centredness, we shall never succeed in building a perfect society. Improvement – yes; perfect justice – no. Utopian dreams are unrealistic; they belong to the world of fantasy. All human plans, though launched with great hopes, have to some degree disappointed the planners, for they have foundered on the rock of human selfishness. Christians have usually remembered this. As William Temple put it, 'Its assertion of Original Sin should make the Church intensely realistic and conspicuously free from Utopianism.'[15] Certainly the evangelical Christians who gathered in Lausanne at the great Inter-national Congress on World Evangelization (1974) declared forthrightly in their Covenant: 'We ... reject as a proud, self-confident dream the notion that man can ever build a utopia on earth.'[16] It is socialists who have tended to be too optimistic about human achievement. Professor C.E.M. Joad is a good example. Having been brought up on the confessions and collects of the Church of England's 1662 Book of Common Prayer, he began by believing in the inherent sinfulness of human beings. But later he discarded this notion in favour of their 'infinite perfectibility', until World War II shattered this illusion and convinced him again that 'evil is endemic in man'. He wrote candidly in his book *Recovery of Belief* (1952): 'It is because we rejected the doctrine of original sin that we on the Left were always being disappointed; disappointed by the refusal of people to be reasonable, by the subservience of intellect to emotion, by the failure of true Socialism to arrive ... above all, by the recurrent fact of war.'[17]

It is difficult to avoid extremes of pessimism and optimism about the possibility of social change. Robert McNamara nearly did, in what has been described as perhaps his 'most eloquent speech' while in office as US Defense Secretary: 'All the evidence of history suggests that man is indeed a rational animal, but with a nearly infinite capacity for folly. His history seems largely a halting but persistent effort to raise his reason above his animality. He draws blueprints for Utopia, but never quite gets it built.'[18] But even this sounds a trifle cynical.

How then can we sum up an attitude to the possibility of social change which reflects 'neither the easy optimism of the humanist, nor the dark pessimism of the cynic, but the radical realism of the Bible'?[19] How can we do equal justice to the truths of the Creation, the Fall, the Redemption and the Consummation? I suggest that the biblical balance is well expressed by Paul in 1 Thessalonians 1:9-10, where he describes the results of conversion from idols to God as being 'to serve the living and true God, and to wait for his Son from heaven'. The combination of 'serving' and 'waiting' is striking, since the former is actively getting busy for Christ on earth, while the latter is passively looking for him to come from heaven. We must serve, but there are limits to what we can achieve. We must wait, but have no liberty to do so in idleness. Thus 'working' and 'waiting' go together. The need to wait for Christ from heaven will rescue us from the presumption which thinks we can do everything; the need to work for Christ on earth will rescue us from the pessimism which thinks we can do nothing. Only a Christian mind which has developed a biblical perspective can enable us to preserve the balance.

I began this chapter by admitting the complexity of the problems of personal and social ethics which confront us today. Neat, cut-and-dried solutions are usually impossible. Simplistic shortcuts, which ignore the real issues, are unhelpful. At the same time, it is not Christian to give up in despair.

We need to remember for our encouragement that God has given us four gifts.

His first gift is a mind with which to think. He has made us rational, intelligent creatures. He still forbids us to behave like horses and mules which lack understanding, and tells us in our thinking to be not babies but adults (Psalm 32:9; 1 Corinthians 14:20).

Secondly, he has given us the Bible and its witness to Christ, in order to direct and control our thinking. As we absorb its teaching, our thoughts will increasingly conform to his. This is not because we memorize a lot of proof texts, which we trot out at appropriate moments, each text labelled to answer its own question. It is rather that we have grasped the great themes and principles of Scripture and the fourfold framework which we have been considering in this chapter.

God's third gift is the Holy Spirit, the Spirit of truth, who opens up the Scriptures to us and illumines our minds so that we can understand and apply them.

Fourthly, God has given us the Christian community as the context in which to do our thinking. Its heterogeneity is the best safeguard against blinkered vision. For the Church has members of both sexes, and of all ages, temperaments, experiences and cultures. And each local church should reflect this colourful diversity. With rich insights contributed to the interpretation of Scripture from different backgrounds, it will be hard to maintain our prejudices.

With these four gifts, used in concert – a mind, a textbook, a Teacher, and a school – it should be possible for us to develop an increasingly Christian mind and to learn to think straight.

An appendix on postmodernity

The very possibility of being able to think straight about contemporary issues, and find solutions to contemporary problems, is being challenged today by postmodernity and its almost total scepticism about truth. A fundamental paradigm shift is taking place around us, as the 'modern' Enlightenment culture, which replaced the 'premodern', is itself being replaced by the 'postmodern'. These are slippery words, however, which elude the firm grasp of precise definition. Different scholars use them in different ways. Perhaps they are most easily understood in relation and reaction to each other.

The *premodern* mindset was essentially medieval and pre-scientific. It was characterized by an unquestioning submission to

feudal authority in church and state, and by an uncritical acceptance of the supernatural, to the point of gross superstition.

The *modern* mindset, which budded in the Renaissance, blos-
somed in the eighteenth-century European Enlightenment. Its
foundation was confidence in man rather than God. It celebrated
the emergence of human beings from the bondage of tradition, and
so from social and intellectual childhood. It sought to replace divine
revelation by human reason; supernatural religion by natural science (the world being a closed, mechanistic system of cause and
effect, with no room for miracles or indeed for an interfering God);
laissez-faire economics by planning; feudalism by human rights;
original sin by the fundamental goodness of human beings and the
inevitability of material and moral progress; and morality by utilitar-
ianism (behaviour is right if it is beneficial).

The *postmodern* mindset is best seen as a reaction against
the 'modernity' of both Renaissance and Enlightenment. Antici-
pated by the romanticism of the early nineteenth century, by the
existentialism of the middle of the twentieth century, and by the
counterculture of the 1960s, postmodernism rejects Enlightenment
self-confidence and optimism. Far from fulfilling its promises,
science has given birth to a dehumanizing technology. The dream of
continuous progress has been shattered by two world wars and the
Holocaust, by the nightmare fears of nuclear and environmental
destruction, and by the spectres of nationalism and tribalism. In
place of the old triumphalism, disillusion now reigns, along with
her twin sisters scepticism and cynicism. In consequence, the postmodern mood distrusts all authorities, and rejects all so-called
'meta-narratives', which propose grandiose, universal solutions.
Where today are the economic liberation promised by Marx, the
evolutionary progress implied by Darwin, and the psycho-analytical
therapy propounded by Freud? Their pretentious theories offered
much but delivered little.

Truth to the postmodernist is purely subjective; it is merely what
happens to make sense to me. Something quite different may make
sense to you; it then becomes your truth. Moreover there are no
documents of law, history, tradition, or religion which can guide or
unite us. For what is decisive in the interpretation of a text is not the
identity and intention of its author (which in any case may not be
discoverable), but rather the impact which it makes on each reader.
Thus it is left to each of us to construct our own reality, believe our

own truth, tell our own story and create our own identity. As Dr Os Guinness has put it: 'Where modernism was a manifesto of human self-confidence and self-congratulation, postmodernism is a confession of modesty, if not despair. There is no truth; only truths. There is no grand reason; only reasons … There is no grand narrative of human progress; only countless stories of where people and their cultures are now … '[20]

The Christian critique of postmodernism is not wholly negative, however, for we share some of its quarrel with modernism. We too reject rationalism, that is, the proclamation of the autonomy and omni-competence of the human mind; yet we affirm the essential rationality of human beings, since God has made us rational in his own image. We also reject modernity's naive confidence in the inevitability of human progress and its dreams of Utopia; yet we refuse to lapse into postmodern cynicism, since through the power of the gospel and through the influence of the Church as salt and light, God can improve society and has in fact done so.

Again, we cannot help acknowledging that the very concept of truth has many limitations. First, ultimate reality has mysteries which science and religion cannot fathom and which language cannot describe. Secondly, the truth we do know is inevitably coloured by our cultural presuppositions and perspectives. Thirdly, the pursuit of truth has sometimes degenerated into a concealed hunger for power to oppress people. Nevertheless, even when these humbling confessions have been made, Christians still affirm that God has revealed himself in Christ and in the biblical witness to Christ, and that the truth of his self-revelation is objective in its character, absolute in its quality and universal in its application. The gospel is, in fact, the authentic meta-narrative.

Chapter 3

PLURALISM: SHOULD WE IMPOSE OUR VIEWS?

We accept that we should get involved, and we struggle to think Christianly about the issues. In consequence, we develop some quite strong convictions, but others do not share them. Indeed, western Christians find themselves increasingly out of step with a post-Christian society. So how can we hope to influence our country into a return to Christian values, in its laws, its institutions and its culture? Should Christians attempt to impose their views on a largely non-Christian nation?

In Europe and America, and in those Commonwealth countries which inherited the 'Christian civilization' of the West, we certainly have to come to terms with the new 'pluralism', meaning a society composed of different ethnic and religious groups. Pluralism is due largely to two factors. The first is the process of secularization, seen as the diminishing influence of the Church on both people and institutions. Accurate statistics are notoriously hard to obtain and to interpret. It seems to be clear, however, that adult membership of the Protestant churches of the UK dropped from 12 per cent of the adult population in 1975 to 9 per cent in 1994. This shows a 19 per cent loss in church membership over the 20-year period in spite of roughly an 8 per cent growth in population.[1] It is significant to note that these declining numbers are part of a larger pattern of decline that has been in place since World War II.

Again, between 1968 and 1990 around 1,200 Church of England churches were declared redundant, and were either demolished or appropriated to other uses (cultural, residential, etc.). While overall church membership has continued to decline in recent years the statistics are not as depressing as they may seem at first glance.

Although just over six churches close down every week, six churches are being opened every week too, with an average of 200 members joining churches every day.[2] Nevertheless, in contrast to half a century ago, let alone the nineteenth century, there can be no doubt that the Church has lost a great deal of ground.

Alongside the Christian decline has gone an increase in non-Christian alternatives. For the second cause of pluralism is the liberal immigration policy of the immediate post-war years. As a result, most western countries now include in their population sizeable ethnic groups from Africa, Asia, the Middle East and the Caribbean. This makes possible for all of us a rich experience of cultural diversity. But it also leads to religious competition and to consequent demands for recognition of other religions in those countries' educational systems, laws and institutions. In 1994 the adult membership of non-Christian religious groups in the United Kingdom was as follows:[3]

- Moslems – 575,000 active members (estimates for the whole community range from 1.15 million to 3 million)
- Sikhs – 325,000 (although the Sikh Cultural Society estimates 500,000)
- Jews – 97,300 (heads of household who represent about one-third of the whole Jewish community)
- Hindus – 144,000 (this is the estimated active membership representing approximately one-third of the Hindu community)
- Mormons – 168,302
- Jehovah's Witnesses – 129,852

If we add together the adult membership of all non-Christian religious minorities in the UK (including Spiritualists, Christian Scientists, Christadelphians, etc.), it comes to over 1.2 million, with the total community (including children, cultural adherents, etc.) nearing 4 million.[4] This is a significant minority, exercising noticeable influence. As for unbelievers, since the most generous estimate of the combined numbers of all religious communities in Britain (including children and non-practising adherents) is 72 per cent of the total population, there must be 28 per cent who make no religious profession at all.[5]

Elsewhere in the world, even if Christians represent a substantial minority, the predominant culture is either Hindu or Buddhist,

Jewish or Islamic, Marxist or secular. So here too, usually in a more acute form, Christians are faced with the same dilemma. In many issues they believe they know the will of God. They also believe it is their Christian duty to pray and work for God's will to be done. Should they hope to impose their Christian convictions on non-Christians? If it is possible, is it desirable? Even if they could, should they try?

The two commonest responses to these questions represent opposite extremes. One is 'imposition', the crusading attempt to co-erce people by legislation to accept the Christian way. The other is '*laissez-faire*', the defeatist decision to leave people alone in their non-Christian ways, and not interfere or try to influence them in any way. We need to look carefully at these alternatives, with some historical examples, before we shall be ready for a third and better option.

Imposition

Here are Christians with a commendable zeal for God. They believe in revelation, and they care deeply about God's revealed truth and will. They long to see society reflecting it. So the desire to achieve this end by force is an understandable temptation.

My first historical illustration is the Inquisition in Europe, which was a special tribunal set up by the Roman Catholic Church in the thirteenth century to combat heresy. Suspected heretics were first hunted out, then invited to confess, and then, if they refused, brought to trial. By Pope Innocent IV's bull *Ad Extirpanda* of 1252, torture was permitted in addition to trial. Impenitent heretics were punished by excommunication or imprisonment or confiscation of goods, or were handed over to the state to be burned alive. The Inquisition lasted about 300 years. It was suppressed in 1542, although the Spanish Inquisition (which was the most cruel), insti-tuted at the end of the fifteenth century by Ferdinand and Isabella for purposes of national security and used especially against Jews, Moors and Protestants, was abolished only in the year 1834.[6] Today, I imagine, Christians of all traditions are deeply ashamed that such methods could ever have been used in the name of Jesus Christ. The Inquisition remains a horrible blot on the pages of Church history, never to be reinstated. Yet dictatorships of the extreme left and right are still guilty of trying by force to abolish opposition and compel assent. All Christians affirm, however, that totalitarianism and torture are both wholly incompatible with the mind and spirit of Jesus.

My second and more recent historical example is that of Prohibition in the United States, namely the legal ban on the manufacture and sale of alcoholic liquor. The National Prohibition Party was formed in 1869 by a group of white Protestants. Their motives were admirable. Dismayed by the increase in heavy drinking and drunkenness, especially among poor immigrants, and perceiving this as a threat to public order, they committed themselves to work for the total prohibition of alcoholic beverages. In 1895 the 'Anti-Saloon League of America' was founded by a group of church leaders, and after a campaign of about 25 years Congress passed in 1919 the Eighteenth Amendment to the Constitution, prohibiting the manufacture, sale and transportation of liquor. It came into force a year later, and 46 out of 48 states had ratified it within about two years.

The result, however, was that the law was widely broken. 'Bootleggers' made, sold and smuggled alcoholic drinks illegally, and 'speakeasies' (stores in which liquor was sold clandestinely) flourished. So in 1933, 13 years after the so-called 'Noble Experiment' began, the Twenty-first Amendment, which voided the Eighteenth, was signed by President Roosevelt, and Prohibition ended. Far from abolishing alcohol abuse, it had provoked and increased it. And the law had been brought into disrepute.

So was Prohibition foisted on the country, or did the people want it? Opinions differ. The 'drys' claim that there was a national consensus; the 'wets' that this was obtained only by legislative action not direct popular vote, and only when the nation's mind was preoccupied with America's entry into World War I. John Kobler writes: 'The accessible evidence confirms neither claim. It precludes any flat answer and leaves the question for ever unsettled.' Nevertheless, this is how he concludes his historical enquiry: 'In sum, it appeared that rural, agricultural America with its large Protestant, native-born population thrust prohibition upon urban, industrial America, with its heterogeneity of races, religions and foreign backgrounds.'[7]

Looking back at these two examples, one European and the other American, the Inquisition was an attempt to impose belief, and Prohibition an attempt to impose behaviour. Both were seen in the end to be unproductive, for you cannot force people to believe what they do not believe, or practise what they do not want to practise. Similarly, to imagine today that we can force Christian convictions and standards on Europe is totally unrealistic. It is a foolish, nostalgic desire for a Christendom which has long since vanished.

Laissez-faire

The opposite to imposition, I suggest, is *laissez-faire*. The term was originally used in the eighteenth century of Free Trade economists, and the concept dominated nineteenth-century society. It had no overtones of the lackadaisical about it. On the contrary, it was a principled belief in the necessity of non-interference by government. The use of the term has changed with the centuries, however, and in popular parlance today it describes a mood of apathy and indifference. It is applied to citizens as much as to governments. Far from imposing our views, we say, we will not even propagate or commend them. We shall leave other people alone to mind their own business, as we devoutly hope they will leave us alone to mind ours. *Laissez-faire* has even sometimes been an attitude adopted by Christian people in the name of tolerance. Tolerant in spirit Christians should certainly be, showing respect towards those who think and behave differently. Socially tolerant too, in the sense that we should want to see political and religious minorities accepted in the community and protected by law, just as the Christian minority in a non-Christian country expects to be legally free to profess, practise and propagate the gospel. But how can we Christians be intellectually tolerant of opinions we know to be false or actions we know to be evil? What kind of unprincipled indulgence is this? Societies smell sweet or acrid in the nostrils of God. He is not indifferent to questions of social justice, so how can his people be? To remain silent and inactive when error or evil is being canvassed has very serious consequences. For the Christian option has then gone by default. Is it not at least partly because Christians have failed to raise their voices for Jesus Christ, that our country has slipped its Christian moorings and drifted away from them?

The gravest modern example of Christian *laissez-faire* is the failure of German churches to speak out against the Nazis' treatment of the Jews. It is a long and dismal story, thoroughly documented by Richard Gutteridge in his book *Open Thy Mouth for the Dumb*.[8] He traces Christian complicity in German anti-Semitism back to the nineteenth century, when Christianity became identified with a mystical German patriotism, which increased after defeat in World War I. It was at this time that several misguided attempts were made to theologize the intrinsic value of the Aryan *Volk*. For example, Paul Althaus wrote in 1932: 'It is God's will that we maintain our Race and our *Volkstum* in purity, that we remain German men, and do not become a bastard-*Volk* of Jewish Aryan blood.'[9] At that time the Church seemed to be in alliance with the National Socialist Movement. Only a few brave voices (like those of Karl Barth and Paul Tillich) were raised in protest. But meanwhile the 'Faith Movement of German Christians', under the patronage of the Nazi Party, affirmed the Aryan Race.

After Hitler came to power in 1933 a law was passed to purge the Civil Service of officials of non-Aryan descent, and, incredible as it may seem, the racially compromised 'German Christians' wanted to apply this 'Aryan Clause' to the Church. Several synods adopted it, against the opposition of men like Martin Niemöller, Walter Künneth, Hans Lilje and Dietrich Bonhoeffer. Yet 'the Evangelical Church never spoke out officially against the Aryan legislation in general.' Bonhoeffer was deeply upset by the Church's silence and frequently quoted Proverbs 31:8: 'Open thy mouth for the dumb.'[10]

In the terrible pogrom of November 1938, 119 synagogues were set on fire (of which 76 were destroyed), 20,000 Jews were arrested, shops were looted and prominent Jewish citizens publicly humiliated. The general public was aghast, and some church leaders protested. But 'there was no chance of the Evangelical Church as a whole voicing her horror and indignation, and the Catholic Church kept almost completely silent, and their hierarchy found no word to say.'[11] Hitler's appalling 'Final Solution', which he had already decided upon before World War II broke out, began to be implemented in 1941. Not until two years later, however, did a conference of Lutheran Church leaders resolve to attack the Reich government for its anti-Jewish atrocities. This is how Richard Gutteridge sums up his thesis: 'The Church as Church did not find a decisive word from Scripture as a whole to embrace the issue as a whole ... Throughout the conflict nobody in a position of authority made a full and plain denunciation of anti-Semitism as such.'[12] Barth called it 'the sin against the Holy Ghost' and a 'rejection of the grace of God'.[13] Some other church officials were equally bold, and paid dearly for their courage. But when evangelical church leaders met soon after the end of the war, and issued their 'Stuttgart Declaration', they had to acknowledge: 'It is our self-indictment that we have not made a more courageous confession.'[14] Gutteridge concludes: 'The ultimate failure of the Church lay not in the inability of bishops and synods to make plain and outspoken pronouncements in public,' though it included that, but rather 'what was missing was a spontaneous outburst at any point by ordinary decent Christian folk ... A really widespread, public, visible expression of righteous indignation would have had to have been taken very seriously indeed by the Nazi leaders, and would assuredly have had a profound effect in curbing the most iniquitous excesses and brutalities, if not in bringing about the downfall of so monstrous and unprincipled a tyranny.'[15]

The story Richard Gutteridge tells speaks for itself. It needs no additional comment from me. The complicity of the 'German Christians', who failed to develop a biblical critique of the Nazis' blatant racism, should be enough to outlaw *laissez-faire* forever. Could they not have prevented the Holocaust?

Persuasion

Better than the extremes of imposition and *laissez-faire* is the strategy of persuasion by argument. This is the way the Christian mind advocates, for it arises naturally from the biblical doctrines of God and human beings.

The living God of the biblical revelation, who created and sustains the universe, intended the human beings he made to live in loving community. Moreover his righteousness is an essential expression of his love. He loves justice and hates oppression. He champions the cause of the poor, the alien, the widow and the orphan. He feeds the hungry, clothes the naked, heals the sick, finds the lost. He wants all humankind to be saved and to come to know the truth in his Son Jesus Christ. Now this biblical vision of God profoundly affects our attitude to society, since God's concerns inevitably become his people's too. We also will respect men and women made in God's image, seek justice, hate injustice, care for the needy, guard the dignity of work, recognize the necessity of rest, maintain the sanctity of marriage, be zealous for the honour of Jesus Christ, and long that every knee will do homage to him and every tongue confess him. Why? Because all these are God's concerns. How can we acquiesce in things which passionately displease him, or affect nonchalance about things he is strongly committed to? The policy of *laissez-faire* is inconceivable to Christians who hold a biblical doctrine of God.

But then the policy of imposition is impossible to those who hold a biblical doctrine of human beings. For God made male and female to be responsible beings. He told them to be fruitful (exercise their powers of procreation), to subdue the earth and rule its creatures, to work and to rest, and to obey him ('you may … you must not …'). These injunctions would be meaningless if God had not endowed humankind with two unique gifts – conscience (to discern between alternatives) and freedom (to choose between them). The rest of the Bible confirms this. It is assumed throughout that human beings are moral beings, who are accountable for their actions. They know the moral law, since it is 'written on their hearts' (Romans 2:14–15), and are exhorted to obedience and warned of the penalties of disobedience. But they are never coerced. No compulsion is ever used. Only persuasion by argument: 'Come now, let us reason together, says the Lord' (Isaiah 1:18).

A basic ground for this is that the human conscience must be treated with the greatest respect. Paul expresses his personal determination 'to keep my conscience clear before God and man' (Acts 24:16). He also has much to say about other people's consciences. They may be 'strong' (well educated and free) or 'weak' (over-scrupulous and full of qualms). But whatever the condition of a person's conscience, even when it is mistaken, it is to be respected. Weak consciences need to be strengthened, and deceiving consciences enlightened, but there must be no bullying of consciences. Only in the most extreme circumstances should people be induced to act against their consciences. In general, consciences are to be educated, not violated. This principle, which arises out of the Christian doctrine of human beings, should affect our social behaviour and institutions. It is the reason why Christians oppose autocracy and favour democracy. Autocracy crushes consciences; democracy (at least in theory) respects them, since democratic governments derive 'their just powers from the consent of the governed' (The American Declaration of Independence).[16] Once laws have been promulgated, however, all citizens (in a democracy as in an autocracy) are under constraint to obey them. They may not do as they please. Yet in matters of great moment (e.g. conscription in time of war) a civilized government will allow 'conscientious objection'. This provision is also the product of Christian thinking.

So both the biblical doctrine of God and that of human beings guide our behaviour in a pluralist society, the former ruling out *laissez-faire*, and the latter ruling out imposition. Because God is who he is, we cannot be indifferent when his truth and law are flouted, but because human beings are who they are, we cannot try to impose them by force.

What, then, should Christians do? We should seek to educate the public conscience to know and desire the will of God. The Church should seek to be the conscience of the nation. If we cannot impose God's will by legislation, neither can we convince people of it merely by biblical quotation. For both these approaches are examples of 'authority from above', which people resent and resist. More effective is 'authority from below', the intrinsic truth and value of a thing which is self-evident and therefore self-authenticating. (Not that the two are incompatible; God's authority is essentially both.) This principle applies equally in evangelism and social action.

In evangelism we should neither try to force people to believe the gospel, nor remain silent as if we were indifferent to their response, nor rely exclusively on the dogmatic proclamation of biblical texts (vital as authoritative biblical exposition is), but rather, like the apostles, we should reason with people from both nature and Scripture, commending God's gospel to them by rational arguments.

In social action, similarly, we should neither try to impose Christian standards by force on an unwilling public, nor remain silent and inactive before the contemporary landslide, nor rely exclusively on the dogmatic assertion of biblical values, but rather reason with people about the benefits of Christian morality, commending God's law to them by rational arguments. We believe that God's laws are both good in themselves and universal in their application because, far from being arbitrary, they fit the human beings God has made. This was God's claim for his laws from the beginning. He gave them, he said, 'for your own good' (Deuteronomy 10:13), and pleaded with the people to obey them 'so that it might go well with them and their children for ever' (Deuteronomy 5:29 etc.). There was thus an essential correspondence between what was 'good and right in the eyes of the Lord' and what was 'well with them' (Deuteronomy 12:28). The 'good' and the 'well' coincided. We believe, moreover, that everybody has an inkling that this is so. But because they may be either unable or unwilling to acknowledge it, we have to deploy arguments to demonstrate that God's laws are for the wellbeing both of individuals and of society.

We therefore need a doctrinal apologetic in evangelism (arguing the truth of the gospel) and an ethical apologetic in social action (arguing the goodness of the moral law). Apologists of both kinds are wanted urgently in today's Church and world.

Examples of persuasion by argument

Let me try to supply some examples. The Christian standards of chastity before marriage and fidelity within it are increasingly challenged and repudiated. Sexual promiscuity is spreading, even though the AIDS scare has provoked a greater degree of self-control in some, and in others even a new celibate lifestyle. At the same time, experimental living together before marriage is not only widely practised, but widely recommended. Cohabitation without marriage, not just in the old sense of *de facto* 'common law marriage' but in the sense of deliberately dispensing with marriage altogether as an obsolete custom, now provokes little if any social displeasure. Wife-swapping is regarded as an amusing suburban game. 'Open marriages', in which the husband knows his wife has other sexual partners, and the wife knows the same about her husband, and both approve of the fact, and even encourage it, are not unusual. In some circumstances a series of successive marriages through easy divorce is regarded as 'enriching' (the suffering of the children being conveniently ignored or rationalized), and a homosexual partnership is more and more considered a legitimate alternative to a heterosexual marriage.

In the face of this sexual revolution, Christians should of course both themselves obey, and make known to others, the unchanging standards of God's law. Nevertheless, it will not be enough to climb Mount Sinai and proclaim the Ten Commandments from that pinnacle of authority. Even when people are converted and regenerated (which remains our paramount concern and the surest route to moral uprightness), they still need reasons for obedience. So what arguments can we deploy? The first is anthropological. It was Raymond Johnston who in his 1978 London Lectures in Contemporary Christianity introduced me to J.D. Unwin's book *Sex and*

Culture (1934). He described it as 'one of the monumental works of comparative anthropology'.[17] Unwin confessed that he began his investigation 'with carefree open-mindedness' and 'in all innocence'. With no axe to grind, and no idea where his researches might lead him, he wanted to test the conjecture that civilization and sexual self-control were related to each other. He studied 80 primitive and 16 civilized societies, and found that a society's cultural energy (art, science, technology, etc.) increases as its sexual energy is controlled.

His study of certain 'vigorous societies' revealed that 'in each case they reduced their sexual opportunity to a minimum by the adoption of absolute monogamy; in each case the ensuing compulsory continence produced great social energy. The group within the society which suffered the greatest continence displayed the greatest energy, and dominated the society.' Conversely, whenever monogamy was modified, the society's cultural energy decreased. The conclusion of his book was that if a vigorous society 'wishes to display its productive energy for a long time', it must regulate relations between the sexes by practising monogamy. Then 'its inherited tradition would be continually enriched; it would achieve a higher culture than has yet been attained; by the action of human entropy (sc. the generation of fresh cultural energy) its tradition would be augmented and refined in a manner which surpasses our present understanding.'[18] Freud had taught similarly that the flourishing of culture and the restraining of instincts belong together.

To this sociological evidence a psychological argument may be added. It is well known that male and female sexual experiences differ. The male sexual appetite is largely physical, is quickly aroused and quickly satisfied. With women, however, sexual intercourse is not *in itself* a wholly satisfying experience, for it arouses other desires which are not so easily met – desires for the security of husband, home and children. For men to arouse such desires, when they have no intention of fulfilling them, can only be described as cruel.[19]

Some years ago I read a confirmation of this in an unlikely place, namely the November 1977 edition of the American magazine *Seventeen*. It carried an article entitled 'The Case Against Living Together', which took the form of an interview with Dr Nancy Moore Clatworthy, a sociologist at Ohio State University in Columbus, Ohio. For 10 years she had been studying the phenomenon of unmarried couples living together. When she began, she was predisposed towards it. Young people had told her it was 'wonderful', and she had believed them. It seemed to her a 'sensible' arrangement, 'a useful step in courtship', during which couples got to know each other. But her research (which involved the testing of hundreds of couples, married and unmarried) led her to change her mind. 'The things people say living together is doing for them, it's not doing,' she said. The problem was specially with the young women, whom she found uptight, fearful, and looking 'past the rhetoric to the possible pain and agony'. She made two points in particular. First, regarding problems. 'In the areas of adjustment, happiness and respect', couples who had lived together before marriage had *more* problems than those who had married first. They also argued more, e.g. about money, friends and sex. 'In *every* area the couples who had lived together before marriage disagreed more often than the couples who had not.' It was evident, she concluded, that living to-gether first does not solve problems. Dr Clatworthy's second point was about commitment. 'Commitment is the expectation a person has about the outcome of a relationship ... Commitment is what makes marriage, living together or any human relationship work.' But 'knowing that something is temporary affects the degree of commitment to it.' So unmarried couples are less than whole-hearted in working to sustain and protect their relationship; and consequently 75 per cent of them break up. It is specially the women who are badly hurt. Dr Clatworthy concludes: 'Statistically, you're much better off marrying than living together.' 'For people who are in love anything less than a full commitment is a cop-out.'

When anthropology, sociology and psychology all point in the same direction, the argument is powerful. We should not be afraid to use it. Nor should we be surprised about this convergence, because God has written his law in two places, on stone tablets and on the tablets of the human heart (Romans 2:14f.). The moral law is not alien to human beings, therefore. There is a fundamental corre-spondence between Scripture and human nature.

Sexual morality is only one example of the need to deploy argu-ments in our defence and commendation of Christian social ethics. We should seek to develop the same strategy in every sphere. The 'just war theory', for instance, is a line of reasoning which is not expressly Christian. Although it has been developed by great Chris-tian thinkers like Augustine and Thomas Aquinas, its origins go back to Plato, Aristotle and Cicero in ancient Greece and Rome. So it is a tradition, although it has been refined and enriched by

Scripture. Many non-Christians agree with its reasonableness, even though they may not accept the authority of Scripture.

Again, we can occupy common ground with non-Christians, and join hands with them, in our desire both to protect human rights and to preserve the natural environment. Respect for human beings is a major concern of secular humanists, who are dedicated to the human cause, even if their reasons differ from those of Christians. As for conservation, it is possible to agree about the unity of space-ship earth, the delicate balance of nature, our common dependence on air, water and earth, and the distinction between capital re-sources (like fossil fuels) and income – without ever quoting a text from Genesis 1 and 2 or from any other part of Scripture.

My last example concerns the use of Sunday. The duty to safe-guard one day in seven for worship and rest is laid down in the fourth commandment, which is still in force. But we shall not secure Sunday observance merely by quoting God's law – or not until peo-ple are converted. Meanwhile, however, we believe that it is God's will to maintain this rhythm, that the nation is well served by legisla-tive protection of Sunday as a different day, that family life is built up by it, that workers are thus protected against being compelled to work, and that at least 'spectator sports' (which demand the trans-portation of large numbers of people and the provision of policing, catering, fire and ambulance services) should be prohibited. For why should some people get their rest and recreation at the expense of others who have to work to provide it? And when the biblical argument is unacceptable, the historical argument may convince. Several attempts have been made to change the one-day-in-seven rhythm, either by cancelling the day of rest altogether or by length-ening the working week. For example, the French revolutionaries, after abolishing the monarchy and setting up the Republic in 1792, introduced a new republican calendar with a 10-day week. But the experiment survived only a few years. People could not last nine days without a break. So in 1805 Napoleon restored the seven-day week. Something similar happened after the Russian revolution a century later. In sweeping away religious institutions, the revolu-tionary leaders turned Sunday into a working day. But again it did not last, and Stalin restored Sunday as a day of rest.

We should not be unduly concerned that the arguments men-tioned in nearly all of my examples are based on self-interest. For when we are looking for reasoning which will appeal to the public at large, we have to be realistic. 'The art of government, in fact,' wrote William Temple, 'is the art of so ordering life that self-interest prompts what justice demands.'[20] People need to be convinced that the laws which govern their lives are for their good, and that it is to their advantage to be law-abiding. This is even more true of groups than it is of individuals. Indeed, the main thesis of Reinhold Niebuhr's book *Moral Man and Immoral Society* is that, whereas 'individual men may be moral in the sense that they are able to consider interests other than their own in determining problems of conduct', we have to recognize 'the brutal character of the behaviour of all human collectives, and the power of self-interest and collective egoism in all inter-group relations'.[21]

Political systems

Social action is not only a question of winning the public debate, but of securing legislation which makes public life more pleasing to God. Not that every sin should be made a crime, and all duty buttressed by legal sanctions. For there are areas of private life into which the law should not intrude. For example, in Moslem countries private sexual immorality is a punishable offence, whereas in Christian countries it is not, unless it harms other people in some way. The main function of the law is to safeguard the accepted values of society and to protect the rights of citizens. Laws must also be enforceable, which means that they must enjoy public approval. To frame and pass such laws requires political power, and in a democracy majority power in Parliament.

It is irrelevant to reply that Jesus and his apostles were not interested in politics, and that they neither required nor even commended political action, let alone engaged in it themselves. This is true. They did not. But we have to remember that they were a tiny, insignificant minority under the totalitarian regime of Rome. The legions were everywhere, and were under orders to suppress dissent, crush opposition, and preserve the *status quo*. The first-century Christians *could* not take political action; is this the reason why they *did* not? At least the fact that they did not because they could not is no reason why we should not – if we can. The question is: would they have been politically active if they had had both the opportunity to be and the likelihood of success? I believe they would. For without appropriate political action some social needs simply cannot be met. The apostles did not demand the abolition of slavery. But are we not glad and proud that nineteenth-century Christians did? Their campaign was based on biblical teaching regarding human dignity, and was a legitimate extrapolation from it. The apostles did not build hospitals either, or require them to be built, but Christian hospitals are a legitimate extrapolation from Jesus' compassionate concern for the sick. Just so, political action (which is love seeking justice for the oppressed) is a legitimate extrapolation from the teaching and ministry of Jesus.

What is necessary now is to take up the three possible attitudes to social change which we have been considering and give them a political twist, at the same time noting what view of human beings each presupposes.

Absolutism is the political expression of imposition. An absolutist government makes and enforces laws without the checks and balances of a constitution or of consultation with the people. Absolutism arises from an entirely *pessimistic* view of human beings. Either they are thought to be too stupid to know what is good for themselves and for society, or, if they do know, it is thought that they cannot agree about it or that they do not want it. In consequence, the argument runs, 'We have to tell 'em; we'll knock their heads together and make 'em conform.' The public justification given is always that tight control is necessary for the sake of social order. And occasionally an autocracy has been genuinely benevolent. Nevertheless, it demeans citizens because it does not trust them to have any share in decision-making.

Anarchy could be regarded as the political expression of *laissez-faire*. Not that it was in the nineteenth century, for its original advocates cherished the vision of an ordered society, with *laissez-faire* economics as the means to that end. But the modern *laissez-faire* attitude would naturally lead to the abolition of all government and law, and would arise from a naively *optimistic* view of human beings. It assumes that they are perfectly capable of governing themselves, and that laws are unnecessary to create a just society. 'Leave people alone,' it is said, 'and all will be well.'

So then absolutism considers rigid control essential because it is pessimistic about human beings, denying their dignity due to their creation in God's image. Anarchy, on the other hand, considers unrestricted freedom safe because it is optimistic about human beings, denying their depravity due to the Fall. Both are politically mistaken because both are theologically mistaken, being based on false doctrines of humanity. They are also disastrous in practice. Absolutism leads to tyranny, not justice, and anarchy leads to chaos, not Utopia.

Democracy is the third option. It is the political expression of persuasion by argument. If absolutism, being pessimistic, imposes law arbitrarily, and anarchy, being optimistic, dispenses with law altogether, then democracy, being realistic about human beings as both created and fallen, involves citizens in the framing of their own laws. At least this is the theory. In practice, especially in countries with a large number of illiterates, the media can too easily manipulate them. And in every democracy there is the constant danger of trampling on minorities.

'The word "democracy" and its derivatives apply to decision-procedures,' writes John R. Lucas in his book *Democracy and Participation*. The word describes three aspects of the decision-making process. The first concerns *who* takes it. 'A decision is democratically taken if the answer to the question "who takes it?" is "more or less everybody", in contrast to decisions taken only by those best qualified to take them, as in a meritocracy, or those taken by only one man, as in an autocracy or monarchy.' Secondly, democracy describes *how* a decision is reached. 'A decision is taken democratically if it is reached by discussion, criticism and compromise.' Thirdly, democracy describes *the spirit* in which a decision is made, namely 'being concerned with the interests of all, instead of only a faction or a party'.[22]

So modern democracy reflects the balanced biblical view of human beings, as we might expect in view of its roots in post-Reformation Christian Europe. It also gives Christians the opportunity to make a constructive contribution in a pluralistic society, by getting into the public debate (whether on disarmament or divorce, abortion or *in vitro* fertilization) and by seeking to influence public opinion until there is a public demand for legislation which would be more pleasing to God. For if democracy is government by consent, consent depends on consensus (or at least does so when electoral procedures are truly democratic), and consensus arises out of a discussion in which the issues become clarified.

Of course the democratic political process is also 'the art of the possible'. Because human beings are fallen there is bound to be a gap between the divine ideal and the human reality, between what

God has revealed and what humans find possible. Jesus himself recognized this distinction within the law of Moses. For Moses' permission of divorce in a case of 'indecency' or 'immorality', he said, was given 'because of the hardness of your hearts' (Mark 10:5). In other words, it was a concession to human weakness. But Jesus immediately added that 'from the beginning it was not so', reminding them of the divine ideal.

There is a great need for more Christian thinkers in contemporary society, who will throw themselves into the public debate, and for more Christian activists who will organize pressure groups to promote the work of persuasion. Their motivation will be thoroughly Christian – a vision of the God who cares about justice, compassion, honesty and freedom in society, and a vision of humanity, made in God's image though fallen, moral, responsible, and with a conscience to be respected. It will be out of zeal for God and love for human beings that they will seek the renewal of society. They will make no attempt to conceal the origins of their concern. Yet in the parry and thrust of debate, and in the policies they develop, they will have to be content with the realities of a fallen world. And all the time, their target will be the shaping of public opinion.

Addressing the need for Christians to live in cheerful protest against the assumptions of the consumer society, John V. Taylor, former Bishop of Winchester, has written: 'It is in the area of public opinion that this battle has to be fought. Nothing can achieve the change of policies which our very salvation demands but a profound reorientation of public opinion.' He went on to quote Reg Prentice, who said in 1972, when Minister of Overseas Development, that the only way to increase Britain's concern for Third World nations was the 'slow, hard grind of public education and political pressure within rich countries'. Bishop Taylor concluded that Christ's 'renewals and revolutions begin quietly, like faith itself. They start growing from one tiny seed, the staggering thought: *things don't have to be like this*. When that idea begins to trickle down into the structures and into the minds of ordinary people in our affluent society, the cry may at last go up: you're nothing but a pack of cards!'[23]

Chapter 4

ALIENATION: HAVE WE ANY INFLUENCE?

No single word captures more accurately, or expresses more eloquently, the modern sense of impotence than the word 'alienation'. To say 'I'm alienated' means 'I can't relate to society any longer and, what's worse, I can't do anything about it.'

Marx popularized the term. But he was referring to an economic order in which the workers, because their products were sold by the factory owner, were thus alienated from the fruits of their labour. Contemporary Marxists give the word a broader application. Jimmy Reid, for example, when a Communist councillor of Glasgow, Scotland, and chief spokesman of the Upper Clyde Shipyard Workers, said in 1972: 'Alienation is the cry of men who feel themselves to be the victims of blind economic forces beyond their control ... the frustration of ordinary people excluded from the process of decision-making.'[1]

So alienation is the feeling of economic and political powerlessness. The juggernauts of institutionalized power roll ruthlessly on their way, but the common man or woman cannot do anything to change their direction or speed, let alone stop them. We are nothing but spectators of a developing situation which we feel helpless to influence in any way. That is 'alienation'.

And in spite of my attempted theological defence of democratic theory, and my plea that Christians should take advantage of the democratic process and join in the public debate, I have to admit that democracy does not always cure alienation, for many are disillusioned with its realities. It is this gulf between theory and practice which lies at the heart of John R. Lucas' book *Democracy and Participation*, from which I quoted in the previous chapter. People exercise their democratic right to vote, and, to be sure, 'the vote constitutes a form of minimal participation' (p. 166). Thereafter, however, 'democracy becomes an autocracy, in which all decisions save one are taken by the autocrat, and the only decision left to the people is the occasional choice of autocrat'. So he renames democracy an 'elective autocracy', because it 'enables people to participate in government only to a derisory extent'. It also 'makes the government singularly insensitive to the wishes of the governed and the requirements of justice' (p. 184). Again, 'although elective autocracy has its democratic aspect, it is deeply undemocratic as regards the way and the spirit in which decisions are taken … It is non-participatory' (p. 198). Without doubt this disenchantment with the actual workings of democracy is widespread. Christians should share with others the concern to broaden the context of public debate, until parliamentary discussions 'reverberate in every inn and workshop in the realm'. Dr Lucas ends his book with the delightful statement that 'democracy can flourish only in a land of pubs' (p. 264).

To me it is sad that many Christians become contaminated by the mood of alienation. 'To be sure,' they agree, 'the quest for social justice is our concern and we cannot escape this fact. But the obstacles are immense. Not only are the issues complex (we claim no expertise), but society is pluralistic (we claim no monopoly of power or privilege), and the forces of reaction dominate (we have no influence). The receding tide of Christian faith in the community has left us high and dry. In addition, human beings are selfish and society is rotten. It is entirely unrealistic to hope for social change.'

The first antidote to this mixture of secular alienation and Christian pessimism is history. History is full of examples of social change as a result of Christian influence. Take England as an example. Social progress, especially as a result of biblical Christianity, cannot be denied. Think of some of the features which marred this country only 200 years ago. Criminal law was so harsh that about 200 offences were punishable by death; it was justly named 'the Bloody Code'. Slavery and the slave trade were still being defended as legitimate, even respectable. Men were 'press-ganged' into the army and navy. No education or health care was provided for the masses. Smallpox killed more than 10 per cent of every generation. Travel by horse and coach was made perilous by highwaymen. Social feudalism imprisoned people in a rigid class system, and condemned millions to abject poverty. Conditions in prisons, factories and mines were unbelievably inhuman. Only Anglicans were eligible to enter university or parliament, although a few dissenters got in through the practice of 'occasional conformity'. One is ashamed that only two centuries ago so much injustice tarnished our national life.

But the social influence of Christianity has been worldwide. K.S. Latourette sums it up at the conclusion of his seven-volume *History of the Expansion of Christianity*. He refers in glowing terms to the effects of the life of Christ through his followers.

> No life ever lived on this planet has been so influential in the affairs of men ... From that brief life and its apparent frustration has flowed a more powerful force for the triumphal waging of man's long battle than any other ever known by the human race ... Through it hundreds of millions have been lifted from illiteracy and ignorance, and have been placed upon the road of growing intellectual freedom and of control over their physical environment. It has done more to allay the physical ills of disease and famine than any other impulse known to man. It has emancipated millions from chattel slavery and millions of others from thraldom to vice. It has protected tens of millions from exploitation by their fellows. It has been the most fruitful source of movements to lessen the horrors of war and to put the relations of men and nations on the basis of justice and peace.[2]

So Christian pessimism is historically unfounded. It is also theologically inept. We have seen that the Christian mind holds together the biblical events of the Creation, the Fall, the Redemption and the Consummation. Christian pessimists concentrate on the Fall ('human beings are incorrigible') and the Consummation ('Christ is coming to put things right'), and imagine that these truths justify social despair. But they overlook the Creation and the Redemption. The divine image in human beings has not been obliterated. Though evil, they can still do good, as Jesus plainly taught (Matthew 7:11). And the evidence of our eyes confirms it. There are non-Christian people who have good marriages, non-Christian parents who love their children and bring them up well, non-Christian industrialists who run factories on a just basis, and non-Christian doctors who still take the Hippocratic standards as their guide and are conscientious in the care of their patients. This is partly because the truth of

God's law is written on all human hearts, and partly because the values of the Kingdom of God, when embodied in the Christian community, are often recognized and to some extent imitated by people outside it. In this way the gospel has borne fruit in western society over many generations.

In addition, Jesus Christ redeems people and makes them new. Are we saying that regenerated and renewed people can do nothing to restrain or reform society? Such an opinion is monstrous. This is the thrust of Charles Colson's book *Kingdoms in Conflict*. The radical values of the Kingdom of God, which was inaugurated by Jesus Christ, confront, challenge and change the kingdoms of men, especially through the agency of what Edmund Burke in the eighteenth century called 'little platoons'. Charles Colson has in mind small voluntary associations of people who love God and their neighbour, exhibit transcendence in the midst of secularism, refuse to acquiesce in evil, oppose injustice, and spread mercy and reconciliation in the world.[3]

The combined witness of history and Scripture is that Christian people have had an enormous influence on society. We are not powerless. Things can be different. Nikolai Berdyaev summed the situation up admirably in these words: 'The sinfulness of human nature does not mean that social reforms and improvements are impossible. It only means that there can be no perfect and absolute social order ... before the transfiguration of the world.'[4]

Salt and light

From history and Scripture I turn to the expectation which Jesus had for his followers. He expressed it most vividly in the Sermon on the Mount by his use of the salt and light metaphors:

> You are the salt of the earth. But if the salt loses its saltiness, how can it be made salty again? It is no longer good for anything, except to be thrown out and trampled by men.
>
> You are the light of the world. A city on a hill cannot be hidden. Neither do people light a lamp and put it under a bowl. Instead they put it on its stand, and it gives light to everyone in the house. In the same way, let your light shine before men, that they may see your good deeds and praise your Father in heaven.
>
> (Matthew 5:13–16)

Everybody is familiar with salt and light. They are found in virtually every household in the world. Jesus himself, as a boy in the Nazareth home, must often have watched his mother Mary use salt as a preservative in the kitchen and light the lamps when the sun went down. He knew their practical usefulness.

So these were the images which Jesus later used to illustrate the influence he expected his disciples to exert in human society. At that time they were very few in number, the initial nucleus of his new society; yet they were to be salt and light to the whole earth. What did he mean? At least four truths cannot be missed.

First, *Christians are fundamentally different from non-Christians*, or ought to be. Both images set the two communities apart. The world is dark, Jesus implied, but you are to be its light. The world is decaying, but you are to be its salt and hinder its decay. In English idiom we might say they are as different as 'chalk from cheese' or 'oil from water'; Jesus said they are as different as light from darkness, and salt from decay. This is a major theme of the whole Bible. God is calling out from the world a people for himself, and the vocation of this people is to be 'holy' or 'different'. 'Be holy,' he says to them again and again, 'because I am holy.'

Secondly, *Christians must permeate non-Christian society*. Although Christians are (or should be) morally and spiritually distinct from non-Christians, they are not to be socially segregated. On the contrary, their light is to shine into the darkness, and their salt is to soak into the decaying meat. The lamp does no good if it is put under a bed or a bowl, and the salt does no good if it stays in the salt cellar. Similarly, Christians are not to remain aloof from society, where they cannot affect it, but are to become immersed in its life. They are to let their light shine, so that their good deeds are seen.

Thirdly, *Christians can influence non-Christian society*. Before the days of refrigeration, salt was the best known preservative. Either it was rubbed into fish and meat, or they were left to soak in it. In this way bacterial decay was retarded, though not of course entirely arrested. Light is even more obviously effective; when the light is switched on, the darkness is actually dispelled. Just so, Jesus must have meant, Christians can hinder social decay and dispel the darkness of evil. William Temple wrote of the 'pervasive sweetening of life and of all human relationships by those who carry with them something of the mind of Christ'.[5]

This prompts the question why Christians have not had a far greater influence for good on the non-Christian world. I hope my American friends will forgive me if I take the United States as my example; of course in principle the situation is the same in Europe. The published statistics of American Christianity are staggering.

According to Gallup polls conducted in 1994 and 1996, 96 per cent of Americans said they believed in 'God or a universal spirit', 28 per cent attended church or synagogue at least once a week, 59 per cent called themselves Protestant, and 41 per cent said they would describe themselves as '"born again" or evangelical'. Why then has this great army of Christian soldiers not been more successful in beating back the forces of evil? This is American futurologist Tom Sine's explanation: 'We have been remarkably effective at diluting his [Christ's] extremist teaching and truncating his radical gospel. That explains why we ... make such an embarrassingly little difference in the morality of our society.'[6] More important than mere numbers of professing disciples are both the quality of their discipleship (maintaining Christ's standards without compromise) and their strategic deployment (capturing positions of influence for Christ).

Our Christian habit is to bewail the world's deteriorating standards with an air of rather self-righteous dismay. We criticize its violence, dishonesty, immorality, disregard for human life, and materialistic greed. 'The world is going down the drain,' we say with a shrug. But whose fault is it? Who is to blame? Let me put it like this. If the house is dark when nightfall comes, there is no sense in blaming the house; that is what happens when the sun goes down. The question to ask is 'Where is the light?' Similarly, if the meat goes bad and becomes inedible, there is no sense in blaming the meat; that is what happens when bacteria are left alone to breed. The question to ask is 'Where is the salt?' Just so, if society deteriorates and its standards decline, till it becomes like a dark night or stinking fish, there is no sense in blaming society; that is what happens when fallen men and women are left to themselves, and human selfishness is unchecked. The question to ask is 'Where is the Church? Why are the salt and light of Jesus Christ not permeating and changing our society?' It is sheer hypocrisy on our part to raise our eyebrows, shrug our shoulders or wring our hands. The Lord Jesus told *us* to be the world's salt and light. If therefore darkness and rottenness abound, it is largely our fault and we must accept the blame

Fourthly, *Christians must retain their Christian distinctness*. If salt does not retain its saltiness, it is good for nothing. If light does not retain its brightness, it becomes ineffective. So we who claim to be Christ's followers have to fulfil two conditions if we are to do any good for him. On the one hand, we have to permeate non-Christian society, and immerse ourselves in the life of the world. On the other, while doing so, we have to avoid becoming assimilated to the world. We must retain our Christian convictions, values, standards and lifestyle. We are back with the 'double identity' of the Church ('holiness' and 'worldliness') which I mentioned in the first chapter.

If it be asked what the 'saltiness' and 'brightness' of Christian holiness are, the rest of the Sermon on the Mount gives us the answer. For in it Jesus tells us not to be like others around us: 'Do not be like them' (Matthew 6:8). Instead, he calls us to a greater righteousness (of the heart), a wider love (even of enemies), a deeper devotion (of children coming to their Father) and a nobler ambition (seeking first God's rule and righteousness.[7] It is only as we choose and follow his way that our salt will retain its saltiness and our light will shine, that we shall be his effective witnesses and servants, and exert a wholesome influence on society.

This purpose and expectation of Christ should be enough to overcome our sense of alienation. We may be ostracized by some at work or in our local community. Secular society may do its best to push us to the circumference of its concerns. But, refusing to be marginalized, we should seek to occupy a sphere of influence for Christ. Ambition is the desire to succeed. There is nothing wrong with it if it is genuinely subordinated to the will and glory of God. True, power can corrupt. True also, the power of Christ is best displayed in our weakness. And indeed we shall continue to feel our personal inadequacy. Yet we should determine by his grace to infiltrate some secular segment of society and raise his flag there, maintaining without compromise his standards of love, truth and goodness.

But how can we exert some influence for Christ? What does it mean in practice to be the world's salt and light? What can we do for social change? I will try to develop six ways, in three pairs.

Prayer and evangelism

First, there is the power of prayer. I beg you not to dismiss this as a pious platitude, a sop to Christian convention. For it really is not.

We cannot read the Bible without being impressed by its constant emphasis on the efficacy of prayer. 'The prayer of a righteous man is powerful and effective,' wrote James (5:16). 'I tell you,' said Jesus, 'that if two of you on earth agree about anything you ask for, it will be done for you by my Father in heaven' (Matthew 18:19). We do not claim to understand the rationale of intercession. But somehow it enables us to enter the field of spiritual conflict, and to align ourselves with the good purposes of God, so that his power is released and the principalities of evil are held back.

Prayer is an indispensable part of the individual Christian's life. It is also indispensable to the life of the local church. Paul gave it priority. 'First of all, then, I urge that supplications, prayers, intercessions, and thanksgivings be made for all men, for kings and all who are in high positions, that we may lead a quiet and peaceable life, godly and respectful in every way. This is good, and it is acceptable in the sight of God our Saviour, who desires all men to be saved and to come to the knowledge of the truth' (Timothy 2:1–4 RSV). Here is prayer for national leaders, that they may fulfil their responsibility to maintain conditions of peace and order, in which the Church is free both to obey God and to preach the gospel.

In theory, we are convinced of this duty to pray. Yet some Christian social activists seldom stop to pray. And some churches hardly seem to take it seriously. If in the community (indeed, in the world), there is more violence than peace, more oppression than justice, more secularism than godliness, is it because Christians and churches are not praying as they should?

This is how the Church's obligation in this matter was expressed in the report of the International Consultation on the Relationship between Evangelism and Social Responsibility (1982):

We resolve ourselves, and call upon our churches, to take much more seriously the period of intercession in public worship; to think in terms of ten or fifteen minutes rather than five; to invite lay people to share in leading, since they often have deep insight into the world's needs; and to focus our prayers both on the evangelization of the world (closed lands, resistant peoples, missionaries, national churches, etc.) and on the quest for peace and justice in the world (places of tension and conflict, deliverance from the nuclear horror, rulers and governments, the poor and needy, etc.). We long to see every Christian congregation bowing down in humble and expectant faith before our Sovereign Lord.[8]

We also rejoice over the growth of parachurch movements whose goal is to stimulate the prayers of the people of God (e.g. in the UK the Lydia Fellowship, Crosswinds, and Intercessors for Britain and in the US Intercessors for America and the AD 2000 movement.)

The successful ousting of President Marcos, the Filipino dictator, is usually referred to as either 'the February Revolution' or 'People Power'. But a number of Christians have been saying, 'It was not people power; it was prayer power.' On 13 February 1986 the Roman Catholic bishops issued a bold statement declaring the 7 February elections fraudulent and the Marcos government illegitimate. Rejecting both extremes of apathy and violence, they went on to call for 'the active resistance of evil by peaceful means', including prayer. At the huge rally in Luneta Park, Cory Aquino also called for prayer and non-violent protest. When, a few days later, Defence Minister Juan Enrile and General Fidel Ramos declared Mrs Aquino the rightful President, and made Camp Aguinaldo their headquarters, Cardinal Archbishop Sin over the radio told his nuns to get to their chapels in order to support and protect Enrile and Ramos. It is estimated that up to two million unarmed civilians, Protestants as well as Catholics, took to the streets and formed human barricades. And when the marines came in their tanks, they were stopped 'not by anti-tank missiles but by the bodies of praying Filipinos.'[9] The soldiers 'could never shoot at people who were praying. They could have shot people who were throwing stones ... But this was the first time that they were confronted with prayers.'[10] The marines withdrew and Marcos fled. 'What is so remarkable about the story of the Philippines,' concludes Charles Colson, 'is that millions of people believed more in the power of prayer than in the power of politics.'[11]

I turn now from the power of prayer to the power of the gospel, and so to evangelism. This book is about Christian social responsibility, not evangelism. Nevertheless, the two belong together. Although different Christians have received different gifts and callings, and although in some situations it is perfectly proper to concentrate on either evangelism or social action without combining them, nevertheless in general and in theory they cannot be separated. Our love for our neighbours will be fleshed out in a holistic concern for all their needs – for the needs of their bodies, souls and community. That is why in the ministry of Jesus words and works were bracketed. As the Grand Rapids Report put it, evangelism and social activity are 'like the two blades of a pair of scissors or the two wings of a bird'.[12]

There are, however, two particular ways in which evangelism should be seen as a necessary prelude to and foundation of social action. First, the gospel changes people. Every Christian should be able to echo Paul's words with conviction: 'I am not ashamed of the gospel, because it is the power of God for the salvation of everyone who believes' (Romans 1:16). We know it in our own lives, and we have seen it in the lives of others. If sin is at root self-centredness, then the transformation from 'self' to 'unself' is an essential ingredient of salvation. Faith leads to love, and love to service. So social activity, which is the loving service of the needy, should be the inevitable result of saving faith, although we have to confess that this is not always so.

There are other situations in which positive social change is taking place apart from explicit Christian initiatives. So we must not bind evangelism and social change together so indissolubly as to say that the former *always* issues in the latter and the latter *never* happens without the former. Nevertheless, these are exceptions which prove the rule. We still insist that evangelism is the major instrument of social change. For the gospel changes people, and changed people can change society. We have seen that society needs salt and light; but only the gospel can create them. This is one way in which we may declare without embarrassment that evangelism takes primacy over social action. Logically speaking, 'Christian social responsibility presupposes socially responsible Christians', and it is the gospel which produces them.[13]

When John V. Taylor, who later became the Bishop of Winchester, was still General Secretary of the Church Missionary Society, he described in his *CMS Newsletter* (May 1972) his reactions to Geoffrey Moorhouse's book *Calcutta*, and indeed to the apparent hopelessness of that city's problems. 'But invariably what tips the balance from despair to faith,' he wrote, 'is the person who rises above the situation.' Such persons are neither 'trapped' in the city, nor have they 'escaped' from it. 'They have *transcended* the situation … Salvation is not the same as solution: it precedes it and makes it a possibility … Personal salvation – salvation in first gear – is still the way in. It is the key to unlock the door of determinism and make possible the "salvation" of corporate organizations and institutions – salvation in second gear – by providing those who can transcend the situation.'

There is another way in which social uplift is facilitated by evangelism. When the gospel is faithfully and widely preached, it not only brings a radical renewal to individuals, but produces what Raymond Johnston once called 'an antiseptic atmosphere', in which blasphemy, selfishness, greed, dishonesty, immorality, cruelty and injustice find it harder to flourish. A country which has been permeated by the gospel is not a soil in which these poisonous weeds can easily take root, let alone luxuriate.

More than this. The gospel which changes people also changes cultures. One of the greatest hindrances to social change is the conservatism of culture. A country's laws, institutions and customs have taken centuries to develop; they have a built-in resistance to reform. In some cases it is the moral ambiguity of culture which is the hindrance. Every political programme, economic system and development plan depends on values to motivate and sustain it. It cannot operate without honesty and some degree of altruism. So progress is effectively blocked if the national culture (and the religion or ideology which shapes it) connives at corruption and selfishness, and offers no incentive to self-control or self-sacrifice. Then culture stands in the way of development.

Professor Brian Griffiths (now Lord Griffiths) applied this principle with great insight to both Capitalism and Marxism in his 1980 London Lectures in Contemporary Christianity, entitled *Morality and the Market Place*. To him Capitalism had lost its legitimacy and Marxism was fatally flawed. 'Capitalism suffers because of inadequate limits on the exercise of freedom', while Communism 'suffers from an inability to put adequate constraints on the urge to control'. But this 'inability to resolve the basic tension between freedom and control' is the crisis of secular humanism. Both Capitalism and Marxism are, in fact, the product of the eighteenth-century Enlightenment: what they lack is Christian values.[14]

Brian Griffiths' last chapter is entitled 'Third World Poverty and First World Responsibility'. He takes issue with a key expression used by Herr Willy Brandt in his Introduction to the Brandt Commission Report: 'We take it for granted that all cultures deserve equal respect, protection and promotion.'[15] 'But they do not' is Brian Griffiths' rejoinder. 'Cultures express values which shape institutions and motivate people – some of which ... promote wealth and justice and liberty, and others of which do not.'[16]

It is entirely logical, therefore, that a book on economics, and in particularly on *Morality and the Market Place*, should conclude with a passionate plea for world evangelism.

Christianity starts with faith in Christ and it finishes with service in the world ... Because of this I believe that evangelism has an indispensable part to play in the establishment of a more just economic order. Obedience to Christ demands change, the world becomes his world, the poor, the weak and the suffering are men, women and children created in his image; injustice is an affront to his creation; despair, indifference and aimlessness are replaced by hope, responsibility and purpose; and above all selfishness is transformed by love.[17]

So the gospel changes both people and cultures. This is not to say that no development is possible without evangelism, but rather that development is hindered without, and greatly facilitated by, the cultural changes which the gospel brings. And the more the gospel spreads, the more hopeful the situation becomes. Even a few Christians in public life can initiate social change. But their influence is likely to be far greater if they have massive grassroots support, as the nineteenth-century British evangelical reformers had. So Christians in every country should pray for a widespread acceptance of the gospel. As the nineteenth-century American evangelicals clearly saw, revival and reform belong together.

Witness and protest

We have seen that the gospel is God's power for salvation. But in fact all truth is powerful. God's truth is much more mighty than the devil's crooked lies. We should never be afraid of the truth. Nor do we ever need to be afraid for the truth, as if its survival hung in the balance. For God watches over it and will never allow it to be completely suppressed. As Paul put it, 'we cannot do anything against the truth, but only for the truth' (2 Corinthians 13:8). And as John put it, 'The light shines in the darkness, and the darkness has not overcome it' (John 1:5, margin). One contemporary Christian thinker who is convinced about this is Solzhenitsyn. His Nobel Speech on Literature (1970) was entitled *One Word of Truth*. He confessed that writers lack all material weapons like rockets and tanks. So 'what can literature do,' he asked, 'in the face of the merciless onslaught of open violence?' First, it can refuse 'to take part in the lie'. Secondly, writers and artists can 'vanquish the lie'. For *'one word of truth outweighs the whole world*. And on such a fantastic breach of the law of conservation of mass and energy are based my own activities and my appeal to the writers of the world.'[18]

All Christians are called like their Master 'to bear witness to the truth'. This, he added, was why he had been born and why he had come into the world (John 18:37). The supreme truth to which we testify is of course Jesus Christ himself, for he is the truth (John 14:6). But all truth – scientific, biblical, theological, moral – is his, and we are to be fearless in defending, maintaining and arguing it. This is the place for developing an ethical apologetic, as I was urging in the last chapter, and for entering into the public debate of contemporary issues. From the pulpit (still a much more influential 'platform' than is commonly realized, especially in the shaping of public opinion), through letters to and articles in national and local newspapers, in discussions at home and work, through opportunities on radio and television, by poetry, drama and popular songs, we are called as Christians to witness to God's law and God's gospel, without fear or apology. Moreover, as with Jesus so with his followers, the true witness (*martus*) must be prepared to suffer, and even if necessary to die, for his testimony. Such costly testimony is the chief weapon of those who are denied the democratic process because they live under an oppressive regime.

In a much-publicized speech in 1974, Sir Keith Joseph spoke about the moral decline of Britain, the possibility of 're-moralizing' the nation, and the power of ideas. 'Are we to be destroyed from inside?' he asked, although we had repelled successive attempts at invasion from outside by Philip of Spain, Napoleon, the Kaiser and Hitler. 'Are we to be destroyed by ideas, mischievous, wrongheaded, debilitating, yet seductive because they are fashionable and promise so much on the cheap?' Later in the speech he answered his own questions, and urged his listeners to go on to the offensive. 'We must fight the battle of ideas,' he cried, 'in every school, university, publication, committee, TV studio, even if we have to struggle for our toe-hold there. We have the truth. If we fail to make it shine clear, we shall be to blame no less than the exploiters, the casuists and the commercializers.'[19]

Here is an illustration of the power of the truth. The World Development Movement, to which many Christians and churches belong, exists to campaign for political changes in Britain's aid and trade policies towards the Third World. In October 1985 it organized the largest ever mass lobby of Parliament, when 20,000 people urged

MPs to fight world poverty. Shortly afterwards the government announced that Britain's aid programme, instead of being reduced, would be increased by £47 million. In January 1987 WDM persuaded the government to double its contribution to UNICEF (the United Nations Children's Fund). The same month Christopher Patten, then Minister for Overseas Development, had the integrity to say: 'WDM has taught me a great deal. As a result of the strength of their intellectual arguments, they have convinced me to change my mind on at least two specific matters of policy.'

Alongside a positive witness to the truth must go its negative counterpart, protest against folly, deceit and wickedness. Many seem to be disenchanted with the weapon of rational protest, but I think they should not be. Public agitation is an effective weapon. Let me give you some examples.

First, before the General Election in 1983, when William Whitelaw as Home Secretary published details of the Police and Criminal Evidence Bill which he intended to introduce into Parliament, there was an immediate outcry against its Clause 10, which would have given police the power to search for and remove confidential records held by clergymen, doctors and social workers. Vigorous protests were made by lawyers and doctors, and 55 Church of England bishops signed a petition. Almost at once the Home Secretary announced that he would amend the clause.

My second example comes from West Germany. When details of the 1983 population census were published, and it became known that respondents would be required to divulge a great deal of private information about themselves, there was a groundswell of protest. A law student and two lawyers used the right of German citizens, when they believe that their civil liberties are being threatened, to appeal to the highest court of the land, the Federal Constitutional Court in Karlsruhe. The Court stopped the census, by what was virtually an interim injunction, in order to create time in which to study its legality in full.

Thirdly, organized protest was very nearly successful in preventing a free-for-all in Sunday trading in England and Wales. The Shops Act of 1950 required Sunday closure, with a few exceptions. Everybody agreed that, as it stood, the law contained anomalies, was difficult to enforce, and needed reform. The Conservative government of the day, however, backed by powerful commercial interests, accepted the Auld Committee's recommendation that all legal restrictions on Sunday should be abolished.

Refusing to be intimidated by this deregulation lobby, a small Christian research group, the Jubilee Centre in Cambridge, launched the 'Keep Sunday Special Campaign'. This became a coalition of the churches of all major denominations, the shop workers' union and several retail trade bodies, who were united in the pursuit of three goals: (1) to protect the special character of Sunday (for rest and recreation as well as worship); (2) to promote family life and social contact; and (3) to prevent hardship for shopworkers, shopkeepers and residents near shopping areas.

The 'Keep Sunday Special Campaign' was at first highly success-ful, not only because it was a grass-roots campaign (more letters were written to MPs on this issue than on any other in 1986), but also because it looked beyond the defeat of deregulation to reform (not the repeal) of the Shops Act. As well as allowing all small shops to open, its positive 'REST' proposals would have allowed for the registering and opening of large shops related to Recreation (e.g. sports and garden centres), Emergencies (e.g. chemists), Social gatherings (e.g. restaurants) and Travel (e.g. garages). All other large shops would have remained closed.

So what happened? The Thatcher government's 'Sunday Trad-ing Bill', providing for total deregulation, was introduced in 1985, but defeated during its second reading in 1986. Following this hu-miliation (the only parliamentary defeat suffered by Mrs Thatcher's government), both sides of the debate rallied their forces, including the giant chainstores. For example, Tescos and Sainsburys tried to gain support for deregulation by openly flouting the laws from December 1991. The John Lewis Partnership, on the other hand, threw its weight behind the 'REST' proposals. In a final twist to the saga, for reasons which remain unclear, the shopworkers' union changed sides shortly before the crucial vote and supported Sunday opening. As a result, the relatively restrictive KSSC proposals were lost in December 1993 by 304 votes to 286. The so-called 'compro-mise' which won the day restricted large shops to opening for six hours on all Sundays except Easter Day (and Christmas when it falls on a Sunday). Although the 'Keep Sunday Special Campaign' eventually salvaged only limited restraints on Sunday opening, it demonstrated that persuasive argument based on biblical values can rally the united support of both Christians and non-Christians. Let no one say that protest and campaigning are a waste of time and effort.

Example and groups

Truth is powerful when it is argued; it becomes even more powerful when it is also exhibited. For people need not only to understand the arguments, but to see its benefits displayed. One Christian nurse in a hospital, teacher in a school, secretary in an office, assistant in a shop, or worker in a factory, can have an influence out of all proportion to numbers and percentages. And who can calculate the influence for good on the whole neighbourhood of a single Christian home, in which husband and wife are faithful to and find fulfilment in each other, their children grow up in the disciplined security of love, and the family are not turned in on themselves but outgoing to the community? Christians are marked people both at work and at home; the world is watching us.

More influential even than the example of Christian individuals and families is that of the local church. For the church is meant by God to be his new and redeemed community, which embodies the ideals of his Kingdom. We must not underestimate, writes Dr John Howard Yoder, 'the powerful ... impact on society of the creation of an alternative social group'. For 'the primary social structure through which the gospel works to change other structures is that of the Christian community.'[20]

But how does the new community change the old? The answer is well expressed in the Grand Rapids Report:

First, the new community should constitute a challenge to the old. Its values and ideals, its moral standards and relationships, its sacrificial life-style, its love, joy and peace – these are the signs of the Kingdom ... and present the world with a radically alternative society ...

Secondly, as the world lives alongside the Kingdom community, some of the values of the Kingdom spill over into society as a whole, so that its industry, commerce, legislation and institutions become to some degree imbued with Kingdom values. So-called 'Kingdomized' or 'Christianized' society is not the Kingdom of God, but it owes a debt to the Kingdom which often is unrecognized.

The 'overspill' model has its limitations, however, because it pictures the two communities as independent of one another, like two vessels standing side by side, the contents of one spilling over into the other. The salt, light and yeast metaphors which Jesus employed are more dynamic, since each implies the penetration of the old community by the new.[21]

Small groups of Christian people can be visible embodiments of the gospel. They can also make use of all the means of influencing society which I have mentioned so far. There is power in prayer and in the gospel; there is even more if we pray and evangelize together. There is power in witness and protest; there is even more if we testify and take action together. The group was our Lord's own chosen way. He began with the Twelve. And the long history of the Church abounds in examples of the strategic influence of small groups. In sixteenth-century Cambridge the early Reformers met in the White Horse Inn to study Erasmus' Greek New Testament; in eighteenth-century Oxford the Holy Club, to which the Wesleys and Whitefield belonged, although at first engaged in barren good works, was the background against which the evangelical revival began; and in nineteenth-century South London the Clapham Sect gave their support to Wilberforce in his anti-slavery campaign and to many other social and religious causes. Today one of the most promising features of modern church life is the hunger for the small group experience. Thousands of congregations have divided their membership into small fellowship or home groups. Many churches also encourage the formation of specialist groups – evangelistic visiting teams, missionary prayer groups, music groups, contemporary issue groups, reading groups, social study and action groups: the list is almost endless.

Then there are communities experimenting in new styles of living, sharing and/or working together – for example, the Kairos Community in Buenos Aires (for theological reflection on discipleship in the secular world), the Sojourners Community in Washington DC (involved in producing the Sojourners' magazine, in promoting its concern for peace and justice, and in serving local black families) and TRACI in New Delhi (The Research and Communication Institute of young Indian thinkers and writers). And in Britain there are groups like CARE Trust and CARE Campaigns (Christian Action, Research and Education) which promote moral standards in society, and I might also mention The Institute for Contemporary Christianity in London, whose goals are to stimulate the integration of consistent Christian thought and action in the world.

A widely respected Roman Catholic leader, long since retired, who believed strongly in the potential of small groups, is Dom Helder Camara, former Archbishop of Recife in north-east Brazil.

Accused of being subversive, forbidden access to the media, under constant threat of assassination, this 'violent peacemaker' (as he has been called) is committed to justice and peace. Having travelled half the world for several years, appealing to institutions, he came to put more faith in groups. He encourages the formation of 'Abrahamic minorities' (so-called 'because like Abraham we are hoping against hope')[22] in neighbourhoods, universities and unions, within the media, in management, among politicians and in the armed forces. Sharing a common thirst for justice and freedom, they gather information; they try to diagnose the problems relating to housing, unemployment, sweated labour and social structures; they pool experiences and carry out whatever form of 'peaceful violence' they deem appropriate. Dom Helder believes that such minority groups have 'the power for love and justice which could be likened to nuclear energy locked for millions of years in the smallest atoms and waiting to be released'.[23] 'All these minorities united could become an irresistible force,' he adds.[24] Some ridicule him, but he perseveres. 'My plan, I am well aware,' he has written, 'may call to mind the combat against Goliath. But the hand of God was with the young shepherd, and David conquered the Philistine with his faith, a sling and five small stones.'[25] 'Keep in mind,' he urges elsewhere, 'that throughout the centuries humanity has been led by daring minorities.'[26]

This contrast between the giant and the boy, the sword and the slingstones, arrogant boasting and humble trust, is characteristic of God's activity in the world. Tom Sine has captured it well in his book *The Mustard Seed Conspiracy*, whose title alludes to the tiny seed out of which a large bush grows. Its subtitle is 'You can make a difference in tomorrow's troubled world.' He writes:

> Jesus let us in on an astonishing secret. God has chosen to change the world through the lowly, the unassuming and the imperceptible … That has always been God's strategy – changing the world through the conspiracy of the insignificant. He chose a ragged bunch of Semite slaves to become the insurgents of his new order … And who would have ever dreamed that God would choose to work through a baby in a cow stall to turn the world right side up! 'God chose the foolish things … the weak things … the lowly things … the things that are not' … It is still God's policy to work through the embarrassingly insignificant to change his world and create his future … [27]

'The embarrassingly insignificant.' I feel the need to underline this topsy-turvy policy which God has adopted. At the same time, I am anxious that we should grasp that it is realistic. What minorities lack in numbers, they can make up in conviction and commitment. In support of this contention I call on the witness of the well-known American sociologist Robert Bellah. Chief author of *Habits of the Heart*, 'a study in American individualism',[28] he is a specialist in 'civil religion', and in the influence of religion and ethics on politics. He lectures in the Department of Sociology at the University of California, Berkeley, and also in its Center for Japanese and Korean Studies. In an interview with Sam Keen in *Psychology Today* (January 1976), he said:

> I think we should not underestimate the significance of the small group of people who have a new vision of a just and gentle world. In Japan a very small minority of Protestant Christians introduced ethics into politics, and had an impact beyond all proportion to their numbers. They were central in beginning the women's movement, labour unions, socialist parties, and virtually every reform movement. The quality of a culture may be changed when two per cent of its people have a new vision.

Christians are less than 1 per cent in Japan, but many more than 2 per cent in a large number of countries. We could have an enormous influence on society, in terms of both evangelism and social action, for the glory of God. There is little justification for a sense of alienation.

PART II

GLOBAL ISSUES

Chapter 5

WARS AND RUMOURS OF WARS

Of all the global problems which confront the human race today none is graver than the threat of a nuclear holocaust. War has always been horrible, whether fought by sticks and stones, bows and arrows, swords and spears, muskets and rifles, or bayonets and bombs. But in the case of these so-called 'conventional' weapons, there has been the possibility of controls and limits, and war has involved an engagement between armies. The arrival of the nuclear age, however, has rendered most military traditions obsolete. 'The unleashed power of the atom,' said Albert Einstein, 'has changed everything save our modes of thinking; and thus we are drifting towards unparalleled catastrophe ... A new type of thinking is essential if mankind is to survive.'[1] He was not exaggerating. Now that we have the power to destroy the total legacy of past civilizations, the present delicate ecological balance of the biosphere, and through radiation the genetic potential of the future, it is the very survival of the human race and of our planet which is at stake.

Contemporary realities

The Christian mind cannot operate in a vacuum. However strongly we hold fast to God's once-for-all revelation of himself in Christ and Scripture, we have to struggle to relate this to the harsh facts of the present situation. Thus revelation and reality belong together as we seek to discern God's will. Consider five such realities.

(1) The end of the cold war

The most notable change in contemporary reality, which at the same time was the most significant event of the twentieth century, and signalled its close, was the dramatic end of the cold war in the late 1980s and early 1990s. Following the relaxation of tension caused by Mr Gorbachev's proclamation of *perestroika* (restructuring) and *glasnost* (openness), event followed event at bewildering speed. In Poland talks between the 'Solidarity' leaders and the government led to free elections. Hungary and Austria opened their border, so that East Germans could cross into freedom. The East German government fell, and Gorbachev refused to intervene. On 9 November 1989 the Berlin wall was dismantled, symbolizing the collapse of a discredited East European socialism. German reunification followed about a year later. Then in 1991 four of the six Soviet republics voted for independence, communism disintegrated in the Soviet Union, and Gorbachev himself fell from power. Thus within two years (1989–91) these so called 'gentle' and 'peaceful' revolutions (apart from some violence in Romania) brought not only political freedom to the Soviet Union and her East European satellites, but also military détente between the USA and the USSR, as both the superpowers turned away from the frantic, competitive arms build-up of the previous era.

Nearly a decade later, however, expectations of peace have proved illusory, and new conflicts have arisen. During the 50 years between 1945 and 1995 there were 80 wars. Yet of these only 28 were 'traditional' wars between the regular armies of nation-states, while 46 were civil or guerrilla wars.

What, then, are the causes of this escalation of violence? Professor Samuel P. Huntington of Harvard, in his book *The Clash of Civilizations and the Remaking of World Order*, develops the thesis that, whereas during the cold war global politics had been 'bipolar' (between the two superpowers), after the cold war it has become 'multipolar *and* multi-civilizational'.[2] In particular, 'in coping with identity crisis, what counts for people are blood and belief, faith and family. People rally to those with similar ancestry, religion, language, values and institutions, and distance themselves from those with different ones.'[3] Thus today the important distinctions between people are not so much ideological and political as cultural. Professor Huntington goes on to divide the world into seven or eight major civilizations, whose chief distinctives are religious and which shape 'the antagonisms and associations of states'.[4]

Robert D. Kaplan, a contributing editor of the *Atlantic Monthly*, develops a similar thesis in his book *The Ends of the Earth*, an expansion of his well-known *Atlantic Monthly* article 'The Coming Anarchy' published in February 1994. In it he reflects on his 'journey at the dawn of the 21st century', which took him to West Africa and the Nile Valley, to Anatolia and the Caucasus, to the Iranian plateau, Central Asia, the Indian Subcontinent and Indochina. In so far as any travelogue may be said to have a theme, his is that nation-states with their neat and rigid borders are the artificial creation of colonial powers. 'Maps, so seemingly objective, are actually propaganda.'[5] They blur the much more fluid realities of ethnicity, which spill over national frontiers. 'In the postcommunist world, discontent [is] no longer ideological but religious – in other words cultural.'[6]

Both authors are pessimistic, even gloomy, about the future. A global war, involving the core states of the world's major civilizations, Professor Huntington declares, is 'highly improbable but not impossible'. He even paints a vivid scenario in which the USA, Europe, Russia and India are aligned against China, Japan and most of Islam.[7] This is his concluding sentence: 'Clashes of civilizations are the greatest threat to world peace, and an international order based on civilizations is the surest safeguard against world war.'[8]

Robert Kaplan does not indulge in speculation about the future. But he quotes former UN Secretary-General Perez de Cuellar's statement that the current proliferation of civil wars is 'the new anarchy'. The fact that in 1993 42 countries were engulfed in major conflicts, and 37 others in lesser ones, certainly seems to demonstrate 'this anarchic trend'.[9] '*We are not in control*,' he concludes, and 'the idea that a global élite like the UN can engineer reality from above is ... absurd ...' We live in 'an age of localized *mini-holocausts*'.[10]

In the light of the changed world situation since the end of the cold war, it is not surprising that western defence specialists have completely revised their strategy. They are no longer preparing for a single large-scale war with the Soviet Union, but rather for multiple regional conflicts. Nevertheless, while nuclear weaponry remains, so does the fear of its use, either in local conflicts or in crazy acts of terrorism.

(2) International nuclear treaties

Before the cold war ended, it was estimated that the two superpowers possessed between them about 50,000 nuclear warheads, with a total destructive power more than a million times greater than that of the Hiroshima bomb. This stockpile represented such a horrendous situation of 'overkill' that George Kennan, in accepting the Einstein Peace Prize in Washington in 1981, called for a 'bold and sweeping' initiative, namely 'an immediate across-the-board reduction by 50 per cent of the nuclear arsenals now being maintained by the two superpowers'. Although his cry went unheeded at the time, in due course it bore fruit.

Ten years later, in 1991, the USA and Russia signed START I (the first 'Strategic Arms Reduction Treaty'), which called for a phased reduction of strategic weapons and for the return to Russia of all warheads held by the other republics of the former USSR. START I came into force in 1994. The previous year the USA and Russia signed START II; it banned all land-based ballistic missiles fitted with 'MIRVs' (Multiple Independently targetable Re-entry Vehicles), and further reduced strategic nuclear weapons. This treaty was ratified by the USA in 1997, but not yet by Russia. Now that START III talks have begun, however, experts believe that Russia may sign the second and third treaties together. It is true that, strictly speaking, this is not disarmament, since the weapons are not destroyed; but at least they are removed from deployment and so are virtually unavailable.

The Comprehensive Test Ban Treaty is a second international initiative which offers hope. In 1994 the UN's 'Conference on Disarmament' commissioned an ad hoc committee to produce a treaty which would ban all further testing of nuclear armaments. This Comprehensive Test Ban Treaty was adopted by the UN's General Assembly in 1996, with 158 votes in favour, 3 against and 5 abstentions. The three against were Bhutan, India and Libya. The treaty will not come into force, however, until 49 states have ratified it in their home legislatures. By 31 July 1997 only five states had ratified it. Critics, crying 'too little, too late', were proved substantially right when in May 1998 first India, then Pakistan, conducted tests of nuclear devices in blatant disregard of the treaty.

The third initiative relates to non-proliferation. It was as long ago as 1968 that the Non-Proliferation Treaty was signed; it called for an eventual, total, global nuclear disarmament. In 1995 the UN decided to extend it indefinitely, and 178 nations pledged themselves to this ultimate goal. Based on it, a movement of over 600 NGOs (non-governmental organizations) on 6 continents, named 'Abolition 2000', is calling for the immediate initiation of negotiations for a phased elimination of all nuclear weapons, beginning in AD 2000.

Now that India and Pakistan have carried out tests seven nations are known to have both nuclear weapons and delivery systems – the United States, Russia, Britain, France, China, India and Pakistan. Israel is almost certainly an eighth member of this deadly club. Doomwatchers are warning that this number may yet increase, which makes movements towards non-proliferation ever more urgent.

In spite of the welcome international efforts described above we still maintain a fearsome level of overkill in our nuclear arsenals. We could take the British Trident programme as an example. Britain has ordered a fleet of four nuclear-powered submarines. Vanguard was launched in 1994 and Victorious in 1995, while Vigilant is due in 1999 and Vengeance in 2001. Each submarine will carry 16 Trident missiles, with a range of 7400 kilometres, each of which has 4–6 independently targeted nuclear warheads, making a maximum of 96. Since each warhead can deliver a blast of 100 kilotons, and since the Hiroshima bomb is calculated at between 12 and 15 kilotons, each Trident carries between 600 and 800 times the blast of the Hiroshima bomb.[11]

(3) The consequences of nuclear war

Probably nothing can bring home to us the ghastly effects of a nuclear explosion more vividly than the eye-witness accounts of what happened at Hiroshima and Nagasaki. Lord Mountbatten quoted one such account shortly before he was himself killed by an act of senseless violence:

> Suddenly a glaring whitish, pinkish light appeared in the sky accompanied by an unnatural tremor which was followed almost immediately by a wave of suffocating heat and a wind which swept away everything in its path. Within a few seconds the thousands of people in the streets in the centre of the town were scorched by a wave of searing heat. Many were killed instantly, others lay writhing on the ground screaming in agony from the intolerable pain of their burns.

Everything standing upright in the way of the blast ... was annihilated ... Hiroshima had ceased to exist.[12]

That was the result of a single, smallish atomic explosion. What the consequences of a nuclear war would be like it is impossible to predict with accuracy because of the many imponderables, such as the number of warheads used, the distribution of people in the target zone, the degree of civil defence available, and the climatic conditions at the time. But the United States' Congress document *The Effects of Nuclear War* (1979) says that 'the minimum consequences would be enormous' and gives four escalating case-studies. Although these belong to the cold war period, they still provide dramatic illustrations of the horror of a nuclear strike.

A single megaton weapon attack on a single big city like Detroit or Leningrad would mean up to two million dead and a further one million injured. 'A very large attack against a range of military and economic targets', in which the USSR struck first and the USA retaliated, would mean the death of up to 77 per cent of the American population (or 160 million people) and up to 40 per cent of the Russian population (being more scattered in rural areas). These casualties would be the immediate effects (within the first 30 days) of the heat, blast, wind, fire storm and direct radiation. Many more millions would die of their injuries (since the medical facilities would be completely inadequate), and of epidemics (due to the breakdown of sewerage and the non-availability of clean water), or would starve or freeze to death during the first winter (because of the collapse of services). A pall of sooty toxic smoke over the devastated area would not only poison many survivors but so completely blot out the warmth and light of the sun as to return the earth to ice-age conditions. In the long term cancer would claim many more victims, and both the genetic consequences and ecological devastation would continue for decades and be incalculable.[13]

(4) Conventional arms expenditure and trade

Another contemporary reality is the appalling level of defence expenditure. In 1995, calculated in billions of dollars, the US spent nearly 278 (3.8 per cent of GDP), while the UK spent just over 34 (3.1 per cent of GDP). Russia's total was 82 and China's nearly 32. The global total spent on defence in 1995 was just over $1,173 billion.[14] President Eisenhower once said: 'Every gun that is made, every warship launched, every rocket fired, signifies … a theft from those who hunger and are not fed, from those who are cold and are not clothed.'[15] Although his concept of 'theft' may have been more rhetoric than economic reality, he was expressing his sense of outrage over the disparity between expenditure on defence and expenditure on development. How should we correlate the thousands of billions spent on arms with the billion or so people in the world who are destitute?

Arms expenditure raises the related question of arms sales. We may agree that every nation has the right to defend itself against an aggressor, and therefore to purchase arms with which to do so. But how far should former colonial powers get embroiled in civil wars? Can they escape the charge of hypocrisy if they call for peace and fund peace-keeping forces even while arming the protagonists? We have reason to be grateful both that since the end of the cold war 'international sales of conventional weapons have declined in value by more than half the average annual level in the 1980s',[16] and that since 1992 the UN Register of Conventional Arms Transfers has been a voluntary means of recording and so to some degree regulating all conventional arms sales. It is believed that approximately 90 per cent of all arms transfers are reported in this way.[17] Nevertheless the figures remain huge. Calculated in billions of dollars, the sales of conventional weapons in 1995 were $19 by the US (approaching 50 per cent of the total), with the UK and France next at $7.8 and $7.4 respectively (19.1 per cent and 18.1 per cent), and with Russia, Germany and China following to form the top six.[18]

(5) The havoc of land mines

The tragic injuries caused by exploding land mines in many parts of the world have recently aroused public concern, not least through the advocacy of Diana, Princess of Wales. The International Committee of the Red Cross estimate that more than 110 million mines remain in the ground, and that approximately 2 million new mines are laid every year; that the cost of clearing the mines already in the ground would be a minimum of $33 billion; that meanwhile 500 people are killed or maimed by land mines every week; and that in Cambodia one person in 236 is an amputee, whereas in the US the ratio is one in 22,000.

We may be very thankful, therefore, that the Vietnam Veterans of America Foundation initiated the International Campaign to Ban Land Mines a few years ago, and enlisted the help of the Canadian government, other countries, voluntary organizations and prominent individuals. In September 1997 an international conference of 50 nations met in Oslo to finalize the terms of a treaty. It calls for (1) a total ban on the future use of all anti-personnel land mines, (2) assistance for land mine victims, (3) the speedy removal of all mines still in the ground, and (4) the destruction of all stockpiles. The Convention to Ban Land Mines was duly signed by 121 countries in Ottawa in December 1997, although the US was unwilling to sign because the conference was unwilling to exempt either South Korea or three anti-tank weapons with anti-personnel devices. As of August 1998, 129 nations had signed the treaty and 32 had ratified it, bringing the total very close to the 40 ratifications needed to make it binding international law for those who have signed.

Theological and moral reflections

Although Christians do not fully agree, and probably have never agreed, about the mind of Christ on war, yet we should neither exaggerate the disagreement between us nor minimize the substantial area in which we are at one. For example, all Christian people affirm that the Kingdom of God inaugurated by Jesus is God's rule of righteousness and peace; that Jesus himself perfectly exemplified in his conduct the ideals of the Kingdom he proclaimed; that the Kingdom community is to hunger for righteousness, to pursue peace, to forbear revenge, to love enemies, in other words to be marked by the cross; and that in the consummated Kingdom 'they will beat their swords into ploughshares and their spears into pruning hooks', for 'nation will not take up sword against nation, nor will they train for war any more' (Isaiah 2:4). All this must mean that, as Christians, we are primarily committed to peace and righteousness. True, the quest for peace with justice is much more costly than appeasement. We also admire the loyalty, self-sacrifice and courage of serving soldiers. Yet we must not glamorize or glorify war in itself, however just we may perceive its cause to be. Some Christians believe that in some circumstances it may be defended as the lesser of two evils, but it could never be regarded by the Christian mind as more than a painful necessity in a fallen world.

Apart from this general biblical background, however, there are three main positions which Christians hold and defend – total pacifism, the just war theory, and relative (or nuclear) pacifism.[19]

(1) The total pacifist position[20]

Pacifists tend to begin with the Sermon on the Mount. At least it is from this part of the teaching of Jesus that many develop their commitment to non-violence. We are not to resist an evil person, Jesus said. Instead, if he strikes us on the right cheek, we are to turn to him the other also. We are to love our enemies, do good to those who hate us and pray for those who persecute us. Only so can we qualify as children of our Heavenly Father, for his love is indiscriminate, and he gives the blessings of rain and sunshine to the evil and the good alike. To hate those who love us is the devil's way. To love those who love us and hate those who hate us is the way of the world. If we would follow Jesus, however, and accept the standards of his Kingdom, we must love those who hate us (Matthew 5:38–48; Luke 6:27–36).

Moreover, Jesus practised what he preached. He exemplified his call to non-resistance. For he resisted neither betrayal nor arrest, neither trial nor sentence, neither torture nor crucifixion. When he was insulted, he did not retaliate. He was the innocent, suffering Servant of the Lord. 'He was led like a lamb to the slaughter, and as a sheep before her shearers is silent, so he did not open his mouth' (Isaiah 53:7). He loved those who despised and rejected him. He even prayed for the forgiveness of those who nailed him to the cross.

Thus, pacifists conclude, the teaching and example of Jesus together commit us to the way of non-resistance and non-violence. For this is the way of the cross, and Jesus calls us to take up our cross and follow him. Moreover, it seems to be historically proven that for two centuries, until the conversion of Constantine, the great majority of Christians refused to serve as soldiers. There is clear evidence that their refusal related to the idolatrous practices associated with life in the Roman army. Pacifists argue that they also perceived war to be incompatible with their Christian obedience. This is not certain.

The pacifist position was adopted by the so-called 'Radical Reformers' of the sixteenth century (the various Anabaptist groups), is preserved by the 'Peace Churches' today (Quakers, Mennonites, United Brethren, etc.), and is also held by considerable minorities in the 'historic' Reformation churches.

(2) The 'just war' tradition[21]

The concept of the 'just war' antedates the Christian era and may be traced back both to the 'holy wars' of the Old Testament and to some Greek and Roman ethical teaching. The notion was Christianized by Augustine in the fourth century, however, systematized by Thomas Aquinas in the thirteenth, further developed by Francisco de Vitoria in the sixteenth, and endorsed by most of the Reformers. It is held by a majority of Roman Catholics and Protestants today.

It has been stated in various forms, although usually seven conditions have been specified, namely formal declaration, last resort, just cause, right intention, proportionate means, non-combatant immunity and reasonable expectation. There is some overlap in these seven criteria, however, and I find it more helpful to reduce them to three, relating to the beginning, the conduct and the end of a war. Thus, for a war to be 'just', first, *its cause must be righteous*. It must be defensive, not aggressive. Its objectives must be to secure justice or remedy injustice, to protect the innocent or champion human rights. It must be undertaken as a last resort only, after all attempts at negotiation and reconciliation have been exhausted, and then only after a formal declaration (following an ultimatum) by a legitimate authority, not by groups or individuals. Moreover, the intention must be as righteous as the cause. Just causes are not served by unjust motives. So there must be no hatred, no animosity, no thirst for revenge.

Secondly, *its means must be controlled*. There must be no wanton or unnecessary violence. In fact two key words are used to describe the legitimate use of violence in a just cause. One is 'proportionate' and the other 'discriminate'. 'Proportionate' signifies that the war is perceived as the lesser of two evils, that the violence inflicted is proportionately less than that which it is intended to remedy, and that the ultimate gains will outweigh the losses. 'Discriminate' means that the war is directed against enemy combatants and military targets, and that civilians are immune. We have to concede that the total immunity of non-combatants is impossible to preserve. But in a 'just war' the distinction must be preserved and the *intentional* killing of civilians outlawed. The principle of non-combatant immunity was implicit in the Hague Conventions (1899 and 1907), became explicit in the Geneva Conventions and their Additional Protocol (1949 and 1977), and has been emphatically reaffirmed by the General Assembly of the United Nations (1970).

Thirdly, *its outcome must be predictable*. That is, like the king in Jesus' little parable who 'counted the cost' before going to war (Luke 14:31–2), there must be a calculated prospect of victory, and so of achieving the just cause for which the war was begun.

To sum up, a 'just war' is one fought for a righteous cause, by controlled means, with a reasonable expectation of success.

The 'just war' theory is only a tradition, however. Can it be commended from Scripture? Some try to do so on the basis of the wars commanded and directed by Yahweh in the Old Testament. But this is a precarious procedure, since these were expressly sanctioned, and no nation can claim today to enjoy Israel's privileged position as a 'holy nation', God's special covenant people, a unique theocracy.

A more secure basis is provided by Paul's teaching about the state in Romans 13:1–7, and its context. It is actually embedded in a passage about neighbour-love, since it is preceded by injunctions to love and serve our enemies (12:14–21) and followed by statements that love never harms our neighbour (13:8–10). We are therefore confronted by a difficult exegetical problem. In particular, the end of Romans 12 and the beginning of Romans 13 appear to be in conflict with one another. The first, echoing the Sermon on the Mount, forbids us to repay anybody evil for evil; the second, echoing rather the Old Testament, describes the state as God's agent for the punishment of evil-doers. The first says that evil-doers are to be served; the second that they are to be punished. How can these instructions be reconciled?

The Peace Churches tend to say that the requirement to love our enemy is primary, that the state's judicial function is incompatible with it, and that therefore the Christian community must keep aloof from the state, and have no share in its work. A recent and eloquent advocate of this view is Dale Aukerman in his book *Darkening Valley*, 'a biblical perspective on nuclear war'. He cannot accept that God 'ordained' or 'instituted' the state ('God does not consecrate and hallow the civil authorities; such hallowing is reserved for the messianic community'),[22] or that the state could be God's minister, except in a secondary sense. He uses two analogies. As in a collapsing marriage husband and wife accuse each other, and 'each is for the other God's agent of retribution', though God is not the author of their quarrel, and as the Assyrian and Babylonian empires were agents of God's judgement, though God was not the author of their arrogant cruelty, so the violence of the civil authorities is not God's intention, yet 'they *are assigned* by God *a place* ... a role in the realm of his wrath'. This is his conclusion: 'Civil authorities in bearing the sword, which represents rule by threatened or inflicted violence, are sinning, going contrary to God's way of love described in the verses immediately before and after the Romans 13:1–7 parenthesis ... But in the retributive dynamisms that emerge under God as he sets himself against sin, civil authorities do have their place along with Assyria and the nagging wife.'[23]

This exegesis is open to serious criticism, however. The apostle Paul asserts that the governing authorities have been established by God, that he has delegated his authority to them, that therefore in submitting to them we are submitting to him and in rebelling against them we are rebelling against him. Further, 'the one in authority' (any official of the state) is 'God's servant' to reward the good citizen and punish the evil-doer. In fact, three times Paul repeats that the state's 'authority' is God's authority and three times that the state's 'ministry' is God's ministry (verses 4a, 4b and 6). It seems clear to me that these are not grudging concessions that God has 'assigned a place' to the state, which when using force to punish evil is nevertheless 'sinning', but genuine affirmations that God has 'established' the state with his authority and that when exercising its authority to punish evil it is doing God's will. This being so, I cannot say that Christian people should remain insulated from public life; they should rather involve themselves in it, knowing that in doing so they are 'ministers of God' just as much as pastors to whom the same expression is applied. There is nothing anomalous about Christians serving in the police force or the prison service, as politicians or magistrates or town councillors. For Christians worship a God who is just and are therefore committed to the quest for justice. The Christian community should not stand aloof from the secular community, but seek to penetrate it for Christ.

Among those who accept the legitimacy of Christian participation in the work of the secular authority are most pacifists who are not members of the Peace Churches. But, like all other Christians, they regard their participation as critical and conditional. For example, they would refuse to obey the state's call to take up arms.

How then should we resolve the apparent discrepancy between Romans 12:17–21, with its call for the loving service of enemies, and Romans 13:1–7, with its call for the punishment of evil-doers? We shall begin to perceive the answer when we notice that the contrast between forgiveness and punishment is not only *between* these paragraphs but embedded *within* the first. For the prohibition 'do not repay anyone evil for evil' is followed by 'I will repay, says the Lord', and the prohibition 'do not take revenge, my friends' is followed by 'leave room for God's wrath, for it is written: "It is mine to avenge"' (verses 17, 19). So the reason why wrath, revenge and retribution are forbidden us is not because they are in themselves wrong reactions to evil, but because they are *God's* prerogative, not ours. Similarly, Jesus himself, when 'they hurled insults at him', not only 'did not retaliate' but also instead 'entrusted himself [and his cause] to him who judges justly' (1 Peter 2:23).

It is better, then, to see the end of Romans 12 and the beginning of Romans 13 as complementary to one another. Members of God's new community can be both private individuals and state officials. In the former role we are never to take personal revenge or repay evil for evil, but rather we are to bless our persecutors (12:14), serve our enemies (12:20) and seek to overcome evil with good (12:21). In the latter role, however, if we are called by God to serve as police or prison officers or judges, we are God's agents in the punishment of evil-doers. True, 'vengeance' and 'wrath' belong to God, but one way in which he executes his judgement on evil-doers today is through the state. To 'leave room for God's wrath' (12:19) means to allow the state to be 'an agent of wrath to bring punishment on the wrongdoer' (13:4). This is not to say that the administration of justice should not be tempered with mercy. It should. And state officials should be concerned not only to 'punish' evil but to 'overcome' it, since retributive and reformative justice should go hand in hand. Nevertheless, what this passage of Scripture emphasizes is that, if evil is to be punished (as it deserves to be), then the punishment must be administered by the state and its officials, and not by individuals who take the law into their own hands.[24]

It should be clear, then, that the state's punishing role is strictly limited and controlled. There is no possible justification in Romans 13:1–7 for an oppressive regime to whom the words 'law and order' have become a synonym for tyranny. No. The state is God's agent to execute his wrath only on evil-doers, that is, on particular and identifiable people who have done wrong and need to be brought to justice. This implies a threefold restriction on the powers of the state. First, the *people* the state punishes must be limited to evil-doers or law-breakers. Secondly, the *force* used to arrest them must be limited to the minimum necessary to bring them to justice. Thirdly, the *punishment* given must be limited in proportion to the evil which they have done. All three – the people, the force and the punishment – must be carefully controlled.

The same principles have to be applied to soldiers as to the police. Indeed, the distinction between them is a comparatively modern one. The enforcement of law, the maintenance of order, and the protection of the innocent, which today are usually the work of the police, were in Paul's day the responsibility of Roman soldiers. Still in our own times there are situations of civil disorder (e.g. during the Mau Mau rebellion in Kenya) in which the army is called in to supplement the police. Whenever this happens, the behaviour of soldiers has to be understood as an extended form of police action and regulated accordingly. The British Ministry of Defence, for example, explains existing law relating to security operations by the 'useful catchphrase "minimum necessary force"': 'No more force may be used than is both necessary and reasonable in the circumstances. The degree of force can never be reasonable if it is more than that required to achieve the immediate aim' – the main aims being the prevention of crime and the arrest of criminals.

What, however, if the disturber of the peace is not an individual or group but another nation? The argument now is that, by legitimate extrapolation, the state's God-given authority to administer justice includes the restraint and resistance of evil-doers who are aggressors rather than criminals, and so the protection of its citizens' rights when threatened from outside as well as from inside. True, the analogy is not exact. For on the one hand, the state which goes to war is acting as judge in its own cause and not as a third party arbitrator, while on the other the cool judicial procedures of the law court have no parallel in the declaration and conduct of war. These differences are due to the fact that acceptable international justice (in arbitration, intervention and peace-keeping) is only in its infancy. Nevertheless, the development of the 'just war' theory 'represented a systematic attempt to interpret acts of war by analogy with acts of civil government', and so to see them as belonging to 'the context of the administration of justice' and as subject to 'the restraining standards of executive justice'.[25]

Executive justice, however, whether in relation to crime or civil disorder or international warfare, must always be both *discriminate* action (limiting the people involved to evil-doers who have to be brought to justice) and *controlled* action (limiting the force used to the minimum necessary to secure this end).

This brings us to the question of whether such a limited justification of the use of force could apply to a war in which nuclear weapons were used (since they appear to be indiscriminate and uncontrolled), and so to the third Christian attitude to war.

(3) Relative or nuclear pacifism[26]

The invention of nuclear weapons brought an entirely new dimension to the debate about war. The old categories of conventional wisdom seemed to become as obsolete as the old weapons of conventional warfare. Both scientists and theologians began to call for new and bold thinking. As the Roman Catholic bishops said at the Second Vatican Council, the Church has 'to undertake a completely fresh appraisal of war'.[27] For everybody knows that if nuclear war were ever to be unleashed, the casualties would be numbered in hundreds of millions, and could not be limited (as they largely have been in the past, though indeed less this century) to armies confronting one another.

The relevant biblical principle, which we need to evoke and apply, seems to be the great evil of 'shedding innocent blood'. The importance of 'blood' in Scripture is that it is the carrier and so the symbol of life (e.g. Genesis 9:4; Leviticus 17:11; Deuteronomy 12:23). To 'shed blood' is therefore to take life by violent means, in other words to kill. But human life, being the life of human beings made in the image of God, is sacrosanct. In the Old Testament the shedding of human blood was strictly forbidden except by specific divine sanction, i.e. in the execution of a murderer and in wars explicitly authorized by God. It is true that in the Mosaic law a small number of other serious offences (e.g. kidnapping, cursing parents, sorcery, bestiality, idolatry and blasphemy, see Exodus 21, 22 and Leviticus 24) were punishable by death. But this does not override the principle: 'Whoever sheds the blood of man, by man shall his blood be shed, for in the image of God has God made man' (Genesis 9:6). That is, the bloodshedding of murder deserves the bloodshedding of capital punishment. For in the latter case it is the blood of the guilty which is shed. In all other cases, the sin of 'shedding innocent blood' has been committed. Hence Abigail's thankfulness that, because David did not avenge himself against Nabal, he did not have 'on his conscience the staggering burden of needless bloodshed' (1 Samuel 25:31).

This understanding was enshrined in the Old Testament provision of six 'Cities of Refuge', three on each side of the River Jordan, carefully sited to cover the whole country. It was based on the distinction between murder (intentional killing) and manslaughter (unintentional), and was designed to protect the manslayer from the 'avenger of blood' and so prevent the shedding of innocent blood (Numbers 35:9–34; Joshua 20:1–9).

A distinction was made in Old Testament times not only between murder and manslaughter, but also between blood shed in war (which was permissible) and blood shed in peace (which was not). Thus when Joab killed both Abner and Amasa, the two commanders of Israel's army, David condemned him for 'avenging in time of peace blood which had been shed in war, and so bringing upon David's house the guilt of shedding innocent blood (1 Kings 2:5, 31–4, RSV).

Against this background of Old Testament law, the prophets uttered fierce denunciations against Israel. Jeremiah warned them of God's coming judgement because they had forsaken him and profaned Jerusalem. How? They had 'burned sacrifices in it' to other gods and 'filled this place with the blood of the innocent' (19:4). Thus idolatry and bloodshed were bracketed. No sin against God was worse than worshipping idols. No sin against man was worse than shedding innocent blood. Similarly, Ezekiel described Jerusalem as bringing doom upon herself 'by shedding blood in her midst' and 'by making idols' (22:1–4; cf. 36:18). Both these prophets coupled worshipping idols and killing the innocent as the two paramount sins.

The same horror over the shedding of innocent blood continues in the New Testament. Judas confessed that he had 'betrayed innocent blood' (Matthew 27:4), and when Pilate claimed to be 'innocent of this man's blood', the people recklessly responded, 'Let his blood be on us and on our children' (Matthew 27:24–5).

The biblical evidence on this matter is an impressively united testimony from the time of the patriarchs through the law and the prophets to the New Testament. Human blood is sacrosanct because it is the life of Godlike human beings. To shed the blood of the innocent is therefore the gravest social sin, whether committed personally in murder or judicially by an oppressive regime. God's judgement fell on Israel in the seventh century BC because they were guilty of shedding much innocent blood, and in the first century AD because they shed the innocent blood of Jesus Christ. 'Hands that shed innocent blood' are among the things which Yahweh is said to hate (Proverbs 6:16–17).

This biblical message must not be evaded. The judicial authority God has given the state, including the use of 'the sword' (Romans 13:4), is strictly limited. In the case of the police it is to be used only to arrest criminals and bring them to justice, in the case of the army only to engage in a just war by just means for a just end. In both cases the immunity of the innocent is to be ensured – of law-abiding citizens in peace-time and of non-combatants in war-time. Therefore any unlimited, uncontrolled or indiscriminate use of force is forbidden. In particular, a distinction has always been recognized in war between combatants and non-combatants, between the army and the civilian population. It is true that the army consists of human beings made in God's image, who may have been conscripted against their will, and who may be entirely innocent of the crimes committed by their government. Nevertheless, if it is legitimate to resist an aggressor nation, it is legitimate to regard its army as its agent in a way that its civilian population are not. This distinction is endorsed both by international law ('the protection of civilian persons in time of war') and by biblical teaching (the prohibition of the shedding of innocent blood). It applies in two ways.

First, the principle of non-combatant immunity condemns the indiscriminate use of 'conventional' (i.e. non-nuclear) weapons. For example, the Christian conscience rebels against the 'obliteration' or 'saturation' bombing of Hamburg, Cologne and Berlin in 1942 and 1943, and especially of Dresden in 1945. British and American leaders (notably Churchill and Roosevelt) had previously denounced the Nazi bombings of cities as odious and shocking, and the British government publicly announced that it was no part of its policy to bomb non-military targets, whatever the Nazis might do. But the Allies went back on their word, as they had reserved the right to do if Germany did not observe the same restrictions. Allied bombs on Hamburg in 1943 and on Dresden in 1945 created a 'fire storm' of unimaginable horror. It was reckoned that about 135,000 people died in two days of raids on Dresden in February 1945 (considerably more than the immediate deaths caused by the atomic bombs dropped on both Hiroshima and Nagasaki); they included thousands of refugees who were fleeing before the Russian advance. I for one am thankful that Bishop George Bell of

Chichester had the courage to protest in the House of Lords against this policy. Obliteration bombing 'is not a justifiable act of war', he said, and 'to justify methods inhumane in themselves by arguments of expediency smacks of the Nazi philosophy that Might is Right'. The report of a Church of England commission *The Church and the Atom* (1948) concurred with his judgement, describing the raids on Dresden as 'inconsistent with the limited ends of a just war: it violates the principles of discrimination'.[28]

Secondly, the principle of non-combatant immunity condemns the use of all indiscriminate weapons. Consider 'chemical' weapons, that is, poison gas. Its use in World War I was a breach of the 1907 Hague Convention. The 1925 Geneva Protocol bound its signatories (by now nearly every nation) not to be the first to use it. And in World War II no signatory nation broke this pledge, although Italy had used it in Abyssinia in the thirties. Stories about 'yellow rain', however, have led to the widespread belief that Soviet troops used it in Afghanistan, and that the Communist forces used it in Kampuchea and Laos. Iraq has certainly used it both against the Kurds and in their war with Iran. In January 1989, however, representatives of nearly 150 nations met in Paris for a Conference on Banning Chemical Weapons, and on 29 April 1997 the Chemical Weapons Convention came into force, with 117 signatories. It calls for the complete elimination of all chemical weapons, and is therefore a true disarmament treaty. There is concern, however, that Russia – with the largest stockpile – has not yet signed the treaty (though their own Chemical Weapons Destruction Act will begin to be implemented in 1998), that North Korea, Iran, Libya and Syria are under suspicion of still producing them, and that the Aum Shinrikyo cult members used a chemical weapon in the Tokyo underground in 1995.

Meanwhile the public needs to understand that modern nerve gases are to the chemist what nuclear weapons are to the physicist. Gas masks would offer no protection, because these gases would penetrate the skin. If they were to be dropped from the air, it is reckoned that 20 civilians would be killed to one combatant, because only combatants would be issued with protective clothing.

'Biological' (sometimes called 'bacterial') weapons were also included in the renunciations of the 1925 Geneva Protocol. Each nation-signatory undertook not to be the first to use either gas or germs. The Biological Weapons Convention of 1971 went further and called for the abolition of stockpiles, although no verification arrangements were agreed. By July 1996 138 nations had ratified this Convention. But still there is no effective means of ensuring compliance, and about a dozen nations are suspected of possessing secret biological weapons programmes.[29]

The third kind of indiscriminate weapon is 'atomic' or 'nuclear'. These three (atomic, biological and chemical) are sometimes referred to as 'ABC' weapons; they surely constitute the most gruesome alphabet ever conceived. The invention and refinement of ABC weapons, especially of nuclear devices, have radically changed the context in which one has to think about the morality of war; they challenge the relevance of the 'just war' theory. A war could still have a just cause and a just goal. But at least if macro-weapons were used ('strategic' or 'tactical'), there would be no reasonable prospect of attaining the goal (since nuclear wars are not winnable) and the means would not be just, since nuclear weapons are neither proportionate, nor discriminate, nor controlled. Millions of non-combatants would be killed. In a nuclear holocaust much innocent blood would be shed. Therefore the Christian conscience must declare the use of indiscriminate nuclear weapons, and also chemical and biological weapons, immoral. A nuclear war could never be a just war. As President Reagan and Mr Gorbachev declared in 1985 in Geneva, 'A nuclear war cannot be won and must never be fought.'

A Christian consensus on this issue seems to be steadily growing. The Second Vatican Council said: 'Any act of war aimed indiscriminately at the destruction of entire cities or of extensive areas along with their population is a crime against God and man himself. It merits unequivocal and unhesitating condemnation.'[30] The British Council of Churches at its November 1980 Assembly passed the following resolution: 'The development and deployment of nuclear weapons has raised new and grave ethical questions for Christians. Because no gain from their use can possibly justify the annihilation they would bring about, and because their effects on present and future generations would be totally indiscriminate as between military and civilians, to make use of the weapons would be directly contrary to the requirements of the so-called just war.'[31]

Similarly, the authors of *The Church and the Bomb*, subtitled 'Nuclear weapons and Christian conscience', though the unofficial report of a Church of England working party which General Synod did not endorse, have carried many of their readers with them in their theological and moral conclusions: 'We must conclude that the use of nuclear weapons cannot be justified. Such weapons cannot be used without harming non-combatants and could never be proportionate to the just cause and aim of a just war.'[32] Again, 'It is in our view proven beyond reasonable doubt that the Just War theory … rules out the use of nuclear weapons. The damage to non-combatants … the havoc made of the environment; and the dangers to generations yet unborn; these things make nuclear weapons indiscriminate and nuclear war almost inevitably disproportionate. The evils caused by this method of making war are greater than any conceivable evil which the war is intended to prevent, and they affect people who have nothing to do with the conflict.'[33] Again, 'We shall have failed wholly in our presentation if we have not made it clear that in our view *the cause of right cannot be upheld by fighting a nuclear war.*'[34]

Evangelical Christians have been slow to catch up with the biblical perspectives of other sections of the Church. In 1980, however, an ecumenical group (with strong evangelical participation) met in the United States, saw a parallel between the nineteenth-century movement to abolish slavery and the need for a twentieth-century movement to abolish nuclear weapons, and issued 'The New Abolitionist Covenant'. It includes these sentences: 'Unlimited in their violence, indiscriminate in their victims, uncontrollable in their devastation, nuclear weapons have brought humanity to an historical crossroads. More than at any previous time in history, the alternatives are peace or destruction. In nuclear war there are no winners.'[35] And what these Christian statements affirm about nuclear weapons is equally applicable to chemical and biological weapons. For all three, being indiscriminate in their effects, are indefensible in their use.

The call for nuclear disarmament

The end of the cold war, together with changing popular attitudes during the 1990s, and not least the growing Christian consensus, have created a new atmosphere which is more conducive to nuclear disarmament than ever before. Already, as we have seen, some progress has been made in the international treaties which limit nuclear stockpiles. So has the time not now come to move on boldly from the reduction, no-testing and non-proliferation of nuclear weapons to their complete elimination? Does the comparative success of the campaigns to ban both chemical and biological weapons not give us solid ground for hope that nuclear weapons could be banned as well? Several recent voices have contributed to this hope.

First, former UN Secretary-General Boutros Boutros-Ghali has said that the safest, surest and swiftest way of dealing with the threat of nuclear arms is to do away with them completely, and that the elimination of all nuclear weapons should be 'humanity's great common cause'.[36]

Secondly, the Canberra Commission on the Elimination of Nuclear Weapons was established as an independent commission by the Australian Government in November 1995. Its brief was to propose practical steps towards a world free of nuclear weapons, while at the same time maintaining international stability and security.

The Canberra Commission's 'statement' begins by describing the present situation, namely that (a) any use of nuclear weapons would be 'catastrophic'; (b) nuclear weapons pose 'an intolerable threat to all humanity and its habitat'; (c) the 'extraordinary time of deep antagonism' in which nuclear arsenals were built up has passed; (d) if the peoples of the world were 'more fully aware' of the danger and consequences of nuclear weapons, 'they would reject them'; (e) the present situation, in which only a handful of states possess nuclear weapons, is 'highly discriminatory and thus unstable'; and (f) the threats of 'nuclear proliferation and nuclear terrorism' are growing. In the light of these things, the opportunity now exists, 'perhaps without precedent or recurrence', to take a new initiative:

> The members of the Canberra Commission call upon the US, Russia, the UK, France and China to give the lead by committing themselves, unequivocally, to the elimination of all nuclear weapons. Such a commitment would propel the process in the most direct and imaginative way. All other governments must join this commitment and contribute to its fulfilment.

Thirdly, in July 1996 the International Court of Justice (the world's highest judicial body), meeting in the Hague, in response to requests from the UN General Assembly and the WHO, ruled by 8 votes to 7 that 'the threat or use of nuclear weapons would generally be contrary to the rules of international law applicable in armed conflicts, and in particular the principles and rules of humanitarian law.'

Many people were disappointed both that the adverb 'generally' made the ruling ambiguous and that the judgement was carried only by the casting vote of the chairman. On the other hand, the Court also reached a unanimous agreement as follows: 'There exists an obligation to pursue in good faith and bring to a conclusion negotiations leading to nuclear disarmament in all its aspects under strict and effective international control.'

The fourth encouragement came in December 1996 from a distinguished international group of more than 60 generals and admirals. Identifying themselves as 'military professionals' who had devoted their lives to the national security of their countries and peoples, they expressed their conviction that nuclear weapons 'represent a clear and present danger to the very existence of humanity'. They went on to appeal for urgent action:

First, present and planned stockpiles of nuclear weapons are exceedingly large and should now be greatly cut back;

Second, remaining nuclear weapons should be gradually and transparently taken off alert ...

Third, long-term international nuclear policy must be based on the declared principle of continuous, complete and irrevocable elimination of nuclear weapons.

How to proceed to eventual abolition, they concede, cannot at present be foreseen. It will necessitate a procedure of surveillance, inspection and, where necessary, forcible intervention. But a movement towards the creation of a world free of nuclear weapons must begin now. 'The end of the cold war makes it possible. The dangers of proliferation, terrorism and a new nuclear arms race render it necessary.'

These four statements, emanating from such different circles (political, legal and military) are very impressive. At the same time, we cannot claim that there is a universal consensus on the possession and use of nuclear weapons. It is necessary to consider, therefore, the questions which are being asked and the qualifications which are being proposed.

Questions and qualifications

First, some are maintaining that *the distinction between combatants and non-combatants is obsolete.* That is, modern war is total war, and there are no non-combatants any longer. The nation's whole population is sucked into the war effort. Every tax payer is helping to finance it. Even people in civilian jobs are thereby releasing others for military service. Therefore, since everybody is involved, the use of indiscriminate weapons is legitimate.

In reply, we agree that the old clear-cut distinction between a country and its small professional army no longer applies, and that certainly everybody engaged in the manufacture, deployment or use of weapons may be regarded as a combatant. Nevertheless, there are still some categories like elderly people, little children, and the physically and mentally sick, who should be guaranteed non-combatant immunity, for to kill such people would clearly be to shed innocent blood.

It will not do to quote Old Testament examples of universal slaughter, since in such cases we are specifically told that the guilt was universal too. They were, therefore, not 'indiscriminate' judgements. Before the Flood 'The Lord saw how great man's wickedness on the earth had become, and that every inclination of the thoughts of his heart was only evil all the time' (Genesis 6:1). Sodom and Gomorrah would have been spared if only 10 righteous people could have been found there (Genesis 18:32), while the Canaanites' practices were so depraved and detestable that the land itself is said to have 'vomited out its inhabitants' (e.g. Leviticus 18:25).

If the universal judgements of the Old Testament supply no precedent for indiscriminate warfare, what about the Old Testament principle of corporate solidarity or responsibility? God described himself as 'punishing the children for the sins of the fathers to the third and fourth generations' of those who hated him (Exodus 20:5), and the humiliated survivors of the destruction of Jerusalem complained: 'Our fathers sinned … and we bear their punishment' (Lamentations 5:7). Does not this divine action, it is asked, justify the slaughter of the innocent with the guilty in war? No. The principle was exemplified in God's dealings with his people as a nation; it was not transferred to the lawcourts, where guilt had to be established. If therefore we are right that a moral defence of the 'just war' is possible only if it can be seen as an extension of the administration of justice, then the distinction between the innocent and the guilty must somehow be preserved.

Secondly, it is pointed out that *not all nuclear weapons are indiscriminate*. During the immediate post-war years and during the Dulles era of the fifties the allied policy was indeed to threaten 'massive retaliation'. But the sixties brought nuclear stalemate, and in 1962 US Defense Secretary Robert McNamara developed the 'counter-force' concept, namely that retaliation would be limited to the destruction of the enemy's military installations, not cities. The key expressions became 'flexible response' and 'graduated response', which (it is claimed) could be contained. Apart from this, during the last two decades both 'tactical' and 'theatre' (as opposed to intercontinental or 'strategic') weapons have become so sophisticated that they could home in on precise targets with incredible accuracy. And the Enhanced Radiation Weapon or 'neutron bomb' can immobilize a single tank by killing its crew. So, as the processes of miniaturization and precision targeting continue, nuclear weapons will become increasingly discriminate in their effects, and their use cannot be given a blanket condemnation. That is the argument.

There is plainly some cogency in this reasoning. The less indiscriminate weapons become, the less unacceptable they are. There might conceivably, therefore, be a situation in which it would be morally permissible to use a very limited nuclear weapon, even though there would be some degree of radioactive fall-out, and therefore some non-combatants would probably be killed. It would have to be a situation of the utmost urgency, in which the only alternative would be the worse evil of surrender to a godless regime.

But before the Christian conscience could depart from its absolute renunciation of nuclear weapons, it would need to be convinced that the use of a limited weapon would almost certainly be effective and cause the enemy to back off. For the alternative is the grave risk of escalation by the losing side. It is true that not all experts consider escalation inevitable. Michael Quinlan claims that 'escalation is not an inexorable scientific process; it is a matter of human decision'.[37] Yet this is the most hazardous speculation. He admits that we do not know what would happen, because (mercifully) we have had no experience of this situation. I think the American Roman Catholic bishops were wiser in their Pastoral Letter to express their 'extreme scepticism about the prospects for control-ling a nuclear exchange, however limited the first use might be'.[38] Similarly, the Public Hearing on Nuclear Weapons and Disarma-ment, organized in Amsterdam in 1981 by the World Council of Churches, reported: 'The weight of the evidence convinces us that the risks are too great, and that there is no moral justification for believing that a limited nuclear war could remain limited.'[39]

The majority of experts and commentators are predicting that, once the nuclear threshold or 'firebreak' has been passed, escalation could not be halted. '*The Church and the Bomb* is fully justified in drawing attention to the central importance of "escalation". It is a metaphor drawn from the moving staircase and implies that once embarked upon the bottom step you can neither get off nor turn back, nor is there any emergency stop button.'[40]

In the Roman Catholic study *Nuclear Deterrence – Right or Wrong?* Roger Ruston quotes Lord Cameron as agreeing that 'in any battlefield use of nuclear weapons the risk of escalation must be immensely high'. Roger Ruston's conclusion is that all uses of nuclear weaponry 'would very probably result in mass slaughter of innocent people'.[41]

The Palme Report (1982) is even stronger: 'We on the Commis-sion are firmly of the mind that there would be virtually no likeli-hood of limiting a nuclear war, once begun.'[42] Therefore, they urge nations 'to maintain a clear nuclear threshold ... a clear distinction between nuclear and conventional weapons' and 'to abstain from deploying weapons which blur the distinction by appearing to be more "usable".'[43]

If the risk of escalation is as great as these quotations indicate, then the only way of safety is to ensure that the nuclear threshold is never crossed.

The third question which people ask nuclear pacifists is this: *If the use of nuclear weapons would be evil, must not their retention as a deter-rent be declared equally evil?* Supposing we agree that the use of macro-nuclear weapons, being agents of indiscriminate destruction, would be immoral, and that the risk of escalation is too great to justify the use of micro-weapons, does that not mean that all Chris-tians should be committed to unilateral nuclear disarmament? No, not all relative (or nuclear) pacifists are unilateralists. For there is a moral distinction between possession, threat and use.[44] It is proba-bly true that if an action is immoral, then the active threat to perform it is immoral too. But the possession of nuclear weapons is more a conditional warning than an aggressive threat. Indeed, since the intention behind possession is not to encourage use but to deter it, possession cannot be pronounced as immoral as use.

Shall we then renounce use but defend possession? This seems to be the conclusion to which we are coming. Of course we can immediately see its logical inconsistency. For the effectiveness of a deterrent depends on the skill (technical) and the will (moral and political) to use it if necessary, and on the belief of the enemy that we intend to do so. A deterrent lacks credibility if the enemy knows we would never use it, and if it lacks credibility it loses its power to deter. So 'retaining possession, renouncing use', though morally defensible, seems practically self-defeating. We are caught between the ineffective and the immoral, or rather between a moral stance which is ineffective and an effective deterrent which (if used) would be immoral, and so between principle and prudence, between what is right and what is realistic. Professor Wolfhart Pannenberg has put his finger on this tension. He writes about 'the conflict ... between two different ethical attitudes: an ethics of conviction that adheres to the purity of moral principles, and an ethics of responsibility that feels obliged to consider the consequences that might follow from the decision embraced'.[45]

Speaking for myself, however, I am not willing to be forced to choose between Christian idealism and Christian realism, if I may use these terms loosely. Nuclear pacifists are certainly idealists, who perceive clearly and refuse to compromise the principle that the use of weapons of indiscriminate destruction would be immoral. But in clinging to this ideal, we must also face the realities of evil in our fallen world and of the current situation which reflects it. How then can we reconcile the ideal and the reality? Is there any escape from the dilemma which I have expressed as 'immoral to use, prudent to keep'?

(1) I accept the argument that immediate unilateral disarmament might well make nuclear war more rather than less likely. It might tempt an enemy to exploit our self-imposed weakness. They might either bully us into surrender by using nuclear missiles without fear of retaliation (in which case we have precipitated use by others through forswearing use ourselves) or blackmail us by threatening to use them (in which case our renunciation will have encouraged an enemy takeover). The question is how to prevent the use of nuclear weapons by

both sides, and at the same time preserve our freedom. It seems to be safer therefore, and more consistent with both ideal and reality, to retain a nuclear deterrent while developing the search for a disarmament which is mutual, progressive and verifiable.

(2) The retention of a deterrent whose weapons it would be immoral to use can be morally justified only as a temporary expedient. As Pope John Paul II said in June 1982 to the UN Second Special Session on Disarmament, the nuclear deterrent 'may still be judged morally acceptable', but only if it is seen 'certainly not as an end in itself, but as a step on the way towards a progressive disarmament'.[46] This should increase the urgency with which the quest for effective disarmament proposals is pursued.

(3) Within the framework of bilateral disarmament there is a place for imaginative unilateral initiatives, which Pope John Paul II has called 'audacious gestures of peace'. Some were earlier taken by the West without being reciprocated (e.g. the American removal from Europe in 1979 of a thousand nuclear warheads, although to be sure, they had long been obsolete). Yet more could surely have been taken without undue danger. Whoever the perceived enemy may be, we should have the courage to declare a 'no first use' commitment.

(4) Whether or not our conscience can accept a distinction between limited and unlimited nuclear weapons, we should be able to agree that the latter should be renounced and abolished as soon as possible. Professor Keith Ward, for example, who on the moral principle that we may 'commit an evil act (one causing harm) in order to prevent a much greater evil' thinks that the use of a limited nuclear weapon might in an extreme situation be the lesser of two evils, nevertheless declares that 'all-out nuclear war must … stand unequivocally condemned … It is morally unjustifiable.' 'It is therefore imperative,' he adds, 'to dismantle the apparatus which makes all-out war possible,'[47] and to retain only 'a limited nuclear deterrent', indeed the minimum necessary to deter. Nuclear 'superiority' is entirely unnecessary; nuclear 'sufficiency' is enough. Moreover, because of the enormous 'overkill' of the superpowers' arsenals, to reduce them further would not appear to entail unacceptable risk. And such a reduction might well be the impetus which is needed to accelerate the downward spiral of disarmament on both sides.

(5) Meanwhile the deterrent must somehow remain credible. If the use of nuclear weapons would be immoral, we cannot threaten

their use. Yet if we want the deterrent to deter, we cannot bluff either. The only alternative seems to be to cultivate uncertainty. We might say to a perceived enemy, 'We believe that the use of weapons of indiscriminate destruction would be both crazy and immoral. We are determined not to use them. We are sure you do not want to use them either. Yet if you attack us, you may provoke us to act against both our reason and our conscience. We beg you not to put us in that position.'

This brings us to the fourth question which is addressed to relative (nuclear) pacifists: *Would not an enemy take-over be a greater evil even than nuclear war?*

The scenario which is frequently envisaged and greatly feared is that we and our allies, threatened with defeat by an invading army equipped with superior conventional weapons, would be tempted in self-defence to resort to nuclear weapons, and so would plunge the world into nuclear war. 'Would that not be justified?' we are asked. Can we seriously envisage the possibility that we would allow our country to be overrun and subjugated? For, if we anticipate the worst that might happen, then the freedom we have come to accept as indispensable to our quality of life would be brutally suppressed. Churches would be closed and Christians harassed. Atheism would be taught in our schools, and the Christian education of children prohibited. Dissidents would be arrested, and without a fair trial consigned to prison, labour camp or psychiatric hospital. The whole hateful apparatus of oppression would be installed. We would find ourselves enslaved. Millions would die. The long dark night of the world would have begun.

Would not such an evil be literally 'intolerable', worse even than the evil of nuclear war? True, the evil of subjugation would be perpetrated by the atheistic aggressor, not by us. Yet if it could be avoided by some moral action on our part, and we do not take action, we would become accomplices in the evil. If something could be done, then to do nothing is to do evil. On the other hand, if the 'something' which could be done to prevent a take-over is a resort to nuclear war, we are back with the original question: which is the greater evil?

Nuclear pacifists, however, are concerned about moral principle, not prudential balance. Our position is this: to start (or share in starting) a nuclear war would be a moral evil of such magnitude that no situation could ever justify it, not even the fear that we ourselves would otherwise be subjugated or destroyed. How can we hope to preserve our values by violating them? Would it not be better to live under an oppressive regime, with all the suffering and slavery that would involve, than be responsible for destroying the whole of human civilization? It would be appalling indeed to allow millions of people to be deprived of liberty; but would we be prepared to incinerate millions in order to prevent it happening? Would it not be better to suffer injustice ourselves than inflict it on others?

In the end, then, we have to decide which blessing we value the more: social freedom, though at the cost of losing our moral integrity by starting a nuclear war; or moral integrity as a nation, though at the cost of losing our social freedom by allowing our country to be overrun. If this might one day be the option before us, I hope we should know which to choose. It would be better to suffer physical defeat than moral defeat; better to lose freedom of speech, of assembly, even of religion, than freedom of conscience before God. For in his sight integrity is yet more valuable than liberty.

Christian peace-making

Jesus spoke of both war and peace. On the one hand, he warned us of 'wars and rumours of wars'; on the other he included in his characterization of the citizens of God's Kingdom the active role of peace-making. He pronounced his peace-making followers both blessed by God and the children of God (Matthew 5:9). For peace-making is a divine activity. God has made peace with us and between us through Christ. We cannot claim to be his authentic children unless we engage in peace-making too.

What practical peace-making initiatives is it possible for us to take?

(1) Christian peace-makers must recover their morale

There are two tendencies in today's Church which undermine Christian morale. Both must be firmly repudiated.

The first is the tendency to trivialize the nuclear horror. We need to watch our vocabulary. Robert W. Gardiner has given examples of the 'ingenious rhetoric' we use to reduce the awfulness of nuclear war. A projectile which destroys millions but deposits little fall-out is called 'a clean bomb'; weapons of mass destruction are given 'diminutive and affectionate labels' like 'nukes'; 'Bambi' is the name of a missile (i.e. 'Don't be afraid of nuclear missiles, they're really cute, harmless little things'); and as for 'nuclear umbrella', what could be 'more suggestive of the safe, ordinary world of daily living than an umbrella?'[48] We might add the 'nuclear club', since a 'club' is normally a place of comfort, privilege and convivial fellowship, not an association of nations whose common denominator is the possession of lethal weaponry.

The second tendency which undermines morale is to be so pessimistic about the future as to acquiesce in the general mood of helplessness. But both indifference and pessimism are inappropriate in the followers of Jesus. We need to recover our sense of indignation about the excessive nuclear stockpile and to resolve to join others in seeking to reduce it further. As Dr David Owen has written in his Introduction to *Common Security*, the Palme Commission Report, 'Governments do respond to popular feeling. They can be influenced, particularly if the pressure is coming from a broadly based public opinion.'[49]

(2) Christian peace-makers must pray

Please do not reject this exhortation as a piece of pietistic irrelevance. For Christian believers it is nothing of the sort. Irrespective of the rationale and the efficacy of praying, we have been commanded to do it. Jesus our Lord specifically told us to pray for our enemies. Paul affirmed that our first duty when we assemble as a worshipping congregation is to pray for our national leaders, so that 'we may live peaceful and quiet lives in all godliness and holiness' (1 Timothy 2:2). Yet today 'often the pastoral prayer in public worship is brief and perfunctory; the petitions are so unimaginative and stale as to border on "vain repetitions"; and the people doze and dream instead of praying'.[50] There is a great need to take seriously the period of intercession in public worship, and to pray for rulers and governments, peace and justice, friends and enemies, freedom and stability, and for deliverance from a nuclear conflagration. The living God hears and answers the sincere prayers of his people.

(3) Christian peace-makers must set an example as a community of peace

God's call to us is not only to 'preach peace' and to 'make peace' but also to embody it. For his purpose, through the work of his Son and his Spirit, is to create a new reconciled society in which no curtains, walls or barriers are tolerated, and in which the divisive influences of race, nationality, rank and sex have been destroyed. He means his Church to be a sign of his Kingdom, that is, a model of what human community looks like when it comes under his rule of righteousness and peace. An authentic Kingdom community will then challenge the value system of the secular community and offer a viable alternative. We can hardly call the world to peace while the Church falls short of being the reconciled community God intends it to be. If charity begins at home, so does reconciliation. We need to banish all malice, anger and bitterness from both church and home, and make them instead communities of love, joy and peace. The influence for peace of communities of peace is inestimable.

(4) Christian peace-makers must contribute to confidence building

During the cold war there was considerable debate in the West about whether the Soviet Union's aggressive postures were a symptom of imperialism or of paranoia. Whichever interpretation was correct, each superpower certainly *perceived* the other as a threat. This is why one of the most important sections of the 'Final Act' (1975) of the Helsinki Conference on Security and Co-operation in Europe (CSCE) was the 'Document on Confidence-Building Measures' ('CBMs'), designed to remove the fear of sudden attack. In order to eliminate the causes of tension, build trust, and so contribute to the strengthening of peace and security in the world, the participating states agreed (1) to give each other notice 21 days in advance of major military manoeuvres and movements, (2) to exchange observers at such manoeuvres, and (3) to promote exchanges among their military personnel. The follow-up CSCE in Stockholm (1986) went further. Participants agreed (1) to share with each other their annual calendar of military activities, (2) to allow each other on-site 'challenge inspections' and (3) to prohibit large-scale troop movements unless announced a year or more in advance.

But there is no reason why the valuable concept of 'CBMs' should be restricted to specifically military matters. In every situation in which people feel threatened, our Christian response should be to seek to remove fear and build confidence. CBMs should include co-operation in commerce, industry, culture and service to the developing world. Tour groups and student exchanges are particularly valuable. For personal contacts break down caricatures and help people to discover one another as human beings. It is even more important for Christians to travel, to serve and to share, so that they may find one another as brothers and sisters in Christ.

(5) Christian peace-makers must promote public debate

Peace movements will contribute to peace-making only if they succeed in stimulating informed discussion. There is always need for a fresh debate with fresh questions. Are nuclear arsenals a deterrent any longer? Is 'moral possession, immoral use' a viable stance or totally self-contradictory? Are we shut up to the straight choice between nuclear deterrence and unilateralism, or are there 'alternative defence policies'?[51] Would the build-up of 'conventional' armies make it safer for nuclear arsenals to be reduced, or can both be reduced simultaneously? Would it ever be justifiable to buy national defence at the cost of millions of civilian lives? Which is the more important in the end: national integrity or national security? Such questions – and many more – need to be raised and debated.

Every Christian is called to be a peace-maker. The Beatitudes are not a set of eight options, so that some may choose to be meek, others to be merciful, and yet others to make peace. Together they are Christ's description of the members of his Kingdom. True, we shall not succeed in establishing Utopia on earth, nor will Christ's Kingdom of righteousness and peace become universal within history. Not until he returns will swords be beaten into plough-shares and spears into pruning hooks. Yet this fact gives no possible warrant for the proliferation of factories for the manufacture of swords and spears. Does Christ's prediction of famine inhibit us from seeking a more equitable distribution of food? No more can his prediction of wars inhibit our pursuit of peace. God is a peace-maker. Jesus Christ is a peace-maker. So, if we want to be God's children and Christ's disciples, we must be peace-makers too.

Chapter 6

OUR HUMAN ENVIRONMENT

In June 1992 over 25,000 people assembled in Rio de Janeiro for the United Nations Conference on Environment and Development. Popularly known as the 'Earth Summit', this gathering of more than 100 heads of state with representatives of other governments, of the scientific community and of special interest groups is thought to have been the largest conference ever held. For in this post-cold-war age it is environmental rather than nuclear destruction which has become for many the greatest threat to the human race.

Environmental studies are a comparatively recent development. Only in 1970 did the British government create a Department of the Environment with a Secretary of State in charge of it, whose responsibilities also included housing, transport and local government.Words like 'ecology', 'habitat', 'conservation' and 'pollution' have not long been part of our everyday vocabulary. One of the most notable features of the 1980s was the rapid, almost worldwide, growth of the 'green movement'.

Public awareness of the critical dangers we face increased, in particular, on account of a series of four disasters: (1) the leak of poisonous gases from a chemical plant at Bhopal (1984), which killed more than 2,000 Indians and blinded or injured over 200,000 more, (2) the catastrophic accident at the nuclear power plant at Chernobyl (1986), which released a huge radioactive cloud over Europe, whose full lethal effects will not be known for years, (3) the release of 30 tons of agricultural chemicals by firemen fighting a blaze at the Sandoz factory in Switzerland (1986), which seriously polluted the Rhine and killed millions of fish, and (4) the grounding of the tanker *Exxon Valdez* in Prince William Sound (1989), which caused the spillage of 10 million gallons of crude oil and the consequent devastation of Alaskan coastline and wildlife.

In 1988 Jonathon Porritt, Director of Friends of the Earth, wrote that 'Green ideas have moved decisively from the fringes of society … into the mainstream', so that now 'there is really no area of social or political concern that hasn't been touched in one way or another by the coming of the Greens'.[1] In 1992 this statement seemed validated in the United States when Senator Al Gore's book *Earth in the Balance* was published, dealing with a host of environmental issues. Now Vice President, he has taken serious environmental concern into the second highest office in the country.

It is remarkable how quickly a dedicated, campaigning minority succeeded in alerting the general public to green concerns. Nearly everybody nowadays seems to be apprehensive about the destruction of the Amazonian rain forest, the depletion of the ozone layer, the greenhouse effect, and the slaughter of whales, elephants and seals. Previously indifferent politicians have become obliged to add green issues to their agendas. Corporations have departments specializing in the ecological aspects of their businesses. Most cars on the road use lead-free petrol, and emissions laws are being tightened. In addition, householders are becoming 'green consumers', using environmentally friendly products, eating 'natural' or 'organic' foods and encouraging the recycling of paper, glass, and metals.[2]

There seem to be four main areas of widespread environmental concern which help to explain this rise in public awareness. They should be seen in relation to one another.

Reasons for environmental concern

First, *population growth*. It has been known for centuries that world population is growing. Only since World War II, however, has the accelerating growth rate been clearly perceived and the potential for disaster in the aftermath of an unchecked population explosion predicted. It is said that in the year AD 1800 there were about 1 billion people on earth. By 1900 this had doubled to 2 billion, and by 1974 doubled again to 4 billion. In 1996 the total reached nearly 6 billion, and the United Nations predicts that world population will approach 8 billion by the year 2015.

Out of 4 billion people in the 1980s, one-fifth of them (800 million) were destitute, and it is being anxiously asked how more than 7 billion people can possibly be fed 35 years later. This is a special problem in the developing world where 90 per cent of population growth is taking place. The earth cannot sustain a larger population which, owing to poverty and even starvation, is forced to use its resources with only short-term gain in mind, often making long-term destruction inevitable. But this is not just a Third World problem. In Britain the population is growing at the comparatively slow rate of 116,000 people per year. However, each new Briton uses more than 30 times the amount of fossil fuel consumed by the average Bangladeshi. Thus, it takes a population growth of 3.39 million Bangladeshis to equal the environmental impact of just over 100,000 Britons.[3] This figure helps to put population growth into context. It is not growth per se that is the problem, for the earth could sustain many more people; it is rather the environmentally unfriendly way in which we live. The wealthy consume too much and are wasteful, while the poor are preoccupied with their immediate survival, rather than with the long-term care of the planet.

There are varying opinions even among Christians about the extent of the population problem and what should be done in response to it. In his Grove booklet entitled *Population Growth and Christian Ethics* (1995) Roy McCloughry, who presented a paper at the 1994 UN International Conference on Population and Development in Cairo, argues that the population problem is primarily neither economic nor environmental but moral, because it is basically about relationships. He pleads for 'a positive vision for human life', in which (1) human beings are seen to have an intrinsic value because they are made in God's image; (2) access to education, especially by women and children, enables them to develop their full potential and to enjoy a quality of life compatible with their human dignity; and (3) the limiting and spacing of children is determined not by coercive governments but by the free decision of the parents.[4] Any discussion of population must begin by reaffirming the dignity of all human life, and the rights of human beings to live out their full potential.

The second cause for concern is *resource depletion* and *loss of biodiversity*. It was the so-called 'Club of Rome' which in 1972 drew the world's attention to the finite nature of the earth's resources. Until then western leaders had confidently been predicting an annual growth rate of 4 per cent. Now continuous growth and finite resources were seen to be incompatible. And that was still a year before the first oil price shock. It was E.F. Schumacher who in 1973 popularized the unpalatable truth in his famous book *Small is Beautiful*, subtitled 'a study of economics as if people mattered'. He wrote of 'the failure to distinguish between income and capital where this distinction matters most … namely the irreplaceable capital which man has not made, but simply found'. His first example of this 'natural capital' was fossil fuels: 'Fossil fuels are not made by men; they cannot be recycled. Once they are gone they are gone for ever.' His other example was 'living nature' (the plankton of the oceans, the green surface of the earth, clean air, etc.), much of which was being destroyed by pollution. 'If we squander our fossil fuels, we threaten civilization,' he wrote, 'but if we squander the capital represented by living nature around us, we threaten life itself.' The folly of 'the modern industrial system', he continued, is that it 'consumes the very basis on which it has been erected. To use the language of the economist, it lives on irreplaceable capital, which it cheerfully treats as income.'[5]

Since Schumacher and the 'Club of Rome' brought the dangers of resource depletion to the discussion table, conversation has also centred on the related problem of loss in biodiversity. Biodiversity is a term that, according to Sir Ghillean Prance, Director of the Royal Botanic Gardens at Kew, encapsulates 'the diversity of species of living organisms on earth, the genes or genetic information which they contain and the complex ecosystems in which they live'.[6] Estimates for the number of different living species on earth range from 5 million to 50 million, with conservative estimates generally around the 10 million mark.[7] Each species contains a unique genetic code, and lives in a certain habitat, often requiring very specific conditions for life. Extinction is a daily part of normal life in a world where species exist in a surprising amount of flux. The concern in the biodiversity discussion, however, is not simply with the natural extinction of species, but with the rate at which human intervention in the natural environment has accelerated those extinctions. Ecologists believe that because of human impact on the environment the current rate of extinction is between 1,000 and 10,000 times the natural rate, representing 20 to 50 species every day![8] The reason why scientists are worried about the loss of biodiversity is not only that individual species become extinct, but that when they do, the delicate balance of their ecosystem is disturbed. And when a so-called 'key-stone' species becomes extinct large-scale problems are quickly encountered. A well-known example is the near extinction of sea otters off the west coast of the United States. Stephen Schneider, a professor in biological sciences at Stanford University, describes what happened. 'After their decline, a major disturbance propa-gated through the offshore marine community. Sea urchins, nor-mally a principal food for otters, multiplied rapidly and in turn decimated the kelp forests leading to biologically impoverished, desert-like stretches of sea floor known as sea-urchin barrens. Only after controversial political pressures to restore the otter were suc-cessful did the urchin populations decline, the kelp grow back, and a new community of fish, squid, and lesser organisms reestablish themselves.'[9]

A third reason for concern is *waste disposal*. An increasing popu-lation brings an increasing problem of how to dispose safely of the undesirable by-products of production, packaging and consump-tion. A glaring example occurred in 1987 when the so-called 'garbage barge' left Long Island, New York and spent six months searching for a port that would take its 3,000 plus tons of garbage. Having been declined entry to numerous ports in the US and elsewhere, the barge eventually returned to New York where the problem had begun.

In January 1994 the British government published an extensive report entitled *Sustainable Development: The UK Strategy*. It recom-mended a four-fold 'hierarchy of waste management', namely 'reduction', 'reuse', 'recovery (including recycling and energy recovery)' and 'disposal without energy recovery by incinerator or landfill'. The last of these options, although the commonest, is the least environmentally productive. It is still unavoidable, however, whenever 'the environmental costs of recycling waste, in terms of energy consumption and emissions, are higher than for disposal'. Clearly the best option in the hierarchy is to reduce the waste which we produce and so have to dispose of.

A fourth major environmental concern, which has been at the forefront of discussion since the 1980s, is our *damaged atmosphere*, owing to a combination of the twin problems of ozone depletion and global warming. Both are the result of atmospheric pollution, to which most of us contribute every day, often without even realiz-ing it.

The depletion of the protective ozone layer exposes us to ultra-violet radiation, which causes skin cancers and upsets our immune system. In consequence, the discovery in 1985 of a continent-sized hole in the ozone over the Antarctic caused widespread public alarm. By 1991 this hole had reached a record size, extending over 21 million square kilometres, and by 1993 the concentration of Antarctic ozone was the lowest ever registered. The neighbouring countries of Argentina and Chile, Australia and New Zealand have been reporting damage to animals and vegetation as well as to humans, and by the mid 1990s serious ozone depletion was recorded in the more temperate regions of the northern hemisphere as well.[10]

Soon after the discovery of the Antarctic ozone hole, its cause was traced to chlorofluorocarbons (CFCs), chemicals which are used in aerosol propellants, air conditioners and refrigerators. Recognizing the gravity of the crisis, the United Nations Environmental Programme took action. The Montreal Protocol (1987) called for the halving of CFC use by 1999, while amendments in 1991 and 1992 resolved that industrialized nations should phase out CFCs completely by 1996 and non-industrialized nations by 2006. The co-operation of many countries in securing this agreement is a great encouragement.

The issue of global warming is a different, though related, problem.[11] The warmth of the earth's surface (which is essential for the planet's survival) is maintained by a combination of the radiation it absorbs from the sun and the infrared radiation it emits into space. This is the so-called 'greenhouse effect'. Atmospheric pollution by so-called 'greenhouse gases', methane, nitrous oxide and specially carbon dioxide (nearly 50 per cent of the total) results in reducing the emission and so increasing the earth's surface temperature.

Scientists are not agreed about the seriousness of the human contribution to the greenhouse effect. Nor is the public's reaction uniform. It ranges from the fear of an imminent catastrophe to a dismissal of the threat as a fiction. There is general agreement, however, that by the year 2100 the average global temperature is likely to rise between 1° and 5° centigrade. Even a 1° increase would be ten times the average rate of temperature change since the last ice age. The long-term effects could include substantial climatic changes, the thermal expansion of the oceans, the flooding of many islands, port cities and low-lying countries like Bangladesh, the drying out of previously fertile regions, and the regional extinction of plants which cannot adjust to the changes. As with ozone depletion, so with global warming, it is urgent to reduce the human augmentation of the problem.

In December 1997 negotiators from all over the world met in Kyoto, Japan, to discuss setting limits and reducing greenhouse gas output. After 11 days of intense debate and multiple compromise by all sides those attending reached a tentative agreement. Thirty-eight industrialized nations, including the USA, the EU, Russia and Japan, all agreed to reduce emissions to 6–8 per cent below 1990 levels by 2008–12. Developing countries are not required to meet these same requirements, but have been given the option to comply and receive technological and material aid in return. As part of reaching their individual reduction goals the industrialized nations are able to 'trade' emissions between themselves. Thus, if the EU, having pledged to reduce emissions to 8 per cent below 1990 levels, were to achieve a 12 per cent reduction, they could then sell the surplus reduction to another country that had been unable to reach its own goal. The country buying the surplus would then be able to apply it towards its own reduction goal. In this way, a potential for economic incentive was worked into the reduction process.

Very few people are happy with the treaty. Environmentalists say it has done far too little to curb emissions, while business and industry advocates, especially in the US, claim it will create economic turmoil if applied. There are no mechanisms in place by which to enforce or even monitor compliance, and the treaty faces uphill battles in many legislatures before it is ratified. Buenos Aires, Argentina, was due to host a follow-up conference in 1998 to work out details of enforcing the treaty, and to cover issues not fully examined in Kyoto. It is at least encouraging that governments have come together and begun the process of seeking to reduce greenhouse gas emissions. This is an achievement which many thought impossible.

These four major reasons for concern – population growth, resource depletion and loss of biodiversity, waste disposal, and atmospheric damage – are integrally related to one another and together constitute a single 'interlocking global crisis'. This expression was used in *Our Common Future*, the official report of the 1987 UN World Commission on Environment and Development. The central notion of the report was that the various environmental, development and energy problems which plague the world are all aspects of the same crisis, whose solution lies in 'sustainable development'. This was reaffirmed at the 1992 Earth Summit in Rio, and given sweeping endorsement in *Agenda 21: A blueprint for action for global sustainable development into the 21st century.* One of the official papers to come out of Rio, *Agenda 21* is a wide-ranging document which has been adopted by 178 governments. It sets environmental, development and economic goals covering a whole spectrum of human and national activities. It does not have the power of a fully legal document, but it has been called 'international soft law', meaning that it carries moral authority and that all nations should adhere to it to the best of their ability. Although the term 'sustainable development' has been variously interpreted, it was defined in *Our Common Future* as development which 'meets the needs of the present without compromising the ability of future generations to meet their own needs'.[12] Indeed the inter-generational responsibility implicit in the word 'sustainable' has been captured in the popular expression 'not cheating on our kids'.

The biblical perspective

The biblical approach to the environmental issue is to ask this basic question: to whom does the earth belong? It is deceptively elementary. For how shall we reply? The first answer is straightforward. It is given in Psalm 24:1: 'The earth is the Lord's, and everything in it.' God is its Creator, and so by right of creation is also its owner. But this is only a partial answer. Here is Psalm 115:16: 'The highest heavens belong to the Lord; but the earth he has given to man.' So then, the balanced biblical answer to our question is that the earth belongs to both God and man – to God because he made it, to us because he has given it to us. Not, of course, that he has handed it over to us so completely as to retain neither rights nor control over it, but that he has given it to us to rule on his behalf. Our possession of the earth is leasehold, therefore, not freehold. We are only tenants; God himself remains (in the most literal sense) the 'landlord', the Lord of all the land.

This double truth (that the earth is both his and ours) is spelled out more fully in Genesis 1 and 2. In several verses of Genesis 1 the word 'earth' occurs:

Verse 10:	'God called the dry ground "earth".'
Verses 11, 12:	'Then God said, "Let the earth produce vegetation" … And it was so. The earth produced vegetation.'
Verse 24:	'And God said, "Let the earth produce living creatures" … And it was so.'
Verse 26:	'Then God said, "Let us make man in our image … and let them rule … over all the earth."'
Verse 28:	'God blessed them and said to them, "… fill the earth and subdue it."'

We may legitimately make three affirmations from this biblical material.

First, *God has given us dominion over the earth.* We note the two divine resolves of verse 26, 'Let us make man in our image' and 'let them have dominion over the earth'. We note also the two divine actions in which his resolves were expressed: 'So God created man in his own image' and 'God … said to them, "… fill the earth and subdue it"' (verses 27–8). Thus from the beginning human beings have been endowed with a double uniqueness: we bear the image of God (consisting of rational, moral, social and spiritual qualities which make it possible for us to know God) and we wield dominion over the earth and its creatures.

Indeed, our unique dominion over the earth is due to our unique relation with God. God arranged an order, even a hierarchy, of creation. He set human beings midway between himself as Creator and the rest of the creation, animate and inanimate. In some ways we are one with the rest of nature, being a part of it and having the status of creatures. In other ways we are distinct from nature, having been created in God's image and given dominion. Biologically, we are like the animals. For example, we breathe like them ('a living being', Genesis 1:21, 24 and 2:7), eat like them (1:29–30) and reproduce like them ('be fruitful and increase', 1:22, 28). But we also enjoy a higher level of experience, in which we are unlike the animals and like God: we are able to think, choose, create, love, pray, and exercise dominion. This is our intermediate position between God and nature, between the Creator and the rest of his creation. We combine dependence on God with dominion over the earth. Gerhard von Rad comments: 'Just as powerful earthly kings, to indicate their claim to dominion, erect an image of themselves in the provinces of their empire, where they do not generally appear, so man is placed upon earth in God's image as God's sovereign emblem.'[13]

Generally speaking, human beings have obeyed God's command to fill the earth and subdue it. At first progress was slow, as they graduated from food-gathering to farming. They learned to cultivate the soil, to protect cultivated areas from marauding animals, and to use the earth's produce to feed, clothe and house themselves and their families. Next they learned to domesticate animals, and to harness them to their service, in order to make their labour lighter and to bring them pleasure as well. Then they learned the secrets of power which God had locked up inside the created world – the power of fire and water, later that of steam, coal, gas and oil, and now that of uranium, the atom and the mighty silicon chip.

In all this, in human research, discovery and invention, in biology, chemistry, physics and other spheres, and in all the triumphs of technology, human beings have been obeying God and exercising their God-given dominion. There is no question (at least in principle) of their having behaved like Prometheus, who stole fire from the gods. In their progressive control of the earth, they have not been invading God's private sphere and wresting power from him, still less imagining that they have stopped up the gaps in which God used to lurk, so that they can now dispense with him. It is foolish to draw these deductions. Human beings may not have known it, or humbly acknowledged it, but in all their research and resourcefulness, far from usurping God's prerogatives or power, they have been exercising the dominion God gave them. Developing tools and technology, farming the land, digging for minerals, extracting fuels, damming rivers for hydro-electric power, harnessing atomic energy – all are fulfilments of God's primeval command. God has provided in the earth all the resources of food, water, clothing, shelter, energy and warmth which we need, and he has given us dominion over the earth in which these resources have been stored.

Secondly, *our dominion is a co-operative dominion*. In exercising our God-given dominion, we are not *creating* the processes of nature, but co-operating with them. It is clear from Genesis 1 that the earth was made fruitful before man was told to fill and subdue it. It is true that we can make the earth more fruitful. We can clear, plough, irrigate and enrich the soil. We can put plants under glass to catch more of the sun. We can manage the soil by rotating our crops. We can improve our stock by selective breeding. We can produce hybrid grains with a fantastic yield. We can mechanize our reaping and threshing by using huge combine harvesters. But in all these activities we are merely co-operating with the laws of fruitfulness which God has already established. Moreover, the 'painful toil' which we experience in agriculture, because of God's 'curse' upon the ground (Genesis 3:17), only modifies and does not override our continuing care of the soil under God's 'blessing' (Psalm 65:9ff.).

True again, we are controlling and even accelerating things artificially. But it is an *artificial* control of essentially *natural* processes. It is humans co-operating with God. It is a recognition that what God gives is 'nature'; whereas what we do with it is 'culture' or 'cultivation'.

True, God has humbled himself to need our co-operation (that is, he needs us to subdue the earth and till the soil). But we must also humble ourselves to acknowledge that our dominion over nature would be entirely fruitless if God had not made the earth fruitful, and if he did not continue to 'give the increase'.

This combination of nature and culture, of human helplessness and human prowess, of resources and labour, of faith and work, throws light on the recent fashion of declaring that 'man has now come of age' and that (in our newly acquired adulthood) we can dispense with God. The truth is that humankind has come of age technologically. We have developed extraordinary expertise in taming, controlling and using nature. In this respect we are *lords*, as God meant and told us to be. But we are also *children* in our ultimate dependence on the fatherly providence of God, who gives us sunshine, rain and fruitful seasons. E.F. Schumacher quotes Tom Dale and Vernon Gill Carter in this respect: 'Man, whether civilized or savage, is a child of nature – he is not the master of nature. He must conform his actions to certain natural laws if he is to maintain his dominance over his environment.'[14]

Thirdly, *our dominion is a delegated, and therefore a responsible dominion.* That is, the dominion we exercise over the earth does not belong to us by right, but only by favour. The earth 'belongs' to us not because we made or own it, but because its Maker has entrusted its care to us.

This has important consequences. If we think of the earth as a kingdom, then we are not kings ruling our own territory, but viceroys ruling it on the king's behalf, since the king has not abdicated his throne. Or if we think of the earth as a country estate, then we are not the landowners, but the bailiffs who manage and farm it on the owner's behalf. God makes us, in the most literal sense, 'caretakers' of his property.

God's continuing ownership and caring supervision of the earth (indeed of the universe) is asserted many times in Scripture. We have already considered the assertion of Psalm 24:1 that 'the earth is the Lord's'. This includes all living things which inhabit the earth: 'every animal of the forest is mine, and the cattle on a thousand hills. I know every bird in the mountains, and the creatures of the field are mine' (Psalm 50:10–11). In the Sermon on the Mount Jesus extended the divine dominion further – from the largest to the smallest of creatures. On the one hand, God makes 'his sun' to rise (it belongs to him), and on the other he feeds the birds, and he clothes the lilies and the grass of the field (Matthew 5:45; 6:26, 28, 30). He thus sustains the whole of his creation; in committing it to us, he has not renounced responsibility for it.

This must be the reason why even Canaan, 'the land of Israel', did not belong to Israel. True, it was 'the promised land' because God had promised to give it to Abraham's descendants, and did in fact do so. Yet individuals owned land only as representatives of their tribe. No one was allowed to transfer land outside the tribe (Numbers 36:5ff.), nor to sell it to anyone in perpetuity. Every 50 years, in the Year of Jubilee, all land was to revert to its original owner. God was teaching that the land was still his, and that no human being had freehold rights. True, property rights were acknowledged, so that not only theft but also covetousness were forbidden in the law. Nevertheless, the proprietors were to remember two fundamental truths. First, they were only temporary residents: 'The land must not be sold permanently, because the land is mine and you are but aliens and my tenants' (Leviticus 25:23).

Secondly, they must not keep all the produce of the land for themselves but provide for their needy neighbour out of it. As Professor Martin Hengel has put it, 'The right to property was in principle subordinated to the obligation to care for the weaker members of society.'[15] It is interesting that Pope John Paul II summed up the Christian tradition on this matter in similar terms. In his Encyclical on 'Human Work' (1981) he distanced himself from both Marxist 'collectivism' and liberal 'capitalism'. In the latter case, he explained, the question is *how* 'the right to ownership or property is understood'. He continued: 'Christian tradition has never upheld this right as absolute and untouchable. On the contrary, it has always understood this right within the broader context of the right common to all to use the goods of the whole creation: *the right to private property is subordinated to the right to common use*, to the fact that goods are meant for everyone.'[16]

If therefore our dominion over the earth has been delegated to us by God, with a view to our co-operating with him and sharing its produce with others, then we are accountable to him for our stewardship. We have no liberty to do what we like with our natural environment; it is not ours to treat as we please. 'Dominion' is not a synonym for 'domination', let alone 'destruction'. Since we hold it in trust, we have to manage it responsibly and productively for the sake of both our own and subsequent generations.

The conservation debate

Trusteeship includes conservation. The greatest threat to humankind may prove in the end to be not a war-time but a peace-time peril, namely the spoliation of earth's natural resources by human folly or greed. All life on earth is dependent on the biosphere, the narrow layer of water, soil and air in which we live. Yet our record in conserving it, especially in the twentieth century, is not good.

Vast areas of America, Africa and Asia, once fertile agricultural land, are now through misuse irrevocable deserts or dustbowls. Worldwide, deserts have increased by 150 per cent during the past 100 years, so that almost 50 per cent of the earth's surface is now desert or semi-desert. The Aral Sea, once the most productive fishing site in central Asia and the fourth largest inland sea in the world, is now at half its volume of 30 years ago. A poorly conceived irrigation scheme to channel water away from the rivers that feed the sea resulted in its virtual drying out. In some places the coast has moved 30 miles, replaced by a desert of sand and salt deposits.[17] In spite of well-publicized concern over the destruction of the rain forests, each year 10 trees are being cut down for every one replanted, which has resulted in the total loss of half the tropical rain forests in the world.[18] Deforestation, among other results, leads to severe soil erosion. It is estimated that 25 billion tons of topsoil are lost each year. Soil has been so abused in parts of the world that 11 per cent of the world's vegetated soil is now beyond recovery. This is an area the size of China and India.[19] Some of this destruction of the environment undoubtedly happens as a result of human ignorance (e.g. the early dustbowls). Nevertheless, the Church of England's Board for Social Responsibility were not exaggerating when they said that 'despoiling the earth is a blasphemy, and not just an error of judgement, a mistake'.[20] It is a sin against God as well as humankind.

At the same time, not all Christians have accepted the responsibility which Scripture lays upon us; some have even used the Genesis story to excuse their irresponsibility. Gavin Maxwell, author of books on otters, especially *Ring of Bright Water*, once wrote how he lost two lovely otter cubs he had brought back from Nigeria: 'A Minister of the Church of Scotland, walking along the foreshore with a shotgun, found them at play by the tide's edge and shot them. One was killed outright, the other died of her wounds in the water. The minister expressed regret, but reminded a journalist that "the Lord gave man control over the beasts of the field." '[21] As Professor C.F.D. Moule rightly comments, 'a crime against sense and sensibility cannot be defended by the appeal to mere texts'.[22]

To be sure, the biblical texts have been variously interpreted. In the middle ages, for example, Thomas Aquinas taught that animals exist entirely for human pleasure and profit, whereas Francis of Assisi treated them as his equals, his brothers and sisters. It was Jeremy Bentham, however, at the end of the eighteenth century, who first maintained that animals have rights, because they are sentient creatures which feel pain. In our day Dr Peter Singer, professor of philosophy at Monash University, Melbourne, has gone much further. In his controversial book *Animal Liberation*,[23] although he concedes that there are differences between humans and animals, he yet argues for the extension of the 'basic principle of equality' to animals (or rather to 'non-human animals', as he calls them). He rejects what he calls 'species-ism' as vigorously as he rejects racism and sexism. He defines it as 'a prejudice or attitude of bias in favor of the interests of members of one's own species and against those of members of other species'.[24] In consequence, the presupposition that 'the human animal' has the right to rule 'over other animals' is in his opinion 'now obsolete'.[25]

This is an extreme over-reaction, however. We cannot possibly surrender the fundamental truth that human beings alone of all God's creatures are made in his image and are given a responsible dominion over the earth and its creatures. It is more meaningful, therefore, to speak of our responsibilities to and for animals than of rights possessed by animals themselves. Since God created them (Genesis 1), since he shows his concern for them by giving them life, food and shelter (Psalm 104), and since Jesus spoke of their intrinsic 'value' (Matthew 10:31; 12:12), we too must be committed to their welfare. The Bible is quite clear on this point. According to the law, the benefits of the sabbath rest were to be enjoyed by animals as well as humans (Exodus 20:10). According to the wisdom literature, 'a righteous man cares for the needs of his animals' (Proverbs 12:10).

Anxious public debate continues, not least among Christians, about the application of these biblical principles to such practices as vivisection, intensive farming, the shipping and slaughter of animals for food, their domestication for work and play, and the keeping of pets. Christians should protest against all perceived cruelty to animals, and campaign for their humane treatment in all circumstances, asking ourselves whether each practice is consonant with their value (as God's creatures) and with our responsibility (as God's stewards).[26]

What about the Genesis texts, however? Are we sure that we have interpreted them correctly? Or are the critics of Christianity right in saying that these verses are to blame for contemporary ecological irresponsibility? For example, the American historian Lynn White, of the University of California, Berkeley, has written: 'Christianity … not only established a dualism of man and nature, but also insisted that it is God's will that man exploit nature for his proper ends … Christianity bears a huge burden of guilt.'[27] More outspoken still is Ian L. McHarg. He is a Scot, who spent his childhood between the ugliness of Glasgow and the beauty of the Firth of Clyde and the Western Highlands and Islands. He became a town planner, an ecologist and the founder and chairman of the Department of Landscape Architecture and Regional Planning at the University of Pennsylvania. In 1969 he wrote that the Genesis story, 'in its insistence upon dominion and subjugation of nature, encourages the most exploitative and destructive instincts in man rather than those that are deferential and creative. Indeed, if one seeks license for those who would increase radioactivity, create canals and harbors with atomic bombs, employ poisons without constraint, or give consent to the bulldozer mentality, there could be no better injunction than this text' (i.e. Genesis 1:26, 28). 'When this is understood,' he continues, 'the conquest, the depredations and the despoliation are comprehensible.'[28] For God's affirmation about man's dominion was 'also a declaration of war on nature'. And he concludes with these words: 'Dominion and subjugation must be expunged as the biblical injunction of man's relation to nature.'[29]

In his Dunning Trust lectures in 1972–3 Ian McHarg further extended his assault. He traced western man's attitude to the natural world to 'three horrifying lines' in Genesis 1 about the dominion which God gave to man. 'Dominion is a non-negotiating relationship,' he said. 'If you want to find one text of compounded horror which will guarantee that the relationship of man to nature can only be destruction, which will atrophy any creative skill … which will explain all of the destruction and all of the despoliation accomplished by western man for at least these 2,000 years, then you do not have to look any further than this ghastly, calamitous text.'[30]

Ian McHarg uses very intemperate language to state his case. Some misguided people (for example, Gavin Maxwell's minister) may have tried to defend their irresponsible use of Genesis 1. But it is absurd to call this text 'horrifying', 'ghastly' and 'calamitous', and then attribute to it two millennia of western man's exploitation of the environment.

A much more temperate judgement is supplied by Keith Thomas, the Oxford University social historian. In his *Man and the Natural World,* he provides meticulously thorough documentation for changing attitudes towards nature in England between 1500 and 1800.[31] His theme is that at the beginning of this period, 'human ascendancy' was taken for granted. People accepted 'the long-established view … that the world had been created for man's sake and that other species were meant to be subordinate to his wishes and needs'.[32] Gradually, however, this 'breathtakingly anthropocentric' interpretation of the early chapters of Genesis was discarded.[33] It is true that some Christians did use the grant of 'dominion' over the creatures as a mandate even for such cruel sports as bear-baiting and cock-fighting.[34] But Dr Thomas also writes that Genesis 1 cannot be blamed for ecological problems, since (a) they exist in 'parts of the world where the Judaeo-Christian tradition has had no influence', (b) Genesis also contains a 'distinctive doctrine of human stewardship and responsibility for God's creatures', and (c) other parts of the Old Testament clearly inculcate care for the animal creation.[35] In fact he concedes that 'the modern idea of the balance of nature ... had a theological basis before it gained a scientific one. It was belief in the perfection of God's design which preceded and underpinned the concept of the ecological chain, any link of which it would be dangerous to move.'[36] So let us look at the Genesis text again.

It is true that the two Hebrew words used in Genesis 1:26 and 28 are forceful. The verb translated 'have dominion' means to 'tread' or 'trample' on, so that the paraphrase in Psalm 8 is 'you have put all things under his feet'. It is often used in the Old Testament of the rule of kings. The other verb, 'subdue', was used of subduing enemies in warfare and of bringing people into subjection or bondage as slaves. So man was commanded to rule the creatures of the sea, sky and earth (verse 26) and to enslave the earth, bringing it into subjection (verse 28). Ian McHarg is right, then? No, he is not. It is an elementary principle of biblical interpretation that one must not establish the meaning of words by their etymology alone, but also and especially by the way they are used in their context. What I have written earlier about this biblical instruction is germane to the interpretation of these texts. We have seen that the dominion God has given us is delegated, responsible and co-operative; that it is intended to express the same sustaining care of the environment as its Creator's; and that, far from exploiting the earth and its creatures, we are to use them in such a way as to be accountable to God and to serve others. We have no liberty to do what Ian McHarg did in one of his lectures, namely to set Genesis 1 and 2 in opposition to each other as if Genesis 2 taught 'cultivation' and Genesis 1 'destruction'. On the contrary, the two passages interpret each other. The dominion God has given humankind is a conscientious and caring stewardship which involves the husbanding of the earth's resources. It would be ludicrous to suppose that God first created the earth and then handed it over to us to destroy it.

Contemporary awareness

Certainly our generation is taking environmental responsibility more seriously than our immediate predecessors did. Scientists are emphasizing the delicate balance of nature. God has established in nature almost unbelievable powers of recuperation and regeneration, and in particular a cycle for the renewal of energy (from sun to plants to animals to bacteria to earth, and back to plants again). It is an example of what Barbara Ward called 'the most majestic unity' of our planet. It is due to natural laws which produce a 'dynamic equilibrium of biological forces held in position by checks and balances of a most delicate sort'.[37] 'They are so intricate,' commented Dr John Klotz, the American conservationist, 'that they could not have developed by chance.'[38] But if we despoil the green surface of the earth, or destroy the plankton of the oceans, we will quickly reach the point of no return in the recycling process. Our immense modern scientific knowledge teaches us 'one thing above all', wrote Barbara Ward, namely the 'need for extreme caution, a sense of the appalling vastness and complexity of the forces that can be unleashed, and of the eggshell delicacy of the agents that can be upset'.[39]

There have been a number of encouragements in recent years. Yet there is also a sense that in some ways the environment has passed out of the international spotlight. Nations have been slow to conform to goals set at Rio. Bureaucracy and red tape clutter the path, and many large environmental organizations are bogged down in fund-raising and bureaucracy of their own. So there remains room for more innovation and personal involvement. Only 1 per cent of the land area of the earth is under cultivation. If only a cheaper and more efficient way to desalinate salt water could be invented, many of the world's deserts could be irrigated and made to blossom like the rose. The sea, which covers two-thirds of the planet's surface, has vast riches in terms of fish protein (not to mention oil, gas and mineral deposits). Yet we have still not learned to farm the oceans; we are still at the stage of primitive hunter-gatherers, and are guilty of over-fishing too. Enormous sums of money have been invested in the space programme; I am not myself convinced, however, that we have a clear mandate to land people on the *moon*, let alone the other planets of our solar system, before we have completed our God-given task of filling and subduing the *earth*.

Have Christians a distinctive contribution to make to the ecological debate? Yes, we believe both that God created the earth, entrusting its care to us, and that he will one day recreate it, when he makes 'the new heaven and the new earth'. For 'the whole creation has been groaning as in the pains of childbirth right up to the present time'. Its groans are due to its 'bondage to decay' and its consequent 'frustration'. In the end, however, it will come to share in 'the glorious freedom of the children of God'. That is, its bondage will give place to freedom, its decay to glory, and its pain to the joy of a new world being born (Romans 8:19–22). These two doctrines, regarding the beginning and the end of history, the Creation and the Consummation, have a profound effect on our perspective. They give us an appropriate respect for the earth, indeed for the whole material creation, since God both made it and will remake it.

In consequence, we must learn to think and act ecologically. We repent of extravagance, pollution and wanton destruction. We recognize that human beings find it easier to subdue the earth than they do to subdue themselves. Ronald Higgins' book *The Seventh Enemy* is significant in this respect. For the first six 'enemies' are the population explosion, the food crisis, the scarcity of resources, environmental degradation, nuclear abuse and scientific technology. The seventh enemy, however, is ourselves, our personal blindness and political inertia in the face of today's ecological challenge. That is why the subtitle of Ronald Higgins' book is 'The Human Factor in the Global Crisis'. The human race needs a new self-awareness, and fresh vision, a reawakening of its moral and religious capabilities.[40] But is this possible? Yes, Christians are convinced it is. One of the particular merits of the late Professor Klaus Bockmuhl's booklet *Conservation and Lifestyle* is that he goes beyond the 'Christian criteria' for environmental responsibility to the 'Christian motives'. And in his conclusion he presses the challenge home: 'What is sought from Christians is the motivation for selfless service, which once distinguished the Christian heritage. We should be pioneers in the care of mankind … We should show whence the power and perspective for such a contribution come. We are charged to give an example.' We have to 'reawaken the heart of the gospel ethic'.[41] We may be thankful that there are now a number of Christian organizations working specifically in the area of care for creation. Among them are the International Evangelical Environmental Network, the A Rocha Trust, the Au Sable Institute, and the Christian Society of the Green Cross.[42]

At the root of the ecological crisis is human greed, what has been called 'economic gain by environmental loss'. Often it is a question of competing commercial interests (though some multinational corporations have an environmental department). It is only logical that the consumer should pay the cost of production without pollution, whether in increased prices or (through a government subsidy to the manufacturer) in increased taxes. Christians should not grudge this, if it is the cost of responsible, ecological stewardship.

A crucial aspect of the economic problems in ecological steward-ship is the race for industrialization occurring in the Third World. As developing countries struggle to raise their standards of living, the environment is often given less priority than the more immedi-ate problems of under-nourishment, disease and poverty. This is understandable, and these deeper issues must be addressed if we are ever to make headway in preserving and enhancing the natural environment. Furthermore, to insist on the protection of tropical forests in the Third World, if we are unwilling to reduce CO_2 output in our own countries, is rank hypocrisy. We must also be willing both to share technologies which can help curb natural destruction and to create economic benefits for environmentally safe business practices. While the vast disparity between wealth and poverty remains, Christians are bound to have an uneasy conscience. We should strenuously avoid all wastefulness and greed, not only out of solidarity with the poor but also out of respect for the living environment.

Chapter 7

NORTH-SOUTH ECONOMIC INEQUALITY

Opinions differ as to what is the principal problem confronting humanity today. For decades following World War II it was the arms race and the fearful spectre of nuclear war. With the end of the cold war, the major global concern became the environment. Now, however, according to the World Bank, 'development is the most important challenge facing the human race'.[1] Indeed, development and the environment are closely related to one another.

In 1964, at the first UNCTAD (United Nations Conference on Trade and Development), the representatives of Third World countries formed themselves into the 'Group of 77' (which has now grown to over 130), in order to promote their economic concerns. Then in 1973, at a meeting of non-aligned countries in Algiers, the concept was formulated of a New International Economic Order (NIEO). This urgent call for a radical restructuring of the world economy in the interests of developing nations was doubtless a flexing of Third World muscle immediately after the quadrupling of the price of oil by the OPEC countries. It also expressed the resolve of countries which had recently obtained their *political* independence to gain their *economic* independence as well.

The following year (1974), to the jubilation of many and the chagrin of some, the General Assembly of the United Nations endorsed the call for an NIEO, and published a few months later a 'Charter of Economic Rights and Duties of States'. This recognized the propriety of NIEO demands, for example for more direct aid and better credit facilities, for the right to regulate (even nationalize) multinational corporations, for the removal of trade barriers to create more favourable trade terms, and for more adequate representation in international decision-making structures like the IMF (International Monetary Fund). But little progress was made to implement these proposals. The next two UNCTADs – in Nairobi (1976) and Manila (1979) – repeated the cry for more credit, aid, trade, power and stability of commodity prices, but the Third World delegates were disappointed that little if anything had been achieved. Then in 1980, at the threshold of the third Development Decade, the Brandt Commission offered new hope in its report entitled *North South: A Programme for Survival*.

The Brandt Commission reports

On any showing *North-South* is a remarkable book. Even its critics (to whom I will come later) concede that it was a great achievement to produce a unanimous report by 18 distinguished independent leaders from five continents and from different political backgrounds after two years' work; that the commission had the courage to draw the world's attention to the need for radical action on a global scale; and that it presented its challenge with an unusual combination of reason and passion. In his personal introduction Herr Willy Brandt, the former West German Chancellor, expressed his conviction 'that the two decades ahead of us may be fateful for mankind'.[2]

The Brandt report was published nearly 20 years ago (in 1980). But it still speaks with relevance today, although its statistics need, of course, to be updated. World population will grow to roughly 8 billion by the year 2015, with five-sixths of people living in the Third World.[3] In spite of three decades of development, with some genuine improvements in economic growth, public health, life expectancy and literacy, still about a quarter of the world population is condemned to absolute poverty.[4] Half the population of the developing world lives on diets which lack essential calories, and every two seconds a child dies of hunger or disease.[5] The Third World has about 80 per cent of the world's population, but subsists on less than 20 per cent of the world's income.[6] It is essential to know these basic statistics; our Christian thinking has to be earthed in reality.

The Brandt Commission saw its task as relating to 'international development issues'. It is important, therefore, to be aware of its understanding of 'development'. The report emphasizes that 'the prime objective of development is to lead to self-fulfillment and creative partnership in the use of a nation's productive forces and its full human potential'.[7]

So, 'development' is much more than 'relief' or 'aid'. Relief is still necessary in emergency situations. Aid is also often needed, especially as a 'pump-priming' operation, although it can both demean people (if it is offered in a patronizing way) and make them more rather than less dependent. Development, on the other hand, does not increase dependence: it aims to end it. Also, true development is wider than mere economic growth; it includes dimensions of human experience which are of great concern to Christians. This is why the 'Wheaton 83' Conference of the World Evangelical Fellowship preferred 'transformation' to 'development', since the transformation Christians desire to promote embraces both individuals and communities, and both the material and the spiritual spheres of human life.

The Villars Statement on Relief and Development (1987) saw 'relief and development' as 'an expression that recognizes two biblical principles. Relief refers to the insistence in both Testaments that the people of God must help the hungry and the oppressed. Development stems from the biblical vision of a people exercising their proper stewardship of God's gifts – of societies that are productive, healthy and governed justly. Together relief and development envision substantial improvement in economic and human well-being.'[8]

At the same time, social transformation is often resisted by a selfish élite who have vested interests in maintaining the status quo. Vishal Mangalwadi, who founded ACRA (the Association for Comprehensive Rural Assistance) in 1976, and has been involved ever since in serving India's rural poor, soon discovered that this reactionary element was the basic cause of continuing poverty. People 'starve, suffer and die because the powerful have other priorities', he writes. Indeed, when he became convinced that 'poverty was planned and perpetuated by powerful people', his emphasis changed 'from development to reform'.[9]

Towards the development goal the Brandt Commissioners called for an immediate 'Emergency Programme: 1980–85'. I summarize it in only the barest outline:

1. A large-scale transfer of resources to developing countries.
2. An international energy strategy.
3. A global food programme.

4. A start on some major reforms in the international economic system, including the creation of a new 'World Development Fund', greater Third World participation in existing international economic institutions, the stabilization of exchange rates and commodity prices, greater access to world markets in more favourable terms, and more regulation of trans-national corporations.[10]

How did the Commissioners imagine that the nations of the North could be persuaded to share their resources, skills and power on such a massive scale? They certainly referred to a sense of 'human solidarity and a commitment to international social justice'.[11] But this was not their main thrust. Instead they wrote, the 'principle of mutuality of interest has been at the centre of our discussions'.[12] That is, 'North and South depend on each other in a single world economy', and now that they are 'increasingly aware of the interdependence, they need to revitalize the dialogue to achieve specific goals, in a spirit of partnership and mutual interest rather than of inequality and charity'.[13]

Critics have not questioned the evident sincerity of the Commissioners, although they have tended to call the report 'visionary' and 'romantic', failing to take sufficient account of human selfishness, and they have drawn attention to the report's emphasis on the distribution of wealth, without a logically prior concern for its creation.

Professor Brian Griffiths (now Lord Griffiths) in his 1980 London Lectures, published as *Morality and the Market Place*, developed a still more fundamental criticism, which indeed I mentioned in Chapter 4. He is a reluctant critic, because he too is deeply disturbed that 'hundreds of millions of our fellow human beings who like us have been created in the image of God ... live in conditions of appalling deprivation'.[14] His main criticism is of the report's omissions. Why did the Commissioners fall into the trap of generalizing about 'the South' or 'the Third World'? Why did they not probe the embarrassing question of why some Third World countries are developing much faster than others? The different pace of development is not due just to the disparity of available natural resources. The reason is deeper than that. For the causes of Third World poverty concern people, Brian Griffiths argues, and their political, economic and cultural behaviour. The political factors include mismanagement, the expulsion of racial minorities, extravagance and corruption on the part of governments and their leaders. Then there is the economic system which they choose and operate. But above all there is the cultural factor, that is, the profound effect of people's cultural background on their motives, thoughts, aspirations and actions.

As a matter of fact, the Brandt Commission did not altogether ignore the cultural factor:

> No matter how enlightened the plans for the economic and social betterment of people's conditions, they will achieve little unless in parallel the battle is fought at the same time in both North and South, to liberate people from outworn ideas, from the grip of narrowly conceived national interests, and from the passions and prejudices inherited from the past. A new international economic order will need men and women with a new mentality and wider outlook to make it work, and a process of development in which their full capacities flourish.[15]

But Brian Griffiths rightly seized on Willy Brandt's own assertion, on behalf of the Commission: 'We take it for granted that all cultures deserve equal respect, protection and promotion.'[16] 'While all cultures deserve respect,' Brian Griffiths responded, 'they do not all deserve equal protection and promotion.' On the contrary, how can we wish to 'protect and promote' cultures which actively hinder development, for example by inculcating a spirit of fatalism and apathy? He continues:

> If we really wish to understand the origins of poverty in Third World countries, I believe we are driven back to an examination of the culture of different countries and to asking basic questions. Why is it that in some societies individual human beings have the views of the physical world, of the importance of work, and the sense of self-discipline which they do? Why is it that in other societies they do not? ... Personally, I find it impossible to answer these questions satisfactorily in purely economic terms. It is at this point that economic analysis needs a religious dimension ... To the extent that any culture contains Judaeo-Christian values, then surely those facets of that culture deserve especial protection and promotion.[17]

Brian Griffiths' main criticism, then, of the Brandt Commission's recommendations is that 'they totally ignore the relationship between economic structures and economic philosophy ... Cultures express values which shape institutions and motivate people – some of which … promote wealth and justice and liberty, and others of which do not.'[18]

So then, '*culture* is central to the whole process [of development],' Dr Herbert Schlossberg has written, 'and central to culture is the religious vision that informs the culture.'[19] It makes a huge difference to the quality and speed of development whether people are characterized by fatalism or confidence, indolence or industry, corruption or integrity, whether they believe the world is ruled by malign spirits who resent any interference with nature or by a good Creator who tells them to transform it, and whether they think of the future in terms of endless reincarnations or of personal accountability to the Judge of all the earth. If the causes of poverty are spiritual as well as material, the remedies must be also. 'The most effective means of spreading economic development, therefore,' Dr Schlossberg continues, 'is a full-orbed mission program' – that is, preaching and teaching the gospel in its fullness.[20] For, as the Villars Statement put it, 'the work of Christian relief and development … must involve spiritual transformation, setting people free from destructive attitudes, beliefs, values and patterns of culture.'[21]

The 1981 London Lectures in Contemporary Christianity, given the year after those by Brian Griffiths, took the form of a symposium published under the title *The Year 2000 AD*.[22] One of the contributors was Donald Hay of Oxford University. Most of his essay was concerned with motivation for development. He pointed out that the Brandt Commissioners tried to induce the North to take action (1) by 'arguments from doom' (that otherwise world war, ecological disaster or economic collapse are inevitable) and (2) by 'arguments from mutual economic interests'. These two sets of arguments he found neither convincing nor fully Christian. In their place he restated 'the Christian moral argument', which is not compassion but justice, especially '*justice* in the access to resources',[23] that is, to the resources of education, technology, land and 'a culture based on hope and not despair about the possibilities for economic development'.[24] By contrast, the North had 'used its power to determine North-South economic relations to its own advantage'.[25]

The publication of the Brandt Commission report, in spite of the criticisms, brought high hopes that at last some action would be taken to redress the North-South economic imbalance. The immediate outcome was minimal, however, and the nations of the North appeared preoccupied with their own economic problems.

So in 1983 the Brandt Commission issued its second document, a memorandum entitled *Common Crisis.*[26] In his introduction Herr Willy Brandt was even more impassioned than before. Three years had elapsed since the publication of *North-South*. Meanwhile, some of the Commissioners' worst fears had been confirmed. The prospects for economic recovery had deteriorated rapidly. Further decline could 'cause the disintegration of societies and create conditions of anarchy in many parts of the world'. So Willy Brandt and his colleagues felt it necessary 'to present an urgent and up-to-date version of our original Emergency Programme',[27] in the hope of breaking the deadlock and averting economic collapse.

They summarized their proposals under five headings:

1. Finance (making more money available to promote recovery).
2. Trade (increasing world trade by resisting protectionist pressures).
3. Food (raising food and agricultural production, to make nations more self-sufficient).
4. Energy (creating a new energy agency to increase energy production).
5. Negotiation (improving the negotiating process between North and South.

I do not think Brandt II contained any proposals of substance which were not in Brandt I. It was the same medicine, though perhaps the mixture was stronger, and certainly the tone of the doctors' appeal was more urgent.

Debt and development

Looking back, it is evident that the 1980s, which had been proclaimed as the Third Development Decade, did not live up to their name. True, there was much idealism. A notable example was Bob Geldof, the Irish pop star who, outraged by television pictures of starving children in Ethiopia, touched the compassion of millions of young people. He did more than raise money (£8 million through Band Aid, £100 million through Live Aid, and more through Sport Aid and later efforts); he raised the issue of development in the public consciousness, produced educational resources for schools, and sought to generate political change by his 'punk diplomacy'.[28] The tragedy is that, in spite of this kind of widespread goodwill, the development process actually went into reverse during the 1980s, disastrously in Africa, seriously too in Latin America, though less so in Asia. During the 1980s and early 1990s the income gap between rich and poor nations widened at a pace faster than it had done in more than three previous decades.[29]

One of the major reasons for this is the debt burden which many Third World countries continue to bear, following the massive lending of the 1970s. Although, of course, in principle all contracts should be kept and debts repaid, one wonders if the present situation does not fall under the Old Testament condemnation of usury. It certainly gives the appearance of the exploitation of the poor through extortionate money-lending by the rich. In 1996 alone Third World debt grew by 7.2 per cent. The debt crisis cannot be attributed in a simplistic way to mismanagement and extravagance by unscrupulous governments and their élite supporters. It is mainly due to factors over which the country's leaders have little if any control – the worldwide recession of the early eighties, rising interest rates in the lending countries, crippling inflation in the borrowing countries, and the instability – in some cases collapse – of commodity prices. So the debts have increased even while the ability to repay them has decreased.

Moreover, whenever the banks have stopped making fresh loans, while the repayment of old debts has continued, the net flow of money has been *out* of the Third World instead of *into* it. For every dollar of aid that goes into the Third World three dollars are paid out in debt repayments. Between 1990 and 1993 debt servicing cost sub-Saharan Africa more than 13 billion dollars, and this was only half of what they needed to pay in order to keep up. As a result, the debts were rolled over and overall debt doubled during this period.[30] Some countries are now paying over half their annual earnings in the servicing of their national debt. A few owe even more in debt repayment and interest than their total income from exports. It is surely unjust that the world's poorest countries should have to stagger under this heavy load; in most cases the lender nations could easily afford more generous rescheduling arrangements, and even remissions.

I am thankful that under Britain's RTA ('Retrospective Terms Adjustment') 21 of the poorest countries (whose per capita GNP was below £300) had by 1985 had their debts cancelled by the conversion of loans into grants, at the cost of nearly £1 billion. At the same time, in rescheduling and cancellation arrangements it is morally wrong for the North to compel debtor governments to reduce their public expenditure on social programmes like education, health and employment, since it is the poor who suffer most from such cuts. Critics claim that this is often what happens under the Structural Adjustment Programs initiated by the World Bank and the IMF's stabilization policies, both of which are aimed at long-term structural change of unproductive economic practices. 'UNICEF estimates that the total additional annual cost of meeting basic human needs for health, education, nutrition ... for everyone in Sub-Saharan Africa is only around $9 billion,' a sum which could easily be found if governments were not struggling to service their debts.[31]

In 1990, at Keele University, Martin Dent decided that there could be a practical way forward in the debt crisis. With the help of others he founded the Jubilee 2000 Campaign. Inspired by the Old Testament jubilee legislation (Leviticus 25), by which every 50 years debts were cancelled and slaves freed, and by the vision of 2,000 million people enjoying a debt-free entry into the new millennium, he called for a one-off cancellation of debt to the world's poorest countries by the year 2000. What began as a simple grass-roots concern has exploded into a worldwide movement with groups in dozens of countries supporting the initiative. It is sponsored in the UK by many different organizations including Tearfund and Christian Aid. If the initiative meets its stated goals, 47 nations will have their foreign debt remitted by the year 2000.[32]

Important fresh thinking in the development debate was contributed by the UN's World Commission on Environment and Development (chaired by Mrs Gro Harlem Brundtland, at that time prime minister of Norway), whose report *Our Common Future* was published in 1987. Characterized by the same urgent tone as the Brandt reports, it called for the integration of the world's environmental and developmental problems (since economics and ecology are inseparable) and for the co-operation of all nations in solving them. It popularized the notion of 'sustainable development', defining it as 'development that meets the needs of the present (in particular, the essential needs of the poor) without compromising the ability of future generations to meet their own needs'.[33] The definition combines 'two key concepts' – meeting needs and setting limits. It thus promotes development and protects the environment simultaneously. Sustainable development became the hallmark of the 1992 United Nations Conference on the Environment and Development in Rio de Janeiro, where details of the interplay between the environment and development were more thoroughly worked out (see Chapter 6).

The decade of the nineties has been marked by a continuous questioning and reformulating of the basic ideas of development. Paul P. Streeten, Director of the World Development Institute, has said, 'Development must be redefined as an attack on the chief evils of the world today: malnutrition, disease, illiteracy, slums, unemployment and inequality.'[34] Alternatively, the same concerns may be expressed more positively. Whereas traditional economics has been concerned mainly with the growth and allocation of resources, development economics is concerned to improve a population's quality of life. Development then becomes a multi-dimensional vision. In particular, the 'three core values of development' are defined as (1) 'sustenance' or the ability to meet one's basic needs (i.e. food, health and shelter), (2) 'self-esteem' or the ability to be a person (with the dignity that comes from education and employment) and (3) 'freedom from servitude' or the ability to make choices (economic, social and political).[35]

In 1990 the United Nations Development Programme launched its now annual publication of the *Human Development Report*, which provides essential insight into the advances and retreats of the development movement.[36] The Human Development Index (HDI) was created and is now a useful tool in analysing the extent to which people are being genuinely helped by the development movement. Based on three general goals of development, the HDI takes into account 'longevity' measured by life expectancy at birth, 'knowledge' measured by adult literacy and mean years of schooling, and 'standard of living' measured by real per capita income adjusted by cost of living and other factors that differ between countries. By looking at facts and figures beyond simple economic growth, the Human Development Index puts a human face on poverty; it helps us to evaluate development in terms of how it affects people in all areas of life.

This specially concerns women. In spite of the designation of 1975 as International Women's Year, and of 1976–85 as the Decade for the Advancement of Women, much development has been 'gender-blind'. That is, it has not noticed that women have been undervalued, disadvantaged, and denied an equal share in the benefits of development. For example, more than 70 per cent of the population's poorest people are women and children, and of the estimated 1 billion illiterate adults in the world, more than 60 per cent are women. These and other imbalances have led some researchers to speak of the 'feminization' of poverty.[37] But if development has to do with human potential, and if men and women have the same potential as human beings created in God's image, no further argument is necessary to secure gender equality. Now, therefore, development is becoming increasingly gender-sensitive, alert to women's rights in law and politics, in access to literacy and education, in paid as well as voluntary work, and so in the personal dignity which these things promote. Alongside HDI (Human Development Index) there is now GDI (Gender-related Development Index), and the search is on for GEMs (Gender Empowerment Measures).[38]

In spite of many failures during the last three decades of the twentieth century, there has been an encouraging increase in international concern for the poor and the oppressed. As a result, many different aid, trade, relief and development organizations have come into existence, and the United Nations itself has a number of independent programmes devoted to aspects of development. Yet we must not allow the quest for social justice to be smothered by politics or bureaucracy. A sobering example of the attempted manipulation of the Third World by the First World took place at the United Nations Conference on Human Settlements (known as Habitat II) in Istanbul in June 1996. Designed to address issues of sustainable urban development in the Third World, it descended into a battle over 'reproductive health', which is liberal language for abortion on demand. Third World countries resisted the political agenda of the European and North American pro-abortion lobby. As a result of their stubbornness, a courageous speech by John Gummer (then British Secretary of State for the Environment), and the support of pro-life non-governmental organizations present, the Third World majority radically modified the pro-abortion vocabulary of some conference resolutions, reaffirmed the family as a cornerstone of society, and left no room for universal abortion on demand.

It is certainly legitimate to conclude this section of the chapter on a note of optimism. At the World Summit for Social Development, held in Copenhagen in 1995, nearly all the nations of the world committed themselves to the goal of eradicating severe poverty during the early decades of the third millennium. What progress has been made since then?

At the launch of the eighth Human Development Report in June 1997 some stirring words were spoken by Richard Jolly, the report's main author, and special adviser to the administrator of the United Nations Human Development Programme:

> The dramatic record of poverty reduction in the twentieth century shows that we should raise our sights, not downsize our vision, for human development ... The resources needed to eradicate poverty are a mere fraction of resources available ... This is a moment of extraordinary hope for people across the world. The nations of the world must reach out, not retreat ... Eradicating absolute poverty in the first decades of the twenty-first century is feasible, affordable and a moral imperative.[39]

Not being an economist or development expert,[40] I lack the expertise to comment either on what shape a 'New International Economic Order' should take, or on the specific proposals of the Brandt, Brundtland and other reports. What I do feel able to do, however, is to offer some biblical thoughts as justification for continuing to seek global economic and environmental co-operation. It is another case of struggling to clarify the principles involved, while leaving the framing of policies to those who have the necessary training, knowledge and influence. It seems to me that two fundamental biblical principles apply to this issue.

The principle of unity

The first is the principle of unity, namely that the planet earth is one, and the human race is also one. Yet this double unity does not control our behaviour. Instead, the basic human predicament is that 'the Earth is one but the world is not'.[41] So nothing is more important than that the two unities God has created should permeate our consciousness.

Some claim that it was Buckminster Fuller, the famous inventor of the geodesic dome, who first coined the term 'Spaceship Earth'. Others attribute the first use of the expression to Ambassador Adlai Stevenson. It is certainly true that, during the last speech he made before the Economic and Social Council in Geneva on 9 June 1965, he referred to the earth as 'a little spaceship' on which we are all travelling together, 'dependent on its vulnerable supplies of air and soil'. The following year Barbara Ward the economist took up the theme in her book *Spaceship Earth*, and a few years later elaborated it with René Dubos in *Only One Earth*.[42] Published in preparation for the 1972 United Nations Conference on the Human Environment in Stockholm, and subtitled 'the care and maintenance of a small planet', the book is addressed to the question of how the growing human population can husband the planet's limited resources, for the common good, and neither exploit, nor waste, nor destroy them. The last chapter, 'Strategies for Survival', ends on a rueful note. Governments have paid lip-service to the notion of planetary interdependence by setting up a whole variety of United Nations agencies to develop worldwide strategies. But these international institutions 'are not backed by any sense of planetary community and commitment ... The planet is not yet a centre of rational loyalty for all mankind.' Yet such a shift of loyalty is possible, and could well be awakened within us by 'a profound and deepening sense of our shared and interdependent biosphere'. After all, the human race has continually enlarged its allegiance – 'from family to clan, from clan to nation, from nation to federation'. So why should it not take the final, logical step? 'Today, in human society, we can perhaps hope to survive in all our prized diversity, provided we can achieve an ultimate loyalty to our single, beautiful and vulnerable Planet Earth.'[43] Christians will want to modify this statement, in that our ultimate loyalty is to God the Creator, who has both made the earth and entrusted it to our care.

This is a clear biblical vision. 'The earth is the Lord's and everything in it, the world, and all who live in it' (Psalm 24:1). I have already quoted this verse in reference to the environment: the earth belongs to God. Now we take note that those who live in it belong to him too. For God has created a single people (the human race) and placed us in a single habitat (the planet earth). We are one people inhabiting one planet. Moreover, these two unities (planet and people) are closely related to one another. For God said, 'Be fruitful, and increase in number; fill the earth and subdue it' (Genesis 1:28). Thus the one people were to populate and tame the one earth, in order to harness its resources to their service. There was no hint at the beginning of the partitioning of the earth or of rivalry between

nations. No, the whole earth was to be developed by the whole people for the common good. All were to share in its God-given riches.
This principle of 'distributive justice' still applies today.

But this divine purpose has been frustrated by the rise of competitive nations who have carved up the earth's surface and now
jealously guard its mineral deposits and fossil fuels for themselves.
Of course the Bible (realistic book that it is) recognizes the existence
of nations, indicates that their developing histories and territorial
frontiers are ultimately under God's sovereign control, welcomes the
cultural diversity (though not all the cultural practices) they have
created, and warns us that 'nation will rise against nation' till the
end. But it does not acquiesce in this international rivalry. On the
contrary, it tells us that the multiplicity of mutually hostile nations
with mutually incomprehensible languages is a consequence of
God's judgement on man's disobedience and pride (Genesis 11).

The Bible also indicates that one of God's major purposes in
redemption will be to overcome the enmity which separates nations
and to reunite the human race in Christ. So, immediately after the
Tower of Babel episode, God promised through Abraham's posterity to bless all the peoples of the earth (Genesis 12:1–3); he predicted through the prophets that all nations would one day 'flow'
like rivers to Jerusalem (e.g. Isaiah 2:2); the risen Jesus told his
followers to go and make disciples of all the nations (Matthew
28:19); the Holy Spirit came upon 'all flesh', the 19 national groups
Luke mentions representing the known world (Acts 2:5–11, 17);
Paul describes the accomplishment of Christ's cross in terms both
of the abolition of the dividing wall of hostility between Jew and
Gentile and of the creation out of the two of 'one new man' or a
single new humanity (Ephesians 2:14–15); and the vision of the
redeemed before God's throne is of a countless multitude 'from
every nation, tribe, people and language' (Revelation 7:9). It would
be impossible to miss this strand of internationalism which appears
right through the biblical revelation.

So then, we cannot evade our responsibility to the world's poor
people on the ground that they belong to other nations and are no
concern of ours. The English tend to exhibit a particularly unpleasant kind of national pride. When we travel on the European continent, we express surprise that other people do not talk our
language, and even annoyance that they expect us to learn theirs.
We also have an obnoxious habit of dismissing foreigners with

contemptuous epithets. It is enough to call somebody a 'wog', 'hun', 'dago', 'frog', 'chink' or 'yank'; this puts him or her beyond the pale of our respect. It should go without saying, however, that Christians should have repented of such conceited attitudes. The main point of the Parable of the Good Samaritan is its racial twist. It is not just that neighbour-love ignores racial and national barriers, but that in Jesus' story a Samaritan did for a Jew what no Jew would ever have dreamed of doing for a Samaritan.

'Patriotism' is good and right. It is a legitimate love for the father-land to which in God's providence we belong. But Sir Alfred Duff Cooper was grievously wrong when he remarked (I think in the early fifties) that 'the love of one's country should be like all true love – blind, prejudiced and passionate'. I hope he had his tongue in his cheek, for what he was describing was not 'patriotism' but 'national-ism', namely a blinkered and exaggerated loyalty to 'my country right or wrong'. It is nationalism, not patriotism, which leads to the framing of trade policies which benefit us at the expense of develop-ing nations. Nationalism is incompatible with the perspective of the Bible and the mind of Christ. We Christians should seek to become more committed internationalists, by reading about other countries, visiting them if possible, welcoming overseas visitors into our homes, learning a second language, and making friends with people of other cultures. These things will enrich our own lives. They will also symbolize our resolve to affirm the biblical principle of unity (one planet, one people), to develop a global perspective, and to recognize everybody's unavoidable interdependence.

Is this a starry-eyed concept? Perhaps Christians can by God's grace become internationalists, since the biblical vision of human unity is very clear. But can we expect this of people who do not pro-fess faith in Jesus Christ? Are not elected governments obliged to consider the national interest first? Otherwise they will not be re-elected. In his useful introduction to the problems of international aid and trade, *Trade, Justice and the Wealth of Nations*, Duncan Munro points out that the expression 'the family of nations', though helpful, is misleading, since 'there is harmony of interests in family life, which nations cannot share ... The family, with its close knit bond between members ... is capable of considerable self-sacrifice ... The nation, however, is incapable of love.' International relationships have to be based on justice instead. 'But,' he continues, 'the moral philosophers are right in saying that there is no logical necessity for men to choose to act justly on the basis of nature alone.' Only the Christian gospel can supply the necessary motivation.[44]

Duncan Monro is justified in drawing our attention to the differ- ences between the nuclear (or extended) family and the family of nations. Yet we must not acquiesce too readily in the distinction. People do recognize that they belong to the worldwide human family. And there is in all human beings, even since the Fall, a basic sense of compassion and justice, which can influence their individual and collective behaviour. There is certainly a very widespread concern in the West to help the developing nations and to eradicate poverty. Let me quote Barbara Ward again, this time from her book *Progress for a Small Planet*. She saw the contemporary world as living in an 'unsteady interregnum between imperial ages which may be dying and a planetary society which struggles to be born'. The 'chief new insight of our century', she claimed, is the 'inescapable physical interdependence' of all human beings.[45] Can this lead to a real co-operation for survival? She commends the theory of 'a global compact based upon the application to the planetary community of certain of the basic principles which govern and harmonize domestic society',[46] namely the redistribution of wealth by taxation not charity. Could we not apply this domestic model to the planet? Barbara Ward asks. The first step would be a commitment of the rich nations to giving 0.7 per cent of their GNP to the Third World, rising to 1 per cent, together perhaps with indirect taxation on international travel. Yet only the Netherlands succeeds in attaining this goal, with 'Official Development Assistance' (ODA) regularly over 1 per cent. Other developed countries are lagging behind, and some have actually reduced their ODA in the last decade. Thus Britain's ODA decreased from 0.34 per cent in 1984 to 0.31 per cent in 1994. The United States' ODA dropped in the 1970s from 0.31 per cent to the low figure (excluding military assistance) of 0.20 per cent in 1989, and further dropped to 0.15 per cent in 1994.[47] We are ready to pay taxes in our own country, Barbara Ward argues, because we are *one nation*, so should we not be willing to pay an international tax because we are *one world*?

The principle of equality

I move now from the first biblical principle (unity) to the second (equality). Consider the following teaching of the apostle Paul in 2 Corinthians 8:8–15:

⁸I am not commanding you, but I want to test the sincerity of your love by comparing it with the earnestness of others. ⁹For you know the grace of our Lord Jesus Christ, that though he was rich, yet for your sakes he became poor, so that you through his poverty might become rich.

¹⁰And here is my advice about what is best for you in this matter: last year you were the first not only to give but also to have the desire to do so. ¹¹Now finish your work, so that your eager willingness to do it may be matched by your completion of it, according to your means. ¹²For if the willingness is there, the gift is acceptable according to what one has, not according to what he does not have.

¹³Our desire is not that others might be relieved while you are hard pressed, but *that there might be equality.* ¹⁴At the present time your plenty will supply what they need, so that in turn their plenty will supply what you need. Then *there will be equality,* ¹⁵as it is written: 'He that gathered much did not have too much, and he that gathered little did not have too little'.

The two references to the goal of equality have been italicized in the text, so that we do not overlook them. Yet we need to see them in the whole context of Paul's instruction about the collection for the poor Judaean Christians which he is organizing in the Greek churches. He begins by assuring them that his teaching is not a command but a test; he is seeking evidence of the genuineness of their love (verse 8). So their giving is to be voluntary. Not in the sense that it is optional (because they are under obligation to share with their more needy Christian brothers and sisters), but in the sense that it is spontaneous and free (an expression of their love for the poor, rather than mere obedience to the apostle).

That leads Paul straight to Christ, and to a sublime statement of his spontaneous grace (verse 9). He grounds his mundane appeal for the disadvantaged on the theology of the Incarnation, and the gracious renunciation which it entailed. He makes two references to wealth, and two to poverty. Christ had been rich, but he became poor; not as a meaningless gesture of asceticism, but 'for your sakes', namely that through his poverty you might become rich. That is to say, because of *our* poverty he renounced his riches, so that through *his* poverty we might share them. It was a renunciation with a view to a certain equalization. Moreover, both his concern to end our poverty and his decision to renounce his riches were expressions of his 'grace' (verse 9), as similar action on our part will be of our 'love' (verse 8). For grace is free, undeserved love.

To his exhortation that they should prove their love Paul adds some practical advice as to how to do so. They should now complete what a year previously they desired and began to do. For desiring and doing must go together, according to their means (verses 10–12). Christian giving is proportionate giving, and is acceptable according to what one has, provided that the willingness is there. Paul is not wanting them to relieve the needs of others by putting themselves in want, for that would be merely to reverse the situation, solving one problem by creating another. No, his desire is rather 'that there might be equality' (verse 13). He puts the affluence of some alongside the want of others, and then calls for an adjustment, that is, an easing of want by affluence (verse 14). Twice he says that this is with a view to *isotēs*, which normally means 'equality', but can also mean 'fairness' or 'justice'. Finally (verse 15), he appeals to an Old Testament quotation about manna. God provided enough for everybody. Larger families gathered a lot, but not too much, for they had nothing over; smaller families gathered only a little, but not too little, for they had no lack. Each family had enough, because they collected according to need, not greed.

Let me try to sum up these instructions, in the reverse order, applying them to the world situation today. (1) God has provided enough for everybody's need (adequate resources in sun and rain, earth, air and water); (2) any great disparity between affluence and want, wealth and poverty, is unacceptable to him; (3) when a situation of serious disparity arises, it ought to be corrected by an adjustment, in order to secure 'equality' or 'justice'; (4) the Christian motive for desiring such 'justice' is 'grace', loving generosity, as in the case of Jesus Christ who, though rich, became poor, so that through his poverty we might become rich; (5) we are to follow his example in this, and so prove the genuineness of our love. Just *how* a worldwide equalization could or should be effected is another question. Economists differ. A massive transfer of aid is not necessarily the long-term solution. Whatever the method, however, the motivation for seeking equality or fairness is love.

It may be objected by some that Paul's instructions related to an equalization within the household of God, Gentile Christians from Greece coming to the aid of Jewish Christians in Judea, and that we have no liberty to extend its application from the Church to the world. But I cannot accept this limitation. The 'poor' for whose sake the rich Christ impoverished himself were unbelieving sinners like us. Besides, the principle that grave disparity should be evened out sounds like a universal truth. And when Paul wrote 'as we have opportunity, let us do good to all people, especially to those who belong to the family of believers' (Galatians 6:10), the purpose of his 'especially' was not to exclude unbelievers, but to remind us that our first responsibility is to our Christian brothers and sisters.

I need now to interpret Paul's teaching with an important qualification: the 'equality' he sets before us as a goal is relative rather than absolute. He is not recommending a total 'egalitarianism', by which all people become precisely the same, receiving an identical income, living in an identical home with identical furniture, wearing identical clothes and developing an identical lifestyle. For the living God is not the Lord of drab uniformity but of colourful diversity. True, he made us equal in dignity and worth (for we all share his life and bear his likeness). True also, he gives the blessings of sunshine and rain to all humankind indiscriminately (Matthew 5:45). But he has not made us equal in ability. On the contrary, by creation we differ from one another – intellectually (we have different IQs), psychologically (our temperaments vary) and physically (some are handsome, others plain, some are strong, others weak). And the new creation extends this disparity. For although we are 'all one in Jesus Christ' (Galatians 3:28), equally God's children, justified by his grace through faith, and although we have all received the same Holy Spirit to indwell us, yet Christ by his Spirit bestows on us different spiritual gifts, whose value differs according to the degree to which they build up the Church.[48]

Personal and economic deductions

How then can we put together what we find in the Bible – this unity and diversity, this equality and inequality? Two answers may be given. First, there is the question of *our personal economic lifestyle*. Is there any criterion by which to decide at what level we should choose to live and how much difference we should permit between ourselves and others in our neighbourhood? It is a question which all missionaries have to face, especially when they go from an affluent situation to a developing country. The Willowbank Report was helpful on this topic: 'We do not believe that we should "go native", principally because a foreigner's attempt to do this may not be seen as authentic but as play-acting. But neither do we think there should be a conspicuous disparity between our lifestyle and that of the people around us. In between these extremes, we see the possibility of developing a standard of living which expresses the kind of love which cares and shares, and which finds it natural to exchange hospitality with others on a basis of reciprocity, without embarrassment.'[49] This strikes me as a very practical rule of thumb. The moment I am embarrassed either to visit other people in their home or to invite them into mine, because of the disparity between our lifestyles, something is wrong. The inequality has broken the fellowship. There needs to be an equalization in one or other direction, or both. President Nyerere applied this challenge to the building of a Tanzanian state in which 'no man is ashamed of his poverty in the light of another's affluence, and no man has to be ashamed of his affluence in the light of another's poverty'.[50]

Secondly, this principle can help us in our thinking about *North-South economic inequality*. Since we all have equal worth (despite our unequal capacity), it must be right to secure equal opportunity for each person to develop his or her God-given potential for the common good. We cannot abolish all inequalities, nor even (because of the diversity of creation) attempt to. It is inequality of privilege we should seek to abolish, in order to create equality of opportunity. For millions of people are unable to develop their human potential. This Christians see to be the real scandal. It is not only an offence to human beings, since they are frustrated and unfulfilled, but also to their Creator who bestowed his gifts on them to be developed and used in service, not to be wasted. Let me comment briefly on equality of opportunity in education, responsibility and trade.

Education must surely come first. Nearly 23 per cent of the world's adult population cannot read. In Africa only 67 per cent of primary-school-aged children are enrolled in school, and the average drop-out rate for students enrolled in primary school in Africa and Asia is 54 per cent.[51] We should therefore support every programme which seeks equality of educational opportunity. Universal education is probably the shortest route to social justice, for it develops people's social awareness, and thus gives them the understanding and the courage to take hold of their own destiny. This is the process of 'conscientization', an ugly word popularized by Paolo Freire of Brazil.

Secondly, the developing nations should be given equality in international responsibility. The International Monetary Fund, the

World Bank and the General Agreement on Trade and Tariffs were all set up as a result of the Bretton Woods conference in 1944, more than 20 years before the first meeting of UNCTAD at which for the first time representatives of Third World countries had a forum of their own. It would seem to be elementary justice (and the Brandt Report argues for it) that developing countries should be given a greater say in these international institutions which control so much of their economic life. Those affected by decisions made should have a share in the decision-making.

Thirdly, I come to the controversial area of international trade. Many are nowadays calling for 'trade not aid'. They are understandably disillusioned that much aid has either financed the wrong things (e.g. prestigious buildings instead of genuine development which creates jobs, increases exports and helps the poor) or been squandered by incompetence or corruption. And they are further frustrated because it is usually thought unacceptable to lay down conditions for the giving of aid. Yet Brandt I and II continue to call for a massive transfer of resources, and it seems to me the duty of givers or lenders (not least because, in the case of a government or bank, it is not their money which is being transferred) to ensure that it is used for the development purposes for which it is given.

Brandt also pleads for less protectionism and more favourable trade terms. Indeed, in principle it is widely acknowledged that justice demands this. It is also recognized, however, that genuine equality in trade is hard to achieve, since the developing nations come to the negotiating table and the market place as unequal partners, with unequal bargaining powers. This is partly because (before industrialization) the products they have to offer are limited by their geography, and partly because they lack the resources (the capital, technology and skill) to be able to diversify their exports. Probably two-thirds of the world come to the international markets disadvantaged in these and other ways.

It is perhaps equality of opportunity in these three areas (education, responsible decision-making and trade) which would ensure, more than anything else, a fairer distribution of the world's wealth.

The present situation of North-South inequality ('a gap so wide that at the extremes people seem to live in different worlds'[52]) is not God's fault (for he has provided ample resources in earth and sea), nor is it the fault of the poor (since they were mostly born into it, though some government leaders are to blame for corruption and for incompetence), nor is it necessarily our fault (although our colonial forefathers may have had a share in creating it). We become personally culpable only if we acquiesce in its continuance. In Jesus' story of the Rich Man and Lazarus there is no hint that the rich man was responsible for the poor man's plight. The rich man was guilty, however, because he ignored the beggar at his gate, did nothing about his destitution, failed to use his affluence to relieve the poor man's need, and acquiesced in a situation of gross economic inequality which had dehumanized Lazarus and which he could have remedied. The pariah dogs who licked the poor man's wounds showed more compassion towards him than the rich man. The rich man went to hell not because he had exploited Lazarus, but because of his scandalous indifference and apathy (Luke 16:19–21).

Our temptation is to use the complexity of macro-economics as an excuse to do nothing. We need to pray that God will call more of his people to develop new international economic policies, work for political solutions, and give their lives in the field of Third World development, practical philanthropy, and evangelism. But these are the callings of only some.

All of us, however, can feel what Jesus felt – the pangs of the hungry, the alienation of the poor, the indignities of the 'wretched of the earth'. Ultimately, the inequalities between North and South are neither political nor economic but moral problems. Until we feel moral indignation over worldwide social injustice, and compassion for worldwide human suffering, we are not likely to act. What action can we take? We can begin by informing ourselves. As Lazarus lay at the rich man's gate, so the Third World lies at ours. The rich man could not plead ignorance; nor can we. We should ensure that our daily paper has adequate Third World coverage, and perhaps subscribe to a magazine devoted to Third World needs and/or join the World Development Movement. We could make friends with somebody from a developing country and perhaps offer for short-term service in a Third World situation. Self-education of this kind may lead to political agitation. It will also undoubtedly affect our pocket. Those who read this book will all be comparatively rich; they could not afford to buy it otherwise. We should be thankful for the good things God has given us, but also remember the biblical principles of unity and equality. Then we shall give generously to both world development and world evangelization. Our personal commitment to a simpler lifestyle will not of course solve the world's economic problems. But it will be an important symbol of Christian obedience, of solidarity with the poor, and of our share in the grace of Jesus Christ which induced him to empty himself and take the form of a servant.

Chapter 8

HUMAN RIGHTS

'**W**hoever wishes to live a quiet life,' Leon Trotsky is said to have remarked, 'should not have been born in the twentieth century.' In this at least he was right.

Human rights violations

This century has been characterized both by violence and by violations of human rights.[1] In the two world wars approximately 60 million people were killed. Six million Jews were exterminated in the 'Holocaust' of Hitler's concentration camps and gas chambers. Millions of dissidents were also liquidated by Stalin in his Siberian labour camps. According to Solzhenitsyn 65 million Russians were killed by their own leaders after 1923. Idi Amin's reign of terror from 1971 to 1979 cost the lives of between half and three-quarters of a million Ugandans, and under President Milton Obote at least 200,000 of his tribal enemies were murdered in the Loweru Triangle. The ruthless killings by the Khmer Rouge between 1975 and 1979 under their leader Pol Pot, carried out under the sick illusion of 'purifying' and 'transforming' Cambodian society, constituted nothing less than genocide; for 3 million Cambodians died by execution, disease or starvation, which was almost half the country's population. In the 1970s Latin America was home to widespread political and ideological oppression with thousands of 'disappearances', killings and arrests in Argentina, Uruguay, Chile, and in the 1980s Peru. These countries were not alone.

In Ethiopia between 1983 and 1985 more than a million died, while approximately 3 million people were displaced. After years of segregation and repression under the racist apartheid regime South Africa held its first non-racial national elections in April of 1994. This was a triumphant moment for human rights supporters around the world, but only after many years of abuses. During the years 1963 to 1988 thousands died in political violence, many while in detention or police custody, mostly in mysterious circumstances, of whom the best known was Steve Biko, the leader of the 'Black Consciousness' movement, who died in 1977. Only recently have his killers confessed to the Truth and Justice Commission the blatant injustices surrounding his (and others') detention and death.

In 1989 we witnessed the unbelievably brutal suppression of the spontaneous democracy movement in China, in which the People's Liberation Army massacred their own unarmed compatriots. Many participants in this movement remain imprisoned or detained to this day.

But in 1989 there was also a glimmer of hope. With the fall of the Iron Curtain many in the West thought we were witnessing the dawn of an era of relative freedom and security for people around the world, as democratic forms of government began to take root in formerly oppressive situations. And this indeed was the case in many Latin American countries, whose records of human rights abuses have steadily improved in the years since. Little did we know that in spite of some improvements, the world was about to embark on a decade of widespread human rights abuses, massive continued exploitation of women and children, the re-emergence of blatant genocide, and a growing persecution of Christians.

In Central Africa we have seen ethnic and tribal disputes erupt into what has been described as the 'systematic planned and condoned' killing of half a million Tutsis in Rwanda in 1994 alone.[2] Moreover, a majority of the Rwandan killings were carried out with clubs or machetes against unarmed citizens, many of whom had gathered together in churches for protection.[3] The story is much the same in the Balkans where 'ethnic cleansing' (a horrible expression) led to severe repression, death and 'disappearance'. Two top Bosnian Serb leaders, Radovan Karadzic and Ratko Mladic, are accused of having personally seen to the executions of 8,000 Moslems in Serbian territory. It will be some years before we can know the exact number of civilian deaths in this conflict.

Women and children, victims of longstanding abuse, have emerged as a priority concern in the human rights community during recent years. It is estimated that over a million children are forced into prostitution each year. Two hundred million children are regular labourers in Asia alone.[4] Child slavery is not uncommon in India and Sudan.[5] Street children are regularly killed and abused by police in Colombia, Brazil, Bulgaria, India, Guatemala, Kenya and Turkey.[6] Female genital mutilation is still widespread in various parts of Africa.[7]

Christians too have been increasingly oppressed in certain parts of the world, and are killed each year by governments or mobs because of their faith. They are especially persecuted in Egypt, Sudan, Iran, Indonesia and China, where kidnapping into slavery, torture and church burning are reported to have taken place.

In such a list of atrocities we run the risk of selective indignation, as if the human rights violations are being perpetrated only by militant ethnic groups, corrupt police and evil dictators. We British need, therefore, to remember with shame that in 1978 the European Court of Human Rights in Strasbourg ruled that the interrogation methods used briefly in 1971 on 14 IRA terrorist suspects by the Royal Ulster Constabulary violated Article 3 of the European Convention on Human Rights. Although the Court cleared Britain of Irish government charges that these techniques amounted to 'torture', it nevertheless described them as 'inhuman and degrading treatment'. The British government accepted the Court's ruling, set up a review committee, and implemented the committee's recommendations.

There are many other ways in which human beings are being oppressed. The United Nations Commission on Human Rights receives about 20,000 complaints every year. There has been, and in some cases still is, the unjust treatment of minorities, for example, of Asians in East Africa, Indians in Brazil, Aborigines in Australia, untouchables in India, Kurds in Turkey, Iran and Iraq, Jews in the former Soviet Republics, Palestinians in Israel, Native Americans in Canada and the United States, Inuit (Eskimos) in Canada, and, perhaps one should add, Roman Catholics in Northern Ireland. There is the plight of refugees, hostages and the victims of terrorists, and the human degradation caused by illiteracy, racism, poverty, hunger and disease. Worse than all these, however, is the continuing use of torture, in spite of its universal condemnation. Dr Emilio Castro has written correctly: 'Torture kills the human in the torturer, and crushes the personality of the one tortured.'[8]

Concern for human rights

Alongside the violation of human rights, even while abuses and outrages have increased, there seems to have been a corresponding growth in the recognition of rights and in concern for their safe-guarding. In a sense this is not new. Being self-conscious creatures, human beings have doubtless thought about themselves and their identity, their duties and their rights, from the beginning. So the concept has had a very long history. Plato and Aristotle wrestled with the notions of freedom and justice, while Thomas Aquinas and other medieval theologians Christianized the thought of the Greeks in terms of 'natural rights'. Britain looks back gratefully to Magna Carta, which King John was induced to sign in 1215, and which King Henry III reissued 10 years later. Among its provisions were the guarantees of freedom for the Church and of fair trial by one's peers. Another milestone in British history was the Bill of Rights (1688–9), which made the crown subject to parliament.

America and France look back to their revolutions towards the end of the eighteenth century as the time when constitutional rights were secured for their citizens. The American Declaration of Independence (1776), drafted by Thomas Jefferson, affirmed as 'self-evident' that 'all men are created equal' and that they 'are endowed by their Creator with certain inalienable rights', especially the rights to 'life, liberty and the pursuit of happiness'. Similar language was used in France's Declaration of the Rights of Man and of Citizens, which was promulgated by its National Assembly in 1789. It speaks of man's 'natural, imprescriptible and unalienable rights' or 'the natural, inalienable and sacred rights of man'. This Declaration was eloquently defended by Thomas Paine in his celebrated book *The Rights of Man* (1791). I shall quote from it presently.

Yet it was World War II, with the horrors of Hitler's savagery and of Japan's brutality, which brought human rights to the top of the world's agenda. In June 1941 President Roosevelt made his famous 'State of the Union' speech, in which he looked forward to the emer-gence of 'a world founded upon four essential freedoms' – freedom of speech and expression, the freedom of every person to worship God in his own way, freedom from want, and freedom from fear – after each of which he added the words 'everywhere in the world'.[9]

The United Nations organization was established in 1945. The preamble to its charter reads: 'We, the people of the United

Nations,' are determined 'to reaffirm faith in fundamental human rights, in the dignity and worth of the human person, the equal rights of men and women and of nations large and small ...' Article 1 speaks of international co-operation 'in promoting and encouraging respect for human rights and for fundamental freedoms for all without distinction as to race, sex, language or religion'. Article 55 goes further and says that the United Nations *shall* promote 'universal respect for, and observance of, human rights and fundamental freedoms for all without distinction as to race, sex, language or religion'.

The following year the United Nations established the Human Rights Commission, under the chairmanship of President Roosevelt's widow, Eleanor, charged with the task of preparing a Universal Declaration of Human Rights as the first element in the international Bill of Rights which it had been commissioned to produce. Its preamble affirms that 'recognition of the inherent dignity, of the equal and inalienable rights, of all members of the human family, is the foundation of freedom, justice and peace in the world.' Article 1 declares that 'all human beings are born free and equal in dignity and rights'. Article 2 adds that 'everyone is entitled to all the rights and freedoms set forth in the Declaration, without distinction of any kind, such as race, colour, sex, language, religion, political or other opinion, national or social origin, property, birth or other status'. The first part of the Declaration covers political and civil rights, and the second part economic, social and cultural rights. It was adopted by the UN General Assembly in Paris on 10 December 1948, though not all nations ratified it.

Writing of the late 1940s, while the draft Declaration was being prepared, the late Dr Charles H. Malik, who belonged to the Christian community of Lebanon, and was later to become President of the UN General Assembly, wrote:

We believed that nothing was more needful in a world that had just emerged from a most devastating war – devastating not only physically, economically, politically, but above all morally, spiritually, humanly – than to recapture and reaffirm the full integrity of man. We loved man and thought him to be wonderful, and we wanted him to be fully himself, enjoying his inherent dignity and freedom, and yet as we looked around, we found only caricatures of humanity – men deprived of their material needs, oppressed by the ideas with which they interpreted themselves and the world, distorted by the arbitrary laws of their governments, warped by the customs and convictions of their societies, diminished and disfigured in their human stature ... Therefore we set about inquiring how much ... we could define and protect what belonged to the essence of man. I never worked harder, I never had a surer sense of self-confidence, I never pulsated with a deeper existential joy, than in those memorable days.[10]

The adoption of the Universal Declaration was only the beginning. The European Convention for the Protection of Human Rights (1950) was followed by the creation of the European Commission on Human Rights (1953) and of the European Court of Human Rights (1958). In 1961 Amnesty International was founded. In 1966 the two International Covenants (one on economic, social and cultural rights, and the other on civil and political rights) were published. 1968 was the International Year for Human Rights. And in 1973 the Helsinki Conference on Security and Co-operation in Europe was held, whose final Act (1975) included a section on 'The Respect of Human Rights and Fundamental Freedoms'. The following year (1976) the two International Covenants came into effect, and so the long dreamed-of International Bill of Human Rights became a reality.

And yet, in spite of half a century of developing standards for human rights, their promotion and protection have been fading as issues of public concern in the West. Although governmental and non-governmental human rights organizations continue to work tirelessly for the oppressed worldwide, the general public seems to be losing interest in the plight of others. The Chicago Council on Foreign Relations and the Gallup Organization, in a recent poll of Americans, show that support for the promotion of human rights around the world has declined 25 per cent between 1990 and 1997.

This, then, is the paradoxical situation (a Universal Declaration of Human Rights, a widespread violation of them, and a growing public apathy) in which Christians need to ask some basic questions. How is it that human beings have any rights? Whence did they acquire them? Have Christians anything distinctive to contribute to continuing debate and action about human rights? It may be good to begin our answers with Thomas Paine. For, although he was a deist and therefore far from being an orthodox Christian, his father was a Quaker and his mother an Anglican, so that he was still

Christian enough in his outlook to know that the rights of man go back to the creation of man. He wrote in 1791:

> The error of those who reason by precedents drawn from antiquity, respecting the rights of man, is that they do not go far enough into antiquity. They do not go the whole way. They stop in some of the intermediate stages of an hundred or a thousand years ... But if we proceed on, we shall at last come out right; we shall come to the time when man came from the hand of his Maker. What was he then? Man. Man was his high and only title, and a higher cannot be given him.[11]

Thomas Paine was correct. The origin of human rights is creation. Human beings have never 'acquired' them. Nor has any government or other authority conferred them. We have had them from the beginning. We received them with our life from the hand of our Maker. They are inherent in our creation. They have been bestowed on us by our Creator.

This is an important principle to understand as the relativistic, secular worldview of our postmodern era threatens to leave the traditional human rights community with little ground to stand on in absolute support of human rights. Gary Haugen, former director of the United Nations' genocide investigation in Rwanda, and current president of the International Justice Mission, sums up the problem:

> The truth is, the secular human rights movement is philosophically committed to cultural relativism, and it is simply a matter of time before repression finds comfort in the moral vacuum. Since World War II, the traditional human rights community has taken a courageous stand for justice out of a passionate moral intuition that is rooted, consciously or not, in the Judaeo-Christian commitment to ethical absolutes. The human rights activists of the nineties, however, are the children of a secular philosophy of moral relativism, multi-culturalism, and radical pluralism. Consequently, when push comes to shove in the new disorderly world of the next century, the international human rights movement may find it increasingly difficult to navigate its way without a moral compass, to avoid moral confusion, or to avoid being captured by the political fashion of the day.[12]

Christians are called to provide that moral compass. The nature of human rights depends on the nature of the human beings whose rights they are. Fundamental, therefore, to human rights is the question of what it means to be human. Since the Bible focuses on the divine purpose for human beings, it has much to say on this topic. Three words seem to summarize it – 'dignity', 'equality' and 'responsibility'.

Human dignity

The dignity of human beings is asserted in three successive sentences in Genesis 1:27–8, which we have already examined in relation to the environment. First, 'God created man in his own image.' Secondly, 'Male and female he created them.' Thirdly, 'God blessed them and said to them, "... fill the earth and subdue it."' Human dignity is here seen to consist of three unique relationships which God established for us by creation, which together constitute a large part of our humanness, and which the Fall distorted but did not destroy.

The first is *our relationship to God*. Human beings are God-like beings, created by his will in his image. The divine image includes those rational, moral and spiritual qualities which separate us from the animals and relate us to God. In consequence, we can learn about him from evangelists or teachers (it is a basic human right to hear the gospel); come to know, love and serve him; live in conscious, humble dependence upon him; understand his will and obey his commands. So then, all those human rights we call the freedom to profess, practise and propagate religion, the freedom of worship, of conscience, of thought and of speech, come under this first rubric of our relationship to God. It is striking that even the deistic leaders of the American and French Revolutions knew this instinctively and referred to the 'Supreme Being' from whom human rights are ultimately derived.

The second unique capacity of human beings concerns *our relationship to one another*. The God who made humankind is himself a social being, one God comprising three eternally distinct modes of personhood. He said: 'Let *us* make man in *our* image,' and, 'It is not good for the man to be alone.' So God made man male and female, and told them to procreate. Sexuality is his creation, marriage is his institution, and human companionship his purpose. So then, all those human freedoms which we call the sanctity of sex, marriage and family, the right of peaceful assembly, and the right to receive respect, whatever our age, sex, race or rank, come under this second rubric of our relationship to each other.

Our third distinctive quality as human beings is *our relationship to the earth* and its creatures. God has given us dominion, with instructions to subdue and cultivate the fruitful earth, and rule its creatures. So then, all those human rights we call the right to work and the right to rest, the right to share in the earth's resources, the right to food, clothing and shelter, the right to life and health and to their preservation, together with freedom from poverty, hunger and disease, come under this third rubric of our relationship to the earth.

In spite of the over-simplification, we may sum up what is meant by human dignity in these three ways: our relationship to God (or the right and responsibility of worship), our relationship to each other (or the right and responsibility of fellowship), and our relationship to the earth (or the right and responsibility of stewardship) – together of course with the opportunity which our education, income and health provide to *develop* this unique human potential.

Thus all human rights are at base the right to be human, and so to enjoy the dignity of having been created in God's image and of possessing in consequence unique relationships to God himself, to our fellow human beings and to the material world. Christians have something important to add to this, namely that our Creator has also redeemed or recreated us, at great personal cost, through the incarnation and atonement of his Son. And the costliness of God's redeeming work reinforces the sense of human worth which his creation has already given us. William Temple expressed this truth with his customary clarity:

> There can be no Rights of Man except on the basis of faith in God. But if God is real, and all men are his sons, that is the true worth of every one of them. My worth is what I am worth to God; and that is a marvellous great deal, for Christ died for me. Thus, incidentally, what gives to each of us his highest worth gives the same worth to everyone; in all that matters most we are all equal.[13]

Our value depends then on God's view of us and relationship to us. As a result of this, human rights are not unlimited rights, as if we were free to be and do absolutely anything we like. They are limited to what is compatible with being the human person God made us and meant us to be. True freedom is found in being our true selves as authentic human beings, not in contradicting ourselves. That is why it has been essential to define 'human being' before defining 'human rights'. This principle will also help to guide us when we come in Chapters 13 and 16 to the demands for 'feminine rights' and 'gay rights'. The question these demands pose is how far feminism and homosexual practices are compatible with the humanness God has created and intends to safeguard.

There is no situation in which it is permissible to forget the dignity of human beings by creation, and their consequent right to respect. Convicted criminals may justly be deprived of their freedom during a period of imprisonment. But the right to incarcerate does not imply the right to inflict solitary confinement on prisoners, or to treat them inhumanly in other ways. I am thankful for the work of Prison Fellowship International, founded by Charles Colson after his personal experience of the brutalizing effects of incarceration. Prison Fellowship now has more than 100,000 volunteers working in over 75 countries with inmates who have been deprived of liberty by a court, but may not be deprived of other rights. 'I was in prison,' Jesus said, 'and you visited me.'

Human equality

The tragedy is that 'human rights' have not always meant 'equal rights'. The good gifts of the Creator are spoiled by human selfishness. The rights God gave to all human beings equally, easily degenerate into *my* rights on which I insist, irrespective of the rights of others or of the common good. So the history of the world has been the story of conflict between my rights and yours, between the good of each and the good of all, between the individual and the community. Indeed, it is when human rights are in conflict with one another that we are presented with a difficult ethical dilemma. It may be the tension between the rights of the mother and her unborn child when an abortion is being considered; or between an individual landowner's right to property and peace on the one hand, and the community's need on the other for a new motorway or airport; or between the freedom of speech and assembly which a civil rights group claims for its demonstration and the freedom which the local inhabitants claim not to have their quiet disturbed or their patience exhausted.

The conflict of rights regularly envisaged in the Bible, however, takes a rather different form. Its emphasis is that no powerful individuals may impose their will on the community, and that no community may violate the rights of an individual or minority. The weak and vulnerable were carefully protected by the Mosaic law. Far from exploiting them, God's people were to be the voice of the voiceless and the champion of the powerless, including their enemies. Paul Oestreicher has put it well:

> When the electrodes are turned on, the torture victim suffers equally when the 'security' think they are saving free enterprise from the revolution or the revolution from reaction ... My own commitment is neither to liberalism nor to Marxism, but to a curious idea put about by a carpenter turned dissident preacher in Palestine that the test of our humanity is to be found in how we treat our enemies ... A society's maturity and humanity will be measured by the degree of dignity it affords to the disaffected and the powerless.[14]

The equality of human beings is clearly expressed in the familiar Authorized Version words 'no respect of persons'. It is a misleading phrase, because of course persons must at all costs be respected. But what the original Greek expression means literally is 'no acceptance of faces'. In other words, we must show 'no partiality' (NIV) in our attitude to other people, and give no special deference to some because they are rich, famous or influential. The biblical authors insist much on this. Moses declared, for example: 'The Lord your God is God of gods and Lord of lords, the great, the mighty, the terrible God, who shows no partiality ...' Therefore Israelite judges were to show no partiality either, but rather give justice 'to the small and to the great alike' (Deuteronomy 10:17; 1:16–17; cf. 16:18, 19).

The same emphasis occurs in the New Testament. God is the impartial Judge. He does not regard external appearances or circumstances. He shows no favouritism, whatever our racial or social background may be (e.g. Acts 10:34; Romans 2:11; 1 Peter 1:17). Jesus was once described (perhaps in flattery, but still with accuracy) in these terms: 'Teacher, we know you are a man of integrity. You are not swayed by men, because you pay no attention to who they are' (Mark 12:14). That is, he neither deferred to the rich and powerful, nor despised the poor and weak, but gave equal respect to all, whatever their social status. We must do the same.

I rather think the best illustration of this principle is to be found in the Book of Job. It is Job's final appeal for justice, after his three comforters have at last stopped their unfair, unkind, untrue accusations. Job clings to his innocence, while at the same time acknowledging that God is a just judge. If he has broken God's laws (by immorality, idolatry or oppression), then indeed let God's judgement fall upon him. He continues: 'If I have denied justice to my servants, when they had a grievance against me, what will I do when God confronts me? What will I answer when called to account? Did not he who made me in the womb make them? Did not the same One form us both within our mother?' (Job 31:13–15). Job continues in a similar vein with reference to the poor and needy, widows and orphans. We have equal rights because we have the same Creator. Both the dignity and the equality of human beings are traced in Scripture to our creation.

This principle should be even more obvious in the New Testament community, since we have the same Saviour also. Paul regulates the behaviour of masters and slaves to each other by reminding both that they have the same heavenly master, and that 'there is no favouritism with him' (Ephesians 6:9; cf. Colossians 3:25). James seeks to banish class distinctions from public worship by urging that there must be no 'favouritism' between rich and poor among believers in Jesus Christ (2:1–9). Yet the same truth is self-evident among unbelievers. Our common humanity is enough to abolish favouritism and privilege, and to establish equal status and rights. All human rights violations contradict the equality we enjoy by creation. 'He who oppresses the poor shows contempt for their Maker' (Proverbs 14:31). If God shows, and if we should show, a 'bias to the poor' (as is now often claimed, and as we shall be considering in Chapter 12), and if such bias is not an infringement of the 'no favouritism' rule, it must be justified either because society as a whole is biased against them, or because they have no one else to champion them.

The fact that 'there is no favouritism with God' is the foundation of the biblical tradition of prophetic protest. The prophets were courageous in denouncing tyranny in leaders, especially in the kings of Israel and Judah. The fact that they were monarchs, and even 'the Lord's anointed', did not make them immune to criticism and rebuke. To be sure, due respect was to be shown to rulers because of their office, but any attempts on their part to convert authority into tyranny or rule into despotism were to be strenuously resisted.

David was the best known of all the kings of Israel, but that gave him no warrant to kill Uriah and steal his wife Bathsheba; God sent the prophet Nathan to rebuke him. When Ahab was king in Samaria, his wife Jezebel thought his power was absolute. 'Do you now govern Israel?' she asked contemptuously, when she found him sulking because Naboth had refused to sell him his vineyard. God sent Elijah to denounce Ahab's later murder of Naboth and seizure of his property. Jehoiakim was king of Judah in the seventh century BC, yet he had no right to build himself a luxurious palace by forced labour. 'Woe to you,' cried Jeremiah. 'Does it make you a king to have more and more cedar?' The prophet then reminded him of his father Josiah. 'He did what was right and just, so all went well with him. He defended the cause of the poor and needy, and so all went well … But your eyes and your heart are set only on dishonest gain, on shedding innocent blood and on oppression and extortion.' No one would lament him when he died, Jeremiah added; he would have the burial of a donkey, and would be dragged away and thrown outside the gates of Jerusalem.[15]

In our day dictators try to defend arbitrary arrest and detention, and even imprisonment or execution without public trial, on the ground of 'national security'. One wonders how a biblical prophet would react. Protest or denunciation within the country concerned would doubtless cost the prophet his life. But at least from outside the kind of work which Amnesty International undertakes is consistent with biblical precedent, and with the recognition that with God 'there is no favouritism'. Human rights are equal rights.

Human responsibility

Christians often cringe when the conversation turns to human rights. For it smacks of one person asserting his or her rights against another person, and so of conflict. It seems also to encourage selfishness. It overlooks the fact that human beings have duties and responsibilities as well as rights. Solzhenitsyn has called recently for this balance to be redressed. 'During these 300 years of Western Civilization, there has been a sweeping away of duties and an expansion of rights. But we have two lungs. You can't breathe with just one lung and not with the other. We must avail ourselves of rights and duties in equal measure.'[16] Let me try, then, to clarify the relationship between rights and responsibilities.

The Bible says much about defending other people's rights, but little about defending our own. On the contrary, when it addresses us, it emphasizes our responsibilities, not our rights. We are to love God and to love our neighbour. These primary requirements comprise our whole duty; for 'all the Law and the Prophets hang on these two commandments,' Jesus said (Matthew 22:40). In fact, what the Bible contains, as Dr Christopher Wright has written, is a 'Universal Declaration of Human Responsibilities' (especially in terms of loving God and neighbour), not of human rights.[17] Indeed, the Bible goes further and links them. It emphasizes that our responsibility is to secure the other person's rights. We must even forgo our own rights in order to do so.

Of this responsible renunciation of rights Jesus Christ is the supreme model. Although eternally 'in very nature God', he 'did not consider equality with God something to be grasped, but made himself nothing, taking the very nature of a servant, being made in human likeness' (Philippians 2:6–7). Throughout his life he was a victim of abuses of human rights. He became a refugee baby in Egypt, a prophet without honour in his own country, and the Messiah rejected by the religious establishment of his own people to whom he had come. He became a prisoner of conscience, refusing to compromise in order to secure his release. He was falsely accused, unjustly condemned, brutally tortured, and finally crucified. And throughout his ordeal he declined to defend or demand his rights, in order that by his self-sacrifice he might serve ours.

'Let this mind be in you, which was also in Jesus Christ,' wrote Paul. And Paul practised what he preached. He had rights as an apostle (the right to marry, the right to receive financial support). But he renounced them for the sake of the gospel, in order to become everybody's slave and so serve their rights (see e.g. 1 Corinthians 9).

The renunciation of rights, however unnatural and idealistic it may seem, is an essential characteristic of God's new society. In the world outside people assert their own rights and exercise authority. 'Not so with you,' Jesus said. On the contrary, in his community those aspiring after greatness must become servants, the leader the slave, and the first last. For love 'is not self-seeking', Paul wrote. And this fundamental stance, learned from Jesus, applies in every situation. For example, believers should not prosecute one another, especially in an unbelieving court. Christian litigation was a scandal in Corinth; it still is in India, Pakistan, Sri Lanka and other countries.

Christians should at the very least settle their own disputes. Better still, 'Why not rather be wronged? Why not rather be cheated?' Is not this the way of Christ? Another first-century application was to Christian slaves with cruel masters. What if they were unjustly beaten? They must bear it patiently, following in the footsteps of Jesus, who did not retaliate, but entrusted himself and his cause to the just Judge of all.[18] This last point, that the non-retaliation of Jesus was accompanied by a commitment of himself to God, is an important addition. To renounce rights is not to acquiesce in wrongs. The reason we do not judge is that this is God's prerogative, not ours (Romans 12:19). Besides, Christ is coming back, and then all evil will be judged, and justice finally and publicly vindicated.

Here then is a Christian perspective on human rights. First, we affirm human dignity. Because human beings are created in God's image to know him, serve one another and be stewards of the earth, therefore they must be respected. Secondly, we affirm human equality. Because human beings have all been made in the same image by the same Creator, therefore we must not be obsequious to some and scornful to others, but behave without partiality to all. Thirdly, we affirm human responsibility. Because God has laid it upon us to love and serve our neighbours, therefore we must fight for their rights, while being ready to renounce our own in order to do so.

Two main conclusions follow. First, we have to accept that other people's rights are our responsibility. We *are* our brother's keeper, because God has put us in the same human family and so made us related to and responsible for one another. The law and the prophets, Jesus and his apostles, all lay on us a particular duty to serve the poor and defend the powerless. We cannot escape this by saying they are not our responsibility. To quote Solzhenitsyn again, 'There are no internal affairs left on this globe of ours. Mankind can be saved only if everybody takes an interest in everybody else's affairs.'[19] We need then to feel the pain of those who suffer oppression. 'Remember those in prison as if you were their fellow prisoners, and those who are maltreated as if you yourselves were suffering' (Hebrews 13:3). In order to do this, we may need to inform ourselves more thoroughly about contemporary violations of human rights.[20] Then whatever action we may believe it right to take, we need to ensure that the methods we use do not infringe the very human rights we are seeking to champion.

Secondly, we have to take more seriously Christ's intention that the Christian community should set an example to other communities. I am not thinking only of our Christian conduct at home and work, in which as husbands and wives, parents or children, employers or employees we are to be submissive to one another out of reverence for Christ (Ephesians 5:21). I am thinking particularly of the life of the local church, which is meant to be a sign of God's rule. The Church should be the one community in the world in which human dignity and equality are invariably recognized, and people's responsibility for one another is accepted; in which the rights of others are sought and never violated, while our own are often renounced; in which there is no partiality, favouritism or discrimination; in which the poor and the weak are defended, and human beings are free to be human as God made them and meant them to be.

An exciting new initiative in the United States gives an excellent example of how Christians can become involved in defending the rights of others. In November 1994 a study was commissioned to examine the need for 'a specialized Christian ministry that could help people overseas who suffer injustice and abuse in circumstances where local authorities cannot be relied upon for relief'.[21]

Eighteen months of extensive research and consultation provided overwhelming evidence that overseas Christian workers all over the world were regularly observing human rights abuses in situations where the local authorities could not be counted on to provide relief. It also showed that the existence of a faith-based ministry with the professional expertise to document human rights abuses and to intervene on behalf of victims without putting missionaries and their agencies in compromising positions was not only a welcome idea but an absolute need. It was in response to this that the International Justice Mission was founded and has begun to work with overseas ministries to support the rights of all people, Christian and non-Christian, in the face of abuse and oppression. Most recently, the IJM's attention has been drawn to cases of child sexual exploitation in Asia, land expropriations in Latin America, and detentions without charge or trial in Africa. In such cases, the IJM is seeking to bring to bear professional expertise in documenting the abuses and securing appropriate relief for the victims.

Initiatives like this indicate to the world that Christians take seriously our commitment to the needs and rights of others.

PART III

SOCIAL ISSUES

Chapter 9

WORK AND UNEMPLOYMENT

Work occupies such a significant place in most people's lives that, if we are Christians, we must know how to think Christianly about it and about the trauma of unemployment. After all, the average worker still divides his or her day into three more or less equal periods – eight hours' sleep, eight hours' work and eight hours' leisure. So our work occupies a third of our day, indeed a half of our waking hours. We also acknowledge the importance of work by our habit of defining people in relation to it. Although convention teaches us to ask '*how* do you do?', the real question which interests us is '*what* do you do?'

Now please let me say it before you think it: a clergyman is the last person in the world to write about work. For, as everybody knows, he has not done an honest day's work in his life. As the old saying goes, he is 'six days invisible and one day incomprehensible'! Some years ago I was travelling by train in South Wales when a rather drunk Communist miner entered my compartment. When he discovered that I was a pastor, he treated me to a lecture (in his sing-song Welsh accent) on work: 'It's time you became productive, man; you're a parasite on the body politic.'

So, then, with the possible exception of the clergy (and of course of the unemployed), we are all workers. In consequence, we need a philosophy of work which will determine our attitude to it.

Attitudes to work

Some people are very negative towards their job and give the impression that, if possible, work is something to be avoided. This view has been well expressed in the following doggerel:

I don't mind work
    If I've nothing else to do;
    I quite admit it's true
That now and then I shirk
Particularly boring kinds of work;
    Don't you?
But, on the whole,
    I think it's fair to say
    Provided I can do it my own way
    And that I need not start on it today –
I quite like work!

The same rather casual attitude to work was illustrated by the following message, which the head of a New York firm put on its notice board: 'Some time between starting and quitting time, without infringing on lunch periods, coffee breaks, rest periods, story-telling, ticket-selling, holiday planning, and the rehashing of yesterday's television programmes, we ask that each employee try to find some time for a work break. This may seem radical, but it might aid steady employment and assure regular pay cheques.'

Other people tolerate their job as a necessary nuisance, a way of earning a living, and a tedious consequence of the Fall. I was astonished to read this latter concept in a serious book: 'The orthodox view of work, which has been accepted by most managers and industrial psychologists, is a simple one, and fifty years of industrial psychology and more than a century of managerial practice have been founded upon it.' What is it? It 'accepts the Old Testament belief that physical labour is a curse imposed on man as a punishment for his sins, and that the sensible man labours solely in order to keep himself and his family alive or … to enable him to do the things he really likes.'[1] The author evidently knows more about industry than Scripture. His concept of work is far from 'the orthodox view' he claims it is. For according to Scripture work is a blessing not a curse, and it is the Creation not the Fall which has made us workers.

This second attitude to work, which regards it as either meaningless in itself or at best a necessary means to some quite different end (e.g. facilitating leisure pursuits), is the same in principle as the view held by some Christians that work is a useful sphere of witness. To be sure, the Christian should be a witness to Christ in every situation, but it is very inadequate to see the workplace as having no Christian significance in itself, but only as a well-stocked lake to fish in.

Yet another group of people have no particular understanding of their work. They have never stopped to think about it. They simply accept it. They are rather like H.L. Mencken, often referred to as 'the sage of Baltimore', who once said: 'I go on working for the same reason that a hen goes on laying eggs.'[2] In other words, work is part of our human nature. We are compulsive workers, as hens are compulsive layers of eggs.

Those who are trying to develop a Christian mind on work, however, look first to Creation. The Fall turned some labour into drudgery (the ground was cursed, and cultivation became possible only by toil and sweat), but work itself is a consequence of our creation in God's image. God himself is represented in Genesis 1 as a worker. Day by day, or stage by stage, his creative plan unfolded. Moreover, when he saw what he had made, he pronounced it 'good'. He enjoyed perfect job satisfaction. His final act of creation, before resting on the seventh day, was to create human beings, and in doing so to make them workers too. He gave them some of his own dominion over the earth and told them to exercise their creative gifts in subduing it. So from the beginning men and women have been privileged stewards of God, commissioned to guard and develop the environment in his name.

Then in the second account of creation, which concentrates on the human perspective, we read: 'Now the Lord God had planted a garden … The Lord God took the man and put him in the Garden of Eden to work it and take care of it' (Genesis 2:8, 15). Thus God planted the garden and God created the man. Then he put the man he had made into the garden he had planted, and told him to cultivate and protect it. As he had put the earth in general into man's charge, now in particular he committed the garden to him. Later (Genesis 4:17ff.) Adam's descendants are pictured as building cities, raising livestock, making and playing musical instruments, and forging tools of bronze and iron. It seems, in fact, to be the Middle Stone Age which is being described.

Here then is God the worker, together with man the worker, who shares God's image and dominion. And (Christians will want to add) there is Jesus the worker, demonstrating at the carpenter's bench the dignity of manual labour. In the light of these revealed truths about God, Christ and human beings, what is the Christian understanding of work?

Self-fulfilment

First, work is intended for the fulfilment of the worker. That is, an important part of our self-fulfilment as human beings is to be found, according to God's purpose, in our work. We can affirm this with confidence in view of the very first instruction which God addressed to man and woman: 'Be fruitful and increase in number; fill the earth and subdue it' (Genesis 1:28). Here are three successive commands, each leading logically to the next. They could not subdue the earth without first filling it, and they could not fill it without first reproducing themselves. This original and composite commandment expresses, then, a basic aspect of our vocation as human beings.

We have already seen, when thinking in Chapter 6 about our responsibility for the environment, that our dominion over nature is due to our likeness to God. Or, to express the same truth in different terms, our potential for creative work is an essential part of our God-likeness. Our Creator has made us creative creatures. Dorothy Sayers was right, then, in her epigram: 'Work is not primarily a thing one does to live, but the thing one lives to do.'[3] Since the Creator has given us gifts, he intends them to be used. He wants us to be fulfilled, not frustrated.

Pope John Paul II is clear and outspoken about the fundamental place of work in human life. In his encyclical on 'Human Work' entitled *Laborem Exercens* he writes: 'Work is one of the characteristics that distinguish man from the rest of creatures, whose activity for sustaining their lives cannot be called work.'[4] From the early chapters of Genesis, 'the Church is convinced that work is a fundamental dimension of man's existence on earth'.[5] For this reason, he continues, 'human work is a *key*, probably *the essential key*, to the whole social question'. If the latter is 'making life more human', as the Second Vatican Council said it was, 'then the key, namely human work, acquires fundamental and decisive importance'.[6] So then, 'work is a good thing for man', not only because through work he transforms nature to serve his needs, but because through it 'he also *achieves fulfilment* as a human being, and indeed, in a sense, becomes "more a human being"'.[7]

It would be an exaggeration, however, to affirm that work is actually 'indispensable' to our humanness, for the climax of Genesis 1 is not the creation of man, male and female, to subdue the earth, but the institution of the sabbath. We human beings are at our most human not so much when we work, as when we lay aside our work in order to worship. Thus the sabbath 'relativizes the works of mankind, the contents of the six working days. It protects mankind from total absorption by the task of subduing the earth, it anticipates the distortion which makes work the sum and purpose of human life, and it informs mankind that he will not fulfil his humanity in his relation to the work which he is transforming but only when he raises his eyes above, in the blessed, holy hour of communion with the Creator.'[8] Here lies a fundamental difference between Marxism and Christianity. In the end a human being is not *homo faber* but *homo adorans*.

Nevertheless, we must say that if we are idle (instead of active) or destructive (instead of creative), we are denying a basic aspect of our humanity, contradicting God's purpose for our lives, and so forfeiting a part of our own fulfilment. This does not mean, of course, that a child, a hospital patient or a retired person is not a human being because he or she cannot work. Yet a child wants to grow up, and a sick person to get well, in order to be able to serve. Similarly, retired people are wise to seek an active retirement, in which they have opportunities for constructive service, even if it is unpaid. I shall come later to the particularly poignant plight of the unemployed. Pessimistic as the Preacher in Ecclesiastes was regarding the meaninglessness of life lived without God, and about 'toilsome labour under the sun', he was able to be positive about our daily work: 'A man can do nothing better than to eat and drink and find satisfaction in his work.' Again, 'there is nothing better for a man than to enjoy his work' (Ecclesiastes 2:24; 3:22).

The concept of self-fulfilment through work is certainly much more difficult in some countries and regions (where the choice of job is extremely limited), and in particular kinds of work. The mining of coal (or for that matter of copper, tin, gold and diamonds) involves dirt, discomfort and danger, and everything should be done by mine owners to reduce risks and unpleasantness. Then there is the tedium of the factory assembly line. E.F. Schumacher did not exaggerate when he wrote about monotonous work: 'Mechanical, artificial, divorced from nature, utilizing only the smallest part of

190 ▶ New Issues Facing Christians Today

man's potential capacities, it sentences the great majority of workers to spending their working lives in a way which contains no worthy challenge, no stimulus to self-perfection, no chance of development, no element of Beauty, Truth or Goodness.'[9] He drives home the anomaly of this by pointing out that 'the modern world takes a lot of care that the worker's body should not accidentally or otherwise be damaged' and, if it *is* damaged, provides for his compensation. But what about 'his soul and his spirit'? 'If his work damages *him*, by reducing him to a robot – that is just too bad.'[10] He then quotes Ananda Coomaraswamy, who says that 'industry without art is brutality'. Why? Because it damages the worker's soul and spirit.[11] Schumacher's solution is in the 'small is beautiful' concept with which his name will always be associated.

Even in large factories attempts have been made to relieve monotony and increase responsibility by job-swapping or job rotation within a team. For example, in 1974 in southern Sweden, a Volvo car manufacturing plant became the first of its kind in the world to operate without a conveyor belt. Through management–union co-operation, flexible working schedules and hours were introduced along with the practice of teamwork. This has become the basis of all of Volvo's new factories and plants. At the newest one in Uddevalla this concept is at its height – teams work on stationary cars so that a sense of craftsmanship rather than tedium is nurtured. In the white collar world as well, which has been the hardest hit by the revolution of information technology, operators may be mesmerized by their computer screen, especially if they are restricted to data entry, and so feel bored and alienated. They need to increase their human contacts. Indeed, we should support every attempt to 'enrich' or 'humanize' working conditions.

Other manual jobs, although not exactly tedious, are thought by some to be 'menial' or 'demeaning'. Take refuse collection as an example. It can involve the handling of rubbish that is filthy or smelly or both. Yet it is, of course, a vital service to public health and hygiene, and as such should provide a measure of job satisfaction. I read in 1970 of Mr Dennis Sibson, a dustman (or in the American tongue 'garbage collector') from Middleton in Lancashire, who was awarded a Churchill travelling fellowship, which he used to study refuse collection and disposal on the European continent. He had previously been a clerk, a coalman, a window cleaner, a toolsetter and a decorator. But he said he found refuse work (he had

had 14 years of it) 'most satisfying to himself and most useful to the public'.[12]

The service of others and of God

Work is intended not only for the fulfilment of the worker, but also for the benefit of the community. Adam did not cultivate the Garden of Eden merely for his own enjoyment, but to feed and clothe his family. Throughout the Bible the productivity of the soil is related to the needs of society. Thus, God gave Israel a 'land flowing with milk and honey', and at the same time issued instructions that the harvest was to be shared with the poor, the alien, the widow and the orphan. Similarly in the New Testament, the converted thief is told to stop stealing and to start working with his own hands, so that he 'may have something to share with those in need' (Ephesians 4:28).

The knowledge that our work is beneficial and appreciated adds considerably to our sense of job satisfaction. I understand that Henri de Man's studies in Germany between the wars, and the Hawthorne experiments which were conducted at the same time at the Chicago plant of the Western Electric Company, were the first pieces of scientific research into this now well-accepted fact. The Hawthorne studies in particular showed 'that workers would increase their output even when the lights were dimmed to the strength of moonlight, if they thought that their labours were considered by other people to be important and significant'.[13]

Certainly the Bible regards work as a community project, undertaken by the community for the community. All work needs to be seen as being, at least to some degree, public service. This principle throws light on the discussion about the purpose(s) of business. It is acknowledged by all that a successful business must: (1) make a profit; (2) provide adequate wages, good prospects and pleasant working conditions for the workforce; (3) invest in research and development; (4) declare a dividend for shareholders; (5) pay taxes to the government; and (6) serve the public. The point of controversy concerns the order in which these six purposes should be placed. Many business people insist that profit must head the list, since otherwise the firm will sink. And everybody agrees that profit is indispensable as an index of efficiency and a condition of survival. But Christians feel uncomfortable about giving priority to profit, lest it seems that the chief end of the company is self-service (although of course there is a distinction between retained profits and distributed profits). It appears more consistent with the Christian emphasis on 'ministry' to give priority to the provision of whatever goods or services the company offers the public. We then of course have to add immediately that in order to serve the public, and so stay in business and/or expand in order to do so, the firm must not only pay its workforce and its taxes, but also make a profit, out of which it can plough something back for research and renewal of equipment, and pay a dividend. In other words, all six obligations of a business dovetail with one another. Some prefer to visualize them as the spokes of a wheel, in which priority is not given to any one purpose, rather than as the layers of a pyramid. Yet the Christian mind still wants to insist that service to the community should come first. After all, it is not only true that a firm cannot serve the public unless it makes a profit and so survives; it is also (and perhaps more) true that it cannot make a profit unless it serves the public acceptably.

More important even than the service of the community is the service of God, though the two cannot be separated. Christians believe that the third and highest function of work is that through it God should be glorified – that is, that his purpose should be revealed and fulfilled. E.F. Schumacher also gives three purposes of human work, as follows:

First, to provide necessary and useful goods and services.
Second, to enable every one of us to use and thereby perfect our gifts, like good stewards.
Third, to do so in service to, and in co-operation with others, so as to liberate ourselves from our inborn egocentricity.[14]

Now it appears that his first purpose is my second, and his second my first. It is when we come to the third that we differ. Schumacher sees life as a school, God as the schoolmaster, and work as one of the chief means by which our chronic self-centredness is reduced, if not eradicated. 'In the process of doing good work,' he writes, 'the ego of the worker disappears.'[15] I do not wish to deny the wholesome ego-diminishing influences of work. But it seems to me that an even higher vision of work is to see it as being for the glory of God. How is this?

God has deliberately arranged life in such a way that he needs the co-operation of human beings for the fulfilment of his purposes. He did not create the planet earth to be productive on its own; human beings had to subdue and develop it. He did not plant a garden whose flowers would blossom and fruit ripen on their own; he appointed a gardener to cultivate the soil. We call this the 'cultural mandate' which God gave to humankind. I like the story of the cockney gardener who was showing a clergyman the beauty of his garden, with its herbaceous borders in full and colourful bloom. Duly impressed, the clergyman broke out into spontaneous praise of God. The gardener was not very pleased, however, that God should get all the credit. 'You should 'ave seen this 'ere garden,' he said, 'when Gawd 'ad it to 'isself!'[16] He was right. His theology was entirely correct. 'Nature' is what God gives us; 'culture' is what we do with it. Without a human cultivator, every garden or field quickly degenerates into a wilderness.

Usually we emphasize the indispensability of *God's* part. We sing at Thanksgiving or Harvest:

We plough the fields and scatter
   The good seed on the land,
But it is fed and watered
   By God's almighty hand.

The opposite, however, would be equally true. We might sing instead:

God plants the lovely garden
   And gives the fertile soil,
But it is kept and nurtured
   By man's resourceful toil.

We should not be shy to declare this. It is not a proud statement; it is true. God does indeed provide soil, seed, sunshine and rain, but we have to do the ploughing, sowing and reaping. God provides the fruit trees, but we have to prune the trees and pick the fruit. As Luther once said in a lecture on Genesis 31:3, 'For God will be working all things through you, he will be milking the cows through you and will be performing the most menial duties through you, and all duties, from the greatest to the least, will be pleasing to him.'

Of what use to us would be God's provision of an udder full of milk, if we were not there to extract it?

So there is co-operation, in which indeed we depend on God, but in which (we add reverently) he also depends on us. God is the Creator; man is the cultivator. Each needs the other. In God's good purpose creation and cultivation, nature and nurture, raw materials and human craftsmanship go together.

This concept of divine–human collaboration is applicable to all honourable work. God has humbled himself and honoured us by making himself dependent on our co-operation. Take the human baby, perhaps the most helpless of all God's creatures. Children are indeed a 'gift of the Lord', although procreation is itself a form of co-operation. After the birth it is as if God drops the newborn child into the mother's arms and says, 'Now you take over.' He commits to human beings the upbringing of each child. In the early days the baby remains almost a part of the mother, so close are they to each other. And for years children depend on their parents and teachers.

Even in adult life, although we depend on God for life itself, we depend on each other for the necessities of life. These include not only the basic needs of physical life (food, clothing, shelter, warmth, safety and health care) but also everything which makes up the richness of human life (education, recreation, sport, travel, culture, music, literature and the arts), not to mention spiritual nurturing. So whatever our job – in one of the professions (teaching, medicine, the law, the social services, architecture or construction), in national or local politics or the civil service, in industry, commerce, farming or the media, in research, management, the services or the arts, or in the home – we need to see it as being co-operation with God, in serving the needs of human beings and so helping them fulfil his purpose and grow into human maturity.

In some jobs the co-operation is direct, and therefore easy to perceive. The farmer plants and sows; God gives the increase. Or take the case of medicine. The words of Ambroise Paré, the sixteenth-century French surgeon, sometimes described as 'the founder of modern surgery', are inscribed on a wall of the École de Médicine in Paris: 'I dressed the wound; God healed him.' In other kinds of work the co-operation is indirect, in which case we need insight to grasp it. When asked whether his doctoral research in solid state physics was 'useful', Robert Newport replied, 'Well, it's not directly related to anything.' But then he went on: 'I hope that later my findings will link up with those of others and the results will be applied in industry.' That is an example of what I mean.[17] And, although I have developed in a specifically Christian way this principle of looking beyond the immediate to the ultimate, it is surely applicable to very many jobs undertaken by non-Christians.

The story is told of a man (in the pre-mechanization era) who, while taking a walk down a country lane, came across a stone quarry in which a number of men were working. He questioned several of them about what they were doing. The first replied irritably, 'Can't you see? I'm hewing stone.' The second answered without looking up, 'I'm earning £100 a week.' But when the same question was put to the third man, he stopped, put his pick down, stood up, stuck out his chest and said, 'If you want to know what I'm doing, I'm building a cathedral.' So it is a matter of how far we can see. The first man could not see beyond his pick, and the second beyond his Friday pay packet. But the third man looked beyond his tools and his wages to the ultimate end he was serving. He was co-operating with the architect. However small his particular contribution, he was helping to construct a building for the worship of God.

So *laborare est orare*, 'work is worship', provided that we can see how our job contributes, in however small and indirect a way, to the forwarding of God's purpose for humankind. Then whatever we do can be done for the glory of God (1 Corinthians 10:31).

Some years ago I was given the opportunity by the Medical Officer of Health for the Port and City of London to see something of his responsibilities. We were shown round by Mr T.L. Mackie, who at that time was the Port of London's Chief Health Inspector. His enthusiasm for his work was infectious, and in a letter he sent me the following week he divulged its origin. He wrote: 'The work covers a rather comprehensive field of preventive medicine and environmental health control. To work for one's own ends, the pay packet, the "perks", security of tenure and eventual pension, is not enough for me. I like to think that I am responsible for a part of the greater human field pattern whereby we all subscribe of our best to the whole effort for human welfare according to our talents, and obey the will of our wonderful Creator. With this trend of thought and outlook, I go into action each day happily.'

So divine–human co-operation in developing the resources of creation is a clear biblical motivation for work.

But Dr Miroslav Volf, in his book *Work in the Spirit*, has challenged this view not as inaccurate but as inadequate. Careful in argument and lucid in style, he has developed a comprehensive theology of work. In essence he bids us look not so much back to the original creation as on to the new creation, whose fullness is yet to come. As there will be a fundamental continuity between our present body and our future resurrection body, so we are looking forward not to the destruction of the world, but to its transformation. It is this expectation which gives human work its significance, since 'through it human beings contribute in their modest and broken way to God's new creation'.[18]

Dr Volf also rejects Luther's teaching on our different 'vocations' in favour of Paul's teaching on our different 'charisms' (charismata, 'gifts of the Spirit'). These, he maintains, include daily mundane work, even that performed by non-Christians, for 'all human work ... is made possible by the operation of the Spirit of God in the working person'.[19] I am left with some uneasy questions, however. Although indeed the Holy Spirit is at work in the world, and although the nations will bring their 'splendour' into the New Jerusalem (Revelation 21:24, 26), does Paul's vision of the *charismata* really embrace the work of non-Christians? And can humans really co-operate with God in the eschatological transformation of the world? Is not the Kingdom of God, both in its present reality and in its future perfection, a gift of God, rather than a human achievement? Nevertheless, as we look to the future regeneration of the world, we are authorized to say that our present 'labour in the Lord is not in vain' (1 Corinthians 15:58).

In the light of the three purposes for work which we have been considering, we are ready to attempt a definition:

> Work is the expenditure of energy (manual or mental or both) in the service of others, which brings fulfilment to the worker, benefit to the community, and glory to God.

Fulfilment, service and worship (or co-operation with God's purpose) all intertwine, as indeed our duties to God, others and self nearly always do. Certainly self-fulfilment cannot be isolated from service. For job satisfaction is not primarily attained by a fair wage, decent conditions, security and a measure of participation in profits, important as these are. It arises from the job itself, and especially from that elusive thing, 'significance'. Moreover, the main component of significance in relation to our job is not even the combination of skill, effort and achievement, but the sense that through it we are contributing to the service of the community and of God himself. It is service which brings satisfaction, discovering ourselves in ministering to others. We need not only to develop this perspective on our own work, but, if we are employers or managers, to do our utmost to develop it in our workforce.

Some years ago I was shown around the Handicrafts Centre in Dacca, Bangladesh, which was operated by HEED (the Health, Education and Economic Development project). Here young people from refugee camps were being taught a skilled trade, carpet making or tapestry, weaving or straw art. What impressed me most was the degree of their concentration on what they were doing. They hardly noticed us, and did not even look up as we walked by. They were absorbed in their craft. Their work had given them dignity, significance, a sense of self-worth through service.

The trauma of unemployment

When we have grasped how central a place work occupies in God's purpose for men and women, we see at once how serious an assault on our humanness unemployment is. Referring to the unemployed in the North of England during the Depression years, William Temple wrote: 'The gravest and bitterest injury of their state is not the animal (physical) grievance of hunger or discomfort, nor even the mental grievance of vacuity and boredom; it is the spiritual grievance of being allowed no opportunity of contributing to the general life and welfare of the community.'[20] It is a shocking experience to be declared 'redundant', and still worse to have to think of oneself thus. Many people live in fear of it happening to them.

In 1963 the total number of unemployed in the United Kingdom (excluding school-leavers) was 500,000. By 1977 this had trebled to 1.5 million, and by 1982 that number doubled to 3 million (13 per cent of the workforce), although the true figure may have been higher still, owing to the non-registration of some unemployed people and the overmanning of some firms. From this shocking peak the figures fell to below 2 million in 1989 and in the 1990s have hovered roughly between 2 and 3 million people, between 6 per cent and 11 per cent of the workforce. Although unemployment in

May 1997 was at a comparatively low figure of 6.9 per cent, these numbers are still too high. In addition, certain groups are particularly hard hit, notably young people in their late teens and early twenties. The percentages are also higher than the average among ethnic (especially coloured) groups, disabled people, and unskilled workers in regions like Northern Ireland, South Wales and the big cities of Scotland and the north of England. There is also the growing problem of long-term unemployment, even inter-generational unemployment, handed down as a cruel birthright from parents to children.

On the European continent the figures vary considerably from country to country. Among European Union nations Spain retains the highest rate of unemployment at 20.9 per cent and Luxembourg the lowest at 3.7 per cent. Unemployment in the European Union remained steady at 10.8 per cent throughout the first six months of 1997. This means that over 18 million people were out of work. Youth unemployment in Europe is twice that of adults, and the number of long-term unemployed has grown to account for over 50 per cent of the currently unemployed. Elsewhere, in April 1997 unemployment was at 3.3 per cent in Japan and 4.9 per cent in the US. In some developing nations the statistics are much higher.[21]

Moreover, the future is unpredictable, and the worldwide problem may well get worse. Although the deregulation and increasing globalization of markets have many advantages, they often make a negative impact on the labour market. Companies are able to search anywhere for cheap labour, which often means lost jobs in the industrialized world, while those who in turn receive new jobs in the developing world do not gain ample benefits from them. Most of the new jobs created in the 1990s have been part-time and, although meeting real needs, often do not bring in sufficient income for a family. By the year 2000 part-time workers will make up a third of the workforce in Britain.[22] Technology continues to race ahead, with many jobs previously performed by humans being efficiently completed by computers and robots. Hand in hand with globalization, new technologies lead to a constant flux in labour markets, with demands for increased minimum skills resulting in rapid obsolescence of both workers and training. There will be no sense in trying to resist these developments, however, like the nineteenth-century Luddites who went round smashing factory machines, beginning in 1811 with the newly installed knitting machines in the hosiery factories of Nottingham. We must learn to face these issues head on.

Unemployment is not a problem of statistics, however, but of people. In the Third World, where no wage-related unemployment benefit is available, it is often a question of actual survival, but in the West the suffering is more psychological than physical. It is a poignant personal and social tragedy. Industrial psychologists have likened unemployment to bereavement, the loss of one's job being in some respects similar to the loss of a relative or friend. They describe three stages of trauma. The first is shock. A young unemployed man in our congregation spoke of his 'humiliation', and an unemployed woman of her 'disbelief', since she had been given assurances that her job was safe. A restaurateur felt 'immediately degraded' and said to himself, 'I've become a statistic, I'm unemployed.' On hearing that they have been sacked or made redundant, some people are angry, others feel rejected and demeaned. Their self-image has suffered a bitter blow, particularly if they have dependants they cannot now provide for. Unemployment brings tension and conflict to their family life. At this stage, however, they are still optimistic about the future.

The second stage is depression and pessimism. Their savings are exhausted and their prospects look increasingly bleak. So they lapse into inertia. As one man summed it up, 'I stagnate.' Then the third stage is fatalism. After remaining unemployed for several months and being repeatedly disappointed in their applications for jobs, their struggle and hope decline, their spirit becomes bitter and broken, and they are thoroughly demoralized and dehumanized. In October 1996 35 per cent of Britain's unemployed had been out of work for over a year and 20 per cent for over two years.[23]

Solutions and palliatives

How should Christians react to the problems of unemployment? The ultimate solution belongs to the realm of macro-economics. Everybody seems to be agreed that unemployment can be overcome only by more trade bringing more demand, bringing more jobs. But experts do not agree on how this growth can be secured. In Britain 'making industry more competitive' is the cry from government, employers and unions. To this end some advocate a massive reflation of the economy by government investment and job creation. Others hope to stimulate a more dynamic economy in private (though government-encouraged) investment. Others accept E.F. Schumacher's 'small is beautiful' dictum and believe we should turn from huge capital-intensive enterprises to modest labour-intensive projects. Yet others believe that new technologies will force this decentralization upon us anyway.

A significant Christian contribution to the macro-economic debate was made in 1997 by the publication of *Unemployment and the Future of Work*, 'an enquiry for the churches', which had been conducted under the auspices of the Council of Churches for Britain and Ireland (CCBI). It is outspokenly Christian in its understanding of the necessity and dignity of work, and of unemployment as 'a social evil of the greatest magnitude',[24] incompatible with both love and justice. Its authors recommend a combination of policies which over a period of years could achieve the goal of full employment. A chapter is devoted to each of the following eight proposals: (1) tax reform to create many more jobs in the private sector; (2) much more employment in the public sector, financed by higher taxation; (3) a fresh start for the long-term unemployed; (4) a national minimum wage; (5) better conditions of work and fairer pay bargaining; (6) reform of the social security benefit system, in order to reduce reliance on means-testing; (7) priority in the education system to be given to basic skills for all young people; and (8) a national employment forum, at which such policies are debated by all interested parties.[25]

We turn now from long-term to short-term remedies, or from solutions to palliatives. Successive governments have done much in their regional policies, training and retraining schemes, and job creation programmes.

Now the new Labour government has publicized its ambitious 'Welfare to Work' plan. Its 'New Deal for 18–24-year-olds' entices private-sector employers with a weekly rebate for up to six months in return for employing them, while offering them either subsidized employment equal to benefit plus a fixed amount, or full-time study, or a job with the environmental task force. New Labour's programme also offers to all 16- and 17-year-olds access to full-time or part-time education or training; to employers who hire the long-term unemployed tax rebates; and to lone parents with young children a 'proactive Employment Service'.

In addition to such government involvement, there is still room for voluntary initiatives. More than 200 Local Enterprise Trusts now exist. These have been formed by leading companies like ICI, Pilkingtons and Marks and Spencer, often with the co-operation of the local authority, to offer expert advice on facilities and finance to those wishing to establish new businesses. 'There are one and one-third million small businesses in Britain,' wrote George Goyder in 1987, 'employing some five million workers. In West Germany there are half as many again, in Japan five times, and in the USA ten times as many. We need to double the number of small businesses in Britain. We could employ another two to three million people in this way.'[26]

Various proposals are also being made not so much to increase demand for labour as to decrease supply. The principle behind them is to redistribute the same amount of work, by spreading it over more people. One arrangement being canvassed is 'job-splitting' or 'job-pairing', by which the same job is shared between two people, who work either a 'week in-week out' or a 'morning-afternoon' rhythm, giving them more freedom, although also of course less pay. Other people are urging the reduction of the weekly total of hours worked, the strict curtailment of overtime, the banning of 'black economy' jobs, the extension of annual leave, the provision of more sabbaticals, and earlier voluntary retirement.

Has the Christian Church any specific contribution to make?

The role of the Church

I have been encouraged by David Bleakley's two books *In Place of Work ... The Sufficient Society,* 'a study of technology from the point of view of people', and *Work: The Shadow and the Substance,* 'a reappraisal of life and labour.' They contain much food for thought and much stimulus to action. David Bleakley believes that in the present transition period the Church should have a key role. In the Industrial Revolution it missed its opportunity, and ever since the working masses of Britain have been alienated from it. This must not happen again. The Church could keep Britain united during the dangerous period of industrial transformation. And, since the unemployed (the chief casualties) have no union to represent them or plead their cause, the Church could be the voice of the voiceless. It is well placed to do so. 'Straddling as it does the whole spectrum of the community, it can be a unique lobby, articulating the Christian social demand and encouraging its people to discover and apply ... such demands through national and local church initiatives.'[27]

Let me spell out at least three ways in which the Church can and should be helping.[28]

First, many of us need to change our attitudes towards the unemployed, and persuade the public to do the same. Those who have been schooled in the values of the so-called 'Protestant Work Ethic' (industry, honesty, resourcefulness, thrift, etc.) tend to despise those who are losers in the struggle to survive, as if it were their fault. No doubt there are a few work-shy people who do not want a job and prefer to sponge on the community. But they must consti-tute a tiny minority. The great majority of unemployed people want to work, but cannot find a job. They are victims of the recession and of the new technology. There is need therefore for more Christian sympathy towards them and more pastoral care. We have to repent of looking down on the unemployed, and of ever imagining that the words 'workless' and 'worthless' might be synonyms. I was cha-grined to hear of a man in our church who, after being unemployed for two years, stayed away from public worship because he was scared of being asked what he was doing and, on the discovery that he was out of work, of being made to feel a failure. But at least within the Christian community no stigma should be attached to unemployment. Paul's dictum 'If a man will not work, he shall not eat' (2 Thessalonians 3:10) was addressed to voluntary not involun-tary unemployment, to the lazy not the 'redundant'. So we need to welcome and support the unemployed in the local church; other-wise our pious talk about 'the Body of Christ' becomes a sick joke.

Secondly, the Church can take its own initiatives. For several decades now an increasing number of local congregations have come to realize that the buildings they inherited from the past are both too large for their needs and unsuitable for their responsibili-ties. Many have therefore developed imaginative plants to preserve (and usually remodel) an area for worship, and convert the rest for other purposes, especially for appropriate service to the local com-munity. Then, in order to indicate its new multi-purpose character, some have dropped the traditional word 'church' and renamed their building (or complex), a 'Christian Centre'. Some such centres accommodate a children's play group or nursery school, a club for 'Mums and Toddlers', a luncheon club and chiropody service for old people, an open youth group, a coffee bar, etc. They are also beginning to be used to serve the unemployed.

CAWTU (Church in Action With The Unemployed),[29] though no longer functioning, was helpful in emphasizing three areas in which local churches can take the initiative. The first is 'Pastoral Care (coping with being out of work)'. Why not open a 'drop-in centre' or 'resource centre' on church premises, where unemployed people can find companionship, information, a library, refreshments and recreation? Secondly, 'Work Experience (a better chance to get jobs)'. Why not sponsor a local initiative which offers training to young people, or provides long-term unemployed people with temporary work which benefits the community? See the examples below for ideas. Thirdly, 'Job Creation (new jobs and permanent work)'. This might involve creating a new job at the church (in administration or maintenance), or starting a neighbourhood co-operative (for odd jobs), or launching a new business (joining with others to set it up).

Here are some examples of local Christian initiatives, which are mostly taken from a wider selection in *Unemployment and the Future of Work* (pp. 182–5).

The Peckham Evangelical Churches Action Network (PECAN) was set up in 1988 in response to long-term unemployment on the local housing estates. PECAN now supports 30 Christian staff and 18 volunteers who are involved in training over 1,000 local unemployed people every year. They take a uniquely proactive approach to recruitment, going door-to-door in the area, and so making personal visits to over 30,000 flats a year. They have an over 70 per cent success rate in getting the unemployed into jobs or further vocational training courses. PECAN's success has inspired similar initiatives such as the Hackney Employment Link Project (HELP), which also helps the unemployed back into work, and has experienced rapid growth in recent years.

Emmaus communities in Cambridge, Coventry, Greenwich, Dover, Belfast and elsewhere are designed to be self-supporting residences for the unemployed homeless. Those who come to live in an Emmaus community agree to work a 40-hour week and to sign off benefits. They are in turn given housing, training, work and weekly wages. Since 1991 Emmaus has responded to the needs of over 500 homeless people, and has a goal of establishing 25 communities in Britain by the year 2000.

New Life Electrics in London (a Quaker project) trains and employs the previously unemployed in the repair and reconditioning of household electrical items. Not only does it provide work for those who need it, but it also performs a valuable service to the community where the replacement of cookers and other appliances is not a viable alternative.

The London Churches' Employment Development Unit is an ecumenical group which gives advice to churches on how to set up and manage projects for the unemployed. Over 20 different projects were active in 1993, with nearly 1,500 people being helped.

As an outgrowth of the Jubilee Centre in Cambridge, the Relationships Foundation is fighting unemployment through local initiatives (City Life). In Teesside a programme is seeking to nurture better relationships between the long-term unemployed and the non-profit sector, between residents in affluent and poorer areas, and among local businesses. By setting up channels of communication the initiative is helping people to connect and understand one another, and is getting the unemployed back into work.

In 1996 the Evangelical Alliance and Tearfund joined forces to launch UK Action, a wide-ranging project which helps support local evangelical initiatives in understanding and fighting poverty. For example, the Toxteth Tabernacle Baptist Church, with help from UK Action, is running a skills training centre for teenagers who are truant, expelled from school or excluded. The centre is building bridges to the community by providing valuable training for the young and unemployed. UK Action serves as both a catalyst and a consultancy; it stimulates and co-ordinates church initiatives in community service and job training. It has so far funded over 25 projects, and is considering many more.

In South Wales, St John's Church, Penydarren, Merthyr Tydfil, developed a large and flourishing programme. Canon Bill Morgan (the Vicar) and his church council decided to demolish two of their buildings, sell the land, buy and modernize a factory, and convert their church's crypt into an operations centre for their project, which they were running in conjunction with the Manpower Services Commission. They formed two companies, the St John's Industry Company, which gives a two-year workshop training to unemployed older teenagers, and the St John's Community Programme Agency, which enables unemployed adults to spend a year in voluntary building, social service, conservation work and urban ministry. By 1988 their workforce had grown to 1,300 people with an annual budget of £6 million.

The third way in which the Church can help is by a determined effort to make, publicize and act on the distinction between 'work' and 'employment'. For although all employment is work (we are not paid for doing nothing), not all work is employment (we can work without being paid for it). What demoralizes people is not so much lack of employment (not being in a paid job) as lack of work (not using their energies in creative service). Conversely, what gives people a sense of self-respect is significant work. Adam was not paid for cultivating the Garden of Eden. The housewife who works at home and students who work at their books are not usually paid (though some of them are agitating to be paid!). I know that the pay packet or salary cheque is important, and that those receiving unemployment benefit tend to feel like parasites (quite falsely, since they have themselves contributed to the National Insurance Scheme). Nevertheless, work significance is more important than wage or salary in giving us a sense of self-worth. To employ people to dig holes and fill them up again brings pay without significance; to work creatively but voluntarily brings significance without pay. Of the unemployed people I have known personally, several have spent time in study, one who had a camera used the opportunity to improve his photographic techniques in the hope that later he would be able to make Christian audio-visuals, while a young woman spent many hours visiting and supporting some alcoholic friends who lived in the flat below her.

The current social revolution will not leave any of us untouched. If the average working week is reduced (which is what the Trades Union Congress are pressing for), how shall we spend our extra free time? Should the Church not be both suggesting and offering some constructive alternatives to television and video? For creative leisure, though unpaid, is a form of work. The possibilities are numerous: 'do-it-yourself' repairs, redecorations and improvements at home; servicing the car, motorbike or bicycle; self-education through evening classes, correspondence courses or Open University; cultivating the garden or allotment, growing your own vegetables, keeping pigs or chickens; working with wood or metal; dressmaking, knitting and embroidery; making music; painting, pottery and sculpting; reading and writing; and where possible doing these things together, spending more time with family and friends.

Then there is the whole sphere of community service, either through the local church or a voluntary organization or on one's own initiative: visiting the sick, the elderly or prison inmates; redecorating an old person's home; working with mentally or physically handicapped people; baby-sitting; collecting other people's children from school; teaching children with learning disabilities, or ethnic families for whom English is a second language, to read and write; helping in the local hospital, school, club or church.

Some readers will doubtless dismiss all this as a typical middle-class reaction, quite impractical for working-class unemployed people in towns. And to some extent this is true. I am not so stupid as to recommend people who live in a council flat in an inner city area to keep pigs! But in principle I still appeal to the great biblical truths on which we have been reflecting. Humankind by creation is creative; we cannot discover ourselves without serving God and our neighbour; we must have an outlet for our creative energies. So, if the unemployed have no facilities for the range of activities I have mentioned, and they are not available elsewhere in the community, should not the Church provide them? Is it impossible for the church to make available a workshop (and tools), a garage or studio, in which people can both learn and practise new skills? And could not most local churches develop a much broader programme of service to the local community? Increasing numbers of unemployed, semi-employed and retired people will need to be encouraged to use their leisure time creatively. As a result of automation, as Marshall McLuhan wrote in 1964, 'we are suddenly threatened with a liberation that taxes our inner resources of self-employment and imaginative participation in society'.[30]

Conclusion

The conclusion of this chapter in the second edition of *Issues* (1990) was entitled 'A More Radical View'. It quoted the pessimistic forecasts of some futurologists in the eighties, who tried to visualize the nature and place of work in the twenty-first century. For example, the International Labour Organisation estimated that in order to achieve worldwide full employment, a billion new jobs would have to be created. This led its Director-General to comment that full employment of the conventional kind would never return. For population growth, the new technologies, the fear of inflation and global trade competition would combine to make the recovery of full employment an impossible dream.

This certainly looks like being the case in Europe. John Palmer, in his book *Trading Places*, has a chapter entitled 'The End of the Old Industrial Order'. In it he documents how the European steel, coal, shipbuilding and textile industries all collapsed before the expanding productivity of Brazil, South Korea, Taiwan and Japan, and how nothing has arisen in Europe to compensate for the huge redundancies involved.[31]

The same basic pessimism lay behind two books which were both published in 1985, the first by a Christian and the second not. They look courageously into a future without full employment and plead for fresh thinking. Michael Moynagh in *Making Unemployment Work* urges us to move from a 'work ethic' (which makes work the basis of worth) to a 'life ethic' (which sees worth as preceding work in the sense of employment, and therefore as independent of it).[32] James Robertson in *Future Work* goes further. He develops three possible scenarios of the future, whose key words are respectively 'employment', 'leisure', and 'ownwork'.[33] The last two scenarios are contrasting visions of a post-industrial society. He calls them 'HE' and 'SHE', 'HE' standing for 'Hyper-Expansionist' and 'SHE' for 'Sane, Humane and Ecological'. 'HE' will acquiesce in an unhealthy polarization between 'a minority of highly skilled and highly responsible people' who will run everything, while 'the rest of us will be living lives of leisure'.[34] 'SHE', by contrast, will be 'sane' (people taking control of their own life and work), 'humane' (nobody exploiting or being exploited) and 'ecological' (everybody living in harmony with their environment). James Robertson's word for this self-organized activity is 'ownwork'. It embraces 'a wide range of flexible options for work and useful activity, including part-time employment, self-employment, irregular and casual employment, co-operative and community work, voluntary work, do-it-yourself activities, and productive leisure as well as full-time employment'.[35]

Michael Moynagh and James Robertson both realize that a society which places equal value on paid work and voluntary service, on 'employment' and 'ownwork', will need a new financial base. They propose that, in place of the present complex system of social security, the government would pay everybody a 'social wage' (Michael Moynagh) or 'Guaranteed Basic Income' (James Robertson). This would be adequate for subsistence, untaxed and unconditional, although for many it would be supplemented by earned income, which would be taxable. So wealth creation would continue as at present. Critics of these proposals, while acknowledging that they would diminish the two-class nature of society, abolish poverty, render the black economy otiose, give everybody a greater freedom of choice and increase the level of voluntary service, nevertheless regard them as somewhat utopian.

Can it be right, however, for Christians, who believe work to be an indispensable element in God's original purpose for human beings, to acquiesce in the problem of large-scale unemployment, and even declare it insoluble? I think not. The books I have read which have been published in the nineties breathe a spirit of optimism. In North-South economic inequality (see Chapter 7), for example, not only has substantial progress been made in the alleviation of poverty but, given a generous influx of capital (comparable to the Marshall Plan after World War II), we are assured that it can be abolished.

The same is true of the problem of unemployment. The tone of the CCBI report *Unemployment and the Future of Work* is splendidly optimistic throughout. It refuses to accept the inevitability of mass unemployment, and insists that an explicit, realistic, national goal should be 'enough good work for everyone',[36] understanding 'good work' as referring to jobs of real value, with fair pay and decent conditions. Whereas the Director-General of the ILO declared full employment to be 'an impossible dream', the authors of the CCBI report contradict him: 'We have heard nothing to convince us that decent paid work for all is an impossible dream.'[37] Unemployment can be solved only by creating more jobs, and more jobs can be created only by greater investment in both the public and private sectors.

So what stands in the way? Sir Fred Catherwood, from his long and wide experience of industry and politics, writes in *Jobs and Justice, Homes and Hope* with refreshing outspokenness: 'Unrestrained greed is well on its way to destroying employment. It is greed which keeps taxes low and interest rates high, crippling the industrial recovery which we need to restore full employment.'[38] He has a later chapter entitled 'Naked Greed', in which he tells us that the selfishness which puts personal profit above social concern is now called 'the new reality'.[39] Political parties touting for votes cannot afford to ignore it.

The CCBI report is equally outspoken. But instead of analysing greed, it issues a positive call for sacrifice. 'It becomes a question of priorities: job creation as against low taxation. Sacrifice is necessary in seeking the common good. We do not think that the deep running sores of unemployment and poverty can be healed without some sacrifice on the part of those of us who are better off.'[40] These stirring words echo the challenge which David Sheppard, until 1997 Bishop of Liverpool, has often addressed to 'comfortable Britain'.

Is such a call realistic? Yes, it is. To be sure, we believe in original sin, namely that our human nature has an inherited twist of self-centredness. In consequence, greed is natural to us, while altruism and sacrifice are unnatural. Nevertheless, we also know that human beings have higher and better instincts, to which it is possible to appeal, especially if it is evident to them that individual unselfishness can benefit the community. In the end, the problem of unemployment is neither economic nor political, but moral and spiritual. Christians should blaze a trail, since sacrifice not greed should characterize those who seek to follow Jesus Christ.

The Christian understanding of work as self-fulfilment through the service of God and neighbour should have several wholesome consequences. We shall value our own work more highly; see to it that those we may employ are able to do the same; feel deeply for the unemployed, and try to ensure that though out of employment they are not out of work. In summary, all of us should expect to remain workers all our lives, so that even after we have retired, we may spend whatever energy we have left in some form of service.[41]

Chapter 10

INDUSTRIAL RELATIONS

Right attitudes to work are essential to our enjoyment of it; right relationships at work are equally important. Management and labour may be highly motivated, and yet at the same time deeply dissatisfied because they are at loggerheads with one another.

Britain has had a bad record of industrial relations. The trough was the winter of 1978–9, which was described at the time as a state of 'industrial civil war'. The Trades Union Congress had agreed with the government to a policy of wage restraint, but had added a warning that this could not be sustained for more than three years. They proved right. There were strikes by bakers, refuse collectors, road haulage and railway workers, hospital workers and ambulance drivers, journalists, teachers and social workers. The number of working days lost through industrial action in 1978 is said to have been 9,306,000. The situation greatly improved in the 1980s, however, and the nineties have been comparatively strike-free.

Industrial peace is of concern to all thoughtful people, but especially to Christians. For we are in the business of right relationships. John V. Taylor, formerly Bishop of Winchester, has justly called God's Kingdom 'the kingdom of right relationships'.[1] Reconciliation is at the top of the Christian agenda, because it lies at the heart of the gospel. Sin disrupts relationships; salvation rebuilds them. Jesus came on a mission of reconciliation. He is the supreme peace-maker; he tells his followers to be peace-makers too.

Moreover, relationships at work are particularly important because God means work, as we have seen, to be a co-operative enterprise, in which we collaborate with him and others for the common good. Britain and her allies experienced this solidarity during World

War II, when united against a common evil, but that unity soon fell apart afterwards, and even the valiant efforts of government, management and unions to co-operate in the sixties and seventies did not altogether restore it.

The biblical principle of mutuality

As in the other topics of this book, my task is not to presume to recommend policies (which is the calling of those involved in government, employment and unions, and for which I have no expertise), but rather to try to clarify biblical principles, so that we can think straight and take whatever action is appropriate to our responsibility.

I invite you therefore to reflect on the situation in Israel after King Solomon died. I recognize that an industry or business is not a kingdom, and that any analogy between them is bound to be only partial. Yet there are some significant parallels. The early united monarchy (under Saul, David and Solomon) had not been uniformly absolutist. At times there had been a reasonable degree of consultation, as when David 'conferred with' his officers, and then with the whole assembly, about bringing the ark to Jerusalem. He did not wish to make a unilateral decision, but to take action only 'if it seems good to you and if it is the will of the Lord our God'. Then after consultation, we are told, 'the whole assembly agreed to do this, because it seemed right to all the people' (1 Chronicles 13:1–4).

David's son and successor Solomon, however, despite all his wisdom and greatness, was a despot. His ambitious building programme was completed only by the use of forced labour. Industrial relations (if I may use this term) were at an all time low. So when he died, the people described his oppressive regime as a 'heavy yoke' and appealed to his son Rehoboam to lighten it. When Rehoboam consulted his father's elder statesmen, they advised him, 'If … you will be a servant to these people and serve them … they will always be your servants' (1 Kings 12:7). This splendid principle was rejected by Rehoboam, and in consequence the kingdom split into two. But it remains the essential basis of every constitutional monarchy (the motto of the Prince of Wales has since the fourteenth century been *Ich dien*, 'I serve') and indeed of every democratic institution, in at least two ways.

First, it embodies the principle of *mutual service*: 'If you will serve them, they will serve you.' Jesus himself went beyond a prudential arrangement (we serve in order to be served) and affirmed that true leadership must be interpreted in terms of service ('Whoever wants to become great among you must be your servant'). Later Paul stated it ('Each of you should look not only to your own interests, but also to the interests of others'), and went on to illustrate it from the incarnation and death of Jesus (Mark 10:43; Philippians 2:4, 5–8).

Secondly, it is mutual service based on *mutual respect*. One might say it is service based on justice, and not on expediency alone. To be sure, expediency enters into it ('you serve them and they will serve you'), but the principle's real foundation is justice, namely that the other party is a group of human beings with human rights, created in God's image as we have been, and therefore deserving our respect, as we deserve theirs. To oppress the poor is to insult their Maker; to serve them is to honour him (see Proverbs 14:31, 17:5, 22:2). It was this truth which lay behind the many detailed social instructions of the Old Testament – for example, the commandment to pay servants their wages the same day, to care for the deaf and the blind, to have compassion on the widow and the orphan, to leave the gleanings of the harvest to the poor and the alien, and to administer justice impartially in the courts. And the same principle also lay behind the New Testament instructions to masters and servants to respect each other. For they served the same Lord and were responsible to the same Judge.

Turning from biblical principle to contemporary reality, the contrast is stark. Wherever there is tension in industrial relations, let alone collision, the fault is seldom if ever limited to one side. Our basic self-centredness skews our vision, so that we see everything from our own perspective. We seek our own interests rather than the other's. It is a situation of conflict born of suspicion and rivalry, instead of a situation of mutual service born of respect and trust. Such a state of affairs, one need hardly say, is wholly incompatible with the mind and spirit of Jesus Christ, and in his name we should set ourselves resolutely against it. But how? How can mutual suspicion be replaced by mutual service, and competition by co-operation?

This is all the more necessary today, because recently a new enemy has appeared and is undermining good relationships between directors, shareholders, managers and workers. This is the corporate shareholder. Because the main shareholders in large companies are nowadays often not individual investors but invisible and impersonal owners like huge investment trusts, insurance and pension funds, whom Sir Fred Catherwood calls 'absentee landlords',[2] their priority concern is to receive unreasonably high short-term dividends. Will Hutton has described this development and its consequences in a chapter entitled 'Tomorrow's Money Today'.[3] In order to satisfy its shareholders' forceful demands, the company is tempted to adopt short-sighted policies, for example trimming their workforce too severely and reducing investment in research and development, which threatens the long-term health and growth of the enterprise. If, on the other hand, the company's directors resist these temptations, they run the risk either of losing their shareholders or of falling victim to a 'hostile take-over', so-called because the predator's motive is often sheer greed and not the good of the company. The fear of a possible take-over then causes a general sense of instability, particularly of job-insecurity, throughout the company from top to bottom. Everybody is under unwelcome pressure: directors to cut corners, managers to serve their own future instead of the firm's, and workers to cling to their job lest they are replaced by others on an insecure short-term contract. In such a situation of uncertainty and anxiety, a preoccupation with healthy relationships would seem to be largely an irrelevance.

Yet relationships of mutual respect can have a transforming influence on the company. This is well illustrated in the experience of the American industrialist Wayne Alderson. For four generations the Aldersons had been coal miners. During his boyhood Wayne's father would come home from the pit saying, 'If only they'd value me as much as they value the mule' (it was easier to replace a miner than a well-trained mule), while his three brothers who had jobs in the local steel works would say, 'If only they would value us as much as they value the machines.' Thus the importance of human *value* was instilled into him in his formative years and was later to flower in his 'Value of the Person' concept. In the early 1970s Wayne Alderson became Vice-President of Operations in the Pittron Corporation, which had a steel foundry in Glassport, Pennsylvania, near Pittsburgh. The firm was struggling to survive after a disastrous 84-day strike, which left an aftermath of implacable bitterness and recrimination between management and men. Mr Alderson conceived a plan for better production, quality, relationships and morale which he called 'Operation Turnaround'. Determined to end the old management style of confrontation, he called for co-operation instead, walked daily through the foundry, greeted the men by name, asked them about their work and home, visited them when they were sick, in fact treated them like human beings. At the request of a few of them he then started a small Bible study, which grew into a brief 'chapel' service in a storage room underneath a furnace. As a result of the mutual confidence which he developed with the men, absenteeism and labour grievances virtually disappeared, while productivity and profits rose substantially. The old sterile days of confrontation were over. People called it 'the Miracle of Pittron'. After nearly two years Pittron was sold and Wayne Alderson lost his job. He started an itinerant ministry as speaker, consultant and peace-maker, to spread his 'Value of the Person' vision. Its three key ingredients, he says, are love (a positive 'I'm for you' attitude), dignity (people count) and respect (appreciation instead of criticism). He goes on: 'Christ is at the centre of the Value of the Person approach. But even an atheist can accept the worth of the person.'[4]

Similarly, 'I am committed,' wrote Kenneth N. Hansen, formerly Chairman of the Board of ServiceMaster Industries Inc., 'to using work to help people develop, rather than to using people to accomplish the work as the end.'

Once there is a desire for mutual respect and mutual service, there will be at least three consequences.

Abolish discrimination

The first is that discrimination will be abolished – both the realities and the symbols, which together perpetuate an unwholesome 'them–us' confrontation.

For example, has there ever been a justification for paying workers by the hour and the week, and higher grades an annual salary? Or for insisting that wage earners clock in, while salaried staff do not have to? Or for restricting workers to the works' canteen, while providing the rest with a posh 'staff restaurant'? In recent years many companies have put an end to such offensive distinctions, but many have not. 'We know there are "untouchables" on other continents,' commented Jock Gilmour, a shop steward in the car industry; 'what we haven't recognised is that our own industrialized society can have its untouchables too.' I know, of course, that my three examples are trivial in themselves, but they are status symbols which appear deliberately to give self-respect to some and deny it to others.

I also understand that many of the old discriminatory practices of 10 or 20 years ago have already been abolished, not least through the influence of the Japanese, who insist on the same conditions for everybody. Nevertheless, bad habits die slowly, and continuing vigilance is needed. Besides, behind the symbols of discrimination there lies the reality of social injustice, namely the excessive disparity between the high paid and the low paid.

As I suggested in Chapter 7 ('North-South economic inequality'), total egalitarianism should not be the Christian goal, for God himself has not made us identical in either our natural or spiritual endowments. What the Christian should oppose is the inequality of privilege, and what we should seek to ensure is that all differentials are due to merit, not privilege. In fact, it is a healthy and confidence-building arrangement when discrimination is both open and limited to pay, and does not extend to hidden perquisites for senior management (e.g. private health care, 'top hat' pension schemes and free theatre tickets).

Human beings have a built-in sense of fair play, so that in all industrial relations arguments there are appeals to 'fairness', and complaints of 'unfair practices'. This concept is the central focus of the book *Social Values and Industrial Relations*, subtitled 'a study of fairness and inequality'.[5] Already in 1881 Engels had described the expression 'a fair day's wage for a fair day's work' as 'the old time-honoured watchword of British industrial relations'.[6]

The incomes policies, which operated in Britain in the sixties and seventies, paid careful attention to wage differentials, and the traditional distinction between 'skilled' and 'unskilled' workers seems to be universally accepted. It should therefore be possible to go further and develop some kind of graduated pay scale, such as was introduced into the Netherlands in the post-war years. It would take into consideration not only skill but such additional factors as length of training, mental and manual effort, risk and responsibility, efficiency and achievement, experience and length of service, together with working conditions (e.g. dirt, discomfort, danger and tedium). The mood of today is against outside interference, but not against a domestic arrangement, worked out by management and labour together, and covering the whole range of employees.

Meanwhile, there is manifest injustice in the status quo. More than 5 million employees in Britain are paid less than £4 an hour, and 1 million of these as little as £2.50. The national minimum wage, to which the new (1997) Labour government is committed, will take care of this. But what about the ridiculously high salary increases which some top directors regularly vote themselves? The Greenbury Committee was set up in 1995 in response to public anger over these, and the Cadbury Committee (set up in 1991) had examined the financial aspects of corporate governance in general. The recommendations of both committees were broadly supported by the TUC, except for two criticisms. First, the codes of practice they produced were voluntary, lacking any enforcement procedure. Secondly, primacy was given to the interest of shareholders, whereas all staff are 'stakeholders'. So what could be done? In 1996, in the colourful language of John Monks, General Secretary of the Trades Union Congress, 'fat cat greed should be curbed by involving employee representatives on the remuneration committees which set top directors' pay. This would bring a sense of reality to their decisions'.[7] He also stated the principle succinctly: 'All staff in a company contribute to its performance, and while roles clearly differ, interdependence is at the heart of all good working relationships.'[8]

I confess that I have admired the Scott Bader Commonwealth, ever since I first read about it in E.F. Schumacher's *Small is Beautiful* (1973) and subsequently corresponded with Mr Ernest Bader. Mr Bader is a Quaker, who came to England from Switzerland before World War I. The company he founded is a leading producer of plastics, and in 1951 he converted it into a 'Commonwealth' in which 'there are no owners or employees' because they are 'all co-owners and co-employees'. In 1979 E.F. Schumacher (who was a director) wrote: 'We have settled the maximum spread between the highest paid and the lowest paid; that is, before tax. It may shock many people [egalitarians, he must mean] that, in spite of a lot of goodwill from all concerned, that spread is still one to seven. There is no pressure from the community that it should be narrowed, because it is understood that this spread is necessary. But of course this includes everybody, the lowest paid juvenile compared with the highest paid senior employee.' The scale is reviewed and fixed by 'a sort of parliament of workers'.[9]

There must be differentials. But unwarranted discrimination in pay, conditions or promotion, 'unwarranted' because based on privilege not merit, must be abjured. It is incompatible with social justice, and with the Christian ideal of mutual respect.

Increase participation

It seems to be increasingly recognized that the workers in any enterprise, on whose skill and labour its success largely depends, should have a share in both decision-making and profits. Although some directors and managers resist this, and naturally feel threatened by it, the principle accords with natural justice. I want to concentrate on the concept of decision-making, since the Christian mind discerns in it a basic component of humanness.

However we define the 'Godlikeness' of humankind, it will surely include the capacity to make choices and decisions. Adam in the Genesis story is certainly regarded, and therefore treated, by God as a morally responsible person. True, the first command addressed to him was identical with that addressed to the living creatures of the sea, namely 'be fruitful and increase in number' (Genesis 1:22, 28), and the injunction to the fish did not denote that they had freedom of choice. Yet, what animals do by instinct, humans do by free decision. The divine mandate to subdue the earth clearly implies responsibility, and a higher degree still is implicit in the words, 'You are free to eat from any tree in the garden; but you must not eat from the tree of the knowledge of good and evil' (2:17). Here side by side are a liberal permission and a single prohibition. It was assumed that Adam was able both to distinguish between 'You may' and 'You may not', and to choose between them. Moreover God held him responsible for his choice.

Christian tradition has always taught this biblical truth, that moral freedom is an essential ingredient in the dignity of human personhood. 'For the supreme mark of a person,' wrote William Temple, 'is that he orders his life by his own deliberate choice.'[10] In consequence, he added, 'society must be so arranged as to give to every citizen the maximum opportunity for making deliberate choices and the best possible training for the use of that opportunity. In other words, one of our first considerations will be the widest possible extension of personal responsibility; it is the responsible exercise of deliberate choice which most fully expresses personality and best deserves the great name of freedom.'[11] Intuitively people know this. They want to be treated as adults with freedom to decide things for themselves; they know that if decision-making is taken away from them, their humanness will be demeaned. They will be reduced either to a child instead of an adult, or to a robot instead of a person.

The essential difference between a 'community' and an 'institution' is that in the former members retain their freedom to choose, while in the latter it is to some degree taken away from them. Erving Goffman's interesting book *Asylums* is, strictly spreaking, an investigation into 'the social situation of mental patients and other inmates'.[12] But he begins with some general observations. What he calls a 'total institution' is a place of residence or work where people 'lead an enclosed, formally administered round of life'.[13] This includes hospitals, orphanages, old people's homes, prisons, army barracks, boarding schools, monasteries and (I would have thought, although they are non-residential) many factories. In such places, the day's activities are 'tightly scheduled' and 'imposed from above by a system of explicit formal rulings and a body of officials'.[14] The key factor is the bureaucratic control, and the existence of a 'basic split between a large managed group, conveniently called "inmates", and a small supervisory staff'.[15] 'Characteristically, the inmate is excluded from knowledge of the decisions taken regarding his fate.'[16] Therefore in 'total institutions' an inmate ceases to be 'a person with adult self-determination, autonomy and freedom of action'.[17]

So important is this principle, if Christians are to help create genuine community life, and to protest against the dehumanizing effects of institutional life, that I will give several examples and then come back to our topic of industrial relations. Before looking at the factory from this perspective, we will look at the school or college, the hospital and the prison.

Christians distinguish sharply between education and indoctrination. Indoctrination is the process by which the leader imposes his or her viewpoint on the malleable mind of the child. In true education, however, the teacher acts as a catalyst to develop the child's ability to learn by observation and reasoning. The former is oppressive, the latter genuinely liberating. To be sure, the teacher cannot and should not adopt a position of complete neutrality, for children need guidance as they grow in discernment. Yet the crucial question is which mind is given pride of place – the teacher's mind as it instructs the children's minds, or the children's minds as they learn how to use them, in order to make their own value judgements and moral decisions. This process of self-education in interaction with teachers should be even more evident in universities and colleges, and also in churches where the preacher should never treat his congregation as nothing more than an absorbent sponge.[18] The students' demands of the 1960s also seemed substantially right, namely that, since it is their education which is at stake, they should have a say in academic questions such as those of curriculum and examinations, and an opportunity to evaluate their teachers' performance. School children and college students, as their age and maturity increase, should be given growing opportunities to make their own decisions.

Prison is very different, of course, because inmates have had their freedom taken from them, following a fair trial, by the judicial authority of a court. It cannot be right to treat prisoners as if they were free citizens. Nevertheless, they should not be treated as if they were slaves or robots either. They are still adult human beings, still persons who bear God's image, even while being punished for their offences. I was struck by Chuck Colson's comments on this in one of the contributions he made to the 1979 London Lectures in Contemporary Christianity. Reflecting on his experience of incarceration, following his involvement in the Watergate cover-up, he said: 'You make absolutely no decisions for yourself. The time of your meals, your work assignments – everything is decided for you. You have an overwhelming sensation of helplessness. Your individual identity is destroyed.'[19]

Turning now to the medical field, there is a constant danger that the doctor–patient relationship, already unnatural because of the awe in which doctors are held, will degenerate further beyond paternalism to control. Patients remain persons, and when decisions have to be made affecting their health and even their life, they should be left free to make them. Although it is obviously difficult for doctors to explain to their patients complex medical conditions and procedures in non-technical language, yet they are under obligation to do their best to do so; otherwise the notion of 'informed consent' to treatment, surgery or research would be meaningless. According to the Nuremberg Code of 1946–9, 'the voluntary consent of the human subject is absolutely essential'. This means not only that there shall be no duress, but that he 'should have sufficient knowledge and comprehension of the elements of the subject matter involved as to enable him to make an understanding and enlightened decision'.[20] Similarly, the 1964 Helsinki Declaration on human experimentation (drawn up by the World Medical Association) included the clause that 'clinical research on a human being cannot be undertaken without his free consent after he has been fully informed'.[21]

Yet patients often feel that they are being bypassed, and even manipulated, because they are kept in the dark about their condition and treatment, and are consequently powerless. Solzhenitsyn gives us a moving example of this in Oleg Kostoglotov, the chief character he created in his book *Cancer Ward*.[22] Like Solzhenitsyn himself, Oleg had been in a concentration camp before he entered the cancer ward. Indeed throughout the book Solzhenitsyn seems to be drawing a subtle parallel between prison and hospital, especially in the fact that neither prisoners nor patients are allowed to make any decisions for themselves. Oleg has a sturdy independence of mind and spirit, however. 'Everything that's gone wrong in my life,' he says, 'has been because I was too devoted to democracy. I tried to spread democracy in the army, that is, I answered my superiors back.'[23] Ludmila Afanasyevna Dontsova, who is in charge of the radiotherapy department, reacts strongly against what she regards as his unco-operative attitude. 'You will go home when I consider it necessary to interrupt your treatment,' she says with great emphasis. 'Ludmila Afanasyevna!' responds Oleg in exasperation. 'Can't we get away from this tone of voice? You sound like a grown-up talking to a child. Why not talk as an adult to an adult? ... You see, you start from a completely false position. No sooner does a patient come to you than you begin to do all his thinking for him ... And once again I become like a grain of sand, just like I was in the camp. Once again nothing *depends* on me.'[24] Then later, writing to his friends, and describing the ward's barred windows, bunk beds, terrified inmates, one-by-one processing, as if he were in prison, Oleg goes on: 'By some right ... they [the doctors] have decided, without my consent and on my behalf, on a most terrible form of therapy – hormone therapy.'[25]

I return at last to industry and to industrial relations. I realize that western hospitals are not like those in the Soviet Union during Stalin's oppressive regime, and that in any case there are differences between factories on the one hand and schools, colleges, prisons and hospitals on the other. Nevertheless, I have been anxious to show that decision-making is a basic right of human beings, an essential component of our human dignity.

The cry for industrial democracy, in order to facilitate a greater participation of workers in their own enterprise, does not make factories a special case, but is the expression within industry of the universal cry for the humanization of society. We now take political democracy for granted, and are grateful to those who struggled long to secure universal suffrage, so that ordinary citizens might share in governing their country and in making the laws they are then required to obey. Is not the propriety of industrial democracy equally self-evident? Already more than 50 years ago William Temple wrote: 'The cause of freedom will not be established till political freedom is fulfilled in economic freedom.'[26] He looked back with feelings of horror to the oppressive beginnings of the Industrial Revolution: 'The pioneers showed little respect for the personality of those who earned their living by working in factories and mills. They were often called "hands", and a hand is by nature a "living tool", which is the classical definition of a slave.'[27] Indeed, in a historic letter to the *Leeds Mercury* in 1830, Richard Oastler, a Christian landowner in Yorkshire, had the courage to draw this very analogy, three years before Wilberforce and his friends had secured the abolition of slavery in the British colonies. 'Thousands of our fellow creatures and fellow subjects, both male and female, are at this moment existing in a state of slavery more horrid than the victims of that hellish system of colonial slavery.' He went on to refer particularly to little children from seven to 14 years of age, who were working 13 hours a day in the factories, with only a half-hour break.[28]

We have come a long way in 170 years, thank God. And yet we still have some way to go. William Temple continued: 'The worst horrors of the early factories have been abolished, but ... the "workers" usually have no voice in the control of the industry whose requirements determine so large a part of their lives.'[29] He states the principle in these clear terms: 'Every citizen should have a voice in the conduct of the business or industry which is carried on by means of his labour.'[30]

At the heart of many industrial disputes (so I understand from my reading) is the question of rules and rule-making – not just *what* the rules require or forbid, but *who* makes the rules and *why*. Management is often dictatorial in making or changing rules, regarding this as 'managerial prerogative'. Workers, on the other hand, usually go by what they call 'C and P' (Custom and Practice), the unwritten but established conventions of the place. The Donovan Report[31] emphasized the tension between these two systems, the 'formal' (official agreements) and the 'informal' (unwritten procedures), and expressed its dislike of this situation. It is the difference between regulations and traditions, and so between two different kinds of authority, power wielded from above and commonsense or custom from below.

Moreover, each side sees the need to legitimize its rules. This necessity is the particular emphasis of the book *Ideology and Shop-Floor Industrial Relations* (1981).[32] It discusses the process of legitimization in industrial relations, the arguments which each side uses to justify or challenge rules, and the ideology, worldview or value-system which lies behind this process. Industrial relations are broader than rules and rule-making, however. The whole policy and programme of the company are concerned. It has to be admitted that in many companies the workers lack self-respect because they lack responsibility. They feel oppressed and powerless. The 'them and us' mentality is enforced because other people make all the decisions (remote, faceless people), while their role is exclusively to react, and indeed to obey. The analogy with slavery, though very inexact, is yet instructive at this point. Christians opposed slavery because human beings are dehumanized by being owned by someone else. Christians now should oppose all forms of labour in which human beings are used by someone else. True, the evil is much smaller, because the work is undertaken voluntarily and is regulated by a contract. Yet it is a contract which diminishes humanness if it involves the relinquishing of personal responsibility and the undertaking to obey without consultation.

Christians will agree that at the very least there should be a procedure of consultation, and, more important, that this should not be a piece of window-dressing but a genuine discussion early in the planning process which is reflected in the final decision. After all, *production* is a team process, in which the workers' contribution is indispensable; should not *decision-making* be a team process too, in which the workers' contribution is equally indispensable? Self-interest undoubtedly lies at the root of each side's viewpoint. Managers tend to begin their thinking with profit, on which the company's survival depends; whereas workers tend to begin with rising costs and therefore wages, on which their personal survival depends. Their different starting points are understandable. But in discussion each side comes to understand the other's legitimate concerns, and then to see that the two, far from being incompatible, are in fact interdependent.

Once the principle of worker-participation has been conceded, there can be a legitimate difference of opinion about the best ways and means to ensure it. The obligation to *inform* employees about the business is already imposed on firms by Company Law; the question is how much to consult them. A variety of structures have been advocated and tried, ranging from thorough consultation at all levels to the election of worker-directors.[33]

In response to a European Commission directive about employee-directors, the British Institute of Management during the chairmanship of Sir Fred Catherwood proposed in 1974 that every company should have a 'works council' elected by all the employees. Two of its members would then be chosen (by agreement between council and board) to sit on the board of directors.[34]

Next, the Labour government appointed the Bullock Committee on Industrial Democracy. Its majority report (1977) recommended a positive partnership between management and labour, both in developing a corporate strategy for the company and in making and implementing decisions. They expressed themselves in favour of the company having employee-directors. But the minority led by Clive Jenkins insisted that the workers could be represented only by their unions and not by elected non-unionized employees. So there was a deadlock.

In May 1978 the Labour Government issued a white paper on *Industrial Democracy,* which accepted the principle of participation. If this Government had had the opportunity to produce legislation on this basis, they would have (1) *obliged* employers in companies of more than 500 employees to discuss with representatives of the workforce all major proposals affecting them, including plans for investment, merger, expansion and contraction; (2) *encouraged* companies to develop a two-tier board structure (a policy board and a management board) and to arrange for employees to be represented on the policy board; and (3) *given a statutory right* to employees in firms of more than 2,000 to be represented on the policy board alongside the shareholders' representatives. A minority report disagreed, on the grounds of lack of evidence and size of risk.

Reactions to these proposals were mixed, though on the whole they were more hostile than friendly. The Confederation of British Industry, representing the employers, said they thought that the Bullock Committee had been given biased terms of reference, and that they were more concerned to give workers control of the company than participation in it. The Unions were negative because they believed board representation and collective bargaining to be fundamentally incompatible. Historically, it has been by collective bargaining that the Trade Unions have undermined the undisputed power of the employers and indeed secured some power of their own over wages and conditions of work. In other words, both sides understandably wanted to preserve their present power, even if this meant a continuing degree of confrontation.

Now the focus of attention has shifted to Europe. In 1989 the European Union's 'Social Charter' (formerly the 'Charter on the Fundamental Social Rights of Workers') was signed by all the member states, except Britain. It called for significant changes, but lacked the power of enforcement.

So in 1991 the 'Social Chapter' of the Maastricht Treaty gave the charter a legal basis. Britain under John Major opted out, but the new (1997) Labour government is committed to opting in. The 'Social Chapter' empowers the European Community to issue 'directives' for the implementation of its policies. Thus, the Working Time Directive (1996) provided for a maximum working week of 48 hours, at least 11 consecutive hours' rest each day, one day's rest in seven, three weeks' paid leave a year, rising to four in 1999, and some other health and safety measures. Still more germane to our topic, the Works Council Directive (1996) requires the creation of works councils in companies which employ (a) more than 1,000 people in one member state and (b) more than 200 people in two. This deliberately includes multinationals. By January 1997, in spite of the British opt-out, the UK already had more than 1,000 seats on nearly 200 European works councils.[35]

I doubt if any Christian would disagree with the way Robin Woods, at that time Bishop of Worcester and Chairman of the Church of England's Board for Social Responsibility, summed the situation up in a letter to *The Times*: 'It is consistent with Christian vision that society should develop in such a way that each person can exercise his God-given ability to make choices, to take responsibility, and to share in shaping his own environment. We believe that employees have a stake in their company which is at least as significant as that of the shareholders.'[36]

The second kind of participation is profit-sharing. Another clear biblical principle seems to be involved, namely that 'the worker deserves his wages' (1 Timothy 5:18). Presumably then there should be some correlation between work and wage. If a company prospers, shared power (responsibility) should bring shared profit. If shareholders benefit from profit, so should workers, whether in bonuses of company stock or deferred benefits (e.g. pensions). The 'pact' between the British Liberal and Labour parties at the end of the 1970s introduced the idea of tax incentives for firms which developed profit-sharing schemes.

The world pioneer in this area appears to have been Karl Zeiss of Jena, Germany, who in 1896 transferred the ownership of his firm to the workforce, while in the United States it was Sears Roebuck, who in 1916 decided to use 10 per cent of his firm's annual pre-tax profits to enable employees to buy its shares in the open market. In Britain, however, the credit for being first in the profit-sharing field seems to belong to the John Lewis Partnership in Oxford Street, London. John Lewis was 28 years old when he opened a small drapery shop there in 1864. By the turn of the century his son Spedan had become troubled in conscience that he, his father and his brother as shareholders were jointly drawing from the business substantially more than all their employees put together. So he determined to devise a more equitable division of the rewards of industry, and in 1920 the first distribution of 'Partnership Benefit' was made, representing an extra seven weeks of pay. Spedan Lewis later made two irrevocable settlements in trust for the benefit of the workers. From 1928 to 1970 the 'Partnership Bonus' (as it is now called) was made in the form of stock, but since 1970 it has been wholly in cash. The company's policy is stated thus: 'After paying preference dividends and interest, and providing for amenities, pensions and proper reserves, the remainder of the profits in any year is distributed to the members of the Partnership in proportion to their pay. In this way the profits are shared among all who work in the business.' The percentage of the total profits applied to the Bonus rose from 12 per cent in 1967 to 20 per cent in 1980, and has been even higher since.

Such an arrangement was innovative in the twenties. Today similar profit-sharing arrangements or profit-linked share plans are multiplying in Britain and continental Europe. The 'Wider Share Ownership Council' was established in 1958 to promote such projects.[37] Also, during the eighties, many large American corporations adopted 'employee stock-ownership plans' (ESOPs), encouraged by tax incentives to do so. Cynics said that their real purpose was to gain the support of employee stockholders in resisting unwelcome take-over bids. But ESOPs also increase the stake which employees have in the company's future, encourage them (and through them their mates) to work harder, and so boost its productivity and profits.

Both aspects of participation (decision-making and profit-sharing) appeal to the Christian mind on the ground not only of expediency (increased industrial peace and productivity) but also of justice (workers have a right to share in power and profits).

Emphasize co-operation

The fundamental concept of mutual respect and mutual service, whose implications for industry we are exploring, should lead not only to the abolition of discrimination, but also to the increase of participation and so of co-operation.

 Trade Unions developed in the nineteenth century (with the active involvement of many Christians) to protect workers against exploitative bosses. Since workers had no rights under British Company Law at that time, they were forced to organize themselves from outside. Over the years they have secured great gains for labour, both in wages and in conditions. They were therefore absolutely necessary; without their sense of collective responsibility and their persistent struggles labour would probably still be exploited today.

Since the end of the 1970s, however, the unions have been steadily losing power in Britain. Various reasons have been given for this: (1) when manual workers are replaced by robots or computers, the skilled technicians who operate them are less unionized and less prone to strike action; (2) the rise of trans-national corporations has made collective bargaining more difficult; (3) so has the spread of flexi-time, especially for women workers; (4) some unions have forfeited public sympathy by taking up a stance which is more political than industrial, by making unreasonable wage demands which further depress the economy, by strike action which causes inconvenience and even suffering to the innocent public, and by violence in the picket lines. The Conservative government took advantage of these factors by introducing what became the Trade Unions Act 1984. Many people will agree that union power needed to be better controlled. At the same time, organized labour must have adequate mechanisms for the redress of injustices, and justice is by no means always on the side of the bosses. Many trade unionists work hard and long to find solutions to conflict in the face of incompetent or intransigent managers, and that patient work often goes unacknowledged.

The tragedy is, however, that the first loyalty of the workers tends to be given to their union rather than their firm, and that confrontation is still built into the very structures of industry. Why should we assume that this structural confrontation is inevitable and therefore everlasting? Why must the language of 'winning' and 'losing', whenever there is an industrial dispute, be perpetuated? Why should we not dream of, and work towards, the day when better structures will be developed which express co-operation? The Labour Government's white paper *Industrial Democracy*, to which I have already referred, defined the goal as 'a positive partnership between management and workers, rather than defensive co-existence'. When management and labour are locked in confrontation, the public also suffers; when they co-operate in the service of the public, their relations to each other improve. But such a partnership is possible only if management and labour feel secure in their jobs, as we considered earlier. Insecurity grows when shareholders have no commitment to the company and behave like 'absentee landlords', for in such a situation the company is very vulnerable to a take-over. Security grows, however, when (as in continental Europe) shareholders become involved in and supportive of the companies they own.

I would like to give you an example of how the atmosphere and attitudes of a whole company can change, which illustrates some of the principles we have been considering.

Towards the end of the 1960s Gerald Snider, an American businessman, worked for a multinational company, whose identity it is not necessary to divulge. He found himself Vice-President and General Manager of a group of European companies. He was in fact Acting President, since the ultimate responsibility for them was his.

He told me the story of one particular company which, when he assumed responsibility for it, was in extremely bad shape. The factory's product was inferior in design and quality. The plant was dirty, the machinery out-of-date and the environment bad. Although wages were competitive, the workers took little interest in their work and were suspicious of management, even hostile. Absenteeism was rampant. As many as 20 per cent of the workforce did not show up on Mondays. In consequence, to make up for absenteeism, the plant was seriously overstaffed. Indeed, one of Gerald Snider's first acts was to declare 400 of the 1,800 workers redundant. It was an extremely unpleasant task, but the only alternative would have been to close the plant down.

As he thought about the whole situation, it became clear to him that the fundamental cause of the factory's malaise was the bad relationships between the workers and their supervisors. To be sure, each employee maintained the required contact with those above and below him. But it was more a ritual than a relationship. The factory was organized by directives which descended from on high through five levels – from managing director through plant manager, personnel manager, supervisor and foreman to the production workers. There was no consultation and no intelligent, willing co-operation. Indeed, there were no genuine relationships at all.

Gerald Snider saw that, if the factory was to survive, it was necessary not only for the quality of its product to be acceptable to the marketplace, but for the employees at every level both to understand the company's objectives and to co-operate in order to achieve them. So he decided to take an unheard-of step. He would call the entire workforce together, in order to take them into his confidence and explain the situation to them. Immediately the most strenuous objections were raised. 'It isn't done,' he was told. 'You fellows in the United States may get away with it, but in our country we don't do things that way.' A whole week of discussion followed, in which managers and supervisors (who felt threatened by what they thought would be the undermining of their authority) advanced every contrary argument they could think of. But the General Manager was adamant.

So one day at 11.45 a.m., for a quarter of an hour of the company's time, everybody assembled in the factory's auditorium. Mr Snider outlined the serious situation which had arisen on account of the poor quality of the product and the poor performance of the workforce. Indeed, of all the companies for which he was responsible in Europe, theirs showed the lowest production and the highest absenteeism. He then propounded his programme for survival. On the one hand, the company was prepared to invest millions of pounds in modernizing equipment and tools, and in improving the work environment. On the other, he asked for their whole-hearted co-operation. Absenteeism would have to stop. There could be no more Saturday work at double or treble time; what had to be done must be done during the working week.

Above all, he added, he was anxious to improve relationships and simplify communication between all levels. He was even now giving them a direct account of the factory's problems, goals and needs. He wanted them to have equally direct access to management and to him personally. For he was convinced that if mutual understanding could grow, mutual responsibility would grow with it. So, when the plant opened at seven o'clock the following morning, he would be there and available to them.

To his surprise, and to the personnel department's astonishment (since they had prophesied that the men would not accept a direct approach from the General Manager), his speech was greeted with loud applause. And when he walked through the factory floor early the following morning, already the old sullenness had gone. Men smiled as he passed. Some also made suggestions, especially the foremen, who occupy a key position between management and labour. A daily meeting between them began, which resulted in a number of useful suggestions. Another important decision was to close the two dining rooms previously reserved for executives and supervisors, so that everybody would eat in the same restaurant, sharing the same conditions and the same food, and having the same opportunity to meet, know and trust one another.

Gradually, too, the General Manager's other promises were fulfilled. Modern equipment was installed. The factory was redecorated. The washrooms were cleaned. The new procedures for open communication continued to be fostered. So as the management's good faith became evident, the workers' good faith increased. Production went up significantly. Absenteeism was reduced from over 20 per cent to under 5 per cent. The quality of the product improved. The crisis was over.

Gerald Snider was brought up in a Christian home, and has remained a practising Christian. Although he modestly disclaims any self-conscious application of Christian principles to his business life, and although he did not put forward his proposals for the survival of his factory as a specifically 'Christian' solution to the problem, nevertheless his actions reflected the teaching of the Bible. On the one hand, he was convinced of the dignity of work in God's intention ('If you can't enjoy your work, you shouldn't be there,' he said to me). On the other, he recognized the value of human beings as God's supreme creation in his own likeness. In the production process, therefore, workers must not be treated as 'objects', who receive directives from the top without explanation or consultation, but rather as 'subjects', who are given the chance to understand their contribution to the whole enterprise, and who participate in it with a good will.

Co-operation cannot be engineered by itself; it is a by-product of a common vision and goal. This fact is increasingly recognized by those who pursue that elusive thing called 'good management'. The main emphasis of Thomas J. Peters and Robert H. Waterman in their best-selling book *In Search of Excellence* is the necessity, if a company is to succeed, of 'shared values', which unite and motivate the entire workforce. After investigating the management techniques of America's 62 best-run companies, they developed the '7-S McKinsey Framework', which they present as an alliterative 'managerial molecule'. The six outer satellites are Strategy, Structure, Systems, Style, Staff and Skills, but the nucleus at the centre, round which all these revolve, is 'Shared values', alternatively described as 'superordinated goals'.[38] One of the most vital of these is respect for people, both employees and customers. 'Treating people – not money, machines or minds – as the natural resource' is of paramount importance.[39]

Japanese management has largely been built on this kind of American foundation. Why, then, is Japanese industry often more productive than American industry? What is the secret of the economic prowess of the Japanese? Richard Tanner Pascale and Anthony G. Athos set out to answer these questions in their book *The Art of Japanese Management*. In particular they investigated the Matsushita Electric Company. They found that this large corporation was using all the American principles of management (Japanese people joke that 'BA' stands for 'Been to America'!). But they also found something else. Matsushita have not only composed an 'employees' creed' (which includes a reference to 'the combined efforts and co-operation of each member of our Company') and seven 'spiritual values' (one of which is 'harmony and co-operation'), but have actually set these to music. 'Matsushita was the first company in Japan to have a song and a code of values. "It seems silly to Westerners," says an executive, "but every morning at 8.00 a.m., all across Japan, there are 87,000 people reciting the code of values and singing together. It's like we are all a community." '[40]

Messrs Pascale and Athos recognize that this emphasis on co-operation has a strongly cultural origin. The Americans prize 'independence', but the Japanese 'interdependence'. Of a person who has difficulties in relating to others Americans say 'he hasn't found himself', the Japanese 'he doesn't belong'.[41] So all members of the workforce belong to a 'work group' of about 10 people, in which harmony is developed, and to which loyalty is expected. It is not suggested that this kind of cultural arrangement can be trans-ferred *tout simple* from Japan to Europe or America. Nevertheless, the contrast between the competitive individualism of the West and the productive co-operation of the East which Richard Pascale and Anthony Athos describe is surely significant. Company morale aris-ing from shared values is easier to develop in small businesses; if huge corporations are to experience it, they may need to break into smaller autonomous units.

The shared values of a company will inevitably include a recog-nition of its multiple responsibilities. In his trail-blazing books *The Future of Private Enterprise* (1951) and *The Responsible Company* (1961), George Goyder considered the alternatives of 'a form of private enterprise based on the profit motive' and 'a form of public enterprise called nationalization', and proposed 'a third and better way through the creation of responsible industrial companies, nei-ther wholly private nor wholly public'.[42] His concern was to make companies accountable not only to their shareholders (which was at that time their only obligation according to Company Law in Britain), but also to their workers, their consumers and the commu-nity at large. Goyder went on to make proposals as to how this could be done legally, in particular by adding to the Company's 'Memorandum of Association' a clause which would define its general purposes. In order to bring private industry under social control without depriving it of freedom, he further suggested that every firm, in addition to an annual financial audit, should establish a triennial 'social audit' relating to pricing policies (affecting con-sumers), labour relations (affecting employees) and local interests (affecting the community). 'The social audit,' he wrote, 'is the nat-ural result of business accepting its full responsibility.'[43] Such a firm, being half way between a private and a public company, might well be called 'a Participating Company'.[44]

In 1987 George Goyder produced a further book entitled *The Just Enterprise*, in which he emphasizes the social responsibilities of the company and defines it not just as 'an instrument for maximiz-ing profit in the interest of shareholders' but as 'a wealth-creating organism in the service of the consumers, employees and the community as well as the shareholders'.[45] It is this balance which makes an enterprise 'responsible' or 'just'. In fact, 'the creation of a sense of partnership in industry and commerce is the most urgent task facing us in domestic politics'.[46] To this end what is needed, he writes, is (1) a general purposes clause relating specially to the company's duties to the customer, (2) an understanding that the directors are trustees, responsible to forward the interests of the company as a whole according to its defined purposes, (3) the opportunity for employees to become shareholders, (4) the transformation of the Annual General Meeting into a genuinely public democratic forum, in which 'freely chosen representatives of the workers, consumers and the community' are allowed 'not only to ask questions but to speak about corporate policy and comment on the chairman's statement',[47] and (5) the 'social audit' which must be an 'independent appraisal of the company's social performance'.[48]

It seems clear, then, that every company should define its goals and assign a priority order to them. In 1975 the Confederation of British Industry approved a report of its Company Affairs Committee entitled 'The Responsibility of the British Public Company'. Its paragraph 22 reads: 'While law establishes the *minimum* standard of conduct with which a company must comply ... a company like a person must be recognized as having functions, duties and moral obligations that go beyond the pursuit of profit and the specific requirements of legislation.' So several organizations, and some individual companies, have issued a 'Code of Practice' which summarizes their ideals and goals. For example, a thorough 'Code of Business Ethics' has been produced by CABE, the Christian Association of Business Executives.[49]

Of course every firm must make a profit, but its priority concern should be the public whom the company (management, shareholders and workers together) exist to serve. Just as the first responsibility of hospital workers is their patients, of teachers their pupils, and of lawyers and social workers their clients, so the first responsibility of every business and industry is their customers – not just because the survival of the enterprise depends on pleasing the public, but because service to the public is its *raison d'être*. 'Put most simply, a company exists to produce goods and services for its customers ... In a free society the consumer is king, and business exists to satisfy his needs.'[50] In addition, the company itself is best served when management, labour and shareholders are united in serving the public. 'If you serve them, they will serve you.'

If the followers of Jesus Christ cannot develop relationships of respect and trust, across social barriers, we can hardly blame the world for failing. But improved relationships need not be limited to the Church. We should work expectantly for greater respect and co-operation in every segment of human society. We should not acquiesce in industrial conflict or be pessimistic about resolving it. For all human beings, though fallen and self-centred, have an in-born sense of dignity and justice. So better relations are possible.

Chapter 11

THE MULTI-RACIAL DREAM

O n 28 August 1963 Martin Luther King, who was committed equally to non-discrimination and to non-violence, in other words to justice and peace, led a march of 250,000 people, three-quarters of whom were black and one quarter white, to Washington DC. And there he shared his dream of a multi-racial America:

> I have a dream that one day on the red hills of Georgia the sons of former slaves and the sons of former slave-owners will be able to sit down together at the table of brotherhood.
>
> I have a dream that one day even the state of Mississippi, a state sweltering with the heat of injustice ... and oppression, will be transformed into an oasis of freedom and justice.
>
> I have a dream that one day in Alabama, with its vicious racists ... little black boys and black girls will be able to join hands with little white boys and white girls as sisters and brothers ...
>
> With this faith we will be able to transform the jangling discords of our nation into a beautiful symphony of brotherhood.
>
> With this faith we will be able to work together, to stand up for freedom together, knowing that we will be free one day ...[1]

A third of a century has passed since then, and still the fulfilment lingers. Yet it is right for Christians to dream this dream. For God has given us in Scripture a vision of the redeemed as 'a great multitude that no one could count, from every nation, tribe, people and language, standing before the throne' (Revelation 7:9). That dream, we know, will come true. Meanwhile, inspired by it, we should seek at least an approximation to it on earth, namely a society characterized by racial justice (no discrimination) and racial harmony (no conflict). Perhaps even the word 'multi-racial' is not specific enough, and 'inter-racial' would be better, since the former South African Nationalist government used to describe its vision of separate 'homelands' as 'multi-racial development', and that is not at all how the word should be used. A helpful definition of racial integration was given by Roy Jenkins when he was Home Secretary: 'I define integration,' he said, 'not as a flattening process of assimilation, but as equal opportunity, accompanied by cultural diversity, in an atmosphere of mutual tolerance.'[2]

Before considering some biblical teaching about race, I think we need to look at some examples of 'racism', both historical and contemporary, and be aware of the false foundations on which it is built.

Slavery and the American racial problem

It is not possible to jump straight to the contemporary problem of race in Europe and America, and ignore the evils of slavery and of the slave trade out of which it has largely sprung. Although slavery was abolished in the British colonies 165 years ago, no sensitive white Briton can meet a West African or West Indian without seeing them as probable descendants of slaves, or visit their countries without remembering the appalling traffic in human beings in which our country engaged for at least 200 years. Similarly, no sensitive American can confront the race issue in the United States today without looking back beyond the Civil War to the cruelty and degradation of life on the plantations.

It is generally accepted that 'the slave has three defining characteristics: his person is the property of another man, his will is subject to his owner's authority, and his labour or services are obtained through coercion.'[3] Being regarded as nothing but movable and disposable property, slaves were normally deprived of elementary human rights, e.g. the right to marry, or to own or bequeath possessions, or to witness in a court of law. Although slavery of different kinds and degrees was universal in the ancient world, it is inexcusable that the professedly Christian nations of Europe (Spain and Portugal, Holland, France and Britain) should have used this inhuman practice to meet the labour needs of their New World colonies. Worse still, practising Christians developed an elaborate defence of slavery on the grounds of social and economic necessity (there was no other source of labour in the colonies to provide raw materials for the Industrial Revolution in Europe), racial superiority (negroes deserved no better treatment), biblical permission (Scripture regulates but nowhere condemns slavery), humanitarian benefit (the trade transferred slaves from African savagery to American civilization), and even missionary opportunity (African infidels would be introduced to Christianity in the New World). The blatant rationalizations of slave-owners make one blush with embarrassment today.

The inherent evil of slavery (which in principle is the evil of racism also) is that it affronts, indeed denies, the Godlike dignity of human beings. Being the property of their owners, slaves were advertised for sale alongside horses and cattle, mules and pigs, corn and plantation tools. Having first been captured, chained and branded in West Africa, they were then shipped across the Atlantic in such overcrowded and unhygienic conditions that about half of them died during the passage. Then on arrival they were auctioned, forced to work, often separated from wife and children, if recalcitrant flogged, if escaped pursued by bloodhounds, and if caught killed.

Some writers argued that the reason why they were property is that they were animals. In his *The History of Jamaica* (1774) Edward Long developed the outrageous argument that in the Creator's 'series or progression from a lump of dirt to a perfect man' African negroes are inferior to human beings. 'When we reflect on … their dissimilarity to the rest of mankind, must we not conclude that they are a different species of the same genus?'[4] The French author J.H. Guenebault went even further in his *Natural History of the Negro Race* (1837). Having given his opinion of the physical form and mental inferiority of negroes, he wrote: 'It is then impossible to deny that they form not only a race, but truly a species, distinct from all other races of men known on the globe.' They belong to 'the ape genus', he declared, and placed them somewhere between orang-outangs and white human beings.[5]

A third inferiority theory, popularized by Ulrich B. Phillips in his *American Negro Slavery* (1918), is that negroes were neither property nor animals but children. He was evidently fond of his slaves in a paternalistic way, but could not take them seriously as adults. Stanley M. Elkins in his book *Slavery* (1959) examines the familiar image of the plantation slave as 'Sambo'. He was 'docile but irresponsible, loyal but lazy, humble but chronically given to lying and stealing ... his relationship with his master was one of utter dependence and childlike attachment: it was indeed the childlike quality that was the very key to his being.'[6] The Sambo stereotype was of 'the perpetual child incapable of maturity'.[7] Professor Elkins goes on to develop the thesis that negro 'infantilism' was due neither to race, nor to culture, nor even to slavery in general, but to the absolutist structure of the North American plantation system. He draws a striking analogy between the victims of North American slavery and those of Nazi concentration camps. For the latter (if they survived) were 'reduced to complete and childish dependence upon their masters', namely the SS guards.[8] Thus, the same mechanism operated in Negro plantation and Nazi concentration camp, since both were hideous forms of slavery, and the victims of both were subjugated into infantilism.[9]

The horror of eighteenth-century slavery, then, was that it regarded adult men and women as tools, animals or children. In consequence, they were thought to have an inborn inferiority. Christian opponents of slavery found it necessary, therefore, to demonstrate that negro slaves were human beings who were in no way inferior to others. So Wilson Armistead, a Quaker businessman from Leeds, subtitled his book *A Tribute for the Negro* (1848) in the following words: 'A vindication of the moral, intellectual and religious capabilities of the coloured portion of mankind, with particular reference to the African race'. He dedicated it to three negroes and 'many other noble examples of elevated humanity in the negro ... beautifully designated "the image of God cut in Ebony" '. His intention, he wrote, was to demonstrate 'from facts and testimonies that the white and the dark coloured races of man are alike the children of one Heavenly Father and in all respects equally endowed by him', and to prove 'that the negro is indubitably and fully entitled to equal claims with the rest of mankind'.[10]

This brief excursus into slavery is far from being irrelevant. For racists, even if they concede the humanness of black people, nevertheless also hold that they have an inborn inferiority. They may defend their position as a so-called 'scientific theory of race', or merely cherish 'vague notions about a unilinear evolution "from monkey to man" ' which encourage them to believe that such 'races' are 'lower' in the 'scale' of evolution than is the group to which they belong; 'that there is a hierarchy of "races" '.[11] It was to demolish this illusion that Dr Ashley Montagu wrote his definitive book

Man's Most Dangerous Myth: The Fallacy of Race. Of course he agrees, as a physical anthropologist, that humankind may be divided into four 'major groups' (Caucasoid, Mongoloid, Negroid and Australoid) and into many smaller 'ethnic groups' (by nationality, language, culture, etc.). But he insists that these groups are arbitrary, overlapping and fluid; that they merely describe populations whose distinctions are due partly to cultural development (as a result of geographical separation) and partly to 'temporary mixtures of genetic materials common to all mankind';[12] and that the differences are definitely *not* due to 'inborn physical and mental traits' which are ineradicable.[13] Indeed, that concept of 'race' is a superstition, 'the witchcraft of our time',[14] and a stratagem invented to justify discrimination.

Columbus Salley and Ronald Behm begin their book *What Color is your God?*[15] with three historical chapters tracing the development of the racial problem in America. The first ('Christianity and Slavery') takes us up to the Civil War (1863). The second ('Christianity and Segregation') runs from 1863 to 1914. This is the period following the Civil War, in which 'Black Codes' were formulated to give blacks some permissions, but to keep them weak and inferior. The Ku Klux Klan was formed, with shameful support from white racist Christians. White churches were segregated and silent, while black churches were conformist and otherworldly. The third period runs from 1914 to about 1980 ('Christianity and Ghettoization'). It began with the mass migration of blacks to the cities of the North and West, and the consequent 'Great White Exodus' from the same cities. 'Institutional racism' restricted blacks to certain areas and certain roles, and gave them inferior education, housing and employment. There were riots and lynchings. Again in this period, as in the previous ones, the Church was largely mute and ineffective. In the 1960s, however, the search for black identity and power led to the more organized Civil Rights movement, and so to the legislation which ended segregation and discrimination. Even this was only a beginning, however. In 1968 the National Advisory Commission on Civil Disorders, which had been appointed by President Lyndon B. Johnson, reported (the 'Kerner Report'). Here is its conclusion: 'Our nation is moving toward two societies, one black, one white – separate and unequal.' Further, 'segregation and poverty have created in the racial ghetto a destructive environment totally unknown to most white Americans ... White institutions created it, white institutions maintain it, and white society condones it.' 'Racism is American society's most exposed weakness,' wrote Ashley Montagu. 'It is America's greatest domestic failure, and the worst of its international handicaps.'[16]

The 1990s opened with the bold experiment called 'Affirmative Action', by which federal law required appropriate representation of black and ethnic minorities in education, employment and other situations. Since it appears to discriminate between Americans solely on racial grounds, however, it is judged by many to be unconstitutional, and is being dismantled in some states in favour of a 'colour-blind' approach.

Two highly publicized trials in the early nineties involved African Americans, namely Rodney King (whose brutal beating by Los Angeles police was captured by a video camera) and O.J. Simpson (who was accused of murdering his ex-wife). The outcome was an almost complete polarization of the American public by colour.

It is extremely regrettable that the Nation of Islam, now led by Louis Farrakhan, is both expressing and fomenting black nationalism. Yet we may be thankful that an increasing number of evangelical Christians are acknowledging racism as a sin and repenting of it. One of the seven promises undertaken by the Promise Keepers, in their huge rallies of men from all ethnic backgrounds, is to reach beyond racial barriers in order to demonstrate their unity in Christ.

German anti-Semitism and South African apartheid

Anti-Semitism in Germany and apartheid in South Africa seem at first sight so different from one another as to be entirely unsuitable for comparison. There is an obvious difference between Jews and blacks, for example, and in the laws relating to them. In particular, the unspeakable outrage of the 'Holocaust' has had no parallel in South Africa. Nevertheless, although it will shock some readers to learn this, the theory of 'race' on which both systems were built is almost identical. So is the sense which many Germans and South Africans have expressed that they are 'destined to rule' and must at all costs preserve their racial 'purity'.

In *Mein Kampf*, published eight years before he came to power, Hitler had already extolled the splendour of the Aryan race. 'Every manifestation of human culture, every product of art, science and technical skill, which we see before our eyes today, is almost exclusively the product of the Aryan creative power ... it was the Aryan alone who founded a superior type of humanity ... he is the Prometheus of mankind, from whose shining brow the divine spark of genius has at all times flashed forth ...'[17] Borrowing his ideas from Wagner's dream of Germanic greatness, Nietzsche's notion of a 'daring ruler race', and Darwin's concept of the ruthless struggle needed for survival, Hitler developed both his illusions of Aryan destiny and his insane phobia of the Jews, who, he declared, were economically, politically, culturally, religiously and morally destroying civilization.[18] The insulting and irrational language he used of them is unrepeatable. He dared even to claim that in dealing with them he would be acting on behalf of the Almighty Creator.[19] In this he was able to quote Christian scholars who had developed a 'Creation Theology' to justify racism. Paul Althaus, for example, recognizing marriage, family, race and *Volk* as God's order of creation, wrote: 'We champion the cause of the preservation of the purity of the *Volk* and of our Race.'[20] Hitler himself knew, it seems, that this racial theory of Aryan *Herrenvolk* ('master race') had no scientific basis. In private he conceded this. Yet he continued to use it because he needed it as a politician: 'With the conception of race, National Socialism will carry its revolution abroad and recast the world.'[21]

The origins of the Afrikaners' sense of divine destiny are bound up with their history. When the Dutch first arrived at the Cape of Good Hope (1652), they saw themselves as the heirs and bearers of European Christian civilization. And when their Great Trek began in 1835, and they travelled in ox wagons North and East to escape from British rule, their conviction of a special destiny increased. They saw a parallel between themselves and the Old Testament people of God. Their trek was a new exodus, a divine deliverance from alien oppression, and on their arduous journey they were tested like Israel in the wilderness. The hostile black nations they had to overcome were their equivalent to the Amalekites and the Philistines. After the Battle of Blood River, in which they defeated the Zulus, they entered into a solemn covenant with God, and henceforth thought of the Transvaal and the Orange Free State as the promised land to which God had brought them. This sacralization of their early history imprinted itself on the Afrikaner consciousness. They thought of themselves as a chosen people, an elect nation. 'Afrikanerdom is not the work of men,' said Dr D.F. Malan, the Nationalist leader who became Prime Minister in 1948, 'but the creation of God.'[22] Thus Afrikaners believed that they had a Messianic vocation, that they were born to rule, and that God had called them to preserve Christian civilization in Africa.

Added to their history (which gave them this sense of destiny) is their theology (which gave them their theory of race). It was this combination of history and theology which undergirded their determination to ensure their distinct survival by means of apartheid. For, said the Dutch Reformed Church (until 1989, see below), 'the Scriptures ... teach and uphold the ethnic diversity of the human race' and regard it as a 'positive proposition' to be preserved. Consequently, 'a political system based on the autogenous or separate development of various population groups can be justified from the Bible'.[23] The way this view of separate development was presented was often even-handed, for an equal concern was expressed that *all* racial groups would be preserved intact. Nevertheless, the impression was clearly given that the Nationalist government's primary concern was the preservation of white Afrikanerdom, and moreover in a position of superiority. Certainly Dr Verwoerd was frank enough to say to Parliament in 1963: 'Keeping South Africa white can mean only one thing, namely white domination; not leadership, not guidance, but "control" supremacy.'

The parallel between German National Socialists and South African Nationalists, then, which some will doubtless find offensive, really cannot be refuted (it is not an accident that a number of South African political leaders studied at German universities in the thirties). It lies in the resolve at all costs to maintain 'racial purity', and to legislate for it by prohibiting mixed marriages. In *Mein Kampf* Hitler wrote that miscegenation was to be opposed with the utmost vigour, in order to preserve the purity of Aryan stock. Intermarriage, he declared, invariably causes physical and mental degeneration. It 'is a sin against the will of the Eternal Creator'.[24] In South Africa the Prohibition of Mixed Marriages Act became law in 1949. It made marriage between 'Europeans and non-Europeans' (i.e. between 'whites' and 'non-whites') illegal, while an Act of 1968 extended this law to include South African male citizens domiciled outside the country. Professor Dupreez tried to give this legislation a theological basis. 'Is it God's will,' he asked, implying that it is not, 'that all the nations he has created in such rich diversity should now be equalized and assimilated, through intermarriage, to a uniform and mixed race?'[25]

In response to this Nazi and South African fear of 'bastardization', two points need to be made. First, there is no such thing as pure racial stock. We are all of us mongrels. 'Not one of the major human groups is unmixed, nor is any one of its ethnic groups pure; all are, indeed, much mixed and of exceedingly complex descent.'[26] 'Pure British blood', for example, is a figment of the imagination. At the very least we are a mixture of Jute, Celt, Goth, Saxon, Roman and Norman. And there is certainly a small percentage (6 per cent) of black blood in Afrikaners. Secondly, as Ashley Montagu puts it,

> one of the most strongly entrenched popular superstitions is the belief that interbreeding or crossing between 'races' ... results in inferior offspring ... The commonly employed stereotype has it that the half-caste inherits all the bad and none of the good qualities of the parental stocks ... There is not a particle of truth in any of these statements ... The truth seems to be that, far from being deleterious to the resulting offspring and the generations following them, interbreeding between different ethnic groups is from the biological and every other standpoint highly advantageous to mankind ... It is through the agency of interbreeding that nature in the form of man's genetic system shows its creative power.[27]

Christians will dislike both Dr Montagu's personification of 'nature' and his references to 'interbreeding' (a word more appropriate to animals than humans), but these expressions in no way affect the point he is making. He goes on to quote Lord Bryce in 1902 that 'all the great peoples of the world are the result of a mixing of races',[28] and then gives numerous examples, like crosses between Tahitian women and the English mutineers from the *Bounty*, between Australian aboriginals and whites, between American Indians and Europeans, between black and white Americans, the ethnic mixture in Hawaii, and so on.[29]

Change in South Africa

During the second half of the eighties in South Africa a number of Christian statements were issued and a number of events took place which, although expressive of different viewpoints, gave ground for hope that the whole apartheid structure would be completely destroyed.

In September 1985 Michael Cassidy and nearly 400 other Christian leaders from a variety of races and denominations launched the National Initiative for Reconciliation. Describing the Church as 'a community of hope', its statement affirmed the sovereignty of God, called for humility, repentance, prayer and fasting before the Cross, espoused non-violence even at the cost of suffering, and urged President Botha to end the State of Emergency, release detainees, and begin talks with representative leaders with a view to eliminating discrimination.

A few weeks later a group of about 150 black theologians issued the *Kairos Document*. Passionate in concern and shrill in tone, it sought to relate liberation theology to the *kairos*, the contemporary South African crisis, and outlined the three options. The first it called the 'State Theology' of the Afrikaner churches, which justified the racist status quo by an appeal to Romans 13, the need for 'law and order' and the threat of communism. This theology, it declared, 'is not only heretical, it is blasphemous'. Secondly, there was the 'Church Theology' of the English-speaking churches which, though cautiously critical of apartheid, sought reconciliation without repentance, and peace without justice. This too was rejected. The third option (which was ardently commended) was a 'Prophetic Theology'. Claiming to return to the Bible and its prophetic tradition, it identified the nationalist government as 'the oppressor' and declared it guilty of such tyranny that it had forfeited its legitimacy. The right stance to adopt towards such a regime, therefore, was not negotiation but confrontation. The document ended with a 'challenge to action' through the Church's solidarity with the oppressed, and through campaigns and protests, civil disobedience, and participation in the armed struggle for liberation.

In July 1986 130 black 'Concerned Evangelicals' published their hard-hitting *Evangelical Witness in South Africa*. Consciously interacting with the *Kairos Document*, although not specifically addressing it, they wrote a courageous, outspoken essay in evangelical self-criticism. For here were black evangelicals deliberately identifying with their white fellow-evangelicals in order to condemn the whole evangelical constituency for its Greek dualism (being concerned for people's 'spiritual', as opposed to their 'material', welfare), its western capitalistic conservatism, its pursuit of reconciliation without repentance, its misuse of Romans 13 to defend the status quo, the patronizing attitude of whites (even many missionaries) to blacks, ulterior motives in evangelism (especially to secure the subservience of black converts to an injust regime), and gospel-preaching which was silent about the brutalities of the apartheid system. Alongside these criticisms, *Evangelical Witness* called for true repentance. That is, it made a radical and comprehensive demand for change.

Then in October 1986 the Dutch Reformed Church issued *Church and Society*, which was a 'Testimony' approved by its synod. It was a thorough exposition of 'Basic Scriptural Principles' and 'Practical Implications', in the course of which the following astonishing statements were made: 'Racism is a grievous sin which no person or church may defend or practise ... As a moral aberration, it deprives a human being of his dignity, his obligations and his rights. It must be rejected and opposed in all its manifestations' (para. 112). Again, 'apartheid ... a forced separation and division of peoples, cannot be considered a biblical imperative. The attempt to justify such a prescription as derived from the Bible must be recognized as an error and be denounced' (para. 305), for it 'contravenes the very essence of neighbourly love and righteousness, and inevitably the human dignity of all involved' (para. 306). This was an extraordinary *volte-face* for a church which previously had supported and defended apartheid.

It seems to be of great significance that in 1985 and 1986 these four Christian documents, in spite of the distinction between so-called 'state', 'church' and 'prophetic' theologies, should all have condemned apartheid as an indefensible system and have committed themselves to its abolition. Their united witness and protest must have had a significant influence on the government.

During this same period some important events, in the state rather than the Church, also took place. In 1986 the hated Pass Laws, which for 40 years had required non-whites to carry their pass books and which had decreed where they might live and work, were abolished. Then in March 1989 a distinguished judicial commission, appointed by the government and chaired by Mr Justice Olivier, called in its report (1) for the total dismantling of apartheid, (2) for the repeal of two of its main legal pillars, the Group Areas Act (which forbade residential integration) and the Population Registration Act (which made classification by race compulsory), both passed in 1950, and (3) for a universal franchise which would inevitably lead to black majority rule. The same year Mr F.W. de Klerk replaced Mr P.W. Botha as President and immediately signalled the direction in which he intended to move by releasing some long-imprisoned leaders of the African National Congress (though not at first intending to release its acknowledged senior leader, Nelson Mandela), and by turning a blind eye to the ANC marches and rallies which followed. Meanwhile, the whole world, outraged by the continuance of apartheid and what Michael Cassidy called 'its de-humanizing awfulness',[30] was waiting, hoping, praying and agitating for the multi-racial society which must one day take its place.

During the 1990s, with almost bewildering speed, the structures of apartheid were dismantled and a democratic South Africa was born. In 1990 Nelson Mandela was released from prison after 26 years, talks began between the Nationalist Party and the African National Congress, the state of emergency was lifted, and the ANC agreed to cease their armed struggle. At the same time violence continued, much of it between the ANC and the Zulu 'Inkatha' movement, fuelled by white police.

In 1991 Nelson Mandela was elected ANC president without opposition, and a significant turning point was reached when official multi-party talks began at the Convention for a Democratic South Africa (CODESA). In 1992 the National Party's referendum resulted in a 69 per cent vote for a continuation of the reform process initiated by President F.W. de Klerk. But CODESA reached a stalemate, and serious Inkatha violence led to strike action by the ANC. By the end of the year, however, official negotiations had resumed, culminating in plans for a five-year power-sharing 'Government of National Unity'. It was fitting that the 1993 Nobel Peace Prize was awarded jointly to Nelson Mandela and F.W. de Klerk. The general election of 27 April 1994 won the ANC 252 of Parliament's 400 seats, brought Nelson Mandela to the presidency, and paved the way for a new constitution.

The Truth and Reconciliation Commission was brought into being in 1995, with Archbishop Desmond Tutu as its chairman. It has been a remarkable initiative inspired by Christian principles, and based on the final clause of the Interim Constitution which reads:

This Constitution provides a historic bridge between the past of a deeply divided society characterised by strife, conflict, untold suffering and injustice, and a future founded on the recognition of human rights, democracy, peaceful co-existence and development opportunities for all South Africans, irrespective of colour, race, class, belief or sex.

The Commission rightly brackets 'truth' and 'reconciliation', since its primary brief has been to investigate, discover and publish the truth about human rights violations, as the only basis on which the perpetrators could be forgiven and their victims (or their relatives) could receive both limited reparation and the restoration of honour and dignity. Reconciliation is offered to those (1) who have offended against human rights between 1960 and 1995, (2) whose offence was politically motivated, (3) who make a full disclosure of all the relevant facts, and (4) who apply for amnesty.

British attitudes and tensions

There is no need to deny that British colonial rule brought some positive good to the countries colonized, not so much in material terms (e.g. roads and railways), as in education, health care and standards of public justice. Yet these benefits have tended to be eclipsed by the offensive attitude of superiority implicit in 'the British Raj mentality'. Sometimes, I regret to say, this was expressed in racial terms ominously reminiscent of the German and South African outlook we have just considered. Cecil Rhodes, for example, spoke of 'the predominance of the Anglo-Saxon race' and of the need to preserve it. And successive British Secretaries of State for the Colonies talked similarly, even using the language of 'destiny', although fortunately such an illusion was never embodied in official policy.

Racial pride remained, however. Consequently, as Margery Perham demonstrated in her 1961 Reith Lectures *The Colonial Reckoning*, Africans felt themselves to be 'humiliated rather than oppressed', and the East African cry for *uhuru* (freedom) was not primarily for political independence but for personal dignity.[31] Similarly, to Jomo Kenyatta the quest for the independence of Kenya was 'not just a question of Africans ruling themselves, though that was the first thing', but also 'an end to the colour bar, to the racist slang of the settler clubs, to the white man's patronizing attitudes of half a century and more'.[32] At a political rally at Wundanyi in January 1962 Kenyatta said about his attitude to Europeans: 'I am not against anyone. I am only against *ubwana*, the boss mentality.'[33]

This British boss mentality was perhaps even more obvious in India. Paul Scott has brought it to life in his 'Raj Quartet' novels on the decline and fall of British India, perhaps specially in the first, *The Jewel in the Crown*. Its hero is Hari Kumar (whose name is anglicized as 'Harry Coomer'), who was sent for a while to a public school in Britain and on his return home experienced a painful tension between his English and Indian identities. The British élite looked through him. He felt he had become invisible to white people, for 'in India an Indian and an Englishman could never meet on equal terms'.[34] It would be hard to resist Arnold Toynbee's verdict that 'the English Protestant rulers of India ... distinguished themselves from all other contemporary Western rulers over non-Western peoples by the rigidity with which they held aloof from their subjects'.[35]

The British colonial record is a necessary background to understanding the last 40 years of racial tensions in Britain. It may be dated from 1958, when racial conflict flared up in Notting Hill, London, and in Nottingham, and may be considered under the headings of immigration, race relations and institutional racism.

(1) Immigration

It was the British Nationality Act of 1948 which defined a British citizen as anybody who had been born in Britain or in a British colony, and which gave citizens freedom of entry and settlement. From then onwards, however, British immigration law has become steadily more restrictive and racially motivated. The Commonwealth Immigrants Act of 1962 removed the automatic right to enter and settle, although the Act of 1968 gave it to some East African Asians during the Kenyan government's programme of Africanization. The Immigration Act of 1971 went further and introduced a distinction between 'patrials' (with at least one grandparent who had been born in the UK) and 'non-patrials', giving the former the right of entry but denying it to the latter even if they had lived in Britain for years. Of course every country has the right and duty to limit the number of immigrants it can welcome. What made many Christians ashamed about this legislation, however, was first that it reduced some former citizens to the status of aliens and secondly that it was weighted against *coloured* immigrants (e.g. no restriction was placed on immigrants from the Republic of Ireland). The churches protested vigorously against this concealed racism, which is what released cabinet papers have shown it to be. At the same time, we were very thankful that in 1972 Ugandan Asians evicted by Idi Amin were granted a free entry into Britain.

The British Nationality Act of 1981, however, travelled further down the road of restriction. It formally abolished the *jus soli* ('law of the soil'), which for hundreds of years had granted British citizenship to all those born on British territory. In its place the Act established three distinct citizenship categories. 'British citizenship' was granted only to those whose parents were British or 'settled' (with unrestricted stay). The other two categories were 'British Dependent Territory citizens' and 'British Overseas citizens', who would be mostly coloured people and would have no right of abode. Despite lobbying by the churches, this Act failed to express the true, multi-racial, character of British society.[36]

These 35 years of restrictive immigration law have caused acute suffering to many innocent people. For example, the abolition of the *jus soli* means that an appreciable number of families, whose children were born in the UK and have been brought up here for even 10–15 years, no longer have the right of abode and have had to face the trauma of deportation. The booklet *Breaking up the Family* (Churches Commission for Racial Justice) provides several case studies. The number of deportations reached a peak of 5,000 in 1993.

Another special case is that of asylum seekers. Church leaders fought hard against the 1996 Asylum and Immigration Bill during its passage through Parliament. They secured some amendments, but in substance it remains unchanged, and is harsh towards innocent people whose only fault is that they are seeking asylum. Many have even been held in detention (i.e. prison) without trial.

The CCRJ paper *The Churches, Immigration Law and Sanctuary* (1995) recommends amnesty as a compassionate alternative to deportation, and supports those churches which – as a last resort – offer sanctuary to people threatened with deportation, provided that (1) there is 'a well-founded fear of persecution' or (2) there is 'a serious threat to family life' or (3) there would be 'a basic denial of justice and compassion'.

New Labour's 1997 election manifesto promised to streamline appeals by visitors denied a visa, and to make their 'immigration and asylum procedures far more fair and efficient'. Jack Straw, Home Secretary, has also promised to recognize a new offence of 'racial harassment'. We now wait hopefully for these promises to be redeemed.[37]

(2) Race relations

The sixties and seventies, in which the British government's immigration policy was developed, were also the period of race relations law. Indeed, Christian observers see a fundamental incompatibility between them, in that the Immigration Acts were racially discriminatory, while the Race Relations Acts aimed at promoting racial harmony. Yet this reflected the inconsistencies of British society in which the voices of both fanaticism and moderation could be heard. On the one hand, racial tension was fomented by Enoch Powell's speeches and by the National Front. On the other, there was a widespread desire for inter-racial respect and peace. Enoch Powell was MP for Wolverhampton South West, near Birmingham. He spoke of the 'madness' of allowing such a large inflow of coloured immigrants, of 'watching the nation heaping up its own funeral pyre', of 'seeing the River Tiber foaming with much blood', and of Britons 'becoming strangers in their own country'.

In 1967 the National Front was formed out of a coalition of extreme right-wing movements. Its declared policy was to halt immigration, promote the repatriation of coloured immigrants, support white Rhodesia and fight communism. Its leaders (Colin Jordan, John Tyndall and Martin Webster) had all been involved in Nazi activities and been ardent admirers of Hitler. Here are some representative statements which these three leaders have made. Colin Jordan said in 1959, 'I loathe the Blacks – we're fighting a war to clear them out of Britain'.[38] John Tyndall (chairman of the National Front until 1974) wrote a pamphlet in 1966 entitled *Six Principles of British Nationalism*, whose fourth was concerned with the preservation of the British 'race': 'We therefore oppose racial integration and stand for racial separateness.'[39] And Martin Webster wrote in 1975 that 'racialism is the only scientific and logical basis for nationalism … we seek to preserve the identity of the British nation … If the British people are destroyed by racial interbreeding, then the British nation will cease to exist.'[40] It is not difficult to detect in these intemperate utterances the same myth of racial purity and racial superiority which found expression in Nazi policy and in the doctrine of apartheid. I am heartily ashamed to have to record that this myth is held by anyone in Britain, even though the National Front is only a tiny minority.

The British National Party, founded in 1982, is larger, however, and even put up more than 50 candidates for the 1997 General Election. Although it avoids the insolent racial rhetoric of the National Front, its manifesto calls for a ban on the immigration of non-whites, and for the repatriation or resettlement of non-whites already here, until Britain becomes 'a white country' again.

But the mood of the country as a whole was much more accurately mirrored in the laws governing race relations. The 1968 Race Relations Act created the Race Relations Board, whose brief was both to investigate complaints of racial discrimination and to promote racial integration. Then the 1976 Race Relations Act created the Commission for Racial Equality, which was given some teeth to enforce the law; made it unlawful to discriminate on the basis of race in such areas as employment and education; made 'incitement to racial hatred' a criminal offence; gave local authorities the responsibility to eliminate discrimination and to promote equal opportunity and racial harmony; and permitted 'positive action' in favour of ethnic minorities, e.g. in training schemes.

Granted the existence of these two contradictory moods (the one inflammatory and the other conciliatory), it is hardly surprising that they came into collision. Already in 1976 and 1979 there were clashes in Southall (West London) fuelled by the National Front. And more serious street riots broke out between 1980 and 1983 in Bristol, Brixton (South London), Toxteth (Liverpool), Manchester, Nottingham, Leeds and other cities. Local social workers attributed the violence to widespread bitterness over the racially prejudiced British Nationality Act (1981) and over the decay and deprivation of the inner city, involving disadvantage to blacks in housing, education and employment.

Lord Scarman was commissioned by the Home Secretary to investigate and report. He concluded that these communal disturbances were not premeditated, but spontaneous, and that 'there was a strong racial element in the disorders'. In short, 'the riots were essentially an outburst of anger and resentment by young black people against the police'.[41] This statement identifies two main problems, the first social and racial, and the second the behaviour of the police. As to the former, Lord Scarman concluded: ' "Institutional racism" does not exist in Britain; but racial disadvantage and its nasty associate, racial discrimination, have not yet been eliminated. They poison minds and attitudes: they are, and so long as they remain will continue to be, a potent factor of unrest.'[42] He recommended temporary reverse discrimination – that is, discrimination in favour of ethnic minorities – in order to redress this balance.

(3) Institutional racism

There was general appreciation for the Scarman Report on account of its candour and lack of bias. Lord Scarman had approached the Brixton situation without prejudice or presuppositions, and had listened carefully to all opinions. This did not prevent people, however, from disagreeing (even incredulously) with his statement that there was no 'institutional racism' in Britain. Our reaction will of course depend on our definition, but 'institutional racism' is normally taken to denote a racial discrimination which goes beyond personal attitudes and is embedded in social structures. This certainly exists in Britain. Two examples will suffice.

The first concerns the police and the whole criminal justice system. Lord Scarman himself alluded to this. He conceded that 'a major cause of the hostility of young blacks towards the police was loss of confidence by significant sections, though not all, of the ... public in the police'.[43] Whether justified or not, criticisms of racial prejudice and harassment were frequently levelled at them. Criticism is directed not only at the personal racist attitudes of some police officers, and at the widespread abuse of their stop-and-search powers, but also at the injustices which black people believe to be ingrained in the system. David Haslam writes: 'Once black people are arrested and charged, it becomes increasingly difficult for them to demonstrate their innocence. Many say it feels as if it is for them to prove their innocence rather than for the police to prove their guilt.'[44]

Here are further aspects of institutional racism in the justice system which are extremely disturbing. (1) Far too few police officers come from ethnic minorities – less than 3 per cent of the Metropolitan Police, for example. There are also too few black judges and magistrates. (2) The Police Complaints Authority is not the entirely independent body it claims to be. Its members are appointed by the Home Secretary, and it is a case of police investigating police. Lord Scarman picked this up. He recommended greater police accountability and the introduction of a genuinely independent element into the police complaints procedure. (3) There have been too many unexplained deaths in police custody, and too many miscarriages of justice. (4) In too many major assaults on, and even murders of, black people the perpetrators have not yet been apprehended several years later. Some are notorious cases of murder like those of Stephen Lawrence, Quddus Ali and Muktar Ahmed.

Unemployment is the second area in which racism is institutional as well as personal. In his 1977 book *Racial Disadvantage in Britain*, David J. Smith stated that in employment 'there is still very substantial racial discrimination against Asians and West Indians', and that this was 'mostly based on colour prejudice'.[45] In the 1980s Bishop David Sheppard reported the same thing: 'Rates of unemployment for black people are generally more than double those for all workers of the same age group.'[46] The same disproportion has continued into the 1990s, and has even deteriorated. *Labour Market Trends* (June 1996) reported that white unemployment was 9.5 per cent for men and 6.5 per cent for women, whereas the corresponding figures for people from ethnic minorities were 20 per cent for men and 17 per cent for women – 'a vast and shocking difference'.[47] Worse still is the unemployment rate among blacks under 25: it is nearly three times higher than among whites. John Monks, General Secretary of the Trades Union Congress, was not exaggerating when he called the level of racial discrimination in the jobs market 'intolerable'.[48] The Churches' Commission for Racial Justice is rightly encouraging companies to adopt the so-called 'Wood-Sheppard Principles on Race Equality in Employment'. Named after Bishop Wilfred Wood of Croydon, the Church of England's first black bishop, and Bishop David Sheppard, formerly bishop of Liverpool, these principles call for 'positive action' to redress the current inequalities.[49]

In sum, racism can be both personal and institutional. It also has two origins. One is a pseudo-scientific myth, and the other is pure prejudice. The myth, which is foundational to Hitler's anti-Semitism, South Africa's apartheid and Britain's National Front, was defined by UNESCO in 1967 as a 'false claim that there is a scientific basis for arranging groups hierarchically in terms of psychological and cultural characteristics that are immutable and innate'. The popular prejudice is not based on any particular theory, but is a psychological reaction to people of other ethnic groups arising usually from resentment, fear or pride.

What is needed is an equally powerful conviction that racism is an affront to the unique dignity of human beings. Nothing I have read has helped me to understand better the damage which racism does to people than *The Autobiography of Malcolm X*. His red-hot anger was due in part to 'the world's most monstrous crime' of slavery, in part to the black American's economic dependence on white America, but above all to the humiliation caused by the white man's 'malignant superiority complex'.[50] The problem, he writes, is not 'civil rights' but 'human rights': 'Human rights! Respect as *human beings*! That's what the American black masses want. That's the true problem. The black masses want not to be shrunk from as though they are plague ridden. They want not to be walled up in slums, in the ghettoes, like animals. They want to live in an open, free society where they can walk with their heads up, like men and women.'[51]

In his well-researched and passionate book *Race for the Millennium*, 'a challenge to church and society', David Haslam has a chapter entitled 'The Necessity of Struggle'. In it he outlines 'three stages through which white people need to go before true reconciliation can occur'. The first is '*listening* to black people', the second '*repenting* of white sin', and the third '*responding* in committed, sacrificial action to the inequalities and injustices to which black people are subject'.[52] Only then, he writes, does 'the opportunity for reconciliation' arise.[53]

There are encouraging signs that we who belong to the Church's evangelical community are at last waking up to our racial responsibilities. Evangelical Christians for Racial Justice was founded in 1972 and over the years has maintained a conscientious witness. Its 'Christian Manifesto on Race' is based on six principles: (1) the human race is one race; (2) the human race is diverse; (3) the human race is fallen; (4) Christ died for all and is Lord of all; (5) the Christian Church is a new humanity in Christ; (6) God's people should seek justice for all.

Moreover, in preparation for the National Assembly of Evangelicals which met in Bournemouth in November 1996, an Evangelical Alliance consultation survey revealed that 62 per cent of member churches and 70 per cent of member societies agreed that 'addressing racial injustice in the UK should be a higher priority for the evangelical churches than at present'. The Bournemouth Declaration also acknowledged our shared responsibility 'to oppose all forms of racism in church and society'.

Biblical foundations for multi-racialism

We turn from the realities of racial mythology, prejudice and tension in the contemporary world to the biblical vision of a multi-racial society. It was thoroughly developed by the apostle Paul in his famous sermon to the Athenian philosophers (Acts 17:22–31). Ancient Athens was a centre of ethnic, cultural and religious pluralism. From the fifth century BC it had been the foremost Greek city-state, and when it was incorporated into the Roman Empire, it became one of the leading cosmopolitan cities in the world. As for religions, it is easy to understand Paul's comment that the Athenians were 'very religious', for according to a Roman satirist, it was 'easier to find a god there than a man'. The city was crammed with innumerable temples, shrines, altars, images and statues.

What then was Paul's attitude to this multi-racial, multi-cultural and multi-religious situation? He made four affirmations.

First, he proclaimed *the unity of the human race*, or *the God of Creation*. God is the Creator and Lord of the world and everything in it, he said. He gives to all human beings their life and breath and everything else. From one man he made every nation of men, that they should inhabit the whole earth, so that human beings would seek and find him, though he is not far from any of us. For 'in him we live and move and have our being' and 'we are his offspring'. From this portrayal of the living God as Creator, Sustainer and Father of all humankind, the apostle deduces the folly and evil of idolatry. But he could equally well have deduced from it the folly and evil of racism. For if he is the God of all human beings, this will affect our attitude to them as well as to him.

Although in terms of an intimate personal relationship God is the Father of those he adopts into his family by his sheer grace, and our brothers and sisters are fellow members of his family, nevertheless in more general terms God is the Father of all humankind, since all are his 'offspring' by creation, and every human being is our brother or sister. Being equally created by him and like him, we are equal in his sight in worth and dignity, and therefore have an equal right to respect and justice. Paul also traces our human origin to Adam, the 'one man' from whom God made us all. This is confirmed by the known homogeneity of the human race, which is asserted even by scholars who have no belief in Adam. Here is the statement of Ashley Montagu, the physical anthropologist: 'Concerning the origin of the living varieties of man we can say little more than that there are many reasons for believing that a single stock gave rise to all of them. All varieties of man belong to the same species and have the same remote ancestry. This is a conclusion to which all the relevant evidence of comparative anatomy, palæontology, serology and genetics points.'[54] As for human blood, apart from the four blood groups and the Rh factor (which are present in all ethnic groups), 'the blood of all human beings is in every respect the same.'[55]

This human unity is not destroyed by interbreeding. We should totally reject the fears of miscegenation entertained by Afrikaners, and Hitler's biological myth which is being revived by the National Front. In 1964 John Tyndall launched the 'Greater Britain Movement', whose official programme said: 'For the protection of British blood, racial laws will be enacted forbidding marriage between Britons and non-Aryans … A pure, strong, healthy British race will be regarded as the principal guarantee of Britain's future.'[56] But there is no such substance as 'British blood'.

Secondly, Paul proclaimed *the diversity of ethnic cultures,* or *the God of History.* The living God not only made every nation from one man, that they should inhabit the earth, but also 'determined the times set for them and the exact places where they should live' (Acts 17:26; cf. Deuteronomy 32:8). Thus the times and the places of the nations are in the hand of God. We may not use this fact to justify the conquest and annexation of foreign territory, although even these historical developments are not beyond God's sovereign control. Probably Paul is alluding to the primeval command to multiply and fill the earth. For such dispersal under God's blessing inevitably resulted in the development of distinctive cultures, quite apart from the later confusing of languages and the scattering under his judgement at Babel.

Now culture is the complement of nature. What is 'natural' is God-given and inherited; what is 'cultural' is man-made and learned. Culture is an amalgam of beliefs, values, customs and institutions developed by each society and transmitted to the next generation. Human cultures are ambiguous because human beings are ambiguous. 'Because man is God's creature, some of his culture is rich in beauty and goodness. Because he is fallen, all of it is tainted with sin and some of it is demonic.'[57]

Scripture celebrates the colourful mosaic of human cultures. It even declares that the New Jerusalem will be enriched by them, since 'the kings of the earth will bring their splendour into it', and 'the glory and honour of the nations will be brought into it' (Revelation 21:24, 26). If they will enrich human life and community in the end, they can begin to do so now. Paul was a product of three cultures. By descent and upbringing a 'Hebrew of the Hebrews', he also possessed Roman citizenship and had absorbed Greek language and concepts. We too can enhance our human life by learning other languages and experiencing other cultures. We need to ensure, therefore, that a multi-racial society is not a mono-cultural society. We must simultaneously assert both the unity of the human race and the diversity of ethnic cultures.

The South African Nationalist Party made much of this diversity. South Africa, they argued, had never been a single nation, but a kaleidoscope of distinct racial groups, each with its own national and cultural identity. What was needed, therefore, they deduced, was not a single integrated state (the 'melting pot' model), but 'multi-national development' or 'separate freedoms' – that is, apartheid – each racial group preserving and advancing its own uniqueness. 'We do not want intermingling of racial groups in South Africa,' wrote Professor Dr J.C.G. Klotze. 'It is in accordance with Scripture that the ideal situation would be for each people to inhabit its own country (Acts 17:26)'.[58] Apart from the question of whether 'nations' and 'racial groups' are the same thing, and whether Acts 17:26 includes the latter, the South African apartheid policy seems to have depended on two other errors. First, the assumption was that distinct cultures could be preserved only if racial groups were segregated from each other. But this is patently untrue, as we know in Britain where the Irish, Welsh, Scots and English intermingle, while their cultural distinctives also survive. Not only is it unnecessary to keep apart in order to preserve our own cultures, but it is impossible to do so if we are to enjoy each other's, as God surely means us to do. Secondly, the assumption underlying the policy to segregate racial groups in order to preserve them was that to integrate them would inevitably mean to destroy them. But integration is not the same as assimilation, and does not necessarily lead to it. On the contrary, although intermarriage should be fully permissible, natural affinities and cultural tensions are likely to keep the number of mixed marriages comparatively small.

Thirdly, Paul proclaimed *the finality of Jesus Christ,* or *the God of Revelation.* He concluded his sermon with God's call to universal repentance because of the coming universal judgement, for which God had both fixed the day and appointed the judge (verses 30–1). Paul refused to acquiesce in the religious pluralism of Athens or applaud it as a living museum of religious faiths. Instead, the city's idolatry provoked him (verse 16) – probably to jealousy for the honour of the living and true God. So he called on the city's people to turn in repentance from their idols to God.

We learn, then, that a respectful acceptance of the diversity of *cultures* does not imply an equal acceptance of the diversity of *religions*. The richness of each particular culture should be appreciated, but not the idolatry which may lie at its heart. For we cannot tolerate any rivals to Jesus Christ, believing as we do that God has spoken fully and finally through him, and that he is the only Saviour, who died, and rose again, and will one day come to be the world's Judge.

Fourthly, Paul proclaimed *the glory of the Christian Church*, or *the God of Redemption*. It is clearer in some of the apostle's letters than it is in Luke's record of this sermon that Jesus died and rose to create a new and reconciled community, his Church. Thus the flow of history is being reversed. The Old Testament is the story of human scattering, of nations spreading abroad, falling apart, fighting. But the New Testament is the story of the divine ingathering of nations into a single international society. It is hinted at here in verse 34, in which we are told that a few men believed, one of whom was named Dionysius, and a woman named Damaris, and a number of others. So here was the nucleus of the new community, in which men and women of all ages, and of all racial, cultural and social origins, find their oneness in Christ.

Since God has made all nations and determines their times and places, it is clearly right for each of us to be conscious of our nationality and grateful for it. But since God has also brought us into his new society, he is thereby calling us into a new internationalism. Every Christian knows this tension, and nobody more keenly than Paul who was at the same time a patriotic Jew and the apostle to the Gentiles. Christian 'internationalism' does not mean that our membership of Christ and his Church obliterates our nationality, any more than it does our masculinity or femininity. It means rather that, while our racial, national, social and sexual distinctions remain, they no longer divide us. They have been transcended in the unity of the family of God (Galatians 3:28). Raymond Johnston was right to say that 'a proper understanding of nationhood calls attention to

258 ▶ New Issues Facing Christians Today

the human need for *roots*, a security and an identity mediated by the community, on the basis of which each individual knows that he "belongs".'[59] Yet it needs to be added that in Christ we have found even deeper roots, and an even stronger security and identity, for through him God has called us into a new and wider unity.

The Church must therefore exhibit its multi-racial, multi-national and multi-cultural nature. There has been considerable debate inrecent years whether a local church could or should ever be culturally homogeneous. A consultation on this issue concluded that no church should ever acquiesce in such a condition: 'All of us are agreed that in many situations a homogeneous unit church can be a legitimate and authentic church. Yet we are also agreed that it can never be complete in itself. Indeed, if it remains in isolation, it cannot reflect the universality and diversity of the Body of Christ. Nor can it grow to maturity. Therefore every homogeneous unit church must take active steps to broaden its fellowship in order to demonstrate visibly the unity and the variety of Christ's Church.'[60] The Statement goes on to suggest how this might be done.

Only a true theology, the biblical revelation of God, can deliver us from racial pride and prejudice. Because he is the God of Creation, we affirm the unity of the human race. Because he is the God of History, we affirm the diversity of ethnic cultures. Because he is the God of Revelation, we affirm the finality of Jesus Christ. And because he is the God of Redemption, we affirm the glory of the Christian Church. Whatever policies for racial integration may be developed, we should try to ensure that they will reflect these doctrines. Because of the unity of humankind we demand equal rights and equal respect for racial minorities. Because of the diversity of ethnic groups we renounce cultural imperialism and seek to preserve all those riches of culture which are compatible with Christ's lordship. Because of the finality of Christ, we affirm that religious freedom includes the right to propagate the gospel. Because of the glory of the Church, we must seek to rid ourselves of any lingering racism and strive to make it a model of harmony between races, in which the multi-racial dream comes true.

Chapter 12

POVERTY, WEALTH AND SIMPLICITY

Wealth increasing for evermore, and its beneficiaries, rich in hire-purchase, stupefied with the telly and with sex, comprehensively educated, told by Professor Hoyle how the world began and by Bertrand Russell where it will end; venturing forth on the broad highways, three lanes a side … blood spattering the tarmac as an extra thrill; heaven lying about them in the supermarket, the rainbow ending in the nearest bingo hall, leisure burgeoning out in multitudinous shining aerials rising like dreaming spires into the sky … many mansions, mansions of light and chromium, climbing ever upwards. This kingdom, surely, can only be for posterity an unending source of wry derision – always assuming there is to be any posterity. The backdrop, after all, is the mushroom cloud; as the Gadarene herd frisk and frolic, they draw ever nearer to the cliff's precipitous edge.[1]

Thus Malcolm Muggeridge satirizes the affluence of the West, its materialism, superficiality and selfishness. It is bad enough in itself and seems to be on the increase. When contrasted with the *barriadas* and *favelas* of Latin America, and the ghettoes, slums and shanty towns of other parts of the world, it becomes inexcusable. Not that the contrast between wealth and poverty corresponds neatly with the North-South divide. For the OPEC countries are rich, and so are some East Asian communities.

Moreover, poverty has not been eliminated from North America or Europe. In the United States in 1995 there were 36.4 million people living below the poverty line, or 13.8 per cent of the population.[2] In Britain in 1995 there were still 9.7 million people, adults and children, living on incomes at or below the level of supplementary benefit, which is the state's definition of the boundary between poverty and subsistence.[3] And more than twice that number live in relative poverty. Hence the launching in Britain in July 1982 of 'Church Action on Poverty'. And three years later Britain was shocked by the carefully researched findings of *Faith in the City*, the report of the Archbishop of Canterbury's Commission on Urban Priority Areas. 'Chapter after chapter of our Report,' its conclusion begins, 'tells the same story: that a growing number of people are excluded by poverty or powerlessness from sharing in the common life of our nation. A substantial minority – perhaps as many as one person in every four or five across the nation, and a much higher proportion in the UPAs – are forced to live on the margins of poverty or below the threshold of an acceptable standard of living.'[4]

The truth is that a grave disparity between wealth and poverty is to be found not only between nations, but within most nations as well. As the Latin American Roman Catholic bishops put it at Puebla in 1979: 'The cruel contrast between luxurious wealth and extreme poverty, which is so visible throughout our continent and which is further aggravated by the corruption that often invades public and professional life, shows the great extent to which our nations are dominated by the idol of wealth.'[5]

Three approaches to poverty

How should Christians approach the harsh fact of poverty in the contemporary world?

First, we could approach the problem *rationally*, with cool statistical detachment. Indeed, this is where we must begin. There are almost 6 billion inhabitants of planet earth, a quarter of whom remain in severe poverty. The 1997 Human Development Report, while enthusiastically recognizing that 'progress in reducing poverty over the 20th century is remarkable and unprecedented', also notes that 'the advances have been uneven and marred by setbacks – and poverty remains pervasive'. Indeed, 'an estimated 1.3 billion people survive on less than the equivalent of $1 a day … Nearly a billion people are illiterate … Some 840 million go hungry or face food insecurity.'[6]

One subject which brings this home to us is that of the provision of clean, safe water. In the West it is piped into our homes and instantly available to us at the turn of a tap. None of us would dream of regarding this as a luxury. We take it for granted. In the developing world only 68 per cent of the population have access to safe drinking water, while in the least developed countries this percentage drops to 38.[7] Almost 2 billion people in the Third World are without access to proper sanitation facilities so that 'waterborne diseases … and a wide array of serious or fatal diarrheal illnesses are responsible for more than 35 per cent of the deaths of young children in Africa, Asia and Latin America.'[8] That is why the United Nations declared the 1980s the International Drinking Water Supply and Sanitation Decade. Although wide-scale improvements were made during the decade and have continued since, the needs continue to be great.

Meanwhile, whereas one-fifth of the world's population lack the basic necessities for survival, rather more than another one-fifth live in affluence and consume about four-fifths of the world's income. In 1988 the 'total disbursements' from these wealthy nations to the Third World 'amounted to $92 billion' (less than 10 per cent of worldwide spending on armaments), 'but this was more than offset by the total debt service of $142 billion, resulting in a net negative transfer of some $50 billion' from the Third World to the developed countries.[9] More recently 'annual losses to developing countries from unequal access to trade, labour and finance have been esti-mated at $500 billion, 10 times what they receive in foreign aid.'[10] The gross disparity between wealth and poverty constitutes a social injustice with which the Christian conscience cannot come to terms.

Secondly, we could approach the phenomenon of poverty *emo-tionally*, with the hotblooded indignation aroused by the sights, sounds and smells of human need. When I recently visited Calcutta airport, the sun had already set. Over the whole city hung a pall of malodorous smoke from the burning of cowdung on a myriad fires. Outside the airport an emaciated woman clutching an emaciated baby stretched out an emaciated hand for *baksheesh*. A man, whose legs had both been amputated above the knee, dragged himself along the pavement with his hands. I later learned that over a quarter of a million homeless people sleep on the streets at night, and during the day hang their blanket – often their only possession – on some convenient railing. My most poignant experience was to see men and women scavenging in the city garbage dumps like dogs. For ex-treme poverty is demeaning; it reduces human beings to the level of animals. To be sure, Christians should be provoked by the *idolatry* of a Hindu city, as Paul was by the idols in Athens, and moved to evangelism. But, like Jesus when he saw the hungry crowds, we should also be moved with compassion to feed them (compare Acts 17:16f. with e.g., Mark 8:1–3).

It is not only the absolute poverty of Third World slums which should arouse our emotions, however, but also the relative (though real) poverty of the decayed and deprived inner-city areas of the West, which the affluent seldom if ever see. This was the emphasis which David Sheppard, Bishop of Liverpool until 1997, made in his Richard Dimbleby Lecture broadcast in 1984. He urged 'Comfortable Britain' to stand in the shoes of the 'Other Britain'. He spoke with deep feeling of youth and long-term unemployment, neglected housing, poor opportunities in schooling, and the sense of alienation, even desertion. He felt indignant, indeed angry, because poverty 'imprisons the spirit', spawns 'sick human relationships' and wastes God-given talent. He then described four 'keys' which could begin to unlock the prison.[11]

The third way, which should stimulate both our reason and our emotion simultaneously, is to approach the problem of poverty *biblically*. As we turn again to that book in which God has revealed himself and his will, we ask: how according to Scripture should we think about wealth and poverty? Is God on the side of the poor? Should we be? What does the Scripture say? Moreover, as we ask these questions, we have to resolve to listen attentively to God's Word, and not manipulate it. We have no liberty either to avoid its uncomfortable challenge, in order to retain our prejudices, or to acquiesce uncritically in the latest popular interpretations.

Psalm 113 seems a good place to begin. It is an invitation to Yahweh's servants, indeed to all people 'from the rising of the sun to the place where it sets', to praise his name, since he 'is exalted over all the nations, his glory above the heavens'. It continues:

> Who is like the LORD our God,
>   the One who sits enthroned on high,
> who stoops down to look
>   on the heavens and the earth?
> He raises the poor from the dust
>   and lifts the needy from the ash heap;
> he seats them with princes,
>   with the princes of their people.
> He settles the barren woman in her home
>   as a happy mother of children.

(verses 5–9)

The psalmist is affirming something distinctive – indeed unique – about Yahweh, which enables him to ask the rhetorical question, 'Who is like the LORD our God?' It is not just that he reigns on high, exalted above both the nations and the sky; nor only that from these lofty heights he condescends to look far below to the heavens and the earth; nor even that on the distant earth he regards with compassion the depths of human misery, the poor discarded on the scrapheaps of life and trampled in the dust by their oppressors. It is more than all these things. It is that he actually exalts the wretched of the earth; he lifts them from the depths to the heights; 'He raises the poor from the dust and … seats them with princes'. For example, he takes pity on the barren woman (whose childlessness was regarded as a disgrace) and makes her a joyful mother. That is the kind of God he is. No other god is like him. For it is not primarily the wealthy and the famous with whom he delights to fraternize. What is characteristic of him is to champion the poor, to rescue them from their misery, and to transform paupers into princes.

This affirmation is many times repeated and exemplified in Scripture, usually with its corollary that the God who lifts up the humble also puts down the proud. This was the essence of Hannah's song when after years of childlessness her son Samuel was born:

> He raises the poor from the dust
> and lifts the needy from the ash heap;
> he seats them with princes
> and has them inherit a throne of honour.

(1 Samuel 2:8)

This too was the theme of the Magnificat, which the Virgin Mary sang after learning that she (and not some famous, noble or wealthy woman) had been chosen to be the mother of God's Messiah. God had looked upon her lowly state, she said; the Mighty One had done great things for her, for which she gave him thanks and praise:

> He has performed mighty deeds with his arm;
> he has scattered those who are proud in their inmost thoughts.
> He has brought down rulers from their thrones
> but has lifted up the humble.
> He has filled the hungry with good things
> but has sent the rich away empty.

(Luke 1:51–2)

In Psalm 113, and in the experiences of Hannah and Mary, the same stark contrast is painted, although the vocabulary varies. The proud are abased and the humble exalted; the rich are impoverished and the poor enriched; the well-fed are sent away empty, and the hungry filled with good things; powerful rulers are toppled from their thrones, while the powerless and the oppressed are caused to reign like princes. 'Who is like the Lord our God?' His thoughts and ways are not ours. He is a topsy-turvy God. He turns the standards and values of the world upside down.

Jesus himself is the greatest example of this. One of his favourite epigrams seems to have been that 'everyone who exalts himself will be humbled, and he who humbles himself will be exalted' (e.g. Luke 18:14). He did not only enunciate this principle, however; he personally exhibited it. Having emptied himself of his glory, he humbled himself to serve, and his obedience took him even to the depths of the cross. 'Therefore God exalted him to the highest place …' (Philippians 2:5–11).

It is this principle, which pledges the reversal of human fortunes, which alone can bring hope to the poor. But who are the 'poor' whom God is said to 'raise'? And what does he do when he 'raises' them? These words demand definition.

Who are the poor? The paradox of poverty

A number of studies of the biblical material have been made and published.[12] They focus on the Old Testament, in which a cluster of words for poverty, deriving from six main Hebrew roots, occur more than 200 times. These may be classified in a variety of ways, but the principal division seems to be threefold. First, and economically speaking, there are *the indigent poor*, who are deprived of the basic necessities of life. Secondly, and sociologically speaking, there are the *powerless poor*, who are oppressed victims of human injustice. Thirdly, and spiritually speaking, there are *the humble poor*, who acknowledge their helplessness and look to God alone for salvation. In each case God is represented as coming to them and making their cause his own, in keeping with his characteristic that 'he raises the poor from the dust'.

The first group, *the indigent poor*, are economically deprived. They may lack food or clothing or shelter, or all three. Sometimes, as the biblical authors recognize, their poverty may be due to their

own sin, whether laziness, extravagance or gluttony. The Book of
Proverbs has much to say about this. The sluggard is exhorted to
study the ways of the ant, in order to learn wisdom. For ants gather
and store food during the summer, while sluggards stay in bed: 'A
little sleep, a little slumber, a little folding of the hands to rest – and
poverty will come on you like a bandit and scarcity like an armed
man' (Proverbs 6:6–11; cf. 24:30–4; similarly, 'lazy hands make a
man poor, but diligent hands bring wealth' (10:4; cf. 19:15; 20:13;
28:19)). Closely linked to laziness, as causing poverty, are greed
and drunkenness: 'drunkards and gluttons become poor, and
drowsiness clothes them in rags' (Proverbs 23:20ff.; cf. 21:17). Not
only did these particular sins bring individual poverty, however.
National poverty also was due to sin. For during the theocracy,
when God ruled over his people in Israel, he promised to bless their
obedience with fruitfulness of field and orchard, and to curse their
disobedience with barrenness. (see e.g. Leviticus 26; Deuteronomy
8 and 28; Isaiah 1:19ff. and 5:8ff. for national blessing and curses).

Generally speaking, however, the Old Testament writers saw
poverty as an involuntary social evil to be abolished, not tolerated,
and represented the poor (who included widows, orphans and aliens)
as people to be succoured, not blamed. They are regarded not as sinners but as 'the sinned against' – an expression popularized at the
1980 Melbourne Conference by Raymond Fung, a Baptist minister
who had spent 11 years serving factory workers in Hong Kong.[13]

In the Law, God's people were commanded not to harden their
hearts or close their hands against their poor brother or sister, but to
be generous in maintaining those who could not maintain themselves, by taking them into their home and feeding them without
charge. Their regular tithes were also to be used to support the
Levites, the aliens, the orphans and the widows (Deuteronomy
15:7ff.; Leviticus 25:35ff.; Deuteronomy 14:29; Leviticus 26:12). If
an Israelite lent money to somebody in need, he was not to charge
interest on it. If he took a pledge to secure his loan, he was not to go
into the house to fetch it, but to stand respectfully outside and wait
for it to be brought out to him. If he took as pledge his neighbour's
cloak, he was to return it before sunset because the poor person
would need it as a blanket to sleep in (Exodus 22:25; Leviticus
25:36f.; Deuteronomy 24:10f.; Exodus 22:26ff.; Deuteronomy
24:12). In particular, the support and the relief of the poor were the
obligations of the extended family towards its own members.

Employers were to pay their workers' wages promptly, the same day that they were earned. Farmers were not to reap their fields 'to the very edges', nor to go back to pick up a dropped or forgotten sheaf, nor to gather the gleanings after harvesting, nor to strip their vineyard bare, nor to gather fallen grapes, nor to go over the branches of their olive trees a second time. For the borders, the gleanings and the fallen fruit were all to be left for the poor, the alien, the widow and the orphan. They too must be allowed to share in the harvest celebrations. Every third year, a tenth of the agricultural produce was to be given to the poor. Every seventh year fields were to lie fallow, and vineyards and olive groves to be unharvested, for the benefit of the poor who could help themselves to the fruit (Leviticus 19:13; Deuteronomy 24:14ff.; Leviticus 19:9f., 23:22; Deuteronomy 16:9ff.; 24:19ff.; 14:28ff.; 26:12ff.; Exodus 23:10ff.; Leviticus 25:1ff.).

The Old Testament Wisdom Literature confirmed this teaching. One of the characteristics of a righteous man is that he 'cares about justice for the poor'; 'he is generous and lends freely', and 'has scattered abroad his gifts to the poor'; whereas 'if a man shuts his ears to the cry of the poor, he too will cry out and not be answered' (Psalm 111:1–9; Proverbs 21:13; 29:7; cf. 14:20ff.; 19:7; 31:20; Job 31:16ff.; Ezekiel 16:49). The wise teachers of Israel also grounded these duties on doctrine, namely that behind the poor Yahweh himself was standing, their Creator and Lord, so that people's attitude to him would be reflected in their attitudes to them. On the one hand, 'He who mocks the poor shows contempt for their Maker'; on the other, 'He who is kind to the poor lends to the Lord' (Proverbs 17:5; 19:17).

Jesus himself inherited this rich Old Testament legacy of care for the poor, and put it into practice. He made friends with the needy and fed the hungry. He told his disciples to sell their possessions and give alms to the poor, and when they gave a party to remember to invite the poor, the crippled, the lame and the blind, who would probably be in no position to invite them back. He also promised that in feeding the hungry, clothing the naked, welcoming the homeless and visiting the sick, they would thereby be ministering to him (Luke 12:33; 14:12ff.; Matthew 25:35–40).

The second group, *the powerless poor*, are socially or politically oppressed. It was clearly recognized in the Old Testament that poverty does not normally just happen. Although sometimes it was due to personal sin or national disobedience, and to God's judgement on them, it was usually due to the sins of others, that is, to a situation of social injustice, which easily deteriorated because the poor were not in a position to change it. We do not understand the Old Testament teaching on this subject unless we see how frequently poverty and powerlessness were bracketed. At the same time, although the poor often had no human helper, they knew that God was their champion. For 'he stands at the right hand of the needy one'. Again, 'I know that the Lord secures justice for the poor and upholds the cause of the needy' (Psalm 109:31; 140:12).

Moses' law laid emphasis on the need for impartial justice in the courts, in particular for the poor and powerless. 'Do not deny justice to your poor people in their lawsuits ... Do not accept a bribe, for a bribe blinds those who see and twists the words of the righteous.' 'Do not pervert justice; do not show partiality to the poor or favouritism to the great, but judge your neighbour fairly.' 'Do not deprive the alien or the fatherless of justice.' Moreover, the reason repeatedly given was that they themselves had been oppressed in Egypt, and the Lord had liberated them (Exodus 23:6,8; Leviticus 19:15; Deuteronomy 24:17; 27:19; 15:15).

The Wisdom books were as explicit as the Law books in demanding justice for the helpless. In Psalm 82 the judges were instructed to 'defend the cause of the weak and fatherless' and 'maintain the rights of the poor and oppressed'. In Proverbs 31 King Lemuel was exhorted by his mother to 'speak up for those who cannot speak for themselves, for the rights of all who are destitute', to 'speak up and judge fairly' and 'defend the rights of the poor and needy' (Psalm 82:1–3; Proverbs 31:8, 9; cf. Job 29:11ff.; Proverbs 22:22ff.; 29:7, 14).

It is well known that the prophets were even more outspoken. They not only urged the people and their leaders to 'seek justice, encourage the oppressed, defend the cause of the fatherless, plead the case of the widow', and conversely forbade them to 'oppress the widow or the fatherless, the alien or the poor', but were fierce in their condemnation of all injustice. Elijah rebuked King Ahab for murdering Naboth and stealing his vineyard. Amos fulminated against the rulers of Israel because in return for bribes they trampled on the heads of the poor, crushed the needy, and denied justice to the oppressed, instead of letting 'justice roll on like a river, and righteousness like a never-failing stream'. Jeremiah denounced King Jehoiakim for using forced labour to build his luxurious palace.

Other examples could be given. The national life of Israel and Judah was constantly tarnished by the exploitation of the poor. And James in the New Testament, sounding just like an Old Testament prophet, also inveighs against the rich. It is not their wealth in itself which he condemns, nor even primarily their self-indulgent luxury, but in particular their fraudulent withholding of wages from their workforce and their violent oppression of the innocent (Isaiah 1:17; Zechariah 7:8ff.; 1 Kings 21; Amos 2:6f.; 4:1ff.; 5:11ff.; 8:4ff.; 5:24; Jeremiah 22:13ff. Other examples of the prophetic stress on justice are Isaiah 3:13ff.; 5:7ff.; 10:1f.; Jeremiah 5:28ff.; Ezekiel 18:10ff.; James 5:1ff.).

In contrast to this dark tradition of the prophets' diatribe against injustice, their predictions of the Messiah's righteous reign shine the more brightly: 'With righteousness he will judge the needy, with justice he will give decisions for the poor of the earth' (Isaiah 11:1–5).

It is abundantly clear from this evidence that the biblical writers saw the poor not only as destitute people, whose condition must be relieved, but as the victims of social injustice, whose cause must be championed. The biblical perspective is not 'the survival of the fittest' but 'the protection of the weakest'. Since God himself speaks up for them and comes to their aid, his people must also be the voice of the voiceless and the defender of the defenceless.

The third group, *the humble poor*, are spiritually meek and dependent on God. Since God succours the destitute and defends the powerless, these truths inevitably affect their attitude to him. They look to him for mercy. Oppressed by human beings, and helpless to liberate themselves, they put their trust in God. It is in this way that 'the poor' came to be synonymous with 'the pious', and their social condition became a symbol of their spiritual dependence. Zephaniah describes them as 'the meek and the humble, who trust in the name of the Lord', and Isaiah calls them the 'humble and contrite in spirit' who tremble at God's Word (Zephaniah 2:3; 3:12; Isaiah 66:2; cf. 49:13).

It is particularly in the Psalms, however, that the otherwise rather blurred portrait of the humble poor comes into sharp focus. For the psalter is the hymnbook of the helpless (see, e.g. Psalms 22, 25, 37, 40, 69, 74, 149). It is here that we listen to their expressions of dependence upon God, and to God's promises to come to their aid. They are 'the lonely and afflicted' who cry to him to be gracious to them; they commit their way to the Lord, are quiet before him, and wait patiently for him to act. They are given the assurance that 'the poor will eat and be satisfied', that 'the meek will inherit the land', and that 'he crowns the humble with salvation' (Psalm 25:16; 37:5, 7; 40:1; 22:26; 37:11; 149:4).

More striking even than these references to the poor and meek as a group, however, are the individual testimonies to Yahweh's salvation. There is Psalm 34, for example: 'This poor man called, and the Lord heard him; he saved him out of all his troubles.' As a result, he determines to 'boast in the Lord' and is confident that others who are 'afflicted' like him will hear and rejoice with him, and will in their turn call upon Yahweh. For, he goes on to affirm, 'The Lord is close to the broken-hearted, and saves those who are crushed in spirit (Psalm 34:1–6, 15–18). Another example occurs in Psalm 86. The psalmist describes himself as savagely assaulted by arrogant, godless and ruthless men. His only hope is in God. 'Hear, O Lord, and answer me,' he cries, 'for I am poor and needy. Guard my life, for I am devoted to you. You are my God; save your servant who trusts in you.' And he goes on to express his confidence that God will rescue him, because he is 'a compassionate and gracious God, slow to anger, abounding in love and faithfulness' (Psalm 86:1–4, 14–17).

All this biblical teaching enables us to affirm that God succours the indigent poor, champions the powerless poor and exalts the humble poor. In each case 'he raises the poor from the dust', whether it be the dust of penury or of oppression or of helplessness.

Good news for the poor

At the risk of oversimplification, however, it will be helpful (especially if we are to grasp what the Christian attitude to poverty should be) if we reduce these three categories to two, namely the material poverty of the destitute and powerless, and the spiritual poverty of the humble and meek. God concerns himself with both. In both cases 'he raises the poor from the dust', but the way he does it is different. For the first kind of poverty is a social evil which God opposes, while the second is a spiritual virtue which he approves. Moreover, there is only one human community in which the two are combined, namely the Kingdom community, the new and redeemed society in which God rules through Christ by his Spirit.

This is clear from the Old Testament expectation of the Kingdom of God. God promised the coming of his ideal king, who would both judge the poor with justice and give the blessing of his rule to the humble and lowly. We meet such people in the first two chapters of Luke's Gospel. Zechariah and Elizabeth, Joseph and Mary, Simeon and Anna were humble, poor believers. They were looking and waiting for the Kingdom of God, in which God would throw down the mighty from their thrones and exalt the humble and meek.

Clearer still was the fulfilment through Jesus Christ. Who are the 'poor' he spoke about, those to whom he had been anointed to preach the good news of the Kingdom and to whom the Kingdom would be given (Luke 4:18ff.; Matthew 11:5; cf. Luke 7:22; Matthew 5:3; cf. Luke 6:20)? They surely cannot be either just the materially poor (for Christ's salvation is not limited to the proletariat) or just the spiritually poor (for this overlooks his ministry to the needy). He must have been referring to both in combination. The 'poor' are those to whom the Kingdom comes as great good news, partly because it is a free and unmerited gift of salvation to sinners, and partly because it promises a new society characterized by freedom and justice.

The Church should exemplify both these truths. On the one hand it consists of the spiritually poor, the 'poor in spirit', who acknowledge their bankruptcy before God. They have no righteousness to offer, no merit to plead, no power to save themselves. They know that the only way to enter God's Kingdom is to humble themselves like little children and receive it as a gift. So they come as beggars, with nothing in their hands, and on their lips the publican's prayer, 'God be merciful to me, a sinner.' To such Jesus says: 'Blessed are the poor in spirit, for theirs is the kingdom of heaven.' By contrast, the rich or self-satisfied, who imagine they have something to offer, are sent away empty.

On the other hand, the Church must proclaim the good news of the Kingdom to the materially poor, welcome them into the fellowship, and share in their struggles. Indeed, the special concern for the poor shown by the biblical authors, and more particularly by Jesus himself, has led some contemporary thinkers to speak of God's 'bias' in their favour. Bishop David Sheppard's 1983 book was entitled *Bias to the Poor*. 'I believe that there is a divine bias to the disadvantaged,' he writes, 'and that the church needs to be much more faithful in reflecting it.'[14] He concludes his analysis of deprivation in Liverpool with these words: 'If we can put ourselves in the shoes of the poor and disadvantaged, we may see how matters appear to their consciousness ... They are to do with the righteousness of God which has a persistent tendency to favour those at a disadvantage. They are to do with God taking flesh in the person of Jesus, living out his life in a special relation to the poor.'[15]

I confess that I am uncomfortable with the word 'bias', since its commonest meaning is 'prejudice', and I do not think God is 'biased' in that sense. Less misleading is the language of the Latin American bishops. At their Second General Conference at Medellín in 1970 they spoke of a 'preference for, and solidarity with, the poor'. At their Third General Conference 10 years later at Puebla in Mexico, they affirmed 'the need for conversion on the part of the whole church to a preferential option for the poor'.[16] It is because of Jesus' ministry to the poor that 'the poor merit preferential attention'.[17] 'Preferential' does not mean 'exclusive', however, for the next chapter of the conference's report is entitled 'A Preferential Option for Young People'. Nevertheless, the option for the poor is 'demanded by the scandalous reality of economic imbalances in Latin America'.[18]

The 1980 Melbourne Conference quoted the Puebla conclusions, and then echoed them in asserting that 'God has a preference for the poor'.[19] It seems to me, however, that better than the vocabulary of personal 'bias' or 'preference' is the language of mission priority. Because of God's own care for the poor, and because of their exploitation by the unscrupulous and their neglect by the Church, they should now receive a 'positive' or 'reverse' discrimination. The Church should concentrate its mission where the need is greatest, and move from the centre out 'towards the periphery',[20] to the 'sinned against', in other words to the poor and the oppressed.

Moreover, the Church should not tolerate material poverty in its own fellowship. When Jesus said, 'The poor you will always have with you' (Mark 14:7), he was not acquiescing in the permanence of poverty. He was echoing the Old Testament statement 'there will always be poor people in the land' (Deuteronomy 15:11). Yet this was intended not as an excuse for complacency but as an incentive to generosity, as a result of which 'there should be no poor among you' (Deuteronomy 15:4). If there is one community in the world in which justice is secured for the oppressed, the poor are freed from the indignities of poverty, and physical need is abolished by the voluntary sharing of resources, that community is the new society of Jesus the Messiah. It happened in Jerusalem after Pentecost, when 'there were no needy persons among them', as Luke is at pains to show, and it can (and should) happen again today. How can we allow our own brothers and sisters in God's family to suffer want?

The Church, then, as the community which is called to exemplify the ideals of the Kingdom of God, should bear witness to the biblical paradox of poverty, by opposing one kind and encouraging the other. We should set ourselves both to eradicate the evil of material poverty and to cultivate the good of spiritual poverty. We should hate injustice and love humility. It is in these two complementary ways that the gospel may be said to be 'good news for the poor', and God may be described as on their side.

Not that our Christian concern should be confined to those poor who are church members. Although we have a special responsibility to 'the family of believers' (or, in older versions of the Bible, 'the household of faith'), we are also required to 'do good to all people' (Galatians 6:10). How will this express itself to the poor? Certainly in terms of personal philanthropy, as we seek to help needy individuals and families in our neighbourhood and further afield. But we cannot allow our duty to stop there. For the Bible itself indicates, as we have seen, that most poverty is the fault rather of society than of the poor themselves. We therefore have a social as well as a personal responsibility towards them, and this will begin with a painful appraisal of the causes of poverty. I call it 'painful' because the tendency of the affluent is to blame the poor, or to find some other scapegoat, whereas the problem may lie in the very structure of society in which we ourselves (willy-nilly) are implicated.

This is the thesis of Robert Holman's carefully researched, well written and overtly Christian book *Poverty: Explanations of Social Deprivation*.[21] He rejects as incomplete three common scapegoat explanations – 'individual' (genetic, economic or psychological inadequacies in the poor themselves), 'cultural' ('the transmission of poverty from one generation to the next'[22]), and 'the deficient agent' (the inefficiency of teachers, social workers and bureaucrats). Instead, he traces the cause of most poverty (at least in Britain) to the stratified structure of society itself, in which resources (especially income, wealth and power) are unequally divided. 'Poverty exists,' he writes, 'in order to support or uphold these social divisions.'[23] It is tolerated, even justified, because it (and therefore its affluent opposite) is made to appear merited, and because it provides a useful pool of workers who have no choice but to undertake the most unattractive occupations.

Bob Holman's approach is sociological. In consequence, he avoids the polarized economic debate between those who blame poverty on capitalism, on the ground that it is inherently covetous and therefore exploits the poor, and those who blame socialism, on the ground that it perpetuates the dependency of the poor and undermines the enterprise of wealth creators. Neither position has a monopoly of truth. Christians should oppose in both systems what they perceive to be incompatible with biblical faith. As we saw in Chapter 2, that faith places an equal emphasis on creativity and compassion, and refuses to foster either at the expense of the other.

Three options for rich Christians

Conscientious Christians have further questions to ask. It is one thing to discern what our attitude to the poor should be; it is another to define our attitude to poverty itself. Involuntary material poverty is a scandal, as we have seen; but what about voluntary poverty? And what is an authentically Christian attitude to money and property? What should rich Christians do?

In the context of western affluence there are three options before us. The first is to become poor, the second to stay rich, and the third to cultivate generosity, simplicity and contentment.

First, should we *become poor*? Paul wrote: 'For you know the grace of our Lord Jesus Christ, that though he was rich, yet for your sakes he became poor, so that you through his poverty might become rich' (2 Corinthians 8:9). This voluntary self-impoverishment of Jesus was the theological ground on which the apostle based his appeal to the Christians of Greece to contribute to the relief of the Christians of Judea. Did he intend them to divest themselves of all their possessions for the sake of their Jewish brothers and sisters? Does he mean us to do the same? At first sight it seems so, and arguments have been advanced for this from the example, teaching and early Church of Jesus.

(1) The example of Jesus
Renouncing the wealth of heaven, Jesus was certainly born into a poor home. When Joseph and Mary came to the Temple to present

their child to the Lord, they availed themselves of the law's provision for poor people and brought as their sacrifice a pair of doves instead of a lamb and a dove. During his public ministry as an itinerant preacher Jesus had no home and few possessions. To an applicant for discipleship he once said: 'Foxes have holes and birds of the air have nests, but the Son of Man has nowhere to lay his head.' He taught from a borrowed boat, rode into Jerusalem on a borrowed donkey, spent his last evening in a borrowed room, and was buried in a borrowed tomb. He and his apostles shared a common purse, and depended for their support on a group of women who sometimes accompanied them (Luke 2:2ff.; cf. Leviticus 12:6ff.; Luke 9:57ff.; Mark 4:1, 11:1ff.; 14:12ff.; 15:42ff.; John 12:6; Luke 8:1ff.). The poverty of Jesus seems to be beyond question.

Yet he was a carpenter by trade, which means that he belonged to the craftsman class. Professor Martin Hengel writes: 'Jesus himself did not come from the proletariat of day-labourers and landless tenants, but from the middle class of Galilee, the skilled workers. Like his father, he was an artisan, a *tekton*, a Greek word which means mason, carpenter, cartwright and joiner all rolled into one ... As far as we can tell, the disciples whom he called to follow him came from a similar social milieu.'[24] Moreover, the women who supported him evidently 'cared for his needs' adequately (Mark 15:41). So he was not destitute.

(2) The teaching of Jesus

To would-be followers Jesus said: 'Any of you who does not give up everything he has cannot be my disciple.' The 12 apostles did this literally. Simon and Andrew 'left their nets and followed him'; James and John 'left their father Zebedee in the boat with the hired men and followed him'; and Levi-Matthew 'got up and followed him', abandoning his tax-collector's booth and work. Similarly, Jesus told the rich young ruler to sell all his possessions, give the proceeds to the poor and then follow him. It was this which prompted Peter to blurt out: 'We have left everything to follow you!' (Luke 14:33; Mark 1:16ff.; 2:13ff., 10:21, 28)

Does Jesus then expect *all* his followers to give up everything in order to follow him? The apostles did it. And the rich young man was challenged to do it. But is it a universal rule? In reply, we must be careful not to whittle down the radical summons of Jesus by a little prudential exegesis. He did say that we should store our treasure in heaven not on earth; that we must put devotion to God's rule and righteousness above material things; that we must beware of covetousness; and that it is impossible to serve God and money simultaneously (Matthew 6:19ff.; cf. Luke 12:33ff.; Matthew 6:33; Luke 12:15; Matthew 6:24). But he did not tell all his followers to get rid of all their possessions. Joseph of Arimathea is described both as 'a rich man' and as 'a disciple of Jesus'. So these two were evidently not incompatible. Zacchaeus the wealthy tax-collector promised both to pay back to people he had cheated four times what he had taken, and to give half of his possessions to the poor, which presumably means that he kept the other half, apart from what he paid back to his victims. Yet Jesus said that salvation had been given to him (Matthew 27:57; Luke 19:8ff.). So then, when he said that no one could be his disciple unless he both 'renounced' all his possessions and 'hated' his parents and other relatives, we shall need to understand both these verbs as dramatic figures of speech. We are not to hate our parents literally, nor to renounce all our possessions literally, What we *are* summoned to is to put Jesus Christ first, above even our family and our property.

(3) The early Church of Jesus

Luke writes of the first Christian community in Jerusalem that they 'had everything in common', that 'no one claimed that any of his possessions was his own', that 'they shared everything they had' and 'gave to anyone as he had need', and that in consequence 'there were no needy persons among them' (Acts 2:44f.; 4:32ff.). Is Luke setting their common life before us as an example for every church to copy? In the sense that the early Spirit-filled believers loved and cared for one another, and eliminated poverty within their fellowship, yes. But is he also advocating the common ownership of goods? Among the Essene groups, especially in their central community of Qumran, this was obligatory, and every novice entering the order had to hand over his property.[25] But it is plain from Luke's narrative that the Christians' selling and sharing were neither universal nor compulsory. For some believers still had houses in which they met. The sin of Ananias and Sapphira was not that they were selfish to withhold some of their property, but that they were deceitful to pretend they had given it all. Peter said to Ananias: 'Didn't it belong to you before it was sold? And after it was sold, wasn't the money at your disposal?'

(Acts 5:4) Thus the Christian's right to property is affirmed, together with the voluntary nature of Christian giving.

The example, teaching and early Church of Jesus all challenge us to renounce covetousness, materialism and luxury, and to care sacrificially for the poor. But they do not establish the case that all Christians must actually become poor.

If the first option for affluent Christians is to become poor, the second and opposite option is to *stay rich*. Some seek to defend this stance by an appeal to biblical arguments. Human beings were commanded in the beginning (they rightly say) to subdue and develop the earth, that is, to extract its animal, vegetable and mineral wealth and to harness it for their use. Wealth, moreover, is a sign of God's blessing, and they intend to claim and enjoy it. 'The Lord will send a blessing on your barns and on everything you put your hand to. The Lord your God will bless you in the land he is giving you ... You will lend to many nations but will borrow from none' (Deuteronomy 28:8, 12). 'What could be clearer than that?' they ask.

The most shameless example of this reasoning which I have come across was in the literature of a certain Pentecostal evangelist. He was appealing for funds to enable him to send Christian materials to the Third World. 'There's no better way to insure your own financial security,' he argued, all in capital letters, 'than to plant some seed-money in God's work. His law of sowing and reaping guarantees you a harvest of much more than you sow ... Have you limited God to your present income, business, house or car? There's no limit to God's plenty! ... Write on the enclosed slip what you need from God – the salvation of a loved one, healing, a raise in pay, a better job, newer car or home, sale or purchase of property, guidance in business or investment ... *whatever you need* ... Enclose your slip with your seed-money ... Expect God's material blessings in return.'

Our first response to this is vigorously to deny what such Christians are affirming, and strenuously to repudiate their false 'prosperity' or 'health and wealth' gospel. When God's people were a nation, he did indeed promise to reward their obedience with material blessings, but in Christ he has blessed us 'with every spiritual blessing' (Ephesians 1:3). Our second response is to draw attention to what they are omitting. For there are other biblical principles which they have overlooked. The earth was to be developed for the common good, and its riches shared with all mankind. The Old Testament economy which promised wealth also commanded the care of the poor. And the rich man in the parable of Jesus found himself in hell not because of his wealth but because of his neglect of the beggar at his gate. That is, Dives indulged himself at the very time when Lazarus was starving.

In the light of these additional biblical truths, and of the contemporary destitution of millions, it is not possible for affluent Christians to 'stay rich', in the sense of accepting no modification of economic lifestyle. We cannot maintain a 'good life' (of extravagance) and a 'good conscience' simultaneously. One or other has to be sacrificed. Either we keep our conscience and reduce our affluence, or we keep our affluence and smother our conscience. We have to choose between God and mammon.

Consider Paul's instruction to Timothy regarding rich people:

> Command those who are rich in this present world not to be arrogant nor to put their hope in wealth, which is so uncertain, but to put their hope in God, who richly provides us with everything for our enjoyment. Command them to do good, to be rich in good deeds, and to be generous and willing to share. In this way they will lay up treasure for themselves as a firm foundation for the coming age, so that they may take hold of the life that is truly life.
>
> (1 Timothy 6:17–19)

We observe at once that the apostle does not tell 'those who are rich in this present world' to 'become poor'. But he does not allow them to 'stay rich' either. Instead, he first warns them of the spiritual dangers of wealth (as Jesus said, it is not impossible for the rich to enter God's Kingdom. but it is hard), and then tells them to be generous with their wealth, which will inevitably result in a lowering of their own standard of living.

The first danger of wealth is pride: 'Command those who are rich … not to be arrogant.' For wealth makes people feel self-important and so 'contemptuous of others' (J.B. Phillips). Rich people are tempted to boast of their home, car, possessions and gadgets. It is easy for wealthy people to become snobs, to emphasize their social 'class' and despise others. James pictures the situation when a rich man enters a Christian assembly wearing fine clothes, and then a poor man in rags comes in. If we behave obsequiously to the rich person and show him to one of the best seats, while rudely telling the poor person to stand on one side or sit on the floor, we have been guilty of class discrimination and so have disrupted the fellowship. It is not difficult to tell whether our affluence has alienated us from our less well-to-do brothers and sisters. If it has, we find ourselves embarrassed in each other's company.

If wealth's first peril is pride, its second is materialism: 'Command those who are rich ... not to put their hope in wealth which is so uncertain, but to put their hope in God.' 'Materialism' is not the mere possession of material things, but an unhealthy obsession with them. It is but a short step from wealth to materialism, from having riches to putting our trust in them, and many take it. But it is foolish. For there is no security in wealth. It is not for nothing that Paul writes of 'uncertain riches'. Burglars, pests, rust and inflation all take their toll. Many have gone to bed rich and woken up poor, or, like the rich fool in Jesus' parable, have not woken up at all.

Trust in wealth is not only foolish, it is also unworthy of human beings, since our trust should not be in a thing but in a Person, not in money but in God 'who richly provides us with everything for our enjoyment'. This is an important addition. For the Christian antidote to materialism is not asceticism; austerity for its own sake is a rejection of the good gifts of the Creator.

Here then are the two main dangers to which rich people are exposed – pride (looking down on the poor) and materialism (enjoying the gift and forgetting the Giver). Wealth can spoil our two noblest relationships. It can make us forget God and despise our fellow human beings. These negative warnings prepare us for the positive instruction which follows.

After considering and rejecting the opposite options of becoming poor and staying rich, we come to the third, which is to *be generous and contented*. The apostle summons Christian believers to be both. I am not, of course, claiming that this approach by itself will solve the problem of world poverty, but at least it is an appropriate expression of solidarity with the poor.

Take generosity. The skeleton of verses 17 and 18 is striking: 'Command those who are rich ... to be rich.' More precisely, 'Command those who are rich in this present world ... to be rich in good deeds.' In other words, let them add one kind of wealth to another. Tell them 'to do good, to be rich in good deeds, and to be generous and willing to share'. Then they will be imitating our generous God 'who richly provides us with everything for our enjoyment'. They will also store up treasure in heaven (verse 19), as Jesus urged us to do.

It would be impossible, however, to describe as 'generous' the voluntary giving to charity of those of us who live in the North of the world. According to the Charities Aid Foundation, in 1993 only 29 per cent of all households in Britain were giving to charity. For these 29 per cent, average weekly giving was £3.89 per week. Although this shows an increase in giving from past years, the number of households participating has dropped.[26] 'The facts appear to be,' comments Michael Brophy, Chief Executive of CAF, 'that a handful of people are very generous, whilst the majority of us are rather mean.' It is interesting to note that UK expenditure on television sets and videos more than doubled between 1976 and 1987.

Next, contentment needs to be added to generosity. For it would be anomalous if generous giving to others resulted in discontent with what we had left. Paul extols contentment in 1 Timothy 6:6–10, as follows:

> But godliness with contentment is great gain. For we brought nothing into the world, and we can take nothing out of it. But if we have food and clothing, we will be content with that. People who want to get rich fall into temptation and a trap and into many foolish and harmful desires that plunge men into ruin and destruction. For the love of money is a root of all kinds of evil. Some people, eager for money, have wandered from the faith and pierced themselves with many griefs.

We notice that, whereas the other paragraph in 1 Timothy 6 which we considered relates to 'those who are rich' (verse 17), this one is addressed to 'people who want to get rich' (verse 9), that is, the covetous. Paul sets covetousness and contentment in contrast to one another. Covetousness is a self-destructive passion, a craving which is never satisfied, even when what has been craved is now possessed. As Schopenhauer said, 'Gold is like sea water – the more one drinks of it, the thirstier one becomes.'[27] 'Beware of covetousness,' warned Jesus. 'Covetousness is idolatry,' added Paul (Luke 12:15 (RSV); Colossians 3:15; cf. Ephesians 5:5). It seduces the heart from love of God and imprisons it in love for money. It brings much pain and many sorrows, for 'the love of money is a root of all kinds of evil' (1 Timothy 6:10).

Contentment, on the other hand, is the secret of inward peace. It remembers the stark truth that 'we brought nothing into the world, and we can take nothing out of it (verse 7). Life, in fact, is a pilgrimage between two moments of nakedness, namely birth and burial. So we should travel light, and live simply. Bishop John V. Taylor has put it well: 'The word "poverty" has come to sound so negative and extreme in our ears that I prefer the word "simplicity", because it puts the emphasis on the right points ... Our enemy is not possessions but excess. Our battle-cry is not "nothing!" but "enough!".'[28] Simplicity says 'if we have food and clothing, we will be content with that' (verse 8). For Christian contentment is coupled with godliness, the knowledge of God in Jesus Christ, and 'godliness with contentment is great gain' (verse 6).

We have looked at the three options which confront all affluent Christians. Should we become poor? No, not necessarily. Though doubtless Jesus Christ still calls some like the rich young ruler to a life of total voluntary poverty, it is not the vocation of all his disciples. Then should we stay rich? No, this is not only unwise (because of the perils of conceit and materialism) but actually impossible (because we are to give generously, which will have the effect of reducing our wealth). Instead of these two, we are to cultivate generosity on the one hand and simplicity with contentment on the other.

At this point the temptation is to lay down rules and regulations, whether for ourselves or others, and so lapse into Pharisaism. This makes three 'isms' for us to avoid – materialism (an obsession with things), asceticism (an austerity which denies the good gifts of the Creator) and Pharisaism (binding one another with rules). Instead, we would be wise to stick to principles.

The principle of simplicity is clear. Its first cousin is contentment. It concentrates on what we need, and measures this by what we use. It rejoices in the Creator's gifts, but hates waste, greed and clutter. It says with the Book of Proverbs 'give me neither poverty nor riches, but give me only my daily bread', for to have either too much or too little may lead to disowning or dishonouring God (30:8ff.). It wants to be free of anything and everything which distracts from the loving service of God and others.

One of the most controversial sections of the Lausanne Covenant, adopted at the conclusion of the International Congress on World Evangelization in 1974, relates to the need for more simple living. It goes like this: 'All of us are shocked by the poverty of millions and disturbed by the injustices which cause it. Those of us who live in affluent circumstances accept our duty to develop a simple lifestyle, in order to contribute more generously to both relief and evangelism.'[29] It was to elucidate the implications of these sentences that an International Consultation on Simple Lifestyle was held in 1980. It issued 'An Evangelical Commitment to Simple Lifestyle', whose nine paragraphs deserve careful study. Paragraph 5 is entitled 'Personal Lifestyle' and develops the concept of 'simplicity'. It includes a general resolve to 'renounce waste and oppose extravagance in personal living, clothing and housing, travel and church buildings'. But it betrays no negative asceticism. On the contrary, it picks up from Dr Ronald Sider's paper 'Living More Simply for Evangelism and Justice' a number of important distinctions: 'We also accept the distinction between necessities and luxuries, creative hobbies and empty status symbols, modesty and vanity, occasional celebrations and normal routine, and between the service of God and slavery to fashion.'[30] The point is that simple living is not incompatible with careful enjoyment.

But simple living *is* incompatible with living beyond one's means, that is, borrowing in order to purchase what one cannot afford. As a result of the steady growth of consumer credit in Britain during the 1980s (approximately 10 per cent per annum in real terms), more and more people (especially younger and poorer people) have been getting into arrears with their mortgage and hire purchase repayments and their credit card bills, and so into serious debt. The Jubilee Centre Research Paper No. 7, *Families in Debt*, documents the results of a sample of 1,043 people with multiple debt problems. It also highlights three major biblical principles which 'provide a coherent and highly reasonable foundation for policy initiatives' covering the prevention and cure of debt problems, namely 'justice' (taking seriously the responsibilities of both lenders and borrowers), 'mercy' (lenders giving good advice and being lenient with defaulters) and 'hope' (the prospect of ultimate rescue from the debt trap).[31]

If the principle of simplicity is clear, so is the principle of generosity. John expresses it in these terms: 'If anyone has material possessions, and sees his brother in need, but has no pity on him, how can the love of God be in him?' (1 John 3:17). Our God is a generous God. If his love indwells us, we shall relate what we 'have' (possessions) to what we 'see' (others' needs) and take action.

May God help us to simplify our lifestyle, grow in generosity, and live in contentment!

PART IV

SEXUAL ISSUES

Chapter 13

WOMEN, MEN AND GOD

A schoolgirl was once asked to write an essay on why women outnumber men in the world. 'God made Adam first,' she wrote. 'When he had finished, he looked at him and said to himself, "Well, I think I could do better than that if I tried again." So then he made Eve. And God liked Eve so much better than Adam that he has been making more women than men ever since.'

The self-confident feminism of that young girl stands out in strong relief against the prevailing attitudes of the centuries. For there is no doubt that in many cultures women have habitually been despised and demeaned by men. They have often been treated as mere playthings and sex objects, as unpaid cooks, housekeepers and child-minders, and as brainless simpletons incapable of engaging in rational discussion. Their gifts have been unappreciated, their personality smothered, their freedom curtailed, and their service in some areas exploited, in others refused.

The rise of feminism

This record of oppression of women has been so longstanding and widespread that there is an evident need for reparation by male-dominated society. Yet in presuming to include a chapter on this topic, I immediately find myself in an unfavourable position. Indeed my maleness, some will say, is more than an initial disadvantage; it constitutes a total disqualification. They may be right. How far can men understand women, let alone make pronouncements about them? Let me make two points in self-defence. First, I have tried to listen carefully to what feminists (both secular and Christian) are saying, have read a number of their books, and have struggled to understand their hurts, frustration and even rage. At the same time, secondly, I am concerned, on this as on every subject, to listen to what Scripture says. This double listening is painful. But it should save us both from denying the teaching of Scripture in a determination at all costs to be modern, and from affirming it in a way that ignores the modern challenges and is insensitive to the people most deeply affected by them.

The ancient world's scorn for women is well known. Plato, who believed that the soul is both imprisoned in the body and released only to be reincarnated, went on to suggest that a bad man's fate would be reincarnation as a woman.[1] Aristotle, although respected as the father of biology because of his two works *The History of Animals* and *The Generation of Animals*, regarded a female as 'a kind of mutilated male'. He wrote: 'Females are imperfect males, accidently produced by the father's inadequacy or by the malign influence of a moist south wind.'[2]

Such crude male chauvinism was not, unfortunately, limited to the pagan world. Even Jewish writers, whose knowledge of the Old Testament should have given them a better understanding, made derogatory remarks about women. Josephus expressed his opinion that 'the woman is inferior to the man in every way'.[3] William Barclay sums up the low view of women expressed in the Talmud in these words: 'In the Jewish form of morning prayer ... a Jewish man every morning gave thanks that God had not made him "a Gentile, a slave or a woman" ... In Jewish law a woman was not a person, but a thing. She had no legal rights whatsoever; she was absolutely in her husband's possession to do with as he willed.'[4]

It is a further tragedy that some of the early Church fathers, influenced more by Greek and Talmudic perspectives than by Scripture, also sometimes spoke disparagingly of women. Tertullian, for example, wrote: 'You are the devil's gateway; you are the unsealer of that (forbidden) tree; you are the first deserter of the divine law; you are she who persuaded him whom the devil was not valiant enough to attack. You destroyed so easily God's image, man. On account of your desert – that, is death – even the Son of God had to die.'[5]

This kind of exaggerated language is incongruous from the pen of a follower of Jesus, to whom the contemporary liberation of women is largely due. The shame is that it did not come earlier, and that the initiative was not taken more explicitly in his name.

At least during this century the status and service of women have been rapidly changing, especially in the West.[6] Women have now been emancipated from nearly all the restrictions which had previously been imposed upon them. They have obtained the franchise, thanks to the courageous agitation of the suffragettes. In many countries (at least in theory) they receive equal pay for equal work. In Britain the Sex Disqualification (Removal) Act of 1919 opened to them virtually every public function, profession and civil post. By the 1960s only two professions were still closed to them, the London Stock Exchange and the ordained ministry of the historic churches. In 1973, however, the Stock Exchange capitulated. Now it is only ordination which, in some churches, is denied to women.

As the feminist movement gathered momentum, especially in the sixties, the utterances of some of its leaders became more strident.

As an example take Germaine Greer, the Australian lecturer and author. She regarded her book *The Female Eunuch* (which *Newsweek* called a 'dazzling combination of erudition, eccentricity and eroticism') as part of 'the second feminist wave'. The first had been that of the suffragettes, but their movement had failed because they had never taken advantage of the freedoms they had won. 'The cage door had opened, but the canary had refused to fly out.' The suffragettes had been content with reform by participation in the existing political system; Germaine Greer called for revolution. Her book contained a chapter entitled 'The middle-class myth of love and marriage', in which she hinted 'that women ought not to enter into socially sanctioned relationships, like marriage, and that once unhappily in, they ought not to scruple to run away'. Women 'are the true proletariat, the truly oppressed majority; they should rebel, and withdraw their labour'.[7]

Christians were offended by her tendency to extreme statement and vulgarity of expression. Yet she was rebelling against the stereotype of a woman as 'the Sexual Object sought by all men', whose value is not in herself but in the demand she excites in others. 'She is not a woman ... She is a doll ... She is an idol ... Her essential quality is her castratedness.'[8] In other words, all that is required of 'the female eunuch' is a sexless submission to the sexual desires of men. Was it not right for Germaine Greer to revolt against this demeaning of women? However, since the publication of *The Female Eunuch* (nearly 30 years ago) she has modified both her position and her tone. Her views of men have changed, and so too have her views of marriage and motherhood.[9]

More persuasive was Janet Radcliffe Richards' *The Sceptical Feminist* (1980). She began by describing her book as 'a battle on two fronts', since she was combating on the one hand the position which said 'there is no justification for the existence of a feminist movement' and on the other hand 'a good deal of common feminist dogma and practice'.[10] Feminism to her was not an irrational movement by women for women, in which on every single issue (however indefensible) women side with women against men. Instead, it had arisen from the conviction that 'women suffer from systematic social injustice because of their sex'. Therefore it was 'a movement for the elimination of sex-based injustice'.[11] This complaint of injustice and cry for justice should be enough to make every Christian sit up and take notice. For justice is concerned with God-given rights.

It would be a mistake, however, to regard feminism as a largely non-Christian movement. Elaine Storkey corrects this error in her fine, largely historical and sociological survey entitled *What's Right with Feminism*.[12] She begins with a thorough, factual account of the inequality and oppression of women in western society. Her case is irrefutable and is calculated to make all readers feel ashamed. She continues with a critical analysis of the three main streams of secular feminism – liberal, marxist and radical. She is prepared to acknowledge what is right in these movements. Yet basically all three are wrong because they have their roots in the Enlightenment and in its fatal confidence in human autonomy. So next she describes the two opposite extremes of Christian response, namely 'Christianity against Feminism' (an uncritical and often uninformed rejection, which refuses to take it seriously) and 'Salvation through Feminism' (ranging from a 'broadly Christian' position, which is selective and even dismissive of Scripture, to a 'post-Christian' stance which has attempted to redefine Christianity as a woman-centred religion). Elaine Storkey ends with 'A Third Way', which traces biblical feminism back to the Reformation and lays down its theological foundations.

It is clear, then, that feminism in all its forms – whether non-Christian, Christian or post-Christian – presents the Church with an urgent challenge. Feminism cannot be dismissed as a secular bandwagon which trendy churches (in their worldliness) jump on board. Feminism is about creation and redemption, love and justice, humanity and ministry. It obliges us to ask ourselves some searching questions. What does 'justice' mean in reference to both men and women? What does God intend our relationships and roles to be? What is the meaning of our masculinity or femininity? How are we to discover our true identity and dignity? In endeavouring to summarize and synthesize the biblical teaching on these sensitive topics, I shall focus on four crucial words – equality, complementarity, responsibility and ministry.[13]

Equality

It is essential to begin at the beginning, namely with the first chapter of Genesis:

> Then God said, 'Let us make man in our image, in our likeness, and let them rule over the fish of the sea and the birds of the air, over the livestock, over all the earth, and over all the creatures that move along the ground.'
>
> So God created man in his own image, in the image of God he created him; male and female he created them.
>
> God blessed them and said to them, 'Be fruitful and increase in number; fill the earth and subdue it. Rule over the fish of the sea and the birds of the air and over every living creature that moves on the ground.'
>
> (1:26–8)

If we put together the divine resolve ('Let us make man ... and let them rule ...'), the divine creation ('So God created ...') and the divine blessing ('Be fruitful ... fill the earth and subdue it ...'), we see that the emphasis seems to be on three fundamental truths about human beings, namely that God made (and makes) them in his own image, that he made (and makes) them male and female, giving them the joyful task of reproducing, and that he gave (and gives) them dominion over the earth and its creatures. Thus from the beginning 'man' was 'male and female', and men and women were equal beneficiaries both of the divine image and of the earthly rule. There is no suggestion in the text that either sex is more like God than the other, or that either sex is more responsible for the earth than the other. No. Their resemblance to God and their stewardship of his earth (which must not be confused, although they are closely related) were from the beginning shared equally, since both sexes were equally created by God and like God.

Moreover, the threefold affirmation of God's creation in verse 27 is not just poetic parallelism. There is surely a deliberate emphasis here, which we are intended to grasp. Twice it is asserted that God created man in his own image, and the third time the reference to the divine image is replaced by the words 'male and female'. We must be careful not to speculate beyond what the text warrants. Yet, if both sexes bear the image of God (as is forcefully asserted), then this seems to include not only our humanity (authentic humanness reflecting divinity), but our plurality (our relationships of love reflecting those which unite the persons of the Trinity) and even, at least in the broadest sense, our sexuality. Is it too much to say that since God, when he made humanity in his own image, made them male and female, there must be within the being of God himself something which corresponds to the 'feminine' as well as the 'masculine' in humankind?

If so, was the National Council of Churches of Christ (USA) justified in publishing *An Inclusive Language Lectionary*, from which all 'sexist' or 'exclusive' vocabulary had been eliminated? We can certainly applaud their desire 'to express the truth about God and about God's inclusive love for all persons' and 'to provide to both reader and hearer a sense of belonging to a Christian faith community in which truly all are one in Christ'. They were right, therefore, to translate 'brethren' as 'sisters and brothers', and the generic 'man' as 'human being' or 'humankind', for in so doing they clarified what these words have always meant. I do not think they had the liberty, however, actually to change the biblical text, on the ground that they regarded its language as sometimes 'male-biased or otherwise inappropriately exclusive'. To call God 'the Father (*and Mother*)' and Jesus Christ his 'only Child' is to set aside the concrete historical reality of the Incarnation. This contradicts both the experience and the teaching of Jesus, who addressed God as 'Abba Father', knew himself as 'the Son', and taught us to call God 'our Father in heaven'.[14]

What we should do, however, is give full weight to those passages of Scripture which speak of God in feminine – and especially maternal – terms. For these texts help to illumine the nature and quality of his 'fatherhood'. For example, according to the Song of

Moses, Yahweh was not only 'the Rock who fathered you' but also 'the God who gave you birth'. This is a remarkable statement that he was simultaneously Israel's Father and Mother. In consequence, Israel could be sure of God's preserving faithfulness. For though a human mother might 'forget the baby at her breast and have no compassion on the child she has borne', yet, Yahweh promised, 'I will not forget you!' Instead, he would unfailingly love and console his people: 'As a mother comforts her child, so will I comfort you.' Moreover, if Yahweh in these texts revealed himself as the mother of his people Israel, the individual Israelite felt at liberty to enter into this relationship. The psalmist dared even to liken his quiet confidence in God to the humble trustfulness of a breast-fed child. Then Jesus himself on occasion used feminine imagery, likening God to a woman who had lost a coin, as well as to a father who had lost a son, and likening himself in his anguish over impenitent Jerusalem to a hen wanting to gather her chicks under her wings (Deuteronomy 32:18; cf. Isaiah 42:14; Isaiah 49:15; 66:13; Psalm 131:1ff.; Luke 15:8ff.; Matthew 23:37).

So then, returning to the creation story, it is clear that from the first chapter of the Bible onwards the fundamental equality of the sexes is affirmed. Whatever is essentially human in both male and female reflects the divine image which we equally bear. And we are equally called to rule the earth, to co-operate with the Creator in the development of its resources for the common good.

This primeval sexual equality was, however, distorted by the Fall. Part of God's judgement on our disobedient progenitors was his word to the woman: 'Your desire will be for your husband, and he will rule over you.' Thus the sexes would experience a measure of alienation from one another. In place of the equality of the one with the other, and of the complementarity of the one to the other (which we have yet to consider), there would come the rule of the one over the other. Even if (according to Paul) sexual complementarity included from the beginning a certain masculine 'headship', to which I will come later, it was never intended to be autocratic or oppressive. The domination of woman by man is due to the Fall, not to the Creation.

Moreover, men have misused this judgement of God as an excuse to maltreat and subjugate women in ways God never intended. Examples could be given from many cultures. I will give four. First, from Gandhi's autobiography: 'A Hindu husband regards himself as lord and master of his wife, who must ever dance attendance upon him.'[15] Next, consider Sura 4 of the Koran, entitled 'Women': 'Men have authority over women because Allah has made the one superior to the other ... As for those from whom you fear disobedience, admonish them and send them to beds apart and beat them ...'[16] My third example comes from the Eskimos. Raymond de Coccola spent 12 years among the 'Krangmalit' in the Canadian Arctic, as a Roman Catholic missionary, and got to know them well. He was shocked when an Eskimo hunter used a word of a woman which was also applied to a she-wolf or a bitch. 'Trained to do all manner of mean tasks,' he reflected, 'the Eskimo woman is used to enduring the weaknesses and appetites of men. But I still could not get used to what appeared to be a master-and-slave relationship between the hunter and his wife.'[17] As my fourth example I choose pornography, a major symbol of western decadence, in which women are made the objects of male abuse and violence.

These are examples of the unlawful exploitation of women, however. In the Old Testament the husband was certainly the patriarch and *ba'al* (lord or ruler) of his clan. Yet his womenfolk were not despised or ill-treated. They were regarded as an integral part of the covenant community, so that 'men, women and children' were together assembled to listen to the public reading of the Torah and to share in the worship (e.g. Deuteronomy 31:12). Marriage was held in high honour, modelled on Yahweh's covenant love to Israel, the beauty of sexual love was celebrated (as in the Song of Songs), the capabilities of a good wife were praised (e.g. Proverbs 31), godly and enterprising women like Hannah, Abigail, Naomi, Ruth and Esther were held up for admiration, and it was constantly emphasized that widows must be cared for.

Yet the prophets looked forward to the days of the New Covenant in which the original equality of the sexes would be reaffirmed. For God would pour out his Spirit on all flesh, including sons and daughters, menservants and maidservants. There would be no disqualification on account of sex.

Then Jesus came in the fullness of time, born of a woman (Galatians 4:4). Although Protestants are anxious to avoid the exaggerated veneration of the Virgin Mary accorded to her in the Roman Catholic and Orthodox Churches, we should also avoid the opposite extreme of failing to honour her. If the angel Gabriel addressed her as 'highly favoured', and if her cousin Elizabeth called her 'blessed ...

among women', we should not be shy to think and speak of her in the same terms, because of the greatness of her Son (Luke 1:28, 42).

It was not only his birth of a woman, however, which restored to women that measure of dignity lost by the Fall, but his attitude to them. In addition to his apostles, who were all men, Jesus was accompanied on his travels by a group of women, whom he had healed and who now provided for him out of their means. Next, he spoke to one at Jacob's Well who, as woman, Samaritan and sinner had a threefold disability, but Jesus actually engaged her in a theological discussion. It was similar with the woman who had been caught in the act of adultery; he was gentle with her and refused to condemn her. Then he allowed a prostitute to come behind him as he reclined at table, to wet his feet with her tears, wipe them with her hair, and cover them with kisses. He accepted her love, which he interpreted as gratitude for her forgiveness. In doing so, he risked his reputation and ignored the silent indignation of his host. He was probably the first man to treat this woman with respect; previously men had only used her (Luke 8:1ff.; Mark 15:41; John 8:1ff.; Luke 7:36ff.).

Here were three occasions on which *in public* he received a sinful woman. A Jewish male was forbidden to talk to a woman on the street, even if she were his wife, daughter or sister. It was also regarded as impious to teach a woman the law; it would be better for the words of the law to be burned, said the Talmud, than that they should be entrusted to a woman. But Jesus broke these rules of tradition and convention. When Mary of Bethany sat at his feet listening to his teaching, he commended her as doing the one thing that was needed, and he honoured another Mary as the very first witness of the Resurrection.[18] All this was unprecedented. Without any fuss or publicity, Jesus terminated the curse of the Fall, reinvested woman with her partially lost nobility, and reclaimed for his new Kingdom community the original creation blessing of sexual equality.

That the apostle Paul had grasped this is plain from his great charter statement of Christian freedom: 'There is neither Jew nor Greek, slave nor free, male nor female, for you are all one in Christ Jesus' (Galatians 3:28). This does not mean that Jews and Greeks lost their physical differences, or even their cultural distinctives, for they still spoke, dressed and ate differently; nor that slaves and free people lost their social differences, for most slaves remained slaves and free people free; nor that men lost their maleness and women their femaleness. It means rather that *as regards our standing before God*, because we are 'in Christ' and enjoy a common relationship to him, racial, national, social and sexual distinctions are irrelevant. People of all races and classes, and of both sexes, are equal before him. The context is one of justification by grace alone through faith alone. It affirms that all who by faith are in Christ are equally accepted, equally God's children, without any distinction, discrimination or favouritism according to race, sex or class. So, whatever may need to be said later about sexual roles, there can be no question of one sex being superior or inferior to the other. Before God and in Christ 'there is neither male nor female'. We are equal.

Sexual equality, then, established by creation but perverted by the Fall, was recovered by the redemption that is in Christ. What redemption remedies is the Fall; what it recovers and re-establishes is the Creation. Thus men and women are absolutely equal in worth before God – equally created by God like God, equally justified by grace through faith, equally regenerated by the outpoured Spirit. In other words, in the new community of Jesus we are not only equally sharers of God's image, but also equally heirs of his grace in Christ (1 Peter 3:7) and equally indwelt by his Spirit. This Trinitarian equality (our common participation in Father, Son and Holy Spirit) nothing can ever destroy. Christians and churches in different cultures have denied it; but it is an indestructible fact of the gospel.

Complementarity

Although men and women are equal, they are not the same. Equality and identity are not to be confused. We are different from one another, and we complement one another in the distinctive qualities of our own sexuality, psychological as well as physiological. This fact influences our different and appropriate roles in society. As J.H. Yoder has written, 'Equality of *worth* is not identity of *role*.'[19]

When we investigate male and female roles, however, we must be careful not to acquiesce uncritically in the stereotypes which our particular culture may have developed, let alone imagine that Moses brought them down from Mount Sinai along with the Ten Commandments. This would be a serious confusion of Scripture and convention.

Feminists are understandably rebelling against the expectation that women must fit into a predetermined role. For who fixed the mould but men? This is what the American author Betty Friedan meant by 'the feminine mystique' in her book of that title (1963). It is the image to which women feel compelled to conform, and which has been imposed on them by a male-dominated society. 'It is my thesis,' she wrote, 'that the core of the problem for women today is not sexual but a problem of identity – a stunting or evasion of growth that is perpetuated by the feminine mystique ... Our culture does not permit women to accept or gratify their basic need to grow and fulfil their potentialities as human beings ...'[20] Motherhood is indeed a divine vocation, and calls for great sacrifices. But it is not woman's only vocation. There are other equally serious and equally unselfish forms of service to society which she may be called to give.

There is nothing in Scripture to suggest, for example, that women may not pursue their own careers or earn their own living; or that married women must do all the shopping, cooking and cleaning, while their husbands remain non-contributing beneficiaries of their labour; or that baby-rearing is an exclusively feminine preserve into which men may not trespass. The German saying which restricts the province of women to *Kinder, Küche und Kirche* ('children, kitchen and church') is an example of blatant male chauvinism. Scripture is silent about this kind of division of labour. Does it then say anything about sexual roles and relationships?

It is without doubt by a deliberate providence of God that we have been given two distinct creation stories, Genesis 2 supplementing and enriching Genesis 1:

> The Lord God said, 'It is not good for the man to be alone. I will make a helper suitable for him.'
>
> Now the Lord God had formed out of the ground all the beasts of the field and all the birds of the air. He brought them to the man to see what he would name them; and whatever the man called each living creature, that was its name. So the man gave names to all the livestock, the birds of the air and all the beasts of the field.
>
> But for Adam no suitable helper was found. So the Lord God caused the man to fall into a deep sleep; and while he was sleeping, he took one of the man's ribs and closed up the place with flesh. Then the Lord God made a woman from the rib he had taken out of the man, and he brought her to the man.
>
> (Genesis 2:18–22)

What is revealed in this second story of creation is that, although God made male and female *equal*, he also made them *different*. For in Genesis 1 masculinity and femininity are related to God's image, while in Genesis 2 they are related to each other, Eve being taken out of Adam and brought to him. Genesis 1 declares the equality of the sexes; Genesis 2 clarifies that 'equality' means not 'identity' but 'complementarity' (including, as we shall soon see, a certain masculine headship). It is this 'equal but different' state which we find hard to preserve. Yet they are not incompatible; they belong to each other as essential aspects of the biblical revelation.

Because men and women are equal (by creation and in Christ), there can be no question of the inferiority of either to the other. But because they are complementary, there can be no question of the identity of one with the other. Further, this double truth throws light on male–female relationships and roles. Because they have been created by God with *equal* dignity, men and women must respect, love, serve, and not despise one another. Because they have been created *complementary* to each other, men and women must recognize their differences and not try to eliminate them or usurp one another's distinctives.

Commenting on the special creation of Eve, Matthew Henry more than 300 years ago wrote with quaint profundity that she was 'not made out of his head to top him, nor out of his feet to be trampled upon by him, but out of his side to be equal with him, under his arm to be protected, and near his heart to be loved'. Perhaps he got this idea from Peter Lombard who in about AD 1157, just before becoming Bishop of Paris, wrote in his *Book of Sentences*: 'Eve was not taken from the feet of Adam to be his slave, nor from his head to be his lord, but from his side to be his partner.'[21]

It is when we try to elaborate the meaning of complementarity, to explain in what ways the two sexes complement each other, and to define the distinctives of men and women, that we find ourselves in difficulties. Feminists become uncomfortable. They are suspicious of attempts to define femininity, partly because the definitions are usually made by men, who have (or at least may have) vested interests in securing a definition congenial to them, and partly because many sexual distinctives, as we have seen, are not intrinsic but established by social pressures. As Janet Radcliffe Richards has put it, feminists consider that it is 'not by *nature* that women are so different from men, but by *contrivance*'.[22]

But inherent sexual differences remain, however much some people wish to abolish them. One author who has emphasized their importance is George F. Gilder in his book *Sexual Suicide* (1973). 'The feminists refer often ... to "human beings",' he wrote, 'but I do not care to meet one. I am only interested in men and women.'[23] Again, 'There are no human beings; there are just men and women, and when they deny their divergent sexuality, they reject the deepest sources of identity and love. They commit sexual suicide.'[24] They also succeed in 'exalting the sexual eccentric – the androgyne'.[25] George Gilder quoted Margaret Mead who had said that 'if any human society ... is to survive, it must have a pattern of social life that comes to terms with the differences between the sexes'. For, he continued, 'the differences between the sexes are the single most important fact of human society'.[26] Then in 1986 a revised edition of George Gilder's book was published under the title *Men and Marriage*. In it his position was consolidated (not least on account of his new, or greater, Christian commitment) rather than changed. He was outspoken not only in his description of men as 'sexual barbarians' needing to be tamed by the disciplines of marriage and family, but also in his insistence on the mutual sacrifice of the sexes in the marriage covenant as the very foundation of a civilized society.

Although this emphasis on mutuality is welcome, the debate about the distinctions between men and women continues. Are they due to sex (unchanging biological differences between male and female) or to gender (changing cultural differences between masculine and feminine)?

It was a recognition of the differences between the sexes (minimized by feminists) which led to the publication in the early nineties of two books which have been sensational bestsellers. The first was Deborah Tannen's *You Just Don't Understand*, subtitled 'Women and men in conversation'.[27] Her field in Georgetown and Princeton universities is linguistics, and her basic thesis is that 'male-female conversation is cross-cultural communication' (p. 42), because men and women speak different languages in different ways for different purposes. The fundamental difference between the sexes is that women use language to secure intimacy, while men use language to secure independence. Failure to recognize this leads to misunderstanding and even confusion.

The second book is Dr John Gray's *Men are from Mars, Women are from Venus*.[28] To him the differences between the sexes are so profound that men and women seem to have come from different planets. 'Martians' (men) value power and achievement, 'Venusians' (women) value love and relationships (pp. 16–18). Like Professor Tannen, Dr Gray illustrates the differences from the way people communicate. When a woman is hurting, 'she wants empathy, but he thinks she wants solutions' (p. 15). They differ too in how they cope with stress. 'Martians go to their caves to solve their problems alone', whereas 'Venusians get together and openly talk about their problems' (p. 31). For men are empowered 'when they feel needed', women 'when they feel cherished' (p. 43). Christians find the book's generalizations somewhat naive, and note that its author is descriptive, not evaluative. He does not recommend that we try to change one another; only that we understand and accept one another. But at least he urges us to remember that we are 'supposed to be different' (pp. 10, 286).

In this connection mention may be made of the remarkable American men's movement called 'Promise Keepers'. Although it is not a self-conscious reaction against feminism, it seems to be responding to the need for men to be men. For example, the second of a Promise Keeper's seven promises is a commitment 'to pursuing vital relationships with a few other men, understanding that he needs brothers to help him keep his promises'. Founded in July 1991, more than 2 million men have now attended Promise Keepers stadium conferences. Many thousands of others have formed small men's groups and participated in educational seminars and conferences on men's ministry, men's leadership and building men of integrity.

Responsibility

All students of Genesis agree that Chapter 1 teaches sexual equality and Chapter 2 sexual complementarity. To these concepts, however, the apostle Paul adds the idea of masculine 'headship;. He writes both that 'the husband is the head of the wife' (Ephesians 5:23) and, more generally, that 'the head of every man is Christ, and the head of the woman is man, and the head of Christ is God' (1 Corinthians 11:3). But what does this 'headship' mean? And how can it possibly be reconciled with sexual equality and complementarity? These questions still seem to me to lie at the heart of the debate about male-female relationships and about the ordination and ministry of women.

Three attempts to resolve the paradox between sexual equality and masculine headship have been made. Some affirm headship so strongly as to contradict equality (or so it seems). Others deny headship because they see it as incompatible with equality. The third group seeks to interpret headship, and to affirm it in such a way as to harmonize with, and not contradict, equality.

The first of these options could perhaps be called 'traditionalist' and even 'hardline'. It assumes that 'headship' equals 'lordship', since the husband is said to be head of his wife as Christ is head of the Church. This view understands Paul's prohibition of women speaking in church or teaching men, and his requirement of female submission and silence, as literal, permanent and universal injunctions. It therefore deduces that, although women do have ministries, leadership and decision-making in both the church and the home are male prerogatives. The most outspoken and persuasive exposition of this viewpoint is David Pawson's *Leadership is Male*. He defines 'the paradox of gender' in terms of 'vertical equality' (equal in relation to God) and 'horizontal inequality' (unequal in relation to each other). But 'inequality' (even when restricted to the horizontal plane) is a misleading term ('complementarity' is better) and seems impossible to reconcile with that full equality of the sexes which has been established by creation, redemption and Pentecost.[29]

Secondly, there are those who go to the opposite extreme. They deny any and every concept of masculine headship as being irreconcilable with the unity of the sexes in Christ. They declare Paul's teaching to be inapplicable on one or other of four grounds, namely that it is mistaken or confusing or culture-bound or purely situational.

As an example of those who consider Paul's teaching on male headship to be erroneous, I cite Dr Paul Jewett in his otherwise admirable book *Man as Male and Female*. His thesis can be simply stated. The original 'partnership' which God intended for men and women was replaced in Old Testament days by a hierarchical model derived from Israel's cultural milieu. But then with Jesus 'a new thing happened: he spoke of women and related to women as being fully human and equal in every way to men. In this respect Jesus was truly a revolutionary.'[30] This dialectic between the Old Testament and Jesus was embodied in Paul, who expressed now the one viewpoint, now the other. As the apostle of Christian liberty he 'spoke the most decisive word … in favour of women's liberation' (namely Galatians 3:28, 'there is neither male nor female'), but as the former Jewish rabbi, following rabbinic interpretation of Genesis 2, he spoke 'the most decisive word … in favour of woman's subjection' (namely 1 Corinthians 11:3, 'the head of the woman is the man'.[31] 'These two perspectives,' Dr Jewett continues, 'are incompatible, there is no satisfying way to harmonize … them.'[32] Indeed, 'female subordination' is 'incompatible with (a) the biblical narratives of man's creation, (b) the revelation which is given us in the life of Jesus, and (c) Paul's fundamental statement of Christian liberty' (i.e. Galatians 3:28).[33] This incongruity, he concludes, is due to the fact that Scripture is human as well as divine, and that Paul's 'insight' has 'historical limitations'.[34] In other words, Paul was mistaken. He did not grasp the full implications of his own assertion that in Christ there is neither male nor female. He did not know his own mind. We are therefore free to choose between the apostle of Christian liberty and the unreformed rabbi, and, says Dr Jewett, we greatly prefer the former.

Now there is much in Dr Jewett's book which is excellent, especially his exposition of the attitudes and teaching of Jesus. But to abandon the task of harmonization and declare the apostle Paul to be double-minded and mistaken is a counsel of despair. It is better to give him credit for consistency of thought. The truth is that submission does not imply inferiority, and that distinct sexual identities and roles are not incompatible with equality of worth.

The second way of rejecting the concept of headship is to declare Paul's teaching to be too confusing to be helpful. This is the position adopted by Gretchen Gaebelein Hull in her book *Equal To Serve*. Her study of Pauline 'hard passages' led her to the discovery that 'there is no scholarly consensus on the meaning or interpretation of these passages'.[35] In consequence, she decided to put them aside as peripheral, and to focus instead on 'the larger truth of women's equal redemption and equal inheritance rights',[36] and 'equal opportunity to serve God'.[37] 'That all believers are equally redeemed,' she writes, 'and therefore equally eligible to serve, forms the basis for any philosophy of Christian life and service. God makes no distinction based on race, class or gender.'[38] I enjoyed reading Mrs Hull's book, and particularly appreciated her repeated emphasis on the sacrificial and suffering servanthood to which all Christ's people are called.[39] Yet I do not myself feel able, in the face of difficult texts, to surrender the tasks of interpretation and harmonization. Nor do I think it logical to argue that our equal redemption necessarily implies equal service.

If Paul's teaching was neither mistaken nor too confusing to understand, then was it culture-bound? That is to say, can we argue that his position on masculine headship was valid for his own day, and so for first-century churches in the Graeco-Roman world, but that it is not binding on us in the modern world? My immediate response to these questions must be to draw attention to the danger inherent in the argument. If we may reject Paul's teaching on men and women on the ground that it is culture-bound, may we not on the same ground also reject his teaching on marriage, divorce and homosexual relationships, indeed on God, Christ and salvation? If the teaching of the apostles was binding only on their own generation, then none of it has any necessary relevance to us or authority over us. But we have no liberty to engage in cultural rejection (i.e. repudiating God's revelation because of its first-century cultural clothing); our task is rather that of cultural transposition (i.e. guarding God's revelation and translating it into an appropriate modern idiom).

The attempt is sometimes made to strengthen the cultural argument by a reference to slavery. For if Paul told wives to submit to their husbands, he also told slaves to submit to their masters. But slaves have long since been liberated; is it not high time that women were liberated too? This parallel between slaves and women, and between abolitionism and feminism, was made as long ago as 1837, when two American books were published, namely, *The Bible Against Slavery* by Theodore Weld and *Letters on the Equality of the Sexes* by Sarah Grimke, his sister-in-law. The key text in their argument was Galatians 3:28, since in it Paul wrote that in Christ on the one hand 'there is neither slave nor free' and on the other 'there is neither male nor female'.[40]

The argument is flawed, however. For the analogy between women and slaves is extremely inexact on two counts. First, women were not chattel property, bought and sold in the market place, as slaves were. And secondly, though Paul sought to regulate the behaviour of slaves and masters, he nowhere appealed to Scripture in defence of slavery, whereas he did base his teaching about masculine headship on the biblical doctrine of creation. He drew his readers' attention to the *priority* of creation ('Adam was formed first, then Eve', 1 Timothy 2:13), the *mode* of creation ('man did not come from woman, but woman from man', 1 Corinthians 11:8) and the *purpose* of creation ('neither was man created for woman, but woman for man', 11:9). Thus, according to Scripture, although 'man is born of woman' and the sexes are interdependent (11:11f.), yet woman was made after man, out of man and for man. One cannot dismiss these three arguments (as some writers try to) as 'tortuous rabbinic exegesis'. On the contrary, as Dr James B. Hurley demonstrates in his *Man and Woman in Biblical Perspective*, they are exegetically well founded. For (a) by right of primogeniture 'the firstborn inherited command of resources and the responsibility of leadership', (b) when Eve was taken out of Adam and brought to him, he named her 'woman', and 'the power to assign ... a name was connected with control', and (c) she was made for him neither as an afterthought, nor as a plaything, but as his companion and fellow worker, to share with him 'in the service of God and in the custodial ruling of the earth'.[41]

It is essential to note that Paul's three arguments are taken from Genesis 2, not Genesis 3. That is to say, they are based on the Creation, not the Fall. And, reflecting the facts of our human creation, they are not affected by the fashions of a passing culture. For what creation has established, no culture is able to destroy. The wearing of a veil or of a particular hair style was indeed a cultural expression of submission to masculine headship,[42] and may be replaced by other symbols more appropriate to the twentieth century, but the headship itself is creational, not cultural.

If we may not reject Paul's teaching on masculine headship on the grounds that it is mistaken, unclear or culture-bound, may we do so because it was situational, that is, because it was addressed to highly specific situations which no longer exist today? This argument is similar to the previous one, but differs from it in one important respect. To declare Paul's teaching 'culture-bound' is a judgement which *we* form, namely that it seems to us dated and therefore irrelevant; to call it 'culture-specific' is to recognize the particularity of the apostle's instruction, and to argue that *he himself* did not regard it as applicable to all times and places.

This suggestion is often made with regard to Paul's requirement that 'women should remain silent in the churches' and be 'not allowed to speak' (1 Corinthians 14:34, 35). Again, 'I do not permit a woman to teach or to have authority over a man; she must be silent' (1 Timothy 2:12). The scholarly attempt to restrict these prohibitions to particular situations in Corinth and Ephesus is associated with the names of Richard and Catherine Clark Kroeger. They wrote a series of articles for *The Reformed Journal* between 1978 and 1980, whose substance was published in 1992 under the title *I Suffer Not a Woman*, 'Re-thinking I Timothy 2:11–15 in Light of Ancient Evidence'.[43] In one article entitled 'Pandemonium and Silence in Corinth'[44] they pointed out that ancient Corinth was a well known centre of the worship of Bacchus (identified by the Greeks with Dionysus), which included frenzied shouting, especially by women. They therefore suggest that Paul was urging self-control in worship, in place of wild ecstasies, and that the *lalein* he was forbidding (an onomatopoetic word) was either the mindless ritual shouting of 'alala' or the babbling of idle gossip.

The Kroegers also suggest in a subsequent article that a different kind of feminist movement had developed in Ephesus, where Timothy was superintending the churches, and where Diana (Artemis) the great mother goddess reigned, served by her numerous fertility priestesses. They point out that there is a strong emphasis in the Pastoral Epistles on the need to 'silence' heretics (e.g. 1 Timothy 1:3; Titus 1:10); that the prohibition of women teaching may well refer to their teaching of heresy; and that the heresy which Paul combats in the Pastorals may have been an incipient Gnosticism, whose later developments 'based their *gnōsis* on a special revelation given to a woman', notably Eve. For she was the first to eat from the tree of knowledge (*gnōsis*), had also (some taught) enjoyed a prior existence, and was even Adam's creator. She was therefore well qualified to instruct Adam. If such a heresy was already current in Ephesus, then Paul's insistence that Adam was created first and Eve deceived – not enlightened – first (1 Timothy 2:13, 14), would certainly take on an extra significance.[45]

As for the verb *authenteō*, whose only New Testament occurrence is in 1 Timothy 2:12, meaning to 'domineer', it is argued that it sometimes had sexual overtones. Some scholars have therefore suggested that what Paul was forbidding was the seduction of men which was doubtless common in Ephesian temple prostitution. Catherine Clark Kroeger, however, prefers to translate it 'to proclaim oneself the author or originator of something' and to understand it as prohibiting the Gnostic mythology that 'Eve pre-dated Adam and was his creator'.[46]

These theories have been developed with considerable learning and ingenuity. They remain speculations, however. Not only is it anachronistic to refer to 'Gnosticism' as if it were already a recognizable system by the sixties of the first century AD, but also there is nothing in the text of either 1 Corinthians 14 or 1 Timothy 2 to indicate that Paul was alluding to specific feminist movements in Corinth and Ephesus. On the contrary, the command to 'silence' in both passages would seem a strangely roundabout way to prohibit the beliefs and practices which these scholars have described. Besides, Paul gives directions about 'a woman' and 'women'; his references are generic, not specific. Finally, even if this apostolic instruction can be proved to have been situational, it remains applicable to similar situations today. After all, every New Testament epistle is an occasional document, which addresses particular problems in particular churches; the epistles nevertheless continue to speak to our condition today.

So far we have looked at the two opposite viewpoints on relationships between men and women. On the one hand, there are those who *affirm* masculine headship (rightly, in my view), but do it so strongly as to seem to deny the full equality of the sexes. On the other hand, there are those who *deny* headship, in order to affirm (rightly, in my view) the equality of the sexes. But, as I have tried to show, all attempts to get rid of Paul's teaching on headship (on the grounds that it is mistaken, confusing, culture-bound or culture-specific) must be pronounced unsuccessful. It remains stubbornly there. It is rooted in divine revelation, not human opinion, and in divine creation, not human culture. In essence, therefore, it must be preserved as having permanent and universal authority.

Is there, then, no way to resolve the paradox between sexual equality and masculine headship, except by denying one of them? Can they not both be affirmed? Many believe that they can, since Scripture itself does so. The right way forward seems to be to ask two questions. First, what does 'headship' mean? Can it be understood in such a way as to be compatible with equality, while at the same time not manipulating it or evacuating it of meaning? Secondly, once headship has been defined, what does it prohibit? What ministries (if any) does it render inappropriate for women? Thus, the meaning and the application of 'headship' are crucial to the ongoing debate.

How, then, can we *interpret* the meaning of headship with care and integrity, and allow Scripture to reform our traditions in this respect? We certainly have to reject the whole emotive language of hierarchy, as if headship means patriarchy or patronizing paternalism, autocracy or domination, and as if submission to it means subordination, subjection or subjugation. We must develop a biblical understanding of masculine headship which is fully consistent with the created equality of Genesis 1, the outpouring of the Spirit on both sexes at Pentecost (Acts 2:17ff.) and their unity in Christ and in his new community (Galatians 3:28).

Two interpretations of headship are being proposed. The first is that *kephalē* ('head') means not 'chief' or 'ruler' but rather 'source' or 'beginning', and that Paul was describing man as woman's 'origin', referring to the priority of his creation. This view goes back to an article by Stephen Bedale entitled 'The Meaning of *Kephalē* in the Pauline Epistles', which appeared in the *Journal of Theological Studies* in 1954. It was taken up and endorsed in 1971 by Professors F.F. Bruce and C.K. Barrett in their respective commentaries on First Corinthians, and has been quoted by many authors since then. In 1977, however, Dr Wayne Grudem published his computerized survey of 2,336 uses of *kephalē* in ancient Greek literature, drawn from 36 authors from the eighth century BC to the fourth century AD. In this article he rejects Bedale's argument that *kephalē* means 'source'; he provides evidence that instead it means 'authority over'.[47] In its turn Dr Grudem's thesis has been both criticized and reaffirmed.[48] So what *Christianity Today* has called 'the battle of the lexicons'[49] continues.

I find myself wondering, however, if this lexical controversy is not to some extent a false trail. To be sure, it is important to determine how *kephalē* was used outside the New Testament. Yet much more important is its meaning in the New Testament, and this is determined less by its etymology than by its use in each context. 'Headship' seems clearly to imply some kind of 'authority', to which 'submission' is appropriate, as when 'God placed all things under his [Christ's] feet and appointed him to be head over everything for the church' (Ephesians 1:22). But we must be careful not to overpress this. It is true that the same requirement of 'submission' is made of wives to husbands, children to parents, slaves to masters and citizens to the state. There must therefore be a common denominator between these attitudes. Yet I cannot believe that anybody conceives the wife's submission to her husband to be *identical* with the obedience expected of children, slaves or citizens. A very different relationship is in mind. Besides, the word 'authority' is never used in the New Testament to describe the husband's role, nor 'obedience' the wife's. Nor does 'subordination' seem to me to be the right word to describe her submission. Although it would be a formally correct translation of the Greek *hupotagē*, it has in modern parlance unfortunate overtones of inferiority, even of military rank and discipline.[50]

How then shall we understand *kephalē*, 'head', and what kind of masculine headship does Paul envisage? It is unfortunate that the lexical debate confines us to the choice between 'source of' and 'authority over'. There is a third option which contains an element of both. On the one hand, headship must be compatible with equality. For if 'the head of the woman is man' as 'the head of Christ is God', then man and woman must be equal as the Father and the Son are equal. On the other hand, headship implies some degree of leadership, which, however, is best expressed not in terms of 'authority' but of 'responsibility'. The choice of this word is not arbitrary. It is based on the way in which *kephalē* is understood in Ephesians 5[51] and on the two models Paul develops to illustrate the head's attitude to the body. The first is Christ's attitude to his body, the Church, and the second is the personal concern which we human beings all have for the welfare of our own bodies.

First, 'the husband is the head of the wife as Christ is the head of the church, his body, of which he is the Saviour' (verse 23). Those last words are revealing. Christ is 'head' of the Church in the sense that he is its 'Saviour'. Changing the metaphor, he loved the Church as his bride, 'and gave himself up for her, to make her holy ... and to present her to himself ... holy and blameless' (verses 25–7). Thus, the very essence of his headship of the Church is his sacrificial love for her.

Secondly, 'husbands ought to love their wives as their own bodies. He who loves his wife loves himself. After all, no one ever hated his own body, but he feeds and cares for it (RSV 'nourishes and cherishes it'), just as Christ does the Church – for we are members of his body' (verses 28–30). The ancient world did not think of the head's relationship to the body in modern neurological terms, for they did not know about the central nervous system. They thought rather of the head's integration and nurture of the body. So Paul wrote elsewhere of Christ as head of the Church, by whom the whole body is 'joined and held together' and through whom it 'grows' (Ephesians 4:16; Colossians 2:19).

The husband's headship of his wife, therefore, is a headship more of care than of control, more of responsibility than of authority. This distinction is of far-reaching importance. It takes our vision of the husband's role away from questions of domination and decision-making into the sphere of service and nurture. I am glad that John Piper and Wayne Grudem, in their massive symposium *Recovering Biblical Manhood and Womanhood*, have opted for the word 'responsibility': 'At the heart of mature masculinity is a sense of benevolent responsibility to lead, provide for and protect women …'[52] Similarly, Roy McCloughry in *Men and Masculinity*, subtitled 'From power to love', lays his emphasis on Christ's call to self-sacrifice. While conceding that there is 'a plurality of masculinities' (p. 249), each shaped by its own culture, yet at all times and in all places masculinity has been associated with power – physical, professional, political and financial. Yet when we see Jesus Christ as 'the key to the understanding of what it means to be a man' (p. 130), then masculinity becomes 'laying down power to express self-giving love' (p. 260).[53]

Accepting responsibility for her as her 'head', her husband gives himself up for her in love, just as Christ did for his body, the Church. And he looks after her, as we do our own bodies. His concern is not to crush her, but to liberate her. As Christ gave himself for his bride, in order to present her to himself radiant and blameless, so the husband gives himself for his bride, in order to create the conditions within which she may grow into the fullness of her womanhood.

But what is 'womanhood' that it needs conditions to be created for its flowering? Can 'manhood' and 'womanhood' be defined in terms of certain invariable distinctives? Many scholars say not, adding that different cultures have arbitrarily assigned different qualities and therefore different roles to their men and women. Margaret Mead, for example, in her classic book *Male and Female*, 'a study of the sexes in a changing world', compared the perceptions of sexuality among seven South Sea peoples with each other and with that of contemporary America. She showed that the diversity of masculine and feminine traits is enormous, the differences and similarities, the vulnerabilities, handicaps and potentialities all varying from culture to culture. Yet there are some regularities, she added, which seem to go back ultimately to the basic physiological distinctions between male and female, and relate to the tension between activity and passivity, initiative and response, potency and receptivity.[54] Janet Radcliffe Richards is understandably concerned with the same question. She has a chapter entitled 'The Feminist and the Feminine', and asks: 'What is it that people are afraid of, when they say they are opposed to feminism because it will result in women's ceasing to be feminine?'[55]

At the risk of causing offence, I think it is necessary for us to face the apostle Peter's description of women as 'the weaker sex' (1 Peter 3:7). Of course we know that women can be extremely strong. In some cultures they perform all the heavy manual jobs. They are capable of astonishing feats of physical endurance. And there were the Amazons, the women warriors of Greek mythology. Yet even such an ardent feminist as Janet Richards feels bound to concede that 'presumably women must in some sense tend to be weaker than men'.[56] And Margaret Mead writes: 'Still in every society men are by and large bigger than women, and by and large stronger than women.'[57] Therefore mining is an occupation reserved for men, and so in most cultures is combatant soldiering. It is also highly significant that in the Olympic Games women do not compete with men. The reason we feel some embarrassment in saying these things is that 'weakness' is not a quality which twentieth-century westerners normally admire, because we have absorbed (unconsciously, no doubt) something of the power-philosophy of Nietzsche. In consequence, we tend like him to despise weakness, whereas Peter tells us that it is to be honoured. Moreover, a recognition that the woman is 'weaker' is not incompatible with Peter's other statement in the same verse that she and her husband are equally 'heirs ... of the gracious gift of [eternal] life'.

Under the rubric of 'weakness' we should probably include those characteristically feminine traits of gentleness, tenderness, sensitivity, patience and devotion. These are delicate plants, which are easily trodden under foot, and which wither and die if the climate is unfriendly. I cannot see that it is demeaning to women to say that male 'headship' is the God-given means by which their womanhood is respected, protected and enabled to blossom.

Of course, men are also weak and needy. Weakness is celebrated in Scripture as the human arena in which Christ's power is best displayed (cf. 2 Corinthians 4:7; 12:9–10). Thus, both sexes are weak, fragile, vulnerable, and therefore dependent upon one another. If women need men, men also need women. Indeed, 'It is not good for the man to be alone,' God said (Genesis 2:18). Without woman, not necessarily as wife but certainly as companion and helper, man is but a pathetic apology for a human being. So we need each other. Yet, because men and women are different, the ways in which we need each other must surely be different too. It seems to me urgent for Christians to research more deeply into the complexity of these differences, in order that we may understand and serve each other better. Meanwhile, 'headship' is the biblical term to describe a major way in which women need men and men may serve women. It is intended not to suppress but to support them, and to ensure that they are – and may more fully become – their true selves.

The heartfelt cry of the feminist has been for 'liberation'. She has felt inhibited by male dominance from discovering her true identity. Letha Scanzoni and Nancy Hardesty, for example, who follow Paul Jewett in his treatment of the biblical material, write this near the beginning of their book *All We're Meant To Be*: 'The liberated Christian woman … is free to know herself, be herself, and develop herself in her own special way, creatively using to the full her intellect and talents.' Then towards the end they write: 'What are the basic issues of women's liberation? Do women want to become men? No, we simply want to be full human beings … We only want to be persons, free to give the world all that our individual talents, minds and personalities have to offer.'[58] The resolute desire of women to know, be and develop themselves, and to use their gifts in the service of the world, is so obviously God's will for them, that to deny or frustrate it is an extremely serious oppression. It is a woman's basic right and responsibility to discover herself, her identity and her vocation. The fundamental question is in what relationship with men will women find and be themselves? Certainly not in a subordination which implies inferiority to men and engenders low self-esteem. Instead, Letha Scanzoni and Nancy Hardesty insist on 'a fully equal partnership'. 'Equality' and 'partnership' between the sexes are sound biblical concepts. But not if they are pressed into denying a masculine headship of protective care. It is surely a distorted headship of domination which has convinced women that they cannot find themselves that way. Only the biblical ideal of headship, which because it is selflessly loving may justly be called 'Christlike', can convince them that it will facilitate, not destroy, their true identity.

Does this truth apply only to married women, whose caring head is their husband? What about single women? Perhaps the reason why this question is not directly addressed in Scripture is that in those days unmarried women were under their father's protective care, as married women were under their husband's. Today, however, at least in the West, it is usual for unmarried women to leave their parents and set up their own home independently. I see no reason to resist this. But I think it would be unnatural for such women to isolate themselves from men altogether, as it would be for single men to isolate themselves from women. For men and women need each other, as we have seen. It would therefore be more conducive to the full flowering of their womanhood if in some context, whether among relatives and friends, or at work, or (if they are Christians) at church, they could experience the respectful and supportive care of a man or men. If it is 'not good for man to be alone', without feminine companionship, it is not good for woman to be alone either, without responsible masculine headship.

Ministry

That women are called by God to ministry hardly needs any demonstration. For 'ministry' is 'service' (*diakonia*), and every Christian, male and female, young and old, is called to follow in the footsteps of him who said he had not come to be served, but to serve (Mark 10:45). The only question is what form women's ministry should take, whether any limits should be placed on it, and in particular whether women should be ordained.

The Roman Catholic and Eastern Orthodox Churches have no women priests; they set themselves firmly against this development. Many Lutheran Churches now have them, for example in Scandinavia, although serious disagreement on the issue continues. The French Reformed Church accepted women ministers in 1965 and the Church of Scotland in 1966. Among the British Free Churches, the Congregationalists have had female ministers since 1917, while Methodists and Baptists have followed suit more recently. In the Anglican Church the pattern is uneven. Bishop R.O. Hall of Hong Kong was the first to ordain a woman priest (that is, presbyter) in 1944. In 1968 the Lambeth Conference (of Anglican bishops) declared that 'the theological arguments as at present presented for and against the ordination of women to the priesthood are inconclusive'. In 1975, however, the Church of England's General Synod expressed the view that there are 'no fundamental objections to the ordination of women to the priesthood'. Nevertheless, no women were yet ordained. Then at the 1978 Lambeth Conference the bishops recognized that some Anglican provinces now had women clergy, and agreed to respect each other's discipline in this matter. Yet a deep division remains, which is partly theological and partly ecumenical, namely the damage which women's ordination would do to Anglican relationships with the Roman Catholic and Orthodox Churches. A sizeable group has broken away from the American Episcopal Church on this issue, and a similar split has been threatened in the Church of England. In other spheres, however, for example as deaconesses and as pioneer missionaries, women have an outstanding record of dedicated service.

Some Christians, anxious to think and act biblically, will immediately say that the ordination of women is inadmissible. Not only were all the apostles and the presbyters of New Testament times men, but the specific instructions that women must be 'silent in the churches' and 'not teach or have authority over a man' (1 Corinthians 14:34; 1 Timothy 2:12) settle the matter.

That is only one side of the argument, however. On the other side, a strong *prima facie* biblical case can be made for active female leadership in the Church, including a teaching ministry. In the Old Testament there were prophetesses as well as prophets, who were called and sent by God to be bearers of his word, women like Huldah, in the time of King Josiah. Before her Miriam, Moses' sister, was described as a 'prophetess', while Deborah was more; she also 'judged' Israel for a number of years, settling their disputes, and actually led them into battle against the Canaanites (2 Kings 22:11ff.; cf. 2 Chronicles 34:19ff.; Exodus 15:20; Judges 4 and 5). In the New Testament, although indeed Jesus had no women apostles, it was to women that he first revealed himself after the Resurrection and entrusted the good news of his victory (John 20:10ff.; Matthew 28:8ff.). In addition, the Acts and the Epistles contain many references to women speakers and women workers. Philip the evangelist's four unmarried daughters all had the gift of prophecy, and Paul refers to women who prayed and prophesied in the Corinthian church. He seems to have stayed on several occasions with Aquila and Priscilla ('my fellow workers in Christ', he called them), and Priscilla was evidently active for Christ in their married partnership, for twice she is named before her husband, and it was together that they invited Apollos into their home and 'explained to him the way of God more adequately' (Acts 21:9; 1 Corinthians 11:5; cf. Joel 2:28; Acts 2:17, Acts 18:26). Paul seems to have had women helpers in his entourage, as Jesus had had in his. It is impressive to see the number of women he mentions in his letters. Euodia and Syntyche in Philippi he describes as 'fellow-workers' (a word he also applied to men like Timothy and Titus), who had 'contended' at his side 'in the cause of the gospel'. And in Romans 16 he refers appreciatively to eight women. He begins by commending 'our sister Phoebe, a servant [or perhaps 'deacon'] of the church in Cenchrea', who had been 'a great help to many people' including Paul himself, and then sends greetings (among others) to Mary, Tryphena, Tryphosa and Persis, all of whom, he says, have worked 'hard' or 'very hard' in the Lord's service (Philippians 4:2ff.; Romans 16:1ff.). Then in verse 7 he greets 'Andronicus and Junias' and describes them as 'outstanding among the apostles'. It seems clear (and was assumed by all the early church Fathers) that Junias (or Junia) was a woman.[59] But was she an apostle? She may have been an 'apostle of the churches' (2 Corinthians 8:23), that is, a kind of missionary, but, since she is otherwise completely unknown, it is extremely unlikely that she belonged to that small and authoritative group, the 'apostles of Christ'. Paul could equally well have meant that she was well known among (that is, to) the apostles.

It is true that all the biblical examples in the preceding paragraph are of women's ministries which were either 'charismatic' rather than 'institutional' (i.e. appointed directly by God, like the prophetesses, not by the church, like presbyters), or informal and private (like Priscilla teaching Apollos in her home) rather than official and public (like teaching during Sunday worship). Nevertheless, if God saw no impediment against calling women into a teaching role, the burden of proof lies with the Church to show why it should not appoint women to similar responsibilities.

There is another argument in favour of women's ministry (including leadership and teaching) which is more general than these specific references, however. It is that on the Day of Pentecost, in fulfilment of prophecy, God poured out his Spirit on 'all people', including 'sons and daughters' and his 'servants, both men and women'. If the gift of the Spirit was bestowed on all believers of both sexes, so were his gifts. There is no evidence, or even hint, that the *charismata* in general were restricted to men, although apostleship does seem to have been. On the contrary, the Spirit's gifts were distributed to all for the common good, making possible what is often called an 'every-member ministry of the Body of Christ' (Acts 2:17ff.; 1 Corinthians 12:44ff.). We must conclude, therefore, not only that Christ gives *charismata* (including the teaching gifts) to women, but that alongside his gifts he issues his call to develop and exercise them in his service and in the service of others, for the building up of his body.

This much is clear. But now we return to the double command to women to be silent in the public assembly. How shall we handle these texts? In 1 Corinthians 14 Paul is preoccupied with the building up of the Church (verses 3–5, 26) and with the 'fitting and orderly' conduct of public worship (verse 40). Perhaps, then, his command to silence is addressed more to loquacious women in the congregation than to all women. It certainly was not absolute, since he assumed that some women would pray and prophesy publicly (1 Corinthians 11:5). Rather, just as tongue-speakers should 'keep quiet in the church' if there is no interpreter (verse 28), and a prophet should stop talking if a revelation is given to somebody else (verse 30), so too talkative women should 'remain silent in the churches' and, if they have questions, put them to their husbands when they get home (verse 34f.). For (and this is the principle which seems to govern all public behaviour in church) 'God is not a God of disorder but of peace' (verse 33). It can hardly be a prohibition of *all* talking by women in church, since Paul has not only referred earlier to prophetesses (11:5) but here allows 'everyone' to contribute 'a hymn, or a word of instruction, a revelation, a tongue or an interpretation' (verse 26), without explicitly restricting these to men.

What about 1 Timothy 2:11–15?[60] The attempt to limit these verses to particular, heretical, feminist movements has not succeeded in gaining widespread acceptance. The apostle is giving directions about public worship and about the respective roles in it of men (verse 8) and women (verses 9ff.). His instruction sounds quite general: 'A woman should learn in quietness and full submission. I do not permit a woman to teach or to have authority over a man; she must be silent.' What strikes me about these sentences (and about 1 Corinthians 14:34), which has not been sufficiently considered by commentators, is that Paul expresses two antitheses, the first between to 'learn in quietness' or 'be silent' and 'to teach', and the second between 'full submission' and 'authority'. The latter is the substantial point, confirms Paul's constant teaching about female submission to male headship, and is firmly rooted in the biblical account of creation ('for Adam was formed first, then Eve'). But the other instruction (the requirement of silence and the prohibition of teaching), in spite of the controversial reference to the fact that Eve was 'deceived', not Adam, seems to be an *expression* of the authority–submission syndrome, rather than an *addition* to it. There does not appear to be anything inherent in our distinctive sexualities which makes it universally inappropriate for women to teach men. So is it possible (I ask myself) whether, although the requirement of 'submission' is of permanent and universal validity, because grounded in creation, the requirement of 'silence', like that of headcovering in 1 Corinthians 11, was a first-century cultural application of it? Is it further possible, then, that the demand for female silence was not an absolute prohibition of women teaching men, but rather a prohibition of every kind of teaching by women which attempts to reverse sexual roles and even domineer over men?

My tentative answer to my own two questions is in the affirmative. I believe that there are situations in which it is entirely proper for women to teach, and to teach men, provided that in so doing they are not usurping any improper authority over them. For this to be so, three conditions need to be fulfilled, relating to the content, context and style of their teaching.

First, the *content*. Jesus chose, appointed and inspired his apostles as the infallible teachers of his Church. And they were all men, presumably because their foundational teaching required a high degree of authority. The situation today is entirely different, however. The canon of Scripture has long ago been completed, and there are no living apostles of Christ comparable to the Twelve or Paul. Instead, the primary function of Christian teachers is to 'guard the deposit' of apostolic doctrine in the New Testament and to expound it. They do not therefore claim authority for themselves, but put themselves and their teaching under the authority of Scripture. This being so, women may surely be numbered among them. Moreover, if the reference to Eve being deceived (1 Timothy 2:14) is intended to mean that women are vulnerable to deception, then their determination to teach only from the Bible should be an adequate safeguard against it.

Secondly, there is the *context* of teaching, which should be a team ministry in the local church. Whether directly or indirectly, Paul appointed 'elders' (plural) in every church (e.g. Acts 14:23; 20:17;

Philippians 1:1; Titus 1:5). Many local churches in our day are repenting of an unbiblical one-man ministry and returning to the healthy New Testament pattern of a plural pastoral oversight. Members of a team can capitalize on the sum total of their gifts, and in it there should surely be a woman or women. But, in keeping with biblical teaching on masculine headship, I still think that a man should be the team leader. The practice of 'cultural transposition' seeks to clothe the unchanged essence of divine revelation in new and appropriate cultural dress. In the first century masculine headship was expressed in the requirement of female head coverings and in the prohibition of women teaching men; could it not be expressed today, in a way that is both faithful to Scripture and relevant to the twentieth century, in terms of female participation in team ministries of which men are leaders? The team concept should also take care of the problem of ecclesiastical discipline. Discipline involves authority, it is rightly said, and should therefore not be exercised by a woman. But then it should not be exercised by a man on his own either. Discipline (especially in its extreme form of excommunication) should ideally be administered by the whole local church membership, and before the ultimate is reached by a team of leaders or elders together (e.g. Matthew 18:17; 1 Corinthians 5:4f.; Hebrews 13:17).

The third condition of acceptable teaching by women concerns its *style*. Christian teachers should never be swashbucklers, whether they are men or women. The humility of Christian teachers is to be seen both in their submission to the authority of Scripture and in their spirit of personal modesty. Jesus warned his apostles against imitating either the vainglorious authoritarianism of the Pharisees, or the power-hungry bossiness of secular rulers (Matthew 23:1ff. and Mark 10:42ff.). And the apostle Peter, sensitive to the temptation to pride which all Christian leaders face, urged his fellow elders to put on the apron of humility, not lording it over those entrusted to their pastoral care, but rather being examples to Christ's flock (1 Peter 5:1ff.). This instruction to men will be even more clearly exemplified in women who have come to terms with their sexual identity and are not trying to be, or behave like, men.

It seems then to be biblically permissible for women to teach men, provided that the content of their teaching is biblical, its context a team and its style humble. For in such a situation they would be exercising their gift without claiming a responsible 'headship' which is not theirs. Does this mean, then, that women could and should be ordained? The difficulty I have in giving a straight answer to this question is due to the layers of muddle which have been wrapped round it. But if ordination publicly recognizes God's call and gifts, and authorizes the person concerned to exercise the kind of ministry described above, there is no *a priori* reason why women should not be ordained. It remains my view that the best way to reconcile women's ministry with masculine headship is to ordain women for ministry in a local team situation. Then they have ample opportunity to exercise their God-given gifts, while at the same time recognizing masculine headship. The fact that in recent years in the Anglican Communion some women have been appointed rectors or vicars and that, at the time of writing, 11 have become bishops (seven diocesan and four suffragan), has not changed my mind about the ideal arrangement. Now that we have been overtaken by events, however, how should we respond? We should surely avoid the two extreme reactions. We should neither make an unprincipled surrender to cultural pressure, nor give up and secede from the Church. What then? We should continue the dialogue, refusing to regard the issue as settled. Meanwhile, we should encourage ordained women to exercise their ministry voluntarily in ways which recognize masculine headship, for example in team situations.

If what I have written above about 'cultural transposition' is correct, then we need to go on searching for appropriate visible symbols of masculine headship. Yet in the end the reality is more important than its symbols, and the reality we need to clarify concerns the essential nature of the ordained ministry and its relationship to masculine headship.

Those who begin with the Catholic view of *the priest* as an icon of Christ (who was male), representing God to us and us to God, conclude that it is impossible for a woman to fulfil this role.[61]

Those who begin instead with the Reformed view of *the presbyter* as a dominant figure, responsible for the teaching and discipline of the Church, conclude that it would be inappropriate for a woman to fulfil such an inherently authoritative role.

Supposing, however, that the Church oversight envisaged by the New Testament is neither priestly in the Catholic sense but pastoral, nor presbyteral in the fixed Reformed sense but more fluid, modest and varied, offering different kinds and degrees of ministry? Supposing that we begin instead with the teaching of Jesus Christ about

the servant-leader? True, pastors are said to be 'over' the congregation in the Lord, and the people are to 'obey' their leaders (1 Thessalonians 5:12; Hebrews 13:17). But this was not Jesus' main
emphasis. He described two communities, secular and godly, each
with its distinctive leadership style. In the world 'rulers of the Gentiles lord it over them, and their high officials exercise authority over
them'. But, he added immediately, 'not so among you'. 'Instead,
whoever wants to become great among you must be your servant',
for he himself had come not to be served, but to serve (Mark
10:42–5). Thus Jesus introduced into the world an altogether new
style of leadership.

If then our fundamental vision of church leadership is neither the
priest of Catholic tradition, nor the presbyter of Reformed tradition,
but the servant described by Jesus, why should women be disquali-
fied? If the essence of pastoral care is love, and its style is humility,
then no biblical principle is infringed if women are welcomed to
share in it. The fundamental issue is neither 'ordination' nor 'priesthood', but the degree of authority which necessarily inheres in the
presbyterate. It may be difficult for us to envisage presbyters (even
rectors and bishops), whose whole lifestyle exemplifies the humble
servanthood of the Kingdom of God, for church history illustrates
the constant tendency towards autocracy and prelacy, and we know
the pride of our own hearts. But this is the reality we should be
seeking, namely a ministry characterized by humility, not authority.
For men it will mean expressing their God-appointed headship in
self-sacrificial service. For women it will mean submitting to this
headship and not attempting to discard or usurp it. Then men
will remain men, and women women, and an unbiblical confusion
will be avoided.

Our Christian struggle, in the midst of and indeed against the
prevailing secularism, is to bear witness to the twin biblical principles of sexual equality and male headship, in Church and society as
well as in the home, even as we continue to debate how this can best
and most appropriately be done. Dr J.I. Packer has expressed this
tension well. Scripture continues to convince him, he writes, 'that
the man-woman relationship is intrinsically non-reversible ... This
is part of the reality of creation, a given fact that nothing will
change. Certainly, redemption will not change it, for grace restores
nature, not abolishes it.' We need, therefore, to 'theologize reciprocity, spiritual equality, freedom for ministry, and mutual submission

and respect between men and women within this framework of non-reversibility ... It is important that the cause of not imposing on women restrictions that Scripture does not impose should not be confused with the quite different goals of minimizing the distinctness of the sexes as created and of diminishing the male's inalienable responsibilities in man-woman relationships as such.'[62]

I conclude with some central simplicities. If God endows women with spiritual gifts (which he does), and thereby calls them to exercise their gifts for the common good (which he does), then the Church must recognize God's gifts and calling, must make appropriate spheres of service available to women, and should 'ordain' (that is, commission and authorize) them to exercise their God-given ministry, at least in team situations. Our Christian doctrines of Creation and Redemption tell us that God wants his gifted people to be fulfilled not frustrated, and his Church to be enriched by their service.

Chapter 14

MARRIAGE
AND DIVORCE

Marriage is in all societies a recognized and regulated human institution. But it is not a human invention. Christian teaching on this topic begins with the joyful affirmation that marriage is God's idea, not ours. As the Preface to the 1662 Prayer Book Marriage Service says, it was 'instituted by God himself in the time of man's innocency'; it was 'adorned and beautified' by Christ's presence when he attended the wedding at Cana; and it symbolizes 'the mystical union betwixt Christ and his church'. In these ways God has shaped, endorsed and ennobled marriage. True, he calls some people to forgo it and remain single in this life (Matthew 19:11ff.; 1 Corinthians 7:7), and in the next world after the Resurrection it will be abolished (Mark 12:25). Nevertheless, while the present order lasts, marriage is to be 'honoured by all'; those who 'forbid people to marry' are false teachers who have been misled by deceiving spirits (Hebrews 13:4; 1 Timothy 4:1ff.). Moreover, because it is a 'creation ordinance', preceding the Fall, it is to be regarded as God's gracious gift to all humankind.

Classical theology has followed the biblical revelation in identifying three main purposes for which God ordained marriage. It has also usually listed them in the order in which they are mentioned in Genesis 1 and 2, while adding that priority of order does not necessarily signify priority of importance. The first command to the male and female whom God had made in his own image was 'Be fruitful and increase in number' (Genesis 1:28). So the procreation of children has normally headed the list, together with their upbringing within the love and discipline of the family.[1]

Secondly, God said, 'It is not good for the man to be alone. I will make a helper suitable for him' (Genesis 2:18). Thus God intended marriage (to quote the 1662 Book of Common Prayer again) for 'the mutual society, help and comfort that the one ought to have of the other both in prosperity and adversity'. Dr Jack Dominian uses more modern phraseology when he writes that husband and wife can give each other 'sustenance' (supporting and 'cherishing' one another), 'healing' (for married life is the best context in which early childhood hurts may be healed by love), and 'growth' or fulfilment (stimulating each other to develop the individual potential of each and so become a mature person).[2]

Thirdly, marriage is intended to be that reciprocal commitment of self-giving love which finds its natural expression in sexual union, or becoming 'one flesh' (Genesis 2:24).

These three needs have been strengthened by the Fall. The loving discipline of family life has become all the more necessary because of the waywardness of children, mutual support because of the sorrows of a broken world, and sexual union because of temptation to immorality. But all three purposes existed before the Fall and must be seen as part of God's loving provision in the institution of marriage.

The higher our concept of God's original purpose for marriage and the family, the more devastating the experience of divorce is bound to be. A marriage which began with tender love and rich expectations now lies in ruins. Marital breakdown is always a tragedy. It contradicts God's will, frustrates his purpose, brings to husband and wife the acute pains of alienation, disillusion, recrimination and guilt, and precipitates in any children of the marriage a crisis of bewilderment, insecurity and often anger.[3]

Changing attitudes

Yet, in spite of the suffering involved, the number of divorces continues to be high. In 1994 in the US there were 2.4 million marriages and 1.2 million divorces. This means that a marriage took place every 13 seconds and a divorce every 26.[4] The total number of divorced people in the US was 17.4 million in 1994.[5] One in every two marriages now ends in divorce. In the UK the picture is not much brighter. In 1994 there were 338,000 marriages, over a third of which were remarriages, and just under 180,000 divorces.[6] Almost four in 10 marriages end in divorce. This is the highest rate in the European Union.[7]

The sociological reasons for the growth in divorce are many and varied. They include the emancipation of women, changes in the pattern of employment (both parents working), the pressures on family life exerted by unemployment and financial anxiety, and of course the provisions of the civil law for easier divorce. But undoubtedly the greatest single reason is the decline of Christian faith in the West, together with the loss of commitment to a Christian understanding of the sanctity and permanence of marriage, and the growing non-Christian assault on traditional concepts of sex, marriage and family. A clear indication of secularization in this area is the fact that, whereas in 1850 only 4 per cent of British marriages took place in a Registry Office (as opposed to a church, chapel or synagogue), by 1993 the percentage had risen to 51. Further, the proportion of women aged 18 to 49 who were co-habiting without being married tripled between 1979 and 1992.[8]

Consider as an example of changed attitudes the book by George and Nena O'Neill entitled *Open Marriage: A New Lifestyle for Couples*. They confidently declare that monogamous marriage is obsolete, and urge their readers to replace an 'archaic, rigid, outmoded, oppressive, static, decaying, Victorian' institution with one that is 'free, dynamic, honest, spontaneous, creative'. They refuse to glorify either traditional marriage or motherhood, and regard partners as equal, independent individuals who enjoy complete and unfettered role reversibility.[9]

If each partner comes to regard marriage as primarily a quest for his or her self-fulfilment, rather than as an adventure in reciprocal self-giving, through which parents and children grow into maturity, the outcome is bound to be bleak. Yet it is this self-centred attitude to marriage which is being canvassed by many today. Here is an unabashed quotation from the book *Divorce: How and When To Let Go* by John H. Adam and Nancy Williamson Adam.[10] It appeared in the June 1982 issue of *New Woman*:

Yes, your marriage can wear out. People change their values and lifestyles. People want to experience new things. Change is a part of life. Change and personal growth are traits for you to be proud of, indicative of a vital searching mind. You must accept the reality that in today's multi-faceted world it is especially easy for two persons to grow apart. Letting go of your marriage – if it is no longer good for you – can be the most successful thing you have ever done. Getting a

divorce can be a positive, problem-solving, growth-oriented step. It
can be a personal triumph.

Here is the secular mind in all its shameless perversity. It celebrates
failure as success, disintegration as growth, and disaster as triumph.

Not only is the Christian view of marriage as a lifelong commitment or contract now a minority view in the West, but the Church is
in danger of giving in to the world. For among Christian people,
too, marriages are no longer as stable as they used to be, and divorces are becoming almost commonplace. Even some Christian
leaders divorce their spouses and remarry, the while retaining their
position of Christian leadership. In this area also the Christian mind
is showing signs of capitulating to secularism. The dominant worldview seems to be one of selfish individualism.[11]

My concern in this chapter is with the Christian understanding
of marriage as set forth in Scripture. Politico-legal issues (like the
place of matrimonial offence in the concept of irretrievable breakdown, justice in financial settlements, custody of and access to
children) are very important. So are social and psychological questions, some of which I have already mentioned. And I shall come to
personal and pastoral matters at the end. But of primary importance for the Christian mind are the biblical questions. Even the
painful trauma of a failed marriage cannot be made an excuse for
avoiding these. What has God revealed to be his will in regard to
marriage, and the possibility of divorce and remarriage? And how
can we frame our policies and practice in accordance with biblical
principles? To be sure, there are no easy answers. In particular, the
Church feels the tension between its prophetic responsibility to bear
witness to God's revealed standards and its pastoral responsibility
to show compassion to those who have been unable to maintain his
standards. John Williams is right to bid us remember that 'the same
God who said through Malachi "I hate divorce" (2:16) also said
through Hosea (whose partner had been blatantly immoral) "I will
heal their waywardness and love them freely, for my anger has
turned away from them" (14:4).'[12]

Old Testament teaching

The nearest the Bible comes to a definition of marriage is Genesis
2:24, which Jesus himself was later to quote, when asked about

permissible grounds for divorce, as a word of God (Matthew 19:4–5). Immediately after Eve has been created and brought to Adam, and Adam has recognized her (in an outburst of love poetry) as his God-given spouse, the narrator comments: 'For this reason a man will leave his father and mother and be united to his wife, and they will become one flesh.'

From this we may deduce that a marriage exists in God's sight when a man leaves his parents, with a view not merely to living apart from them but to 'cleaving' to his wife, and becomes one flesh with her. The 'leaving' and the 'cleaving' belong together, and should take place in that order. They denote the replacement of one human relationship (child–parent) by another (husband–wife). There are some similarities between these relationships, for both are complex and contain several elements. These are physical (in one case conception, birth and nurture; in the other sexual intercourse), emotional ('growing up' being the process of growing out of the dependence of childhood into the maturity of partnership) and social (children inheriting an already existent family unit, parents creating a new one). Yet there is an essential dissimilarity between them too. For the biblical expression 'one flesh' clearly indicates that the physical, emotional and social unity of husband and wife is more profoundly and mysteriously personal than the relationship of children to parents. It is increasingly recognized that development as a human being necessitates a measure of emotional separation from parents, and that, as Dr Jack Dominian has put it, 'the failure to achieve a minimum of emotional independence is one of the main causes of marital breakdown'.[13]

So Genesis 2:24 implies that the marriage union has at least five characteristics. It is an exclusive man–woman relationship ('a man … his wife …'), which is publicly acknowledged at some social event ('leaves his parents'), permanent ('cleaves to his wife'), and consummated by sexual intercourse ('they will become one flesh'). A biblical definition of marriage might then be as follows: 'Marriage is an exclusive heterosexual covenant between one man and one woman, ordained and sealed by God, preceded by a public leaving of parents, consummated in sexual union, issuing in a permanent mutually supportive partnership, and normally crowned by the gift of children.'

With this definition of marriage in our minds, we are in a position to evaluate cohabitation, that is, the practice of living together as man and wife without being married. This has become an increasingly popular lifestyle. In fact, 'it is estimated that by the year 2000 four out of five couples (in the UK) will cohabit before they marry'.[14] The report of a Church of England working party entitled *Something to Celebrate* (1995), and subtitled 'Valuing Families in Church and Society', included a ten-page section on this topic. It is a great pity that serious reflection on it has been inhibited by a diversion tactic on the part of the media. They seized on the statement that the Church should 'abandon the phrase "living in sin" ', but failed to appreciate the reason for the report's recommendation, namely that the expression reduced a complexity of issues to 'a single sensationalist category'.[15] The working party deserved better treatment, and in my view was right to listen open-mindedly, even sympathetically, to those who are unwilling to condemn cohabitation out of hand.

For cohabitation is at least to some degree a protest by the rising generation against the marriage conventions, hypocrisies and failures of their parents' generation. They have no wish to repeat their mistakes. 'Marriage is only a piece of paper,' they cry dismissively, meaning that the quality of their relationship is more important. We could perhaps affirm their concern as follows. If a man and a woman find themselves marooned on a desert island, they can undoubtedly enter into a valid marriage in the sight of God, even though all the trappings of a traditional wedding are unavailable to them. For what constitutes marriage before God is neither a legal document, nor a church service, nor an elaborate reception, nor a shower of gifts, but a reciprocal covenant, pledging lifelong fidelity and consummated in sexual union.

In the light of this, some cohabitation may almost be regarded as marriage by another name, since the essence of marriage (a covenant commitment) is there. Nevertheless, two essential elements are usually missing from a situation of cohabitation. The first is the promise of a *life-time commitment*. Too much cohabitation is an open-ended arrangement, a kind of trial marriage, in which the permanent commitment of marriage has been replaced by a temporary experiment. This cannot be called marriage; moreover, its provisional nature is bound to destabilize the relationship. 'The period of cohabitation tends to be short-lived. One third of couples cohabit for less than a year, and only 16 per cent live with their partner for more than 5 years'.[16] Further, the commonly made claim that a trial period will make a later marriage more stable is not borne out by the facts. 'Those couples marrying in the 1980s, having first cohabited, were 50 per cent more likely to have divorced within 5 years of marrying than those who did not previously cohabit.'[17] No relationship may be called marriage which does not include the intention to be faithful to one another for life. 'What God has joined together,' Jesus said, 'let nobody separate' (Matthew 19:6.)

The second missing element in cohabitation is the *public context* in which marriage is undertaken. We have seen that the biblical definition of marriage (Genesis 2:24) includes the leaving of parents. In the culture of those days such a departure will not have been private, let alone clandestine, but public. In our day it cannot be applied to a casual leaving of home, as when a single student goes up to university. It indicates rather a definitive move away from dependence on parents in the home of one's childhood, in order to marry and so establish a new and independent home. A public relationship like this (a man and a woman living together as partners) needs to have a public beginning. This would of course be impossible on a desert island, but in society family and friends have a right to know what kind of relationship exists, so that they can adjust to it. They would naturally also desire an opportunity to say goodbye, to celebrate, and to promise support in the future. It is neither fair nor kind to leave the families in the dark and in the cold.

It is not parents only, however, nor only a wider circle of family and friends, who have a right to know about and share in the new relationship, but society as a whole. Sexual intimacy is of course essentially private, but not the relationship within which it takes place. Yet cohabitees do not make this distinction, and make the mistake of regarding their whole relationship as an entirely private affair. Marriage, however, is public – both the event which initiates it and the relationship to which it leads. And although its due recognition by the law is not essential to the marriage itself (desert island marriages being registered in heaven but not on earth), its legal enactment is certainly advantageous. For a solemn pledge can hardly be regarded as 'binding' without the sanctions of law. Moreover, a couple who commit themselves to each other need the protection which the law gives them.

From the family and the law we come to the Church. To be sure, a church service is no more essential to a marriage in God's sight than the corresponding secular formalities. Neither church nor registry office is to be found on a desert island. Nevertheless, since lifelong vows are solemn and should if possible be made publicly, a church service is most appropriate, especially for Christian believers. For it sets the reciprocal pledges in the presence of God and his people. Although marriage is not a 'sacrament' in the sense that baptism is, yet both include a public commitment, which should be made in the presence of chosen witnesses.

To sum up, we should be able to agree that a couple could marry validly in the sight of God on a desert island, provided that they make lifelong vows to one another, even though no representatives of family, law or church are present to witness them. But in the real world in which we live, a couple's commitment needs to be public as well as permanent, and the role of the family, the law and the Church make the difference between marriage and cohabitation.

In my view, therefore, *Something to Celebrate* was unwise to take a 'both-and' approach, and to recommend Christians 'both to hold fast to the centrality of marriage and at the same time to accept that cohabitation is, for many people, a step along the way towards that fuller and more complete commitment'.[18] In their both-and approach, and in their laudable desire to be sympathetic and non-judgemental, the authors of the report have blurred the distinction between marriage and cohabitation. It is more accurate and more helpful to speak of cohabitation as falling short of marriage, than as a stepping-stone towards it. Our imaginary visit to a desert island should have helped us to clarify theologically what the essence of marriage is in the sight of God. But our responsibility is to stay in the real world and to maintain without compromise the biblical definition of marriage, including its public and permanent nature.

Then we can affirm what Dr George Carey, Archbishop of Canterbury, said during the General Synod debate on *Something to Celebrate*: 'Cohabitation is not, and cannot be, marriage in all but name. Marriage is public and formal, whereas … cohabiting relationships … remain private and provisional in status … Marriage, not cohabitation, is the institution which is at the heart of the good society, and let us not be reluctant to say so. I do not say this in condemnation, I say it as an invitation to a better way …'[19]

We come now in our survey of biblical teaching to Deuteronomy 24:1–4, which is of particular importance because it is the only Old Testament passage which refers to grounds or procedures for divorce.

¹If a man marries a woman who becomes displeasing to him because
he finds something indecent about her; and he writes her a certificate
of divorce, gives it to her and sends her from his house, ²and if after
she leaves his house she becomes the wife of another man, ³and her
second husband dislikes her and writes her a certificate of divorce,
gives it to her and sends her from his house, or if he dies, ⁴then her
first husband, who divorced her, is not allowed to marry her again
after she has been defiled. That would be detestable in the eyes of
the Lord. Do not bring sin upon the land the Lord your God is giving
you as an inheritance.

Three particular points need to be clarified about this legislation.
The first concerns its thrust and purpose. It neither requires, nor
recommends, nor even sanctions divorce. Its primary concern is not
with divorce at all, nor even with certificates of divorce. Its object is
to forbid a man to remarry his former spouse, if he has divorced
her, since this would be 'detestable in the eyes of the Lord'. It is
thought that the ruling was intended to protect the woman from a
capricious and perhaps cruel former husband. At all events, the first
three verses are all the protasis or conditional part of the sentence;
the apodosis or consequence does not begin until verse 4. The law is
not approving divorce; what it says is that *if* a man divorces his wife,
and *if* he gives her a certificate, and *if* she leaves and remarries, and
if her second husband dislikes and divorces her, or dies, *then* her
first husband may not marry her again.

Secondly, although divorce is not encouraged, yet if it happens,
the ground on which it takes place is that the husband finds 'something shameful' (NEB, RSV) or 'something indecent' (NIV) in his wife.
This cannot refer to adultery on her part, for this was punishable by
death, not divorce (Deuteronomy 22:20ff.; cf. Leviticus 20:10). So
what was it? During the first century BC the rival Pharisaic parties
led by Rabbi Shammai and Rabbi Hillel were debating this very
thing. Shammai was strict and understood 'something indecent'
(whose Hebrew root alludes to 'nakedness' or 'exposure') as a sexual offence of some kind which, though left undefined, fell short of
adultery or promiscuity. Rabbi Hillel, by contrast, was lax. He
picked on the phrases which said that the wife 'becomes displeasing' to her first husband (verse 1) or that her second husband
'dislikes' her (verse 3), and interpreted them as including even the
most trivial misdemeanours, for example, if she spoiled the food she

was cooking for him, or was quarrelsome, or if he came across a woman more beautiful than she, and so lost interest in her.[20] In fact, according to Hillel, 'anything which caused annoyance or embarrassment to a husband was a legitimate ground for a divorce suit'.[21]

A third point from these Deuteronomy verses, which is noteworthy, is that if divorce was allowed, so evidently was remarriage. For the text presupposes that, once the woman had received her certificate of divorce and been sent from the house, she was free to remarry, even though in this case she was the guilty party, having done 'something indecent' on account of which she had been divorced. In fact, so far as is known, the cultures of the ancient world all understood that divorce carried with it the permission to remarry; *divortium a thoro et mensa* (from bed and board), namely a legal separation, without being also *a vinculo matrimonii* (from the marriage bond itself), was not contemplated. Dr James B. Hurley summarizes the marriage and divorce laws of the Code of Hammurabi, who was king of Babylon in the early eighteenth century BC when Abraham left Ur, and also the harsher Assyrian laws at the time of Israel's exodus from Egypt.[22] And Dr Gordon Wenham has added information from the fifth century BC papyri at Elephantine, a small Jewish garrison town in southern Egypt, as well as from Philo, Josephus and the Greek and Roman world.[23] All these cultures supply evidence for divorce by the husband, and in some cases by the wife as well, with liberty to remarry. Usually the divorced wife had her dowry returned to her, and received some divorce-money as well. If divorce was comparatively infrequent in the ancient world, it was because the termination of one marriage and the arrangement of a second would have been financially crippling.

The teaching of Jesus

Our Lord's instruction on marriage and divorce was given in response to a question from the Pharisees. Mark says they posed their question in order to 'test' him (10:2), and Matthew elaborates what the test question was: 'Is it lawful for a man to divorce his wife for any and every reason?' (19:3). Perhaps behind their question was the public scandal of Herodias, who had left her husband Philip in order to marry King Herod Antipas. John the Baptist had courageously denounced their union as 'unlawful' (Mark 6:17ff.), and had been imprisoned as a result. Would Jesus be equally outspoken, especially when, as seems probable, he was at the time within the jurisdiction of Herod (Mark 10:1)? Certainly the Pharisees wanted to embroil him in the Shammai–Hillel debate, already mentioned. Hence the emphasis in their question on the 'reasons' or 'causes' which justify divorce.

> ³Some Pharisees came to him to test him. They asked, 'Is it lawful for a man to divorce his wife for any and every reason?'
> ⁴'Haven't you read,' he replied, 'that at the beginning the Creator "made them male and female", ⁵and said, "For this reason a man will leave his father and mother and be united to his wife, and the two will become one flesh"? ⁶So they are no longer two, but one. Therefore what God has joined together, let man not separate.'
> ⁷'Why then,' they asked, 'did Moses command that a man give his wife a certificate of divorce and send her away?'
> ⁸Jesus replied, 'Moses permitted you to divorce your wives because your hearts were hard. But it was not this way from the beginning. ⁹I tell you that anyone who divorces his wife, except for marital unfaithfulness, and marries another woman commits adultery.'
> ¹⁰The disciples said to him, 'If this is the situation between a husband and wife, it is better not to marry.'
> ¹¹Jesus replied, 'Not everyone can accept this teaching, but only those to whom it has been given. ¹²For some are eunuchs because they were born that way; others were made that way by men; and others have renounced marriage because of the kingdom of heaven. The one who can accept this should accept it.'
>
> (Matthew 19:3–12)

It is clear that Jesus disassociated himself from the laxity of Rabbi Hillel. He had already done so in the Sermon on the Mount. His teaching on divorce in that passage was given as one of his six antitheses, introduced by the formula 'you have heard that it was said … but I tell you …' What he was opposing in these antitheses was not Scripture ('it has been written') but tradition ('it has been said'), not the revelation of God but the perverse interpretations of the Scribes. The object of their distortions was to reduce the demands of the law and make them more comfortable. In the divorce antithesis the scribal quotation ('It has been said, "Anyone who divorces his wife must give her a certificate of divorce" ' appears to be a deliberately misleading abbreviation of the Deuteronomy 24 passage. It gives the impression that divorce was readily permissible, even for trivial reasons (as Hillel taught), provided only that a certificate was given. Jesus categorically rejected this. What did he teach?

First, *Jesus endorsed the permanence of marriage.* It is significant that he did not give the Pharisees a direct answer to their question about divorce. Instead, he spoke to them about marriage. He referred them back to Genesis 1 and 2, and asked incredulously if they had not read these chapters. He drew their attention to the two facts that human sexuality was a divine creation and that human marriage was a divine ordinance. For he bracketed two texts (Genesis 1:27 and 2:24) and made God the author of both. For the same Creator who 'at the beginning ... "made them male and female"', also said (in the biblical text) '"For this reason a man will leave his father and mother and be united to his wife, and the two will become one flesh."' 'So,' Jesus went on, adding his own explanatory assertion, 'they are no longer two, but one.' And, 'Therefore,' adding his own prohibition, 'what God has joined together (literally, "yoked together"), let man not separate.'

The teaching is unambiguous. The marriage bond is more than a human contract: it is a divine yoke. And the way in which God lays this yoke upon a married couple is not by creating a kind of mystical union but by declaring his purpose in his Word. Marital breakdown, even the so-called 'death' of a relationship, cannot then be regarded as being in itself a ground for dissolution. For the basis of the union is not fluctuating human experience ('I love you, I love you not') but the divine will and Word (they 'become one flesh').

Secondly, *Jesus declared the Mosaic provision of divorce to be a concession to human sinfulness.* The Pharisees responded to his quotations from Genesis by asking a second question: 'Why then did Moses command that a man give his wife a certificate of divorce and send her away?' To this Jesus replied: 'Moses permitted you to divorce your wives because your hearts were hard. But it was not this way from the beginning.' Thus, what they had termed a 'command' Jesus called a 'permission', and a reluctant permission at that, due to human stubbornness rather than divine intention.[24]

Since Jesus referred to the Mosaic provision as a concession to human sin, which was also intended to limit its evil effects, it cannot possibly be taken as indicating God's approval of divorce. To be sure, it was a *divine* concession, for according to Jesus whatever

Moses said, God said. Yet the divine concession of divorce was contrary to the divine institution of marriage 'from the beginning'. The Rabbis' error lay in ignoring the distinction between God's will (Genesis 1 and 2) and his legal provision for human sinfulness (Deuteronomy 24). 'Human conduct which falls short of the absolute command of God is sin and stands under the divine judgement. The provisions which God's mercy has designed for the limitation of the consequences of man's sin must not be interpreted as divine approval for sinning.'[25]

Thirdly, *Jesus called remarriage after divorce 'adultery'*. Putting together his teaching from the Synoptic Gospels, and leaving aside for the moment the exceptive clause, we may summarize it as follows: a man who divorces his wife, and then remarries, both commits adultery himself (Matthew 19:9; Mark 10:11; Luke 16:18) and, because it is assumed that his divorced wife will also remarry, causes her to commit adultery as well (Matthew 5:32). A woman who divorces her husband and remarries similarly commits adultery (Mark 10:12). Further, a man (and presumably a woman too, assuming reciprocity in this situation as in others) who marries a divorcee commits adultery (Matthew 5:32; Luke 16:18). These are hard sayings. They expose with candour the logical consequences of sin. If a divorce and remarriage take place, which have no sanction from God, then any new union which follows, being unlawful, is adulterous.

Fourthly, *Jesus permitted divorce and remarriage on the sole ground of immorality (porneia)*. It is well known that Matthew 5:32 and 19:9 both contain an 'exceptive clause', whose purpose is to exempt one category of divorce and remarriage from being branded 'adultery'. Much controversy has raged round this clause. I do not think I can do more than indicate three conclusions which I have reached about it.

(1) *The exceptive clause should be accepted as an authentic utterance of Jesus*. Because it does not occur in the parallel sayings in Mark and Luke, many scholars have been too ready to dismiss it. Some suggest that it was an early scribal interpolation and no part of Matthew's original text. But there is no manuscript evidence that it was a gloss; even the alternative reading of Codex Vaticanus, retained in the RSV margin, does not omit the clause. Other scholars attribute the clause to Matthew himself, and/or to the church in which he was writing, but deny that Jesus ever spoke it. But its omission by Mark and Luke is not in itself a sufficient ground for rejecting it as an editorial

invention or interpretation by the first evangelist. It is perfectly possible to suppose that Matthew included it for his Jewish readership who were very concerned about the permissible grounds for divorce, whereas Mark and Luke, writing for Gentile readers, did not have the same concern. Their silence is not necessarily due to their ignorance: it may equally well be that they took the clause for granted. Pagan cultures regarded adultery as a ground for divorce. So did both the Jewish schools of Hillel and Shammai, in spite of their disagreements on other points. This was not in dispute.

(2) *The word 'porneia' means sexual immorality.* In deciding how to translate *porneia*, we need to avoid both extremes of too much laxity and too much rigidity.

Several 'rigid' views have been held, which identify *porneia* as one particular sexual sin – either 'fornication' in the sense of the discovery of pre-marital immorality, or a marriage within prohibited familial relationships, or post-marriage adultery. The main reason for rejecting any of these translations is that, although *porneia* could mean all of them, it would not be understood as referring to any one of them if there were no further qualification. *Porneia* was, in fact, a generic word for sexual infidelity or 'marital unfaithfulness' (NIV), and included 'every kind of unlawful sexual intercourse' (Arndt-Gingrich).

The 'lax' view is that *porneia* includes offences which may be regarded as broadly 'sexual' in psychological rather than physical terms and so embraces even a basic temperamental incompatibility. Now it may be possible to use other arguments for the legitimacy of divorce on such grounds as these, but it is not possible to do so from the meaning of the word *porneia*. *Porneia* means physical sexual immorality; the reason why Jesus made it the sole permissible ground for divorce must be that it violates the 'one flesh' principle which is foundational to marriage as divinely ordained and biblically defined.

(3) *Divorce for immorality is permissible, not mandatory.* Jesus did not teach that the innocent party *must* divorce an unfaithful partner, still less that sexual unfaithfulness *ipso facto* dissolves the marriage. He did not even encourage or recommend divorce for unfaithfulness. On the contrary, his whole emphasis was on the permanence of marriage in God's purpose and on the inadmissibility of divorce and remarriage. His reason for adding the exceptive clause was to clarify that the only remarriage after divorce which is not tantamount to adultery is that of an innocent person whose

partner has been sexually unfaithful, for in this case the infidelity has already been committed by the guilty partner. Jesus' purpose was emphatically not to encourage divorce for this reason, but rather to forbid it for all other reasons. As John Murray wrote: 'It is the one exception that gives prominence to the illegitimacy of every other reason. Preoccupation with the *one* exception should never be permitted to obscure the force of the negation of all others.'[26]

After this long excursus on the meaning of the exceptive clause and the permissible ground for divorce, it is important to come back to where we began. Although Jesus knew the realities of the Fall and of the hardness of human hearts, he recalled his contemporaries to the norm of the Creation and the unchanging purpose of God. He stressed reconciliation not separation, marriage not divorce. We must never move out of earshot of his ringing cry: 'What God has joined together, let no one separate.'

The teaching of Paul

The teaching of Paul which we have to consider occurs in 1 Corinthians 7:10–16, and concerns in particular the so-called 'Pauline privilege':

> [10]To the married I give this command (not I, but the Lord): A wife must not separate from her husband. [11]But if she does, she must remain unmarried or else be reconciled to her husband. And a husband must not divorce his wife.
> [12]To the rest I say this (I, not the Lord); If any brother has a wife who is not a believer and she is willing to live with him, he must not divorce her. [13]And if a woman has a husband who is not a believer and he is willing to live with her, she must not divorce him. [14]For the unbelieving husband has been sanctified through his wife, and the unbelieving wife has been sanctified through her believing husband. Otherwise your children would be unclean, but as it is, they are holy.
> [15]But if the unbeliever leaves, let him do so. A believing man or woman is not bound in such circumstances; God has called us to live in peace. [16]How do you know, wife, whether you will save your husband? Or, how do you know, husband, whether you will save your wife?

We need to observe, first, that *Paul is giving authoritative, apostolic instruction.* The antithesis he makes between verse 10 ('I give this command – not I, but the Lord') and verse 12 ('To the rest I say this – I, not the Lord') has been much misunderstood. It is quite mistaken to imagine that he is setting Christ's teaching and his own in opposition to each other, with the further implication that Christ's has authority, whereas his has not. No, his contrast is not between divine, infallible teaching (Christ's) and human, fallible teaching (his own), but between two forms of divine and infallible teaching, the one dominical (the Lord's) and the other apostolic (his own). There can be no doubt that this is correct, for Paul continues to use the authoritative apostolic *ego* 'I' in this chapter, in verse 17 ('This is the rule I lay down in all the churches'), verse 25 ('I have no command from the Lord', i.e. no recorded saying of Jesus, 'but I give judgement as one who by the Lord's mercy is trustworthy') and verse 40 ('I think that I too have the Spirit of God'). Later and similarly, he puts his authority above that of prophets and declares his instruction to be the Lord's command: 'If anybody thinks he is a prophet or spiritually gifted, let him acknowledge that what I am writing to you is the Lord's command' (14:37).

Secondly, *Paul echoes and confirms Jesus' prohibition of divorce.* In verses 10 and 11, as in his teaching in Romans 7:1–3, and as in the Lord's teaching recorded by Mark and Luke, the prohibition of divorce is stated in absolute terms. 'A wife must not separate from her husband … And a husband must not divorce his wife.' This is because he is expressing the general principle. It is not necessary to suppose that he knew nothing of the Lord's exceptive clause.

In verse 11 he adds an important parenthesis to the effect that if a wife does 'separate' from her husband, 'she must remain unmarried or else be reconciled to her husband'. Now the verb Paul uses for separate (*chōrizō*) could refer to divorce and was so used both in marriage contracts in the papyri and by some early Church Fathers (Arndt-Gingrich). But the context suggests that Paul is not referring to divorce. He seems rather to be envisaging a situation in which the husband has not been sexually unfaithful and the wife is therefore not at liberty to divorce him. Some other reason (unstated) has prompted her to 'separate' from him. So Paul emphasizes that in this case she is not free to remarry. Her Christian calling is either to remain single or to be reconciled to her husband, but not to remarry.

Thirdly, *Paul permits divorce after a believer has been deserted by an unbelieving partner.* He addresses three successive paragraphs 'to the unmarried and the widows' (verses 8, 9), 'to the married' (verses 10, 11) and 'to the rest' (verses 12–16). The context reveals that by 'the rest' he has in mind a particular kind of mixed marriage. He gives no liberty to a Christian to marry a non-Christian, for a Christian woman 'is free to marry anyone she wishes, but he must belong to the Lord' (verse 39). And the converse is equally true of Christian men (2 Corinthians 6:14ff.). Paul is rather handling the situation which arises when two non-Christians marry, one of whom is subsequently converted. The Corinthians had evidently sent him questions about this. Was the marriage unclean? Should the Christian partner divorce the non-Christian? What was the status of their children? Paul's reply is clear.

If the unbelieving partner 'is willing to live with' the believing, then the believer must not resort to divorce. The reason given is that the unbelieving partner 'has been sanctified' through his or her be-lieving spouse, and so have the children. The 'sanctification' in mind is clearly not a transformation of character into the likeness of Christ. As John Murray puts it, 'the sanctification of which Paul speaks … must be the sanctification of privilege, connection and relationship'.[27]

But if, on the other hand, the unbelieving partner is unwilling to stay, and decides to leave, then 'let him do so. A believing man or woman is not bound in such circumstances.' The reasons given are that God has called us to live in peace, and that the believer cannot guarantee to win the unbeliever by insisting on perpetuating a union which the unbeliever is not willing to continue.[28]

It is important to grasp the situation which the apostle envisages, and not to draw unwarrantable deductions from his teaching. He affirms that, if the unbeliever refuses to stay, the believer 'is not bound', that is, bound to hold on to him or her, indeed, bound to the marriage itself.[29] Several negative points need to be made about the freedom which the believing partner is here given.

(1) The believer's freedom is not due to his or her conversion, but rather to the partner's non-conversion and unwillingness to remain. Christians sometimes plead for what they call 'gospel real-ism', arguing that because conversion makes all things new, a mar-riage contracted in pre-conversion days is not necessarily still binding and in its place a new beginning may be made. This is dangerous reasoning, however. Are all pre-conversion contracts can-celled by conversion, including all one's debts? No, Paul's teaching

lends no possible support to such a view. On the contrary, he contradicts it. His teaching is not that after conversion the believing partner is defiled by the unbeliever, and should therefore extricate himself or herself from the relationship. It is the opposite, that the unbelieving partner has been 'sanctified' by the believer, and that therefore the believer should not seek to escape. Further, Paul urges in verses 17–24 that Christians should remain in the state in which they were when God called them, and that we are able to do so because now we are there 'with God'.

(2) The believer's freedom is not due to any resolve of his own to begin divorce proceedings, but only to his reluctant acquiescence in his partner's 'desertion', or unwillingness to stay. The initiative must not be the believer's. On the contrary, if the unbelieving partner is willing to remain, 'he must not divorce her' and 'she must not divorce him' (verses 12, 13). The furthest Paul goes is to say that if the unbeliever insists on leaving, 'let him do so' (verse 15). Perhaps this is the way to reconcile the apparently inconsistent statements that (a) Jesus permitted divorce on one ground only and (b) Paul added another. The first is a case of divorce; the second is an acquiescence in desertion.

(3) The believer's freedom is not due to 'desertion' of any and every kind, nor to desertion for any form of unbelief (e.g. the Roman Catholic Church's view that marriage is not *ratum* if a partner is unbaptized), but only to the specific unwillingness of an unconverted person on religious grounds to continue living with his or her now-converted partner. The 'Pauline privilege' provides no basis, therefore, for divorce on the general grounds of desertion; this is not a Christian option.

Summing up what Scripture teaches in the passages so far considered, we may make the following three affirmations:

(1) God created humankind male and female in the beginning, and himself instituted marriage. His intention was and is that human sexuality will find fulfilment in marriage, and that marriage will be an exclusive, loving and lifelong union. This is his purpose.

(2) Divorce is nowhere commanded, and never even encouraged, in Scripture. On the contrary, even if biblically justified, it remains a sad and sinful declension from the divine norm.

(3) Divorce and remarriage are permissible (not mandatory) on two grounds. First, an innocent person may divorce his or her partner if the latter has been guilty of serious sexual immorality.

Secondly, a believer may acquiesce in the desertion of his or her unbelieving partner, if the latter refuses to go on living with him or her. In both cases, however, the permission is given in negative or reluctant terms. Only if a person divorces his or her partner on the ground of marital unfaithfulness is his or her remarriage not adulterous. Only if the unbeliever insists on leaving, is the believer 'not bound'.

Irretrievable breakdown

My position, as defined above, was criticized by Dr David Atkinson in his book *To Have and To Hold* (1979). He called it 'legislative' and expressed his uneasiness in the following terms: 'The difficulty with this view is that in pastoral practice it can lead to the sort of casuistry which can become negatively legalistic. It concentrates on physical adultery but neglects other "unfaithfulness", and can mean that the Church's blessing for second marriage is reserved only for those who are fortunate (!) enough to have had their former partner commit adultery against them. It raises the question as to what breaks the marriage bond.'[30]

It is, indeed, because of the practical problems which beset us when we insist on a 'matrimonial offence' as the only legitimate ground for divorce, that an alternative and more flexible approach has been sought. The Church of England report *Putting Asunder* (1966) recommended the concept of 'irretrievable breakdown' as an alternative, and the 1969 Divorce Reform Act was based upon it. It nevertheless required that irretrievable breakdown be proved by one of five evidences, three being faults (adultery, desertion and unreasonable behaviour), and two indicating de facto separation (for two years if the couple agree to divorce, and for five years if they do not). Then the Church of England Commission which was presided over by Canon Professor Howard Root, and which reported in *Marriage, Divorce and The Church* (SPCK, 1971), investigated further the concept that some marriages 'die' even while both married partners are still alive. And a few years later the Commission chaired by Bishop Kenneth Skelton of Lichfield, which reported in *Marriage and the Church's Task* (CIO, 1978), took a similar line.

In 1990 the Law Commission's report *Family Law: The Ground for Divorce* proposed that all reference to fault be dropped; that irretrievable breakdown become the sole ground for divorce; and that such breakdown be proved by the passage of 12 months (mini-mum) in which the couple may reflect, voluntarily seek counsel and conciliation, and make adequate arrangements for custody, home and finance. These proposals with modifications were embodied in the Family Law Act, which became law in 1996 and comes into effect in 1998. It is based on the no-fault principle, and extends the minimum period of waiting for reflection and consideration to 18 months. Lord Mackay emphasized that the purpose of the Act is to support marriage and stem the rising tide of divorce. The Church of England's General Synod debated and approved his proposals.

One can understand the motives behind this development, in particular the desire to avoid the need to establish culpability. But the arguments against it do not seem to have been adequately con-sidered. The concept of 'irretrievable breakdown' has undesirable consequences. (1) It makes divorce too easy; it virtually opens the door to divorce on demand. (2) It represents marriage in terms of self-fulfilment, instead of self-giving. If it does not deliver what we had expected, then, instead of working at it, we declare that it does-n't work for us. (3) It gives the impression that marriages break down by themselves. It makes marriage the scapegoat and exoner-ates the married partners. But if the essence of marriage is a com-mitment of love and faithfulness, then only a failure in these will threaten it. By adopting the secular approach of no-fault break-down, Dr Alan Storkey has written, the churches have locked them-selves into a contradiction, 'affirming ... one view of marriage, while accepting a competely different dynamic behind divorce reform'.[31] (4) It is an expression of secular pessimism. If two persons are 'in-compatible', and a breakdown is 'irretrievable', what has become of the grace of God and the gospel of reconciliation?

Here then are two different approaches to the vexed question of divorce – 'fault' and 'no fault', human culpability and irretrievable breakdown. Are we obliged to choose between them? Or is there a third way which embraces the best in both concepts? Perhaps the answer lies in the biblical notion of 'covenant' and 'covenant faith-fulness'. It could be described as a third way in the sense that the ground for divorce is neither a breakdown for which nobody accepts responsibility, nor a particular individual fault which has to be proved, but rather a culpable breach of the marriage covenant.

It is clear that Scripture regards marriage as a covenant, indeed – although between two human beings – as a 'covenant of God'

(Proverbs 2:17 literally), instituted and witnessed by him. In a letter which I received some years ago Roger Beckwith, Warden of Latimer House, Oxford, summarized what he saw to be the five terms of the marriage covenant: (1) Love (as in every covenant), but married love involving specific obligations; (2) living together as a single household and family; (3) faithfulness to the marriage bed; (4) provision for the wife by the husband; and (5) submission to the husband by the wife.

In his book *To Have and To Hold*, subtitled 'The Marriage Covenant and the Discipline of Divorce', David Atkinson develops the covenant idea further. He defines a covenant as 'an agreement between parties based on promise, which includes these four elements: first, an undertaking of committed faithfulness made by one party to the other (or by each to the other); secondly, the acceptance of that undertaking by the other party; thirdly, public knowledge of such an undertaking and its acceptance; and fourthly, the growth of a personal relationship based on and expressive of such a commitment.'[32] It is not difficult to apply such a definition of 'covenant' to marriage, especially because human marriage is used in Scripture as a model of God's covenant with his people, and God's covenant as a model for human marriage.[33] David Atkinson goes on to quote Professor G.R. Dunstan's development of this analogy, in that God's covenant and human marriage both have (1) an *initiative of love*, inviting a response, and so creating a relationship, (2) a *vow of consent*, guarding the union against the fitfulness of emotion, (3) *obligations of faithfulness*, (4) the *promise of blessing* to those who are faithful to their covenant obligations, and (5) *sacrifice*, the laying down of life in death, especially in this case death to the old independence and self-centredness.[34]

David Atkinson goes on to argue that 'the covenant structure of marriage lends weight to the view … that marriage is not a metaphysical status which cannot be destroyed; it is rather a moral commitment which should be honoured.'[35] Yet a covenant can be broken. 'Covenants do not just "break down",' however, 'they are broken; divorce expresses sin as well as tragedy.' So then 'from a biblical moral perspective, we cannot dissolve the category of "matrimonial offence" without remainder into the less personally focused concept of "irretrievable breakdown"'.[36] Instead, 'the covenant model for marriage places the question of divorce in the area of moral responsibility.'[37] And his conclusion is that 'any action which constitutes unfaithfulness to the marriage covenant so persistent and unrepentant that reconciliation becomes impossible may be sufficient to break the bond of marriage and so may release the other partner from their covenant promise.'[38]

There is much in the covenant model of marriage which is compelling. To begin with, it is a thoroughly biblical notion. It also emphasizes the great solemnity both of covenant making and of covenant breaking – in the former case emphasizing love, commitment, public recognition, exclusive faithfulness and sacrifice, and in the latter the sin of going back on promises and rupturing a relationship of love. I confess, however, that my problem is how to fuse the concepts of covenant loyalty and matrimonial offence. I can understand the reasons for not wanting to build permission to divorce on two offences. But if Scripture regards the marriage covenant as capable of being broken in several ways, how shall we explain the single offence mentioned in our Lord's exceptive clause? Certainly the covenant relationship envisaged in marriage (the 'one flesh' union) is far deeper than other covenants, whether a suzerainty treaty, a business deal or even a pact of friendship. May it not be, therefore, that nothing less than a violation (by sexual infidelity) of this fundamental relationship can break the marriage covenant?

God's marriage covenant with 'Jerusalem' (personifying his people), described at length in Ezekiel 16, is germane to this issue. God says to her: 'I gave you my solemn oath and entered into a covenant with you … and you became mine' (verse 8). But Jerusalem 'played the harlot', or rather (because she gave hire rather than receiving it) was a wife guilty of promiscuous adultery (verses 15–34). Therefore, God said he would sentence her to 'the punishment of women who commit adultery' (verse 38). Nevertheless, although her behaviour was worse even than her 'younger sister Sodom' (verses 46–52), and although she had despised God's oath 'by breaking the covenant' (verse 59), yet God said: 'I will remember the covenant I made with you in the days of your youth, and I will establish an everlasting covenant with you' (verse 60), bringing forgiveness and penitence.

It seems to me that we must allow these perspectives of God's covenant to shape our understanding of the marriage covenant. The marriage covenant is not an ordinary human contract which, if one party to it renegues, may be renounced by the other. It is more like God's covenant with his people. In this analogy (which Scripture develops) only fundamental sexual unfaithfulness breaks the covenant. And even this does not lead automatically or necessarily to divorce; it may rather be an occasion for reconciliation and forgiveness.

Personal and pastoral realities

This has been a long chapter. Some readers will have been provoked by it, finding it drily academic, or unfeeling towards the profound sufferings of those whose marriages break down, or remote from the realities of the contemporary western world, or all three. I can understand their reactions. Yet it has been necessary to give the biblical material a thorough examination. For this book is about developing a Christian mind on current issues. Conscientious disciples of Jesus know that Christian action is impossible without Christian thought; they resist the temptation to take short cuts. At the same time, the process of 'making up one's mind' means reaching a decision which has practical consequences. What then are these likely to be? Because of the great seriousness with which Scripture views both marriage and divorce, I conclude with four urgent pastoral needs.

First, there is *the need for thorough biblical teaching about marriage and reconciliation.* Pastors must give positive instructions on both these subjects. In sermons, Sunday School and confirmation classes we have to hold before the congregation we serve the divine intention and norm of exclusive, committed, lifelong faithfulness in marriage. We ought also to give clear and practical teaching on the duty and the way of forgiveness. For reconciliation lies at the very heart of Christianity. For some years now I have followed a simple rule, that whenever anybody asks me a question about divorce, I refuse to answer it until I have first talked about two other subjects, namely, marriage and reconciliation. This is a simple attempt to follow Jesus in his own priorities. When the Pharisees asked him about the grounds for divorce, he referred them instead to the original institution of marriage. If we allow ourselves to become preoccupied with divorce and its grounds, rather than with marriage and its essentials, we lapse into Pharisaism. For God's purpose is marriage not divorce, and his gospel is good news of reconciliation. We need to see Scripture as a whole, and not isolate the topic of divorce.

Secondly, there is *the need for preparation for marriage.* Couples preparing for marriage usually cherish high ideals for the future, and are ready, even anxious, for help. Yet hard-pressed clergy can often manage to give each couple no more than a single interview, and even then legal and social questions sometimes crowd out the spiritual and moral dimensions of marriage. Some clergy arrange courses for groups of engaged couples, or encourage them to attend appropriate weekend conferences. Others give couples a book[39] or a short annotated list of recommended reading. Best of all, perhaps, is the resolve to harness the services of mature lay couples in the congregation, who would be willing to spend several evenings with an engaged couple, meet them again after the wedding, and continue to keep in touch with them during the early days of adjustment.

Thirdly, there is *the need for a reconciliation ministry*. In the UK, during the eighties both in-court and out-of-court conciliation services were developed, and there has been a growing desire to see conciliation attempts built into the initial stages of legal proceedings, so that an adversarial approach is avoided. At present probation officers appear to be more involved than anybody else with married couples and families who need help. There are also voluntary organizations like RELATE, the Catholic Marriage Advisory Council, the Family Discussion Bureau, and Marriage Resource (a network of Christian marriage-support groups, which sponsor National Marriage Week). I wish the churches were yet more actively involved in this ministry, especially at the local level. Christians are supposed to be in the reconciliation business. Many more people would seek help, and seek it early when it is most needed, if they knew where they could turn for sympathy, understanding and advice. Sometimes expert marital therapy will be necessary, but at other times a listening ear may be enough. As Dr Jack Dominian writes, 'Marital reconciliation ultimately depends on the ability of the spouses to change sufficiently to meet each other's minimal needs.'[40] But a friend can often be the catalyst to help people see the need for change and want it.

American Christians are in advance of Britain in this area. Partly as a result of the epidemic of suing (in 1982 22,000 law suits were being filed every day), the Christian Legal Society took the initiative in 1977 to set up 'the Christian Conciliation Service'. Responding to Christ's call to his followers to be peace-makers, to his teaching in Matthew 18:15–17 and to Paul's in 1 Corinthians 6:1–8, they are seeking to resolve conflicts and settle disputes (in business, marriage and other fields) out of court. So they offer mediation, reconciliation and (if these fail) arbitration, as alternatives to the adversarial approach of the civil courts.[41]

Fourthly, there is *the need for pastoral ministry to the divorced.* Because marriage is a 'creation ordinance', God's purposes for it do not vary; they are the same for the world as for the Church. The non-Christian world will often be unable and unwilling to fulfil them because of the hardness of human hearts, and so is likely to have its own legislation for divorce. It is right, however, to expect higher standards in the new community of Jesus. He repeatedly told his followers not to follow the way of the world. 'It shall not be so among you,' he said. In marriage, therefore, the Church's calling is not to conform to popular trends, but to bear witness to God's purpose of permanence.

Nevertheless, 'hardness of heart' is not confined to the non-Christian world. As with the Old Testament people of God, so with the people of the New Covenant, some concession to human fallibility and failure will be needed, and each church or denomination will have to make its own regulations. The sustained policy of the Church of England for several decades has been to refuse to marry in church any person who has a previous spouse still living, while at the same time seeking to offer a ministry of pastoral compassion and care to those who have been divorced. In 1981, however, reversing a vote taken in 1978, the General Synod resolved that 'there are circumstances in which a divorced person may be married in church during the lifetime of a former partner'. What those 'circumstances' are has until now not been agreed. Yet it is hoped that the deep division in the Church on this issue will be overcome, and that the Church will distinguish between those who cause divorce and those who are victims of it. For if Jesus and his apostle Paul did allow divorce and remarriage in certain circumstances, then this permission of a new beginning needs what Professor Oliver O'Donovan has called 'institutional visibility'.[42]

What institutional arrangements should the Church make? Professor O'Donovan continues: 'The primary question is how it may find *some* arrangement that will give adequate form both to its beliefs about the permanence of marriage and to its belief about the forgiveness of the penitent sinner.'[43] It could express this ambivalence either by permitting the remarriage in church (emphasizing the gospel of redemption), while adding some kind of discipline (recognizing God's marriage norm), or by refusing the remarriage in church (emphasizing the norm), while adding some expression of acceptance (recognizing the gospel). I myself incline to the former. But before any church service for the marriage of a divorced person is permitted, the Church must surely exemplify its adherence to the revelation of God in two ways. It must satisfy itself first that the remarriage comes within the range of the biblical permissions, and secondly that the couple concerned accept the divine intention of marriage permanence.

In this case the church service could not with integrity be identical with a normal marriage ceremony. Some expression of penitence should be included, either in a private preliminary (as suggested by the Root Report in paragraphs 143–7) or in the public service itself. Either way would be an acknowledgement that every divorce, even when biblically permissible, is a declension from the divine norm. This is not to stand in judgement on the people concerned in any proud or paternalistic way; it is rather to confess the universal taint of sin, in which we ourselves, as well as they, are personally involved.

In all this we continue to be caught in the tension between law and grace, witness and compassion, prophetic ministry and pastoral care. On the one hand, we need the courage to resist the prevailing winds of permissiveness and to set ourselves to uphold marriage and oppose divorce. The state will continue to frame its own divorce laws, but the Church also has its own witness to bear to the teaching of its divine Lord, and must exercise its own discipline. On the other hand, we shall seek to share with deep compassion in the suffering of those whose marriages have failed, and especially of those whom we cannot conscientiously advise to seek an escape by divorce. We may on occasion feel at liberty to advise the legitimacy of a separation without a divorce, or even a divorce without a re-marriage, taking 1 Corinthians 7:11 as our warrant. But we have no liberty to go beyond the permissions of our Lord. He knew his Father's will and cared for his disciples' welfare. Wisdom, righteousness and compassion are all found in following him.

Chapter 15

ABORTION AND EUTHANASIA

The debates over abortion and euthanasia are admittedly complex. They have medical, legal, theological, ethical, social and personal aspects. They are highly emotional subjects, for they touch on the mysteries of human sexuality and reproduction, life and death. Both often involve acutely painful dilemmas.

Yet Christians cannot opt out of personal decision-making or public discussion regarding these topics merely because of their complexity. Instead, two factors should bring them to the top of our agenda.

First, what is involved in the abortion and euthanasia debate is nothing less than our Christian doctrines of both God and humanity, or, more precisely, the sovereignty of God and the sanctity of human life. All Christian people believe that Almighty God is the only giver, sustainer and taker-away of life. On the one hand 'he himself gives all men life and breath and everything else', and 'in him we live and move and have our being'. On the other, as the psalmist says to God, 'when you take away their breath, they die and return to the dust'. Indeed, whenever anybody dies, Christian faith struggles to affirm with Job: 'The Lord gave and the Lord has taken away; may the name of the Lord be praised' (Acts 17:25, 28; Psalm 104:29; Job 1:21). To the Christian, then, both life-giving and life-taking are divine prerogatives. And although we cannot interpret 'You shall not kill' as an absolute prohibition, since the same law which forbade killing also sanctioned it in some situations (e.g. capital punishment and holy war), yet the taking of human life is a divine prerogative which is permitted to human beings only by specific divine mandate. Without this, to terminate human life is the height of arrogance. Hence Mother Teresa's strong feelings about the evil of abortion:

> ... only God can decide life and death ... That is why abortion is such a terrible sin. You are not only killing life, but putting self before God; yet people decide who has to live and who has to die. They want to make themselves almighty God. They want to take the power of God in their hands. They want to say, 'I can do without God. I can decide.' That is the most devilish thing that a human hand can do ...[1]

The questions of abortion and euthanasia concern our doctrine of humanity as well as our doctrine of God. For, however undeveloped the embryo may still be, and however mentally absent an elderly person may be, everybody agrees that they are living and that the life they possess is human. So in whatever way we decide to formulate the relationship between newborn and unborn children, or those with a life 'worth living' and those 'not worth living', our evaluation of human life is inevitably involved. Abortion and euthanasia reflect a rejection of the biblical view of human dignity. It is this aspect of the situation which most concerned Francis Schaeffer and C. Everett Koop in their book and film *Whatever Happened to the Human Race?*, which dealt with abortion, infanticide and euthanasia. They rightly traced 'the erosion of the sanctity of human life' to 'the loss of the Christian consensus'.[2]

So then, if both divine sovereignty and human dignity are being challenged by the abortion and euthanasia debates, no conscientious Christian can stand aside from them. We will look primarily at abortion and the discussion that surrounds it, returning at the end of the chapter to euthanasia and some of the particular problems which it raises.

The revolution in public attitudes

The second reason for taking these questions seriously concerns the revolution which has recently taken place in public attitudes. Whether or not doctors have actually subscribed to the ancient Hippocratic Oath (fifth century BC), it has been generally assumed that they took its main undertakings for granted:

I will follow that method of treatment which, according to my ability and judgement, I consider for the benefit of my patients, and abstain from whatever is deleterious and mischievous. I will give no deadly drug to anyone if asked, nor suggest any such counsel; and in like manner I will not give to a woman a pessary to procure abortion.

Since some other clauses of the Oath are decidedly antiquated, the Declaration of Geneva (1948) updated it, while at the same time taking care to include the promise: 'I will maintain the utmost respect for human life from the time of conception.'

One would not necessarily expect a country like Japan, whose Christian population numbers less than 1 per cent, to reflect a biblical view of the sanctity of human life (although of course the Buddhist tradition professes all life to be sacred). So we are not altogether surprised by the statistics which followed their liberaliza-tion of abortion legislation in 1948. In the first eight years no fewer than 5 million abortions were performed, and in the year 1972 1.5 million were carried out.[3]

But one's expectations of the situation in the West, the heir of many centuries of Christian tradition, are naturally higher. In Britain abortion remained illegal until the Infant Life (Preservation) Act of 1929 provided that no action would be punishable 'when done in good faith with the intention of saving the life of the mother'. David Steel's 1967 Abortion Act appeared to many to be only a cautious extension of this. Two registered medical practition-ers were required to express their opinion, 'formed in good faith', that the continuance of the pregnancy would involve either (1) risk to the life of the pregnant woman, or (2) and (3) risk of injury to her or her existing children's physical or mental health, 'greater than if the pregnancy were terminated', or (4) 'substantial risk that if the child were born it would suffer from such physical or mental abnor-malities as to be seriously handicapped'. Whatever the intentions were of the Abortion Law Reform Association (who master-minded the Bill), it seems clear that its catastrophic consequences were not foreseen by its parliamentary sponsors. Before the Act became law, the number of legal abortions carried out annually in the hospitals of the National Health Service in England and Wales had crept up slowly to 6,100 (1966).[4] In 1968, however, the number was al-ready 24,000, in 1973 it was 167,000 and in 1983 over 184,000, an increase on the previous year of about 8 per cent. By 1983 over

2 million legal abortions had been performed since the 1967 Act was passed, and by 1995 over 4.5 million.[5]

Since 1967 several unsuccessful attempts have been made to tighten our much-too-liberal abortion legislation. But in April 1990 the time limit was successfully reduced from 28 weeks to 24. This victory was extremely modest, however, (1) because very few abortions are performed after 24 weeks anyway (only 23 in 1988) and (2) because at the same time (by an oversight, it seems) no abortion time limit at all was set where there is substantial risk that, if born, the child would suffer serious physical or mental handicap.

The situation in the United States is worse. In 1970 a Texan woman (who used the pseudonym Jane Roe) became pregnant and decided to fight the anti-abortion legislation of her state. She took Henry Wade, the Dallas district attorney, to court. In January 1973 in the now notorious Roe v. Wade case, the United States Supreme Court declared by seven votes to two that the Texas law was unconstitutional.[6] Its judgement inhibited all regulation of abortion during the first three months of pregnancy, and during the second and third trimesters regulated it only in relation to the mother's physical or mental health. This ruling implicitly permitted abortion on demand at every stage of pregnancy. The number of legal abortions in the United States in 1969 was less than 20,000. In 1975 it passed the million mark, and in 1980 reached more than 1.5 million. Throughout the 1980s it remained at about this number every year. This means that during this period, for every 1,000 'births' (natural and induced), 300 were abortions. In fact, over 4,250 babies are aborted daily, 177 hourly, or three every minute. In 1996 1,400,000 abortions were performed, bringing the total since 1972 to an estimated 32.5 million.[7]

Although Roe v. Wade has not been overturned, in July 1989 a divided Supreme Court, hearing the case of Webster v. Reproductive Health Services, decided to allow states to limit a woman's access to abortion and outlawed it in all public institutions. Meanwhile, the nationwide debate has grown into a deeply held confrontation. Abortion is always a major election issue, and both pro-life and pro-choice groups have annual marches on Washington. The March for Life in 1996 had an estimated attendance of 125,000.

The total number of legal and illegal abortions throughout the world was estimated in 1968 to be between 30 million and 35 million.[8] Today the estimate is that as many as 55 million abortions take place each year,[9] which means that more than one abortion occurs every second.

These figures are so staggering as to defy the imagination. I do not think Francis Schaeffer and Everett Koop were exaggerating when they wrote of 'The Slaughter of the Innocents', or John Powell SJ when he entitled his moving book *Abortion: The Silent Holocaust*.[10] To make his point yet more forcefully, he introduced his book with a chart of 'war casualties', on which each cross represented 50,000 American combatants killed. The Korean and Vietnam wars had only one cross each. World War I had two and a half, and World War II eleven. But 'the War on the Unborn' had no fewer than 240 crosses, representing the 12 million legal American abortions up to the beginning of 1981.

Any society which can tolerate these things, let alone legislate for them, has ceased to be civilized. One of the major signs of decadence in the Roman Empire was that its unwanted babies were 'exposed', that is, abandoned and left to die.[11] Can we claim that contemporary western society is any less decadent because it consigns its unwanted babies to the hospital incinerator instead of the local rubbish dump? Indeed modern abortion is even worse than ancient exposure because it has been commercialized, and has become, at least for some doctors and clinics, an extremely lucrative practice. But reverence for human life is an indisputable characteristic of a humane and civilized society.

The key issue[12]

Those who campaign for a lax policy on abortion, and those who campaign for a strict one, begin their argument from opposite positions.

Pro-abortionists emphasize the rights of the mother, and especially her right to choose; anti-abortionists emphasize the rights of the unborn child, and especially his or her right to live. The first see abortion as little more than a retroactive contraceptive, the second as little less than pre-natal infanticide. The appeal of pro-abortionists is often to compassion (though also to the justice of what they see as a woman's right); they cite situations in which the mother and/or the rest of the existing family would suffer intolerable strain if an unwanted pregnancy were allowed to come to term. The appeal of anti-abortionists is usually also and especially to justice; they stress the need to defend the rights of unborn children who are unable to defend themselves.

Those who oppose easy abortion are not lacking in compassion, however. They recognize the hardships, and even tragedies, which the arrival of an unplanned baby often brings. Consider some examples. An expectant mother is already worn out by a large and demanding family. Their home is already over-crowded and their budget over-stretched. It would be financially crippling to have another mouth to feed. The family simply could not cope with another child. Or the mother is herself the wage earner (because she is widowed or divorced, or her husband is sick or unemployed); to have another child would ruin the family. Or the husband is violent or cruel, perhaps an alcoholic or even a psychopath, and his wife dare not allow another child to come under his influence. Or she is unmarried and feels she cannot face either the stigma or the disadvantage which she and her child would have to endure as a single-parent family. Or she is a schoolgirl or student, and a continued pregnancy would interfere with her education and her career. Or perhaps her pregnancy is due to adultery or incest or rape, and these tragedies are great enough in themselves without adding to them an unplanned, unwanted child. Or she has contracted rubella, or had a prenatal scan, and fears that her child will have Down's Syndrome or be defective in some other way.

All these cases, and many more, cause great personal suffering, and arouse sincere Christian compassion. It is easy to understand why some women in such situations opt for the abortion which seems to them the only escape, and why some doctors interpret the law as liberally as they can, in order to justify one.

But Christians who confess Jesus as Lord, and who desire to live under the authority of his truth, justice and compassion, can never be pure pragmatists. We have to ask ourselves what principles are involved. Our compassion needs both theological and moral guidelines. If it is expressed at the expense of truth or justice, it ceases to be genuine compassion.

The key issue, then, is a moral and theological one. It concerns the nature of the fetus (*foetus* is Latin for 'offspring'). How are we to think of the embryo in the mother's womb? For it is our evaluation of the fetus which will largely determine our attitude to abortion.

The first view (which Christians reject as totally false and utterly abhorrent) is the notion that the fetus is merely a lump of jelly or blob of tissue, or a growth in the mother's womb, which may therefore be extracted and destroyed like teeth, tumours or tonsils. Yet some adopt this extreme position. For example, K. Hindell and Madelaine Simms (pro-abortion campaigners) have written that 'medically and legally the embryo and fetus are merely parts of the mother's body, and not yet human'.[13] Such people insist that the fetus belongs to the woman who bears it; that it cannot be regarded as in any sense independent of her or as human in its own right; that to have it removed is no more significant than the surgical removal of some other unwanted tissue; and that the decision to abort or not to abort rests entirely with the woman. Since it is her body, it is also her choice. Nobody else (and certainly no man, feminists would add) has any say in the matter. A liberated woman cannot be forced to bear a child; she has absolute control over her own reproductive powers and processes.

After a mass rally in Hyde Park, arranged by the Society of the Protection of Unborn Children in June 1983, we were walking to 10 Downing Street, in order to present a petition to the Prime Minister, when at the top of Whitehall a group of young women started chanting:

Not the Church, not the State,
Let the woman decide her fate.

I went over to talk to them, and quietly remonstrated that it was not the woman's fate we were concerned about in our rally and march, so much as her unborn child's. Their only reply was to shout unprintable obscenities at me, and to make the rather obvious point that I would not be able to give birth to a child in a million years. I am not saying that they were wholly wrong. For I recognize that abortion is more a woman's issue than a man's. It is she who has been made pregnant, perhaps without her consent, who has to bear the pregnancy, and who will carry the burden of early child care. It is all too easy for men to forget these facts. But we should remember them. We should also be 'pro-choice' in the sense that we recognize a woman's right to decide whether to have a baby or not. But the time for her to exercise her right and make her choice (still assuming that she has not been forced) is before conception, not after. Once she has conceived, her child has independent rights both before and after birth, and it was these rights which those young women in Whitehall did not acknowledge.

That an embryo, though carried within the mother's body, is nevertheless not a part of it, is not only a theological but a physiological fact. This is partly because the child has a genotype distinct from the mother's, but also because the whole process of gestation, from ovulation to birth, may be seen as a kind of 'expulsion' of the child with a view to its ultimate independence.

A second group of people seeks the decisive moment of the embryo's 'humanization' at some point between conception and birth. Some opt for implantation when the egg, six days after fertilization, descends the fallopian tube and becomes attached to the wall of the uterus. And it is true both that implantation is an indispensable stage in the development of the fetus, and that the greatest number of spontaneous abortions (often due to fetal abnormality) take place before this moment. Nevertheless, implantation changes only the environment of the fetus, not its constitution. In former generations 'quickening' was regarded by many as the moment of, or at least the evidence for, the 'ensoulment' of the embryo, but we now know that this new beginning is not of the child's movement but of the mother's perception of it. A third option is 'viability', the time when the fetus, if born prematurely, would be able to survive. But modern medical techniques are constantly bringing this moment forward. The fourth option is to regard birth itself as the crucial moment. This was the position adopted by Rex Gardner in his *Abortion: The Personal Dilemma* (1972). 'My own view,' he wrote, 'is that while the fetus is to be cherished increasingly as it develops, we should regard its first breath at birth as the moment when God gives it not only life, but the offer of Life.' He quoted Genesis 2:7 as biblical evidence, when God breathed into man's nostrils 'the breath of life'. He appealed also to common human experience: 'An audible sigh of relief goes round the delivery room when the baby gives that first gasp.'[14] It is certainly true that no funeral is held for a stillborn child, and that Scripture usually speaks of 'new life' beginning at 'new birth'. Yet this does not settle the matter, since Scripture also speaks of God 'begetting' us and of the implanted 'seed' which leads to new birth (see, for example, James 1:18; 1 Peter 1:23–5; and 1 John 3:9). In addition, pictures of the child just before birth reveal that there is no fundamental difference between the unborn and the newly born: both are dependent on their mother, even if in different ways.

The third group of people, which I think should include all Christians, although they use different formulations and draw different deductions, looks back to conception or fusion as the decisive moment when a human being begins. This is the official position of the Roman Catholic Church. Pope Pius XII, for example, in his Address to the Italian Catholic Society of Midwives in 1951, said, 'The baby, still not born, is a man (that is, a human being) in the same degree and for the same reason as the mother.'[15] Similarly, many Protestants, although some find difficulty with the non-recognition of 'degree', yet similarly affirm that there is no point between conception and death at which we can say, 'After that point I was a person, but before it I was not.' For certainly the conceptus is alive, and certainly the life it possesses is human life. Indeed, many medical people who make no Christian profession recognize this fact. Thus the First International Conference on Abortion, meeting in 1967 in Washington DC, declared: 'We can find no point in time between the union of sperm and egg and the birth of an infant at which point we can say that this is not a human life.'[16]

There is now a fourth view, which deliberately avoids making a decision about the precise identity of the fetus. It has been persuasively put forward by Professor Ronald Dworkin in his influential book *Life's Dominion* (HarperCollins 1993), subtitled 'An argument about abortion and euthanasia'. What readers have found appealing about Professor Dworkin's approach is that he tries to break the deadlock between the 'conservative' pro-life and the 'liberal' pro-choice lobbies, to get behind the 'screaming rhetoric' of the debate, and to reformulate the fundamental moral issue.

There is both agreement and disagreement between the two positions, he claims. On the one hand, both (he alleges) believe that 'our lives have intrinsic, inviolable value' (p. 28), so that to extinguish a human life is 'intrinsically a bad thing, a kind of cosmic shame' (p. 13). On the other hand, the crucial difference between them lies in their understanding of the 'value' of human life. Conservatives tend to regard the fetus as being from conception 'a person with rights and interests of its own', whereas liberals affirm 'the sanctity of life understood in a more impersonal way' (p. 39). The former he calls the 'derivative' view, because it is derived from the nature of the fetus and its supposed rights. The latter he calls the 'detached' view, because it regards human life as sacred in itself, without any presupposition about rights and interests (pp. 11, 21).

When Professor Dworkin comes to explain the 'value' of human life, however, he seems to be in difficulties. Human lives are intrinsically valuable as great paintings are. Their value is measured by the degree of 'investment' contributed to their creation (both natural and human) and by the degree of 'waste' involved in their destruction. For example, should a seriously deformed fetus be allowed to be born or be aborted? Either way there would be a serious 'frustration of life'. Abortion would mean the destruction of life. Birth 'would add, to the sad waste of a deformed human's biological creation, the further heartbreaking waste of personal emotional investment made in that life by others, but principally by the child himself before his inevitable early death' (p. 90). Which is the greater 'investment'? Which would be the greater 'waste'?

While appreciating Professor Dworkin's emphasis on the 'value' of the fetus, Christians will feel very uneasy about the way he develops his thesis. (1) He is much too optimistic in his assessment of the liberals' position. They do not appear to affirm (as he says they do) the 'sanctity', let alone the 'inviolability', of the life of the unborn. (2) His personification of 'nature' (e.g. 'not destroying what nature has created', p. 76) lacks plausibility. The better and biblical way of explaining the intrinsic value of the human fetus is to acknowledge God as Creator and ourselves as the bearers of his image. It is not 'investment' but 'creation' which establishes the innate worth of human beings. (3) Professor Dworkin's vocabulary of 'investment' and 'waste' seem inappropriate in relation to human beings. 'Waste' suggests the loss of a commodity. and an 'investment' is an outlay with a view to a profit. But it is of the essence of love to give without expecting any return.

The biblical basis

To me the firmest foundation in Scripture for the third view is to be found in Psalm 139, in which the author marvels at God's omniscience and omnipresence, and in the course of his meditation makes important statements about our pre-natal existence. To be sure, Psalm 139 makes no claim to be a textbook of embryology. It employs poetical imagery and highly figurative language (e.g. verse 15, 'I was woven together in the depths of the earth'). Nevertheless, the psalmist is affirming at least three important truths.

The first concerns his *Creation*. 'You created my inmost being; you knit me together in my mother's womb' (verse 13). Two homely metaphors are used to illustrate God's creative skill, namely those of the potter and the weaver. God is like a skilled artisan, who 'created' him ('formed' is a better word) as the potter works the clay. The same thought recurs in Job 10:8, where Job affirms that God's hands had 'fashioned and made' him (RSV) or 'shaped and modelled' him (JB). The other picture is that of the weaver who 'knit' him together (verse 13), which the NASB renders 'thou didst weave me'. Similarly Job asks: 'Did you not … clothe me with skin and flesh, and knit me together with bones and sinews?' (10:10–11). In consequence, the psalmist goes on: 'For all these mysteries I thank you, for the wonder of myself, for the wonder of your works' (verse 14, JB).

Though not intending to give a scientific account of fetal development, the biblical authors are nevertheless affirming (in the familiar imagery of the ancient Near East) that the process of embryonic growth is neither haphazard nor even automatic, but a divine work of creative skill.

The psalmist's second emphasis is on *Continuity*. He is now an adult, but he looks back over his life until before he was born. He refers to himself both before and after birth by the same personal pronouns 'I' and 'me', for he is aware that during his ante-natal and post-natal life he was and is the same person. He surveys his existence in four stages. First (verse 1), 'you have searched me' (the past). Secondly (verses 2–3), 'you know when I sit and when I rise … you are familiar with all my ways' (the present). Thirdly (verse 10), 'your hand will guide me, your right hand will hold me fast' (the future). And fourthly (verse 13), 'you knit me together in my mother's womb' (the pre-natal stage). Yet in all four stages (before birth, from birth to the present, at the present moment, and in the future), he refers to himself as 'I'. He who is thinking and writing as a grown man has the same personal identity as the fetus in the womb. He is aware of no discontinuity between his ante-natal and post-natal being. On the contrary, in and out of his mother's womb, before and after his birth, as embryo, baby, youth and adult, he is conscious of being the same person.

The third truth the psalmist expresses I will term *Communion*, for he is conscious of a very personal and particular communion between God and himself. It is the same God who created him, who now sustains him, knows him and loves him, and who will forever hold him fast. Psalm 139 is perhaps the most radically personal statement in the Old Testament of God's relationship to the individual believer. The 'I–you' relationship is expressed in almost every line. Either the pronoun or the possessive in the first person ('I–me – my') comes 46 times in the psalm, and in the second person ('you – your') 32 times. More important than the 'I–you' relationship is his awareness of the 'you–me' relationship, of God knowing him, surrounding him, holding him (verses 1–6), and of God sticking to him in covenant faithfulness and never leaving him or letting him go (verses 7–12).

Indeed, 'Communion' may not be the best description of this third awareness, because the word implies a reciprocal relationship, whereas the psalmist is bearing witness to a relationship which God has established and which God sustains. Perhaps therefore 'Covenant' would be a better word, indeed a unilateral covenant, or covenant of 'grace' which God initiated and which God maintains. For God our Creator loved us and related himself to us long before we could respond in a conscious relationship to him. What makes us a person, then, is not that we know God, but that he knows us; not that we love God but that he has set his love upon us. So each of us was already a person in our mother's womb, because already then God knew us and loved us.

It is these three words (Creation, Continuity and Communion or Covenant) which give us the essential biblical perspective from which to think. The fetus is neither a growth in the mother's body, nor even a potential human being, but already a human life who, though not yet mature, has the potentiality of growing into the fullness of the individual humanity he or she *already* possesses.

Other biblical passages express the same sense of personal continuity due to divine grace. Several times in the Wisdom Literature of the Old Testament the conviction is expressed that it is God who 'made me in the womb' (Job 31:15; Psalm 119:73), even though we do not know how (Ecclesiastes 11:5), who 'brought me out of the womb', and who therefore 'from my mother's womb' has been my God (Psalm 22:9–10; 71:6). The prophets shared the same belief, whether of the individual like Jeremiah ('before I formed you in the womb I knew you', 1:5), or of 'the Servant of the Lord' (whom the Lord both formed and called in the womb, Isaiah 49:1, 5) or by analogy of the nation of Israel (Isaiah 46:3–4). The implications of these texts for personal continuity cannot be avoided by analogy with New Testament assertions that God 'chose' us in Christ and 'gave' us his grace in Christ 'before the creation of the world' (e.g. Ephesians 1:4; 2 Timothy 1:9). The argument would then be that, just as we did not exist before the beginning of time except in the mind of God, so we had no personal existence in the womb, although God is said to have 'known' us in both cases. The analogy is inexact, however, for the situations are different. In passages which relate to *election*, the emphasis is on salvation by grace not works, and therefore on God's choice of us before we existed or could do any good works. In passages which relate to *vocation*, however (the calling whether of prophets like Jeremiah or of apostles like Paul – cf. Galatians 1:16), the emphasis is not only on God's gracious choice but on his 'forming' or 'fashioning' them for their particular service. This was not 'before the creation of the world', nor even 'before conception', but rather 'before birth', before they were yet fully 'formed', that is, while they were still being 'fashioned' in the womb. Personal continuity before and after birth is integral to this teaching.

There is only one Old Testament passage which some interpreters have thought devalues the human fetus, namely Exodus 21:22–5.[17] The situation envisaged is not in dispute. While two men are fighting, they accidentally hit a pregnant woman with the result that she either miscarries or 'gives birth prematurely' (NIV). The penalty laid down depends on the seriousness of any injury sustained. If the injury is not serious, a fine is to be imposed; if it is serious, there is to be exact retribution, 'life for life' etc. Some have argued that the first category (no serious injury) means the death of the child, while the second is serious harm to the mother, and that therefore the mere imposition of a fine in the former case indicates that the fetus was regarded as less valuable than the mother. This is a gratuitous interpretation, however. It seems much more probable that the scale of penalty was to correspond to the degree of injury, whether to the mother or to her child, in which case mother and child are valued equally.

Turning to the New Testament, it has often been pointed out that when Mary and Elizabeth met, both being pregnant, Elizabeth's baby (John the Baptist) 'leaped in her womb' in salutation of Mary's baby (Jesus) and also that Luke here uses the same word *brephos* of an unborn child (1:41, 44) as he later uses of the newborn baby (2:12, 16) and of the little ones whom people brought to Jesus to be blessed by him (18:15).

It is fully in keeping with all this implied continuity, that Christian tradition affirms of Jesus Christ in the Apostles' Creed that he was 'conceived by the Holy Spirit, born of the Virgin Mary, suffered under Pontius Pilate, was crucified, dead and buried ... and on the third day he rose again.' Throughout these events, from beginning to end, from conception to resurrection, it is the very same person, Jesus Christ, in whom we believe.

Modern medical science appears to confirm this biblical teaching. It was only in the 1960s that the genetic code was unravelled. Now we know that the moment the ovum is fertilized by the penetration of the sperm, the 23 pairs of chromosomes are complete, the zygote has a unique genotype which is distinct from both parents, and the child's sex, size and shape, colour of skin, hair and eyes, temperament and intelligence are already determined. Each human being begins as a single fertilized cell, while an adult has about 30 million million cells. Between these two points (fusion and maturity) 45 generations of cell division are necessary, and 41 of them occur *before birth*.

Pre-natal medical photography has further disclosed the marvels of fetal development. I have in mind particularly the strikingly beautiful pictures in the Swedish photographer Lennart Nilsson's book *A Child is Born*.[18] At three to three and a half weeks the tiny heart begins to beat. At four, though the fetus is only about a quarter of an inch long, the head and body are distinguishable, as are also the rudimentary eyes, ears and mouth. At six or seven weeks brain function can be detected, and at eight (the time most abortions begin to be performed) all the child's limbs are apparent, including fingers, fingerprints and toes. At nine or ten weeks the baby can use his or her hands to grasp and his mouth to swallow, and can even suck his thumb. By 13 weeks, the completion of the first trimester, the embryro is completely organized, and a miniature baby lies in the mother's womb; he can alter his position, respond to pain, noise and light, and even get a fit of hiccups. From then on the child merely develops in size and strength. By the end of the fifth month and beginning of the sixth (before the second trimester is complete, and while the pregnancy is not yet two-thirds complete), the baby has hair, eyelashes, nails and nipples, and can cry, grip, punch and kick (which sometimes happens after an abortion has been performed by hysterotomy, to the extreme distress of the medical team).

Expectant mothers endorse from their own experience their sense of bearing a living child. True, parents sometimes give their little one a humorous nickname, especially if they do not know which sex it will turn out to be. But they also say with pride, 'We have a baby on the way.' During pregnancy one mother said she 'felt herself to be the mother of a person, with certain motherly responsibilities before birth, and others after birth'. Another wrote: 'My feelings know that this is a person, and thus has his or her own independent rights before God.'

A contemporary Christian debate

It would not be honest to claim that all Christians see eye to eye on this issue, even all Christians who seek to submit to the authority of Scripture. An apparently sharp difference of opinion surfaced when an interdisciplinary seminar of theologians and doctors was held in 1983, jointly sponsored by the London Institute for Contemporary Christianity and the Christian Medical Fellowship. The keynote address was given by Canon Oliver O'Donovan, Regius Professor of Moral and Pastoral Theology at Oxford, under the title 'And Who is a Person?' His starting point was the Parable of the Good Samaritan. Just as Jesus declined to answer the question 'And who is my neighbour?' by providing a set of criteria, so there are no criteria (whether self-consciousness or reason or responsive love) by which to decide who is a 'person'. Instead, the Good Samaritan identified his neighbour by caring for him, since 'the truth of neighbourhood is known in engagement'. Just so, the question, 'Who is a person?' cannot be answered speculatively. Instead, we come to *recognize* someone as a person 'only from a stance of prior moral commitment to treat him or her as a person'. Then later we come to *know* him or her as a person, as he or she is disclosed to us in personal relationships. It is not that personhood is *conferred* on someone by our resolve to treat him as a person, but that personhood is *disclosed* that way. Personhood becomes apparent in personal relationships, although it is not established by them. At the same time, before we commit ourselves to the service of a person, it is right to look for evidence that it is appropriate to do so, either by appearance or (in the case of a fetus) by our scientific knowledge of its unique genotype. There are thus three stages. First, there must be recognition, making it appropriate to engage with a person as person. Next follows commitment, caring for him as a person. And thirdly there comes encounter: 'Those whom we treat as persons when they are yet unborn, become *known* to us as persons when they are children.'

These three stages acknowledge the gradualness of development into personal encounter, while affirming the reality of personhood from the moment of conception.[19]

In an unpublished essay entitled 'The Logic of Beginnings' the late Professor Donald MacKay, formerly director of the Research Department of Communication and Neuroscience at Keele University, took issue with Professor O'Donovan's argument. 'Things come into existence in various ways,' he wrote. For example, artefacts (like a car) are assembled piece by piece, rain clouds form by condensation, an explosive mixture of gas and air develops gradually, while plants and animals grow. Each of these processes has an end product (a car, a rain cloud, an explosion, a mature plant or an animal), but it is difficult for us to perceive either the exact moment when this comes into being or the exact nature of the change which takes place when it does. This led Donald MacKay to criticize the language of 'potentiality'. To be sure, the beginning of every process has the potentiality to reach the end product, granted the enabling conditions, but this does not justify ontological assertions about the earlier stages. For example, various components will become a car, if they are assembled properly, but we do not refer to them as a 'potential car', because they might instead end up on the scrapheap. May we then refer to a fertilized ovum as a 'potential human being'? Yes, in the sense that it will lead to maturity if gestation proceeds normally, but not if this leads us to attribute to the ovum specific properties of the end product. The value of 'potentiality' language is that it emphasizes the importance of beginnings, expectations and resulting obligations; its danger is to imagine that all the attributes and rights of the end product already belong to the beginning. They do not, even if there is a direct line of continuity between the two.

In particular, Donald MacKay concluded, before the fetus may rightly be considered a 'conscious personal agency', there are certain information-processing requirements which are necessary for human self-supervision. This is not to reduce a person to a brain, but to say that a person cannot be embodied in a structure which lacks a self-supervisory system, because it lacks adequate brain development. 'The capacity to sustain conscious personhood is a systemic property of the central nervous system.' On the one hand, the fertilized ovum is a 'physical structure with the richest and most strangely mysterious repertoire known to man', for it can develop into 'the embodiment of a new human being in the image of God, loved by God, replete with potentialities of not merely earthly but eternal significance'. On the other, to treat it as 'a person with the rights of a person' is a conspicuous example of 'thin-end-of-the-wedgery'.[20]

In summary, Oliver O'Donovan insisted that the fetus has 'personhood' from the moment of fusion, and that therefore we must commit ourselves to its care, although only later will its personhood be revealed in personal relationships. Donald MacKay agreed that from the moment of fusion the conceptus has biological life and a marvellous repertoire of potentiality, but added that it only becomes a person possessing rights and demanding care when brain development makes self-supervision possible.

The conflict between the two learned professors sounds irreconcilable. Yet I believe that there may be more common ground between them than appears at first sight, and I do not believe that either is altogether denying what the other affirms. Donald MacKay emphasizes the development of the fetus, while not denying that already the fertilized ovum has a rich repertoire. Oliver O'Donovan emphasizes that from the very beginning the conceptus has a unique and complete genotype, and indeed personhood, while not denying that its destiny is to reach human maturity. Is this not at base the old tension (with which the New Testament has made us familiar) between the 'already' and the 'not yet'? Tertullian expressed it as early as the end of the second century: 'He also is a man who is about to be one; you have the fruit already in its seed.'[21] In our own day Paul Ramsey has put it like this: 'The human individual comes into existence as a minute informational speck ... His subsequent prenatal and postnatal development may be described *as a process of becoming what he already is* from the moment he was conceived.'[22] Lewis Smedes calls the status of a fetus a 'deep ontological ambiguity – the ambiguity of not being something yet and at the same time having the makings of what it will be'.[23] It is the language of 'potentiality' in relation to the embryo which has confused us. Professor Thomas F. Torrance has clarified it by explaining that 'the potentiality concerned is not that of becoming something else but of becoming what it essentially is'.[24]

This brings me back to Psalm 139 and to the reason for the psalmist's sense of continuity of being, namely God's steadfast love. Indeed, it is God's loving, personal commitment to the unborn child which makes me uncomfortable with Donald MacKay's non-personal analogies (material artefacts, clouds, gases, plants and animals). The sovereign initiative of God in creating and loving is the biblical understanding of grace. Donald MacKay declines to attribute personhood to the newly conceived fetus because as yet it has no brain to sustain either self-supervision or conscious relationships. But supposing the vital relationship which confers personhood on the fetus is God's conscious, loving commitment to him, rather than his to God? Such a one-sided relationship is seen in parents who love their child, and commit themselves to its care and protection, long before it is able to respond. And a unilateral initiative is what makes grace to be grace. It is, in fact, God's grace which confers on the unborn child, from the moment of its conception, both the unique status which it already enjoys and the unique destiny which it will later inherit. It is grace which holds together this duality of the actual and the potential, the already and the not yet.

Human fertilization

The ethical debate has to some extent shifted from the deliberate destruction of unwanted fetuses to the artificial creation of embryos for married couples who desperately want to have a child. One feels instinctive sympathy for a couple who began their married life with the intention and expectation of having children, only to discover that they cannot. Scripture itself speaks positively of parenthood as the natural crown of marriage, summons us to praise the God who 'settles the barren woman in her home as a happy mother of children' (Psalm 113:9), and views childlessness as a painful, personal tragedy.

It is understandable, therefore, that fertility clinics have been set up and that a variety of techniques have been developed, not only medical and surgical but also biogenetic, in order to help infertile couples to have children. These procedures have provoked public reactions ranging from 'pride' in technological achievement and 'pleasure' in overcoming infertility to 'unease' over the lack of social controls.[25] What should Christians think of modern fertilization techniques?

At the risk of serious oversimplification, one might say that normal and natural procreation depends on four parental contributions – the father's sperm, the mother's egg, fallopian tubes which connect her ovaries to her womb and where fusion takes place, together with her womb in which the embryo develops. But one or more of these four (sperm, egg, tubes and womb) may be in some way defective. For example, a common cause of infertility is the blocking of the fallopian tubes, which in many cases can be rectified by surgery. In other situations artificial insemination may be used, namely the insertion of the husband's sperm ('AIH') through a plastic tube directly into his wife's cervix or uterus.

An alternative way of bringing about the fusion of sperm and ovum, outside rather than inside the mother's body, is *in vitro* fertilization ('IVF'), followed by embryo transfer ('ET'). This double technique was first developed in Britain by Dr Robert Edwards, a Cambridge University physiologist, and Mr Patrick Steptoe, a gynaecologist. Their first 'test-tube baby' was Louise Brown, who was born in 1978, and they celebrated their one hundredth birth by this means in 1983. It was reckoned at that time that perhaps another 100 IVF babies had been born worldwide. By now the number is much higher, since IVF is also practised in Australia, the United States, France, West Germany, Israel and other countries.[26]

The moral dicussion surrounds not only the IVF technique itself, but also the uses to which it is being put. If damage to the fallopian tubes is one cause of infertility, others are a defect or deficiency in the husband's sperm or in the wife's ova or womb, so that the proposed solution involves in each case the 'donation' by an outside or third party of the missing component.

First, if it is the husband who is infertile, *sperm donation* is possible, either by direct insemination ('AID') or by IVF. In the latter case the wife's egg is fertilized by an outside donor's sperm, followed a few days later by ET into the wife's womb.

Secondly, if it is the wife who is infertile, then *egg donation* by another woman (perhaps her sister) is possible, the outside donor's egg being fertilized by the husband's sperm through IVF, followed again by ET into the wife's womb.

Thirdly, if both husband and wife are infertile, it is possible for them to commission another married couple to contribute their sperm and ovum, which would then be fused through IVF and placed in the wife's womb. This would be a case of *embryo donation*.

Fourthly, it may be that, although neither husband nor wife is infertile, her womb has been damaged so that she cannot bear her own child. In this case, it is suggested, his sperm and her egg could through IVF and ET be inserted into another woman, who would carry and in due course give birth to their child and then surrender him or her to them, the genetic parents. This could be called *womb donation*, although it is commonly referred to as 'surrogate motherhood'.

These are the four main procedures which are being recommended, although additional permutations and combinations are possible. What is common to all four is the use of IVF together with the donation (which IVF makes possible) of sperm, egg, embryo or womb, in each case by a third party or outside donor.

Although the brief of the Warnock Committee included 'consideration of the social, ethical and legal implications' of the new technologies for assisted reproduction, the weakest feature of its Report is its failure to contribute a coherent or comprehensive moral basis for its proposals. The Committee even acknowledges its decision to go 'straight to the question of *how it is right to treat the human embryo*' without first considering 'when life or personhood begin'.[27] Before we are ready, however, to enter into the moral debate, here is a summary of those main recommendations of the Report which are germane to our discussion. It was recommended

– that sperm, egg and embryo donation should be permitted, provided that they are properly controlled by a statutory licensing authority (A 4–7);

– that couples and donors (of sperm and ova) should remain permanently unknown to each other, although a confidential central register should be maintained (B 18, 24);

– that donors should have no parental rights or obligations (E 51, 54, 55);

– that children born as a result of donation should have their birth registered as if the couple were their parents (though with 'by donation' added if desired) and should never be entitled to know the identity of their biological parents except, on reaching the age of eighteen, their 'ethnic origin and genetic health' (E 53–4); 4.17, 21, 25);

– that, although surrogate motherhood should not be made a criminal offence, surrogacy agencies, arrangements and contracts should (E 56–8);

– that research on human embryos (both 'spare' and specially pro-
cured embryos) should be permitted under licence for up to 14 days
after fertilization and on condition of informed parental consent. However, three committee members opposed all experimentation, and
four more were opposed to the deliberate production of embryos for
research purposes (A 11–14, D 43–4).

A few months after the publication of the Warnock Report Mr
Enoch Powell MP tabled his private member's Unborn Children
(Protection) Bill, which would have prohibited the production of
human embryos by IVF solely for research and subsequent destruction. Although it attracted considerable support, it ran out of parliamentary time. In 1987 the government published a White Paper
which prepared the way for its Human Fertilization and Embryology Research Bill, which was first introduced to Parliament in
November 1989. Then in April 1990 in a free vote MPs endorsed
by almost two to one the practice of research on human embryos up
to 14 days old.

What, then, are the ethical issues which make Christians uneasy
about (to say the least), and even totally hostile to, these developments? The question of fertilization is a debate about relationships –
between husband and wife, parents and children, doctors and family, donors and recipients, the natural and the artificial. In particular, Christians see in the new reproductive technologies a threefold
intrusion or interference.

First, IVF may involve *an intrusion into the process of procreation*.
Some Christians are just able to come to terms with IVF and ET
when they concern the husband's sperm and the wife's ovum and
womb. Yet even in this case, when no external donation is involved,
the sacredness of human reproduction has been moved from the
bedroom into the laboratory, and from a God-designed process to
a human technique, as fusion takes place no longer unwitnessed
within the mother's body but on a glass dish carefully monitored by
scientists. It was this which led Professor Oliver O'Donovan to enti-
tle his 1983 London Lectures *Begotten Or Made?* 'That which we
beget,' he said, 'is *like* ourselves ... But that which we make is *unlike*
ourselves.' Consequently, 'that which is made rather than begotten
becomes something that we have at our disposal, not someone with
whom we can engage in brotherly fellowship.'[28] It is, in fact, on account of 'the extent of medical intervention and control' in the

process of IVF, that Dr Richard Higginson called his fine book on the ethics of IVF *Whose Baby?* Is an IVF child in some sense 'the *doctor's* baby' or 'the *donor's* baby', or still truly '*God's* baby'?[29]

Moreover, IVF separates what God has united. His purpose from the beginning was that marriage, love, sex and procreation should belong together, and in particular that 'baby-making' (better, 'baby-getting') should be the consequence of 'love-making'. The Vatican's 1987 *Instruction* makes this one of the main grounds of its unequivocal rejection of IVF. It quotes from Pope Paul VI's Encyclical *Humanae Vitae* (1968) that there is an 'inseparable connection, willed by God and unable to be broken by man on his own initiative, between the two meanings of the conjugal act: the unitive meaning and the procreative meaning'.[30] Protestants are less dogmatic, however, on the inseparability of sexual intercourse and the procreation of children. Since contraception (which they tend to allow), whether natural or mechanical, separates sex from procreation, it would be illogical to condemn IVF for separating procreation from sex. Nevertheless, we agree that God did unite the two. In consequence, parents who decide on IVF will want to ensure (as far as possible) that its whole context is one not of clinical efficiency only but of caring, conjugal love.[31]

Secondly, IVF may involve *an intrusion into the bonds of marriage and parenthood*. Marriage is a permanent covenant between one man and one woman, which demands uncompromising faithfulness. But all forms of donation introduce a third party (the donor) into this relationship. When sperm or egg donation by outside donor is achieved by sexual intercourse, we condemn it as 'adultery'. If the donation is made externally, without intercourse, is it entirely free from the taint of adultery? It is certainly incompatible with the view of marriage as an exclusive relationship which admits of no third-party intrusion. In surrogacy too, even if both sperm and ovum are contributed by the married couple, a physical and emotional bonding takes place between the 'mother' and the child she is carrying, which may later be hard to break.

The fundamental inappropriateness of all donation arrangements is seen in the consequent muddle between biological and social parents and the tensions which this is bound to cause either between husband and wife (since one has contributed to their child's procreation while the other has not), or between the two mothers, or between the parents and the child. As for the secrecy which surrounds these transactions, it is enough in itself to outlaw them. All children have a fundamental right to know their own identity, which includes the identity of their parents. It would certainly be shameful to lie to them about their genetic parents. The Warnock Report at least provides, as we have seen, for the optional addition of the words 'by donation' on the birth certificate and for the availability to the child when 18 years old of some information. But children should surely have access to all the information they wish to be given. One reason why fostering and adoption belong to a different category is that they are not shrouded in secrecy or spoiled by deception.

Thirdly, IVF may involve *an intrusion into the integrity of the embryo*, since a living human embryo is now available for research and/or experimentation outside the mother's body and in a laboratory. Indeed, several embryos are usually available, since the custom is to induce super-ovulation in the mother so that the doctor can recover about half a dozen eggs, either in case first attempts at fertilization or implantation fail or in order that some eggs may be frozen for possible future use. Should spare embryos be used for research? Two arguments are used to defend this practice. First, research is necessary, the pioneers are saying, in order to perfect the IVF technique, to discover the causes of infertility, early miscarriage, genetic disorders and hereditary diseases, to be able to use embryonic tissue for transplant and to test drugs. However, Professor Jerome Lejeune, the French geneticist, wrote to *The Times* on 26 March 1985 that equivalent research could be performed on laboratory mammals instead, and that in any case the human embryo of less than 14 days is too underdeveloped for some research into genetic disabilities. It is true that Dr Andrew Huxley, President of the Royal Society, expressed his disagreement in a letter which appeared on 6 April. But other scientists have sided with Professor Lejeune. So the experts are not at one on the necessity of embryonic research.

The second argument is that up to 14 days the embryo is so minute as to be invisible to the naked eye, and that therefore it should not be given the total or absolute protection which is given to a mature human being or even to the fetus at later stages of its development. But this begs the question of the status of the embryo from the moment of fusion.

The Warnock Report agreed 'that the embryo of the human species ought to have a special status', which 'should be enshrined in legislation' and should carry with it 'some protection in law'.[32] That is good, but not enough, as the three dissentients saw. They rightly said that the embryo's special status and legal protection should not be made dependent on a technical decision about 'personhood': 'Clearly, once that status [of personhood] has been accorded, all moral principles and legal enactments which relate to persons will apply. But before that point has been reached the embryo has a special status because of its potential for development to a stage at which everyone would accord it the status of a human person.'[33] So then, both those who accord 'personhood' to human embryos and those who do not should be able to agree (1) that they are at least in the process of developing into their full potential (which indeed is the popular understanding of the adjective 'embryonic') and (2) that they are therefore inviolable.

Once this special status of the human embryo is acknowledged, it will follow that 'experimentation' should be forbidden and that permissible 'research' should be most carefully defined. The Vatican's *Instruction* (1987) is quite clear: 'No objective, even though noble in itself, such as a foreseeable advantage to science, to other human beings or to society, can in any way justify experimentation on living human embryos.'[34] The only justification would be when the work 'is clearly therapeutic for the subject himself'.[35] This is in keeping with the fundamental principle that human beings must be regarded and treated as ends in themselves, and not as means to some other end, however good.

Techniques and exceptions

How will our evaluation of the uniqueness of the human fetus (however we decide to formulate it) affect our thinking and acting, especially in relation to abortion?

To begin with, it will change our attitudes. Since the life of the human fetus is a human life, with the potential of becoming a mature human being, we have to learn to think of mother and unborn child as two human beings at different stages of development. Doctors and nurses have to consider that they have two patients, not one, and must seek the well-being of both. Lawyers and politicians need to think similarly. As the United Nations' 'Declaration of the Rights of the Child' (1959) put it, the child 'needs special safeguards and care, including appropriate legal protection, before as well as after birth'. Christians would wish to add 'extra care before birth'. For the Bible has much to say about God's concern for the defenceless, and the most defenceless of all people are unborn children. They are speechless to plead their own cause and helpless to protect their own life. So it is our responsibility to do for them what they cannot do for themselves.

All Christians should therefore be able to agree that the human fetus is in principle inviolable. Lord Ramsey, when as Archbishop of Canterbury he was addressing the Church Assembly in 1967, said, 'We have to assert as normative the general inviolability of the fetus ... We shall be right to continue to see as one of Christianity's great gifts to the world the belief that the human fetus is to be reverenced as the embryo of a life capable of coming to reflect the glory of God ...'

It is the combination of what the human fetus already is and what it one day could be which makes the realities of abortion so horrific. How can anybody possibly reconcile the brutal techniques of abortion with the concept of the abortus as a potential mirror of God's glory?

The most common method of abortion is vacuum aspiration, which is used in pregnancies up to 12–14 weeks. In this operation the cervix is dilated and a tube connected to a suction pump is inserted into the womb. The fetus is sucked from the womb and collected in a jar where body parts must be accounted for to ensure full removal.

A second, older method is 'D and C', dilation and curettage. The cervix is dilated to facilitate the insertion of an implement, either a 'curette' with which the wall of the womb is scraped until the fetus is cut into pieces and removed, or, in later pregnancies, sponge forceps and a plier-like instrument by which it is torn into pieces. In either case a violent and bloody dismemberment takes place.

A third method (employed between 12 and 16 weeks) is to inject a toxic (usually saline) solution by a long needle inserted through the mother's abdomen into the amniotic sac enveloping the fetus, which is thus poisoned, burned and killed, and then 'spontaneously' ejected. At a later stage of pregnancy surgery is used, either a hysterotomy which resembles a Caesarean section (except that in this case the baby is taken from the womb to be killed, not saved) or a complete hysterectomy by which womb and fetus are removed together and discarded together (this is rarely used).

Yet another method, developed in the United States but legal in Britain as well, is dilation and extraction (D and X), commonly known as 'partial birth abortion'. This procedure is performed in late-term pregnancies when fetal tissues have become too strong for easy dismemberment. In this abortion the child is manipulated into a breech birth position and partially delivered feet-first until the head alone remains in the womb. The doctor then inserts a pair of scissors into the base of the skull, followed by a suction catheter that removes the brain, causing the skull to collapse and facilitating the removal of the now dead baby. Because of the barbaric nature of this method it is currently under intense debate in the United States, and the discussion grows louder in Britain.

An alternative to surgery in the first few months of pregnancy is the use of the drug RU 486 in conjunction with prostaglandins. The RU 486 drug was licensed for use in 1991 by the Department of Health and is now in fairly common use. It can be taken up to nine weeks of pregnancy and procures an abortion by destroying the lining of the womb. RU 486 is used in conjunction with prostaglandin, a drug which facilitates the evacuation of the contents of the womb.

A final method of abortion is the 'morning after' pill. If a woman has had intercourse without contraception and fears pregnancy she can be prescribed a 'morning after' pill to be taken within 72 hours of intercourse. This is a high-dose oestrogen pill that prevents implantation by disrupting the lining of the womb. Because this method is not covered by the Abortion Act the pill can be prescribed by a single doctor, even one's GP.

A factual knowledge of these procedures should lead us to revise our vocabulary. For the popular euphemisms make it easier for us to conceal the truth from ourselves. The occupant of the mother's womb is not a 'product of conception' or 'gametic material', but an unborn child. Even 'pregnancy' tells us no more than that a woman has been 'impregnated', whereas the truth in old-fashioned language is that she is 'with child'. How can we speak of 'the termination of a pregnancy' when what is terminated is not just the mother's pregnancy but the child's life? And how can we describe the average abortion today as 'therapeutic' (a word originally used only when the mother's life was at stake), when pregnancy is not a disease needing therapy, and what abortion effects nowadays is not a cure but a killing? And how can people think of abortion as no more than a kind of contraceptive, when what it does is not prevent conception but destroy the conceptus? We need to have the courage to use accurate language. Induced abortion is feticide, the deliberate destruction of an unborn child, the shedding of innocent blood.

Is abortion, then, never justified? To answer this question in a way that is both faithful and realistic, theologians and doctors need each other. More interdisciplinary consultation is necessary. For doctors are understandably impatient with theologians because they tend to be unpractical, making ivory-tower pronouncements unrelated to painful clinical dilemmas. Theologians, on the other hand, are understandably impatient with doctors because they tend to be pragmatists, making clinical decisions uncontrolled by theological principle. The principle on which we should be able to agree is well expressed as the first aim of the Society for the Protection of Unborn Children, namely 'that human life ought not to be taken except in cases of urgent necessity'. Professor G.R. Dunstan is probably right that there is an ethic of 'justifiable feticide', by analogy with 'justifiable homicide'.[36] But if we accept the general inviolability of the human fetus, then every exception has to be rigorously and specifically argued. Ever since the Infant Life (Preservation) Act (1929) an abortion to save the mother's life has been legal in England, though not condoned by the Roman Catholic Church. With improved modern medical techniques, however, this case seldom arises, although one could imagine a borderline situation in which an unwanted pregnancy threatened an overburdened and neurotic mother with such a complete breakdown that she would become 'a physical and mental wreck',[37] or would be in imminent danger of taking her own life. According to Christian tradition human life may be taken to protect and preserve another life – for example, in self-defence; but we have no liberty to introduce death into a situation in which it is not already present, either as a fact or as a threat.

What about the 'substantial risk' of the child to be born being 'seriously handicapped', which is the fourth clause of the 1967 Abortion Act? Ante-natal screening and amniocentesis (tapping and testing the amniotic fluid) can now reveal abnormalities in the fetus at about the fourth month. Is an abortion then morally justified? Many think so. Dr Glanville Williams has expressed himself forcefully on this issue: 'To allow the breeding of defectives is a horrible evil, far worse than any that may be found in abortion.'[38] In discussing the tragic predicament of a mother who gives birth to 'a viable monster or an idiot child', he even wrote: 'An eugenic killing by a mother, exactly paralleled by the bitch that kills her misshapen puppies, cannot confidently be pronounced immoral.'[39] How should a Christian conscience react to this possibility? Surely with horror. The only exceptions might be an anencephalic child (born without a brain) or a child so completely malformed as to be incapable of independent survival; these could be allowed to die.

But there are at least three reasons why such a drastic procedure must be reserved for only the most exceptional cases and must not be extended to other – even severe – abnormalities. First, it is now frequently said that the issue is not the 'sanctity' of life but the 'quality' of life, and that the life of a severely handicapped person is not worth living. But who can presume to decide this? To me the most moving speech at the Hyde Park Rally in June 1983, which I have already mentioned, was made by Alison Davis, who described herself as 'a happy spina bifida adult' and spoke from a wheelchair. 'I can think of few concepts more terrifying,' she said, 'than saying that certain people are better off dead, and may therefore be killed *for their own good*.' One doctor, on hearing her say that she was glad to be alive, 'made the incredible observation that no one can judge their own quality of life, and that other people might well consider a life like mine miserable!' On the contrary, she insisted, 'most handicapped people are quite contented with the quality of their lives'. After all, it is love which gives quality to life and makes it worth living, and it is we – their neighbours – who can choose whether to give love to the handicapped or withhold it. The quality of their life is in our hands.

Secondly, once we accept that a handicapped child may be destroyed before birth, why should we not do it also after birth? Indeed, the practice of infanticide has already begun. Doctors of course do not use this word, and some try to persuade themselves that starving babies to death is not killing them, but 'I'd like to bet they'd change their minds,' said Alison Davis, 'if we did it to them!' The solemn fact is that if society is prepared to kill an unborn child on the sole ground that it will be handicapped, there is no logical reason why we should not go on to kill the deformed newborn, the comatose victim of a car crash, the imbecile and the senile. For the handicapped become disposable when their lives are judged 'worthless' or 'unproductive', and we are back in Hitler's horrible Third Reich.

Christians will rather agree with Jean Rostan, the French biologist, who wrote: 'For my part I believe that there is no life so degraded, debased, deteriorated or impoverished that it does not deserve respect and is not worth defending with zeal and conviction … I have the weakness to believe that it is an honour for our society to desire the expensive luxury of sustaining life for its useless, incompetent, and incurably ill members. I would almost measure society's degree of civilization by the amount of effort and vigilance it imposes on itself out of pure respect for life.'[40]

A third reason for not aborting the handicapped is that to do so would be for fallible mortals to play God. We do not have that authority, and those who arrogate it to themselves are bound to make grave mistakes. Maurice Baring used to tell the story of one doctor who asked another: 'About the termination of a pregnancy, I want your opinion. The father was syphilitic, the mother tuberculous. Of the four children born the first was blind, the second died, the third was deaf and dumb, and the fourth also tuberculous. What would you have done?' 'I would have ended the pregnancy.' 'Then you would have murdered Beethoven.'[41]

In this whole discussion we have to be on our guard against selfish rationalizations. I fear that the real reason why we say that serious handicap would be an unbearable burden for a child, if it were allowed to be born, is that it would be an unbearable burden for us. But Christians must remember that the God of the Bible has expressed his special protective care for the handicapped and the weak.

A call to action

What then shall we do? First, *we need to repent*. I agree with Raymond Johnston, the late founder director of CARE Trust, when he wrote in a newspaper article: 'I personally am convinced that the destruction of the unborn on this massive, deliberate scale is the greatest single offence regularly perpetrated in Britain today, and would be the first thing an Old Testament prophet *redivivus* would reproach us for.' Dr Francis Schaeffer and Dr Everett Koop dedicated their book and film *Whatever Happened to the Human Race?* 'to those who were robbed of life, the unborn, the weak, the sick, the old, during the dark ages of madness, selfishness, lust and greed for which the last decades of the twentieth century are remembered'. Were they right to condemn our 'enlightened' western civilization as 'the dark ages'? At least in this matter I think they were, and I for one am ashamed that we Christians have not been 'the light of the world' which Jesus intended us to be. We also need to repent of our tendency to selective campaigning. We lack integrity if we fight for the life of the unborn and care little for the life of the born – for example, of abused or neglected children, battered and abandoned mothers, slum dwellers or refugees. Christians are committed to human life, both to defending its sanctity and to promoting its quality.

Secondly, *we need to accept full responsibility for the effects of a tighter abortion policy*, if it can be secured. To agitate for it without being prepared to bear its costs would be sheer hypocrisy. We must not occasion an increase of illegal 'back-street' abortions. Instead, we shall want to help the pregnant woman to overcome any reluctance she feels to have her baby, and see that she is given every possible personal, medical, social and financial support. For God tells us to 'carry each other's burdens, and in this way … fulfil the law of Christ' (Galatians 6:2). We shall want to ensure that, although some babies are unwanted (and even unloved) by their parents, no baby is unwanted by society in general and by the Church in particular. We should not hesitate to oppose the abortion, and urge the birth, of every child. Pregnancy is a time of emotional instability, so that the minds and feelings of expectant mothers sometimes change. Rex Gardner refers to two reports about women who have been refused an abortion. In one case 73 per cent of them, in the other 84 per cent, said they were glad the pregnancy had not been terminated. He also quotes Sir John Stallworthy, who has said that some of the happiest people he knows are those who have said to him: 'You don't remember, but the first time I came wanting an abortion. Thank God you did not agree, because this child has brought the greatest joy into our home that we have ever known.'[42] As for those who would find the strain of keeping their child too great, there is a lengthy queue of married but infertile couples who are longing for the chance to adopt. As Mother Teresa used to say, 'We are fighting abortion by adoption.'

I thank God for the organizations which have been pioneering a supportive ministry for pregnant women, like 'Birthright' and Care Net in Canada and the United States, 'Alternatives to Abortion International' (whose publication is called *Heartbeat*), and LIFE and SPUC (Society for the Protection of Unborn Children) in Britain.[43] In different ways they are offering a caring service, such as counselling women with an unplanned pregnancy, offering emergency help to those in despair, giving advice on practical problems, finding accommodation for mothers both before and after their child's birth, helping to secure employment for them, granting financial help, and providing personal support groups. As Louise Summerhill, founder of 'Birthright', has written, 'We help rather than abort, we believe in making a better world for babies to come into, rather than killing them.'[44]

Thirdly, *we need to support a positive educational and social campaign*, not least in schools. Christians must not be shy to teach thoroughly and constantly the biblical understanding of humanness and of the value, indeed the sacredness, of human life. We have to recognize that all abortions are due to unwanted pregnancies, and that all unwanted pregnancies are due to a failure of some kind.

Often it is sexual failure, whether lack of sexual self-control (especially in men, who usually escape the tragic consequences of their action) or lack of a responsible use of contraceptives. The Church of England General Synod's Board for Social Responsibility has called for 'a major effort at social education' (and moral education too, we might add), in order 'to reduce the number of unwanted pregnancies', 'to undermine the habit of mind which leads straight from the recognition of pregnancy to resort to an abortionist', and to move the public 'to find a better solution'.[45] This is 'The Better Way' of which Rex Gardner writes in his chapters 28 and 29.[46]

Unwelcome pregnancies are also often due to social failure, to such conditions as poverty, unemployment and overcrowding. So for this reason we too should be working for a better society. Social evils are to be fought; they will not be solved by more abortions.

In the Third World large families are a kind of insurance against old age. Only a measurable reduction of infant mortality will give parents confidence to have smaller families, and only the development of a simple, safe, cheap contraceptive will help them to do so.

More important in the end than either social education or social action, vital as they both are, is the good news of Jesus Christ. He came to bind up the broken-hearted and support the weak. He calls us to treat all human life with reverence, whether in the unborn, the infant, the handicapped or the senile.

I have no desire to stand in personal judgement either on the women who have resorted to an abortion, or on the men whose sexual self-indulgence is responsible for most unwanted pregnancies. I want to say to them instead, 'There is forgiveness with God' (Psalm

130:4). For Christ died for our sins and offers us a new beginning. He rose again and lives, and by his Spirit can give us a new, inward power of self-control. He is also building a new community characterized by love, joy, peace, freedom and justice. A new beginning. A new power. A new community. This is the gospel of Christ.

Euthanasia

The obvious parallels between abortion and euthanasia make it appropriate for them to be discussed in the same chapter. For, although abortion relates to the beginning of a human life, and euthanasia to its end, both are decisions for death. Both therefore raise the same urgent question whether it may ever be morally justifiable to terminate life and precipitate death.

The euthanasia debate can be traced back at least to the heyday of Greek philosophy. But a number of factors have combined to bring it to the forefront of public concern in our day – advances in medical technology which prolong life and so are responsible for an ageing population, the AIDS epidemic, some particularly poignant and well publicized cases which seemed to cry out for euthanasia on compassionate grounds, and the persuasive campaigning of EXIT (previously the Voluntary Euthanasia Society) in the UK and the Hemlock Society, its equivalent in the US.

A widely accepted definition of euthanasia, which has been adopted for example by HOPE ('Healthcare opposed to Euthanasia'), is as follows: 'Euthanasia is the intentional killing by act or omission of a person whose life is considered not to be worth living.'

This is popularly called 'mercy-killing', and is divided between 'voluntary euthanasia' ('assisted suicide', the death occurring at the explicit plea of the patient) and 'involuntary euthanasia' (the death occurring by someone else's decision when the patient is incapable of giving consent). It is essential to clarify that euthanasia, whether voluntary or involuntary; is intentional killing. It deliberately introduces death into a situation in which it did not previously exist. But to withhold or withdraw useless treatment from a terminally ill patient is not euthanasia. Nor is the administration of painkillers to a dying patient which may incidentally accelerate death, but whose primary intention is to relieve pain. In both these cases death is already irreversibly present. To intervene with further treatment would only prolong the process of dying. Although this distinction is not always amenable to precise definition, there is a fundamental difference between causing somebody to die (which is euthanasia) and allowing him or her to die (which is not). During Dr Martyn Lloyd-Jones' final illness in hospital, there came a moment when he refused further treatment, complaining to his doctor 'You are keeping me from the glory!'

There seem to be three basic issues in the euthanasia debate, which I will call 'value' (what value has a human life?), 'fear' (what are the main fears which euthanasia is intended to relieve?) and 'autonomy' (what right do we have over our own life?).

First, there is the question of *value*. Some contemporary non-Christian writers flatly deny that human life has any absolute or intrinsic value. Notable among them is Professor Peter Singer in his book *Rethinking Life and Death, 'the collapse of our traditional ethics'* (1994, OUP 1995). He is well known for his rejection of 'speciesism', namely 'discrimination against or exploitation of certain animal species by human beings, based on an assumption of mankind's superiority' (OED). Accepting both the Darwinian view that 'we are animals too' (p. 176) and the corresponding view that the higher animals are 'persons' too (pp. 180–3), he argues that we must 'abandon the distinction between humans and non-human animals'. Since then 'neither a newborn human infant nor a fish is a person' (p. 220), we can imagine the logical consequences of such a position for both abortion and euthanasia.

There are other non-Christian scholars, however, who still maintain, albeit not on biblical grounds, that human beings have a unique value. For example, as with abortion so with euthanasia, Professor Dworkin is able to affirm 'the intrinsic cosmic importance of human life itself' (p. 217). So far we have seen that, in relation to abortion, he has formulated a person's value in terms of the 'investment', both natural and human, which has been made in him or her, adding that the natural investment in a human life is more important than the human. It can therefore be argued that death would frustrate nature's investment and so 'cheat nature' (p. 214). Now, however, in relation to euthanasia, Professor Dworkin develops a view of human 'value' which is based on our 'best interests', distinguishing between 'experiential' interests (what causes pleasure or pain) and 'critical' interests (what gives life meaning). Only after he has made this distinction is he able to ask the question whether death could ever be in someone's 'best interests'? Certainly our life's

conclusion needs to be consonant with the convictions and commitments which have motivated it throughout, since 'none of us wants
to end our lives out of character' (p. 213). On the contrary, this
would compromise our dignity, our sense of being 'someone with
critical interests' (p. 237).

These concepts of 'investment' and 'critical interests' are valiant
attempts to construct a secular understanding of human value.
They fail to convince, however, and seem too abstract to have popular appeal. The Christian alternative, which we need to defend and
promote with increasing determination, is that we have intrinsic
value because God has created us in his own image. Human beings
are God-like beings, possessing a cluster of unique faculties
(rational, moral and social) which distinguish us from animals. In
particular, there is our capacity for the relationships of love, since
God is love.

But this raises a problem. Is not love an essentially reciprocal
relationship? How can we love a person who is unable to respond to
our love, for example somebody in a 'persistent vegetative state' or
indeed an unborn fetus? Does not their unresponsiveness disqualify
them from being regarded and treated as a human being? No, this is
where grace comes in. For grace is precisely love to the unrespon-
sive. Grace is love taking a unilateral initiative. Grace is God's free,
spontaneous, unsolicited, even unreturned love, which finds its
origin in itself, not in its object. We looked earlier at Psalm 139,
in which the psalmist affirms that at every stage of his life (as fetus,
baby, youth and adult) he is the same person with the same identity.
He is also aware of a special personal relationship to God, which
God has initiated and which God sustains. He finds his humanity
and dignity not in his knowing and loving God, but in the fundamental truth that God knows and loves him, whether he responds to
God or not. This same divine unilateral love binds a mother to her
unborn child, and young people to their frail, elderly, and perhaps
demented relatives. It is not responsiveness which makes people
human; it is love, not loving only but being loved.

Secondly, the spectre of *fear* haunts the euthanasia debate. One of
the strongest incentives of those campaigning for euthanasia is that
(understandably) they are afraid of what they see as the only
alternative, namely having to endure (or see loved ones endure) the
horrors of a lingering, distressing, anguished, messy end. Professor
John Wyatt, consultant neo-natal paediatrician at University College

Hospital, in his 1997 London Lectures in Contemporary Christianity (*Matters of Life and Death*) analysed this often inarticulate fear. First, it is fear of uncontrollable and unbearable pain. Secondly, it is fear of indignity, of being subjected to the dehumanizing effect of modern medical technology, 'with tubes in every orifice'. Thirdly, it is fear of dependence. We want to 'write our own script and determine our own exit' and not suffer the ultimate humiliation of total helplessness.

Further, if we are to have a balanced understanding of the place of fear in the euthanasia debate, we need to add a fourth fear, although this is experienced not by those who advocate euthanasia, but by those who oppose it. It is the fear that their doctor might become their killer. A crucial clause in the Hippocratic Oath is the following: 'I will use treatment to help the sick according to my judgement and ability, but I will never use it to injure or wrong them.' This general promise to heal and not to hurt accounts for the two particular rejections which follow, namely assisted suicide and abortion, although both were very common in the ancient world: 'I will not give poison to anyone, even though asked to do so ... I will not give a pessary to a woman to cause abortion.' Here is a clear recognition that the vocation of a doctor is to be a healer. There is therefore a fundamental anomaly about a healer becoming a killer at either end of human life. It undermines the doctor–patient relationship, which is based on trust, not fear. Doctors are the servants of life; they must not become the agents of death.[47]

Reverting to the fears which surround the process of dying, many see euthanasia as the only way to escape this threefold trauma (pain, indignity and dependence). But there is an alternative, which Christians want to promote, namely modern palliative care. One of its Christian pioneers was Dame Cicely Saunders, founder of the St Christopher's Hospice in South London.[48] Another is Dr Robert Twycross, who since 1971 has been a full-time hospice doctor. He says to his patients: 'Not only will we enable you to die with dignity, but we will enable you to live before you die.' But it appears that large numbers of doctors do not know about this development. It is significant that Dr Nigel Cox, who in 1992 gave a lethal injection to his longstanding patient Lilian Boyes, was rebuked by the General Medical Council for being unaware of the available resources of palliative medicine and was ordered to take a course in this area. It is now claimed that more than 90 per cent of pain can be controlled by analgesia. And Christian people can and should be more actively involved in giving love and support to terminally ill patients in their nearest hospice.

The third issue involved in the euthanasia debate is the question of human *autonomy* or self-determination. The advocates of euthanasia insist, often in strident tones, that all human beings (provided that they are rational and competent) have the right to make their own decisions and dispose of their own life, and that no institution or individual has the authority to deny them that right.

It is certainly a fundamental biblical truth that God has made us rational and volitional beings. That is, we have a God-given mind and will of our own. Consequently, it is an essential aspect of our identity and maturity as human beings that we live by choice and not by coercion, and that we are accountable to God for our decisions. Indeed, this is the meaning of freedom. Freedom presupposes choice, and 'freedom is the cardinal absolute requirement of self-respect'.[49] While stating in general terms the goodness of choice, however, we need immediately to qualify our assertion in relation to freedom, dependence and life.

First, *freedom has limits*. The notion of absolute freedom is an illusion. Even God, who is perfect in his freedom, is not free to do absolutely anything. This is not the meaning of his omnipotence. Scripture itself mentions several things God 'cannot' (because he will not) do, especially that he cannot deny or contradict himself (2 Timothy 2:13). For God's freedom is limited by his nature. He is free to do absolutely anything which it is consistent with his nature to do. The same principle applies to human beings. Human freedom is not unlimited. We find our freedom only in living according to our God-given nature, not in rebellion against it. The notion of total human autonomy is a myth.

Secondly, *dependence can be good*, even though it is the opposite of autonomy. It is highly significant that Jesus chose little children as his model of humility. For the 'humility' of children is not in their character (which is often self-centred and stubborn) but in their status (dependent on their parents). Just so, we human beings are to acknowledge humbly our dependence on God, not only for the sustaining of our physical existence, but also for our salvation, which is due to his grace, not our achievement. The proclamation of our autonomy in this area, claiming that we can know and reach God by our own effort, is the essence of sin, not of maturity. Dependence is far from being the unmitigated, undignified evil some fear.

Thirdly, *life is a gift of God.* 'I know, O Lord,' cried Jeremiah, 'that a man's life is not his own' (Jeremiah 10:23). He was right; it is God's. According to a long, consistent, biblical tradition, God is the creator, giver, sustainer and taker away of life. He said in the Song of Moses: 'There is no god besides me. I put to death and I bring to life (Deuteronomy 32:39; cf. Genesis 39:2; 1 Samuel 2:6; Job 1:21). Similarly, the king of Israel was indignant when the king of Syria wrote to him about Naaman's leprosy: 'Am I God? Can I kill and bring back to life?' (2 Kings 5:7). Moreover, having received this gift from his hands, we are trustees and guardians of it, and he invites us to co-operate with him in fostering it. This includes curing and caring, looking after those who cannot look after themselves, and seeking to restore to health those who are sick. For human beings are not animals, *pace* Professor Peter Singer and others who reject 'speciesism'. When necessary, we 'put down' or 'put to sleep' a favourite pet, but we may not use this vocabulary in relation to the handicapped or the senile, the unborn or the dying. The doctor must not think or behave like a vet.

Yet 'there exists in contemporary culture,' Pope John Paul II has written, 'a certain Promethean attitude which leads people to think that they can control life and death by taking the decisions about them into their own hands.'[50] The proper name for this frame of mind is not autonomy but *hubris*, presumption before God. Although the lines of demarcation between God's responsibility and ours are not always sharp, and although God does call us into a privileged partnership with himself, yet we human beings may not trespass into his territory or assume his prerogatives. Instead, we must let God be God in his unique majesty and power, and humble ourselves before him in worship.

Chapter 16

SAME-SEX PARTNERSHIPS?

Because of the explosive nature of this topic, let me begin by describing the proper context of our thinking about it and by affirming a number of truths about my readers and myself which I am taking for granted as I write.

The context for discussion

First, *we are all human beings.* That is to say, there is no such phenomenon as 'a homosexual'. There are only people, human persons, made in the image and likeness of God, yet fallen, with all the glory and the tragedy which that paradox implies, including sexual potential and sexual problems. However strongly we may disapprove of homosexual practices, we have no liberty to dehumanize those who engage in them.

Secondly, *we are all sexual beings.* Our sexuality, according to both Scripture and experience, is basic to our humanness. Angels may be sexless; we humans are not. When God made humankind, he made us male and female. So to talk about sex is to touch a point close to the centre of our personality. A vital part of our identity is being discussed, and perhaps either endorsed or threatened. So the subject demands an unusual degree of sensitivity.

Moreover, not only are we all sexual beings, but we all have a particular sexual inclination. The American zoologist Alfred C. Kinsey's famous investigation into human sexuality led him to place every human being somewhere on a spectrum from 0 (an exclusively heterosexual bias, attracted only to the opposite sex) to 6 (an exclusively homosexual bias, attracted only to the same sex, whether homosexual males or 'lesbians', as homosexual females are usually called). In between these poles he plotted varying degrees of bisexuality, referring to people whose sexual inclination is either dual or indeterminate or fluctuating.

Since the publication in 1948 of Kinsey's report on male sexual behaviour,[1] he has been widely quoted as having found that 10 per cent of American men (at least of white American males) are exclusively homosexual throughout their lives. This is a serious misquotation, however. Ten per cent was his figure for men who are predominantly homosexual for up to three years between the ages of 16 and 65. His figure for lifelong and exclusive homosexual men was 4 per cent, and even this has been challenged on the ground that his sampling was not representative. More recent studies have found the incidence of homosexual practice to be lower still. According to four surveys conducted by the US National Opinion Research Center between 1970 and 1990, the number of men who had ever had a homosexual encounter was 6 per cent and during the previous year 1.8 per cent, while the percentage of the population who had adopted a consistently homosexual lifestyle was between 0.6 and 0.7 per cent. A 1990-1 British survey found similarly that 1.1 per cent had had a homosexual partner during the previous year. These studies suggest that in the western world less than 2 per cent of the male population, and less than 1 per cent of the female, are exclusively homosexual in inclination and practice.

Thirdly, *we are all sinners*. We are frail and vulnerable. We are pilgrims on our way to God. We are very far from having arrived. We are engaged in an unremitting conflict with the world, the flesh and the devil. Not yet have we conquered. Perfection awaits the Parousia. In addition and in particular, we are all sexual sinners. The doctrine of total depravity asserts that every part of our human being has been tainted and twisted by sin, and that this includes our sexuality. Dr Merville Vincent, of the Department of Psychiatry at Harvard Medical School, was surely correct when he wrote: 'In God's view I suspect we are all sexual deviants. I doubt if there is anyone who has not had a lustful thought that deviated from God's perfect ideal of sexuality.'[2] Nobody (with the sole exception of Jesus of Nazareth) has been sexually sinless. There is no question, therefore, of coming to this study with a horrid 'holier-than-thou' attitude of moral superiority. Because all of us are sinners, we all stand under the judgement of God and we are all in urgent need of the grace of

God. Besides, sexual sins are not the only sins, nor even necessarily the most sinful; pride and hypocrisy are surely worse.

Fourthly, in addition to being human, sexual and sinful creatures, I take it that *we are all Christians*. At least the readers I have in mind in this chapter are not people who reject the lordship of Jesus Christ, but rather those who earnestly desire to submit to it, believe that he exercises it through Scripture, want to understand what light Scripture throws on this topic, and have a predisposition to seek God's grace to follow his will when it is known. Without this kind of commitment, it would be more difficult for us to find common ground. To be sure, God's standards are the same for everybody, but non-Christian people are less ready to accept them.

Having delineated the context for our discussion, I am ready to ask the question: are same-sex partnerships a Christian option? I phrase my question advisedly. It introduces us to three necessary distinctions.

First, at least since the Wolfenden Report of 1957 and the resultant Sexual Offences Act of 1967, we have learned to distinguish between sins and crimes. Adultery has always (according to God's law) been a sin, but in most countries it is not an offence punishable by the state. Rape, by contrast, is both a sin and a crime. What the Sexual Offences Act of 1967 did was to declare that a homosexual act performed between consenting adults over 21 in private should no longer be a criminal offence. 'The Act did not in fact "legalize" such behaviour,' wrote Professor Sir Norman Anderson, 'for it is still regarded by the law as immoral, and is devoid of any legal recognition; all the Act did was to remove the criminal sanction from such acts when performed in private between two consenting adults.'[3]

Secondly, we have grown accustomed to distinguish between a homosexual inclination or 'inversion' (for which people may not be responsible) and homosexual physical practices (for which they are). The importance of this distinction goes beyond the attribution of responsibility to the attribution of guilt. We may not blame people for what they are, though we may for what they do. And in every discussion about homosexuality we must be rigorous in differentiating between this 'being' and 'doing', that is, between a person's identity and activity, sexual preference and sexual practice, constitution and conduct.

But now we have to come to terms with a third distinction, namely between homosexual practices which are casual (and probably anonymous) acts of self-gratification and those which (it is claimed) are just as expressive of authentic human love as is heterosexual intercourse in marriage. No responsible homosexual person (whether Christian or not) is advocating promiscuous 'one-night stands', let alone violence or the corruption of young people and children. What some are arguing, however, especially in the Lesbian and Gay Christian Movement, is that a heterosexual marriage and a homosexual partnership are 'two equally valid alternatives',[4] being equally tender, mature and faithful. In May 1989 Denmark became the first country to legalize homosexual marriages. The previous year Bishop John S. Spong of Newark, New Jersey, urged the Episcopal Church 'to bless and affirm the love that binds two persons of the same gender into a life-giving relationship of mutual commitment'.[5]

The question before us, then, does not relate to homosexual practices of a casual nature, but asks whether homosexual partnerships – lifelong and loving – are a Christian option. Our concern is to subject prevailing attitudes (which range from total revulsion to equally uncritical endorsement) to biblical scrutiny. Is our sexual 'preference' purely a matter of personal 'taste'? Or has God revealed his will regarding a norm? In particular, can the Bible be shown to sanction homosexual partnerships, or at least not to condemn them? What, in fact, does the Bible condemn?

The biblical prohibitions

The late Derrick Sherwin Bailey was the first Christian theologian to re-evaluate the traditional understanding of the biblical prohibitions. His famous book, of which all subsequent writers on this topic have had to take careful account, namely *Homosexuality and the Western Christian Tradition*, was published in 1955. Although many have not been persuaded by his attempted reconstruction, in particular his reinterpretation of the sin of Sodom, there are other writers, less cautious in scholarly standards than he, who regard his argument as merely preliminary and build on his foundations a much more permissive position. It is essential to consider this debate.

There are four main biblical passages which refer (or appear to refer) to the homosexual question negatively: (1) the story of Sodom (Genesis 19:1–13), with which it is natural to associate the very similar story of Gibeah (Judges 19); (2) the Levitical texts

(Leviticus 18:22 and 20:13) which explicitly prohibit 'lying with a man as one lies with a woman'; (3) the apostle Paul's portrayal of decadent pagan society in his day (Romans 1:18–32); and (4) two Pauline lists of sinners, each of which includes a reference to homosexual practices of some kind (1 Corinthians 6:9–10 and 1 Timothy 1:8–11).

(1) The stories of Sodom and Gibeah

The Genesis narrative makes it clear that 'the men of Sodom were wicked and were sinning greatly against the Lord' (13:13), and that 'the outcry against Sodom and Gomorrah' was 'so great and their sin so grievous' that God determined to investigate it (18:20–1), and in the end 'overthrew those cities and the entire plain, including all those living in the cities' (19:25) by an act of judgement which was entirely consistent with the justice of 'the Judge of all the earth' (18:25). There is no controversy about this background to the biblical story. The question is: what was the sin of the people of Sodom (and Gomorrah) which merited their obliteration?

The traditional Christian view has been that they were guilty of homosexual practices, which they attempted (unsuccessfully) to inflict on the two angels whom Lot was entertaining in his home. Hence the word 'sodomy'. But Sherwin Bailey challenged this interpretation on two main grounds. First, it is a gratuitous assumption (he argued) that the demand of the men of Sodom, 'Bring them out to us, so that we may know them' meant 'so that we can have sex with them' (NIV). For the Hebrew word for 'know' ($y\bar{a}\underline{d}a\acute{}$) occurs 943 times in the Old Testament, of which only 10 occurrences refer to physical intercourse, and even then only to heterosexual intercourse. It would therefore be better to translate the phrase 'so that we may get acquainted with them'. We can then understand the men's violence as due to their anger that Lot had exceeded his rights as a resident alien, for he had welcomed two strangers into his home 'whose intentions might be hostile and whose credentials – had not been examined'.[6] In this case the sin of Sodom was to invade the privacy of Lot's home and flout the ancient rules of hospitality. Lot begged them to desist because, he said, the two men 'have come under the protection of my roof' (verse 8).

Bailey's second argument was that the rest of the Old Testament nowhere suggests that the nature of Sodom's offence was homosexual. Instead, Isaiah implies that it was hypocrisy and social injustice,

Jeremiah adultery, deceit and general wickedness, and Ezekiel arrogance, greed and indifference to the poor (Isaiah 1:10ff.; Jeremiah 23:14; Ezekiel 16:49ff.; cf. the references to pride in Ecclesiasticus 16:8 and to inhospitableness in Wisdom 19:8). Then Jesus himself (though Bailey does not mention this) on three separate occasions alluded to the inhabitants of Sodom and Gomorrah, declaring that it would be 'more bearable' for them on the day of judgement than for those who reject his gospel (Matthew 10:15, 11:24; Luke 10:12). Yet in all these references there is not even a whiff or rumour of homosexual malpractice! It is only when we reach the Palestinian pseudepigraphical writings of the second century BC that Sodom's sin is identified as unnatural sexual behaviour.[7] And this finds a clear echo in the Letter of Jude, in which it is said that 'Sodom and Gomorrah and the surrounding towns gave themselves up to sexual immorality and perversion' (verse 7), and in the works of Philo and Josephus, Jewish writers who were shocked by the homosexual practices of Greek society.

Sherwin Bailey handled the Gibeah story in the same way, for they are closely parallel. Another resident alien (this time an anonymous 'old man') invites two strangers (not angels but a Levite and his concubine) into his home. Evil men surround the house and make the same demand as the Sodomites, that the visitor be brought out 'so that we may know him'. The owner of the house first begs them not to be so 'vile' to his 'guest', and then offers his daughter and the concubine to them instead. The sin of the men of Gibeah, it is again suggested, was not their proposal of homosexual intercourse but their violation of the laws of hospitality.

Although Bailey must have known that his reconstruction of both stories was at most tentative, he yet made the exaggerated claim that 'there is not the least reason to believe, as a matter of either historical fact or of revealed truth, that the city of Sodom and its neighbours were destroyed because of their homosexual practices.'[8] Instead, the Christian tradition about 'sodomy' was derived from late, apocryphal Jewish sources.

But Sherwin Bailey's case is not convincing for a number of reasons: (1) The adjectives 'wicked', 'vile' and 'disgraceful' (Genesis 18:7; Judges 19:23) do not seem appropriate to describe a breach of hospitality; (2) the offer of women instead 'does look as if there is some sexual connotation to the episode',[9] (3) although the verb *yāḏaʿ* is used only 10 times of sexual intercourse, Bailey omits to mention that six of these occurrences are in Genesis and one in the Sodom story itself (about Lot's daughters, who had not 'known' a man, verse 8); (4) for those of us who take the New Testament documents seriously, Jude's unequivocal reference to the 'sexual immorality and perversion' of Sodom and Gomorrah (verse 7) cannot be dismissed as merely an error copied from Jewish pseude-pigrapha. To be sure, homosexual behaviour was not Sodom's only sin; but according to Scripture it was certainly one of its sins, which brought down upon it the fearful judgement of God.

(2) The Leviticus texts

Both texts in Leviticus belong to the 'Holiness Code' which is the heart of the book, and which challenges the people of God to follow his laws and not copy the practices either of Egypt (where they used to live) or of Canaan (to which he was bringing them). These prac-tices included sexual relations within the prohibited degrees, a vari-ety of sexual deviations, child sacrifice, idolatry and social injustice of different kinds. It is in this context that we must read the follow-ing two texts:

> Do not lie with a man as one lies with a woman; that is detestable (18:22)
> If a man lies with a man as one lies with a woman, both of them have done what is detestable. They must be put to death; their blood will be on their own heads (20:13).

'It is hardly open to doubt,' wrote Bailey, 'that both the laws in Leviticus relate to ordinary homosexual acts between men, and not to ritual or other acts performed in the name of religion.'[10] Others, however, affirm the very point which Bailey denies. They point out that the two texts are embedded in a context preoccupied largely with ritual cleanness, and Peter Coleman adds that the word trans-lated 'detestable' or 'abomination' in both verses is associated with idolatry. 'In English the word expresses disgust or disapproval, but in the Bible its predominant meaning is concerned with religious truth rather than morality or aesthetics.'[11] Are these prohibitions merely religious taboos, then? Are they connected with that other prohibition, 'No Israelite man or woman is to become a temple prostitute' (Deuteronomy 23:17)? For certainly the Canaanitish fertility cult did include ritual prostitution, and therefore provided both male and female 'sacred prostitutes' (even if there is no clear evidence that either engaged in homosexual intercourse). The evil kings of Israel and Judah were constantly introducing them into the religion of Yahweh, and the righteous kings were constantly expelling them (see, for example, 1 Kings 14:22ff.; 15:12; 22:46 and 2 Kings 23:7). The homosexual lobby argues therefore that the Levitical texts prohibit religious practices which have long since ceased, and have no relevance to same-sex partnerships today. The burden of proof is with them, however. The plain, natural interpretation of these two verses is that they prohibit homosexual intercourse of every kind. And the requirement of the death penalty (long since abrogated, of course) indicates the extreme seriousness with which homosexual practices were viewed.

(3) Paul's teaching in Romans 1

> Because of this, God gave them over to shameful lusts. Even their women exchanged natural relations for unnatural ones (verse 26). In the same way the men also abandoned natural relations with women and were inflamed with lust for one another. Men committed indecent acts with other men, and received in themselves the due penalty for their perversion (verse 27).

All are agreed that the apostle is describing idolatrous pagans in the Graeco-Roman world of his day. They had a certain knowledge of God through the created universe (verses 19–20) and their own moral sense (verse 32), yet they suppressed the truth they knew in order to practise wickedness. Instead of giving to God the honour due to him, they turned to idols, confusing the Creator with his creatures. In judgement upon them, 'God gave them over' to their depraved mind and their decadent practices (verses 24, 26, 28), including 'unnatural' sex. It seems at first sight to be a definite condemnation of homosexual behaviour. But two arguments are advanced on the other side: (1) although Paul knew nothing of the modern distinction between 'inverts' (who have a homosexual disposition) and 'perverts' (who, though heterosexually inclined, indulge in homosexual practices), nevertheless it is the latter he is condemning, not the former. This must be so, it is urged, because they are described as having 'abandoned' natural relations with women, whereas no exclusively homosexual male would ever have had them. (2) Paul is evidently portraying the reckless, shameless, profligate, promiscuous behaviour of people whom God has judicially 'given up'; what relevance has this to committed, loving homosexual partnerships? These two arguments can be rebutted, however, especially by the apostle's reference to 'nature', that is, the created order, as I hope to show later.

(4) The other Pauline texts

> Do you not know that the wicked will not inherit the kingdom of God? Do not be deceived: Neither the sexually immoral, nor idolaters nor adulterers nor male prostitutes (*malakoi*) nor homosexual offenders (*arsenokoitai*) nor thieves nor the greedy nor drunkards nor slanderers nor swindlers will inherit the kingdom of God (1 Corinthians 6:9–10).
>
> We also know that law is made not for good men but for lawbreakers and rebels, the ungodly and sinful, the unholy and irreligious; for those who kill their fathers or mothers, for murderers, for adulterers and perverts (*arsenokoitai*), for slave traders and liars and perjurers – and for whatever else is contrary to the sound doctrine that conforms to the glorious gospel of the blessed God ... (1 Timothy 1:9–10).

Here are two ugly lists of sins which Paul affirms to be incompatible in the first place with the Kingdom of God and in the second with either the law or the gospel. It will be observed that one group of offenders are called *malakoi* and the other (in both lists) *arsenokoitai*. What do these words mean? To begin with, it is extremely unfortunate that in the original Revised Standard Version translation of 1 Corinthians 6:9 they were combined and translated 'homosexuals'. Sherwin Bailey was right to protest, since the use of the word 'inevitably suggests that the genuine invert, even though he be a man of irreproachable morals, is automatically branded as unrighteous and excluded from the Kingdom of God'.[12] Fortunately, the revisers heeded the protest, and the second edition (1973), though still combining the words, rendered them 'sexual perverts'. The point is that all 10 categories listed in 1 Corinthians 6:9–10 (with the possible exception of 'the greedy') denote people who have offended by their *actions* – for example, idolaters, adulterers and thieves.

The two Greek words *malakoi* and *arsenokoitai* should not be combined, however, since they 'have precise meanings. The first is literally "soft to the touch" and metaphorically, among the Greeks, meant males (not necessarily boys) who played the passive role in homosexual intercourse. The second means literally "male in a bed", and the Greeks used this expression to describe the one who took the active role.'[13] The Jerusalem Bible follows James Moffatt in using the ugly words 'catamites and sodomites', while among his conclusions Peter Coleman suggests that 'probably Paul had commercial paederasty in mind between older men and post-pubertal boys, the most common pattern of homosexual behaviour in the classical world'.[14] If this is so, then once again it can be (and has been) argued that the Pauline condemnations are not relevant to homosexual adults who are both consenting and committed to one another. This is not, however, the conclusion which Peter Coleman himself draws. His summary is as follows: 'Taken together, St Paul's writings repudiate homosexual behaviour as a vice of the Gentiles in Romans, as a bar to the Kingdom in Corinthians, and as an offence to be repudiated by the moral law in 1 Timothy.'[15]

Reviewing these biblical references to homosexual behaviour, which I have grouped, we have to agree that there are only four of them. Must we then conclude that the topic is marginal to the main thrust of the Bible? Must we further concede that they constitute a rather flimsy basis on which to take a firm stand against a homosexual lifestyle? Are those protagonists right who claim that the biblical prohibitions are 'highly specific'[16] – against violations of hospitality (Sodom and Gibeah), against cultic taboos (Leviticus), against shameless orgies (Romans) and against male prostitution or the corruption of the young (1 Corinthians and 1 Timothy), and that none of these passages alludes to, let alone condemns, a loving partnership between genuine homosexual inverts? This is the conclusion reached, for example, by Letha Scanzoni and Virginia Mollenkott in their book *Is The Homosexual My Neighbour?* They write:

> The Bible clearly condemns certain kinds of homosexual practice (... gang rape, idolatry and lustful promiscuity). However, it appears to be silent in certain other aspects of homosexuality – both the 'homosexual orientation' and 'a committed love-relationship analogous to heterosexual monogamy'.[17]

But no, plausible as it may sound, we cannot handle the biblical material in this way. The Christian rejection of homosexual practices does not rest on 'a few isolated and obscure proof texts' (as is sometimes said), whose traditional explanation (it is further claimed) can be overthrown. And it is disturbing that those who write on this subject, and include in their treatment a section on the biblical teaching, all seem to deal with it in this way. For example, 'Consideration of the Christian attitude to homosexual practices,' wrote Sherwin Bailey, 'inevitably begins with the story of the destruction of Sodom and Gomorrah.'[18] But this beginning is not at all 'inevitable'. In fact, it is positively mistaken. For the negative prohibitions of homosexual practices in Scripture make sense only in the light of its positive teaching in Genesis 1 and 2 about human sexuality and heterosexual marriage. Yet Sherwin Bailey's book contains no allusion to these chapters at all. And even Peter Coleman, whose *Christian Attitudes to Homosexuality* is probably the most comprehensive biblical, historical and moral survey which has yet been published, mentions them only in a passing reference to 1 Corinthians 6 where Paul quotes Genesis 2:24. Yet without the wholesome positive teaching of the Bible on sex and marriage, our perspective on the homosexual question is bound to be skewed.

Sexuality and marriage in the Bible

The essential place to begin our investigation, it seems to me, is the institution of marriage in Genesis 2, although we have already looked at it in Chapters 13 and 14. Since members of the Lesbian and Gay Christian Movement deliberately draw a parallel between heterosexual marriages and homosexual partnerships, it is necessary to ask whether this parallel can be justified.

We have seen that in his providence God has given us two distinct accounts of creation. The first (Genesis 1) is general, and affirms the *equality* of the sexes, since both share in the image of God and the stewardship of the earth. The second (Genesis 2) is particular, and affirms the *complementarity* of the sexes, which constitutes the basis for heterosexual marriage. In this second account of creation three fundamental truths emerge.

First, *the human need for companionship*. 'It is not good for the man to be alone' (verse 18). True, this assertion was later qualified when the apostle Paul (surely echoing Genesis) wrote: 'It is good for a man not to marry' (1 Corinthians 7:1). That is to say, although marriage is the good institution of God, the call to singleness is also the good vocation of some. Nevertheless, as a general rule, 'It is not good for the man to be alone.' For God has created us social beings. Since he is love, and has made us in his own likeness, he has given us a capacity to love and be loved. He intends us to live in community, not in solitude. In particular, God continued, 'I will make a helper suitable for him.' Moreover, this 'helper' or companion, whom God pronounced 'suitable for him', was also to be his sexual partner, with whom he was to become 'one flesh', so that they might thereby both consummate their love and procreate their children.

Secondly, Genesis 2 reveals *the divine provision to meet this human need*. Having affirmed Adam's need for a partner, the search for a suitable one began. God first paraded the birds and beasts before him, and Adam proceeded to 'name' them, to symbolize his taking them into his service. But (verse 20) 'for Adam no suitable helper was found', who could live 'alongside' or 'opposite' him, who could be his complement, his counterpart, his companion, let alone his mate. So a special creation was necessary.

The debate about how literally we are intended to understand what follows (the divine surgery under a divine anaesthetic) must not prevent us from grasping the point. Something happened during Adam's deep sleep. A special work of divine creation took place. The sexes became differentiated. Out of the undifferentiated humanity of Adam, male and female emerged. And Adam awoke from his deep sleep to behold before him a reflection of himself, a complement to himself, indeed a very part of himself. Next, having created the woman out of the man, God himself brought her to him, much as today the bride's father gives the bride away. And Adam broke spontaneously into history's first love poem, saying that now at last there stood before him a creature of such beauty in herself and similarity to him that she appeared to be (as indeed she was) 'made for him':

> This is now bone of my bones
>   and flesh of my flesh;
> She shall be called 'woman',
>   for she was taken out of man.

There can be no doubting the emphasis of this story. According to Genesis 1 Eve, like Adam, was created in the image of God. But as to the manner of her creation, according to Genesis 2, she was made neither out of nothing (like the universe), nor out of 'the dust of the ground' (like Adam, verse 7), but out of Adam.

The third great truth of Genesis 2 concerns the *resulting institution of marriage*. Adam's love poem is recorded in verse 23. The 'therefore' or 'for this reason' of verse 24 is the narrator's deduction:

> For this reason a man will leave his father and mother, and be united to his wife, and they will become one flesh.

Even the inattentive reader will be struck by the three references to 'flesh': 'this is ... flesh of my flesh ... they will become one flesh'. We may be certain that this is deliberate, not accidental. It teaches that heterosexual intercourse in marriage is more than a union; it is a kind of reunion. It is not a union of alien persons who do not belong to one another and cannot appropriately become one flesh. On the contrary, it is the union of two persons who originally were one, were then separated from each other, and now in the sexual encounter of marriage come together again.

It is surely this which explains the profound mystery of heterosexual intimacy, which poets and philosophers have celebrated in every culture. Heterosexual intercourse is much more than a union of bodies; it is a blending of complementary personalities through which, in the midst of prevailing alienation, the rich created oneness of human being is experienced again. And the complementarity of male and female sexual organs is only a symbol at the physical level of a much deeper spiritual complementarity.

In order to become one flesh, however, and experience this sacred mystery, certain preliminaries are necessary, which are constituent parts of marriage. 'Therefore' (verse 24),

> 'a man' (the singular indicates that marriage is an exclusive union between two individuals)
> 'shall leave his father and mother' (a public social occasion is in view)
> 'and cleave to his wife' (marriage is a loving, cleaving commitment or covenant, which is heterosexual and permanent)
> 'and they will become one flesh' (for marriage must be consummated in sexual intercourse, which is a sign and seal of the marriage covenant, and over which no shadow of shame or embarrassment had yet been cast, verse 25)

It is of the utmost importance to note that Jesus himself later endorsed this Old Testament definition of marriage. In doing so, he both introduced it with words from Genesis 1:27 (that the Creator 'made them male and female') and concluded it with his own comment ('so they are no longer two, but one. Therefore, what God has joined together, let man not separate' – Matthew 19:6). He thus made three statements about God the Creator's activity. First, God 'made' them male and female. Secondly God 'said' that a man must leave his parents and cleave to his wife. Thirdly, he 'joined' them together in such a way that no human being might put them apart. Here then are three truths which Jesus affirmed: (1) heterosexual gender is a divine creation; (2) heterosexual marriage is a divine institution; and (3) heterosexual fidelity is the divine intention. A homosexual liaison is a breach of all three of these divine purposes.

It is in this context of the creation narratives of Genesis 1 and 2 that I need to respond to Michael Vasey's sincere but misguided attempt, in his 1995 book *Strangers and Friends*, to combine evangelical faith with homosexual advocacy. In regard to his historical thesis, that there was 'widespread acceptance of homosexual desire and behaviour among Christians until about the thirteenth century',[19] he is dependent on the writings of John Boswell.[20] The scholarly assessment of Boswell's work by his fellow historians, however, has ranged 'from the sharply critical to the dismissive to the devastating'.[21] Dr David Wright of Edinburgh University ends his article on homosexuality in *The Encyclopedia of Early Christianity* with these words: 'The conclusion must be that, for all its interest and stimulus, Boswell's book provides at the end of the day not one firm piece of evidence that the teaching mind of the early church countenanced homosexual activity.'[22]

Michael Vasey's handling of the biblical material is even less plausible. He virtually dismisses any appeal to the implications of Genesis 2:24 on the ground that 'it imposes on scripture the domestic ideals of the nuclear family',[23] isolated, self-contained and self-centred. He evinces a surprising degree of hostility to marriage and the family, caricaturing them as destructive 'idols' of modern society.[24] Jesus did not marry, he reminds us, and implies by this that he disapproved of marriage, for 'it is precisely the passage in which Jesus quotes Genesis 2:24 that commends the renunciation of marriage'.[25] Indeed, he suggests, there is a fundamental conflict between marriage and the gospel in the teaching of Jesus and his apostles.

'For them the family was part of the present world order which was characterized by rebellion against God.'[26] Hence 'withdrawal from the social institutions and responsibilities of marriage and the family was a step into Christian freedom', so that people need not 'continue as slaves within the present transient order'.[27] In such an analysis the way is opened for homosexual partnerships as another, even a better, option.

But Michael Vasey has twisted the biblical material to suit his purpose. Neither Jesus' own singleness, nor his teaching that singleness is a divine vocation for some (Matthew 19:11, 12), may be taken as evidence that he opposed marriage and family, for they belong to the created order. Nor is the family envisaged in Genesis 1 and 2 'nuclear' in a negative or selfish sense. To be sure, Jesus did inaugurate a new order, refer to his new community as his family (Mark 3:34), and warn that if an unavoidable conflict arises between our loyalty to him and our loyalty to our natural family, then our loyalty to him takes precedence (Matthew 10:37, Luke 14:26). But Jesus and his apostles also insisted that Christians have a continuing obligation to their natural family, including reciprocal duties between parents and children, and between husbands and wives (e.g. Mark 7:9–13; Ephesians 5:22—6:4). The new creation restores and redeems the old; it does not reject or replace it. As for idols, every good gift of God can become an idol, including marriage and family; but in themselves neither is idolatrous or enslaving. A homosexual partnership, however, is essentially incompatible with marriage as the God-ordained context for one-flesh intimacy.

Thus Scripture defines the marriage God instituted in terms of heterosexual monogamy. It is the union of one man with one woman, which must be publicly acknowledged (the leaving of parents), permanently sealed (he will 'cleave to his wife') and physically consummated ('one flesh'). And Scripture envisages no other kind of marriage or sexual intercourse, for God provided no alternative.

Christians should not therefore single out homosexual intercourse for special condemnation. The fact is that every kind of sexual relationship and activity which deviates from God's revealed intention is *ipso facto* displeasing to him and under his judgement. This includes polygamy and polyandry (which infringe the 'one man – one woman' principle), cohabitation and clandestine unions (since these have involved no decisive public leaving of parents), casual encounters and temporary liaisons, adultery and many divorces (which conflict with 'cleaving' and with Jesus' prohibition, 'let man not separate'). and homosexual partnerships (which violate the statement that 'a man' shall be joined to 'his wife'.

In sum, the only 'one flesh' experience which God intends and Scripture contemplates is the sexual union of a man with his wife, whom he recognizes as 'flesh of his flesh'. As George Carey, Archbishop of Canterbury, said in an address at Virginia Theological Seminary on 10 February 1997, 'I do not find any justification, from the Bible or from the entire Christian tradition, for sexual activity outside marriage.'

Contemporary arguments considered

Homosexual Christians are not, however, satisfied with this biblical teaching about human sexuality and the institution of heterosexual marriage. They bring forward a number of objections to it, in order to defend the legitimacy of homosexual partnerships.

(1) The argument about Scripture and culture

Traditionally, it has been assumed that the Bible condemns all homosexual acts. But are the biblical writers reliable guides in this matter? Were their horizons not bounded by their own experience and culture? The cultural argument usually takes one of two forms.

First, the biblical authors were addressing themselves to questions relevant to their own circumstances, and these were very different from ours. In the Sodom and Gibeah stories they were preoccupied either with conventions of hospitality in the Ancient Near East which are now obsolete or (if the sin was sexual at all) with the extremely unusual phenomenon of homosexual gang rape. In the Levitical laws the concern was with antiquated fertility rituals, while Paul was addressing himself to the particular sexual preferences of Greek paederasts. It is all so antiquarian. The biblical authors' imprisonment in their own cultures renders their teaching on this topic irrelevant.

The second and complementary culture problem is that the biblical writers were not addressing themselves to *our* questions. Thus the problem of Scripture is not only with its teaching but also with its silence. Paul (let alone the Old Testament authors) knew nothing of post-Freudian psychology. They had never heard of 'the homosexual condition'; they knew only about certain practices.

The difference between 'inversion' and 'perversion' would have been incomprehensible to them. The very notion that two men or two women could fall in love with each other and develop a deeply loving, stable relationship comparable to marriage simply never entered their heads.

If the only biblical teaching on this topic were to be found in the prohibition texts, it might be difficult to answer these objections. But once those texts are seen in relation to the divine institution of marriage, we are in possession of a principle of divine revelation which is universally applicable. It was applicable to the cultural situations of both the Ancient Near East and the first-century Graeco-Roman world, and it is equally applicable to modern sexual questions of which the ancients were quite ignorant. The reason for the biblical prohibitions is the same reason why modern loving homosexual partnerships must also be condemned, namely that they are incompatible with God's created order. And since that order (heterosexual monogamy) was established by creation, not culture, its validity is both permanent and universal. There can be no 'liberation' from God's created norms; true liberation is found only in accepting them.

This argumentation is the opposite of the 'biblical literalism' of which the gay lobby tend to accuse us. It is rather to look beneath the surface of the biblical prohibitions to the essential positives of divine revelation on sexuality and marriage. It is significant that those who are advocating same-sex partnerships usually omit Genesis 1 and 2 from their discussion, even though Jesus our Lord himself endorsed their teaching.

(2) The argument about creation and nature

People sometimes make this kind of statement: 'I'm gay because God made me that way. So gay must be good. I cannot believe that God would create people homosexual and then deny them the right to sexual self-expression. I intend, therefore, to affirm, and indeed celebrate, what I am by creation.' Or again, 'You may say that homosexual practice is against nature and normality; but it's not against *my* nature, nor is it in the slightest degree abnormal for *me*.' Norman Pittenger was quite outspoken in his use of this argument a couple of decades ago. A homosexual person, he wrote, is 'not an "abnormal" person with "unnatural" desires and habits'. On the contrary, 'a heterosexually oriented person acts "naturally" when he acts heterosexually, while a homosexually oriented person acts equally "naturally" when he acts in accordance with his basic, in-built homosexual desire and drive.'[28]

Others argue that homosexual behaviour is 'natural' (a) because in many primitive societies it is fairly acceptable, (b) because in some advanced civilizations (ancient Greece, for example) it was even idealized and (c) because it is said to be quite widespread in animals. Yet, according to Thomas E. Schmidt, the research consensus is that 'no evidence has as yet emerged to suggest that any non-human primate ... would rate a 6 (exclusively homosexual) on the Kinsey scale ...'[29]

In any case these arguments express an extremely subjective view of what is 'natural' and 'normal'. We should not accept Norman Pittenger's statement that there are 'no eternal standards of normality or naturalness'.[30] Nor can we agree that animal behaviour sets standards for human behaviour! For God has established a norm for sex and marriage by creation. This was already recognized in the Old Testament era. Thus, sexual relations with an animal were forbidden, because 'that is a perversion' (Leviticus 18:23), in other words a violation or confusion of nature, which indicates an 'embryonic sense of natural law'.[31] The same verdict is passed on Sodom by the second century BC *Testament of Naphtali*: 'As the sun and the stars do not change their order, so the tribe of Naphtali are to obey God rather than the disorderliness of idolatry. Recognizing in all created things the Lord who made them, they are not to become as Sodom which changed the order of nature ...'[32]

The same concept was clearly in Paul's mind in Romans 1. When he wrote of women who had 'exchanged natural relations for unnatural ones', and of men who had 'abandoned natural relations', he meant by 'nature' (*physis*) the natural order of things which God has established (as in 2:14, 27 and 11:24). What Paul was condemning, therefore, was not the perverted behaviour of heterosexual people who were acting against their nature, as John Boswell argued, [33] but any human behaviour that is against 'Nature', that is, against God's created order. Richard B. Hays has written a thorough rebuttal of John Boswell's exegesis of Romans 1. He provides ample contemporary evidence that the opposition of 'natural' (*kata physin*) and 'unnatural' (*para physin*) was 'very frequently used ... as a way of distinguishing between heterosexual and homosexual behaviour.'[34]

British commentators confirm his conclusion. As C.K. Barrett puts it: 'In the obscene pleasures to which he [Paul] refers is to be seen precisely that perversion of the created order which may be expected when men put the creation in place of the Creator.'[35] Similarly, Charles Cranfield writes that by 'natural' and 'unnatural' 'Paul clearly means "in accordance with the intention of the Creator" and "contrary to the intention of the Creator", respectively.' Again, 'the decisive factor in Paul's use of it [*physis*, "nature"] is his biblical doctrine of creation. It denotes that order which is manifest in God's creation and which men have no excuse for failing to recognize and respect.'[36]

An appeal to the created order should also be our response to another argument which is being developed by a few people today, especially in the Church of England. They point out that the early Church distinguished between primary and secondary issues, insisting on agreement about the former but allowing freedom to disagree about the latter. The two examples of Christian liberty which they usually quote are circumcision and idol-meats. They then draw a parallel with homosexual practice, suggesting that it is a second-order issue in which we can give one another freedom. But actually the early Church was more subtle than they allow in its argumentation. The Jerusalem Council (Acts 15) decreed that circumcision was definitely not necessary for salvation (a first-order question), but allowed its continuance as a matter of policy or culture (second-order). The Council also decided that, although of course idolatry was forbidden (first-order), eating idol-meats was not necessarily idolatrous, so that Christians with a strong, educated conscience might eat them (second-order). Thus the second-order issues, in which Christian liberty was allowed, were neither theological nor moral but cultural. But this is not the case with homosexual practice.

A second parallel is sometimes drawn. When the debate over women's ordination was at its height, General Synod agreed that the Church should not be obliged to choose between the two positions (for and against), declaring one to be right and the other wrong, but should rather preserve unity by recognizing both to have integrity. In consequence, we are living with 'the two integrities'. Why, it is asked, should we not equally acknowledge 'two integrities' in relation to same-sex partnerships, and not force people to choose? The answer should be clear. Even if women's ordination is a second-order issue (which many would deny), homosexual partnerships are not. Gender in relation to marriage is a much more fundamental matter than gender in relation to ministry. For marriage has been recognized as a heterosexual union from the beginning of God's creation and institution; it is basic to human society as God intended it, and its biblical basis is incontrovertible. Dr Wolfhart Pannenberg, professor of theology at Munich University, is outspoken on this subject. Having declared that 'the biblical assessments of homosexual practice are unambiguous in their rejection', he concludes that a Church which were to recognize homosexual unions as equivalent to marriage 'would cease to be the one, holy, catholic and apostolic church' (*Christianity Today*, 11 November 1996).

(3) The argument about quality of relationships

The Lesbian and Gay Christian Movement borrows from Scripture the truth that love is the greatest thing in the world (which it is) and from the 'new morality' or 'situation ethics' of the 1960s the notion that love is an adequate criterion by which to judge every relationship (which it is not). Yet this view is gaining ground today. One of the first official documents to embrace it was the Friends' Report *Towards a Quaker View of Sex* (1963). It included the statements 'One should no more deplore "homosexuality" than lefthandedness'[37] and 'Surely it is the nature and quality of a relationship that matters'.[38] Similarly in 1979, the Methodist Church's Division of Social Responsibility, in its report *A Christian Understanding of Human Sexuality*, argued that 'homosexual activities', are 'not intrinsically wrong', since 'the quality of any homosexual relationship is ... to be assessed by the same basic criteria which have been applied to heterosexual relationships. For homosexual men and women, permanent relationships characterized by love can be an appropriate Christian way of expressing their sexuality.'[39] The same year (1979) an Anglican working party issued the report *Homosexual Relationships: a contribution to discussion*. It was more cautious, judicious and ambivalent than the Quaker and Methodist reports. Its authors did not feel able to repudiate centuries of Christian tradition, yet they 'did not think it possible to deny' that in some circumstances individuals may 'justifiably choose' a homosexual relationship in their search for companionship and sexual love 'similar' to those found in marriage.[40]

In his *Time for Consent* Norman Pittenger lists what he sees to be the six characteristics of a truly loving relationship. They are

(1) commitment (the free self-giving of each to the other), (2) mutuality in giving and receiving (a sharing in which each finds his or her self in the other, (3) tenderness (no coercion or cruelty), (4) faithfulness (the intention of a lifelong relationship), (5) hopefulness (each serving the other's maturity), and (6) desire for union.[41]

If then a homosexual relationship, whether between two men or two women, is characterized by these qualities of love, surely (the argument runs) it must be affirmed as good and not rejected as evil? For it rescues people from loneliness, selfishness and promiscuity. It can be just as rich and responsible, as liberating and fulfilling, as a heterosexual marriage.

More recently, in the spring of 1997, in a lecture delivered at St Martin-in-the-Fields in London, Bishop John Austin Baker gave his own version of this argument. Formerly Bishop of Salisbury, chairman of the Church of England's Doctrine Commission, and chairman of the drafting group which produced the moderate report *Issues in Human Sexuality* (1991), he astonished the Church by his apparent volte-face. The goal of Christian discipleship, he rightly affirmed, is 'Christlikeness', that is, 'a creative living out of the values, priorities and attitudes that marked his humanity', especially of love. Now sex in marriage can be 'a true making of love', and 'erotic love can and often does have the same beneficial effects in the life of same-sex couples'.

There are three reasons, however, why this claim for the quality of same-sex love is flawed. First, the concept of lifelong, quasi-marital fidelity in homosexual partnerships is largely a myth, a theoretical ideal which is contradicted by the facts. The truth is that gay relationships are characterized more by promiscuity than by fidelity. A number of researches have been made. 'One of the most carefully researched studies of the most stable homosexual pairs,' writes Dr Jeffrey Satinover, namely *The Male Couple*, 'was researched and written by two authors who are themselves a homosexual couple ...' They found that 'of the 156 couples studied, only seven had maintained sexual fidelity; of the hundred couples that had been together for more than five years, none had been able to maintain sexual fidelity'. They added that 'the expectation for outside sexual activity was the rule for male couples and the exception for heterosexuals.'[42] The result of these research studies led Thomas Schmidt to conclude: 'Promiscuity among homosexual men is not a mere stereotype, and it is not merely the majority experience – it is virtually the *only* experience ... In short, there is practically no comparison possible to heterosexual marriage in terms of either fidelity or longevity. Tragically, lifelong faithfulness is almost non-existent in the homosexual experience.'[43] There seems to be something inherently unstable about homosexual partnerships. The quality of relationships argument does not hold water.

Secondly, it is difficult to maintain that homosexual partnerships are just as much an expression of love as heterosexual marriages in the light of the known damage and danger involved in usual gay sexual practices. Dr Satinover has the courage to give us 'the brute facts about the adverse consequences of homosexuality', based on the most recent medical studies. He writes of infectious hepatitis which increases the risk of liver cancer, of freqently fatal rectal cancer, and of a 25–30-year decrease in life expectancy.[44] Thomas Schmidt is even more explicit, describing seven non-viral and four viral infections which are transmitted by oral and anal sex. It is true that some diseases can also be transmitted by similar activity between heterosexual people, but 'these health problems are rampant in the homosexual population because they are easily spread by promiscuity and by most of the practices favoured by homosexuals'. And these diseases are apart from AIDS, to which we will come shortly. Thomas Schmidt justly calls this chapter 'The Price of Love'.[45] If these physical dangers attend common gay sexual activities, can authentic lovers engage in them?

But, thirdly, the biblical Christian cannot accept the basic premise on which this case rests, namely that love is the only absolute, that besides it all moral law has been abolished, and that whatever seems to be compatible with love is *ipso facto* good, irrespective of all other considerations. This cannot be so. For love needs law to guide it. In emphasizing love for God and neighbour as the two great commandments, Jesus and his apostles did not discard all other commandments. On the contrary, Jesus said, 'If you love me you will keep my commandments,' and Paul wrote, 'Love is the fulfilling [not the abrogating] of the law.' (John 14:15; Romans 13:8–10).

So then, although the loving quality of a relationship is an essential, it is not by itself a sufficient criterion to authenticate it. For example, if love were the only test of authenticity, there would be nothing against polygamy, for a polygamist could certainly enjoy a relationship with several wives which reflects all Dr Pittenger's six characteristics. Or let me give you a better illustration, drawn from my own pastoral experience. On several different occasions a married man has told me that he has fallen in love with another woman. When I have gently remonstrated with him, he has responded in words like these: 'Yes, I agree, I already have a wife and family. But this new relationship is the real thing. We were made for each other. Our love for each other has a quality and depth we have never known before. It *must* be right.' But no, I have had to say to him, it is not right. No man is justified in breaking his marriage covenant with his wife on the ground that the quality of his love for another woman is richer. Quality of love is not the only yardstick by which to measure what is good or right.

Similarly, we should not deny that homosexual relationships can be loving (although *a priori* they cannot attain the same richness as the heterosexual complementarity which God has ordained). As the 1994 Ramsey Colloquium put it, 'Even a distorted love retains traces of love's grandeur.'[46] But the love-quality of gay relationships is not sufficient to justify them. Indeed, I have to add that they are incompatible with true love because they are incompatible with God's law. Love is concerned for the highest welfare of the beloved. And our highest human welfare is found in obedience to God's law and purpose, not in revolt against them.

Some leaders of the Lesbian and Gay Christian Movement appear to be following the logic of their own position, for they are saying that even monogamy could be abandoned in the interests of 'love'. Malcolm Macourt, for example, has written that the Gay Liberationist's vision is of 'a wide variety of life patterns', each of which is 'held in equal esteem in society'. Among them he lists the following alternatives: monogamy and multiple partnerships; partnerships for life and partnerships for a period of mutual growth; same-sex partners and opposite sex partners; living in community and living in small family units.[47] There seem to be no limits to what some people seek to justify in the name of love.

(4) The argument about justice and rights

If some argue for homosexual partnerships on the basis of the love involved, others do so on the basis of justice. Desmond Tutu, for example, formerly Archbishop of Cape Town, and universally admired for his courageous stand against apartheid and for racial equality, has several times said that for him the homosexual question is a simple matter of justice. Others agree. The justice argument runs like this: 'Just as we may not discriminate between persons on account of their gender, colour, ethnicity or class, so we may not discriminate between persons on account of their sexual preference. For the God of the Bible is the God of justice, who is described as loving justice and hating injustice. Therefore the quest for justice must be a paramount obligation of the people of God. Now that slaves, women and blacks have been liberated, gay liberation is long overdue. What civil rights activists were in the 1950s and '60s, gay rights activists are today. We should support them in their cause and join them in their struggle.'

The vocabulary of oppression, liberation, rights and justice, however, needs careful definition. 'Gay liberation' presupposes an oppression from which homosexual people need to be set free, and 'gay rights' imply that homosexual people are suffering a wrong which should be righted. But what is this oppression, this wrong, this injustice? If it is that they are being despised and rejected by sections of society on account of their sexual inclination, are in fact victims of homophobia, then indeed they have a grievance which must be redressed. For God opposes such discrimination and requires us to love and respect all human beings without distinction. If, on the other hand, the 'wrong' or 'injustice' complained of is society's refusal to recognize homosexual partnerships as a legitimate alternative to heterosexual marriages, then talk of 'justice' is inappropriate, since human beings may not claim as a 'right' what God has not given them.

The analogy between slaves, blacks, women and gays is inexact and misleading. In each case we need to clarify the Creator's original intention. Thus, in spite of misguided attempts to justify slavery and racism from Scripture, both are fundamentally incompatible with the created equality of human beings. Similarly, the Bible honours womanhood by affirming that men and women share equally in the image of God and the stewardship of the environment, and its teaching on masculine 'headship' or responsibility may not be interpreted as contradicting this equality (see Chapter 13). But sexual intercourse belongs, according to the plain teaching of Scripture, to heterosexual marriage alone. Therefore homosexual intercourse cannot be regarded as a permissible equivalent, let alone a divine right. True gay liberation (like all authentic liberation) is not freedom from God's revealed purpose in order to construct our own morality; it is rather freedom from our self-willed rebellion in order to love and obey him.

(5) The argument about acceptance and the gospel

'Surely,' some people are saying, 'it is the duty of heterosexual Christians to accept homosexual Christians. Paul told us to accept – indeed welcome – one another. If God has welcomed somebody, who are we to pass judgement on him (Romans 14:1ff.;15:7)?' Norman Pittenger goes further and declares that those who reject homosexual people 'have utterly failed to understand the Christian gospel'. We do not receive the grace of God because we are good and confess our sins, he continues; it is the other way round. 'It's always God's grace which comes *first* ... his forgiveness awakens our repentance.'[48] He even quotes the hymn 'Just as I am, without one plea', and adds: 'The whole point of the Christian gospel is that God loves and accepts us just as we are.'[49]

This is a very confused statement of the gospel, however. God does indeed accept us 'just as we are', and we do not have to make ourselves good first, indeed we cannot. But his 'acceptance' means that he fully and freely forgives all who repent and believe, not that he condones our continuance in sin. Again, it is true that we must accept one another, but only as fellow-penitents and fellow-pilgrims, not as fellow-sinners who are resolved to persist in our sinning. Michael Vasey makes much of the fact that Jesus was called (and was) 'the friend of sinners'. And indeed his offer of friendship to sinners like us is truly wonderful. But he welcomes us in order to redeem and transform us, not to leave us alone in our sins. No acceptance, either by God or by the Church, is promised to us if we harden our hearts against God's Word and will. Only judgement.

The AIDS epidemic

Is AIDS, then, the judgement of God on practising homosexual men? This is what some evangelical Christians have confidently declared, and is the reason why I have included a section on AIDS in this particular chapter. Before we are in a position to decide, however, we need to know the basic facts.

AIDS (the Acquired Immune Deficiency Syndrome) was identified and described for the first time in 1981 in the United States. It is spread through HIV (the Human Immuno-deficiency Virus), which may then lie dormant and unsuspected in its human host for 10 years or even longer. But eventually it will in most cases manifest itself by attacking and damaging the body's immune and nervous systems, and so making it defenceless against certain fatal diseases. The origin of this human virus is unknown, although the accepted wisdom is that it developed as a spontaneous mutation of a virus which had long infected African monkeys.

Many myths surround AIDS (specially in relation to its transmission and its extent), which need to be dispelled.

First, AIDS is not an easily caught infectious disease. The virus is transmitted only in body fluids, particularly in semen and blood. The commonest ways of getting it are through sexual intercourse with an infected partner and through an injection either of contaminated blood or with an unsterilized needle (the sharing of needles by drug addicts is a very dangerous practice). A child in the womb is also greatly at risk if the pregnant mother is HIV positive.

Secondly, AIDS is not a specifically 'gay plague'. It was given that inaccurate designation in the early 1980s because it first appeared in the male homosexual communities of San Francisco and New York. But the virus is transmitted by heterosexual as well as homosexual intercourse (overwhelmingly so in Africa, where homosexual behaviour is almost unknown), and AIDS sufferers include many women and babies as well as men. It is promiscuous sexual behaviour which spreads the disease most rapidly; whether this takes place with same-sex or opposite-sex partners is largely irrelevant. 'The greater the numbers, the greater the risk,' writes Dr Patrick Dixon, founder of ACET (AIDS Care Education and Training), whose well-researched and compassionate book *The Truth About AIDS* I recommend.[50]

Thirdly, AIDS is not a peculiarly western phenomenon. It seemed in the early eighties to be so, because American and European hospitals, possessing the necessary resources, were the first to diagnose it. But it is increasingly a world-wide disease. In East and Central Africa it has already reached epidemic proportions.

Fourthly, AIDS is not a problem which is going to be quickly solved. It is an incurable disease, with neither preventative vaccine nor therapeutic drug in sight. The drug known as AZT can prolong an AIDS victim's life by about a year, and alleviate suffering, but it has unpleasant side-effects and is a treatment, not a cure. Meanwhile, the statistics are growing at an alarming rate. The American Psychiatric Association Press reports that '30% of all 20-year-old gay men will be HIV positive or dead of AIDS by the time they are age 30.'[51] In 1996 alone there were an estimated 3.1 million new HIV infections around the world. In sub-Saharan Africa there are

14 million people living with HIV/AIDS. In parts of East Africa over 10 per cent of women attending ante-natal clinics are HIV infected, with some clinics reporting numbers over 40 per cent. Almost 1 million children in Kenya, Rwanda, Uganda and Zambia have been orphaned as a result of AIDS, with approximately 8 per cent of these children infected themselves. AIDS is also spreading with incredible ferocity in some parts of India: with up to 10 per cent of truck drivers infected it is moving beyond the urban centres and into the countryside. The 10,000 estimated cases of HIV infection in China in 1993 increased to 100,000 in 1995. But the most appalling figure of all was given by a 1997 joint UN and WHO report. Confessing that the scale of the global epidemic had been 'grossly underestimated', they reckoned that the total number of people living with HIV/AIDS was then more than 30 million and would reach 40 million by AD 2000.[52]

Fifthly, AIDS cannot be avoided merely by the use of a condom, which is known to be an unreliable contraceptive. Dr Dixon sums the matter up succinctly: 'Condoms do not make sex safe, they simply make it safer. Safe sex is sex between two partners who are not infected! This means a lifelong, faithful partnership between two people who were virgins and who now remain faithful to each other for life.'[53] Or, to quote the United States Catholic Conference, 'Abstinence outside of marriage and fidelity within marriage, as well as the avoidance of intravenous drug abuse, are the only morally correct and medically sure ways to prevent the spread of AIDS.'[54]

A threefold Christian response to these sobering facts and figures would seem to be appropriate.

First, *theological*. Reverting to the question whether AIDS is a divine judgement on practising homosexual men, I think we have to answer 'Yes and no.' 'No' because Jesus warned us not to interpret calamities as God's specific judgements upon evil people (Luke 13:1–5). 'No' also because AIDS victims include many women, especially faithful married women who have been infected by their unfaithful husbands, with a substantial minority of innocent haemophiliacs and children. But 'yes' in the sense that Paul meant when he wrote: 'Do not deceive yourselves; no-one makes a fool of God. A person will reap exactly what he sows' (Galatians 6:7 GNB). The fact that we reap what we sow, or that evil actions bring evil consequences, seems to have been written by God into the ordering of his moral world. Christians cannot regard it as an accident, for example, that promiscuity exposes people to venereal diseases, that heavy smoking can lead to lung cancer, excessive alcohol to liver disorders, and overeating (directly or indirectly) to heart conditions. Moreover, this cause-and-effect mechanism is viewed in Scripture as one of the ways in which God's 'wrath', that is, his just judgement on evil, is revealed (Romans 1:18–32). Before the day of judgement arrives, Jesus taught, a process of judgement is already taking place (John 3:18–21; 5:24–9). AIDS may rightly be seen, then, as 'part of God's judgement on society'. 'It is calling the bluff of the permissive society that there is any such thing as sexual liberation in promiscuity.'[55]

Our second Christian response must be *pastoral*. We do not deny that many people have contracted AIDS as a result of their own sexual promiscuity. But this provides us with no possible justification for shunning or neglecting them, any more than we would those who damage themselves through drunken driving or other forms of recklessness. As the American Roman Catholic bishops have put it, 'Stories of persons with AIDS must not become occasions for stereotyping or prejudice, for anger or recrimination, for rejection or isolation, for injustice or condemnation.' Instead, 'they provide us with an opportunity to walk with those who are suffering, to be compassionate towards those whom we might otherwise fear, to bring strength and courage both to those who face the prospect of dying as well as to their loved ones'.[56] 'Don't judge me,' an American AIDS patient called Jerome said. 'I'm living under my own judgement. What I need is for you to walk with me.'[57] Local churches need specially to reach out to AIDS sufferers in their own fellowship and in their wider community. The Terrence Higgins Trust, named after the first person in Britain who is known to have died of AIDS (in 1982), teaches high standards of counselling and care, especially through the 'buddy' service of volunteers which it has pioneered.[58] At the same time, we may be thankful that both the origins of the hospice movement, and its extension from terminal cancer patients to AIDS victims, have been due largely to Christian initiatives.[59]

Our third response must be *educational*. It is true that some people scorn this as a hopelessly inadequate reaction to the AIDS crisis, and propose instead the compulsory isolation of all virus carriers. But the Christian conscience shrinks from such a ruthless measure, even if it could be democratically accepted and successfully imposed. Mandatory regular screening is also advocated by some, and the arguments for and against were well developed by Dr David Cook in his 1989 London Lectures entitled *Just Health.*[60] But Christians are likely to prefer a thoroughgoing educational programme as the most human and Christian way to combat ignorance, prejudice, fear and promiscuous behaviour, and so turn back the AIDS tide. Certainly the current complacency and indifference, which are helping to spread the disease, can be overcome only by the relentless force of the facts. Dr Patrick Dixon, in his 'Ten Point Plan for the Government', urges that they 'get an army of health educators on the road', to visit and address all the country's schools and colleges, factories and shops, clubs and pubs. In such a preventive education programme the churches should have a major role. Is it not the failure of the churches to teach and exemplify God's standards of sexual morality which, more than anything else, is to blame for the current crisis?[61] We must not fail again, but rather challenge society to sexual self-control and faithfulness, and point to Jesus as the source of forgiveness and power. Several Christian groups have been set up to alert the churches to their responsibilities, to provide educational resources and to encourage support groups.[62]

Above all, 'the AIDS crisis challenges us profoundly to be the Church in deed and in truth: *to be the Church as a healing community*'. Indeed, because of our tendency to self-righteousness, 'the healing community itself will need to be healed by the forgiveness of Christ'.[63]

Faith, hope and love

If homosexual practice must be regarded, in the light of the whole biblical revelation, not as a variant within the wide range of accepted normality, but as a deviation from God's norm; and if we should therefore call homosexually inclined people to abstain from homosexual practices and partnerships, what advice and help can we give to encourage them to respond to this call? I would like to take Paul's triad of faith, hope and love, and apply it to homosexually inclined people.

(1) The Christian call to faith

Faith is our human response to divine revelation; it is believing God's Word.

First, *faith accepts God's standards.* The only alternative to hetero-sexual marriage is singleness and sexual abstinence. I think I know the implications of this. Nothing has helped me to understand the pain of homosexual celibacy more than Alex Davidson's moving book *The Returns of Love.* He writes of 'this incessant tension be-tween law and lust', 'this monster that lurks in the depths', this 'burning torment'.[64]

The secular world says: 'Sex is essential to human fulfilment. To expect homosexual people to abstain from homosexual practice is to condemn them to frustration and to drive them to neurosis, despair and even suicide. It's outrageous to ask them to deny themselves what to them is a normal and natural mode of sexual expression. It's "inhuman and inhumane".[65] Indeed, it's positively cruel.'

But no, the teaching of the Word of God is different. Sexual experience is not essential to human fulfilment. To be sure, it is a good gift of God. But it is not given to all, and it is not indispensable to humanness. People were saying in Paul's day that it was. Their slogan was, 'Food for the stomach and the stomach for food; sex for the body and the body for sex' (1 Corinthians 6:13). But this is a lie of the devil. Jesus Christ was single, yet perfect in his humanity. So it is possible to be single and human at the same time! Besides, God's commands are good and not grievous. The yoke of Christ brings rest, not turmoil; conflict comes only to those who resist it.

At the very centre of Christian discipleship is our participation in the death and resurrection of Jesus Christ. 'The Saint Andrew's Day Statement' on the homosexuality debate (1995), commis-sioned by the Church of England Evangelical Council, emphasized this. We are 'called to follow in the way of the cross'. For 'we all are summoned to various forms of self-denial. The struggle against dis-ordered desires, or the misdirection of innocent desire, is part of every Christian's life, consciously undertaken in baptism.' But after struggle comes victory, out of death resurrection.[66]

So ultimately it is a crisis of faith: whom shall we believe? God or the world? Shall we submit to the lordship of Jesus, or succumb to the pressures of prevailing culture? The true 'orientation' of Chris-tians is not what we are by constitution (hormones), but what we are by choice (heart, mind and will).

Secondly, *faith accepts God's grace.* Abstinence is not only good, if God calls us to celibacy; it is also possible. Many deny it, however. 'You know the imperious strength of our sex drive,' they say. 'To ask us to control ourselves is just not on.' It is 'so near to an impossibility', writes Norman Pittenger, 'that it's hardly worth talking about'.[67]

Really? What then are we to make of Paul's statement following his warning to the Corinthians that male prostitutes and homosexual offenders will not inherit God's Kingdom? 'And that is what some of you were,' he cries. 'But you were washed, you were sanctified, you were justified in the name of the Lord Jesus Christ and by the Spirit of our God' (1 Corinthians 6:11). And what shall we say to the millions of heterosexual people who are single? To be sure, all unmarried people experience the pain of struggle and loneliness. But how can we call ourselves Christians and declare that chastity is impossible? It is made harder by the sexual obsession of contemporary society. And we make it harder for ourselves if we listen to the world's plausible arguments, or lapse into self-pity, or feed our imagination with pornographic material and so inhabit a fantasy world in which Christ is not Lord, or ignore his command about plucking out our eyes and cutting off our hands and feet, that is, being ruthless with the avenues of temptation. But, whatever our 'thorn in the flesh' may be, Christ comes to us as he came to Paul and says: 'My grace is sufficient for you, for my power is made perfect in weakness' (2 Corinthians 12:9). To deny this is to portray Christians as the helpless victims of the world, the flesh and the devil, to demean them into being less than human, and to contradict the gospel of God's grace.

(2) The Christian call to hope

I have said nothing so far about 'healing' for homosexual people, understood not now as self-mastery but as the reversal of their sexual bias. Our expectation of this possibility will depend largely on our understanding of the aetiology of the homosexual condition, and no final agreement on this has yet been reached. Many studies have been conducted, but they have failed to establish a single cause, whether inherited or learned. So scholars have tended to turn to theories of multiple causation, combining a biological predisposition (genetic and hormonal) with cultural and moral influences, childhood environment and experience, and repeatedly reinforced personal choices. Dr Jeffrey Satinover concludes his investigation with an appeal to common sense: 'One's character traits are in part innate, but are subject to modification by experience and choice.'[68] So, if homosexuality is at least partly learned, can it be unlearned?

Just as opinions differ on the causes of homosexuality, so they also differ on the possibilities and the means of 'cure'. This issue divides people into three categories – those who consider healing unnecessary, and those who consider it possible or impossible.

First, we have to recognize that many homosexual people categorically reject the language of 'cure' and 'healing'. They see no need, and they have no wish, to change. Their position has been summed up in three convictions. Biologically, their condition is innate (being inherited), psychologically it is irreversible, and sociologically it is normal.[69] They regard it as a great victory that in 1973 the trustees of the American Psychiatric Association removed homosexuality from its official list of mental illnesses. Michael Vasey declares that this decision was not the result of some 'liberal' conspiracy.[70] But that is exactly what it was. Seventy years of psychiatric opinion were overthrown not by science (for no fresh evidence was produced) but by politics.[71] At least the Roman Catholic Church was neither impressed nor convinced. The American bishops in their 1986 'Pastoral Letter' continued to describe homosexuality as 'intrinsically disordered' (paragraph 3).

Secondly, there are those who regard 'healing', understood as the reversal of sexual orientation, as impossible. 'No known method of treatment or punishment,' writes D.J. West, 'offers hope of making any substantial reduction in the vast army of adults practising homosexuality'; it would be 'more realistic to find room for them in society'. He pleads for 'tolerance', though not for 'encouragement', of homosexual behaviour.[72]

Are not these views, however, the despairing opinions of the secular mind? They challenge us to articulate the third position, which is to believe that at least some degree of change is possible. Christians know that the homosexual condition, being a deviation from God's norm, is not a sign of created order but of fallen disorder. How, then, can we acquiesce in it or declare it incurable? We cannot. The only question is *when* and *how* we are to expect the divine deliverance and restoration to take place. The fact is that, though Christian claims of homosexual 'healings' are made, either through regeneration or through a subsequent work of the Holy Spirit, it is not easy to substantiate them.[73]

Martin Hallett, who before his conversion was active in the gay scene, has written a very honest account of his experience of what he calls 'Christ's way out of homosexuality'. He is candid about his continuing vulnerability, his need for safeguards, his yearning for love and his occasional bouts of emotional turmoil. I am glad he entitled his autobiographical sketch *I am Learning to Love* in the present tense, and subtitled it 'A personal journey to wholeness in Christ'. His final paragraph begins: 'I have learnt; I am learning; I will learn to love God, other people and myself. This healing process will only be complete when I am with Jesus.'[74]

True Freedom Trust have published a pamphlet entitled *Testimonies*. In it homosexual Christian men and women bear witness to what Christ has done for them. They have found a new identity in him, and have a new sense of personal fulfilment as children of God. They have been delivered from guilt, shame and fear by God's forgiving acceptance, and have been set free from thraldom to their former homosexual lifestyle by the indwelling power of the Holy Spirit. But they have not been delivered from their homosexual inclination, and therefore some inner pain continues alongside their new joy and peace. Here are two examples: 'My prayers were not answered in the way I had hoped for, but the Lord greatly blessed me in giving me two Christian friends who lovingly accepted me for what I was.' 'After I was prayed over with the laying on of hands a spirit of perversion left me. I praise God for the deliverance I found that afternoon ... I can testify to over three years of freedom from homosexual activity. But I have not changed into a heterosexual in that time.'

Similar testimonies are given by ex-gay ministries in the United States. Over 200 of them belong to the coalition called Exodus International.[75] Tim Stafford in the 18 August 1989 edition of *Christianity Today* describes his investigation into several of them. His conclusion was one of 'cautious optimism'. What ex-gays were claiming was 'not a quick 180-degree reversal of their sexual desires' but rather 'a gradual reversal in their spiritual understanding of themselves as men and women in relationship to God'. And this new self-understanding was 'helping them to relearn distorted patterns of thinking and relating. They presented themselves as people in process ...'

Is there really, then, no hope of a substantial change of inclination? Dr Elizabeth Moberly believes there is. She has been led by her researches to the view that 'a homosexual orientation does not depend on a genetic pre-disposition, hormonal imbalance, or abnormal learning process, but on difficulties in the parent-child relationships, especially in the earlier years of life'. The 'underlying principle', she continues, is 'that the homosexual – whether man or woman – has suffered from some deficit in the relationship with the parent *of the same sex*; and that there is a corresponding drive to make good this deficit through the medium of same-sex or "homosexual" relationships.'[76] The deficit and the drive go together. The reparative drive for same-sex love is not itself pathological, but 'quite the opposite – it is the attempt to resolve and heal the pathology'. 'The homosexual condition does not involve abnormal needs, but normal needs that have, abnormally, been left unmet in the ordinary process of growth.' Homosexuality 'is essentially a state of incomplete development' or of unmet needs.[77] So the proper solution is 'the meeting of same-sex needs without sexual activity', for to eroticize growth deficits is to confuse emotional needs with physiological desires.[78] How, then, can these needs be met? The needs are legitimate, but what are the legitimate means of meeting them? Dr Moberly's answer is that 'substitute relationships for parental care are in God's redemptive plan, just as parental relationships are in his creative plan'.[79] What is needed is deep, loving, lasting, same-sex but non-sexual relationships, especially in the Church. 'Love,' she concludes, 'both in prayer and in relationships, is the basic therapy … Love is the basic problem, the great need, and the only true solution. If we are willing to seek and to mediate the healing and redeeming love of Christ, then healing for the homosexual will become a great and glorious reality.'[80]

Even then, however, complete healing of body, mind and spirit will not take place in this life. Some degree of deficit or disorder remains in each of us. But not for ever! For the Christian's horizons are not bounded by this world. Jesus Christ is coming again; our bodies are going to be redeemed; sin, pain and death are going to be abolished; and both we and the universe are going to be transformed. Then we shall be finally liberated from everything which defiles or distorts our personality. And this Christian assurance helps us to bear whatever our present pain may be. For pain there is, in the midst of peace. 'We know that the whole creation has been groaning as in the pains of childbirth right up to the present time. Not only so, but we ourselves, who have the firstfruits of the Spirit, groan inwardly as we wait eagerly for our adoption as sons, the redemption of our bodies' (Romans 8:22f.). Thus our groans express the birthpangs of the new age. We are convinced that 'our

416 ► New Issues Facing Christians Today

present sufferings are not worth comparing with the glory that will be revealed in us' (Romans 8:18). This confident hope sustains us.

Alex Davidson derives comfort in the midst of his homosexuality from his Christian hope. 'Isn't it one of the most wretched things about this condition,' he writes, 'that when you look ahead, the same impossible road seems to continue indefinitely? You're driven to rebellion when you think of there being no point in it and to despair when you think of there being no limit to it. That's why I find a comfort, when I feel desperate, or rebellious, or both, to remind myself of God's promise that one day it will be finished ...'[81]

(3) The Christian call to love

At present we are living 'in between times', between the grace which we grasp by faith and the glory which we anticipate in hope. Between them lies love.

Yet love is just what the Church has generally failed to show to homosexual people. Jim Cotter complains bitterly about being treated as 'objects of scorn and insult, of fear, prejudice and oppression'.[82] Norman Pittenger describes the 'vituperative' correspondence he has received, in which homosexuals are dismissed even by professing Christians as 'filthy creatures', 'disgusting perverts', 'damnable sinners' and the like.[83] Pierre Berton, a social commentator, writes that 'a very good case can be made out that the homosexual is the modern equivalent of the leper'.[84] Rictor Norton is yet more shrill: 'The church's record regarding homosexuals is an atrocity from beginning to end: it is not for us to seek forgiveness, but for the church to make atonement.'[85]

The attitude of personal antipathy towards homosexuals is nowadays termed 'homophobia'.[86] It is a mixture of irrational fear, hostility and even revulsion. It overlooks the fact that the majority of homosexual people are probably not responsible for their condition (though they are, of course, for their conduct). Since they are not deliberate perverts, they deserve our understanding and compassion (though many find this patronizing), not our rejection. No wonder Richard Lovelace calls for 'a double repentance', namely 'that gay Christians renounce the active lifestyle' and that 'straight Christians renounce homophobia'.[87] Dr David Atkinson is right to add: 'We are not at liberty to urge the Christian homosexual to celibacy and to a spreading of his relationships, unless support for the former and opportunities for the latter are available in genuine love.'[88] I rather think that the very existence of the Lesbian and Gay Christian Movement is a vote of censure on the Church.

At the heart of the homosexual condition is a deep loneliness, the natural human hunger for mutual love, a search for identity, and a longing for completeness. If homosexual people cannot find these things in the local 'church family', we have no business to go on using that expression. The alternative is not between the warm physical relationship of homosexual intercourse and the pain of isolation in the cold. There is a third option, namely a Christian environment of love, understanding, acceptance and support. I do not think there is any need to encourage homosexual people to disclose their sexual inclinations to everybody; this is neither necessary nor helpful. But they do need at least one confidante to whom they can unburden themselves, who will not despise or reject them, but will support them with friendship and prayer; probably some professional, private and confidential pastoral counsel; possibly in addition the support of a professionally supervised therapy group; and (like all single people) many warm and affectionate friendships with people of both sexes. Same-sex friendships, like those in the Bible between Ruth and Naomi, David and Jonathan, and Paul and Timothy, are to be encouraged. There is no hint that any of these was homosexual in the erotic sense, yet they were evidently affectionate and (at least in the case of David and Jonathan) even demonstrative (e.g. 1 Samuel 18:1–4; 20:41 and 2 Samuel 1:26). Of course sensible safeguards will be important. But in African and Asian cultures it is common to see two men walking down the street hand in hand, without embarrassment. It is sad that our western culture inhibits the development of rich same-sex friendships by engendering the fear of being ridiculed or rejected as a 'queer'.

The best contribution of Michael Vasey's book *Strangers and Friends*, in my view, is his emphasis on friendship. 'Friendship is not a minor theme of the Christian faith,' he writes, 'but is integral to its vision of life.'[89] He sees society as 'a network of friendships held together by bonds of affection'. He also points out that Scripture does 'not limit the notion of covenant to the institution of marriage'.[90] As David and Jonathan made a covenant with each other (1 Samuel 18:3), we too may have special covenanted friendships.

These and other relationships, both same-sex and opposite-sex, need to be developed within the family of God which, though universal, has its local manifestations. He intends each local church to be a warm, accepting and supportive community. By 'accepting' I do not mean 'acquiescing'; similarly, by a rejection of 'homophobia' I do not mean a rejection of a proper Christian disapproval of homosexual behaviour. No, true love is not incompatible with the maintenance of moral standards. On the contrary, it insists on them, for the good of everybody. There is, therefore, a place for church discipline in the case of members who refuse to repent and wilfully persist in homosexual relationships. But it must be exercised in a spirit of humility and gentleness (Galatians 6:1f.); we must be careful not to discriminate between men and women, or between homosexual and heterosexual offences; and necessary discipline in the case of a public scandal is not to be confused with a witch-hunt.

Perplexing and painful as the homosexual Christian's dilemma is, Jesus Christ offers him or her (indeed, all of us) faith, hope and love – the faith to accept both his standards and his grace to maintain them, the hope to look beyond present suffering to future glory, and the love to care for and support one another. 'But the greatest of these is love' (1 Corinthians 13:13).

CONCLUSION

Chapter 17

A CALL FOR CHRISTIAN LEADERSHIP

There is a serious dearth of leaders in the contemporary world. Massive problems confront us, some of which we have looked at in this book. Globally, there are still the terrifying size of nuclear arsenals, the widespread violations of human rights, the environmental and energy crises, and North-South economic inequality. Socially, there are the tragedy of long-term unemployment, the continuance of conflict in industrial relations, and the outbreaks of racial violence. Morally, Christians are disturbed by the forces which are undermining the stability of marriage and the family, the challenges to sexual mores and sexual roles, and the scandal of what is virtually abortion on demand. Spiritually, I might add, there are the spread of materialism and the corresponding loss of any sense of transcendent reality. Many people are warning us that the world is heading for disaster; few are offering us advice on how to avert it. Technical know-how abounds, but wisdom is in short supply. People feel confused, bewildered, alienated. To borrow the metaphors of Jesus, we seem to be like 'sheep without a shepherd', while our leaders often appear to be 'blind leaders of the blind'.

There are many kinds and degrees of leadership. Leadership is not restricted to a small minority of world statesmen, or to the national top brass. In every society it takes a variety of forms. Clergy are leaders in the local church and community. Parents are leaders in their home and family. So are teachers in school and lecturers in college. Senior executives in business and industry, judges, doctors, politicians, social workers and union officials all have leadership responsibilities in their respective spheres. So do the opinion-formers who work in the media – authors and playwrights, journalists, sound and vision broadcasters, artists and producers. And student leaders, especially since the 1960s, have been exercising influence beyond their years and their experience. There is a great need in all these and other situations for more clearsighted, courageous and dedicated leaders.

Such leaders are both born and bred. As Bennie E. Goodwin, a black American educationist, has written: 'Although potential leaders are born, effective leaders are made.'[1] In Shakespeare's famous lines, 'Be not afraid of greatness! Some are born great, some achieve greatness, and some have greatness thrust upon them.'[2] Books on management refer to 'BNLs' (born natural leaders'), men and women endowed with strong intellect, character and personality. And we would want to add with Oswald Sanders that Christian leadership is 'a blending of natural and spiritual qualities',[3] or of natural talents and spiritual gifts. Nevertheless, God's gifts have to be cultivated, and leadership potential has to be developed.

What, then, are the marks of leadership in general, and of Christian leadership in particular? How can we give up sitting around, waiting for somebody else to take the initiative, and take one ourselves? What is needed to blaze a trail which others will follow?

Although many different analyses of leadership have been made, I want to suggest that it has five essential ingredients.

Vision

'Where there is no vision, the people perish' is a proverb from the King James' Version of the Bible, which has passed into common usage. And although it is almost certainly a mistranslation of the Hebrew, it is nonetheless a true statement.[4] Indeed, it has been a characteristic of the post-Pentecost era that 'your young men will see visions' and 'your old men will dream dreams' (Acts 2:17). Monsignor Ronald Knox of Oxford concluded his critical though somewhat wistful book *Enthusiasm* with these words:

> Men will not live without vision; that moral we do well to carry away with us from contemplating, in so many strange forms, the record of the visionaries. If we are content with the humdrum, the second-best, the hand-over-hand, it will not be forgiven us.[5]

'Dreams' and 'visions', dreamers and visionaries, sound somewhat unpractical, however, and remote from the harsh realities of life on earth. So more prosaic words tend to be used. Management experts tell us we must set both long-term and short-term goals. Politicians publish election manifestos. Military personnel lay down a campaign strategy. But whether you call it a 'goal', a 'manifesto' or a 'strategy', it is a *vision* that you are talking about.

So what is vision? It is an act of seeing, of course, an imaginative perception of things, combining insight and foresight. But more particularly, in the sense in which I am using the word, it is compounded of a deep dissatisfaction with what *is* and a clear grasp of what *could be*. It begins with indignation over the status quo, and it grows into the earnest quest for an alternative. Both are quite clear in the public ministry of Jesus. He was indignant over disease and death, and the hunger of the people, for he perceived these things as alien to the purpose of God. Hence his compassion for their victims. Indignation and compassion form a powerful combination. They are indispensable to vision, and therefore to leadership.

It will be remembered that Bobby Kennedy was assassinated in 1968 at the age of 42. In an appreciation of him which appeared 10 years later, David S. Broder wrote that 'his distinguishing quality was his capacity for what can only be called moral outrage. "That is unacceptable," he said of many conditions that most of us accepted as inevitable … Poverty, illiteracy, malnutrition, prejudice, crookedness, conniving – all such accepted evils were a personal affront to him.'[6] Apathy is the acceptance of the unacceptable; leadership begins with a decisive refusal to do so. As George F. Will wrote in December 1981, after the declaration of martial law in Poland, 'What is outrageous is the absence of outrage.' There is a great need today for more righteous indignation, anger, outrage over those evils which are an offence to God. How can we tolerate what he finds intolerable?

But anger is sterile if it does not provoke us to positive action to remedy what has aroused our anger. 'One must oppose those things that one believes to be wrong,' writes Robert Greenleaf, 'but one cannot *lead* from a predominantly negative posture.'[7] Before Robert McNamara retired in 1981 as President of the World Bank after 13 years, he addressed its annual meeting for the last time, and in his speech he quoted George Bernard Shaw: 'You see things as they are and ask "Why?" But I dream things that never were, and ask "Why not?"'

History abounds in examples, both biblical and secular. Moses was appalled by the cruel oppression of his fellow-Israelites in Egypt, remembered God's covenant with Abraham, Isaac and Jacob, and was sustained throughout his long life by the vision of the 'Promised Land'. Nehemiah heard in his Persian exile that the wall of the Holy City was in ruins, and its inhabitants in great distress. The news overwhelmed him, until God put into his heart what he could and should do. 'Come, let us rebuild the wall of Jerusalem,' he said. And the people replied, 'Let us start rebuilding' (Nehemiah 2:12, 17, 18).

Moving on to New Testament times, the early Christians were well aware of the might of Rome and the hostility of Jewry. But Jesus had told them to be his witness 'to the ends of the earth', and the vision he gave them transformed them. Saul of Tarsus had been brought up to accept as inevitable and unbridgeable the chasm between Jews and Gentiles. But Jesus commissioned him to take the gospel to the Gentile world, and he was 'not disobedient to the heavenly vision'. Indeed the vision of a single, new, reconciled humanity so captured his heart and mind, that he laboured, suffered and died in its cause (see e.g. Acts 26:16–20; Ephesians 2:11—3:13. for Paul's vision).

In our own generation Presidents of the United States have had noble visions of a 'New Deal' and of a 'Great Society', and the fact that their expectations did not altogether materialize is no criticism of their vision. Martin Luther King, incensed by the injustices of segregation, had a dream of dignity for blacks in a free, multi-racial America; he both lived and died that his dream might come true.

There can be little doubt that the phenomenal early success of Communists (within 50 years from the Russian Revolution of 1917 they had won over a third of the world) was due to the vision of a better society which they were able to inspire in their followers. This, at least, was the considered opinion of Douglas Hyde who in March 1948 resigned both from the British Communist Party (after 20 years' membership) and from being News Editor of the *Daily Worker*, and became a Roman Catholic. The subtitle he gave to his book *Dedication and Leadership* was 'Learning from the Communists', and he wrote it to answer the question 'Why are Communists so dedicated and successful as leaders, whilst others so often are not?' Here is how he put it: 'If you ask me what is the distinguishing mark of the Communist, what is it that Communists most outstandingly have in common ... I would say that beyond any shadow of doubt it is their idealism ...'[8] They dream, he continued, of a new society in which (quoting from Liu Shao-chi) there will be 'no oppressed and exploited people, no darkness, ignorance, backwardness' and 'no such irrational things as mutual deception, mutual antagonism, mutual slaughter and war'.[9] Marx wrote in his *Theses on Feuerbach* (1888): 'The philosophers have only in various ways *interpreted* the world: the point, however, is to change it.' That slogan 'change the world', comments Douglas Hyde, 'has proved to be one of the most dynamic of the past 120 years ... Marx concluded his *Communist Manifesto* with the words: "You have a world to win".'[10] This vision fired the imagination and zeal of young idealistic Communists. Because of it, Hyde wrote about the first half of this century, 'the recruit is made to feel that there is a great battle going on all over the world', and 'that this includes his own country, his own town, his own neighbourhood, the block of flats in which he lives, the factory or office where he works'.[11] 'One reason why the Communist is prepared to make his exceptional sacrifices,' Douglas Hyde argued, 'is that he believes he is taking part in a crusade.'[12]

But Jesus Christ is a far greater and more glorious leader than Karl Marx could ever be, and the Christian good news is a much more radical and liberating message than the Communist Manifesto. The world can be won for Christ by evangelism, and made more pleasing to Christ by social action. Why then does this prospect not set our hearts on fire? Where are the Christian people today who see the status quo, who do not like what they see (because there are things in it which are unacceptable to God), who therefore refuse to come to terms with it, who dream dreams of an alternative society which would be more acceptable to God, and who determine to do something about it? 'Nothing much happens without a dream. And for something great to happen, there must be a great dream. Behind every great achievement is a dreamer of great dreams.'[13]

We see with our mind's eye the 2 billion people who may never even have heard of Jesus, and the further 2 billion who have heard but have had no valid opportunity to respond to the gospel;[14] the poor, the hungry and the disadvantaged; people crushed by political, economic or racial oppression; the millions of babies aborted and incinerated; and the so-called 'balance' of nuclear terror. We see these things; do we not care? We see what is; do we not see what could be? Things could be different. The unevangelized could be reached with the good news of Jesus; the hungry could be fed, the oppressed liberated, the alienated brought home. We need a vision of the purpose and power of God.

David Bleakley writes about such visionaries, 'the people with a "hunch" alternative, those who believe that it *is* possible to build a better world'. He calls them 'Pathfinders', who are 'lovers of our planet, who feel a responsibility for God's creation, and wish to give true meaning to the lives of all his people'. Indeed, he is confident, as I am, that such 'Pathfinders represent a growing ground-swell of change in our society and in societies elsewhere'.[15]

Industry

The world has always been scornful of dreamers. 'Here comes that dreamer!' Joseph's older brothers said to one another. 'Come now, let's kill him … Then we'll see what comes of his dreams' (Genesis 37:19ff.). The dreams of the night tend to evaporate in the cold light of the morning.

So dreamers have to become in turn thinkers, planners and workers, and that demands industry or hard labour. Men of vision need to become men of action. It was Thomas Carlyle, the nineteenth-century Scottish writer, who said of Frederick the Great that genius means first of all 'the transcendent capacity of taking trouble', and it was Thomas Alva Edison, the inventor of electrical devices, who defined genius as '1% inspiration and 99% perspiration'. All great leaders, not least great artists, find this to be true. Behind their apparently effortless performance there lies the most rigorous and painstaking self-discipline. A good example is the world-renowned pianist, Paderewski. He spent hours in practice every day. It was not unknown for him to repeat a bar or phrase 50 times to perfect it. Queen Victoria once said to him, after she had heard him play, 'Mr Paderewski, you are a genius.' 'That may be, Ma'am,' he replied, 'but before I was a genius, I was a drudge.'[16]

This addition of industry to vision is an evident hallmark of history's great leaders. It was not enough for Moses to dream of the land flowing with milk and honey; he had to organize the Israelite rabble into at least the semblance of a nation and lead them through the dangers and hardships of the desert before they could take possession of the Promised Land. Similarly, Nehemiah was inspired by his vision of the rebuilt Holy City, but first he had to gather materials to reconstruct the wall and weapons to defend it. Winston Churchill loathed the Nazi tyranny and dreamed of Europe's liberation. But he was under no illusions about the cost of the enterprise. On 13 May 1940, in his first speech to the House of Commons as Prime Minister, he warned members that he had 'nothing to offer but blood, toil, tears and sweat', and 'many long months of struggle and suffering'.

Moreover the same combination of vision and industry is needed in our more ordinary individual lives. William Morris, who became Lord Nuffield the public benefactor, began his career repairing bicycles. What was the secret of his success? It was 'creative imagination wedded to indomitable industry'.[17] Thus dream and reality, passion and practicalities must go together. Without the dream the campaign loses its direction and its fire; but without hard work and practical projects the dream vanishes into thin air.

Perseverance

Thomas Sutcliffe Mort was an early nineteenth-century settler in Sydney, Australia, after whom the 'Mort Docks' are named. He was determined to solve the problem of refrigeration, so that meat could be exported from Australia to Britain, and he gave himself three years in which to do it. But it took him 26. He lived long enough to see the first shipment of refrigerated meat leave Sydney, but died before learning whether it had reached its destination safely. The house he built in Edgecliffe is now Bishopscourt, the residence of the Anglican Archbishop of Sydney. Painted 20 times round the cornice of the study ceiling are the words 'To persevere is to succeed', and engraved in stone outside the front door is the Mort family motto (a play on their Huguenot name) 'Fidèle à la Mort'.

Perseverance is certainly an indispensable quality of leadership. It is one thing to dream dreams and see visions. It is another to convert a dream into a plan of action. It is yet a third to persevere with it when opposition comes. For opposition is bound to arise. As soon as the campaign gets under way, the forces of reaction muster, entrenched privilege digs itself in more deeply, commercial interests feel threatened and raise the alarm, the cynical sneer at the folly of 'do-gooders', and apathy becomes transmuted into hostility.

But a true work of God thrives on opposition. Its silver is refined and its steel hardened. Of course those without the vision, who are merely being carried along by the momentum of the campaign, will soon capitulate. So it is that the protesting youth of one decade become the conservative establishment of the next. Young rebels lapse into middle-class, middle-aged, middle-of-the-road mediocrity. Even revolutionaries, once the revolution is over, tend to lose their ideals. But not the real leader. He has the resilience to take setbacks in his stride, the tenacity to overcome fatigue and discouragement, and the wisdom (in a favourite phrase of John Mott's) to 'turn stumbling-blocks into stepping stones'.[18] For the real leader adds to vision and industry the grace of perseverance.

In the Old Testament Moses is again the outstanding example. On about a dozen distinct occasions the people 'murmured' against him, and he had the beginnings of a mutiny on his hands. When Pharaoh's army was threatening them, when the water ran out or was too bitter to drink, when there was no meat to eat, when the scouts brought back a bad report of the strength of the Canaanite fortifications, when small minds became jealous of his position – these were some of the occasions on which the people complained of his leadership and challenged his authority. A lesser man would have given up and abandoned them to their own pettiness. But not Moses. He never forgot that these were *God's* people by *God's* covenant, who by *God's* promise would inherit the land.

In the New Testament the man who came to the end of his life with his ideals intact and his standards uncompromised was the apostle Paul. He too faced bitter and violent opposition. He had to endure severe physical afflictions, for on several occasions he was beaten, stoned and imprisoned. He suffered mentally too, for his footsteps were dogged by false prophets who contradicted his teaching and slandered his name. He also experienced great loneliness. Towards the end of his life he wrote 'everyone in the province of Asia has deserted me' and 'at my first defence ... everyone deserted me' (2 Timothy 1:15, 4:16). Yet he never lost his vision of God's new, redeemed society, and he never gave up proclaiming it. In his underground dungeon, from which there was to be no escape but death, he could write: 'I have fought the good fight, I have finished the race, I have kept the faith' (2 Timothy 4:7). He persevered to the end.

In recent centuries perhaps nobody has exemplified perseverance more than William Wilberforce. Sir Reginald Coupland wrote of him that, in order to break the apathy of parliament, a would-be social reformer 'must possess, in the first place, the virtues of a fanatic without his vices. He must be palpably single-minded and unself-seeking. He must be strong enough to face opposition and ridicule, staunch enough to endure obstruction and delay.'[19] These qualities Wilberforce possessed in abundance.

It was in 1787 that he first decided to put down a motion in the House of Commons about the slave trade. This nefarious traffic had been going on for three centuries, and the West Indian slave-owners were determined to oppose abolition to the end. Besides, Wilberforce was not a very prepossessing man. He was little and ugly, with poor eyesight and an upturned nose. When Boswell heard him speak, he pronounced him 'a perfect shrimp', but then had to concede that 'presently the shrimp swelled into a whale'.[20] In 1789 in the House Wilberforce said of the slave trade: 'So enormous, so dreadful, so irremediable did its wickedness appear that my own mind was completely made up for Abolition … Let the consequences be what they would, I from this time determined that I would never rest until I had affected its Abolition.'[21] So Abolition Bills (which related to the trade) and Foreign Slave Bills (which would prohibit the involvement of British ships in it) were debated in the Commons in 1789, 1791, 1792, 1794, 1796 (by which time Abolition had become 'the grand object of my parliamentary existence'), 1798 and 1799. Yet they all failed. The Foreign Slave Bill was not passed until 1806 and the Abolition of the Slave Trade Bill until 1807. This part of the campaign had taken 18 years.

Next, soon after the conclusion of the Napoleonic wars, Wilberforce began to direct his energies to the abolition of slavery itself and the emancipation of the slaves. In 1823 the Anti-Slavery Society was formed. Twice that year and twice the following year Wilberforce pleaded the slaves' cause in the House of Commons. But in 1825 ill-health compelled him to resign as a Member and to continue his campaign from outside. In 1831 he sent a message to the Anti-Slavery Society, in which he said: 'Our motto must continue to be *perseverance*. And ultimately I trust the Almighty will crown our efforts with success.'[22] He did. In July 1833 the Abolition of Slavery Bill was passed in both Houses of Parliament, even though it included the undertaking to pay £20,000,000 in compensation to the slave-owners. 'Thank God,' wrote Wilberforce, 'that I have lived to witness a day in which England is willing to give

£20,000,000 sterling for the abolition of slavery.'[23] Three days later he died. He was buried in Westminster Abbey, in national recognition of his *45 years* of persevering struggle on behalf of African slaves.

Mind you, perseverance is not a synonym for pig-headedness. True leaders are not impervious to criticism. On the contrary, they listen to it and weigh it, and may modify their programme accordingly. But they do not waver in their basic conviction of what God has called them to do. Whatever the opposition aroused or the sacrifice entailed, they persevere.

Service

A note of caution needs to be added at this point. 'Leadership' is a concept shared by the Church and the world. We must not assume, however, that Christian and non-Christian understandings of it are identical. Nor should we adopt models of secular management without first subjecting them to critical Christian scrutiny. For Jesus introduced into the world an altogether new style of leadership. He expressed the difference between the old and the new in these terms:

> You know that those who are regarded as rulers of the Gentiles lord it over them, and their high officials exercise authority over them. Not so with you. Instead, whoever wants to become great among you must be your servant, and whoever wants to be first must be slave of all. For even the Son of Man did not come to be served, but to serve, and to give his life as a ransom for many.
>
> (Mark 19:42–5)

Among the followers of Jesus, therefore, leadership is not a synonym for lordship. Our calling is to be servants not bosses, slaves not masters. True, a certain authority attaches to all leaders, and leadership would be impossible without it. The apostles were given authority by Jesus, and exercised it in both teaching and disciplining the Church. Even Christian pastors today, although they are not apostles and do not possess apostolic authority, are to be 'respected' because of their position 'over' the congregation (1 Thessalonians 5:12f.), and even 'obeyed' (Hebrews 13:17). Yet the emphasis of Jesus was not on the authority of a ruler-leader but on the humility of a servant-leader. The authority by which the Christian leader leads is not power but love, not force but example, not coercion but reasoned persuasion. Leaders have power, but power is safe only in the hands of those who humble themselves to serve.

What is the reason for Jesus' stress on the leader's service? Partly, no doubt, because the chief occupational hazard of leadership is pride. The Pharisaic model would not do in the new community which Jesus was building. The Pharisees loved deferential titles like 'Father', 'Teacher', 'Rabbi', but this was both an offence against God to whom these titles properly belong, and disruptive of the Christian brotherhood (Matthew 23:1–12).

Jesus' main reason for emphasizing the servant role of the leader, however, was surely that the service of others is a tacit recognition of their value. I have been troubled recently to observe that the 'service' model of leadership is being borrowed by the world and commended for the wrong reasons. Robert K. Greenleaf, for example, a specialist in the field of management research and education, wrote in 1977 a long book called *Servant Leadership*, to which he gave the intriguing subtitle 'A journey into the nature of legitimate power and greatness'. He tells us that the concept of 'the servant as leader' came to him from the reading of Hermann Hesse's *Journey to the East*, in which Leo, the menial servant of a group of travellers, turns out in the end to have been their leader. The 'moral principle' which Mr Greenleaf draws from this is that 'the great leader is seen as the servant first'. Or, expressed more fully: 'The only authority deserving one's allegiance is that which is freely and knowingly granted by the led to the leader in response to, and in proportion to, the clearly evident servant stature of the leader. Those who choose to follow this principle ... will freely respond only to individuals who are chosen as leaders because they are proven and trusted as servants.'[24] I do not deny the truth of this, that leaders have first to win their spurs by service. But the danger of the principle as thus stated is that it regards service as being only a means to another end (namely qualifying one as a leader), and is therefore commended only because of its pragmatic usefulness. This is not what Jesus taught, however. To him service was an end in itself. T.W. Manson expressed the difference beautifully when he wrote: 'In the Kingdom of God service is not a stepping-stone to nobility: it *is* nobility, the only kind of nobility that is recognised.'[25]

Why then did Jesus equate greatness with service? Must not our answer relate to the intrinsic worth of human beings, which was the presupposition underlying his own ministry of self-giving love, and which is an essential element of the Christian perspective? If human beings are Godlike beings, then they must be served not exploited, respected not manipulated. As Oswald Sanders has expressed it, 'True greatness, true leadership, is achieved not by reducing men to one's service but in giving oneself in selfless service to them.'[26] Herein also lies the peril of seeing leadership in terms of projects and programmes. Leadership will inevitably involve the development of these, but people take precedence over projects. And people must be neither 'manipulated' nor even 'managed'. Though the latter is less demeaning to human beings than the former, yet both words are derived from *manus*, meaning a hand, and both express a 'handling' of people as if they were commodities rather than persons.

So Christian leaders serve, indeed serve not their own interests but rather the interests of others (Philippians 2:4). This simple principle should deliver the leader from excessive individualism, extreme isolation and self-centred empire-building. For those who serve others serve best in a team. Leadership teams are more healthy than solo leadership, for several reasons. First, team members *supplement* one another, building on one another's strengths and compensating for one another's weaknesses. No leader has all the gifts, so no leader should keep all the reins of leadership in his or her own hands. Secondly, team members *encourage* one another, identifying each other's gifts and motivating each other to develop and use them. As Max Warren used to say, 'Christian leadership has nothing whatever to do with self-assertion, but everything to do with encouraging other people to assert themselves.'[27] Thirdly, team members are *accountable* to one another. Shared work means shared responsibility. Then we listen to one another and learn from one another. Both the human family and the divine family (the Body of Christ) are contexts of solidarity in which any incipient illusions of grandeur are rapidly dispelled. 'The way of a fool seems right to him, but a wise man listens to advice' (Proverbs 12:15).

In all this Christian emphasis on service, the disciple is only seeking to follow and reflect his teacher. For though he was Lord of all, Jesus became the servant of all. Putting on the apron of servitude, he got down on his knees to wash the apostles' feet. Now he tells us to do as he did, to clothe ourselves with humility, and in love to serve one another (John 13:12–17; 1 Peter 5:5; Galatians 5:13). No leadership is authentically Christlike which is not marked by the spirit of humble and joyful service.

Discipline

Every vision has a tendency to fade. Every visionary is prone to discouragement. Hard work begun with zest can easily degenerate into drudgery. Suffering and loneliness take their toll. The leader feels unappreciated and gets tired. The Christian ideal of humble service sounds fine in theory but seems impractical. So leaders may catch themselves soliloquizing: 'It is quicker to ride roughshod over other people; you get things done that way. And if the end is good, does it really matter what means we employ to attain it? Even a little prudent compromise can sometimes be justified, can't it?'

It is evident, then, that leaders are made of flesh and blood, not plaster or marble or stained glass. Indeed, as Peter Drucker has written, 'Strong people always have strong weaknesses too.'[28] Even the great leaders of the biblical story had fatal flaws. They too were fallen and fallible and frail. Righteous Noah got drunk. Faithful Abraham was despicable enough to risk his wife's chastity for the sake of his own safety. Moses lost his temper. David broke all five commandments of the second table of the law, committing adultery, murder, theft, false witness and covetousness, in that single episode of moral rebellion over Bathsheba. Jeremiah's lonely courage was marred by self-pity. John the Baptist, whom Jesus described as the greatest man who had ever lived, was overcome by doubt. And Peter's boastful impetuosity was doubtless a cloak for his deep personal insecurity. If those heroes of Scripture failed, what hope is there for us?

The final mark of Christian leaders is discipline, not only self-discipline in general (in the mastery of their passions, their time and their energies), but in particular the discipline with which they wait on God. They know their weakness. They know the greatness of their task and the strength of the opposition. But they also know the inexhaustible riches of God's grace.

Many biblical examples could be given. Moses sought God, and 'the Lord would speak to Moses face to face, as a man speaks with his friend'. David looked to God as his shepherd, his light and salvation, his rock, the stronghold of his life, and in times of deep distress 'found strength in the Lord his God'. The apostle Paul, burdened with a physical or psychological infirmity which he called his 'thorn in the flesh', heard Jesus say to him, 'My grace is sufficient for you', and learned that only when he was weak was he strong.

But our supreme exemplar is our Lord Jesus himself. It is often said that he was always available to people. This is not true. He was not. There were times when he sent the crowds away. He refused to allow the urgent to displace the important. Regularly he withdrew from the pressures and the glare of his public ministry, in order to seek his Father in solitude and replenish his reserves of strength. Then, when it came to the end, he and his apostles faced the final test together. How is it, I have often asked myself, that they forsook him and fled, while he went to the cross with such serenity? Is not the answer that he prayed while they slept? (For Moses see Exodus 33:11 and Deuteronomy 34:10; for David Psalm 23:1, 27:1 and 1 Samuel 30:6; for Paul 2 Corinthians 12:7–10; and for Jesus Mark 4:36, 6:45, 14:32–42 and 50.)

It is only God who 'gives strength to the weary and increases the power of the weak'. For 'even youths grow tired and weary, and young men stumble and fall'. But those who 'hope in the Lord', and wait patiently for him, 'will renew their strength. They will soar on wings like eagles; they will run and not grow weary, they will walk and not be faint' (Isaiah 40:29–31). It is only those who discipline themselves to seek God's face who keep their vision bright. It is only those who live before Christ's cross whose inner fires are constantly rekindled and never go out. Those leaders who think they are strong in their own strength are the most pathetically weak of all people; only those who know and acknowledge their weakness can become strong with the strength of Christ.

I have tried to analyse the concept of Christian leadership. It appears to consist of five main ingredients – clear vision, hard work, dogged perseverance, humble service and iron discipline.

In conclusion, it seems to me that we need to repent of two particularly horrid sins. The first is *pessimism*, which is dishonouring to God and incompatible with Christian faith. To be sure, we do not forget the fallenness, indeed the depravity, of human beings. We are well aware of the pervasiveness of evil. We are not so foolish as to imagine that society will ever become perfect before Christ comes and establishes the fullness of his rule.[29] Nevertheless, we also believe in the power of God – in the power of God's gospel to change society. We need to renounce both naive optimism and cynical pessimism, and replace them with the sober but confident realism of the Bible.

The second sin of which we need to repent is *mediocrity*, and the acceptance of it. I find myself wanting to say, especially to young people: 'Don't be content with the mediocre! Don't settle for anything less than your full God-given potential! Be ambitious and adventurous for God! God has made you a unique person by your genetic endowment, upbringing and education. He has himself created you and gifted you, and he does not want his work to be wasted. He means you to be fulfilled, not frustrated. His purpose is that everything you have and are should be stretched in his service and in the service of others.'

This means that God has a leadership role of some degree and kind for each of us. We need, then, to seek his will with all our hearts, to cry to him to give us a vision of what he is calling us to do with our lives, and to pray for grace to be faithful (not necessarily successful) in obedience to the heavenly vision.

Only then can we hope to hear from Christ those most coveted of all words, 'Well done, good and faithful servant!'

NOTES

1 Involvement: is it our concern?

1   *Evangelism and Social Responsibility: An Evangelical Commitment*,
    The Grand Rapids Report, in John Stott (ed.) *Making Christ
    Known*, 'Historic mission documents from the Lausanne movement
    1974–1989' (Paternoster, 1996; Eerdmans, 1997), p. 179.

2   The adjective 'evangelical' is used in different ways by different
    people, but in this book it denotes those Christians who, as heirs
    of the Reformation, emphasize Scripture as having supreme
    authority in the Church and the cross of Christ as being the only
    ground of salvation.

3   G.M. Trevelyan endorsed the opinion of the French historian
    Elie Halevy that evangelical religion in England 'was the chief
    influence that prevented our country from starting along the path
    of revolutionary violence', *English Social History* (Longmans Green,
    1942), p. 477. See also W.E.H. Lecky, *A History of England in the
    Eighteenth Century*, vol. VI (Longmans Green, 1919), p. 376.

4   J. Wesley Bready, *England: Before and After Wesley* (Hodder &
    Stoughton, 1939), pp. 11, 14.

5   ibid. p. 126.

6   ibid. p. 405.

7   ibid.

8   ibid. p. 327.

9   ibid. p. 316.

10 Ernest Marshall Howse, *Saints in Politics*, 'The "Clapham Sect"
    and the growth of freedom' (George Allen & Unwin, 1953), p. 26.
    See also Kenneth Hylson-Smith, *Evangelicals in the Church of
    England 1734–1984* (T & T Clark, 1989), Chapter 5.

11 Howse, *Saints in Politics*, p. 27.

12 Georgina Battiscombe, *Shaftesbury*, 'A biography of the 7th Earl 1801–1885' (Constable, 1974), p. 334.

13 Quoted by David O. Moberg in *The Great Reversal*, 'Evangelism versus social concern' (1972; Scripture Union, 1973), p. 184. For an account of evangelical social work in Britain in the nineteenth century, see also Kathleen Heasman, *Evangelicals in Action* (Geoffrey Bles, 1962).

14 Donald W. Dayton, *Discovering an Evangelical Heritage* (Harper & Row, 1976), pp. 15–24. See also Timothy L. Smith, *Revivalism and Social Reform*, 'American Protestantism on the eve of the Civil War' (1957; John Hopkins University Press, 1980). Dr Smith begins his preface by saying that Thomas Paine, if he had visited New York in 1865, would have been amazed to discover that 'the emancipating glory of the great awakenings had made Christian liberty, Christian equality and Christian fraternity the passion of the land' (p. 7).

15 Dayton, *Discovering an Evangelical Heritage*, p. 25.

16 From an article by Donald W. Dayton in *The Post-American* (March 1975).

17 From the Introduction by R. Pierce Beaver in Samuel Escobar and John Driver, *Christian Mission and Social Justice* (Herald, 1978), pp. 7–9.

18 See also George Marsden, *Fundamentalism and American Culture* (Oxford University Press, 1980), pp. 85–93.

19 Michael Cassidy, *The Passing Summer*, 'A South African pilgrimage in the politics of love' (Hodder & Stoughton, 1989), pp. 253–4.

20 Walter Rauschenbusch, *Christianity and the Social Crisis* (Macmillan, London, 1907).

21 ibid. pp. 391–400.

22 ibid. p. 357.

23 ibid. p. 65.

24 ibid. p. xiii.

25 ibid. p. 149.

26 ibid. p. 420.

27 ibid. p. 210.

28 ibid. p. 380.

29 Walter Rauschenbusch, *A Theology for the Social Gospel* (1917; Macmillan, New York, 1918).

30 ibid. p. 1.

31 ibid. p. 131.
32 ibid. p. 142.
33 ibid. p. 145.
34 George Marsden, 'An Overview' in Michael Cromartie (ed.), *No Longer Exiles* (Ethics and Public Policy Center, Washington DC, 1993), p. 14.
35 Moberg, *The Great Reversal*, pp. 53–7.
36 The National Evangelical Anglican Congress (ed. Philip Crowe), *Keele 67* (Falcon, 1967), para. 20.
37 Stott (ed.), *Making Christ Known*, p. 185.
38 ibid. p. 196.
39 ibid. pp. 197–8.
40 Dr Edward Norman, *Christianity and the World Order* (Oxford University Press, 1979).
41 Stott (ed.), *Making Christ Known*, p. 202.
42 Tom Sine, *The Mustard Seed Conspiracy* (Word, 1981), pp. 69–71.
43 I think it was Dr Carl Henry who coined this phrase. See his autobiography, *Confessions of a Theologian* (Word, 1986), p. 257.
44 John Gladwin, *God's People in God's World*, 'Biblical motives for social involvement' (Inter-Varsity Press, 1979), p. 125.
45 H.J. Blackham, *Humanism* (Penguin, 1968). He writes: 'Humanism is the human case and the human cause, an age-old conviction about the human case … which will induce men and women … to espouse the human cause with head and heart and with two hands' (p. 9).
46 Sir Julian Huxley (ed.), *The Humanist Frame* (George Allen & Unwin, 1961), p. 47.
47 Summarized from Sir Frederick Treves, *The Elephant Man and other Reminiscences* (Cassell, 1923). For a thoroughly researched account of the whole affair, see Michael Howell and Peter Ford, *The True History of the Elephant Man* (Penguin, 1980).
48 Quoted by Charles Smyth in *Cyril Forster Garbett* (Hodder & Stoughton, 1959), p. 106.
49 A.R. Vidler, *Essays in Liberality* (SCM, 1957), pp. 95–112. Dr Vidler contrasted it with 'unholy worldliness', which is 'to conform uncritically and complacently to the standards and fashions that prevail' (p. 96).
50 A.N. Triton, *Whose World?* (Inter-Varsity Press, 1970), pp. 35–6.

51   CARE, Jubilee Trust, Tearfund and the Institute for
     Contemporary Christianity (among others) all sponsor groups
     which seek to blend Christian thought on specific issues with
     action. See M.A. Eden and E.C. Lucas, *Being Transformed*
     (Marshall, 1988), especially Appendix 3; and Roy McCloughry,
     The Eye of the Needle (Inter-Varsity Press, 1990).

2 Complexity: can we think straight?

1   William Temple, *Citizen and Churchman* (Eyre & Spottiswoode,
    1941), p. 82.
2   ibid. p. 83.
3   ibid. p. 84.
4   William Temple, *Christianity and the Social Order* (Penguin, 1942),
    p. 29.
5   ibid. p. 31.
6   Harry Blamires, *The Christian Mind* (SPCK, 1963), p. 70.
7   ibid. p. 43.
8   ibid. p. 3.
9   ibid. p. 50.
10 David W. Gill, *The Opening of the Christian Mind*, 'Taking every
    thought captive to Christ' (Inter-Varsity Press, US, 1989), pp.
    65–75 and 91. See also Arthur Holmes, *Contours of a World View*
    (Eerdmans, 1983) and Oliver R. Barclay, *Developing a Christian
    Mind* (Inter-Varsity Press, 1984).
11 Theodore Roszak, *Where the Wasteland Ends*, 'Politics and
    transcendence in post-industrial society' (1972; Anchor, 1973),
    pp. xxi and 67.
12 J.S. Whale, *Christian Doctrine* (1941; Fontana, 1957), p. 33.
13 Reinhold Niebuhr, *The Children of Light and the Children of
    Darkness* (Nisbet, 1945), p. vi.
14 Sine, *The Mustard Seed Conspiracy*, p. 70.
15 Temple, *Christianity and the Social Order*, p. 54.
16 *The Lausanne Covenant*, para. 15. See Stott (ed.), *Making Christ
    Known*, p. 49.
17 C.E.M. Joad, *The Recovery of Belief* (Faber & Faber, 1952), p. 82.
18 From *The Essence of Security*, quoted by Gavin Reid in *The
    Elaborate Funeral* (Hodder & Stoughton, 1972), p. 48.
19 Whale, *Christian Doctrine*, p. 41.
20 Os Guinness, *Fit Bodies, Fat Minds* (Hodder & Stoughton, 1994),
    p. 105.

3 Pluralism: should we impose our views?

1 Peter Brierley and Heather Wright (eds), *UK Christian Handbook 1996/1997*, p. 240.

2 ibid. p. 23.

3 ibid. pp. 281–4.

4 ibid.

5 ibid. p. 283.

6 The standard work on the Inquisition is still H.C. Lea, *A History of the Inquisition of the Middle Ages*, 3 vols (1887; Macmillan, 1906). Bernard Hamilton gives a briefer account in *The Medieval Inquisition* (Edward Arnold, 1981).

7 John Kobler, *Ardent Spirits*, 'The rise and fall of prohibition' (Michael Joseph, 1974), pp. 216–17.

8 Richard Gutteridge, *Open thy Mouth for the Dumb*, 'The German Evangelical Church and the Jews 1870–1950' (Basil Blackwell, 1976).

9 ibid. p. 48.

10 ibid. p. 128.

11 ibid. p. 181.

12 ibid. p. 268.

13 ibid. p. 298.

14 ibid. p. 299.

15 ibid. p. 304.

16 Abraham Lincoln concluded his famous Gettysburg Address (1863) with the resolve 'that this nation, under God, shall have a new birth of freedom, and that government of the people, by the people, for the people, shall not perish from the earth'. He seems to have borrowed this definition of democracy from the Rev. Theodore Parker, who used it in a speech in Boston in 1850.

17 O.R. Johnston, *Who Needs the Family?*, 'A survey and a Christian assessment' (Hodder & Stoughton, 1979). pp. 43–6.

18 J.D. Unwin, *Sex and Culture* (Oxford University Press, 1934), pp. 411–12 and 431–2.

19 See, for example, Hugh Arthur, *Sex and Society* (Presbyterian Church of England, 1969): 'There is no doubt, physiologically and psychologically speaking, that whereas for men intercourse is a pleasure and an end in itself, it is a pleasure and a beginning for a woman ... the basic feminine sexual need really is security.'

20 Temple, *Christianity and the Social Order*, p. 59.

21 Reinhold Niebuhr, *Moral Man and Immoral Society* (Scribner's, 1932; revised ed., 1960), pp. xi and xx.

22 John R. Lucas, *Democracy and Participation* (1975; Pelican, 1976), p. 10. Also recommended is Reinhold Niebuhr, *The Children of the Light and the Children of the Darkness* (Nisbet, 1945). He wrote it 18 months before the end of World War II, in which he saw 'bourgeois civilization' collapsing before the onslaught of Nazi barbarism. He subtitles his book 'A vindication of democracy and a critique of its traditional defenders'. His faith in democracy was not the blind optimism of liberals who, having no conception of original sin, held a 'fatuous and superficial view of man' (p. 15). It was rather that democracy is the best way to resolve the tension between the individual and the community, self-interest and the common good, freedom and order.

23 John V. Taylor, *Enough is Enough* (SCM, 1975), pp. 64 and 114.

4 Alienation: have we any influence?

1   From his Inaugural Address to students on 28 April 1972, when installed as Rector of Glasgow University.

2   K.S. Latourette, *History of the Expansion of Christianity*, (Eyre & Spottiswoode, 1945), vol. 7, pp. 503–4.

3   Charles W. Colson, *Kingdoms in Conflict*, 'An insider's challenging view of politics, power and the pulpit' (William Morrow/ Zondervan, 1987), e.g. pp. 238, 253–64, 371. Fran Beckett, in her book *Called to Action* (Fount, 1989), emphasizes the responsibility of each church to get to know its local community and to mobilize teams to serve the needs it has discovered.

4   Nikolai Berdyaev, *The Destiny of Man* (Geoffrey Bles, 1937), p. 281.

5   Temple, *Christianity and the Social Order*, p. 27.

6   Sine, *The Mustard Seed Conspiracy*, p. 113.

7   Matthew 5—7. I try to develop this exposition in *The Message of the Sermon on the Mount*, 'Christian counter-culture' (Inter-Varsity Press, 1978).

8   *Evangelism and Social Responsibility*, in Stott (ed.), *Making Christ Known*, p. 200.

9   Colson, *Kingdoms in Conflict*, p. 327.

10 Quoted in Ronald J. Sider, *Exploring the Limits of Non-Violence* (Spire, 1988), p. 70. See also Dr Isabelo Magalit, 'The Church and the Barricades', in *Transformation*, April–June 1986.

11 Colson, *Kingdoms in Conflict*, p. 333.

12 *Evangelism and Social Responsibility*, in Stott (ed.), *Making Christ Known*, p. 182.

13   ibid. p. 183.

14   Brian Griffiths, *Morality and the Market Place*, 'Christian
      alternatives to capitalism and socialism' (Hodder & Stoughton,
      1982), p. 69.

15   *North-South*, 'A programme for survival', the report of the
      Independent Commission on International Development Issues
      under the chairmanship of Willy Brandt (Pan Books, 1980), p. 25.

16   Griffiths, *Morality and the Market Place*, pp. 148–9.

17   ibid. pp. 154–5.

18   Alexander Solzhenitsyn, *One Word of Truth* (Bodley Head, 1972),
      pp. 22–7.

19   Speech by Sir Keith Joseph in Birmingham, October 1974.

20   John Howard Yoder, *The Politics of Jesus* (Eerdmans, 1972),
      pp. 111 and 157.

21   *Evangelism and Social Responsibility*, in Stott (ed.), *Making Christ
      Known*, p. 189.

22   Dom Helder Camara, *Spiral of Violence* (1970; Sheed & Ward,
      1971), p. 69.

23   Dom Helder Camara, *The Desert is Fertile* (Sheed & Ward, 1974),
      p. 3.

24   Camara, *Spiral of Violence*, p. 43.

25   Dom Helder Camara, *Race Against Time* (Sheed & Ward, 1971),
      pp. vii–viii.

26   ibid. p. 17.

27   Sine, *The Mustard Seed Conspiracy*, pp. 11–12.

28   Harper & Row, 1985.

5 Wars and rumours of wars

1   Albert Einstein, in a telegram asking prominent persons for funds
     for the Atomic Scientists' Emergency Committee, cited in the
     New York Times, 25 May 1946.

2   Samuel Huntington, *The Clash of Civilizations and the Remaking
     of World Order* (Simon & Schuster, 1997), p. 21.

3   ibid. p. 126.

4   ibid. p. 29.

5   Robert D. Kaplan, *The Ends of the Earth*, 'A journey at the dawn of
     the 21st century' (Random House, 1996; Papermac, 1997), p. 5.

6   ibid. p. 134.

7   Huntington, *The Clash of Civilizations*, pp. 312–16.

8   ibid. p. 321.

9   Kaplan, *The Ends of the Earth*, pp. 8, 9.

10 ibid. p. 436.

11 SIPRI Yearbook 1997 (Stockholm International Research
    Institute, 1997), pp. 398–9.

12 From Earl Mountbatten's 'The Final Abyss?' speech, May 1979,
    published in *Apocalypse Now?* (Spokesman Books, 1980), p. 11.

13 See also *The Long-Term Consequences of Nuclear War* (1983), the
    report of an international conference sponsored by 31 groups.
    Two imaginative scenarios, written by military men, were
    published in 1978. *World War 3*, 'A military projection founded
    on today's facts', edited by Brigadier Shelford Bidwell (Hamlyn,
    1978) predicted that in 1983 the third world war would start 'as a
    result of some intolerable provocation' (p. xiii), e.g. the invasion of
    West Germany by Soviet tanks to prevent her becoming a nuclear
    power. The last chapter is entitled 'Doomsday' and describes the
    final, total devastation. *The Third World War* by General Sir John
    Hackett, assisted by top-ranking American and German generals
    (Sidgwick & Jackson, 1978), calls itself 'A future history'. It also
    describes an invasion of West Germany by Soviet tanks, though in
    1985, which steadily escalates until first Birmingham and then in
    retaliation Minsk are obliterated by nuclear missiles. This time,
    however, the final holocaust is averted by the uprising against the
    Soviet Union of her satellites.
       The ghastly consequences of a nuclear explosion are factually
    described by Donald B. Kraybill in *Facing Nuclear War* (Herald
    Press, 1982) and in *Common Security* (the Palme Commission
    Report, 1982), pp. 49–70.

14 International Institute for Strategic Studies, *The Military Balance
    1996/1997* (Oxford University Press, 1996), pp. 306–11.

15 From an address entitled 'The Chance for Peace', delivered on 16
    April 1953. See *Public Papers of the Presidents of the United States:
    Dwight Eisenhower, 1953* (Washington DC: US Government
    Printing Office, 1960), p. 182.

16 *The Military Balance 1996/1997*, p. 273.

17 ibid. p. 289.

18 ibid. p. 273.

19 For a debate between eight Christian thinkers, who assess the
    arguments for and against these three positions, see Oliver R.
    Barclay (ed.), *Pacifism and War*, 'When Christians Disagree' series
    (Inter-Varsity Press, 1984). Similar ground is covered in Robert
    G. Clouse (ed.), *War: Four Christian Views* (Inter-Varsity Press,
    US, 1981). See also J. Andrew Kirk (ed.), *Handling Problems of
    Peace and War* (Marshall Pickering, 1988).

20 For recent statements of the pacifist position see Jean Lasserre, *War and the Gospel* (E.T. James Clarke, 1962), Ronald J. Sider, *Christ and Violence* (Herald Press, Canada, 1979), and Ronald J. Sider and Richard K. Taylor, *Nuclear Holocaust and Christian Hope* (Inter-Varsity Press, US, 1982).

21 The theory of the 'just war' is carefully argued in two books by Paul Ramsey: *War and the Christian Conscience* (Duke University Press, 1961) and *The Just War* (Scribner's, 1968). For more recent statements of the 'just war' position, see Arthur F. Holmes in Clouse (ed.), *War: Four Christian Virtues*, pp. 120–1; *The Church and the Bomb* (Hodder & Stoughton, 1982), pp. 81–98; and *The Challenge of Peace: God's Promise and Our Response*, the US Bishops' Pastoral Letter (CTS/SPCK, 1983), pp. 24–32. For a similar position based on the justice of God, see Jerram Barrs, *Peace and Justice in the Nuclear Age* (Garamond Press, 1983).

22 Dale Aukerman, *Darkening Valley*, 'A biblical perspective on nuclear war' (Seabury, 1981), Chapter 15, p. 95.

23 ibid. pp. 92–4.

24 It needs to be added that in some emergency situations when no policeman is present, it may be right for a citizen to intervene in a fight, protect an innocent person against assault or arrest a burglar. But in such cases the citizen is temporarily constituting himself an arm of the law; he is not acting as a private individual, nor is he justified in feeling personal animosity or taking personal revenge.

25 Oliver O'Donovan, *In Pursuit of a Christian View of War*, Grove Booklet on Ethics No. 15 (Grove Books, 1977), pp. 13–14. This booklet is a valuable enquiry into the legitimacy of the analogy between domestic justice and warfare.

26 Dana Mills-Powell (ed.), *Decide for Peace*, 'Evangelicals against the bomb', is a symposium of 16 contributions by both nuclear and total pacifists (Marshall Pickering, 1986).

27 *Pastoral Constitution*, para. 80.

28 *The Church and the Atom*, the report of a Church of England Commission (1948), p. 43. For a factual account of the bombing of German and Japanese cities, see Brigadier Peter Young (ed.), *The Almanac of World War II* (Hamlyn, 1981). Bishop Bell's speech in the House of Lords is recorded in *Hansard* (9 February 1944), vol. 130, pp. 738–46. It is also referred to in Ronald C.D. Jasper, *George Bell, Bishop of Chichester* (Oxford University Press, 1967), pp. 276–7.

29 International Institute for Strategic Studies, *Strategic Survey 1996/1997* (Oxford University Press, 1997), p. 38.

30 *Gaudium et Spes* ('The Church in the Modern World'), 1965, para. 80, in W. M. Abbott and J. Gallagher, *The Documents of Vatican II* (Geoffrey Chapman, 1966).

31 British Council of Churches resolution.

32 *The Church and the Bomb*, 'Nuclear weapons and Christian conscience', an unofficial report of a Church of England working party (Hodder & Stoughton, 1982), p. 97.

33 ibid. pp. 143–4.

34 ibid. p. 162.

35 'The New Abolitionist Covenant' is printed in Jim Wallis (ed.), *Waging Peace*, 'A handbook for the struggle to abolish nuclear weapons' (Harper & Row, 1982), pp. 17–21. See also Jim Wallis (ed.), *Peace-makers*, 'Christian voices from the New Abolitionist Movement' (Harper & Row, 1983).

36 Quoted by William Epstein in 'The ABCs of Disarmament', an article on the home page for the NGO Committee for Disarmament, at <www.igc.apc.org/disarm/>.

37 Michael Quinlan, 'The Meaning of Deterrence', in Francis Bridger (ed.), *The Cross and the Bomb* (Mowbray, 1983), p. 143.

38 US Bishops' Pastoral Letter, *The Challenge of Peace*, see endnote 12, pp. 43–6.

39 Paul Abrecht and Ninan Koshy (eds), *Before It's Too Late*, 'The challenge of nuclear disarmament' (WCC, 1983), p. 10.

40 Hugh Beach, 'Where Does the Nuclear-Free Path Lead?', in Bridger (ed.), *The Cross and the Bomb*, p. 126.

41 Roger Ruston, OP, *Nuclear Deterrence – Right or Wrong?*, a study prepared for the Roman Catholic Commission for International Justice and Peace (Catholic Information Services, 1981), pp. 35–6, 58.

42 *Common Security* (Palme Commission Report, 1982), p. 105.

43 ibid. pp. 141, 149.

44 See, e.g., Walter Stein (ed.), *Nuclear Weapons and Christian Conscience* (Merlin Press, 1961 and 1980), and Geoffrey Goodwin (ed.), *Ethics and Nuclear Deterrence* (Croom Helm, 1982). See also Richard Harries, 'The Strange Mercy of Deterrence', in John Gladwin (ed.), *Dropping the Bomb* (Hodder & Stoughton, 1985), pp. 64–73, and Richard Harries, *Christianity and War in a Nuclear Age* (Mowbray, 1986), especially pp. 134–44.

45 Ernest Lefever and Stephen Hunt (eds), *The Apocalyptic Premise: Nuclear Arms Debated* (Ethics and Public Policy Center, Washington DC, 1982), pp. 351–9. See also Anthony Kenny, *The Logic of Deterrence* (Firethorn Press, 1985).

46 Quoted in US Bishops' Pastoral Letter, *The Challenge of Peace*. The bishops elaborated the Pope's statement, declaring that they had 'arrived at a strictly conditional, moral acceptance of deterrence'.

47 Bridger (ed.), *The Cross and the Bomb*, pp. 50, 60, 64–5.

48 Robert W. Gardiner, *The Cool Arm of Destruction* (Westminster, 1974), quoted by Robert G. Clouse in *War: Four Christian Views*, pp. 193–4.

49 From Dr David Owen's introduction to *Common Security* (Palme Commission Report), p. xxi.

50 *Evangelism and Social Responsibility*, in Stott (ed.), *Making Christ Known*, p. 200.

51 See, e.g., *Defence without the Bomb*, the Report of the Alternative Defence Commission (Taylor and Francis, 1983).

6 Our human environment

1 Jonathon Porritt and David Winner, *The Coming of the Greens* (Fontana/Collins, 1988), pp. 267, 7.

2 Many 'green' consumer guides are available in most bookshops.

3 Ghillean Prance, *The Earth Under Threat* (Wild Goose Publications, 1996), p. 31.

4 Roy McCloughry, *Population Growth and Christian Ethics*, Grove Ethical Studies No. 98 (Grove Books Ltd, 1995).

5 E.F. Schumacher, *Small is Beautiful* (1973; Abacus, 1974), pp. 11–16. The vision of unlimited growth has been pertinently criticized by Bishop Lesslie Newbigin in *Foolishness to the Greeks* (SPCK, 1986). 'Growth … for the sake of growth', he writes, which 'is not determined by an overarching social purpose', is 'an exact account of the phenomenon which, when it occurs in the human body, is called cancer' (p. 114).

6 Prance, *The Earth Under Threat*, p. 45.

7 ibid.

8 ibid. p. 47. For other figures see also Jessica Tuchman Matthews, 'Grasping the Concept of Environmental Insecurity', in Gwyn Prins (ed.), *Threats without Enemies* (Earthscan Publications, 1993), p. 27; and Stephen H. Schneider, *Laboratory Earth* (Weidenfeld & Nicolson, 1996), p. 112.

9 Schneider, *Laboratory Earth*, p. 107.

10   Prance, *The Earth Under Threat*, p. 41.
11   See Sir John Houghton (chairman of the Royal Commission on Environmental Pollution), *Global Warming*, 'The complete briefing' (Lion, 1994).
12   World Commission on Environment and Development, *Our Common Future* (Oxford University Press, 1987), pp. 8, 43.
13   Gerhard von Rad, *Genesis* (1956; SCM, 1963), p. 58.
14   Tom Dale and Vernon Gill Carter, *Topsoil and Civilisation* (1955), quoted in Schumacher, *Small is Beautiful*, p. 84.
15   Martin Hengel, *Property and Riches in the Early Church* (1973; Fortress and SCM, 1974), p. 12.
16   *Laborem Exercens*, Pope John Paul II's Encyclical Letter on 'Human Work' (Catholic Truth Society, 1981), pp. 50–1.
17   Jessica Tuchman Matthews, 'Nations and Nature: A New View of Security', in Prins, *Threats without Enemies*, p. 36.
18   Prance, *The Earth Under Threat*, p. 47.
19   ibid. pp. 48–9.
20   *Man in his Living Environment*, 'An ethical assessment', a report from the Board for Social Responsibility (Church Information Office, 1970), p. 61. See also *Our Responsibility for the Living Environment*, a report from the Board for Social Responsibility's Environmental Issues Reference Panel (Church House Publishing, 1986).
21   Gavin Maxwell's article appeared in *The Observer*, 13 October 1963.
22   C.F.D. Moule, *Man and Nature in the New Testament*, 'Some reflections on biblical ecology' (Athlone, 1964; Fortress, 1967), p. 1. See also Andrew Linzey, *Christianity and the Rights of Animals* (SPCK, 1988).
23   Peter Singer, *Animal Liberation* (1990; 2nd ed., Pimlico Books, 1995). See also his more recent work *Rethinking Life and Death*, 'The collapse of our traditional ethics' (Oxford University Press, 1995), in which he attempts to narrow the difference between humans and animals.
24   ibid. p. 6.
25   ibid. p. 185.
26   For a good discussion of animal rights, see *Green Cross*, Winter 1996, vol. 2, no. 1. This issue is devoted to the discussion of Christian responsibility for animals. See also Richard Griffiths, *The Human Use of Animals* (Grove Booklets, 1982), and Tony Sargent, *Animal Rights and Wrongs, a Biblical Perspective* (Hodder & Stoughton, 1996).

27 From an address to the American Association for the Advancement of Science, which was published as 'The Historical Roots of our Ecological Crisis', in *Science* 155 (1967), pp. 1203–7, and was reprinted as Chapter 5 of his *Machina ex Deo: Essays in the Dynamism of Western Culture* (MIT Press, Cambridge, Mass., and London, 1968).

28 Ian L. McHarg, *Design with Nature* (Doubleday, 1969), p. 26.

29 ibid. p. 197.

30 These extracts from Ian McHarg's Dunning Trust Lectures were quoted in the *Ontario Naturalist*, March 1973.

31 Keith Thomas, *Man and the Natural World* (1983; Penguin, 1984). See also Edward Echlin, *The Christian Green Heritage*, 'World as creation' (Grove Ethical Studies, no. 74, 1989), and Colin A. Russell, *The Earth, Humanity and God* (UCL Press, 1994), especially pp. 86–93.

32 Thomas, *Man and the Natural World*, p. 17.

33 ibid. p. 18.

34 ibid. p. 22.

35 ibid. p. 24; cf. p. 151.

36 ibid. p. 278.

37 Barbara Ward and Rene Dubos, *Only One Earth*, 'The care and maintenance of a small planet' (Penguin, 1972), p. 83.

38 ibid. p. 45.

39 ibid. p. 85.

40 Ronald Higgins, *The Seventh Enemy* (Hodder & Stoughton, 1978).

41 Klaus Bockmuhl, *Conservation and Lifestyle* (1975, translated by Bruce N. Kaye; Grove Books, 1977), pp. 23–4. For a more recent Christian evaluation of environmental issues, see Ron Elsdon, *Greenhouse Theology* (Monarch, 1992); Stan LeQuire (ed.), *The Best Preaching on Earth*, a collection of sermons on care for creation (Judson Press, 1996); and Colin A. Russell, *The Earth, Humanity and God* (UCL Press, 1994). See also the quarterly magazine *Green Cross*, a publication of the Christian Society of the Green Cross, a ministry of Evangelicals for Social Action – Green Cross, 10 East Lancaster Avenue, Wynnewood, PA 19096-3495, USA.

42 These organizations can be reached at the following addresses. The Evangelical Environmental Network c/o The Institute for Contemporary Christianity, St Peter's Church, Vere St, London W1M 9HP, or 10 East Lancaster Avenue, Wynnewood

PA 19096-3495, USA. The Au Sable Institute at Messiah College,
Grantham PA 17027, USA. The A Rocha Trust, 3 Hooper St,
Cambridge CB1 2NZ, UK.

7 North-South economic inequality

1 World Development Report, 1991.
2 *North-South*, 'A programme for survival', the Report of the
Independent Commission on International Development Issues,
pp. 7, 8.
3 Michael P. Todaro (ed.), *Economic Development* (Longman, 1997),
p. 189.
4 ibid. pp. 43–4.
5 Brandt Commission, *Common Crisis*, 'North-South: co-operation
for world recovery' (Pan Books, 1983), pp. 9–10.
6 *Human Development Report*, 1997 (Oxford University Press,
1997), and *Economic Development*, p. 32.
7 *North-South*, p. 23.
8 The Villars Statement is included in Marvin Olasky (ed.),
Freedom, Justice and Hope, 'Towards a strategy for the poor and
the oppressed' (Crossway Books, 1988), pp. 141–6.
9 Vishal Mangalwadi, *Truth and Social Reform* (Hodder &
Stoughton, 1989), e.g. pp. 5–6, 25, 32, 115.
10 *North-South*, pp. 276–80.
11 ibid. p. 64.
12 ibid.
13 ibid. p. 30.
14 Griffiths, *Morality and the Market Place*, p. 127.
15 *North-South*, p. 63.
16 ibid. p. 25.
17 Griffiths, *Morality and the Market Place*, p. 143.
18 ibid. pp. 148–9.
19 'Imperatives for Economic Development', in Olasky (ed.),
Freedom, Justice and Hope, p. 112.
20 ibid. pp. 116–17.
21 ibid. p. 145.
22 John Stott (ed.), *The Year 2000 AD* (Marshall, Morgan & Scott,
1983), pp. 72–102. Donald Hay elaborated and recast his lecture
in Chapter 7, 'Rich Nation, Poor Nation', of his book *Economics
Today*, 'A Christian critique' (Apollos, Inter-Varsity Press, 1989).
23 Hay, ibid. pp. 92–3.
24 ibid. p. 94.

25   ibid. p. 95.
26   Brandt Commission, *Common Crisis.* Three years later, Willy Brandt wrote another book, angry in tone and popular in appeal, entitled *World Armament and World Hunger,* 'A call for action' (Pantheon, 1986). In it he drew attention to global military spending, which was estimated at 1 trillion dollars annually, and argued that defence and development expenditure could no longer be segregated. Indeed, the former should be subordinated to the latter.
27   *Common Crisis,* p. 1.
28   See Bob Geldof with Paul Vallely, *Is That It?* (Penguin, 1986).
29   Todaro, *Economic Development,* p. 41.
30   *Human Development Report 1996* (Oxford University Press, 1996), p. 73.
31   ibid.
32   Jubilee 2000's international petition calls for lending nations to 'cancel the backlog of unpayable debts of the most impoverished nations ... by the year 2000 ... [and] to take effective steps to prevent such high levels of debt building up again'. The petition will be presented to the G7 nations when they meet in 1998 and 1999. Jubilee 2000 can be reached at PO Box 100, London SE1 7RT, UK, or on the internet at <www.oneworld.org/jubilee2000>. Other development agencies share the 'oneworld' site and it can be a useful site to visit for more information.
33   World Commission on Environment and Development, *Our Common Future,* pp. 8, 43.
34   Quoted in Todaro, *Economic Development,* p. 69.
35   ibid. pp. 7–19.
36   Visit <www.undp.org> for the most up to date information on this report as it is published each year.
37   For example, 'Poverty has become feminized to a significant degree', *Christian Faith and the World Economy Today,* a 1992 study document from the World Council of Churches, p. 26.
38   See Ruth Pearson, 'Gender Matters in Development', in Tim Allen and Alan Thomas (eds), *Poverty and Development in the 1990s* (Oxford University Press, 1992), pp. 291–312; 'Women in Poverty', in Todaro, *Economic Development,* pp. 156–9; and the quarterly update from June 1997 entitled BRIDGE (Briefings on Development and Gender), produced by the Institution of Development Studies in Sussex, on <www.ids.ac.uk/ids/research/bridge/dgb.html>.

39 Quotations extracted from press releases related to the publication of the *Human Development Report 1997.*

40 I have read that there are at least 'five major and often competing development theories'. See Todaro, *Economic Development*, pp. 69–95.

41 World Commission on Environment and Development, *Our Common Future*, p. 27.

42 Ward and Dubos, *Only One Earth*, an unofficial report commissioned by the Secretary-General of the United Nations Conference on the Human Environment, prepared with the assistance of a 152-member Committee of Corresponding Consultants in 58 countries.

43. ibid. p. 298.

44 Duncan Munro, *Trade, Justice and the Wealth of Nations* (Grove Books, 1976), pp. 11, 24.

45 Barbara Ward, *Progress for a Small Planet* (Penguin, 1979), p. 277.

46 ibid. p. 257.

47 Roger D. Hansen and others, *US Foreign Policy and the Third World: Agenda 1982* (Praeger, 1982), p. 234, and *The Human Development Report 1996*, p. 199.

48 For the same Spirit, see e.g. Romans 8:9; 1 Corinthians 12:13. For different spiritual gifts, see e.g. Romans 12:3–8 and 1 Corinthians 12:4–31.

49 *Gospel and Culture*, the Willowbank Report, in Stott (ed.), *Making Christ Known*, pp. 77–113.

50 From a 1967 speech on the Arusha Declaration, published in *Freedom and Socialism, uhuru na ujamaa*, 'A selection from the writings and speeches of Julius Nyerere 1965–1967' (Oxford University Press, Dar-es-Salaam, 1968), p. 326.

51 Todaro, *Economic Development*, p. 382.

52 *North-South*, p. 30.

8 Human rights

1 Statistics of human rights violations are readily available from a variety of sources. I have culled mine mostly from Amnesty International's annual reports and Human Rights Watch world reports. The United Nations and US government are also good sources of information.

2 Amnesty International Annual Report 1995, p. 249.

3 Gary Haugen, 'Rwanda's Carnage', in *Christianity Today*, 6 February 1995, pp. 52–4.

4 'Statistics Concerning the Needs of Children Worldwide', *Action International,* January 1997.

5 Human Rights Watch World Report 1997, p. 333.

6 ibid. p. 334.

7 ibid. p. 339.

8 From the editorial by Emilio Castro in *International Review of Mission,* vol. LXVI, no. 263, devoted to 'Human Rights' (July 1977), p. 218.

9 The most handy collection of these texts is Ian Brownie (ed.), *Basic Documents on Human Rights* (Clarendon, 2nd ed. 1981).

10 From Dr Malik's introduction to O. Frederick Nolde, *Free and Equal,* 'Human rights in ecumenical perspective' (WCC, 1968), p. 7.

11 Thomas Paine, *The Rights of Man* (1791), 8th ed., pp. 47–8.

12 From personal communication to the author.

13 Temple, *Citizen and Churchman,* pp. 74–5.

14 Paul Oestreicher, *Thirty Years of Human Rights* (the British Churches' Advisory Forum on Human Rights, 1980).

15 The prophetic protest against these three kings is found in 2 Samuel 11–12 (Nathan and David), 1 Kings 21 (Elijah and Ahab) and Jeremiah 22:13–19 (Jeremiah and Jehoiakim).

16 From an interview published in *TIME* magazine, 24 July 1989.

17 Christopher J.H. Wright, *Human Rights: A Study in Biblical Themes,* Grove Booklet on Ethics no. 31 (Grove Books, 1979), p. 16.

18 For this renunciation of rights, see Mark 10:42–5 ('not so with you'); 1 Corinthians 13:5 (love); 1 Corinthians 6:1–8 (litigation) and 1 Peter 2:18–25 (slaves).

19 Nobel Prize speech, 1970.

20 For information about human rights violations in general, and about imprisonment and torture in general, write to Amnesty International, 1 Easton Street, London WC1X 8DJ.

21 'A Christian Witness for Justice, a Needs Assessment and Operational Outline' (November 1996, p. 1), conducted by the International Justice Mission, PO Box 58147, Washington DC, 20037-8147, USA; or on the internet at <www.ijm.org>.

9 Work and unemployment

1 James A.C. Brown, *The Social Psychology of Industry* (Penguin, 1954), p. 186.

2 H.L. Mencken, quoted by David Weir in *Men and Work in Modern*

Britain (Fontana, 1973), p. 75.

3 Quoted from Dorothy Sayers' *Creed or Chaos?*, in Ted W. Engstrom and Alec Mackenzie, *Managing Your Time* (Zondervan, 1967), pp. 21–3.

4 Pope John Paul II, *Laborem Exorcens*, p. 4.

5 ibid. p. 13.

6 ibid. p. 12.

7 ibid. p. 33.

8 Henri Blocher, *In the Beginning*, 'The opening chapters of Genesis' (Inter-Varsity Press, 1984), p. 57.

9 E.F. Schumacher, *Good Work* (Abacus, 1980), p. 27.

10 ibid. pp. 119–20.

11 ibid. p. 121.

12 Report in the *Guardian Weekly*, 14 February 1970.

13 From Henri de Man, *Joy in Work* (1929), quoted in Sherwood E. Wirt, *The Social Conscience of the Evangelical* (Scripture Union, 1968), p. 38.

14 Schumacher, *Good Work*, pp. 3–4.

15 ibid. p. 122.

16 The story is told by Basil Willey in *Religion Today* (A & C Black, 1969), p. 74.

17 From one of 13 interviews in David Field and Elspeth Stephenson, *Just the Job* (Inter-Varsity Press, 1978), pp. 93–4.

18 Miroslav Volf, *Work in the Spirit* (Oxford University Press, 1991), p. 92.

19 ibid. p. 114.

20 Quoted in F.A. Iremonger, *William Temple* (Oxford University Press, 1948), p. 440. See also Chapter 1, 'The Unemployment Experience', in Michael Moynagh, *Making Unemployment Work* (Lion, 1985), and Ann Warren, *Living with Unemployment* (Hodder & Stoughton, 1986).

21 These figures were taken from the European Union web-site at <www.europa.int.eu>.

22 TUC press release, 6 June 1997.

23 *Unemployment and the Future of Work* (CCBI, 1997), p. 33.

24 ibid. p. 30.

25 ibid. pp. 11, 174.

26 George Goyder, *The Just Enterprise* (Andre Deutsch, 1987), p. 93.

27 David Bleakley, *Work: The Shadow and the Substance*, 'A reappraisal of life and labour' (SCM, 1983), p. 56. See also

In Place of Work … the Sufficient Society, 'A study of technology from the point of view of people' (SCM, 1981), p. 3.

28 Peter Elsom and David Porter, *Four Million Reasons to Care*, 'How your church can help the unemployed' (MARC Europe and CAWTU, 1985), is a mine of information and practical suggestions on how local churches can get into action.

29 Church in Action with the Unemployed published a book entitled *Action on Unemployment*, which describes 100 church projects for and with the unemployed.

30 Marshall McLuhan, *Understanding Media* (1964; Abacus, 1973), p. 381.

31 John Palmer, *Trading Places*, 'The future of the European Community' (Radius, 1988), pp. 133–71.

32 Moynagh, *Making Unemployment Work*, pp. 89–93.

33 James Robertson, *Future Work*, 'Jobs, self-employment and leisure after the industrial age' (Gower/Maurice Temple Smith, 1985), p. 1.

34 ibid. pp. 14–15.

35 ibid. pp. x and 130–1.

36 *Unemployment and the Future of Work*, pp. 8, 171.

37 ibid. p. 79.

38 Sir Fred Catherwood, *Jobs and Justice, Homes and Hope*, 'Analysing the state of the nation' (Hodder & Stoughton, 1997), p. xiv.

39 ibid. pp. 75, 85.

40 *Unemployment and the Future of Work*, p. 101.

41 Two further books that deal helpfully with many practical and pastoral issues relating to work and unemployment are Mark Greene's *Thank God it's Monday* (Scripture Union, 1994), and David Westcott's *Work Well: Live Well*, 'Rediscovering a biblical view of work' (Marshall Pickering, 1994).

10 Industrial relations

1 Taylor, *Enough is Enough*, p. 102. For the central importance of relationships, see Michael Schluter and David Lee, *The R Factor* (Hodder & Stoughton, 1993).

2 Catherwood, *Jobs and Justice, Homes and Hope*, pp. 77–9.

3 Will Hutton, *The State We're In* (1995; revised ed. Vintage, 1996), pp. 132–68.

4 From a news report in *Christianity Today* in 1979, a tape-recorded conference address, and especially R.C. Sproul's *Stronger than Steel*, 'The Wayne Alderson story' (Harper & Row, 1980).

5   Richard Hyman and Ian Brough, *Social Values and Industrial Relations*, 'A study of fairness and inequality' (Blackwell, 1975).
6   ibid. p. 11.
7   TUC press release, 16 September 1996.
8   TUC press release, 20 December 1996.
9   Schumacher, *Good Work*, p. 79.
10 Temple, *Christianity and the Social Order*, p. 87.
11 ibid. p. 61.
12 Erving Goffman, *Asylums*, 'Essays on the social situation of mental patients and other inmates' (Anchor Books, Doubleday, 1961).
13 ibid. p. xiii.
14 ibid. p. 6.
15 ibid. p. 7.
16 ibid. p. 9.
17 ibid. p. 43.
18 See my *I Believe in Preaching* (Hodder & Stoughton, 1981), pp. 174–8.
19 From Charles Colson's lecture entitled 'The Rehabilitation of Prisoners', published in *Crime and the Responsible Community* (Hodder & Stoughton, 1980), p. 156.
20 The Nuremberg Code (1947); reproduced in A.S. Duncan, G.R. Dunstan and R.B. Welbourn (eds), *Dictionary of Medical Ethics* (DLT, 1981), pp. 130–2.
21 Declaration of Helsinki (1964, revised 1975); ibid. pp. 132–5.
22 Alexander Solzhenitsyn, *Cancer Ward* (1968; Penguin 1971).
23 ibid. p. 240.
24 ibid. pp. 85–6.
25 ibid. p. 320.
26 Temple, *Christianity and the Social Order*, p. 96.
27 ibid.
28 Quoted in Bleakley, *In Place of Work … the Sufficient Society*, pp. 16, 17.
29 Temple, *Christianity and the Social Order*, p. 87.
30 ibid. p. 99.
31 *The Donovan Report* (1968) was produced by the fifth Royal Commission on Trade Unions and Employers' Associations, which was set up by the Labour government and sat between 1965 and 1968.
32 P.J. Armstrong, J.F.B. Goodman and J.D. Hyman, *Ideology and Shop-Floor Industrial Relations* (Croom Helm, 1981).
33 The principle of 'co-determination', first developed in the 1930s,

was put into practice in West Germany after World War I. In essence it advocated (1) a 'works council', which represented the workers, (2) a 'supervisory board' (two-thirds of whose members being owners and one-third workers' representatives), which appointed (3) the Executive board, which ran the company. West Germany's post-war economic progress and good record of labour relations are thought by many to be at least partly due to this arrangement. See H.F.R. Catherwood, *A Better Way*, 'The case for a Christian social order' (IVP, 1975), p. 121.

34 Sir Fred Catherwood, *At the Cutting Edge* (Hodder & Stoughton, 1996), pp. 130–2.

35 For facts and figures about Europe, see Timothy Bainbridge with Anthony Teasdale, *The Penguin Companion to European Union* (Penguin, 1995).

36 Bishop Robin Woods of Worcester, letter to *The Times*, 16 February 1977.

37 See *Employee Share Schemes*, published in 1979 by the Wider Share Ownership Council, Juxon House, St Paul's Courtyard, London EC4M 8EH. The booklet also explains the profit-sharing provisions of the 1978 Finance Act. Other businesses which early adopted dividend limitation and profit-sharing were ICI, Courtaulds and Rowntrees.

38 Thomas J. Peters and Robert H. Waterman, *In Search of Excellence*, 'Lessons from America's best-run companies' (Harper & Row, 1982).

39 ibid. p. 39.

40 Richard Tanner Pascale and Anthony G. Athos in *The Art of Japanese Management* (Simon & Schuster, 1981; Penguin, 1982), p. 50.

41 ibid. p. 122.

42 George Goyder, *The Responsible Company* (Basil Blackwell, 1961), p. ix.

43 ibid. pp. 109–11.

44 ibid. pp. 118, 126.

45 Goyder, *The Just Enterprise*, p. xi.

46 ibid. p. 5.

47 ibid. p. 79.

48 ibid. p. 82.

49 The Christian Association of Business Executives, 12 Palace Street, London SW1E 5JA.

50 Goyder, *The Just Enterprise*, p. 16.

11 The multi-racial dream

1 Martin Luther King's 'I have a dream' speech is recorded in Coretta Scott King's *My Life with Martin Luther King, Jr* (Hodder & Stoughton, 1969), p. 249.

2 From an address by Roy Jenkins, Home Secretary, May 1966 to a meeting of Voluntary Liaison Committees.

3 David Brion Davies, *The Problem of Slavery in Western Cultures* (Cornell University Press, 1966), p. 31.

4 Edward Long, *The History of Jamaica* (Lowndes, London, 1774), pp. 351–6.

5 J.H. Guenebault, *The Natural History of the Negro Race* (English translation published by Dowling, Charleston, South Carolina, 1837), pp. 1–19. See also the references to this book in Wilson Armistead, *A Tribute for the Negro* (Manchester, 1848), e.g. p. 36.

6 Stanley M. Elkins, *Slavery*, 'A problem in American institutional and intellectual life' (1959; 2nd ed. University of Chicago Press, 1968), p. 82.

7 ibid. p. 84.

8 ibid. p. 113.

9 ibid., especially Chapter III, 'Slavery and Personality'.

10 Armistead, *A Tribute for the Negro*, p. 5.

11 M.F. Ashley Montagu, *Man's Most Dangerous Myth: the Fallacy of Race* (1942; 5th ed. revised and enlarged, Oxford University Press, 1974), p. 101.

12 ibid. p. 67.

13 ibid. p. 416.

14 ibid. p. 3.

15 Columbus Salley and Ronald Behm, *What Color is Your God?*, 'Black Consciousness and the Christian faith', first published 1970 under the title *Your God is Too White* (Inter-Varsity Press, revised ed. 1981).

16 Montagu, *Man's Most Dangerous Myth*, p. 420.

17 Adolf Hitler, *Mein Kampf* (1925, translated by James Murphy; Hutchinson, 1940), p. 150.

18 ibid. p. 284.

19 Gutteridge, *Open thy Mouth for the Dumb*, p. 69.

20 ibid. p. 48.

21 Quoted in Montagu, *Man's Most Dangerous Myth*, p. 50.

22 Quoted in John W. de Gruchy, *The Church Struggle in South Africa* (Eerdmans, 1979), pp. 30–1. For recent assessments of Christian

attitudes to racism in South Africa, see Zolile Mbali, *The Churches and Racism*, 'A Black South African perspective' (SCM, 1987), and Cassidy, *The Passing Summer*.

23 *Human Relations and the South African Scene in the Light of Scripture*, a 1974 report of the Dutch Reformed Church (Dutch Reformed Publishers, 1976), pp. 14, 32, 71.

24 Hitler, *Mein Kampf*, p. 248.

25 Professor Dr A.B. Dupreez, *Inside the South African Crucible* (HAUM, Kapstaad-Pretoria, 1959), p. 63.

26 Montagu, *Man's Most Dangerous Myth*, p. 10.

27 ibid. p. 190–3.

28 ibid. p. 202.

29 ibid. pp. 204–34.

30 Cassidy, *The Passing Summer*, p. 154.

31 Margery Perham, *The Colonial Reckoning*, the 1961 Reith Lectures (Collins, 1961), p. 39.

32 Jeremy Murray-Brown, *Kenyatta* (Allen & Unwin, 1972), p. 306.

33 Mzee Jomo Kenyatta, *Suffering without Bitterness* (East African Publishing House, 1968), p. 166. For similar African reactions to French colonial rule, see Frantz Fanon, *Black Skin, White Masks* (1952).

34 Paul Scott, *The Jewel in the Crown* (1966; Granada, 1973), p. 260.

35 Arnold Toynbee, *A Study of History*, vol. 1, p. 213, quoted by Archbishop Cyril Garbett in *World Problems of Today* (Hodder & Stoughton, 1955), p. 135.

36 See Anne Owers, *Sheep and Goats*, 'British nationality law and its effects', and *Families Divided*, 'Immigration control and family life' (CIO, 1984).

37 See also *The Churches' Charter for Racial Justice in Europe* (1996).

38 Martin Walker, *The National Front* (Collins, 1977), p. 34.

39 ibid. pp. 78–84.

40 ibid. p. 185.

41 Lord Scarman, *The Scarman Report*, 'The Brixton Disorders 10–12 April 1981' (Penguin, 1981), pp. 77–8.

42 ibid. p. 209.

43 ibid. p. 196.

44 David Haslam, *Race for the Millennium*, 'A challenge to church and society' (Church House, 1996).

45 Penguin, 1977, Part 2, 'Employment', pp. 109–10.

46 David Sheppard, *Bias to the Poor* (Hodder & Stoughton, 1983), p. 69.

47 *Unemployment and the Future of Work*, p. 106.

48 TUC news release, April 1997.

49 See Haslam, *Race for the Millennium*, pp. 121–2, and *Unemployment and the Future of Work*, pp. 116–17.

50 *The Autobiography of Malcolm X* (Grove Press, 1964), pp. 175, 275.

51 ibid. pp. 179, 272.

52 Haslam, *Race for the Millennium*, p. 167.

53 ibid. p. 175.

54 Montagu, *Man's Most Dangerous Myth*, p. 74.

55 ibid. p. 307.

56 Quoted in Walker, *The National Front*, p. 47.

57 *The Lausanne Covenant*, para. 10, 'Evangelism and Culture', *Making Christ Known*, pp. 39–42.

58 J.C.G. Klotze, *Principle and Practice in Race Relations According to Scripture* (SCA Publications, Stellenbosch, 1962), p. 55.

59 O.R. Johnston, *Nationhood: Towards a Christian Perspective* (Latimer Studies, no. 7, 1980), p. 14.

60 *The Pasadena Statement* on the Homogeneous Unit Principle, *Making Christ Known*, p. 64. For a black Christian's experience of living in Britain, see Philip Mohabir, *Building Bridges* (Hodder & Stoughton, 1988). Also recommended is the 'Study Pack for Christians in a Multi-Racial Society', entitled *New Humanity* and produced by Evangelical Christians for Racial Justice, 29 Trinity Road, Aston, Birmingham B6 6AJ.

12 Poverty, wealth and simplicity

1 From an article by Malcolm Muggeridge which first appeared in *The Observer* on 26 June 1966 and was subsequently published in *Jesus Rediscovered* (Collins Fontana, 1969), p. 57.

2 US Census Bureau press release, 26 September 1996.

3 *Social Security Statistics 1996* (HMSO 1996), p. 17.

4 *Faith in the City*, 'A call for action by church and nation' (Church House Publishing, 1985), p. 359.

5 *Puebla*, 'Evangelization at present and in the future of Latin America', Conclusions of the Third General Conference of Latin American bishops (St Paul Publications, 1980), p. 107, para. 494.

6 UN *Human Development Report 1997*, executive summary, taken from web-site <www.undp.org>.

7 UN *Human Development Report 1996* (Oxford University Press, 1996), pp. 148–9.

8   Todaro, *Economic Development*, p. 46.

9   The World Bank Annual Report 1989, p. 27.

10 UNDP press release, 12 June 1997, from *Human Development Report 1997* launch.

11 Bishop David Sheppard's Richard Dimbleby Lecture, 'The Poverty that Imprisons the Spirit', was published in *The Listener* (19 April 1984). See also Paul Harrison, *Inside the Inner City* (Penguin, 1983).

12 See, e.g., Albert Gelin, *The Poor of Yahweh* (1964; English translation by the Liturgical Press, Minnesota); Julio de Santa Ana, *Good News to the Poor* (WCC, 1977), and Julio de Santa Ana (ed.), *Towards a Church of the Poor* (Orbis, 1979); Conrad Boerma, *Rich Man, Poor Man and the Bible* (1978; SCM, 1979); Atholl Gill, *Christians and the Poor* (Zadok Centre Series, Canberra, no. 9, undated); *Christian Witness to the Urban Poor* (Lausanne Occasional Paper no. 22, 1980), a group report from the Consultation on World Evangelization at Pattaya, Thailand, which incorporates as an Appendix Jim Punton's analysis of the nine Hebrew words for the poor; *Your Kingdom Come*, the report of the World Conference on Mission and Evangelism, held in Melbourne in 1980; Vinay Samuel and Chris Sugden, *Evangelism and the Poor* (Partnership in Mission, Asia, Bangalore, revised ed. 1983); Redmond Mullin, *The Wealth of Christians* (Paternoster, 1983); and Peter Lee, *Poor Man, Rich Man*, 'The priorities of Jesus and the agenda of the church' (Hodder & Stoughton, 1986).

13 Raymond Fung's speech, 'Good News to the Poor', is published in *Your Kingdom Come* (WCC, 1980), pp. 83–92.

14 Sheppard, *Bias to the Poor*, p. 16.

15 ibid. p. 225.

16 *Puebla*, p. 178, para. 1134.

17 ibid. p. 179, paras. 1141–2.

18 ibid. p. 180, para. 1154.

19 *Your Kingdom Come*, p. 171.

20 This was Professor Kosuke Koyama's expression at Melbourne (*Your Kingdom Come*, p. 161).

21 Robert Holman, *Poverty: Explanations of Social Deprivation* (Martin Robertson, 1978).

22 ibid. p. 134.

23 ibid. p. 188.

24 Martin Hengel, *Property and Riches in the Early Church*, 'Aspects of a Social History of the Early Church' (1973; English

translation SCM and Fortress, 1974), pp. 26–7.

25 ibid. pp. 32–3.

26 Cathy Pharaoh (ed.), *Dimensions of the Voluntary Sector* (CAF, 1997), p. 60.

27 Quoted by Bishop Otto Dibelius in his autobiography, *In the Service of the Lord* (Holt, Reinhart & Winston, 1964), p. 31.

28 Taylor, *Enough is Enough,* pp. 81–2.

29 See *The Lausanne Covenant – An Exposition and Commentary,* in Stott (ed.), *Making Christ Known.*

30 *An Evangelical Commitment to Simple Lifestyle,* ibid. pp. 139–53. See also the papers prepared for the 'International Conference on Simple Lifestyle', published in Ronald J. Sider (ed.), *Lifestyle in the Eighties* (Paternoster, 1982), pp. 16 and 35–6.

31 Andrew Hartropp (ed.), *Families in Debt,* 'The nature, causes and effects of debt problems, and policy proposals for their alleviation' (Jubilee Centre Publications, 1987). See also Roy McCloughry and Andrew Hartropp, *Debt* (Grove Ethical Studies no. 71, 1988); Michael Schluter and David Lee, *Credit and Debit,* 'Sorting it out' (Marshalls, 1989), and the study pack on debt produced by The Institute for Contemporary Christianity for use by church groups (St Peter's Church, Vere Street, London W1M 9HP).

13 Women, men and God

1 Plato, *Timaeus,* Loeb Classical Library, translated by R.G. Bury (Heinemann, 1929), p. 249, para. 91a.

2 Aristotle, *The Generation of Animals,* II, iii, Loeb Classical Library, translated by A.L. Peck (Heinemann, 1943), p. 175.

3 Josephus, *Against Apion,* or *On the Antiquity of the Jews,* Book II, Loeb Classical Library, translated by H.St.J. Thackeray (Heinemann, 1926), p. 373, para. 201.

4 William Barclay, *Ephesians,* Daily Study Bible (St Andrews Press), pp. 199ff.

5 Tertullian, *On the Apparel of Women,* Book 1, Chapter 1, The Ante-Nicene Fathers, vol. IV (Eerdmans, reprinted 1982), p. 14.

6 Claiming that the twentieth century 'has brought greater change to women's lives than any other period in human history', Helen Wilkinson and Melanie Howard summarize what they call 'the long march to equality' (*Tomorrow's Women,* Demos, 1997, pp. 14–49). They then paint five different portraits of tomorrow's women, who represent a variety of feminisms (pp. 50–158). They are uncertain, however, whether the future will be an

extrapolation from current trends or will slow down and even halt 'the forward march of women' (pp. 159–70).

7   Germaine Greer, *The Female Eunuch* (Paladin, 1971), pp. 12, 18, 22. In her more recent book *Sex and Destiny*, 'The politics of human fertility' (Secker & Warburg, 1984), while retaining her power to startle and shock by her unconventional opinions, Germaine Greer is much more positive towards the human family. Indeed, she almost romanticizes the parent–child relationships which are traditional in Asia and Africa, in contrast to the tendency of the western nuclear family which (in her view) despises and neglects children.

8   ibid. pp. 59–60.

9   See *Sex and Destiny*, and note 6 above.

10 Janet Radcliffe Richards, *The Sceptical Feminist*, 'A philosophical enquiry' (1980; Penguin, 1982), p. 11.

11 ibid. pp. 13–14, 16.

12 SPCK/Third Way Books, 1985.

13 A recommended symposium which opens up the issues fairly is Shirley Lees (ed.), *The Role of Women* (Inter-Varsity Press, 1984), in which eight prominent Christians debate with one another. Its American equivalent is Bonnidell Clouse and Robert G. Clouse, *Women in Ministry: Four Views* (Inter-Varsity Press, US, 1989).

14 *An Inclusive Language Lectionary: Readings for Year A* (Cooperative Publications Association, 1983). The quotations are from the Preface and the Introduction. See also Graham Leonard, Iain Mackenzie and Peter Toon, *Let God Be God* (Darton, Longman & Todd, 1989). The Church of England General Synod's Liturgical Commission produced a judicious report in 1988 entitled *Making Women Visible*, subtitled 'The use of inclusive language with the Alternative Service Book'. They did not recommend any changes in the biblical and traditional ways of referring to God. In relation to 'the use of male terms to include both genders' (e.g. 'man', 'men', 'mankind'), they avoided the two extremes of those wishing to eliminate them all as inherently offensive to the dignity of women and those wishing to retain them all as deeply embedded in culture and literature. The Commission has recommended a sensitive and flexible way forward, accepting many of the theological arguments of the former group and some of the linguistic arguments of the latter (see especially paras 81–3).

15 *Gandhi: An Autobiography* (1949; Jonathan Cape, 1966), p. 155.

16 *The Koran*, translated by N.J. Dawood (Penguin, 1956), pp. 360ff.

17 Raymond de Coccola, *Ayorama* (1955; Paper Jacks, Ontario, 1973), p. 212.

18 Luke 10:38ff.; John 20:10ff. John Wenham argues cogently in *Easter Enigma* (Paternoster, 1984) that 'Mary of Bethany' was in fact Mary Magdalene (pp. 22–33).

19 Yoder, *The Politics of Jesus*, p. 177, footnote 23.

20 Betty Friedan, *The Feminine Mystique* (Pelican, 1963), p. 68. In her subsequent book, *The Second Stage* (1981; Abacus, 1983), Betty Friedan declares the first stage of the feminist battle to be over. Women have been liberated from feminine role stereotypes into equality with men. The second stage will transcend the male–female polarization and involve a restructuring of society, especially of the family. The *feminine* mystique has been overcome; now the *feminist* mystique must be renounced, which denied the need for the nurturing environment of the family.

21 Leslie F. Church (ed.), *Matthew Henry's Commentary* (1708; Marshall Morgan & Scott, 1960), p. 7.

22 Richards, *The Sceptical Feminist*, p. 65.

23 George F. Gilder, *Sexual Suicide* (1973; Bantam, 1975), p. v.

24 ibid. p. 46.

25 ibid. p. 246.

26 ibid. p. 63.

27 William Morrow & Co., 1990; Vintage, 1991.

28 HarperCollins, 1992.

29 David Pawson, *Leadership is Male*, 'A challenge to Christian feminism' (Highland Books, 1988), pp. 17, 18, 57, 58.

30 Paul K. Jewett, *Man as Male and Female* (Eerdmans, 1975), p. 86. A somewhat similar uncertainty about how to interpret the Pauline texts is to be found in the Second Report of the House of Bishops of the General Synod of the Church of England, entitled *The Ordination of Women to the Priesthood* (GS829, 1988), especially its Chapter 3, 'Priesthood, Headship and the Exercise of Authority'.

31 ibid. p. 86.

32 ibid. p. 112.

33 ibid. p. 134.

34 ibid. p. 138.

35 Gretchen Gaebelein Hull, *Equal to Serve*, 'Women and men in the Church and home' (Revell, 1987), p. 65.

36 ibid. p. 229.

37 ibid. p. 210.

38 ibid. pp. 73–4.

39 ibid. pp. 55–6, 128, 210, 240, 244.

40 See Dayton, *Discovering an Evangelical Heritage*. In his chapter entitled 'The Evangelical Roots of Feminism' (pp. 85–98), Dr Dayton traces the roots of the American feminist movement to the revivals of Charles G. Finney, whose Oberlin College 'became the first co-educational college in the world' (p. 88).

41 James B. Hurley, *Man and Woman in Biblical Perspective*, 'A study in role relationships and authority' (Inter-Varsity Press, 1981), pp. 206–14.

42 James B. Hurley gives us a thorough treatment of 'veils'. He points out that the Old Testament contains no law about wearing a veil, and that the Hebrew and Graeco-Roman custom was for women to be normally unveiled. In both cultures too it was usual for women to put their hair up: loosed or hanging hair was a sign either of mourning or of separation from the community (e.g. because of leprosy, Nazirite vows or being suspected of adultery). Dr Hurley argues, therefore, that the 'covering' and 'uncovering' Paul mentions refers to the putting up and letting down of the hair. The NIV margin also adopts this interpretation (ibid. pp. 45–7, 66–8, 162–71, 178–9, 254–71).

43 See my appreciative critique of this book in *The Message of 1 Timothy and Titus* (Inter-Varsity Press, 1996), pp. 76–7.

44 Vol. 28, no. 6, June 1978.

45 'May Women Teach? Heresy in the Pastoral Epistles', in *The Reformed Journal*, vol. 30, no. 10, October 1980. See also Catherine Clark Kroeger, '1 Timothy 2:12 – A Classicist's View', in Alvera Mickelson (ed.), *Women, Authority and the Bible* (1986; Marshalls, 1987), pp. 225–44.

46 Mickelson (ed.), *Women, Authority and the Bible*, pp. 229–32. See also C.C. Kroeger, 'Ancient Heresies and a Strange Greek Verb', in *The Reformed Journal*, vol. 29, no. 3, March 1979.

47 'Does *kephale* (head) mean "source" or "authority over" in Greek literature? A survey of 2,336 examples', first published in 1977, reprinted in *Trinity Journal*, no. 6, 1985.

48 See, e.g., Berkeley and Alvera Mickelson, 'What does *kephale* mean in the New Testament?', in *Women, Authority and the Bible*, pp. 97–110, and especially Philip Barton Payne in his response to their paper, ibid. pp. 118–32. See also Gilbert Bilezikian, *Beyond Sex Roles* (Baker, 1985), and C.C. Kroeger, 'The Classical Concept of *Head* as "Source" ', Appendix III of Hull, *Equal to*

Serve, although in these works neither author betrays any
knowledge of Dr Grudem's survey. Dr Bilezikian directly
challenged Dr Grudem's thesis, however, at a meeting of the
Evangelical Theological Society in Atlanta in November 1986. See
also Dr Grudem's paper, 'The Meaning of *Kephale* ("Head"):
A Response to Recent Studies', published as Appendix I in John
Piper and Wayne Grudem, *Recovering Biblical Manhood and
Womanhood* (Crossway Books, 1991), pp. 425–68.

49 16 January 1987.

50 Stephen B. Clark opts for this word in his magisterial survey *Man
and Woman in Christ*, an examination of the roles of men and
women in the light of Scripture and the social sciences (Servant
Books, 1980), pp. 23–45. Despite his distinctions between
'coercive', 'mercenary' and 'voluntary' subordination, I remain
uncomfortable with the word, and have written further about
'authority' and 'submission' (1 Timothy 2:11–15) in *The Message
of 1 Timothy and Titus*, pp. 73–88.

51 For a fuller exposition of Ephesians 5:21–33, and of its
implications for marriage, see *The Message of Ephesians* in the 'Bible
Speaks Today' series (Inter-Varsity Press, 1979), pp. 213–36.

52 Crossway Books, pp. 36–45.

53 Hodder & Stoughton, 1992.

54 Margaret Mead, *Male and Female* (1949; Penguin, 1962), e.g.
pp. 41, 71, 86 and 192ff. Consider also the very ancient Chinese
teaching about the equilibrium between Yin (the feminine or
passive principle) and Yang (the masculine or active). Stephen B.
Clark summarizes the findings of psychology and anthropology
on the differences between the sexes (*Man and Woman in Christ*,
pp. 371–465).

55 Richards, *The Sceptical Feminist*, p. 192.

56 ibid. p. 175.

57 Mead, *Male and Female*, p. 88.

58 Letha Scanzoni and Nancy Hardesty, *All We're Meant To Be*,
'A biblical approach to women's liberation' (Word, 1974),
pp. 12 and 206.

59 See, e.g., C.E.B. Cranfield, *Commentary on Romans* (T & T Clark,
1979), vol. II, p. 788.

60 See my fuller exposition of these crucial verses in *The Message of
1 Timothy and Titus*, pp. 73–88.

61 For a thorough defence of the Catholic doctrine of priesthood, see
Manfred Hauke, *Women in the Priesthood?*, 'A systematic analysis

in the light of the order of creation and redemption' (first published in German in 1986; English translation Ignatius, 1988).

62 Mickelsen (ed.), *Women, Authority and the Bible*, p. 299.

14 Marriage and divorce

1 See O. Raymond Johnston's 1978 London Lectures in Contemporary Christianity, published under the title *Who Needs the Family?* (Hodder & Stoughton, 1979).

2 Jack Dominian, *Marriage, Faith and Love* (Darton, Longman & Todd, 1981), pp. 49–83. See also his earlier book, *Christian Marriage* (Darton, Longman & Todd, 1965).

3 See Judson J. Swihart and Steven L. Brigham, *Helping Children of Divorce* (Inter-Varsity Press, US, 1982).

4 1996 Statistical Abstract of the USA by the Census Bureau. Taken from the web-site of the Census Bureau: <www.census.gov>.

5 Census Bureau press release, 13 March 1996.

6 *Social Trends 1997* (HMSO, 1997), p. 46.

7 *Something to Celebrate*, 'Valuing families in Church and society', the report of a working party of the Church of England Board for Social Responsibility (Church House, 1995), p. 35.

8 Figures from *Social Trends 1996* (HMSO, 1996), p. 34, and *Social Trends 1997*, p. 47.

9 George and Nena O'Neill, *Open Marriage: A New Lifestyle for Couples* (Evans, NY, 1972). This book is referred to and quoted in Gilder, *Sexual Suicide*, pp. 47ff.

10 Prentice-Hall, 1979.

11 For a lyrical meditation on married love, and its call to self-giving, see Mike Mason, *The Mystery of Marriage* (Triangle, SPCK, 1997). He writes: 'Love is an earthquake that relocates the centre of the universe' (p. 26).

12 John Williams, *For Every Cause?*, 'A biblical study of divorce' (Paternoster, 1981), p. 12.

13 Jack Dominian, *Marital Breakdown* (Penguin, 1968), p. 42.

14 *Something to Celebrate*, p. 109.

15 ibid. p. 117.

16 ibid. p. 34.

17 ibid. p. 114.

18 ibid. pp. 115–16.

19 London, 30 November 1995.

20 The details may also be found in the tract *Gittin* in the Babylonian Talmud. See also Ecclesiasticus 25:26.

21 William L. Lane, *The Gospel of Mark*, New International Commentary Series (Eerdmans and Marshall Morgan & Scott, 1974), p. 353.

22 Hurley, *Man and Woman in Biblical Perspective*, pp. 22–8.

23 'The Biblical View of Marriage and Divorce', three articles published in *Third Way*, October and November 1977 (vol. 1, nos. 20–22).

24 It is true that in Mark 10:3ff. Jesus is recorded as having used the verb 'command', but there he seems to have been referring either to the Mosaic legislation in general or in particular to the issuing of the divorce certificate.

25 C.E.B. Cranfield, *The Gospel According to Mark*, Cambridge Greek Testament Commentary (Cambridge University Press, 1959), pp. 319–20.

26 John Murray, *Divorce* (Committee on Christian Education, Orthodox Presbyterian Church, 1953), p. 21. It is only fair to add that the moderate position developed in these pages, although based on careful exegesis, has not been acceptable to all. Some understand Jesus as having been more lenient than I have suggested, and others as more strict. The more lenient view was expressed by Ken Crispin, an Australian lawyer, in *Divorce: The Forgivable Sin?* (1988). Incensed by 'callous and irresponsible' church leaders, he interpreted *porneia* so broadly as to include every kind of misconduct which undermines a marriage. The stricter position was presented by William A. Heth and Gordon J. Wenham in *Jesus and Divorce* (1984). They argued from Scripture and Church history that Jesus placed an absolute ban on divorce and remarriage. Andrew Cornes in *Divorce and Remarriage* (1993) takes a similarly strict position. He concedes that Jesus permitted divorce in the case of a serious sexual offence, and that Paul permitted a Christian to acquiesce if his/her non-Christian partner insists on leaving. But, he urges, Jesus did not permit a remarriage to the divorcee. This is 'not because he is divorced but because he is still married. It is because God yoked him and his original partner together. It is because in God's eyes they became, in marriage, no longer two but one' (pp. 307–8). Although I am not myself convinced about the total ban on remarriage, Andrew Cornes combines biblical scholarship and pastoral experience, courage and compassion. His book will provoke some furious rethinking; it is indispensable reading for those anxious to develop a Christian mind on these topics.

27 Murray, *Divorce*, p. 65.

28 RSV and NIV translate 'how do you know ... whether you will save your wife/husband?', understanding the question to express doubt, even resignation. It may well be, however, that the apostle is rather expressing hope. The GNB renders the verse: 'how can you be sure ... that you will not save your wife/husband?' The NEB is even stronger: 'think of it: as a wife you may be your husband's salvation...' As F.F. Bruce comments, 'a mixed marriage had thus missionary potentialities' (*New Century Bible*, 1971, p. 70). So the Christian partner must do his/her utmost to preserve the marriage.

29 In *The Teaching of the New Testament on Divorce* (William & Norgate, 1921), R.H. Charles argued that, since in 1 Corinthians 7:39 the opposite of 'bound' is 'free to marry', therefore in verse 9 'the right of remarriage is here conceded to the believing husband or wife who is deserted by an unbelieving partner' (p. 58).

30 David Atkinson, *To Have and To Hold*, 'The marriage covenant and the discipline of divorce' (Collins, 1979), p. 28.

31 Alan Storkey, *Marriage and its Modern Crisis* (Hodder & Stoughton, 1996), p. 197.

32 Atkinson, *To Have and To Hold*, p. 70.

33 ibid. p. 71.

34 ibid. pp. 75–6.

35 ibid. p. 91.

36 ibid. p. 151.

37 ibid. p. 152.

38 ibid. p. 154.

39 I especially recommend a book by Bishop Michael and Mrs Myrtle Baughen, *Your Marriage* (Hodder & Stoughton, 1994; US edition entitled *Christian Marriage*, Baker Book House).

40 Dominian, *Marital Breakdown*, p. 61.

41 See Lynn R. Buzzard and Laurence Eck, *Tell It to the Church: Reconciling out of Court* (David C. Cook, 1982). The Christian Legal Society's address is 4208 Evergreen Ln., Suite 222, Annandale Va., 22003, USA. See also *Reconciliation and Conciliation in the Context of Divorce* (the Order of Christian Unity, 1982) and *Marriage Breakdown and Conciliation* (Board for Social Responsibility, Newsletter no. 111, December 1982).

42 Oliver O'Donovan, *Marriage and Permanence*, Grove Booklet on Ethics no. 26 (Grove Books, 1978), p. 20.

43 ibid. p. 21.

15 Abortion and euthanasia

1 Desmond Doig, *Mother Teresa: Her People and Her Work* (Collins, 1976), p. 162.

2 Francis A. Schaeffer and C. Everett Koop, *Whatever Happened to the Human Race?* (Revell, 1979; revised British ed. by Marshall Morgan & Scott, 1980). See particularly Chapter 1, 'The Abortion of the Human Race', pp. 2–27, and Chapter 4, 'The Basis for Human Dignity', pp. 68–99.

3 The Japanese abortion statistics are given by C. Everett Koop in his *The Right to Live; the Right to Die* (Tyndale House, US, and Coverdale House, UK, 1976), p. 46.

4 Report of the Committee on the Working of the Abortion Act 1967, vol. 1 (HMSO Cmnd, 5579, April 1974), p. 11.

5 The Registrar General's Statistical Review of England and Wales for the years 1968–73; Supplement on 'Abortion' (HMSO). The more recent statistics were supplied in 1996 by the Society for the Protection of Unborn Children.

6 A full description and discussion of the Roe v. Wade case may be found in Harold O.J. Brown, *Death Before Birth* (Thomas Nelson, 1977), pp. 73–96.

7 These figures are taken from (1) *Statistical Abstract of the United States: 1982–83* (US Bureau of the Census, 1982), p. 68, (2) 'Intercessors for America Newsletter', vol. 10, no. 2, February 1983, and (3) the Family Research Council, Washington DC.

8 Quoted from Daniel Callahan's *Abortion: Law, Choice and Morality*, p. 298, in Lewis B. Smedes, *Mere Morality* (Eerdmans, 1983), p. 267, footnote 21.

9 See, e.g., Richard Winter, *Choose Life*, 'A Christian perspective on abortion and embryo experimentation' (Marshall Pickering, 1988), p. 8.

10 John Powell, SJ, *Abortion: the Silent Holocaust* (Argus Communications, Allen, Texas, 1981), e.g. pp. 20–39.

11 For ancient perspectives and practices, see Michael J. Gorman, *Abortion and the Early Church*, 'Christian, Jewish and Pagan attitudes in the Graeco-Roman world' (Inter-Varsity Press, 1982).

12 One of the most thorough treatments of this topic is *Abortion: A Christian Understanding and Response* (Baker, 1987). It is an American symposium, edited by James K. Hoffmeier. Fifteen of its contributors are members of the faculty of Wheaton College. See also Nigel M. de S. Cameron, *Is Life Really Sacred?* (Kingsway, 1990).

13   Quoted from *Abortion Law Reformed* (1971) in R.F.R. Gardner, *Abortion: The Personal Dilemma* (Paternoster Press, 1972), p. 62.

14   Gardner, *Abortion: The Personal Dilemma*, p. 126.

15   Quoted by John T. Noonan in *The Morality of Abortion* (Harvard University Press, 1970), p. 45.

16   Quoted in Koop, *The Right to Live; the Right to Die*, pp. 43–4.

17   John M. Frame discusses this passage fully, including the meaning of the Hebrew words used, in his chapter in Richard L. Ganz, *Thou Shalt Not Kill*, 'The Christian case against abortion' (Arlington House, 1978), pp. 50–7.

18   First published by Faber in 1965.

19   For Oliver O'Donovan's position, see his *The Christian and the Unborn Child* (Grove Booklets on Ethics, no. 1, 1973), and his 1983 London Lectures in Contemporary Christianity, *Begotten or Made?*, 'Human procreation and medical technique' (Oxford University Press, 1984). See also Paul Fowler, *Abortion: Toward an Evangelical Consensus* (Multnomah, 1987).

20   Donald MacKay wrote up his position in an essay entitled 'The Beginnings of Personal Life', which was published in the Christian Medical Fellowship's magazine *In the Service of Medicine*, no. 30(2), 1984, pp. 9–13. See also his 1977 London Lectures in Contemporary Christianity, *Human Science and Human Dignity* (Hodder & Stoughton, 1979), especially pp. 64–5 and 98–102. The two positions represented by Professors O'Donovan and MacKay were given further expression in the Church of England Board for Social Responsibility report *Personal Origins* (CIO, 1985). The minority emphasized the *continuity* of the individual from the moment of fusion, while the majority stressed *consciousness* as necessary for personhood, and a certain brain structure as necessary for consciousness. Then in 1987 Professor Gareth Jones contributed a full discussion of 'personhood' in relation to the fetus in his *Manufacturing Humans*, 'The challenge of the new reproductive technologies' (Inter-Varsity Press), Chapter 5, pp. 125–67.

21   Tertullian's *Apology*, Chapter ix. Michael J. Gorman gives a popular but thorough account of the unanimous pro-life, anti-abortion stance of the first five centuries of Christianity in his *Abortion and the Early Church*. His references to Tertullian are on pp. 54–8.

22   Paul Ramsey, *Fabricated Man*, 'The ethics of genetic control' (Yale University Press, 1970), p. 11.

23 Smedes, *Mere Morality*, p. 129.

24 Quoted in the Church of Scotland's Board of Social Responsibility 1985 report to the General Assembly. See Professor Torrance's booklet *Test-tube Babies* (Scottish Academic Press, 1984).

25 *Report of the Committee of Enquiry into Human Fertilisation and Embryology*, chaired by Dame Mary Warnock (HMSO, 1984), 1.1.

26 A recent alternative to IVF is GIFT (Gamete Intra Fallopian Transfer). In this case ovum and sperm, after being mixed, are immediately transferred to the end of the fallopian tube, where conception takes place as normal. Many consider GIFT preferable to IVF. Technically, it is simpler and cheaper. Ethically, it precludes the production of 'spare' embryos for research.

27 *Report … into Human Fertilization and Embryology*, para. 11.9.

28 O'Donovan, *Begotten or Made?*, pp. 1–2, 65.

29 Richard Higginson, *Whose Baby?*, 'The ethics of *in vitro* fertilization' (Marshall Morgan & Scott, 1985), p. x.

30 *Instruction on Respect for Human Life in its Origin and on the Dignity of Procreation*, written by the Congregation for the Doctrine of the Faith (Catholic Truth Society, 1987), p. 26.

31 Paul Ramsey, the distinguished American ethicist, also wrote about God's intention that sexual intercourse be simultaneously an act of love and procreation. See his *Fabricated Man*. Richard Higginson helpfully compares and contrasts Roman Catholic and Protestant positions in his *Whose Baby?*, pp. 19–40.

32 *Report … into Human Fertilization and Embryology*, para. 11.17.

33 ibid. pp. 90–1.

34 *Instruction on Respect for Human Life*, p. 17.

35 ibid. p. 16.

36 From Professor G.R. Dunstan's contribution to the article on 'Abortion' in Duncan, Dunstan and Welbourn (eds), *Dictionary of Medical Ethics*.

37 The expression used by Mr Justice McNaughten in the Rex v. Bourne case of 1938.

38 Glanville Williams, *The Sanctity of Life and the Criminal Law* (Faber, 1958), p. 212.

39 ibid. p. 31.

40 Quoted from his book *Humanly Possible*, at the beginning of Koop, *The Right to Live; the Right to Die*.

41 Quoted by Norman St John Stevas in *The Right to Life* (Hodder & Stoughton, 1963), p. 20.

42 Gardner, *Abortion: The Personal Dilemma*, pp. 225–6.

43 The addresses of these organizations are as follows. 'Birthright', 777 Coxwell Avenue, Toronto, Ontario, Canada M4C 3C6. Alternatives to Abortion, International, 2606 1/2 West 8th Street, Los Angeles, California 90057, USA. LIFE, 7 The Parade, Leamington Spa, Warwickshire. SPUC, 7 Tufton Street, London SW1. CARE Trust, 53 Romney Street, London SW1P 3RF. CARENET, 109 Carpenter Dr., Suite 100, Sterling, Virginia 20164, USA.

44 Quoted in Gardner, *Abortion: The Personal Dilemma*, p. 276. See also Louise Summerhill, *The Story of Birthright: the Alternative to Abortion* (Prow Books, Kenosha, 1973).

45 *Abortion: An Ethical Dilemma*, a report of the Board for Social Responsibility (CIO, 1965), p. 57.

46 Gardner, *Abortion: The Personal Dilemma*, pp. 248–62.

47 See Nigel Cameron, *The New Medicine*, 'Life and death after Hippocrates' (Crossway, 1991).

48 See, e.g., her contribution 'Euthanasia: the Hospice Alternative', in Nigel M. de S. Cameron (ed.), *Death Without Dignity* (Rutherford House Books, 1990).

49 Dworkin, p. 239

50 From the Encyclical *Evangelium Vitae*, March 1995.

16 Same-sex partnerships?

1 See A.C. Kinsey's *Sexual Behaviour in the Human Male* (1948) and *Sexual Behaviour in the Human Female* (1953).

2 From an article entitled 'God, Sex and You', in *Eternity* magazine, August 1972.

3 J.N.D. Anderson, *Morality, Law and Grace* (Tyndale Press, 1972), p. 73.

4 Malcolm Macourt (ed.), *Towards a Theology of Gay Liberation* (SCM Press, 1977), p. 3. The quotation comes from Mr Macourt's own introduction to the book.

5 See his *Living in Sin?*, 'A bishop rethinks human sexuality' (Harper & Row, 1988).

6 Derrick Sherwin Bailey, *Homosexuality and the Western Christian Tradition* (Longmans, Green, 1955), p. 4.

7 Sherwin Bailey gives references in the *Book of Jubilees* and the *Testaments of the Twelve Patriarchs*, ibid. pp. 11–20. There is an even fuller evaluation of the writings of the inter-testamental period in Peter Coleman's *Christian Attitudes to Homosexuality* (SPCK, 1980), pp. 58–85.

8   Bailey, ibid. p. 27.
9   See James D. Martin in Macourt (ed.), *Towards a Theology of Gay Liberation* (SCM, 1977), p. 53.
10 Bailey, *Homosexuality and the Western Christian Tradition*, p. 30.
11 Coleman, *Christian Attitudes to Homosexuality*, p. 49.
12 Bailey, *Homosexuality and the Western Christian Tradition*, p. 39.
13 Coleman, *Christian Attitudes to Homosexuality*, pp. 95–6.
14 ibid. p. 277.
15 ibid. p. 101.
16 Rictor Norton, in Macourt (ed.), *Towards a Theology of Gay Liberation*, p. 58.
17 Letha Scanzoni and Virginia R. Mollenkott, *Is the Homosexual My Neighbour?* (Harper & Row and SCM, 1978), p. 111.
18 Bailey, *Homosexuality and the Western Christian Tradition*, p. 1.
19 Michael Vasey, *Strangers and Friends* (Hodder & Stoughton, 1995), pp. 46, 82–3.
20 See *Christianity, Social Tolerance and Homosexuality* (Chicago University Press, 1980), and *Same-sex Unions in Pre-Modern Europe* (Villard Books, 1994).
21 Richard John Neuhaus, 'The Case Against John Boswell', excerpted in Julie Belding and Bruce Nicholls (eds), *A Reason for Hope, Christian Perspectives on Homosexuality and Healing* (The Human Relationships Foundation, Auckland, New Zealand, 1996), p. 14.
22 Everett Ferguson (ed.), *The Encyclopedia of Early Christianity* (Garland, 1990).
23 Vasey, *Strangers and Friends*, p. 116.
24 ibid. pp. 176–7.
25 ibid. p. 117 (Vasey is referring to Matthew 19:11–12).
26 ibid. p. 33.
27 ibid. p. 34.
28 Norman Pittenger, *Time for Consent* (3rd ed., SCM, 1976), pp. 7, 73.
29 Thomas E. Schmidt, *Straight and Narrow?*, 'Compassion and clarity in the homosexuality debate' (Inter-Varsity Press, 1995), pp. 134–5.
30 Pittenger, *Time for Consent*, p. 7.
31 Coleman, *Christian Attitudes to Homosexuality*, p. 50.
32 Chapter 3.3–5, quoted in Coleman, ibid. p. 71.
33 John Boswell, *Christianity, Social Tolerance and Homosexuality*, pp. 107ff.

34 Richard B. Hays, 'A Response to John Boswell's Exegesis of Romans 1', *Journal of Religious Ethics*, Spring 1986, p. 192. See also his *The Moral Vision of the New Testament* (T & T Clark, 1996), pp. 383–9.

35 C.K. Barrett, *Commentary on the Epistle to the Romans* (A & C Black, 1962), p. 39.

36 C.E.B. Cranfield, Commentary on Romans in the *International Critical Commentary* (T & T Clark, 1975), vol. 1, p. 126. He attributes the same meaning to *physis* in his comment on 1 Corinthians 11:14. What NIV translates 'the very nature of things' Professor Cranfield renders 'the very way God has made us'.

37 The Friends' Report *Towards a Quaker View of Sex* (1963), p. 21.

38 ibid. p. 36.

39 Methodist Church's Division of Social Responsibility, *A Christian Understanding of Human Sexuality* (1979), Chapter 9.

40 Chapter 5.

41 Pittenger, *Time for Consent*, pp. 31–3.

42 Jeffrey Satinover, *Homosexuality and the Politics of Truth* (Baker, 1996), p. 55. He is quoting from D. McWhirter and A. Mattison, *The Male Couple: How Relationships Develop* (Prentice-Hall, 1984).

43 Schmidt, *Straight and Narrow?*, p. 108.

44 Satinover, *Homosexuality and the Politics of Truth*, p. 51. See the whole of his Chapter 3.

45 Schmidt, *Straight and Narrow?*, p. 122. See the whole of his Chapter 6.

46 *The Homosexual Movement: A Response by the Ramsey Colloquium*, first published in *First Things*, March 1994.

47 Macourt (ed.), *Towards a Theology of Gay Liberation*, p. 25.

48 Pittenger, *Time for Consent*, p. 2.

49 ibid. p. 94.

50 Kingsway, 1987, p. 78.

51 Quoted in Satinover, *Homosexuality and the Politics of Truth*, p. 17. See also p. 57.

52 Statistics on AIDS taken from the UNAIDS web-site on <www.unaids.org>. This is a good source for up-to-date information on AIDS around the world.

53 Dixon, *The Truth About AIDS*, p. 113. See also p. 88 and the whole chapter entitled 'Condoms are Unsafe', pp. 110–22.

54 *The Many Faces of AIDS*, 'A gospel response' (United States Catholic Conference, 1987), p. 18.

55 Roy McCloughry and Carol Bebawi, *AIDS: A Christian Response*

(Grove Ethical Studies no. 64, 1987), pp. 4, 18. See the theological discussion 'Is AIDS the Judgment of God?', pp. 12–19.

56 *The Many Faces of AIDS*, p. 6.
57 Quoted in *Christianity Today*, 7 August 1987, p. 17.
58 The Terrence Higgins Trust, BM/AIDS, London WC1N 3XX.
59 For example, The London Lighthouse (a 26-bed AIDS hospice), 178 Lancaster Road, London W11 1QU, and the internationally known 32-suite AIDS ward at the Mildmay Mission Hospital, Hackney Road, London E2 7NA. Both hospices also arrange home care. ACACIA (AIDS Care, Compassion in Action) cares for about 75 people with HIV/AIDS in their own homes in Manchester.
60 These were never published.
61 So Gavin Reid rightly argues in his *Beyond AIDS*, 'The real crisis and the only hope' (Kingsway, 1987).
62 For example, Christian Action on AIDS was established in 1986 (PO Box 76, Hereford, HR1 1JX). Also ACET (AIDS Care Education and Training), with an aim of developing a nationwide network of hospices, home care volunteers and church support groups. Its address is PO Box 3693, London SW15 2BQ.
63 *AIDS*, a report by the Church of England Board for Social Responsibility (GS 795, 1987), p. 29.
64 Alex Davidson, *The Returns of Love* (Inter-Varsity Press, 1970), pp. 12, 16, 49.
65 Norman Pittenger, in Macourt (ed.), *Towards a Theology of Gay Liberation*, p. 87.
66 The St Andrew's Day Statement (published 30 November 1995) begins with three theological 'Principles' relating to the Incarnate Lord (in whom we come to know both God and ourselves), the Holy Spirit (who enables us to interpret the times) and God the Father (who restores the broken creation in Christ). The Statement's second half consists of three 'Applications' relating to such questions as our human identity, empirical observations, the reaffirmation of the good news of salvation, and the hope of final fulfilment in Christ. Two years later *The Way Forward?* was published, with the subtitle 'Christian voices on homosexuality and the Church'. This symposium, edited by Tim Bradshaw, consists of 13 responses to the St Andrew's Day Statement, from a wide range of different viewpoints. One appreciates the call to patient and serious theological reflection. But it is inaccurate to

write of 'dialogue' and 'diatribe' as if they were the only options. Some of us have been listening and reflecting for 30 or 40 years! How long must the process continue before we are allowed to reach a conclusion? In spite of claims to the contrary, no fresh evidence has been produced which could overthrow the clear witness of Scripture and the longstanding tradition of the Church. The St Andrew's Day Statement says that the Church recognizes two vocations (marriage and singleness), and adds that 'there is no place for the Church to confer legitimacy upon alternatives to these'. Further, the authors of the Statement do not consider that 'the considerable burden of proof to support a major change in the Church's teaching and practice has been met' by the contributors to the book (p. 3). Yet the book makes a more uncertain sound than the Statement. So by all means let there be serious theological reflection, but then let the Church make up its mind.

67 Pittenger, *Time for Consent*, p. 7. Contrast *The Courage to be Chaste*, 'An uncompromising call to the biblical standard of chastity' (Paulist Press, 1986). Written by Benedict J. Groeschel, a Capuchin friar, the book contains much practical advice.

68 Satinover, *Homosexuality and the Politics of Truth*, p. 117.

69 ibid. pp. 18, 19, 71.

70 Vasey, *Strangers and Friends*, p. 103.

71 See Satinover, *Homosexuality and the Politics of Truth*, pp. 31–40.

72 D.J. West, *Homosexuality* (1955; 2nd ed. Pelican, 1960; 3rd ed. Duckworth, 1968), pp. 266, 273.

73 Nelson Gonzalez's article 'Exploding Ex-Gay Myths', in *Regeneration Quarterly*, vol. 1, no. 3, Summer 1995, challenged the aims and claims of the ex-gay movement. In 1991 Charles Socarides founded the National Association for Research and Therapy of Homosexuality (NARTH), which investigates the possibilities for 'healing'.

74 Marshall Morgan & Scott, 1987, p. 155. Martin Hallett's organization is called 'True Freedom Trust' (PO Box 3, Upton Wirral, Merseyside, L49 6NY). It offers an inter-denominational teaching and counselling ministry on homosexuality and related problems.

75 PO Box 2121, San Rafael, California 94912.

76 Elizabeth R. Moberly, *Homosexuality: A New Christian Ethic* (James Clarke, 1983), p. 2. See also Lance Pierson, *No-Gay Areas*, 'Pastoral care of homosexual Christians' (Grove Pastoral Studies no. 38,

1989), which helpfully applies Elizabeth Moberly's teaching.

77 Moberly, ibid. p. 28.

78 ibid. pp. 18–20.

79 ibid. pp. 35–6.

80 ibid. p. 52.

81 Davidson, *The Returns of Love*, p. 51.

82 Macourt (ed.), *Towards a Theology of Gay Liberation*, p. 63.

83 Pittenger, *Time for Consent*, p. 2.

84 Quoted from *The Comfortable Pew* (1965) by Letha Scanzoni and Virginia Mollenkott.

85 Macourt (ed.), *Towards a Theology of Gay Liberation*, p. 45.

86 The word seems to have been used first by George Weinberg in *Society and the Healthy Homosexual* (Doubleday, 1973).

87 Richard R. Lovelace, *Homosexuality and the Church* (Revell, 1978), p. 129, and cf. p. 125.

88 David J. Atkinson, *Homosexuals in the Christian Fellowship* (Latimer House, 1979), p. 118. See also Dr Atkinson's more extensive treatment in his *Pastoral Ethics in Practice* (Monarch, 1989). Dr Roger Moss concentrates on pastoral questions in his *Christians and Homosexuality* (Paternoster, 1977).

89 Vasey, *Strangers and Friends*, p. 122.

90 ibid. p. 233.

17 A call for Christian leadership

1 Bennie E. Goodwin II, *The Effective Leader: a Basic Guide to Christian Leadership* (Inter-Varsity Press, US, 1971), p. 8.

2 William Shakespeare, *Twelfth Night*, II, iv, 158.

3 J. Oswald Sanders, *Spiritual Leadership* (Marshall Morgan & Scott, 1967; Lakeland ed. 1981), p. 20.

4 Proverbs 29:18. The NIV rendering is, 'Where there is no revelation, the people cast off restraint.'

5 Ronald A. Knox, *Enthusiasm*, 'A chapter in the history of religion' (Oxford University Press, 1950), p. 591.

6 From the *Washington Post*, republished in *The Guardian Weekly*, June 1978.

7 Robert K. Greenleaf, *Servant Leadership*, 'A journey into the nature of legitimate power and greatness' (Paulist Press, 1977), p. 236.

8 Douglas Hyde, *Dedication and Leadership*, 'Learning from the Communists' (University of Notre Dame Press, 1966), pp. 15–16.

9 ibid. p. 121.

10 ibid. pp. 30–1.

11   ibid. p. 52.

12   ibid. p. 59.

13   Greenleaf, *Servant Leadership*, p. 16.

14   See *The Manila Manifesto*, 1989, para. 11, in Stott (ed.), *Making Christ Known*, pp. 245–6.

15   David Bleakley, *Work: the Shadow and the Substance*, 'A reappraisal of life and labour' (SCM, 1983), p. 85.

16   Quoted by William Barclay in his *Spiritual Autobiography*, or *Testament of Faith* (Mowbray and Eerdmans, 1975), p. 112.

17   From a review by Canon R.W. Howard of James Leasor, *Wheels to Fortune*, 'The life and times of Lord Nuffield' (1955).

18   Basil Matthews, *John R. Mott*, 'World citizen' (SCM, 1934), p. 357.

19   Reginald Coupland, *Wilberforce* (Collins, 1923; 2nd ed. 1945), p. 77.

20   John C. Pollock, *Wilberforce* (Lion, 1977), p. 27. (Sir Reginald Coupland recounts the same incident in different words, ibid. p. 9.)

21   ibid. p. 56.

22   ibid. p. 304.

23   ibid. p. 308.

24   Greenleaf, *Servant Leadership*, pp. 7–10.

25   T.W. Manson, *The Church's Ministry* (Hodder & Stoughton, 1948), p. 27.

26   Sanders, *Spiritual Leadership*, p. 13.

27   M.A.C. Warren, *Crowded Canvas* (Hodder & Stoughton, 1974), p. 44.

28   Peter F. Drucker, *The Effective Executive* (Harper & Row, 1966), p. 72.

29   See *The Lausanne Covenant*, para. 15, in Stott (ed.), *Making Christ Known*, pp. 49–53.